Perspectives from *Historical Archaeology*

Mortuary and Religious Sites

Compiled by
Richard F. Veit
Alasdair M. Brooks

No. 4

SOCIETY *for* HISTORICAL ARCHAEOLOGY

Compiled by: Richard F. Veit and Alasdair M. Brooks

Contact Information:
Richard F. Veit
Department of History and Anthropology
Monmouth University
400 Cedar Avenue
West Long Branch NJ 07764

Alasdair M. Brooks
School of Archaeology and Ancient History
University of Leicester
University Road
Leicester
LE1 7RH
United Kingdom

Cover: Bernini, Gian Lorenzo. *Ecstasy of St. Theresa.* 1652. Santa Maria della Vittoria, Rome.
　　　Armstrong, Douglas V. *Sculpted Face No. 1.* 2006.
　　　Jodoin, Lise, and Andrée Héroux. *Three Types of Religious Medallions at Intendant's Palace.* 2003. Québec City.
　　　McEachen, Patty, and Laura D. Cushman. *Raritan-in-the-Hills Site Base Map.* 1999.

Perspectives from Historical Archaeology is a reader series providing collected articles from the journal of the Society for Historical Archaeology (SHA). Published since 1967, <u>Historical Archaeology</u> is the oldest North American scholarly publication on the archaeology of sites and materials from the historic past, and one of the world's premier publications on this subject. Each volume in the *Perspectives* series is developed on either a subject or regional basis by a compiler, who selects the articles for inclusion and their order. The compilers also provide an introduction that presents an overview of the substantive work on that topic. *Perspectives* volumes offer non-archaeologists a convenient source for important publications on a subject or a region; an excellent resource for students interested in developing a specialization in a specific topic or area; as well as a convenient reference for archaeologists with an interest in the material.

The *Perspectives* series is managed by the SHA's Journal Editor and Co-Publications Editor and is published through the SHA's Print-On-Demand Press. Individuals interested in compiling a volume for publication through this series are encouraged to contact the Series Editors:

J. W. Joseph, PhD, RPA
Journal Editor, SHA
New South Associates, Inc.
6150 East Ponce de Leon Avenue
Stone Mountain, GA 30083
jwjoseph@newsouthassoc.com

Annalies Corbin, PhD
Co-Publications Editor, SHA
The PAST Foundation
1929 Kenny Road, Suite 200
Columbus, OH 43210
annalies@pastfoundation.org

Formed in 1967, the SHA is the largest scholarly group concerned with the archaeology of the modern world (A.D. 1400-present). The main focus of the society is the era since the beginning of European exploration. SHA promotes scholarly research and the dissemination of knowledge concerning historical archaeology. The society is specifically concerned with the identification, excavation, interpretation, and conservation of sites and materials on land and underwater. Geographically the society emphasizes the New World, but also includes European exploration and settlement in Africa, Asia, and Oceania. To learn more about the SHA and historical archaeology, visit www.sha.org.

Contents

Part V: Commemoration

Part VI: Human Remains and Grave Goods

Richard F. Veit and Alasdair M. Brooks

Religious Sites in Historical Archaeology: An Introduction

This volume brings together some of the best scholarship published in *Historical Archaeology* on religious and mortuary sites. It is neither all-encompassing nor encyclopedic; the volume provides a useful compendium of studies on significant sites, topics, and approaches that would be valuable to individuals hoping to learn more about the archaeology of historic religious sites, or teach about such sites. The scope is intentionally wide-ranging, from Quaker burial practices in Rhode Island to Moravian mission landscapes in Australia, Native American commemoration in British Columbia, and Catholic churches in Venezuela. The volume begins by exploring the investigative methods that historical archaeologists have employed on these sites. Then it examines some significant religious sites and landscapes. The third section of the volume focuses on material culture reflective of religious beliefs. Next, commemoration as seen in gravemarkers is examined, and then finally the treatment of human remains and grave goods is explored. These categories are inevitably somewhat arbitrary, and there is considerable overlap between them; however, they provide a framework for organizing and understanding the historical archaeology of religious sites, including mortuary sites and cemeteries.

Archaeologists and anthropologists have always been interested in the material traces of religious practices. Anthropologists have long recognized that religious beliefs are an important manifestation of human culture, though the method by which 'religion' had been categorized and identified has inevitably changed since the first 19th-century anthropological studies of religion (Steadman 2009:21-35). In the 1930s Ruth Benedict observed that "there is no monograph in existence that does not group a certain class of facts as religion, and there are no records of travelers, provided they are full enough to warrant such a judgment, that do not indicate this category" (1938:629). Perhaps this is no longer as true as it was in 1938; not every individual feels a need to worship, and the strength of religious

feeling can undoubtedly fluctuate both within and between societies (Davis 2003:xx). Nonetheless, though many western industrialized societies have undoubtedly become more secular in recent decades, many anthropological studies have recognized that some form of religious belief has traditionally been fundamental to human culture.

In archaeology, mortuary sites in particular have often provided a powerful lens through which to examine religious behavior. Early archaeologists documented and at times dismantled Greek and Roman temples to develop museum collections; explorers and antiquarians in the Middle East searched for sites associated with the Old Testament; Egyptologists explored pharaoh's tombs and drew and documented temples; while medievalists documented churches, abbeys, and other religious sites (Daniel 1967; Willey and Sabloff 1993; Bahn 1996; Fagan 2005). Perhaps because of archaeology's fascinating history, aided and abetted by the stereotypes of popular culture, many people wrongly assume that the primary concerns of archaeologists are uncovering lost temples, excavating the graves of god kings, and documenting ancient religions. C.W. Ceram's well-known history of archaeology, *Gods, Graves and Scholars* (1951) is one of several works from decades past that have served to popularize this perspective. More recently, filmmakers such as Stephen Spielberg have made a host of movies drawing on this stock theme, with Indiana Jones searching for a Lost Ark, entering a Temple of Doom, and engaging in a Last Crusade. Infamously, Erich von Daniken (1968), apparently disappointed by the prosaic nature of the past, concocted outlandish arguments about how space aliens influenced ancient human cultures and their religious beliefs.

Historical archaeologists, who study the material remains of the modern world, have also shown a longstanding interest in religious sites. As early as the mid-19th century, the Jesuit priest Father Felix Martin documented an early Jesuit mission to the Huron at Sainte Marie I in Ontario, Canada in the hopes of commemorating its martyred founders (Kidd 1994). Mary Jeffery Gault, a founding member of the Association for the Preservation of Virginia Antiquities who conducted pioneering excavations at Jamestown Island for a decade starting in 1893, focused much of her work on the standing ruins of a church (Noël Hume 1996:111). In the southwest, the archaeology of mission churches has long been a major theme. J.O. Brew carried out pioneering work at Arizona's Awatovi Pueblo in the 1930s (Brew 1994:27-47), and other missions soon felt the probe of the archaeologist's trowel (Cordell 1992; Costello and Hornbeck 1992; Hester 1992; Deetz 1978). The missions of La Florida, though less visible than those of the west, have also seen extensive study (McEwan 1993; Thomas 1993). There was also pioneering archaeological research at Mormon sites in the American West. This research has been well synthesized by Benjamin Pykles in his 2010 book, *Excavating Nauvoo: The Mormons and the Rise of Historical Archaeology in America*. In the 1970s Mark Leone carried out important interpretive work on Mormon Town Plans (1973) and on the new Mormon Temple in Washington D.C. (Leone 1977). Other historical archaeologists have focused on communal religious groups such as the Harmony Society and the Shakers (De Cunzo et al. 1996; Starbuck 1984, 1990).

In a series of now-iconic studies in the 1960s, James Deetz and Edwin Dethlefsen drew the attention of archaeologists to New England gravemarkers and their implications for understanding religion's change, as well as colonial artisanship, trade patterns, and urban and rural differences (Deetz and Dethlefsen 1965, 1967, 1971; Dethlefsen and Deetz 1966). Art historians (Ludwig 1966; Benes 1977), historians of religion (David Hall 1976), cultural geographers (Zelinsky 1976, 2007), and folklorists (Glassie 1969) rediscovered them within the span of a decade. Deetz and Dethlefsen's research had an immense impact. Their theory provided a coherent, logical explanation for the iconographic change seen in New England gravemarkers. Although scholars continue to test their theory (Crowell 1981, 1983; Crowell and Mackie 1984; Gorman and DiBlasi 1976; Stone 1978; Baugher and Winter 1983; Gradwohl 1998; Mytum 2009; Veit 1991) and have noted many exceptions to the patterns they first recorded, their work remains compelling.

Despite this robust body of work, religious sites – whether houses of worship, religious communities, or burial grounds – have often been overshadowed by other themes in historical archaeology, such as race, gender, economics, plantations, domestic, industrial, and military sites, and even certain artifact types, most notably ceramics, glass bottles, and tobacco pipes. Furthermore, much of the historical archaeology of religious sites has tended to focus on religion within the context of marginalized or minority (whether ethnic or religious) social groups. The contributions in the present volume to a certain extent epitomize this phenomenon. There are multiple papers on marginalized ethnicities, such as Native Americans and African Americans, or religious minorities, such as Quakers and Theosophists. Some groups discussed in this volume, such as Moravians, Doukhobors and Jews, were (and indeed still are) both ethnic and religious minorities.

These are all important topics that have added substantially to our understanding of the role of religion in the North American past, but there have been comparatively few studies in historical archaeology that seek to illuminate the role of religious belief within the 'mainline' Protestants (Episcopalians, Methodists, Baptists, Lutherans, etc.) and Catholics who would have formed the plurality of socially dominant faith communities within historical North America. The contributions in this volume from Lawrence et al., Riordan, and Stone are important exceptions in this regard, but it remains noticeable that historical archaeologists working outside the United States, such as Mytum and Zucchi, are more likely to explore religious belief within the context of the local dominant social groups, or as an integral element across and within local communities and cultures, than their North American counterparts.

Studies of religious sites in historical archaeology therefore face a dual paradox: a relative lack of interest across the discipline, and a tendency to focus on the socially marginal when religion is studied. Why this relative lack of interest in religious and sacred sites? Some archaeologists have argued that they are not particularly edifying to study. In the 1980s, one British archaeologist wrote "Churches are particularly unedifying as archaeological sites: the structural sequence is difficult to read and usually impossible to date… artifacts are rare, and the only biological deposits susceptible to analysis are generally those of human bones" (quoted in Rodwell 1981). One recent study has argued that the anthropological perspective central to North American archaeology may have predisposed some North American researchers towards studying religion in the context of social groups that can be overtly characterized as an 'other' rather than as belonging to the 'self' (Brooks et al. 2011). Other scholars believe that the scientific focus of the New Archaeology drew researchers away from the topics of religion and toward more materialistic concerns (Trigger 1989:327). Indeed, several important recent synthesis of historical archaeology make only infrequent mention of religious topics (De Cunzo and Jamieson 2005; Hicks and Beaudry 2006; Hall and Silliman 2006). There are, however, important exceptions, such as Ralph Merrifield's fine book, *The Archaeology of Ritual and Magic* (1987).

Nonetheless, the tide is turning. Historical and Post-Medieval archaeologists have shown renewed interest in religious sites and gravemarkers. For the first time in its history, an archaeologist is serving as President of the Association for Gravestone Studies. Historical and post-medieval archaeologists (Gradwohl 1997, 1998; Tarlow 1999; Mytum 2000, 2004, 2009; Baugher et al. 2009) and historians (Jackson and Vergara 1989; Sloane 1991; Faust 2008) are writing extensively about memory and commemoration. In the United Kingdom, church archaeology has become a recognized sub-discipline with defined procedures and methodologies (Lane 2001:159-160), and traditional British topics such as the archaeology of landscapes and standing structures increasingly consider the role of religion (Bond 2003; Derek Hall 2006; Aston 2009).

After existing as a minor cord since the inception of the field, the archaeology of religion and commemoration is becoming an increasingly important theme in historical archaeology. This volume assembles some of the critical pieces on these topics that have been published in the journal *Historical Archaeology* over the past three decades. It seems inevitable, given the degree of interest in this topic and the expansion of scholarship that new articles will soon appear that would have been appropriate inclusions here. Nevertheless, the present articles reflect well on some of the important themes within the historical archaeology of religion.

Investigative Methods

The section on investigative methods begins with a fine example of public archaeology, stemming from Sherene Baugher's study of the John Street Methodist Church in New York City's Lower Manhattan (2009). For too long, archaeologists were arguably insufficiently aware of the wishes of descendant communities, or even ignored their perspectives (Price 1991; Watkins 2003). In some cases, well-organized descendant groups were able to draw attention to their concerns through protest, as seen at the African American Burial Ground in New York, but more often their wishes were overlooked. Legislation such as the Native American Graves Protection and Repatriation Act (NAGPRA) and the advent of more inclusive perspectives within archaeology are increasingly coming to the fore and correcting these longstanding problems, but there is still much work to be done.

The article by Baugher, the former New York City Archaeologist, provides a model for productive collaboration between archaeologists and descendant communities. Her work at the John Street Methodist Church is an impressive example of public archaeology carried out despite considerable constraints; she was excavating within the cellar of a church, working with a very limited budget, and to a strict deadline. The small but noteworthy project began after construction workers accidentally unearthed human remains. It was not clear whether these remains were Native American, but given the context in which they were found it seemed possible that they were. Baugher, working cooperatively with Church leaders and members of New York City's American Indian Community House, developed a program of archaeological excavations that investigated the possibility that other burials might be present under the church. Careful historical research indicated that skeletal remains had been found during earlier construction episodes at the church and in some cases reburied. Although Baugher's excavations did not unearth other human remains, they did document extensive archaeological deposits, including artifacts relating to activities frowned upon by Methodists, including clay smoking pipes, and bottles for alcoholic beverages (Baugher 2009:59). The implications for understanding human behavior, which Baugher explores, are fascinating. However, as important as her discoveries were, this study also highlights the potential and indeed the power of working with descendant communities, in this case Native American and Methodist. Finally, her work demonstrates the extent to which even small projects with limited budgets can have a significant impact.

A very different sort of excavation is presented in John Lawrence, Paul Schopp, and Rob Lore's article, "'They Even Threaten the Sick That They will Not Be Buried in the Churchyard': Salvage Archaeology of the Raritan-in-the-Hills Cemetery, Somerset County, New Jersey" (2009). This article also begins with the unexpected discovery of human remains, in this case associated with an extinct German Lutheran Congregation in Bernards Township, Somerset County, New Jersey. The blasting of basalt bedrock in preparation for the construction of a housing development unearthed fragmentary human remains. Using ground penetrating radar and surface stripping, archaeologists were able to locate 68 burials in a heavily disturbed burial ground. Although any gravemarkers that had once existed were gone, Lawrence and his colleagues were able to document the organization of the burial ground and inferred from the pattern of burials that the congregation's social cohesion gradually disintegrated, something corroborated by the historical record. They frame their study using Ferdinand Tönnes' (1957) concepts of *Gemeinschaft* and *Gesellschaft*: corporate unity and individual survival (Wilcox 2004:124).

Their study is important not just as an example of salvage archaeology, but also for what it reveals about the varied religious practices found in 18th century New Jersey. Daniel Falckner, the Pastor of the Raritan-in-the Hills Congregation was also, perhaps paradoxically, the husband of Anna Maria Schuchart, the Erfurt prophetess who was accused by some of her husband's congregants of being a witch (Lawrence et al. 2009:98). The article also highlights the differences between pietists who believed in a profound individual religious experience and more orthodox ministers in the Lutheran Faith. These religious divisions ultimately split the Raritan-in-the-Hills congregation asunder. Lawrence, Schopp, and Lore see the evidence for this division in the burial ground. They argue that the changing patterns of burials over time reflects a move from the burial

of adults in one section of the cemetery and children in another to the creation of dispersed family plots as the ties that bound the community together weakened and family allegiances became paramount (Lawrence et al. 2009:111).

Shannon Novak and Derinna Kopp's article, "To Feed a Tree in Zion: Osteological Analysis of the 1857 Mountain Meadows Massacre" (2003) examines skeletal remains from a mass grave in Utah. The grave contained 28 victims of this 1857 massacre. The massacre occurred at a time when the Mormon hierarchy was involved in a tense disagreement with the Federal Government. A company of immigrants crossing through Mormon territory during this period of religious and political tension rested their animals in Mountain Meadows, where they were attacked by a force of Mormons and their Native American allies. After an extended siege, the surviving immigrants surrendered, only to be massacred. Only a small group of children survived. As might be imagined, the site remains controversial.

Novak and Kopp recount the excavation of the mass grave, and use the available skeletal and taphonomic evidence to examine the victim's lives and the physical traces of the assault and its aftermath (Novak and Kopp 2003:87-88). The remains of at least 28 victims were present, primarily young adult males who had been shot. Today the site is both a sacred spot and contested ground, with powerful meanings for both members of the LDS Church and for descendant communities. The remains provide a new source of evidence about this tragic incident in the history of the American West.

Ross Jamieson's article, "Material Culture and Social Death: African-American Material Culture" (1995) is based on a premise proposed by sociologist Orlando Patterson (1982) that states that slavery caused the social death of slaves in that the inherited meanings of their ancestors were denied to them through the control of their cultural practices by slave owners and overseers. Based on the archaeological evidence, however, Jamieson contends that this was not entirely the case (Jamieson 1995:39). Jamieson correctly notes that "Archaeologists of the African-American past have a social responsibility constantly to remind themselves of 'who controlled the quality of life,' and what interests they have in their cultural heritage and how these can be related to archaeological research" (Potter 1991:98-100 in Jamieson 1995:39). Archaeologists studying skeletal remains have examined such topics as culture areas and cultural diffusion, mortuary practices, socio-economic status of the deceased, group affiliations, and a variety of other historical and anthropological issues. In Jamieson's view, slavery, while leading to a sort of social death for the cultural practices of enslaved Africans, did not lead to the extinguishment of all aspects of African tradition. However, studying this period and discerning these traditions is made challenging by the relatively lack of work on contemporary sites, especially in Africa; a limited body of ethnohistoric data; and the diversity of cultural beliefs that enslaved Africans brought to America. Jamieson's article is both a useful review of the state of knowledge regarding African-American burial practices and also a trumpet call to further and more careful research.

Leslie Stewart-Abernathy and Barbara L. Ruff's article, "A Good Man in Israel: Zooarchaeology and Assimilation in Antebellum Washington, Washington, Arkansas" (1989) uses a rich deposit of household trash associated with a mid-19th century Jewish family, the Blocks, to examine the issue of ethnic and in this case ethno-religious signatures. The Blocks were prominent southern merchants. The deposit is interesting, in part because of the presence of a large collection of faunal material, from which Stewart-Abernathy and Ruff are able to examine issues of diet, and also because of the substantial changes in Jewish practice that occurred during this period as new immigrants brought their traditions to the New World, and the foundations of modern Reform and Conservative Judaism developed. Perhaps not surprisingly, there were no artifacts of specifically Jewish origin or use in the deposit. Furthermore, there was no clear dietary evidence of the family's Jewish faith. The documentary evidence, in contrast, provides a more complicated story, and seems to indicate some maintenance of tradition, even in a situation of relative isolation from co-religionists.

Places and Landscapes

Another major theme in the archaeology of religious sites relates to places and landscapes.

Churches, temples, mosques, burial grounds, cemeteries, pilgrimage sites, pilgrimage routes, religious communities, shrines, oracle sites, and numerous other sacred sites make up the landscapes of religion. There are still many unexplored and underexplored themes in the historical archaeology of this period. Here we examine case studies of distinctive religious communities, missions, Catholic burial places in Latin America, and sites associated with abolition, resistance, and commemoration.

Brian Thomas' article, "Inclusion and Exclusion in the Moravian Settlement in North Carolina, 1770-1790" (1994:15-29) provides a probing analysis of a distinctive ethno-religious community in colonial America, the Moravians, and explores the question of how Moravian leaders balanced maintaining the integrity of their community with the participation in the larger Anglo-American society they were situated within. Thomas argues that the Moravian leadership employed "The built environment, mortuary practices, language, and the regulation of marriage to maintain social cohesion" but could, when necessary, deemphasize these practices to "give the appearance of Moravian inclusion in the larger Anglo-American society" (Thomas 1994:15).

The 18th-century Moravians established settlements in Georgia, North Carolina, New Jersey, and Pennsylvania. A Protestant Christian sect, their faith developed in Moravia and Bohemia, now part of the Czech Republic. Harshly persecuted during the 16th and 17th centuries, some families sought refuge with Count Nicholas Ludwig von Zinzendorf in Saxony, and built their own community called Herrnhut. Encouraged by Zinzendorf to spread their faith, missionaries were dispatched to much of the known world. The Moravians in North Carolina hoped to establish an independent church-based settlement (Thomas 1994:17). English and Scots-Irish settlers were also moving into this region of the Piedmont of North Carolina. One way the Moravians reinforced their ideas of community was through the built environment. This is particularly true in the earlier buildings they constructed, often half-timbered structures that clearly reflected their Germanic heritage. Later buildings, in contrast, hewed closer to the norms of their Anglo-American neighbors. The Moravian cemetery, where individuals were buried with their choir or social group, rather than their family, and had small uniform undecorated grave markers, speaks to their distinctiveness. A strangers' graveyard was also constructed so that the Moravians would not have to share their burial ground with outsiders.

Despite these clear efforts at exclusion, the community was a major center for trade and of manufacturing, particularly of pottery. Moravian potters made their own distinctive wares and also copied British wares with some success. The strength of Thomas' article is that he uses a variety of sources to examine his central thesis regarding maintenance of conformity in a unique ethno-religious community. The 19th century saw the decline of the distinctive Moravian community and its cultural absorption into the larger Carolina Piedmont community.

Halfway across the world from North Carolina, a later group of Moravians allows us to see how Christian missions have acted major nodes of culture change and have often been important components of the colonial enterprise. Jane Lydon's study, "Imagining the Moravian Mission: Space and Surveillance at the Former Ebenezer Mission, Victoria, Southeastern Australia" (2009), examines the history of a Moravian mission established in 1859 in Victoria, Australia. The site contains original mission buildings and a substantial archaeological record. Lydon's work in this article focuses on the mission as part of a landscape of power that was intended to coerce Aboriginal Australians into behaving like Europeans, and also embodied aspects of these power relationships in the landscape. While highlighting the influence of the Moravians in structuring Aboriginal policy, the article also suggests that they faced resistance from an Aboriginal population that was able and willing to maintain some traditional practices.

Alberta Zucchi's work at the San Francisco Church in Coro, Venezuela focuses on commemorative landscapes rather than landscapes of power, and provides interesting insights into changing Catholic burial practices (2006:57-68). She begins by outlining the history of Catholic burial from ancient catacombs, to the first burials of religious leaders in churches through to the burial of nobility, and eventually other parishioners in churches. The San Francisco Church was founded in 1527, although the current structures date from the early 1600s and later. Fifteen small excavation units were dug within the church in order

to locate subsurface features. These revealed a series of buried floors and numerous burials, including crypts and ossuaries. Remains of a few primary burials and some secondary burials were also noted. The excavations provided considerable new information about the evolution of the church and changing burial practices. Ossuaries and crypts for families were first constructed during the 19th century. Tombstones also became common during the 19th century. It was not until the early 20th century that in-church burial ceased in Venezuela. Zucchi's work is useful for providing a glimpse of burial practices in predominantly Catholic Latin America during the 17th, 18th, and 19th centuries, practices that stand in sharp contrast with those seen in contemporary North America.

In "Clay Faces in an Abolitionist Church: The Wesley and Methodist Church in Syracuse, New York" Douglas Armstrong and LouAnn Wurst examine an enigmatic series of sculpted clay faces found in a curious tunnel beneath the former Wesleyan Methodist Church in Syracuse New York. The historic importance of religion in African-American life was profound. Churches provided spiritual solace, safe havens for individuals escaping slavery for freedom, and provided educational opportunities for the disenfranchised, and even medicine for the sick. In Armstrong and Wurst's article, these faces, which were hidden beneath the church but known to congregants, may relate to the church's role as a local center for abolitionist activities. The church was founded by disaffected members of the local Methodist Episcopal Church. The new church was utilized as a station on the Underground Railroad (Armstrong and Wurst 2003:19). The origins of the clay faces are mysterious. Recent research indicates that they likely were created during the 19th century. Investigations at the site were carried out in the hopes of unearthing evidence of the basement passage's role in hiding escaping slaves; however, no clear evidence was uncovered linking the sculptures to the Underground Railroad. The preservation of the faces also became a major conservation challenge, but ultimately resulted in their preservation. Although the case for their having been created during the antebellum period is circumstantial, it is still convincing. Moreover, the faces came to be seen as symbols of an era in American history where individuals struggled for their freedom, often against daunting odds.

"Small Things" Material Culture

Historical archaeology's basic building blocks are artifacts, material expressions of cultural behavior, the detritus of past lives that James Deetz, quoting from a colonial household inventory called "…Small Things Forgotten" (1977). Material culture can reveal, confirm, and yet also obfuscate issues of religious behavior. The following case studies use material culture to examine issues of identity, a utopian society that rejected the dominant culture's values, the persistence of traditional African-American religious beliefs, and the layered meanings of Roman Catholic religious medals found on Native American sites in French North America.

Archaeology has the potential to provide considerable information about issues such as group identity. Stacy Kozakavich's study "Doukhobor Identity and Communalism at Kilovka Village Site in western Saskatchewan" (2006:119-132) is a particularly good example. The Doukhobor were immigrants from the Russian Empire who arrived on the Canadian prairies in the early 20th century. In some ways, they resembled Quakers in their belief in the guidance of an inner spirit and emphasis on equality and rejection of worldly government (Kozakavich 2006:19). They developed out of a split in the Russian Orthodox Church and, after considerable persecution and several changes of location within Russia, many emigrated to Canada lured by free homestead land and the opportunity for religious freedom. Their individual houses were identical, reflecting a belief in social equality. Due to internal and external factors, their communities were abandoned in the early 20th century. Kozakavich investigated a Doukhobor community called Kirilovka as part of a cultural resource management project associated with a highway improvement project. The Doukhobors were pacifists, vegetarians, and abstained from tobacco and alcohol. Interestingly, archaeological remains indicate that drinking may have played a role in village life as gin, wine, beer, and cognac bottles were recovered. Similarly, there was some evidence for meat consumption. While the community's layout spoke to issues of communalism, diverse ceramics may reflect individual purchases. Kozakavich argues that artifact patterns, which appear to indicate the abandonment of tradition, may instead reflect dynamic complex

processes shaping Doukhobor identity in a new land (2006:131). As such, her study is both informative in its own right and a cautionary tale for others studying similarly distinctive communities.

A different sort of utopian vision is provided by the headquarters of the Theosophical Society's headquarters at Point Loma, near San Diego, California (Van Wormer and Gross 2006:100-118). The 18th and 19th centuries saw the rise of a wide variety of alternative religious and utopian philosophies. Groups as diverse as Christian Scientists and Koreshans provided alternatives to more traditional Christian denominations. Some, such as the Shakers, began in the 18th century, while others, such as the Church of Jesus Christ of Latter Day Saints, date from the 19th century. Utopian groups, such as the followers of John Humphrey Noyes, who founded the Oneida Community in New York and was the first to use the term 'free love,' also thrived in this period. Charles Fourier's Fourierists founded utopian communities, or 'phalanxes' across the northeast, notably Brook Farm in Massachusetts and the North American phalanx in New Jersey.

One interesting alternative group that has seen archaeological investigation is the Theosophical Society, founded in 1875 by Madame Helena Petrovna Blavatsky and Henry Olcott. They hoped "to achieve a universal brotherhood of man through an ever increasing awareness of the relationship between the spirit of man and the universe" (Wormer and Gross 2006:101), and their surprisingly wide-ranging contemporary cultural influence reached as far as the Russian modernist composer Alexander Scriabin (Samson 1977). Their philosophy drew from the traditions of several major schools of religious thought, including Buddhism, Christianity, Hinduism, and Judaism. The society's California headquarters, founded by Madame Katherine Tingley, functioned as an agricultural commune, boarding school, and art colony (Wormer and Gross 2006:115). The school closed in 1940.

Stephen Wormer and G. Timothy Gross studied a sizeable dump associated with the community as part of a cultural resource management project. They were interested in learning how the Theosophical Society differed from the broader American society of the time, and in particular whether artifact patterns could be discerned that reflected the inhabitants' unique lifestyle. They compared their finds to those recovered from contemporary urban dumps in California and Arizona. The assemblage was quite distinctive, and does indeed seem to reflect the Theosophist's distinctive lifestyle. For instance, medicines largely consisted of homeopathic vials. There were fewer consumer goods, but larger quantities of beads and even art supplies, likely reflecting the distinctive curriculum of the school. Food remains also seem to reflect the distinctive foodways of the community. It appears that the Theosophists were successful in their rejection of the dominant consumer culture. Wormer and Gross' project provides a fascinating study of a successful early 20th century religious movement.

Laurie A. Wilkie's article "Secret and Sacred: Contextualizing the Artifacts of African-American Magic and Religion" (1997:81-106) examines the persistence of African American magical and religious practices in North America. Wilkie's work examines how magic and religion fulfilled different needs in African and African American society. Magic, especially magic intended to harm, provided African Americans with a means of retaliating against Euro-American violence (Wilkie 1997:83). While magical and religious beliefs provided a means or resistance, they simultaneously helped provide an explanation for how the world worked, and as such served to construct a community's cosmology.

Wilkie also discusses the role of magical and medical practitioners in the African American community: root doctors, conjurers, or Hoodoos. Wilkie's own research at an African American midwife's house site in Mobile, Alabama unearthed a collection of artifacts that may be related to midwifery (Wilkie 1997:85-86). Similarly, Kenneth Brown's work at the Levi-Jordan plantation revealed artifacts that may relate to traditional African American healing and magical practices (Brown and Cooper 1990). Wilkie's work is important for exploring the contexts of various magical practices among African and African American immigrants. She also deals with issues of death, gender, religious syncretism, and the continuance of traditional African religious systems in America. Her far-reaching work provides an excellent introduction to an important topic.

Marcel Moussette's article, "An Encounter in the Baroque Age: French and Amerindians in North America," does not emphasize the persistence of traditional beliefs, but instead uses material culture, and in particular religious medals, to explore areas of compatibility between French/Roman Catholic and Native American beliefs during the colonial period (2003:29-39). He situates his study by examining late Medieval France's move towards a capitalist economy, away from a feudal system that he contrasts with Native American modes of production based upon kinship ties. He employs the key concept of *métissages,* mixture or hybridity (Moussette 2003:30), to examine the exchange between Native Americans and Europeans and their descendants, the Creoles or métis of the colony. Mousette argues that for one cultural group to accept elements of another functional group, they must be able to integrate it into their system. Each group must have reasons for doing so. Moussette notes that "For the Amerindians, it is clear that such motives included commerce and power linked to the acquisition of European goods and technologies." Mousette also notes that the interaction must create a system in flux or crisis, but one in which there is some compatibility (2003:31). This interaction between Native Americans and the French occurred in the Baroque age, the period of the Counterreformation. Moussette views this period through the lens of religious medallions and draws parallels between Catholic religious iconography and Native Americans appropriation of these designs, resulting in a distinctive negotiated identity that spoke to both traditions, and was also uniquely Canadian.

Commemoration

Gravemarkers are a particularly important category of material culture as they were, and are, intentionally designed to convey information, with various levels of detail, to future generations. Following the pioneering work of James Deetz and Edwin Dethlefsen, numerous other scholars attempted to replicate their work in other locations. One of the first of these studies was carried out by Gaynell Stone in the 1970s and 1980s. Stone's specific focus was on 17th and 18th-century gravemarkers from Long Island, New York. Long Island is a particularly fruitful location to study early American gravemarkers as it is situated on a cultural fault line between New England and New Netherland, and due to its sandy soils was dependent upon imported stones. Stone's encyclopedic study, summarized in her article "Sacred Landscapes: Material Evidence of Ideological and Ethnic Choice in Long Island, New York Gravestones, 1680-1800" resulted in the recordation of more than 4,300 markers (2009:142-159).

Settlement of Long Island began in the early 1600s. Western Long Island fell within the culturally diverse Dutch colony of New Netherland, while eastern Long Island was settled in large part by New Englanders moving south and west. Stone was particularly interested in the trade patterns reflected by the gravemarkers and their connections with various ethnic and religious groups. Although, generally speaking, the number of gravemarkers increased over time, some groups were poorly represented, particularly enslaved African Americans. Curiously, while Long Island has a rich Native American heritage, gravemarkers for Native Americans were virtually nonexistent for the time period studied. Gravemarkers for Dutch settlers and English Quaker settlers are also underrepresented, Quakers particularly so. The latter were late in adopting formally carved markers and on Long Island seem to have preferred undecorated markers. Dutch language markers persisted into the early 19th century. Moreover, Dutch women continued to use their natal names, a traditional Dutch practice. The Dutch also seem to have eschewed mortality images, though they were quite popular with the English in eastern Long Island. Stone's meticulous work shows that gravemarkers have much to say about gender, ethnicity, religion, and trade networks. Although in a very general sense the tripartite Deetzian scheme works on Long Island, there are significant differences. Building from the work of cultural geographers, Stone employs the idea of a cultural hearth, the area where a culture "displays most strongly its essential features" (Zelinksy 1973:89 in Stone 2009:156). She concludes that "Gravestones are an enduring and traditional part of a people's culture and the cemetery is a nodal point of the social landscape. Both represent choices illustrating their beliefs; their presence provides a fuller record of an area's history" (Stone 2009:156-157).

Another important study of early American gravemarkers is James Garman's research on African American gravemarkers in Newport, Rhode Island. It provides a fascinating glimpse of commemorative practices in a distinctive and often forgotten early American community. Newport, Rhode Island, is perhaps best known for its Gilded Age mansions. It is also the home of the Touro Synagogue, America's oldest synagogue, an unparalleled collection of early American gravemarkers, and the John Stevens Shop, a gravestone carving business that has been in continuous operation since 1705. Garman's work, which builds on earlier research on New England gravemarkers, is unusual and important in that it focuses on race, or to quote W. E.B. Du Bois, the color line, and the dual consciousness of African Americans (Garman 1994:74). Garman's article examines what gravemarkers can tell us about attitudes towards race in colonial Newport, how the symbolic meanings of these artifacts be read, and how "reception theory enables historical archaeologists to link African American pasts with the sociopolitics of practicing historical archaeology in the present" (Garman 1994:75). More than ten percent of the population of colonial Newport was enslaved, and many slaves lived in urban white households. Some authors have seen this as evidence of a "kinder, gentler, Northern slavery" (Mason 1884:104). In contrast, others have noted that household slavery of this form would have resulted in very high degree of surveillance, and perhaps heightened tension.

Garman's study focuses on the African American section of Newport's Common Burying ground, a segregated space within a larger burial ground. Garman examines the size, placement, cost, and inscriptions of the markers, and probes what these markers might have meant, to the individuals interred there, the carvers who produced the stones, and the slaveholders who purchased them. The late 18th and early 19th centuries saw the Rhode Island General Assembly taking gradual steps to stop the important of slavery, and emancipate those already enslaved. The result was a confusing system of free and enslaved. During this period, markers for African American men and women grew larger and became less distinctive from those of their Euro-American contemporaries. Markers tended not to mention the ethnicity of the deceased (Garman 1994:88). Garman's work is important for expanding the vision of archaeologists studying the lives of enslaved African Americans, helping to create a more inclusive view of the past, while at the same time looking at the distinctive and shifting position African Americans held in early Rhode Island and the insights gravemarkers can provide into their lives and times.

Harold Mytum's work on 18th century memorials in western Ulster, Ireland, illustrates how gravemarkers may reinforce or challenge religious beliefs (2009:160-182), and these memorials present a fascinating counterpoint to the somewhat better known gravemarkers of colonial New England. This is particularly true because of the dynamics of class, ethnicity, and of course, religion being played out in Ireland during this period. As Mytum notes, "gravemarkers are potent artifacts, consciously created to serve private commemorative purposes but also to act as a public and visible statement regarding both the deceased and their families" (2009:160). Data from both Catholic and Protestant burial grounds were recorded. Some of the markers were decorated with mortality symbols, and Mytum makes the important point that they could be read in very different ways. He demonstrates mortality images were not solely the domain of Protestants; indeed, the Catholic Counterreformation, which had its own iconography, sometimes employed them as a means of creating an environment for prayer, thereby reducing the deceased's time in purgatory (Mytum 2009:164; Ariès 1985:463). This article is important for highlighting the many different messages regarding class, ethnicity, and religion embodied by gravemarkers, and could provide a model for fruitful work elsewhere.

Another important contribution to understanding of practices of commemoration and memorial landscapes is Paul Prince's article (2002:50-65), "Cultural Coherence and Resistance in Historic-Period Northwest-Coast Mortuary Practices at Kimsquit." This article examines mortuary practices among the Kimsquit on the central coast of British Columbia, using a late 19th-century Kimsquit cemetery as its focal point. This is a tale of resistance, viewed through the lens of material culture, particular burial practices, grave goods, and mortuary monuments. Prince shows that the Kimsquit maintained their traditional values during a period of intense cultural change. Despite the known resistance of the Kimsquit people to Euro-Canadian attempts to impose their religious and cultural ideas, the cemetery shows significant change in burial mode, form of monuments, and occurrence of European grave goods (Prince 2002:53).

Drawing from photographs, and documentation of the extant cemetery, Prince shows that changes did occur in burial practices. Essentially, changes in acculturative forces led to new technology being employed in traditional ways to mark and commemorate their dead. As the Kimsquits were encouraged to move into smaller dwellings they put more effort into the construction of conspicuous dwellings for the dead.

Grave goods also prove revealing. Typically the deceased's personal possessions were burned after their death to prevent sickness among the living and to send these goods on the underworld. The remaining goods were placed in a grave house (Prince 2002:56). The persistence of traditional beliefs and indeed the disposal of expensive goods show a desire to send wealth to the deceased in the underworld. Markers also evolved from posts or planks carved with lineage information to plain poles commemorating ceremonies the deceased had hosted. They show the continued importance of the potlatch even after it was banned in 1884. Prince's fascinating article shows that although changes in mortuary practice at Kimsquit were rapid, they were consistent with and indeed served to reinforce traditional beliefs, rather than reflecting assimilation into Euro-Canadian society.

David Burley's study of Tongan burial practices brings us fully into the 20th century (1995:75-83). His topic is the social meaning of gravemarkers found in the Polynesian kingdom of Tonga. What is particularly interesting about the study is how different Tongan interpretations of the gravemarkers are from those posited by the archaeologist. Tonga's history is discussed from first contact with the outside world in the 17th century, to its transformation into a constitutional monarchy in 1875. Traditionally Tongan leaders were buried in elaborate earthen mounds, often faced with blocks of beach stone. As Burley describes them, Tongan burial grounds or *mala'e* contain a wide range of burial markers from grave houses to tombstones, but share the fact that all graves are covered with white sand and often decorated with beer bottles (Burley 1995:77). The beer bottles are used to mark the outline of the grave.

Kava, a mildly fermented drink made from the crushed root of the pepper shrub, is the favorite national drink. Western alcoholic beverages were introduced to Tonga by explorers, and by the early

20th century had become quite popular; however, they were very expensive. Today, with the establishment of a domestic brewery and increasing travel by Tongans, alcoholic beverages have become much more common. According to Burley, beer drinking could potentially be seen as part of modernity and progress, and given the expense of alcoholic beverages, the beer bottle encrusted graves might therefore be seen as marking the lifestyles of the deceased. The form of the graves is also interesting in that the bottles and cans form tiered boundaries, much like stone facing on chiefly burial mounds (Burley 1995:79). There also seems to be a color preference for brown over green bottles.

It would seem that the bottle-decorated gravemarkers are replete with meaning; however, as Burley notes, discussions with Tongan informants did not corroborate the beliefs of the archaeologists. Indeed, the Tongans claimed the bottles were just decorations (Burley 1995:80), and the prevalence of brown bottles over green was merely predicated on the local bottle recycling plant only accepting green glass. Burley's study intentionally serves as a cautionary tale, juxtaposing the views of anthropologists with those of the practitioners themselves, with very different results.

Human Remains and Grave Goods

In addition to gravemarkers and other forms of above-ground commemoration, human remains and grave goods have the potential to provide volumes of information about past religious beliefs. The orientation of graves, the presence or absence of grave goods, the use and ornamentation of coffins, and the remains within them all are sources of information about past cultural beliefs.

St. Mary's City in Maryland is one of North America's most intensively studied 17th-century sites. Timothy Riordan has carried out extensive research at the cemetery associated with the ca. 1667 Brick Chapel that has recently been reconstructed at the site. His work has provided considerable insights into the evolution of the site (Riordan 1997, 2009). Riordan's article, "The 17th-Century Cemetery at St. Mary's City: Mortuary Practices in the Early Chesapeake" focuses on grave shaft orientation and

wooden gravemarkers. Although grave shafts may seem decidedly less interesting than the skeletal remains that may be recovered from them, their location, orientation, fill, and associated features can provide important insights into a society's beliefs. St. Mary's City's first chapel was constructed in the 1640s and was an earthfast structure. A substantial brick chapel replaced it in the 1660s. In 1704 the Brick Chapel was closed, and is believed to have been torn down shortly thereafter. Aside from the extensive subterranean archaeological traces of the chapel, there were no aboveground remains associated with the structure present, though a modern reconstruction now stands on the site.

Initially excavated in the 1930s (Forman 1938:249-251), the chapel was completely exposed by archaeologists from Historic St. Mary's City in 1989-1990 (Riordan 1997:29). The property was excavated using a 5% random sample followed by block excavations around known or suspected buildings. The graves themselves were recorded, their fill content sampled, and evidence of markers was noted (Riordan 1997:30). Generally speaking, in traditional English Christian burial, graves were oriented with their long axes on an east-west line, with the deceased's head to the west. Riordan found that while many of the graves were oriented east west, there is some variation, which he attributes in part to these graves being oriented parallel to some of the structures and other landscape features present in the cemetery. Indeed, he is able to demonstrate that some graves predate, while others postdate, the chapel based on their orientation. Riordan hypothesized that grave shaft forms may provide evidence of burial in coffins or shrouds. Finally, unlike New England burial grounds, Maryland's early burial places have very few gravemarkers. Indeed, carved tombstones were not common at all before the mid-18th century. Roughly 16 percent of the burials found in the cemetery show evidence of what were likely wooden markers. These may have been crosses, grave rails, or dead boards. Some were oriented parallel and above the graves others were perpendicular to the heads of the graves. So even in sites where it appears there is very little to say about the burials considerable information can be gleaned from the stains in the soil as seen at the Chapel Burying Ground. Riordan's subsequent publications on the site have emphasized the variety of coffin forms and their cultural derivation (Riordan 2009). This work shows a movement towards more regular coffin construction, and an emphasis on non-Catholic English practices over Catholic traditions in areas such as the placement of deceased's hands.

Few religious groups had such a strong impact on early American life and culture as the Religious Society of Friends or Quakers. Founded in the 17th century, they believed in a doctrine of inner light, the idea that all humans carried within them the spark of the divine and that there was no need for priests, ministers, or a sacraments as God spoke directly to the individual. They were also strong advocates for abolition, the rights of women, prisoners, and the mentally ill. Furthermore, Quakers are famous for their plain style, reflected in architecture, clothing, speech, and gravemarkers. Persecuted in England as non-conformists, many emigrated to the Delaware Valley, where the prominent Quaker, William Penn, founded Pennsylvania, in part, as a safe haven for religious dissidents. Quaker settlement was not, however, limited to Pennsylvania, and also occurred in New Jersey, Maryland, Delaware, Virginia, Rhode Island, the Caribbean, and indeed many other locations. In their article, "The Quaker Burying Ground in Alexandria, Virginia: A Study of Burial Practices of the Religious Society of Friends" (2006:57-88) Francine Bromberg and Steven Shepard examine the Quaker Burying Ground in Alexandria, Virginia in light of Quaker beliefs. Their study focused on an 18th and 19th century burial ground that was to be impacted by the construction of an addition to a library.

Quaker burials, fitting their faith, were described by contemporaries as restrained, lacking the ostentation seen in some other denominations, with plain coffins, and were often unmarked. Although some meetings later relented and allowed gravemarkers, those that were used were minimalist so as not to condone social distinctions (Bromberg and Shepard 2006:63).

Alexandria's Quaker community began in the mid-18th century, and was deeply concerned with abolition. Their meeting ground was established in the late 18th century and burials were certainly occurring by the early 19th century. The 19th century saw a revolution in attitudes towards death and

burial in early America. This is sometimes called the beautification of death movement (Bromberg and Shepard 2006:64). The trappings of this movement included increasingly elaborate gravemarkers, elaborate caskets, ornate mourning clothes, and the like. Mass production of hardware, and the increasingly mechanized production of gravemarkers, allowed this movement to permeate nearly all classes of society.

Although the cemetery had long since stopped being used as a burial ground, and the Quaker community encouraged the use of the property for a socially beneficial purpose, such as a library, they decided to allow limited examination of the human remains. One hundred fifty nine burial features were identified and 66 were excavated. The addition to the library was also designed so as to minimally impact the burial ground. The majority of burials were in wooden coffins, with one in a cast iron coffin and one in a wooden coffin placed in a brick vault. These appear to be exceptions to the Quaker ethos discussed earlier, but may relate to the need to move the deceased from some other location or perhaps how ubiquitous iron coffins had become by the mid-19th century. Several coffins had also been covered with gray clay that acted as a shield around the burial. Coffins indicate that the Friends preferred simple traditional forms (Bromberg and Shepard 2006:73). However, hinges, which would have allowed the deceased to be viewed, were present on several of the coffins, which accords with the Beautification of Death concept. Generally speaking, the early 19th century burials showed little evidence for elaborate mourning trappings, although some decorative coffin hinges, and handles, associated with later burials speak to the growing cult of commemoration. The recovered artifacts highlight the attempts of Alexandria's Friends to uphold the value of simplicity during the 18th and 19th centuries. Moreover, the collection as a whole reflects the value of material culture for examining issues of cultural beliefs and change.

Another important article dealing with burial practices is Christina J. Hodge's "Faith and Practice at an Early-Eighteenth-Century Wampanoag Burial Ground: The Waldo Farm Site in Dartmouth, Massachusetts" (2005:73-94). The interaction of Native American and Euro-American populations in early America has seen intensive archaeological study. Many of the best-known sites from this period in the northeast are cemeteries (Grumet 1995:113, 177 in Hodge 2005:73). Early scholars focused on documenting the presence and quantity of trade goods in an effort to trace the supposed decline of Native American communities and their increasing level of acculturation. Hodge notes that Native American burial grounds differ from those of Euro-Americans in their spatial organization, choice of grave markers, and in the presence of grave goods. Hodge's study focused on the Waldo Farm site in southern Massachusetts. It was used by Christianized Wampanoag's during the early 18th century (Hodge 2005:74). Unlike many Native American burial grounds from this period, the individuals interred in the Waldo Farm burial ground holds few grave goods. How is this to be interpreted? By employing a holistic approach including folk history, historical documentation, tribal oral histories, and archaeological data, Hodge is able to "explain the absence of grave goods in light of accommodation, ambivalence, and a persistent Wampanoag identity" (Hodge 2005:75). The area's earliest European settlers were Quakers who arrived in the mid-16th century. During King Philip's War, the area saw considerable conflict, and it seems likely that captured Wampanoags from the area were sent to the West Indies as slaves (Hodge 2005:76).

Excavations at the site first occurred in 1924 under the direction of Harry Shapiro, after property owner John Lincoln Waldo unearthed the remains of three individuals. Shapiro unearthed an additional 34 graves. The site is likely associated with a burial ground donated by Quaker John Slocum to the local Native American population, and was used for the first half of the 18th century. With the exception of shroud pins, no grave goods were recovered with the bodies. This is noteworthy, as Quakers employed shrouds for burials while Native Americans during this period often buried individuals fully clothed. Simple fieldstone grave markers are present which fits well with Quaker beliefs that eschewed elaborate grave markers. The cemetery appears irregular in form and grave orientation is somewhat variable, though over 17% of the Waldo burials have the head to the west, thereby conforming with contemporary Christian practices (Hodge 2005:80). Complicating matters, this would also fit with Native beliefs, which placed the dwelling of the creator to the southwest.

Hodge employs postcolonial theory in her interpretation of the burial ground. As she notes, "Postcolonial theory mandates the critical investigation of colonizer and colonized interaction in its multiple, dynamic, and situationally dependant forms" (Hodge 2005:84). This is not a straightforward but rather a conflicted discourse. Mimicry and imitation of European cultural norms, may not simply indicate the acculturation of the Natives, but a subversive employment. Rather the colonizer and the colonized must be seen as linked as unified, but at the same time divided from their larger societies. Unlike the authoritative Puritans, the Quakers had no single message, they established no missions and oversaw no praying towns; rather they preached the gospel to both Native Americans and Euro-Americans. The lack of gave goods may reflect a lack of tension regarding social structures. Hodge concludes by citing Kathleen Bragdon who has argued that "Christianity played a positive role in the maintenance of distinct native communities in the eighteenth century" (Hodge 2005:88). Quakers in particular may have found their beliefs particularly attractive to Native Americans during a period of redefinition and change.

Another important study of a burial ground, indeed one of the best known excavations of a historic burial ground in North America, is the excavation of New York City's African Burial Ground. This study began in 1991 when excavations for a new Federal Building in lower Manhattan unearthed the remains of a large burial ground used by African Americans and other disenfranchised members of colonial New York City's population. Ultimately, over 400 burials were excavated from the site, as well as a significant collection of artifacts. The burials were later reinterred and the site designated as a National Historic Landmark. The recovery of a substantial collection of African American skeletal remains from an urban setting, dating to the 17th and 18th centuries provided an unprecedented opportunity to study the population's geographic origins, investigate the physical quality of life for these people who were primarily enslaved, and learn about "the biocultural transformations of these people from African to African American identities" (Mack and Blakey 2004:10). Also of interest was the issue of modes of resistance. The approach taken by the team investigating these burials is best termed "biocultural and biohistorical" in that "it examines the historical interactions of biology and culture such that data on each inform the other and... that human biology is interpreted within historically specific, sociocultural contexts" (Mack and Blakey 2004:11). Even at a preliminary level, DNA and skeletal evidence shows similarities to populations in Benin, Nigeria, and other parts of West Africa. There are also cultural modifications generally found in sub-Saharan Africa, such as dental modifications. One challenge that the researchers have faced is that earlier scholars tended to lump African American materials together rather than treating them as representative of distinct populations.

The skeletal remains show the effects of heavy labor. Physical traces of anemia, infection, and torn muscle attachments are all present. However, the story of the African Burial Ground is not simply about what the bones may tell us. It is also a story of a negotiated past, where we see the initial reluctance of the U.S. General Services Administration to adequately study the remains, and the role of an engaged and politically active public and descendant community, which mounted a concerted effort to carefully excavate and analyze the remains. The scholars involved in the study characterize themselves as activist scholars. Their research provides a model for other scholars working with descendant communities and indeed highlights the importance of communities in shaping the interpretation of such sites and even their excavation.

Edward Bell's study of coffin hardware from Uxbridge, Massachusetts examines changing 19th century American attitudes towards death. In Bell's words, "Deathways encompasses the whole cultural system of mortuary behavior, involving emotion, ideology, symbolism, technology, and economy" (Bell 1990:54). His focus is on a particular aspect of the material culture of death, coffin hardware, especially mass- produced coffin hardware and what it reveals about changing attitudes towards death in 19th-century America. Previous studies have presented coffin hardware as an indication of socioeconomic rank. As Bell notes, this is an unsatisfactory explanation for the materials recovered from a pauper's burial ground. Bell provides an alternative yet convincing explanation. Rather than seeing these mass market objects reflecting true wealth, Bell views them as material evidence of the pervasive cultural notion of the beautification of death, and also objects designed to impart of a sense of socioeconomic stature otherwise not attainable for these individuals (Bell 1990:55). This was a cultural shift that was tectonic in scale, and was linked to new romantic views of death and mourning, which came together with the rise of the funeral industry and mass production of coffin hardware in sentimental styles. There was a trend towards more decorative coffins, and indeed caskets that might be seen as display boxes rather than simply coffins.

Bell's case study, the burial ground associated with the Uxbride Alsmhouse, apparently provided for economic but respectable burial of the dead. The archaeological evidence provides some collaboration of this minimal investment in burials. Gravemarkers were simple granite spalls, coffins were minimalist and often ill made; however, several did display embellishments associated with the beautification of death. Bell's work cautions us that mass-produced coffin hardware should not be used as an unequivocal indication of socioeconomic rank. Rather, the coffin hardware may have been used to mask the nature of socioeconomic distance between classes (Bell 1990:72).

Conclusions

These articles illustrate just some of the topics that historical archaeologists interested in religion and its material correlates have studied. They examine different investigative methods, from the technical, such as the use of forensic analysis to unravel the last moments of massacre victims; to faunal analysis, employed by Abernathy and Ruff as they explore the religiosity of an antebellum southern Jewish family; through public archaeology as seen in the work of Sherene Baugher at the John Street Methodist church; and finally, spatial analysis as employed by John Lawrence and his colleagues to better understand the disintegration of an 18th-century religious community.

Studies of landscapes and places are also important. The Ebenezer Mission provides an example of a Moravian mission to Australia's Aborigines and how its organization was used to shape lives and in turn became part of the meaningful landscape for the area's original inhabitants. Zucchi explores burial practices in a Catholic Church. Issues of ethnicity, the Underground Railroad, abolitionism, and memory are all present in Armstrong and Wurst's article on curious clay faces found beneath an abolitionist church. Thomas' study of the Moravian settlement shows how one distinctive ethno-religious community strove to maintain its traditions.

Material culture provides clues to peoples' belief systems. From the struggles of the Doukhobor's to maintain their identity to an unusual cult's refuse, and what it tells us about their philosophy, artifacts reveal beliefs and practices. Material culture also informs the study of the traces of African American magic and religion in Laurie Wilkie's work, and the interaction of Roman Catholic beliefs in the Counterreformation with Native American beliefs through Mousette's study of religious medals.

Gravemarkers can be sensitive indicators of trade networks, religious beliefs, and issues of race, though as David Burley points out, meanings that seem obvious to the archaeologist may not resonate with the people who created the sites. Finally, to quote Hebrews 11:4, "he being dead yet speaketh," so too do the human remains unearthed at the burial grounds studied by Riordan in Maryland, Bromberg and Shepherd in Virginia, Mack and Blakey in New York, and Bell in Massachusetts. Over the past three decades, historical archaeologists have drawn considerable insights into the past religious beliefs and behaviors from their studies. Nonetheless, there are still many topics that bear further exploration, and it is hoped that this volume will serve to inspire those future studies by offering an overview of what has gone before.

References

ARIÈS, PHILIPPE
1985   *Images of Man and Death*. Janet Lloyd, translator. Harvard University Press, Cambridge, MA.

ARMSTRONG, DOUGLAS, AND LOUANN WURST
2003   Clay Faces in an Abolitionist Church: The Wesleyan Methodist Church in Syracuse, New York. *Historical Archaeology* 37(2):19-37.

ASTON, MICK
2009   *Monasteries in the Landscape*. Amberley Publishing, Stroud, United Kingdom.

BAHN, PAU. G. (EDITOR)
1996   *The Cambridge Illustrated History of Archaeology*. Cambridge University Press, Cambridge, United Kingdom.

BAUGHER, SHERENE
2009   The John Street Methodist Church: An Archaeological Excavation with Native American Cooperation. *Historical Archaeology* 43(1):46-64.

BAUGHER, SHERENE B., GERARD P. SCHARFENBERGER, AND RICHARD F. VEIT (GUEST EDITORS)
2009   Historical Archaeology of Religious Sites and Cemeteries. *Historical Archaeology* 43(1).

BAUGHER, SHERENE, AND FREDERICK WINTER
1983   Early American Gravestones: Archaeological Perspectives on Three Cemeteries of Old New York. *Archaeology* 36(5):46-53.

BELL, EDWARD L.
1990   The Historical Archaeology of Mortuary Behavior: Coffin Hardware from Uxbridge, Massachusetts. *Historical Archaeology* 24(3):54-78.

BENEDICT, RUTH
1938   Religion. In *General Anthropology*, F. Boas, (editor), pp. 628-629. D.C. Heath and Co., New York, NY.

BENES, PETER
1977   *The Masks of Orthodoxy: Folk Gravestone Carvings in Plymouth County Massachusetts 1689-1805*. The University of Massachusetts Press, Amherst.

BOND, JAMES
2003   *Monastic Landscapes*. Tempus, Stroud, United Kingdom.

BREW, J. O.
1994   St. Francis at Awatovi. In *Pioneers in Historical Archaeology: Breaking New Ground*, edited by Stanley South, pp. 27-47. Plenum Press, New York, NY.

BROMBERG, FRANCINE W., AND STEVEN J. SHEPHARD
2006   The Quaker Burying Ground in Alexandria, Virginia: A Study of Burial Practices of the Religious Society of Friends. *Historical Archaeology* 40(1):57-88.

BROOKS, ALASDAIR, SUSAN LAWRENCE, AND JANE LENNON
    2011   The Parsonage of the Reverend Willoughby Bean: Church, State and Frontier Settlement in 19th-Century Colonial Australia. *Historical Archaeology* 45(2) in press

BROWN, KENNETH L., AND DOREEN C. COOPER
    1990   Structural Continuity in an African-American Slave and Tennant Community. *Historical Archaeology* 24(4):7-19.

BURLEY, DAVID V.
    1995   Contexts and Meaning: Beer Bottles and Cans in Contemporary Burial Practices in the Polynesian Kingdom of Tonga. *Historical Archaeology* 29(1):75-83.

CERAM, C. W.
    1951   *Gods, Graves, and Scholars: The Study of Archaeology*. Knopf, New York, NY.

CORDELL, LINDA S.
    1992   Durango to Durango: An Overview of the Southwest Heartland. In *Columbian Consequences, Vol. 1 Archaeological and Historical Perspectives on the Spanish Borderlands West*. David Hurst Thomas, editor, pp. 17-41. Smithsonian Institution Press, Washington, DC.

COSTELLO, JULIA G., AND DAVID HORNBECK
    1992   Alta California: An Overview. In *Columbian Consequences, Vol. 1, Archaeological and Historical Perspectives on the Spanish Borderlands West*, David Hurst Thomas, editor, pp. 303-333. Smithsonian Institution Press, Washington, DC.

CROWELL, ELIZABETH ANNE
    1981   Philadelphia Gravestones: 1740-1820. *Northeast Historical Archaeology*. 10:23-29.
    1983   Migratory Monuments and Missing Motifs: Archaeology Analysis of Mortuary Art in Cape May County, New Jersey, 1740-1810. Ph.D. disertation, Department of Anthropology, University of Pennsylvania.

CROWELL, ELIZABETH A., AND NORMAN VARDNEY MACKIE III
    1984   "Depart From Hence and Keep This Thought in Mind": The Importance of Comparative Analysis in Gravestone Research. *Northeast Historical Archaeology* 13: 9-16.

DANIEL, GLYNN
    1967   *The Origins and Growth of Archaeology*. Pelican, Harmondsworth, United Kingdom.

DAVIS, NATHANIEL
    2003   *A Long Walk to Church; a Contemporary History of the Russian Orthodox Church*. Westview Press, Boulder, CO.

DE CUNZO, LU ANN, THERESE O'MALLEY, MICHAEL J. LEWIS, GEORGE E. THOMAS, AND CHRISTA WILLMANNS-WELLS
    1996   Father Rapp's Garden at Economy: Harmony Society Culture in Microcosm. In *Landscape Archaeology*, Rebecca Yamin and Karen Bescherer Metheny, editors, pp, 99-117. University of Tennessee Press, Knoxville.

DE CUNZO, LUANN AND JOHN H. JAMESON, JR.
    2005   *Unlocking the Past: Celebrating Historical Archaeology in North America*. University of Florida Press, Gainesville.

DEETZ, JAMES, AND EDWIN DETHLEFSEN
    1965   The Doppler Effect and Archaeology: A Consideration of the Spatial Aspects of Seriation. *Southwestern Journal of Anthropology* 21(3):196-206.
    1967   "Death's Head, Cherub, Urn and willow" *Natural History*. Vol. 76, No. 3, 29-37.
    1971   Some Social Aspects of New England Colonial Mortuary Art. *American Antiquity* 36:30-38.

DEETZ, JAMES
    1977   *In Small Things Forgotten*. Anchor Books, New York, NY.
    1978   Archaeological Investigations at La Purisima Mission. In *Historical Archaeology: A Guide to Substantive and Theoretical Contributions*, Robert L. Schuyler, editor, pp. 160-190. Baywood Publishing Company, Farmingdale, NY.

DETHLEFSEN, EDWIN, AND JAMES DEETZ
    1966   Deaths Heads, Cherubs and Willow Trees: Experimental Archaeology in Colonial Cemeteries. *American Antiquity* 31:4, 502-510.

FAGAN, BRIAN M.
    2005   *A Brief History of Archaeology, Classical Times to the Twenty-First Century*. Pearson/Prentice Hall, Upper Saddle River, NJ.

FAUST, DREW GILPIN
    2008   *This Republic of Suffering: Death and the American Civil War*. Alfred A. Knopf, New York, NY.

FORMAN, HENRY CHANDLEE
    1938   *Jamestown and St. Mary's, Buried Cities of Romance*. The Johns Hopkins Press, Baltimore, MD.

GARMAN, JAMES C.
    1994   Viewing the Color Line through the Material Culture of Death. *Historical Archaeology* 28(3):74-92.

GLASSIE, HENRY H.
    1969   *Pattern in the Material Folk Culture of the Eastern United States*. Philadelphia, University of Pennsylvania Press, Philadelphia.

GORMAN, FREDERICK, AND MICHAEL DIBLASI
1976   Nonchronological Sources of Variation in the Se-riation of Gravestone Motifs in the Northeast and Southeast Colonies. In *Puritan Gravestone Art*, edited by Peter Benes, pp. 79-87. Boston University Press, Boston, MA.

GRADWOHL, DAVID MEYER
1997   Cemetery Symbols and Contexts of American Indian Indentity: The Grave of Painter and Poet T. C. Cannon. *Markers: Annual Journal of the Association for Gravestone Studies* 14:1-34.
1998   "Bendichta Sea Vuestra Memoria": Sephardic Jewish Cemeteries in the Caribbean and Eastern North America. *Markers: Annual Journal of the Association for Gravestone Studies* 15:vi,1-29.

GRUMET, ROBERT
1995   *Historic Contact: Indian Peoples and Colonists in Today's Northeastern United States in the Sixteenth through Eighteenth Centuries.* University of Oklahoma Press, Norman, OK.

HALL, DAVID D.
1976   The Gravestone Image as a Puritan Cultural Code. In *Puritan Gravestone Art*, edited by Peter Benes, pp. 23-32. Boston University Press, Boston, MA.

HALL, DEREK
2006   *Scottish Monastic Landscapes.* Tempus, Stroud, United Kingdom.

HALL, MARTIN, AND STEPHEN W. SILLIMAN (EDITORS)
2006   *Historical Archaeology.* Blackwell Publishing, Malden, MA.

HESTER, THOMAS R.
1992   Texas and Northeastern Mexico: An Overview. In *Columbian Consequences, Vol. 1, Archaeological and Historical Perspectives on the Spanish Borderlands West.* David Hurst Thomas, editor, pp. 191-211. Smithsonian Institution Press, Washington, DC.

HICKS, DAN, AND MARY C. BEAUDRY (EDITORS)
2006   *The Cambridge Companion to Historical Archaeology.* Cambridge University Press, Cambridge, United Kingdom.

HODGE, CHRISTINA J.
2005   Faith and Practice at an Early Eighteenth-Century Wampanoag Burial Ground: The Waldo Farm Site in Dartmouth, Massachusetts. *Historical Archaeology* 39(4)73-94.

JACKSON, KENNETH AND CAMILLO VERGARA
1989   *Silent Cities: The Evolution of the American Cemetery.* Princeton Architectural Press, Princeton, NJ.

JAMIESON, ROSS W.
1995   Material Culture and Social Death: African American Burial Practices. *Historical Archaeology* 29(4):39-58.

KIDD, KENNETH E.
1994   The Phoenix of the North. In *Pioneers in Historical Archaeology: Breaking New Ground*, edited by Stanley South, pp. 48-66. Plenum Press, New York, NY.

KOZAKAVICH, STACY C.
2006   Doukhobor Identity and Communalism at Kirilovka Village Site. *Historical Archaeology* 40(1):119-132.

LANE, PAUL
2001   The Archaeology of Christianity in Global Perspective. In *Archaeology and World Religion*, T. Insoll, editor, pp. 148-171. Routledge, London, United Kingdom.

LAWRENCE, JOHN W., PAUL W. SCHOPP, AND ROBERT J. LORE
2009   "They Even Threaten the Sick That they will Not be Buried in the Churchyard": Salvage Archaeology of the Raritan-in-the-Hills Cemetery, Somerset County, New Jersey. *Historical Archaeology* 43(1):93-114.

LEONE, MARK P.
1973   Archaeology as the Science of Technology: Mormon Town Plans and Fences. In *Research and Theory in Current Archaeology*, Charles Redman, editor, pp. 125-150. John Wiley and Sons, New York, NY.
1977   The New Mormon Temple in Washington, D.C. In *Historical Archaeology and the Importance of Material Things.* Leland G. Ferguson, editor, pp. 43-61. Special Publication Series 2. The Society for Historical Archaeology, California, PA.

LUDWIG, ALLAN
1966   *Graven Images.* Wesleyan University Press, Middletown, CT.

LYDON, JANE
2009   Imagining the Moravian Mission: Space and Surveillance at the Former Ebenezer Mission, Victoria, Southeastern Australia. *Historical Archaeology* 43(3):5-19.

MACK, MARK E., AND MICHAEL L. BLAKEY
2004   The New York African Burial Ground Project: Past Biases, Current Dilemmas, and Future Research Opportunities. *Historical Archaeology* 38(1):10-17.

MASON, GEORGE CHAPMAN
1884   *Reminiscences of Newport.* Charles E. Hammett Jr., Newport, Rhode Island.

McEwan, Bonnie (editor)
    1993   *The Missions of La Florida*. University of Florida Press, Gainesville.

Merrifield, Ralph
    1987   *The Archaeology of Ritual and Magic*. New Amsterdam, NY.

Mousette, Marcel
    2003   An Encounter in the Baroque Age: French and Amerindians in North America. *Historical Archaeology* 37(4):29-39.

Mytum, Harold
    2000   *Recording and Analysing Graveyards*. Council for British Archaeology Handbook 15. Council for British Archaeology, York, United Kingdom,.
    2004   *Mortuary Monuments and Burial Grounds of the Historic Period*. Kluwer Academic/Plenum, New York, NY.
    2009   Mortality Symbols in Action: Protestant and Catholics Memorials in Early-Eighteenth-Century West Ulster. *Historical Archaeology* 43(1):160-182.

Noël Hume, Ivor
    1996   *In Search of this and That: Tales from an Archaeologist's Quest*. Colonial Williamsburg Foundation, Williamsburg, VA.

Novak, Shannon A., and Derinna Kopp
    2003   To Feed a Tree in Zion: Osteological Analysis of the 1857 Mountain Meadows Massacre. *Historical Archaeology* 37(2):85-108.

Potter, Parker B., Jr.
    1991   What is the Use of Plantation Archaeology? *Historical Archaeology* 25(3):94-108.

Price, H. Marcus III
    1991   *Disputing the Dead: U.S. Law on Aboriginal Remains and Grave Goods*. University of Missouri Press, Columbia.

Prince, Paul
    2002   Cultural Coherency and Resistance in Historic-Period Northwest-Coast Mortuary Practices at Kimsquit. *Historical Archaeology* 36(4):50-65.

Pykles, Benjamin C.
    2010   *Excavating Nauvoo: The Mormons and the Rise of Historical Archaeology in North America*. University of Nebraska Press, Lincoln.

Riordan, Timothy
    1997   The 17th-Century Cemetery at St. Mary's City: Mortuary Practices in the Early Chesapeake. *Historical Archaeology* 31(4):28-40.
    2009   "Carry Me to Yon Kirk Yard": An Investigation of Changing Burial Practices in the Seventeenth-Century Cemetery at St. Mary's City, Maryland." *Historical Archaeology* 43(1):81-92.

Rodwell, Warwick
    1981   *Archaeology of the English Church: The Study of Historic Churches and Churchyards*. B. T. Batsford, London, United Kingdom.

Samson, Jim
    1977   *Music in Transition: A Study of Tonal Expansion and Atonality, 1900–1920*. W. W. Norton & Company, New York, NY.

Sloane, David Charles
    1991   *The Last Great Necessity, Cemeteries in American History*. Johns Hopkins University Press, Baltimore, MD.

Starbuck, David R.
    1984   The Shaker Concept of Household. *Man in the Northeast* 28:73-86.
    1990   Canterbury Shaker Village: Archaeology and Landscape. *The New Hampshire Archaeologist* 31(1):1-163.

Steadman, Sharon R.
    2009   *The Archaeology of Religion; Cultures and Their Beliefs in Worldwide Context*. Left Coast Press, Walnut Creek, CA.

Stewart-Abernathy, Leslie C. and Barbara Ruff
    1989   A Good Man in Israel: Zooarchaeology and Assimilation in Antebellum Washington, Arkansas. *Historical Archaeology* 23(2):96-112.

Stone, Gaynell
    2009   Sacred Landscapes: Material Evidence of Ideological and Ethnic Choice in Long Island, New York, Gravestones, 1680-1800. *Historical Archaeology* 43(1): 142-159.

Tarlow, Sarah
    1999   *Bereavement and Commemoration: An Archaeology of Mortality*. Cambridge University Press, Cambridge, United Kingdom.

Thomas, Brian W.
    1994   Inclusion and Exclusion in the Moravian Settlement in North Carolina, 1770-1790. *Historical Archaeology* 28(3):15-29.

Thomas, David H.
    1993   The Archaeology of Santa Catalina de Guale: Our First 15 Years. In *The Missions of La Florida*. Bonnie McEwan, editor, pp. 1-34. University of Florida Press, Gainesville.

TRIGGER, BRUCE
    1989   *A History of Archaeological Thought.* Cambridge University Press, Cambridge, United Kingdom

VAN DÄNIKEN, ERICH
    1968   *Chariots of the Gods.* Bantam Books, New York.

VAN WORMER, STEPHEN R., AND G. TIMOTHY GROSS
    2006   Archaeological Identification of an Idiosyncratic Lifestyle: Excavation and Analysis of the Theosophical Society Dump, San Diego, California. *Historical Archaeology* 40(1):100-118.

VEIT, RICHARD
    1991   Middlesex County New Jersey Gravestones 1687-1799: Shadows of a Changing Culture. Master's thesis, Department of Anthropology, the College of William and Mary, Williamsburg, VA.

WATKINS, JOE
    2003   Archaeological Ethics and American Indians. In *Ethical Issues in Archaeology*, Larry J. Zimmerman, Karen D. Vitelli, and Julie Hollowell-Zimmer, editors, pp. 129-141. AltaMira Press, Walnut Creek, CA.

WILCOX, CLIFFORD
    2004   *Redfield and the Development of American Anthropology.* Lexington Books, Lanham, MD.

WILKIE, LAURIE A.
    1997   Secret and Sacred: Contextualizing the Artifacts of African-American Magic and Religion. *Historical Archaeology* 31(4):81-106.

WILLEY, GORDON R. AND JEREMY A. SABLOFF
    1993   *A History of American Archaeology.* 3rd edition. W.H. Freeman, New York, NY.

ZELINSKY, WILBUR
    1973   Unearthly Delights: Cemetery Names and the Map of the Changing American Afterworld, In *Geographies of the Mind*, David Lowenthal and Martyn J. Bowden, editors, pp. 171-195. Oxford University Press, Oxford, United Kingdom.
    2007   The Gravestone Index: Tracking Personal Religiosity Across Nations, Regions, and Periods. *The Geographical Review.* 9:441-446.

ZUCCHI, ALBERTA
    2006   Churches as Catholic Burial Places: Excavations at the San Francisco Church, Venezuela. *Historical Archaeology* 40(2):57-68.

RICHARD VEIT
DEPARTMENT OF HISTORY AND ANTHROPOLOGY
MONMOUTH UNIVERSITY
400 CEDAR AVENUE
WEST LONG BRANCH NJ 07764

ALASDAIR BROOKS
SCHOOL OF ARCHAEOLOGY AND ANCIENT HISTORY
UNIVERSITY OF LEICESTER
UNIVERSITY ROAD
LEICESTER
LE1 7RH
UNITED KINGDOM

Sherene Baugher

The John Street Methodist Church: An Archaeological Excavation with Native American Cooperation

ABSTRACT

During construction work at the historic John Street Methodist Church in Lower Manhattan in New York City, workers found human bones near the foundation wall of the church. The minister and church leaders voluntarily halted the project so that archaeological work could be undertaken. Since the property had the potential to contain Native American or European American burials, the City Archaeology Program and the American Indian Community House undertook a joint excavation of the site. This was the first time in New York City that Native Americans worked on an archaeological excavation. No other human remains were found, but many artifacts from the mid-19th century were uncovered. The artifacts provide glimpses into the social behavior of the congregation.

Introduction

During remodeling at the 1841 John Street Methodist Church in Lower Manhattan, New York City, construction workers found small fragments of human bones buried under the basement floor near a foundation wall. The minister and church leaders voluntarily halted the project so that archaeological work could be undertaken. Since the property had the potential to contain Native American as well as European American burials, the City Archaeology Program and the American Indian Community House (New York City's urban Native American center) undertook a joint excavation of the site in January 1986.

Even though non-Native American archaeologists have worked on sites in New York City since the late-19th century, American Indians have not been involved in these excavations. In 1920, Arthur C. Parker, a Seneca archaeologist, compiled an archaeological history of New York State using data from both professional and amateur archaeologists (Parker 1920). There is no evidence, however, that Parker ever excavated within New York City; consequently, the John Street Church project was the first time that Native Americans worked on an archaeological excavation in Manhattan. While journal articles and book chapters have described cooperative efforts on precontact sites, it was unusual to have Native Americans and archaeologists excavating together at an historic period site (Swidler et al. 1997; Dongoske et al. 2000). This project can hopefully serve as a model for others working on historic sites.

Although no other human remains were found, many artifacts from the mid-19th-century church were uncovered. The 19th-century artifacts provide glimpses into the social behavior of the Methodist congregation. This article discusses the cooperative effort of archaeologists and the Native Americans who worked alongside them, and it also analyzes what all of them found.

Cooperation without Legal Mandates

The John Street project was a totally voluntary effort among Native Americans, church officials, and archaeologists. No federal, state, or city laws mandated this work:

1. New York City Landmarks Law (1965) did not apply because the landmark designation for the historic church only applied to the façade; because the project only involved work inside the church; and because the church's interior was not covered by the landmark designation report.

2. National Historic Preservation Act (1966) did not apply because the project did not involve federal monies, a federal project, or federal permits.

3. New York City Environment Quality Review Act (1977) did not apply because the project did not involve city funds, city property, or require actions by city agencies.

4. New York State Environmental Quality Review Act (1978) did not apply because

the construction did not involve state money, a state agency, or a state permit.

5. Native American Grave Protection and Repatriation Act (1990) did not apply because the project occurred four years before Congressional passage.

The significance of the voluntary cooperation is that the John Street Church project was carried out harmoniously during the 1980s in the midst of a raging controversy over American Indian reburials.

Controversy over Native American Burial Grounds

Lawyer H. Marcus Price III, in his 1991 book *Disputing the Dead,* analyzed all federal and state laws prior to the 1990 NAGPRA regarding the protection (or lack of protection) of Native American burial grounds and concluded that most state laws offered little or no protection for Native American burial grounds. Price (1991:118) noted that prior to NAGPRA, the major goal of many archaeologists working on burial sites was to excavate the site without consulting Native Americans and then send any human remains or burial goods to a university or a museum—not to keep a burial site intact or to return the remains and burial goods to an American Indian "tribal government." This well-established archaeological approach to American Indian burial grounds pitted archaeologists against Native Americans.

Because there are more than 300 American Indian cultures and religions in North America, there is no single pan-Indian response in terms of the treatment of the dead (Baugher 1998:98). Since the arrival of the Europeans, most Native Americans who followed a traditional religion have always supported the preservation of burial grounds and sacred sites (Baugher 2005:253). There are some exceptions: the Navajos and the Eskimos, for example, do not want bodies returned because of their cultures' specific beliefs about the negative powers of the dead (Thomas 2000:218–219). Some assimilative Native Americans view museums as a viable alternative for the preservation of human remains and burial goods (Baugher 2005:253). The traditional Native Americans who opposed interference with sacred sites were given additional support in the

1960s because of that era's American Indian political activism, including the rise of "Red Power." Native Americans became increasingly vocal in their opposition to the removal of human remains and grave goods and to their placement in museums (Deloria 1969, 1994; Echo-Hawk and Echo-Hawk 1991; Jemison 1997; Mihesuah 2000).

The Native American Grave Protection and Repatriation Act (NAGPRA) only covers sites existing on federal property or projects that receive federal money, so many American Indian burial grounds remain unprotected if they are on private property. The John Street Church is private property and does not receive any federal funding. An additional significance of the John Street site excavation is that even today it would have to rely on an entirely voluntary cooperation among archaeologists, Native Americans, and church officials.

The professional archaeological community, like Native American communities, was and is divided over the burial issue. If a Native American burial is discovered on private land and thus not protected by federal, state, or municipal laws, some archaeologists still favor the removal of bodies and grave goods to museums or universities to become part of permanent collections (Meighan 1996, 2000). Others, however, will open a dialogue with the local Native American community to decide jointly what to do with any body or burial site (Watkins 2003). Within this dialogue, one of the options is to decide to excavate a site and remove any bodies temporarily so that they can be analyzed for indications of diet, disease, and other factors that are of interest to both the archaeologists and the Indian communities (Watkins 2000). After any analysis, the bodies are reburied. Another option is to leave the site completely undisturbed; while this option will not provide new historical information to anyone, the local Indian community may already have an established reverence for the history of the site (Zimmerman 1996, 2000). Some states also play a part in this process. For example, in New Jersey, state museum staff coordinate the reburial of accidentally discovered Native American remains (Veit 2004, pers. comm.).

As noted above, when the "reburial controversy" was heating up in the 1980s, the accepted approach in archaeology was the excavation and removal of bodies and grave goods to museums or universities to become part of permanent collections (Quick 1985; Klesert and Powell 2000:200–201). Some archaeologists strongly defended this position (Buikstra 1981; Meighan 1984; Turner 1986). Others tried to look for a middle ground that allowed some input from Native Americans but insured that archaeologists "retain for themselves the 'final court of appeal' on the disposition of human remains" (Klesert and Powell 2000:201). A minority advocated an equal partnership with Native Americans in the decision-making process, with Native Americans having the final say (Zimmerman 1985). When it began to appear that federal and state politicians were becoming seriously interested in the controversy and sympathetic to the Native American side, tensions mounted within the archaeological community. It was in these tumultuous times, four years before NAGPRA, that the John Street Methodist Church site was excavated.

After the passage of NAGPRA in 1990, archaeologists had to deal with the legal reality that they had to communicate with Native Americans. By the late 1990s, two federally funded journals, *CRM* and *Common Ground* (formerly the *Federal Archaeologist*), and the Society for American Archaeology's newsletter published positive examples of the cooperation between Native communities and archaeologists (Baugher 2005:256). Overall, these journals have shown an enlightened and culturally sensitive approach by archaeologists toward Native burial grounds. In *Native Americans and Archaeologists: Stepping Stones to Common Ground* (Swidler et al. 1997), produced by the Society of American Archaeology, the articles provide detailed examples of cooperative efforts. *Working Together: Native Americans and Archaeologists* (Dongoske et al. 2000) republished columns from the *SAA Bulletin* from 1993 to 1999. The edited book detailed both the cooperative efforts and tensions that still exist regarding the excavation of Native American sites and burial grounds. While the number of culturally sensitive archaeologists is growing, some archaeologists still do not agree with NAGPRA and only reluctantly comply with the law (Watkins 2000). Reluctant archaeologists (both in the past and today) often notify American Indian communities of the discovery of burial grounds at the last possible

moment the law allows, causing their work to take on crisis management proportions (Abatelli 1993; Watkins 2000, 2003; Baugher 2005). These continuing problems may have escalated with the ongoing legal battles between some Native American tribal governments and some archaeologists surrounding disposition of the remains of Kennewick Man, the approximately 9,000 year old skeleton found in Washington in 1996 (Thomas 2000; Zimmerman 2000). In light of these growing tensions, additional articles and books have been published that emphasize professional responsibilities to Native Americans (Lynott and Wylie 2000; Thomas 2000; Watkins 2000, 2003).

Unfortunately, some archaeological projects still involve "reactive planning"; that is, planning how to deal with a burial crisis *after* it has happened. Some of these confrontational situations can be avoided if Native American communities are treated with respect and are informed at the beginning rather than the end of the process (Baugher 2005:256). To have "proactive planning," all sides need to discuss the issues and arrive at a jointly agreed-upon plan of action *before* archaeological excavations begin. This can be done both in university settings and in cultural resource management cases. The John Street Methodist Church project provides an early positive proactive example that still has relevance for the 21st century.

Archaeologists and Native Americans Working Together in New York City

As early as 1982 (eight years before the passage of NAGPRA), the New York City Archaeology Program, housed within the New York Landmarks Preservation Commission, was already including Native Americans in discussions regarding the excavation of Native American sites within New York City. The commission regularly contacted the American Indian Community House, which represented 14,000 Native Americans living in the city. If a phase I CRM project uncovered a potential Native American site or burial ground, the city archaeologist, planners, representatives of the American Indian Community House, and the developers' representatives would all discuss the various scenarios for action if a burial was uncovered. The Native American representatives had a voice at the negotiating table. While that voice was not legally binding, it was a calm, convincing, and strong expression for the ethical treatment of burial sites. Together, the representatives planned exactly how the discovery of a burial ground would be handled. Because these discussions were being undertaken early in the planning process, in situ preservation of a burial ground was possible. If necessary, the redesign or the re-siting of a new building could be undertaken without major time delays in construction. The Native American community in New York was not "either/or" in its approach. A middle ground was reached that would have permitted the excavation and analysis of any bodies, followed by a reburial of the bodies. As it turned out, however, none of these early projects uncovered a burial site.

After all these planning efforts, human remains were finally found by construction workers at the John Street Methodist Church during restoration, stabilization, and remodeling work. The minister, Reverend Warren Danskin, who was interested both in Native Americans and in the history of his church grounds, voluntarily contacted the author, who was the city archaeologist. The very small collection of bones was human, but additional information was needed. The bones were taken to Thomas McGovern, director of the Hunter College Bioarchaeological Laboratory. McGovern evaluated the bones and identified them as adult human remains. He added that the bones had been in the ground for at least 100 years and perhaps much longer. From prior documentary research, the archaeologists in the City Archaeology Program knew that the bones at this site could have been associated with either white Methodists from the 18th century or Native Americans buried prior to European contact (Baugher et al. 1982; New York City Landmarks Preservation Commission 1986).

Because the bones could be either European American or Native American, the author met on separate occasions with Michael Bush and Rosemary Richmond, the director and assistant director of the American Indian Community House and then with Reverend Danskin, the minister of the John Street Methodist Church and his superiors. Later all parties met together. Religious leaders from both the Methodist and Native American communities agreed that they wanted the bones eventually to be reburied, but they were willing to have physical anthropologists study the bones as long as none of the bones were destroyed or treated in a disrespectful manner. Both communities wanted the City Archaeology Program to undertake an emergency excavation to determine if any additional bones or intact bodies were on the site. Danskin and members of the board of trustees wanted the archaeologists to test only in the small area of the basement that would be impacted by the new renovations and was still untouched by the construction work. The archaeologists and Native Americans worked in this undisturbed area to insure that no human burials would be disturbed by further construction and in the hopes of discovering stratified deposits associated with either the church or a Native American settlement.

The Site

The John Street Methodist Church is at 44 John Street in Lower Manhattan, just three blocks east of the former World Trade Center (Figure 1). The current building, built in 1841, is the third Methodist church on this site (Figure 2). In 1768, on this lot, the Methodists in New York City constructed Wesley Chapel, the first

Figure 1. The John Street Methodist Church in New York City. (Drawing by Daniel Costura.)

Figure 2. John Street Methodist Church (the 1841 church). (Photo by Carl Forster.)

permanent Methodist meetinghouse in America (Rogers 1984:35). Prior to 1768, a one and one-half story building, of unknown use, fronted on John Street on a Bradford map of 1730; however, most of the lot was empty. Later that building was used as the Methodists' parsonage (Rogers 1984:10). An 1824 painting by J. B. Smith and P. C. Smith depicted the 1768 church and the parsonage, a courtyard in front of the church, and a fenced side yard along the east side of the church (Figure 3). The colonial church kept attracting new members until it had outgrown its space. In 1817, the congregation demolished the old Wesley Chapel and parsonage and built a second and larger church in its place in 1818 (Rogers 1984:22–26). In 1835, a great fire destroyed much of Lower Manhattan. Although the church survived, much of the surrounding neighborhood was damaged. As part of the rebuilding, the city decided to widen John Street, which meant the 1818 church would have to be moved or demolished. After much discussion regarding the merits of moving or rebuilding, the church leaders decided to demolish the 1818 church and build the third and final church

in 1841 (John Street United Methodist Church [JSUMC] 1838–1858). This third church is a designated New York City landmark.

In 1970, the Federal Reserve Bank of New York wished to purchase the "air rights" over the church, meaning that the bank could transfer those air rights from the church to an adjacent property in order to build a taller building than normally allowed. If the church agreed to the sale, the church property would have a restrictive covenant that would limit the height of any future buildings on the church property to the height of the existing church. As a result of the negotiations, the church agreed to sell their air rights to the bank (JSUMC 1960–1980). The bank subsequently sold the adjacent property and the church's former air rights to Park Tower Realty Corporation, which then constructed a 28-story office tower next to the church (JSUMC 1984). Unfortunately, the church sustained structural damage to its west wall due to the construction of new office tower. To determine the extent of the damage, the western portion of the finished basement floor was removed in 1986. It was during the course of trenching by construction workers that human bone fragments, as well as some animal bone fragments, were found next to a possible foundation footing from the second church that had been built in 1818 (Baugher et al. 1991:53). The discovery of human remains beneath the church resulted in a request by Danskin to the author to conduct an archaeological excavation.

To determine if a Native American site might have been located on the property, members of the City Archaeology Program examined early maps to analyze the topography and physiography of the area prior to its development as a church property. The site was on an elevated terrace at the juncture of two streams, with a marsh located a short distance to the northeast. The East River is nearby as well. Based on his previous research, City Archaeology Program member Edward Lenik (1992:11) knew that Native American sites in New York City have been found on river and stream banks, adjacent to ponds and marshes, and on terraces. The pre-urban landscape of the John Street site is identical to the American Indian settlement pattern found elsewhere in New York City, and this site would have been very attractive to Native Americans. There was a high probability that a

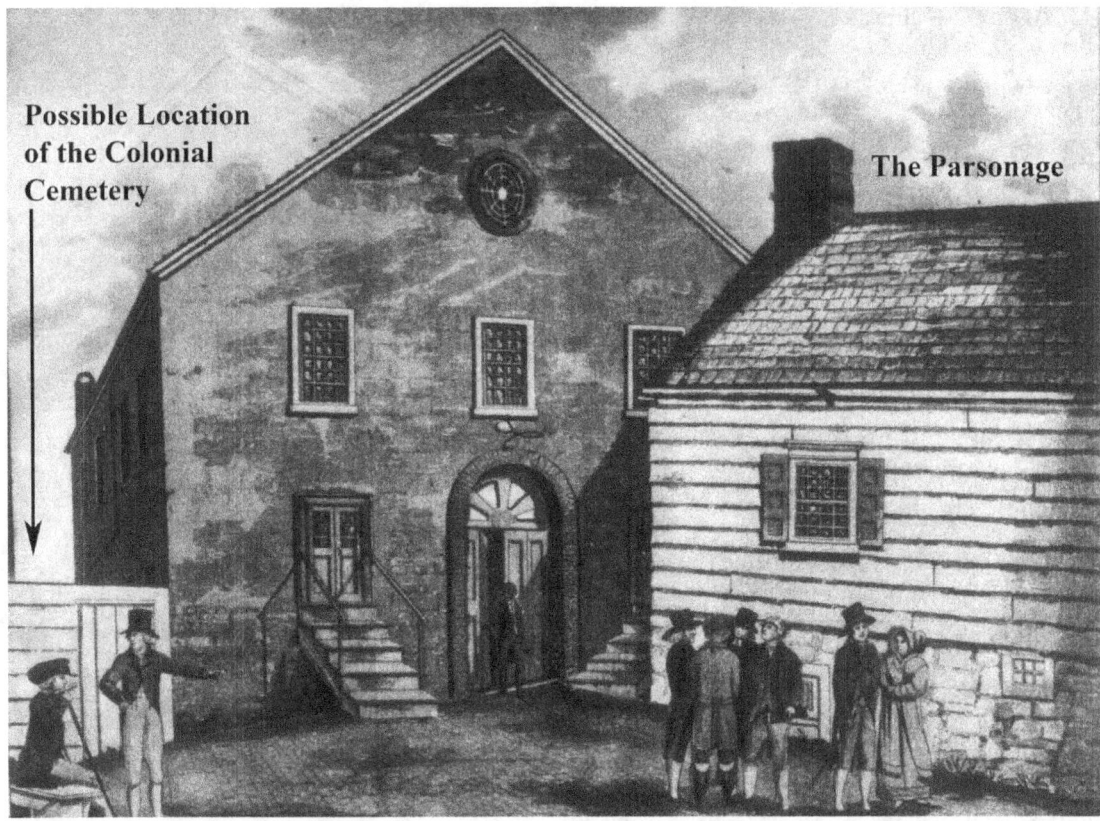

Figure 3. "A Correct View of the Old Methodist Church in John Street N. York." Colored aquatint by I. (J.) B. and P. C. Smith, 1824, depicting 1768. (from Stokes 1915, Vol. I:plate 43.)

Native American occupation could have occurred near the present-day John Street Church (Guston et al. 1991:11).

At the same time, evidence indicated the possibility of European American burials. In Reverend J. B. Wakeley's (1858:451) history of the church, he notes that next to the first (1768) church "… was the first place the Methodists used for a bury-ground in New–York." Unfortunately, the graveyard is not mentioned in any other primary sources. In the 18th century, the only location for a graveyard on the property would be on the east side of the lot (Figure 3 and Figure 4). The construction work that uncovered the bones was along the western wall, however, and at least 35 ft. west of the possible 18th-century cemetery.

The Excavation

Members of the American Indian Community House, including Director Michael Bush

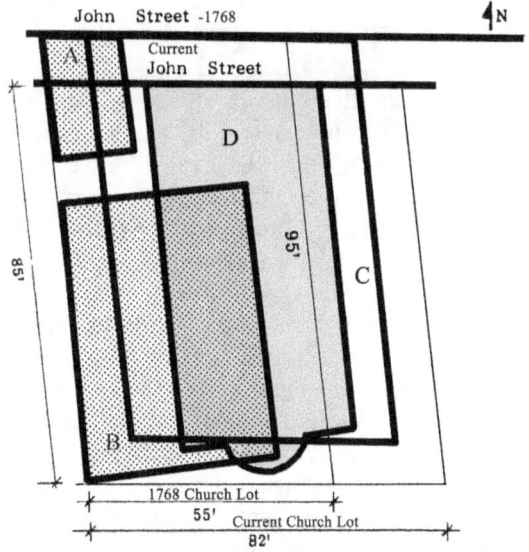

Figure 4. (*A*) Footprints of the 1768 parsonage, (*B*) 1768 church, (*C*) 1818 church, and (*D*) 1841 church. (Drawing by Daniel Costura, based on data from Rogers 1984:10,22,33,48.)

(Mohawk), volunteered to participate in the excavation with the archaeologists (Figure 5). Archaeologists and Native Americans worked side by side, troweling and screening the site (Figure 6). This was an opportunity to discuss and teach methods of archaeology. More importantly, it was a valuable time for archaeologists to listen to Native Americans and to truly hear their concerns about burials.

The archaeological excavation took place in the current kitchen of the church. This area was located within the footprint of the 1818 church and the walkway between the 1768 church and its parsonage (Figure 7). The building contractor removed the kitchen tile floor and a 3-in. concrete floor prior to archaeological work. Two shovel tests were excavated to determine the depth of 20th-century disturbance and to ascertain if there were any intact deposits. In spite of all this 20th-century construction, some intact stratified deposits remained. Four units were excavated (Figure 8). Although some of the artifacts from these stratified deposits could be associated with the eras of the second or third churches, most were associated with the third church and dated primarily from 1840 to 1870. No intact burials or other bones were unearthed. Excavations were only undertaken in the area where future construction was going to take place.

The Stratified Deposit

Underneath the kitchen tile floor and the concrete floor was almost 4 ft. of 20th-century fill, and below the fill were intact 19th–century deposits. Under the 20th-century kitchen floor was a 3 in. base of fine cinders (Figure 9). Below the cinders was an additional 4 in. base of small chunks of cement, mixed with cinders, that was used in the 1940s to form a base for the recent kitchen floor (Baugher et al. 1991:58). Below this base was between 31 and 38 in. of fill that contained bricks, cinders, slag, plaster, and 20th-century building debris. The building debris included cut electric cables, electric brackets, fragments of iron pipes, fragments of rusted unidentifiable metal, nails, and wood fragments. By the age of this fill, it seems that the 1940s workers had discarded material, including a water tank. Below this 20th–century layer were the intact 19th-century deposits.

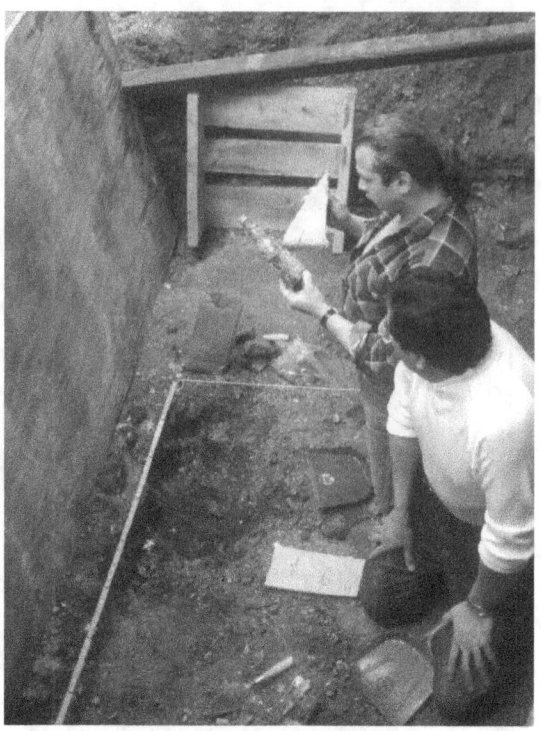

Figure 5. Michael Bush (*left*), director of the American Indian Community House, excavates with fellow Native American Paul Kataquatit. (Photo by Carl Forster.)

Figure 6. Volunteers from the American Indian Community House screening artifacts with a staff member from the City Archaeology Program. (Photo by Carl Forster.)

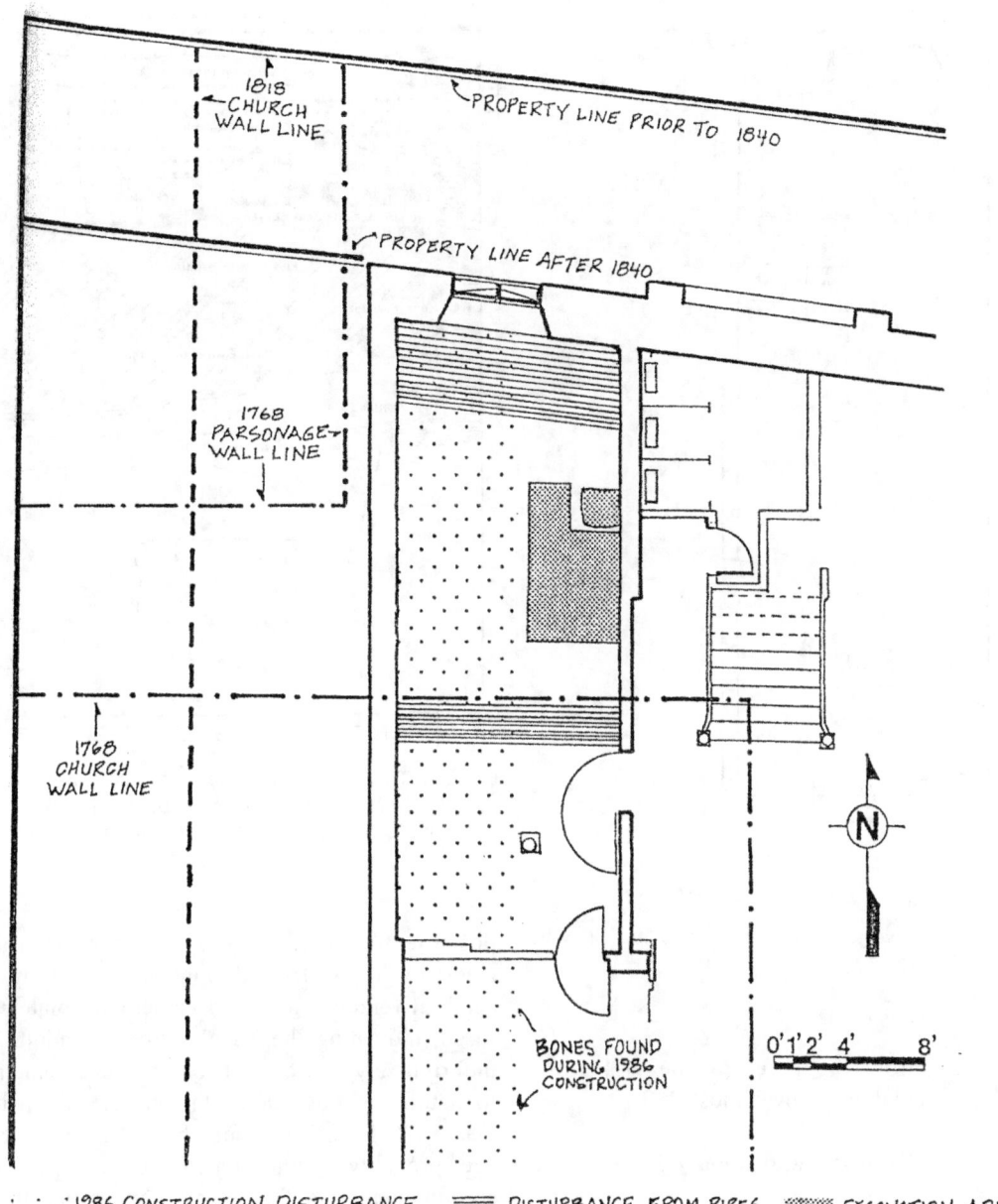

·.·.·1986 CONSTRUCTION DISTURBANCE ≡≡≡ DISTURBANCE FROM PIPES ▓▓▓ EXCAVATION AREA

Figure 7. Wall lines of the 1768 church and the 1818 church are superimposed over an outline of a part of the basement of the contemporary church. (Drawing by Louise De Cesare and Eric Rich.)

When the level of intact 19th-century deposits was reached, the archaeologists widened the fill layer by one foot in order to put protective shoring around the excavation units. The shoring protected the excavators and prevented fill from slipping into the units. The entire fill, including the fill from the enlarged units, was screened through 1/4 in. mesh screens. Trowels were used to excavate all of the layers below the fill, and all deposits were screened.

All units were excavated well into sterile soil. The deepest test was shovel test no. 2, which was excavated to 84 in. below the concrete basement floor; the last 22 in. were in sterile soil. Excavation unit no. 1 was excavated to 74 in., the last 22 in. were sterile soil. The excavation

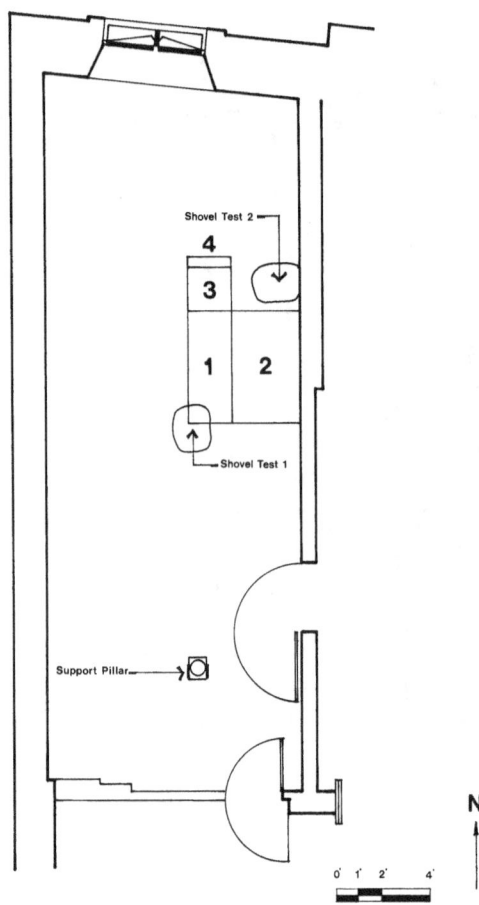

Figure 8. The shovel tests and excavation units. (Drawing by Louise De Cesare.)

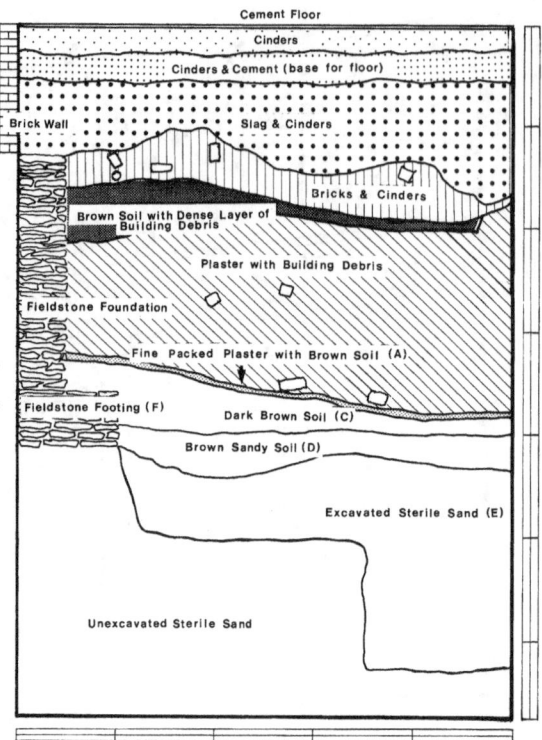

Figure 9. The south wall profile from units 1 and 2; (*A–E*) various layers of 20th-century fill cover the 19th-century deposits. (Drawing by Louise De Cesare.)

was also below the level of the fieldstone foundation and footing by almost 2 ft.

The Bones and Reburial

After the archaeological excavation was completed, the author consulted with Bobbi Brickman, a physical anthropologist and a consultant in the 1980s to some of the large CRM projects in New York City. Brickman undertook a more in-depth study of the six very small human bones found by the construction workers (if an elementary school student cupped both hands, the six bones would easily rest in them). Brickman (1991:153) compared the bones to skeleton collections at Hunter College and noted, "due to the fragmentary nature of the skeletal material, traditional methods of age, sex, and race were not possible." Some identification was

possible. A small section of the supraorbital ridge of a left frontal bone showed that the cerebral (endocranial) and ectocranial plate was fused, indicating the bone is from an adult, but unfortunately not enough of the bone remained to determine the sex of the individual (Brickman 1991:153). The bone showed recent breakage, probably by the construction workers. The second bone is a fragment of either the 4th or 5th thoracic vertebra. The partial bone is very worn, and there are several shovel cut marks on the bone. Brickman (1991:154) notes that these were old cut marks because of "the presence of microscopic dirt in the deep recess of the cut as well as the patina on the cut bone surface." The third bone is the head of a femur. This bone had the "remnant of the epiphyseal line on the external surface," which indicates the bone is from an adult, but unfortunately the sex could not be determined (Brickman 1991:155). In addition, there are salt deposits "within the spaces of the trabecular bone of the femur head," and Brickman (1991:155) notes that since the bone fragment was found in a plaster layer, the salt deposits were "probably due to the composition of the plaster." The fourth bone is another head of a femur. A subchondral bone on the second head of a femur is very pitted and worn. The bone is so damaged that age and sex determination was not possible (Brickman 191:155). The fifth bone is a small section of a shaft of a femur that has a heavily developed linea aspera. Brickman (1991:154) notes, "the extent to which the linea aspera is developed indicates an adult individual who did a lot of stooping and bending," but there is not enough of the bone to indicate the sex of the individual. This bone contains cut marks with a patina over them, similar to the marks on the vertebra, which also indicates a past historic disturbance. The last bone is in very poor condition, making identification difficult. The age of the individual could not be determined from this bone. The bone could be a metacarpal. Brickman (1991:155) said "the upper tables of the compact bone are cracked," and the bone has a recent cut mark. No intact burial was found. Two of the bones indicate prior historic disturbances and may have been moved from their original site and later either discarded or reburied. Due the fragmentary quality of the bones, they could have been from the same individual; however, because six bones were found, it is also possible that they were from as many as six separate individuals. Brickman (1991:156) could not determine racial identity.

Brickman noted that she found dissociated human bones on other New York City sites where there was major construction and land alteration (Brickman 1984 and 1987; also Geismar 1983). She added, "the pattern of secondary deposition exhibited by these (John Street) fragments is consistent with human bone fragments recovered from other New York City excavations" (Brickman 1991:156). The various phases of construction on this site with the building of three churches and the alteration of the landscape could certainly account for the historic disturbance of the burials and the subsequent secondary deposition of the bones.

As agreed before the archaeological excavation, the John Street Church bones were reburied underneath the basement floor. Because the religious leaders did not want any intrusive tests performed, the exact age or race of the bones could not be determined. Since both the bones' race and age were not known, the religious leaders decided to have the bones reburied on the Methodist church property in a joint Native American and Methodist reburial ceremony. All parties involved, including the archaeologists and physical anthropologists, agreed this was acceptable. There was sufficient time for Brickman's analysis, and then the bones were reburied. The process worked because all views were heard and respected.

Additional Research on Burial Practices

Two years after Brickman's study was completed, additional funds from a grant from the Park Avenue Methodist Trust Fund enabled archaeologist Judith Guston to undertake additional research in various Methodist archives to determine if there was any further documentary evidence of burials on the John Street Church property. Guston did find important evidence of human bones being found during earlier construction projects on the church property and then being reburied under the church (Guston et al. 1991). The first example comes from demolition of the 1768 church; Wakeley (1858:330) notes, "In 1817, when the old church edifice was torn down ... they disturbed the dead .... Some of their bones were gathered together and buried under one end of the church ..." Unfortunately, there is no indication if these were intact burials. Furthermore, Wakeley provides no mention of grave goods or any clues to the age or cultural affiliation of these bones. In the 1817 example, the bones were reburied under the second church. In a sense, the reburial ceremony in 1988 was continuing a practice that had begun in 1817.

Later, in the 19th century, construction work again uncovered more human bones. In 1882, the owners of the property to the rear of the church undermined the church wall when they were digging a foundation for a new building. During these excavations, "Four sculls [sic] and portions of four skeletons were uncovered. Brother Davis, our sexton, was instructed to suitably bury all bones uncovered under the church" (JSUMC 1869–1947:94). In 1882, the newly disturbed bones were reburied in the basement of the third church. Unfortunately, there is no indication of the positions of the bodies, such as flexed burials, no mention of any indication of coffins, nor mention of any associated grave goods that might indicate if they were Native American or European American.

The final recorded example of the discovery of bones in connection with the church took place during World War II. In 1944, the church was closed for repairs, and bones were unearthed in the cellar near the east wall (Guston et al. 1991:51–52). The report of the bones being found in 1944 comes from Architect Raynor Rogers's interview with Arthur Moss, former pastor of the John Street Church, now deceased. Rogers had conversations with Moss when Rogers was researching his book on the history of the church. The bones were reinterred "in a new vault constructed beneath the altar in the Wesley Chapel Museum" in the basement of the extant church (Rogers 1984:48). Interestingly, the bones buried in 1988 were near the burial of the 1944 bones. The basement of the church has become a burial ground and, in a sense, a sacred site.

Guston also found evidence for colonial vaults. In the 18th century, vaults were under the church (Wakeley 1858:451). Underground burial vaults were a regular feature of early Methodist churches, but this practice stopped by the end of the 18th century (Seaman 1892:181,491). In addition, church oral tradition states that members of the John Street church put their family treasures in these underground vaults for safe keeping during the American Revolution (Wakeley 1858:433). William Lupton, one of the 18th-century trustees of the John Street Methodist Church, provided the church with funds for the construction of his own vault (JSUMC 1768:1). It is unknown how many burials or vaults may have existed in the basement of the church. Unfortunately, there is no description of these vaults. These colonial vaults, if they still exist, would be under the footprint of the original chapel in the southernmost part of the current basement and outside of the area excavated.

Both the documentary and archaeological evidence raise the question of whether the burying and reburying of human bones under the basement of John Street Church was unique or whether other churches in the northeast also had similar practices. The answer is that this activity is not unique. In New Jersey, human bones have

also been found under the basement of historic churches. Richard Veit (2002:108) notes that at the 18th-century Christ Episcopal Church in Shrewsbury, New Jersey, construction workers found three grave shafts under the floor along with "a group of disarticulated bones buried in a pit, probably a mass reburial associated with previous alterations to the church." Thomas Crist (1998), the forensic anthropologist who excavated and analyzed the burials, found that the bones in the pit represented several individuals. Veit (2002:109) notes that when the church "was erected in 1769, several burials predating the new structure were left in place, and the tombstones commemorating them ... were incorporated into the church floor." Another example is in Trenton, New Jersey, when archaeologists from Hunter Research (1998) found several standing tombstones in the crawl space under the Parish House of St. Michael's Episcopal Church. Veit (2002:109) notes that the Parish House, constructed in 1892, covered much of an old cemetery and that "some burials may have been reinterred in Riverview cemetery, but others were not."

Burials underneath churches were also found in the Tidewater area of Virginia and Maryland. In the early-20th century, Mary Jeffrey Galt, one of the founders of the Association for the Preservation of Virginia Antiquities, undertook extensive excavations at the brick church at Jamestown, unearthed an earlier church inside it, and found more than 50 burials (Kelso et al. 1998:26). She found some burials in separate areas inside the church. William Kelso and colleagues (1998:26) note, "it seems likely that some of the bones generally were left undisturbed and the shafts backfilled, where today they rest beneath a reconstructed brick floor in the 1907 church." Archaeologists from St. Mary's City, Maryland, found that "dozens of people were interred under the floor" of the 17th-century Catholic church (Miller et al. 2004: 352). Only three of the numerous burials had lead coffins; these coffins (burials of a man, a woman, and a child) were found underneath what would have been the floor of the church (Miller et al. 2004). Archaeologists were able to identify the man as Philip Calvert, governor of Maryland and the "youngest son of George Calvert, first Lord Baltimore"; the woman was his first wife, Anne Wolsley Calvert (Riordan 2004:329,345). The infant girl (approximately 6 months old) may have been the only child of Philip Calvert and his second wife Jane Sewell Calvert (Miller et al. 2004:366). Studies of the burial practices of this early Catholic community are ongoing (Hurry 2004).

Burying bodies within a church was not an unusual or unique colonial practice. What is the probable explanation for the bones found within the John Street Methodist Church? The bones uncovered by construction workers in 1986 were found along the west wall of the church. The workers also uncovered a possible footing from the second (1818) church. The bones were found near this 1818 footing. Brickman (1991:153–155) notes that two of the bones, the vertebra and the partial shaft of the femur, have cut marks with a patina over them, providing evidence of past historic disturbance. These two bones may have been part of the disturbed bones that were reinterred in the church basement in either 1818 or 1882. Based on this additional documentary evidence, it is possible that the 1986 bones are bones from individuals originally buried in the 18th-century Methodist Church cemetery or in the vaults within the 1768 church. Probably some were disturbed by 19th-century construction on the site. Because racial identity could not be determined, it is still also possible that they are bones from Native American burials, disturbed during earlier constructions on the site.

Artifacts at the Church Site

The American Indian Community House members of the excavation were relieved that the group did not uncover any other bones or burials. The Native American connection with the excavation did not end with the reburial ceremony. The American Indian Community House members were quite interested in the process of doing archaeology and in learning more about the 19th-century material they had uncovered. This belies the perception by some archaeologists who think that Native Americans are only interested in American Indian artifacts. The American Indian Community House team wanted to be kept up-to-date on the laboratory work, to see some of the washed and reconstructed artifacts, and to hear about the analysis of the materials.

Architectural Artifacts

Not surprisingly, with all of the demolition and rebuilding in the 19th century, most of the 19th-century artifacts are related to architecture (78% of the assemblage), including nails and window glass plus hinges, screws, tacks, brackets, and hooks. Several fragments from glass lamps and even fragments from a glass chandelier were also found.

Kitchenwares

Kitchenwares (bottles, table glass, ceramics, and cutlery) make up the second largest category of artifacts (16%). The church had social functions within the building throughout its history, so it was not surprising to find kitchen-related artifacts and food remains. Most of the artifacts date from 1830 to 1870.

The ceramics sherds represent 10 separate vessels. The assemblage includes ceramics for both food preparation and tableware. Four utilitarian wares include a yellowware bowl, a brown stoneware bowl, a buff-colored stoneware jar, and a gray stoneware bottle. The six tablewares include two plain undecorated ironstone dishes, one ironstone bowl (soup or salad), one creamware plate, one undecorated ironstone cup, and one undecorated whiteware cup. A small sherd of Jackfield-like redware was found. The sherd is too small to determine its exact function; perhaps it is from a tea set. Since this is an assemblage for a church, it was not surprising to find that the tablewares are primarily undecorated items. The stoneware could have been purchased at one of the local New York City potteries, perhaps as inexpensive "seconds" from the pottery.

Faunal

Daniel Russell and Thomas Amorosi (1991) analyzed the faunal remains. The bones are butcher cuts and are primarily from sheep/goat (42.28%). Sixty percent of the sheep bones are from mature animals (over two years of age), thus the Methodists were serving inexpensive mutton, perhaps in soups and stews. Twenty percent of the ovis/capra bones are from animals between one-half and one year in age, so some more expensive cuts of meat were served. There was a preference for sheep. Almost 53% of the ovis/capra collection is from vertebra; the other sheep bones are from diverse body parts and cuts of meat. The Methodists also served a small amount of chicken (1.75%), beef (6.17%), pig (1.34%), and, curiously, deer (1.34%). Was this a food preference or the result of economic limitations? Research in the church archives indicates that this congregation had a long history of helping and feeding the poor (Baugher et al. 1991:110). If the dietary remains were associated with meals for the poor, it would have been economical to purchase the least expensive meat to serve in quantity. These meats, used primarily in stews, may have been standard fare for the poor who came to eat at the church. The documentary record does not clarify whether the congregation's charitable giving included meals served at the church. Perhaps the dietary remains are linked to the ethnic preferences of the congregation and were associated with social, not charitable, meals. Churches in both the 19th and 20th centuries have hosted meals, and food remains have been found on other 19th-century church sites. More research on the ethnic and economic background of the congregation is needed before any conclusions can be drawn.

Russell and Amorosi (1991) also note that 69% of the animal bones shows gnaw marks from rodents. In the levels of this 19th-century basement were also the remains of rats; in fact, rat bones make up 40% of the entire faunal collection. Four rat mandibles were found and almost one complete rat skeleton. The rats were between two and three years old. Finding the bones of mature rats on an urban site is consistent with the findings from other New York City excavations (Russell and Amorosi 1991:129). There were also a few bones from one cat.

Personal Items

A variety of buttons were unearthed. The buttons consist of two milk glass buttons, two shell buttons, one ivory button, and one metal snap-type button, probably from a pair of overalls. Perhaps members of the congregation lost these buttons. One straight pin and one small piece of cloth were also uncovered. Other items include a rubber comb and a fragment of a rubber comb, which would provide a date of post-1851. Finally, the six clay marbles were found in the room that, coincidentally, is currently used as the children's playroom.

Alcohol and Smoking in the Church

There were some surprises in the collection, such as a beer bottle, wine bottle fragments, and smoking pipe fragments. The Methodists had strong prohibitions against drinking, except for communal wine. Although smoking was not prohibited outright, it is referred to in admonitions against wasting one's time in "frivolous activities," and it is linked to banned activities such as drinking liquor, gambling, card playing, and horse racing (Baugher et al. 1991:87).

A number of decorated and undecorated 19th-century pipe stems and bowls were unearthed and were analyzed by pipe expert Diana Dallal (1991), archaeology curator at the South Street Seaport Museum in Manhattan. Of the five undecorated stems, one mouthpiece is smudged with the pipe maker's fingerprints and one crudely made, brown clay stem may have been made locally. Two of the decorated stems have parallel ribs and raised bands, and both have the initials "C.P." Dallal (1991:90) notes that throughout the 19th-century fluted/ribbed pipes are the most common of the decorated pipe stems. She also believes the initials "C.P." do not refer to any known maker but may refer to a model name such as "cutty pipe," which was a popular 19th-century style (Dallal 1991:90).

The decoration on another stem has opposing lines of "V"s, which combine to create the illusion of fish scales. Dallal (1991:90) notes that this pipe is "reminiscent of 17th-century pipes which represent Sir Walter Raleigh being swallowed by a crocodile who spat him out because he was rank with the smell of tobacco"—these pipes were known as "Jonah" pipes. Raleigh was a Protestant hero who was executed by the Catholic King James I of England. Did this 19th-century pipe evoke these religious themes? Perhaps it was used by a member of the congregation rather than by a non-Methodist worker or visitor. Unfortunately, it is not clear from the records if the church hired members of the congregation to undertake this work.

The most expensive pipe bowl is a beautifully molded bowl in an "apple" shape. It has large broad leaves in graduated sizes with veins running down the middle of the leaves (Figure 10). Dallal notes that the leaves look like stylized "Prince of Wales feathers." Above the leaves are small flowers. Dallal (1991:95) believes that the fine and careful execution of the details on this pipe suggest that it was made by either the Fiolet or Gambier companies in France.

By far the most interesting pipe from the church assemblage is a "Jacob" pipe (Figure 11). The famous French Gambier firm initially made the religiously themed Jacob pipes, but they were later produced by numerous other firms (Walker 1983:32). Dallal (1991:93) notes that the John Street Church Jacob pipe is a crude copy of the finer French Jacob pipes: "The details of the John Street pipe are not as sharp ... the lips cannot be seen, the eyes are not deeply set and the features are not clearly delineated." She suggests that the pipe was not made by any of the French firms known for their excellent quality but was more likely made by one of the Glasgow firms that produced numerous affordable products for the American market. The discovery (beneath the floor of the church) of a pipe depicting a biblical figure may suggest some meaningful link between the artifact and a member of the congregation. On the other hand, a non-Methodist worker could have discarded the pipe.

The small but diverse clay smoking-pipe assemblage suggests material left by people of different social classes, from the simple undecorated pipes (including the crudely made local pipe) to the finely made French pipe bowl. The majority of the collection are inexpensive pipes and could have been discarded by non-Methodist workers and by the poor who may have come to the church for alms or for food. The French pipe suggests either an owner of more substantial means or someone who saved up to purchase a status pipe. Did visitors discard all of these smoking pipes? Both the Jacob pipe and the Raleigh-inspired pipe have religious themes and may have been connected to a member of the congregation.

Smoking could be connected to class distinctions. Smoking among middle-class men usually involved cigars or fancy pipes with long stems, whereas working-class members smoked clay

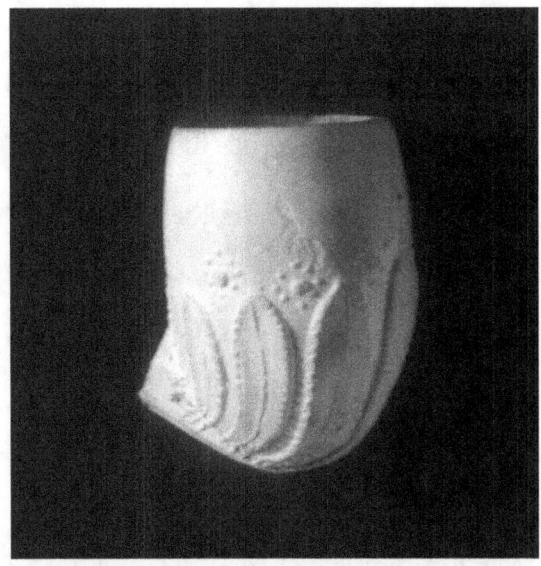

Figure 10. Beautifully molded 19th-century smoking pipe bowl, decorated with leaves and flowers; the carefully executed design suggests that a French manufacturer probably made the pipe. (Photo by Carl Forster.)

Figure 11. A "Jacob" pipe. The French firm Gambier was famous for making these Biblical portrait pipes; however, this John Street site pipe was a crude imitation of the French Jacob pipes, and a Glasgow firm probably made it. (Photo by Carl Forster.)

pipes, especially ones with short stems called "cutties" (Mrozowski et al. 1996:68). The historical documents indicate that the John Street Church was not an economically and socially united congregation. By the 1850s the church had a mixed congregation of "uptowners" and "downtowners" (as they called themselves at that time). The uptowners were in favor of selling the church and building a new structure in their uptown neighborhood, which unfortunately would have left the poorer members without a church in Lower Manhattan (JSUMC 1838–1858:188,212–223). This factionalism caused tension in the church for years. Finally, Bishop James headed a movement to protect the church because of its significance as one of the first two Methodist Churches in America. In 1866, the legislature of New York State passed an act granting a special charter to the John Street Church, whereby "the property must permanently remain, and the church edifice be forever kept open in its present location" (Rogers 1984:36).

Methodist Prohibitions

In terms of "prohibited activities," the one beer bottle and the clay smoking pipes could have been discarded by non-Methodist workers who helped build or renovate the third church. The wine bottle fragments from four separate bottles could be associated with communal wine. It is also possible that some of these items, especially the smoking pipes, could have been used by poor people who were not Methodists and who came to eat a meal at the church. Members of the congregation, however, may also have discarded these objects. There is even an intriguing record of alcohol being used by members of the church. In 1856, during a dispute over whether to move the church uptown, some members of the congregation protested by barricading themselves inside the church. The police had to remove the protestors. The *New York Daily Times* (26 June 1856) noted that when police searched the church for damages, they found "sundry bottles which had contained schnapps and rot-gut " (Guston et al. 1991:47). While this is not indisputable evidence regarding the origin of the alcohol bottles, it does provide evidence of alcohol use by Methodists at the John Street Church. The presence of artifacts

from "prohibited activities" at the John Street Church raises the question of whether similar finds have been made at other church sites or if these artifacts are simply unique to this site.

Do What We Say, Not What We Do

Archaeologists also unearthed 19th-century clay smoking pipes and alcohol bottles in the basement of another church, the Old First Church, in Middletown, New Jersey (Scharfenberger and Baugher 2000). No Baptist minister or caretaker lived on the church property in the 19th century, and therefore the material must have been associated with people who worked in or used the church (Scharfenberger 2000). The liquor bottles were not used to hold communion wine (Scharfenberger and Baugher 2000:52). During the 19th century, the Old First Church congregation adopted a strict anti-alcohol policy. Richard A. Leonard, deacon and trustee of the church for more than 15 years, was the vice president of the New Jersey State Temperance Alliance (Ellis 1885:557). His brother, Thomas, had been a leading figure in the temperance movement since the 1830s (Ellis 1885:566). Not everyone in the congregation agreed, however, with this total ban on alcohol. Archaeologists Scharfenberger and Baugher (2000:53) raise the question of whether these alcohol bottles are evidence of defiance by the congregation for this controversial policy.

In Red Wing, Minnesota, another example of alcohol bottles and smoking pipes were uncovered on church property. The Methodist Church established Hamlin University in 1854 and was one of a small number of antebellum colleges that admitted women (McCarthy and Ward 2000:1–4). Archaeologists John McCarthy and Jeanne Ward (2000:8) found 19th-century alcohol bottles and clay pipes associated with a dormitory at Hamlin, even though the school had prohibitions against drinking alcohol and smoking. Were the students smoking and drinking behind closed doors? McCarthy and Ward (2000:8) note, "neither the student body nor the faculty were composed entirely of Methodists." Were non-Methodists participating in these forbidden activities or were some Methodists simply ignoring these prohibitions?

Archaeologists excavated the trash pit of Father Philibert Turnell in Skagway, Alaska. The archaeologists note that some Catholics believed that the state did not have the right to interfere in individual lives, but many Catholics accepted prohibition (Spude et al. 1993:101–104). During prohibition, Father Turnell, a leading citizen, signed a petition to close the saloons in Skagway. Did his public image as an opponent of drinking reflect his personal choices in the privacy of his home? Even though there was public garbage collection, it appears that the priest chose to bury a large number of beer, wine, and brandy bottles in his backyard (Spude et al. 1993:105–106). Was burying the bottles a way to prevent citizens from seeing evidence of his drinking? Were other people disposing of their alcohol bottles in the priest's backyard? Alternatively, were these bottles buried symbolically as the testimony of those who had, at the priest's direction, given up drinking?

In early-20th-century deposits associated with the Troy Corners Parsonage site in Troy, Michigan, students volunteering on an excavation, co-directed by archaeologists Suzanne Spencer-Wood and Richard Stamps, found beer bottles. Two of the bottles were found in fill from around the parsonage, but one was lying intact on the floor in a corner of the basement of the Methodist parsonage (Spencer-Wood 2006, pers. comm.). Ironically, a temperance poster was found in the attic of the Methodist Church next to the parsonage after the buildings were moved to the Troy Historical Museum (Spencer-Wood 2006, pers. comm.). The archaeologists suggest that someone in the parson's family, or perhaps friends, may have been illicitly drinking in the basement and burying bottles in the yard. The bottle in the basement postdates the construction of the parsonage and seems unlikely to have been subsequently deposited by any workers in the basement. Further, church records reveal that the congregation was poor, and parishioners performed much maintenance work on the church and probably the parsonage as well. In the 1960s the Methodist Church was transformed into an antique store, but it seems unlikely that valuable antique bottles would be stored next door in the parsonage basement because it frequently flooded. Although the parson's family probably had some non-Methodist friends, how likely is it that they would have insisted on bringing beer to drink in front of the supposedly teetotaler parson's family? If the parson's family did allow friends to drink at their house,

it seems unlikely that friends would bury beer bottles in the yard or leave one in the basement instead of taking bottles away when they left (Spencer-Wood 2006, pers. comm.).

In summary, forbidden alcohol bottles were found at three 19th-century sites (John Street Methodist Church, Old First Church, and Hamlin University) and at two early-20th-century sites (Father Turnbull's trash pit and the Troy Corners Parsonage). Did workers or other outsiders discard all of these bottles? Perhaps, rather, archaeologists are uncovering a pattern in mid-19th to early-20th-century America of individual congregations (and perhaps even ministers) ignoring social policies that were established by a national-level church hierarchy, such as prohibitions against smoking and drinking. Perhaps this is evidence of individual church members ignoring church policy. Whatever the answer is, archaeologists are uncovering more and more evidence of "prohibited activities" (smoking and drinking) on church grounds.

Conclusion: The Role of Cooperation

Although some archaeologists still believe that problems with a Native American community are bound to occur whenever human remains are discovered during the excavation or construction phase of a project, this excavation provided a wonderful opportunity for archaeologists and Native Americans to collaborate on an archaeological project. In addition, it provided a glimpse of this Methodist congregation in the mid-19th century. The New York City example shows that if Native Americans are given a vote in the decision-making process, it is more likely that problems can be resolved. If a project involving a Native American site is going to be harmonious, the conditions surrounding the excavation *must* be negotiated with leaders of the Native American community *before* the archaeological excavation starts. A cooperative spirit will allow all stakeholders to decide vital issues, including whether to excavate or leave a site untouched and how to proceed if human remains are found.

Acknowledgments

For their enthusiastic support of this project, I thank Michael Bush, former director of the

American Indian Community House in New York City; Rosemary Richmond, director of the American Indian Community House; and Reverend Warren Danskin, former minister of the John Street Methodist Church. I also greatly appreciate all the fieldwork provided by the volunteers from the American Indian Community House. I thank all members and volunteers of the City Archaeology Program for their diligent work at the excavation and in the laboratory. The laboratory work and site report was funded by grants from the Park Avenue Methodist Church Trust Fund and the John Street United Methodist Church Trust Fund Society. The 1991 site report could not have been completed without a team of specialists working with me as part of the City Archaeology Program: Edward Lenik, Diane Dallal, and Judith Guston and consultants Thomas Amorosi, Bobbi Brickman, and Daniel Russell. I thank Daniel Costura, Louise De Cesare, and Eric Rich for their meticulous work on all the maps and drawings. I thank Carl Forster for his excellent photographs and generous cooperation. I appreciate the helpful suggestions made to drafts of this article by Gerald Scharfenberger, Suzanne Spencer-Wood, Richard Veit, and the two anonymous reviewers. Lastly, I thank my husband, historian Robert W. Venables, for his insightful suggestions on drafts of this article and for leaving his library to participate fully in the "dirt" side of archaeology at the John Street Church excavation.

References

ABATELLI, CAROL
1993 Ethics of Reburial: Two Case Studies from Southern New England. *Man in the Northeast* 45:87–100.

BAUGHER, SHERENE
1998 Who Determines the Significance of American Indian Sacred Sites and Burial Grounds? In *Preservation of What, for Whom? A Critical Look at Historical Significance*, Michael Tomlan, editor, pp. 97–108. National Council for Preservation Education, Ithaca, NY.
2005 Sacredness, Sensitivity, and Significance: The Controversy over Native American Sacred Sites. In *Heritage of Value, Archaeology of Renown: Reshaping Archaeological Assessment and Significance*, Clay Mathers, Tim Darvill, and Barbara Little, editors, pp. 248–275. University Press of Florida, Gainesville.

BAUGHER, SHERENE, JUDITH GUSTON, EDWARD LENIK, DIANE DALLAL, THOMAS AMOROSI, DANIEL RUSSELL, AND BOBBI BRICKMAN
1991 John Street Methodist Church: An Archaeological Investigation. Manuscript, New York City Landmarks Preservation Commission, New York, NY.

BAUGHER, SHERENE, META JANOWITZ, MARC KODACK, AND KATE MORGAN
1982 Towards an Archaeological Predictive Model for Manhattan: A Pilot Study. Manuscript, New York City Landmarks Preservation Commission, New York, NY.

BRICKMAN, BOBBI L.
1984 Appendix A. Human Remains. In Fifty-Third at Third, Report of Test Excavations for Gerald D. Hines Interest, Frederick A. Winter, editor. Report to the New York City Landmarks Preservation Commission, from Key Perspectives, New York, NY.
1987 The Human Remains from Site 1 of the Washington Street, Urban Renewal Area. In Archaeological Investigations of Site 1 of the Washington Street Urban Renewal Area, New York City, Appendix 1 of Appendix E, pp. 1–3. Report to the New York City Landmarks Preservation Commission, from Louis Berger and Associates, the Cultural Resources Group, East Orange, NJ.
1991 John Street Church Human Remains. In The John Street Methodist Church: An Archaeological Investigation, by Sherene Baugher, Judith Guston, Edward Lenik, Diane Dallal, Thomas Amorosi, Daniel Russell, and Bobbi Brickman, pp. 153–156. Manuscript, New York City Landmarks Preservation Commission, New York, NY.

BUIKSTRA, JANE
1981 A Specialist in Ancient Cemetery Studies Looks at the Reburial Issue. *Early Man* 3(3):26–27.

CRIST, THOMAS A. J.
1998 Report on the Bioarchaeological Excavation and Analysis of Human Remains Discovered beneath Christ Episcopal Church, Shrewsbury Borough, Monmouth County, New Jersey. Manuscript, Christ Episcopal Church, Shrewsbury, NJ.

DALLAL, DIANE
1991 Clay Smoking Pipes. In The John Street Methodist Church: An Archaeological Investigation, by Sherene Baugher, Judith Guston, Edward Lenik, Diane Dallal, Thomas Amorosi, Daniel Russell, and Bobbi Brickman, pp. 85–96. Manuscript, New York City Landmarks Preservation Commission, New York, NY.

DELORIA, VINE, JR.
1969 *Custer Died for Your Sins.* Macmillan, New York, NY.
1994 *God Is Red: A Native View of Religion*, updated edition. Fulcrum Publishing, Golden, CO.

DONGOSKE, KURT E., MARK ALDENDERFER, AND KAREN DOEHNER (EDITORS)
2000 *Working Together: Native Americans and Archaeologists.* Society for American Archaeology, Washington, DC.

ECHO-HAWK, WALTER E., AND ROGER C. ECHO-HAWK
1991 Repatriation, Reburial, and Religious Rights. In *Handbook of American Indian Religious Freedom,* Christopher Vecsey, editor, pp. 63–80. Crossroad Publishing Company, New York, NY.

ELLIS, FRANKLIN
1885–1886 *History of Monmouth County.* R.T. Peck & Co., Philadelphia, PA.

GEISMAR, JOAN
1983 Archaeological Investigations of 175 Water Street Block: New York City. Report to the New York City Landmarks Preservation Commission, from Professional Service Industries, Soils Systems Divisions, Atlanta, GA.

GUSTON, JUDITH M., DIANE DALLAL, AND EDWARD J. LENIK
1991 The History of the John Street Church Site. In The John Street Methodist Church: An Archaeological Investigation, by Sherene Baugher, Judith Guston, Edward Lenik, Diane Dallal, Thomas Amorosi, Daniel Russell, and Bobbi Brickman, pp. 9–55. Manuscript, New York City Landmarks Preservation Commission, New York, NY.

HUNTER RESEARCH, INC.
1998 Archaeological Investigations in Connection with the St. Michael's Parish House Restoration and Rehabilitation, City of Trenton, Mercer County, New Jersey. Report to the New Jersey Historic Trust, Trenton, from Hunter Research, Trenton, NJ.

HURRY, SILAS D.
2004 Recreating the Chapel. Historic St. Mary's City, St. Mary's City, MD <http://www.stmaryscity.org/History/the%20Brick%20Chapel.html>. Accessed 30 Nov. 2004.

JEMISON, G. PETER
1997 Who Owns the Past? In *Native Americans and Archaeologists: Stepping Stones to Common Ground,* Nina Swidler, Kurt E. Dongoske, Roger Anyon, and Alan S. Downer, editors, pp. 57–63. AltaMira Press, Walnut Creek, CA.

JOHN STREET UNITED METHODIST CHURCH (JSUMC)
1768–1796 The Old Book. Manuscript, John Street United Methodist Church, New York, NY.
1838–1858 Minutes of the Board of Trustees. Records, John Street United Methodist Church, New York. NY.
1869–1947 Minutes of the Board of Trustees. Records, John Street United Methodist Church, New York, NY.
1960–1980 Records of the Trustees. Records, John Street United Methodist Church, New York, NY.

1984 Trustees Report for the 1984 Conference. Manuscript, John Street United Methodist Church, New York, NY.

KELSO, WILLIAM M., NICHOLAS M. LUCCKETTI, AND BEVERLY A. STRAUBE
1998 *Jamestown Rediscovery, Vol. 4.* The Association for the Preservation of Virginia Antiquities, Richmond.

KLESERT, ANTHONY L., AND SHIRLEY POWELL
2000 A Perspective on Ethics and the Reburial Controversy. In *Repatriation Reader: Who Owns American Indian Remains?* Devon A. Mihesuah, editor, pp. 200–210. University of Nebraska Press, Lincoln.

LENIK, EDWARD J.
1992 Native American Archaeological Resources in Urban America: A View from New York City. *The Bulletin, Journal of the New York State Archaeological Association* 103:20–29.

LYNOTT, MARK J., AND ALISON WYLIE (EDITORS)
2000 *Ethics in American Archaeology,* 2nd edition. Society for American Archaeology, Washington, DC.

MCCARTHY, JOHN P., AND JEANNE A. WARD
2000 Higher Education on the Frontier: Hamline University, Red Wing, Minnesota, 1854–1869. Paper presented at the Conference for The Society of Historical Archaeology, Quebec City, Quebec, Canada.

MEIGHAN, CLEMENT W.
1984 Archaeology: Science or Sacrilege? In *Ethics and Values in Archaeology,* E. L. Green, editor, pp. 208–233. Free Press, New York, NY.
1996 Burying American Archaeology. In *Archaeological Ethics,* Karen D. Vitelli, editor, pp. 209–213. AltaMira Press, Walnut Creek, CA.
2000 Some Scholars' Views on Reburial. In *Repatriation Reader: Who Owns American Indian Remains?* Devon A. Mihesuah, editor, pp. 190–199. University of Nebraska Press, Lincoln.

MIHESUAH, DEVON A. (EDITOR)
2000 *Repatriation Reader: Who Owns American Indian Remains?* University of Nebraska Press, Lincoln.

MILLER, HENRY M., SILAS D. HURRY, AND TIMOTHY B. RIORDAN
2004 The Lead Coffins of St. Mary's City: An Exploration of Life and Death in Early Maryland. *Maryland Historical Magazine* 99(3):351–373.

MROZOWSKI, STEPHEN A., GRACE H. ZIESING, AND MARY C. BEAUDRY
1996 *Living on the Boot: Historical Archaeology at the Boot Mills Boardinghouses, Lowell, Massachusetts.* University of Massachusetts Press, Amherst.

NEW YORK CITY LANDMARKS PRESERVATION COMMISSION
1986 John Street Methodist Church, Archaeology. Records, New York City Landmarks Preservation Commission, New York, NY.

PARKER, ARTHUR C.
1920 The Archaeological History of New York, Parts I and II. *New York State Museum Bulletin*, nos. 235–238:2–743.

PRICE, H. MARCUS III
1991 *Disputing the Dead: U.S. Law on Aboriginal Remains and Grave Goods*. University of Missouri Press, Columbia.

QUICK, POLLY McW. (EDITOR)
1985 *Proceedings: Conference on Reburial Issues*. Society for American Archaeology and Society of Professional Archeologists, Newberry Library, Chicago, IL.

RIORDAN, TIMOTHY B.
2004 Philip Calvert: Patron of St. Mary's City. *Maryland Historical Magazine* 99(3):329–349.

ROGERS, RAYNOR R.
1984 *The Story of the Old John Street Church*. The John Street Press, New York, NY.

RUSSELL, DANIEL H., AND THOMAS AMOROSI
1991 John Street Church Fauna. In The John Street Church: An Archaeological Investigation, by Sherene Baugher, Judith Guston, Edward Lenik, Diane Dallal, Thomas Amorosi, Daniel Russell, and Bobbi Brickman, pp. 125–152. Manuscript, New York City Landmarks Preservation Commission, New York, NY.

SCHARFENBERGER, GERARD P.
2000 The Baptists of Middletown: An Ethnoarchaeological Study of New Jersey's Earliest Congregation. Master's thesis, Department of Anthropology, Hunter College, New York, NY.

SCHARFENBERGER, GERARD P., AND SHERENE BAUGHER
2000 Preliminary Archaeological Report on the Old First Church Site, Middletown, Monmouth County, New Jersey. *Bulletin of the Archaeological Society of New Jersey* 55:44–56.

SEAMAN, SAMUEL A.
1892 *Annals of New York Methodism*. Hunt and Eaton, New York, NY.

SPUDE, CATHERINE H., DOUGLAS D. SCOTT, FRANK NORRIS, DAVID R. HULESBECK, LINDA S. CUMMINGS, AND KATHRYN PUSEMAN
1993 *Archaeological Investigations in Skagway Alaska, Vol. 4, Father Turnell's Trash Pit, Klondike Gold Rush National Park, Skagway, Alaska*. U.S. Department of the Interior, National Park Service, Denver, CO.

STOKES, I. N. PHELPS
1915 *The Iconography of Manhattan Island, 1498–1909*, Vol. 1. Robert H. Dodd, New York, NY.

SWIDLER, NINA, KURT E. DONGOSKE, ROGER ANYON, AND ALAN S. DOWNER (EDITORS)
1997 *Native Americans and Archaeologists: Stepping Stones to Common Ground*. AltaMira Press, Walnut Creek, CA.

THOMAS, DAVID HURST
2000 *Skull Wars: Kennewick Man, Archaeology, and the Battle for Native American Identity*. Basic Books, New York, NY.

TURNER, C. G., II
1986 What Is Lost with Skeletal Reburial? *Quarterly Review of Archaeology* 7(1):1–3.

VEIT, RICHARD
2002 *Digging New Jersey's Past: Historical Archaeology in the Garden State*. Rutgers University Press, New Brunswick, NJ.

WAKELEY, J. B.
1858 *Lost Chapters Recovered from the Early History of American Methodism*. Carlton & Porter, New York, NY.

WALKER, IAIN C.
1983 Nineteenth-Century Clay Tobacco-Pipes in Canada. In *The Archaeology of the Clay Tobacco Pipe*, Vol. 7., Peter Davey, editor, pp. 1–88. BAR International Series, No. 175. America, Oxford, England, UK.

WATKINS, JOE
2000 *Indigenous Archaeology: American Indian Values and Scientific Practice*. AltaMira Press, Walnut Creek, CA.
2003 Archaeological Ethics and American Indians. In *Ethical Issues in Archaeology*, Larry J. Zimmerman, Karen D. Vitelli, and Julie Hollowell-Zimmer, editors, pp. 129–141. AltaMira Press, Walnut Creek, CA.

ZIMMERMAN, LARRY J.
1985 A Perspective on the Reburial Issue from South Dakota. In *Proceedings: Conference on Reburial Issue*, Polly McW. Quick, editor, pp. 1–4. Society for American Archaeology and Society of Professional Archeologists, Newberry Library, Chicago, IL.
1996 Sharing Control of the Past. In *Archaeological Ethics*, Karen D. Vitelli, editor, pp. 214–218. AltaMira Press, Walnut Creek, CA.
2000 A New and Different Archaeology? With a Postscript on the Impact of the Kennewick Dispute. In *Repatriation Reader: Who Owns American Indian Remains?* Devon A. Mihesuah, editor, pp. 294–306. University of Nebraska Press, Lincoln.

SHERENE BAUGHER
ARCHAEOLOGY PROGRAM
CORNELL UNIVERSITY
261 McGRAW HALL
ITHACA, NY 14853

John W. Lawrence
Paul W. Schopp
Robert J. Lore

"They Even Threaten the Sick That They Will Not Be Buried in the Churchyard": Salvage Archaeology of the Raritan-in-the-Hills Cemetery, Somerset County, New Jersey

ABSTRACT

This article discusses the chance discovery and subsequent salvage archaeology of an early-18th-century German Lutheran burying ground in the mountains north of Pluckemin, Somerset County, New Jersey. The project began purely as a salvage operation wrought by residential development; excavation techniques employed under less-than-ideal conditions and a description of the cemetery are presented. Documentary research revealed that the congregation had only lasted from ca. 1714 to 1756, during which time it endured a great deal of internal conflict. Osteological analysis permitted age/sex identification of most of the individuals interred in the cemetery, and the artifactual record provided an opportunity to explore some aspects of the burial practices employed. These data, together with observed variation in the location of individual graves within the cemetery, are used to formulate a possible interpretation that links the variations observed in the physical remnants of the cemetery with the historical record that speaks in detail about the social breakdown of the community during its brief 50-year existence. In brief, the interpretation offered here argues that the principal of social organization within Raritan-in-the-Hills shifted from one of corporate unity (*Gemeinschaft*) to individual survival (*Geschellschaft*) prior to its final dissolution.

Introduction

By the afternoon of 30 July 1998, the charges had been set. The blast needed to crumble the bedrock that lay just beneath the surface of the hilltop had been scheduled for that afternoon. Located on a hilltop in the Second Watchung range in Bernards Township, Somerset County, dense basalt underlay the site (Figure 1). The bedrock would have to be removed to lay utility trenches and build house foundations for the planned subdivision. The blast that afternoon created a semicircular crater 2 to 3 ft. deep with a maximum diameter of 50 ft.

The developer called archaeologists to the site the following day to examine the situation. Human bones, highly fragmented and in poor condition, could be seen at the site of the detonation, along with the faint outlines of a grave shaft in the wall of the blast crater. Local and county police officials arrived to remove the bones to the Regional Medical Examiner's office for examination.

As an unregistered cemetery with no affiliation with Native Americans or African Americans, the site lacked the protective umbrella normally afforded significant cultural resources by state or federal regulatory agencies. Nevertheless, the office of the New Jersey State Attorney General assumed oversight. By its order, the developer sealed off a wide area surrounding the blast crater, and construction activities halted until the identification and removal of all human remains had occurred. Over the next five months, archaeologists successfully recovered the remains of 68 individuals and associated artifacts from this site, while at the same time recording precise provenience information for all recovered materials.

At initial discovery, no markers indicated the presence of a cemetery, and very little was known about the site. Historical research began concomitantly with the archaeological salvage operation, and preliminary documentation quickly established that the burial ground was the site of Raritan-in-the-Hills, one of several Lutheran churches established in the Raritan River valley by German immigrants early in the 18th century and which had disappeared before the Revolutionary War.

Historical research also revealed that this was a deeply troubled community, riven by internal dissent and fueled by factionalism within the Lutheran church—all this exacerbated by personal animosities and ambitions. This article attempts to link the documented dissolution of the community with patterns observed in coffin type and the placement of individual graves within the cemetery. Ultimately, it is argued, changing patterns

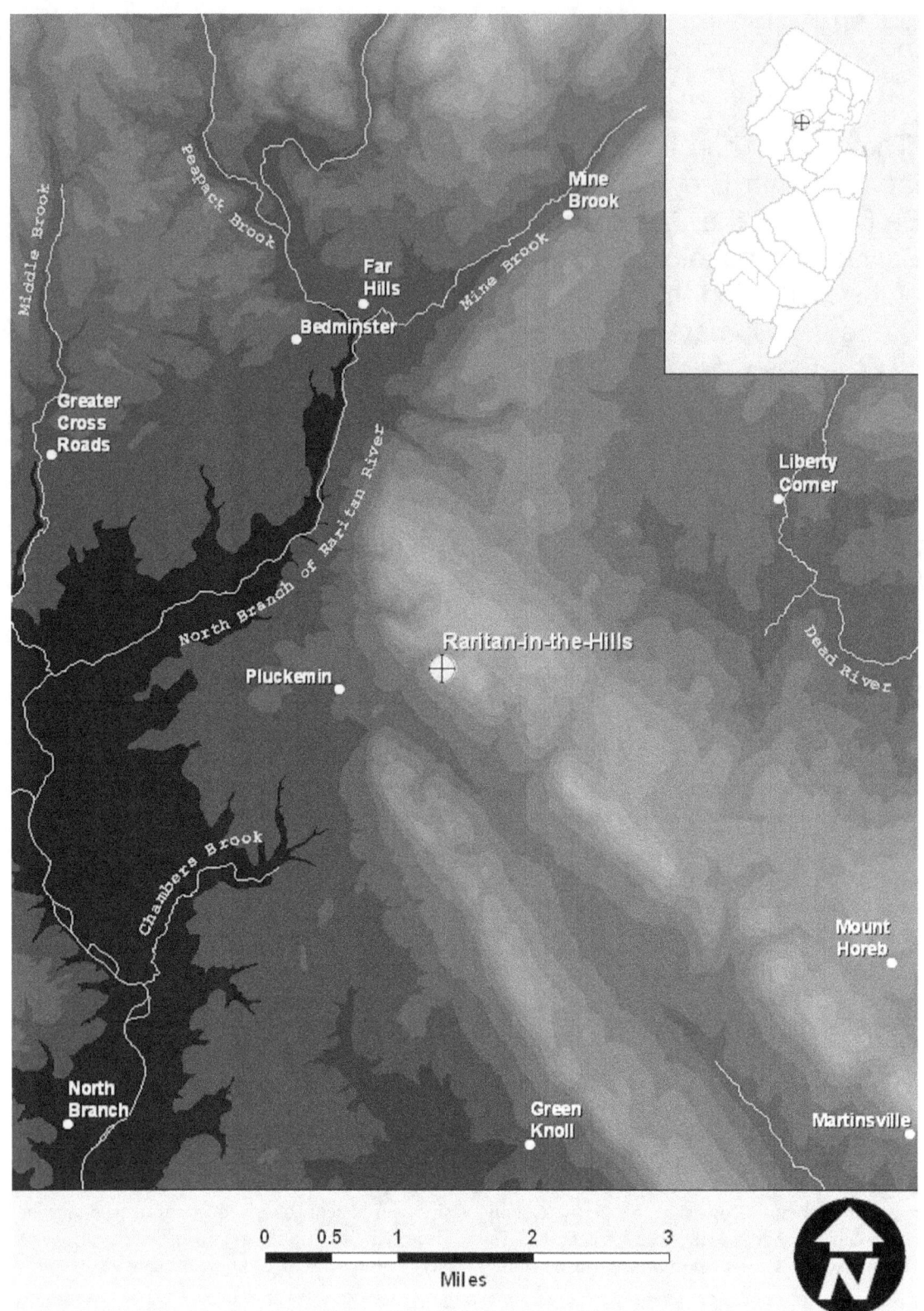

FIGURE 1. Raritan-in-the-Hills (28So128). (Map by Laura D. Cushman, 1999.)

of coffin placement from one of orderly rows and columns to one of individual or individual family groups is indicative of a transformation in the principal of social order from *Gemeinschaft*, a social strategy of survival based on corporate unity and corporate action, to *Geschellschaft*, adaptation taken at the level of the individual or individual family.

History of Raritan-in-the-Hills

Establishment of the Community

The Raritan-in-the-Hills congregation dates to the early years of the 18th century when German immigrants, generally called Palatinates, began to settle in the Somerset and Hunterdon counties area of New Jersey. Named for the Palatine region of Germany, these transplants represent just one sector of ongoing German migration to North America. According to Philip Otterness (1999), the people who departed southwest Germany during 1709 for London and eventually North America were a diverse group, both ethnically and religiously. A number of British officials and organizations, ranging from the Earl of Sunderland (England's secretary of state) to the Anglican Society for the Propagation of the Gospel, grouped these people together as "Germans" to engender empathy for their plight. A carefully crafted portrayal of this group as "Palatine refugees" served as an appeal to wealthy Britons for underwriting the Germans' cause. Conditions in the camps established for these peoples in England soon elicited a backlash, however, and Queen Anne wished them gone from England.

How the Germans arrived in the Raritan River valley region is not precisely known, but it is probable that they arrived from north-central New York State. Robert Hunter, governor of New York, proposed relocating the Palatine refugees that were in England to the Schorarie region of the New York colony to produce supplies for the British Navy. In April 1710, 3,000 Germans departed London for New York (Otterness 1999). Their relationship with Hunter deteriorated quickly. The most likely scenario has them fissioning from the New York settlement and traveling south to Hunterdon and northern Somerset counties in New Jersey (Otterness 1999:19). Many of these emigrants became squat-ters, establishing farms on unappropriated and untitled land that actually belonged to the East Jersey Proprietors.

The earliest record of a Lutheran service in northern Somerset County is dated 1714 (Banta 1903:57). In that year, the Reverend Justus Falckner, head of the Lutheran Church in New York and New Jersey, established a continuing pattern of visiting the region every summer to lead religious services for German residents. He did so until his death in 1723 (Kreider 1942:33–34) (Figure 2). Falckner held these religious services in various homes as no church building existed. In 1724, the year after Justus Falckner's death, his brother, Daniel, assumed responsibility for the Raritan congregations, since Daniel reportedly already resided in the Raritan River valley (Kreider 1942:38–39). Sometime during the early 1730s, the Raritan-in-the-Hills congregation erected a sanctuary—reportedly a log structure—on a 100-acre lot of land that Peter Sonmans, a large landholder in East Jersey, donated to the congregation (Honeyman 1913:96; Hart and Kreider 1962:66,157). Daniel continued serving at least four Raritan River valley congregations until he was reportedly overtaken with a brain disorder in 1731 (Honeyman 1913:162). Both Justus and Daniel held pietistic beliefs, although contemporary records report Daniel as anything but pious.

According to Christoph Wilhelm Berkenmeyer, the leader of the New York-New Jersey Lutheran Church beginning in 1725, Daniel "was the leader of the 'inspired maidens' whom he brought into this country, of whom Anna Maria Schuchart is now his wife, for he made her pregnant during the voyage" (Hart and Kreider 1962:16–20). Little has been found concerning the radical pietistic "inspired maidens," except that authors Simon Hart and Harry Kreider (1962:414) note, "Anna Maria Schuchart, wife of Daniel Falckner, was known as 'the Erfurt prophetess,' a visionary pietist." On his deathbed, Justus reportedly "warned his whole parish not to have anything to do with this drunkard," referring to his brother. Constantly intoxicated, Daniel accosted women on the street and even threatened to slit the throat of one of his parishioners. Similarly, some communicants deemed Daniel's "inspired maiden" wife to be a witch. An incident is reported where Anna Maria was accused of having caused the bride to faint and scream in pain, and to make

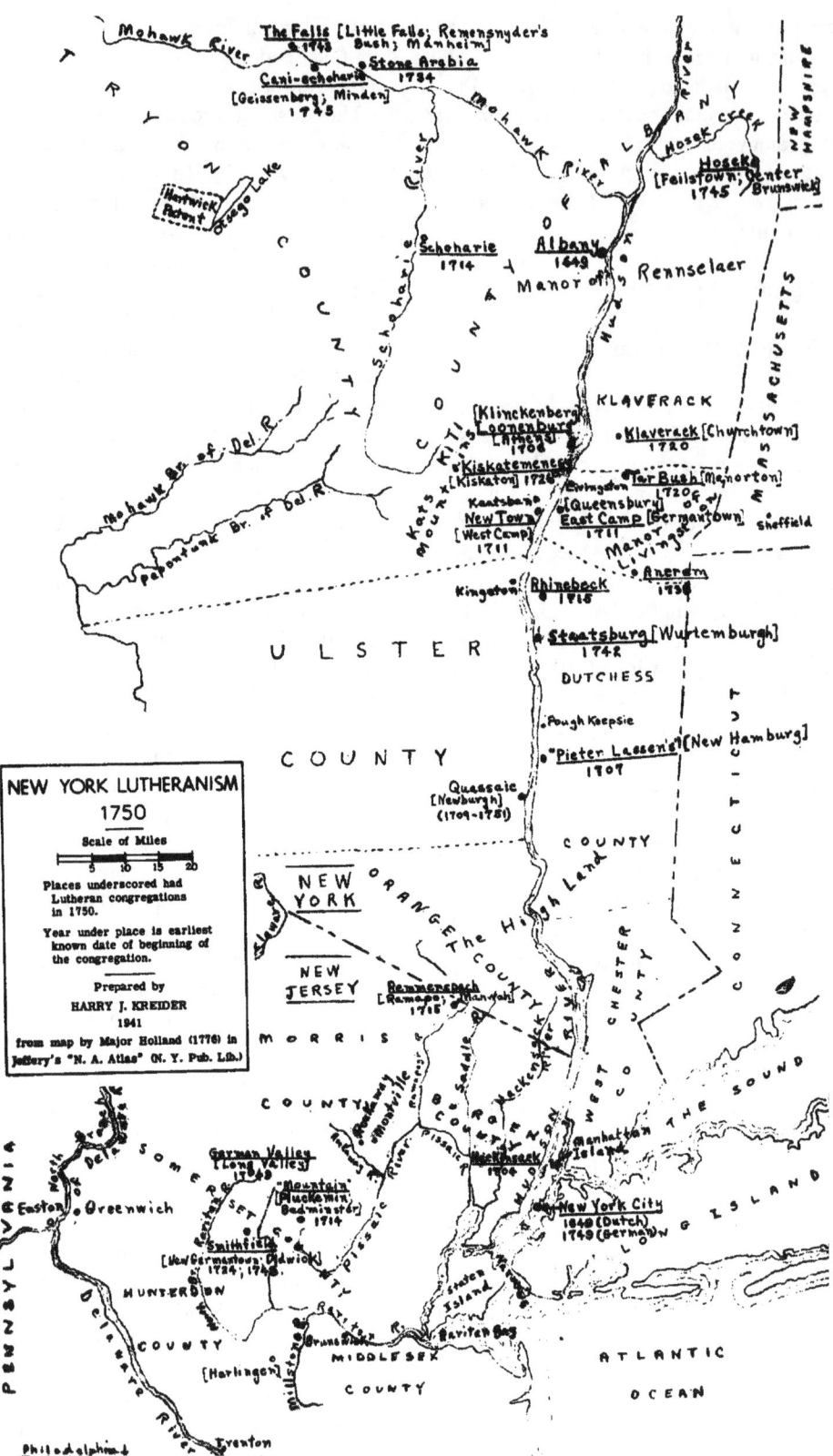

FIGURE 2. Early-eighteenth-century Lutheran settlements in Northern New Jersey. (Adapted from Kreider 1942 by Laura D. Cushman, 1999.)

Perspectives from *Historical Archaeology*

animal sounds and rend her clothes during her wedding ceremony. The account relates that Anna Maria cured the affected women by gathering some herbs and throwing them on the cookhouse fire. Anna Maria then threatened to send her husband and his entire parish "to the devil" (Hart and Kreider 1962:16–20).

Daniel and Anna Maria agreed to leave their congregations and retire, but the couple continued to live nearby (Honeyman 1913:162–163; Hart and Kreider 1962:14). In 1731, the Raritan Parish sent a formal request to the Hamburg Ministerium for a new German pastor to tend to its needs, but the consistory did not select a candidate until 1734. For the period between 1731 and 1734, a number of visiting pastors held services for the congregations (Honeyman 1913:162–163; Hart and Kreider 1962:14). The Hamburg Ministerium selected Johann August Wolf, a graduate of an orthodox university, as pastor of the Raritan Parish. Wolf arrived in New York during September 1734 and made his way to Raritan to begin his ministerial assignment. Upon reaching Raritan, Wolf was not immediately prepared to preach, and members of the congregation requested that Daniel deliver a farewell message (Hart and Kreider 1962:53,65). This lack of preparation provides an early indication of Wolf's problems and his chaotic relationship with the Raritan community that would haunt both for more than a decade.

Raritan-in-the-Hills and the Dynamics of Lutheran Factionalism

Not only did the English find the Palatines a "turbulent race of men" requiring "a strong hand and severe discipline" (Otterness 1999:19), the Raritan congregation's localized problems played out the much larger debate between those who subscribed to pietistic doctrine and the orthodox leadership within the Evangelical Lutheran Church. Not a "distinct sect or creedal statement," pietism is defined as "the interpretation of Christianity in terms of meaningful relationship of the believer with God which resulted in a feeling of contentment and a state of righteousness ... [and a] ... personal commitment to a moral life lived in accord with the will of God" (Riforgiato 1980:27). Other authors indicate that elements of pietism included religious idealism, a strong emphasis placed upon biblical law, good

works, personal experience of salvation, and individual responsibility in faith (Feuerhahn 1998; Gordon 1998). Orthodoxy, "under the influence of rationalism, gradually reduced faith to intellectual assent to abstract theological propositions," in contrast to pietism, which defined "faith existentially, as practice and personal commitment" (Riforgiato 1980:28).

As described above, the death of Justus in 1723 caused the New York and New Jersey congregations to issue a formal call to Germany for a new senior pastor to provide collective congregational and pastoral oversight throughout the region, which resulted in Berkenmeyer arriving in America during September 1725. Berkenmeyer fulfilled the role of a Lutheran bishop without owning the title. Among other roles, he served as the liaison between the region's congregations and the Hamburg Ministerium. He had studied theology at the orthodox university of Altdorf and was "... a firm adherent to the orthodox order" (Kreider 1942:41). Berkenmeyer found his workload in America almost overwhelming, with most congregations in disarray, worshiping in decaying sanctuaries, and involved in intercongregational disputes. In response, he applied his orthodox-based rationalism to his seemingly desperate pastoral situation and grouped the 10 congregations into four parishes with a pastor assigned to each parish. During the process of creating the parishes, Berkenmeyer transcended his role as a pastor and assumed the mantle of a superintendent, dedicating himself to the welfare of all the congregations and their members (Kreider 1942:39–48).

Subsequent to establishing the parishes, Berkenmeyer continued applying orthodoxy-based hierarchical order to his American charge by creating a church constitution based on one the Dutch drafted in Amsterdam. His revised copy, completed in 1734, "... would be 'more applicable' to colonial needs ... , ... signed by all the pastors, present and future, and permanently 'deposited with the Church Council at New York [City]'" with a copy "furnished to every congregation or parish" (Kreider 1942:84). All pastors had signed this document by 1746, thereby indicating approval. Berkenmeyer wrote his liturgical constitution with exactness concerning congregational conformity to orthodox practices while he "carried to an extreme" the condemnation of pietistic customs. The constitution forbid "all private conventicles and secret meetings" without the church council having full knowledge of such meetings (Kreider 1942:88). Other sections of the document also reflected Berkenmeyer's staunch orthodox stance, particularly in the way the church would secure its pastors, in which he admonished that congregations could "... accept only those pastors who were 'orthodox' Lutherans, coming from consistories of Hamburg, London, or Amsterdam, 'or other orthodox Academies and Ministeriums'" (Kreider 1942:89). Because Berkenmeyer had pastoral oversight, he accepted Wolf upon his arrival as a fellow pastor in every sense of the word, particularly since Wolf had received orthodox training in preparation for the ministry. Berkenmeyer remained steadfast in his full support throughout Wolf's tenure at Raritan-in-the Hills.

In 1742, the Reverend Henry Melchior Muhlenberg, a pietist pastor, emigrated to Pennsylvania to begin administering Lutheranism in that colony. Within a year of his arrival, the Raritan communicants implored him to assist them in removing Wolf as their pastor. By 1745, Muhlenberg accomplished ridding the congregation of Wolf and won the hearts of the Raritan Parish, thereby releasing the congregations from Berkenmeyer's control by 1750. During the same year, Muhlenberg also claimed two more of Berkenmeyer parishes for the pietists, leaving the orthodox leader with just two parishes. Berkenmeyer died a broken man in 1751 (Kreider 1942:106–121).

The Wolf Controversy

Wolf's problems with the Raritan-in-the-Hills community consisted of personal, financial, and religious issues. Perhaps due to his orthodox training, he arrived unprepared to present his scriptural exegesis from memory and retreated to reading all his sermons from prepared notes. This contradicted the extemporaneous style the Raritan-in-the-Hills congregation expected, and they quickly became outraged. Other examples of Wolf's deficiencies in the eyes of community followed, reaching a point where Wolf indicated that if the church would remit the six months salary due him, he would resign his pastorate.

In an effort to quell the growing unrest in the parish, Berkenmeyer called a "classical assembly" at Raritan-in-the-Hills for August 1735

(Hart and Kreider 1962:105–109,121–122). One 20th-century source indicates the congregation sought redress for "... the conduct of the Rev. Johann Wolf, who it was said, had been charging exorbitant rates for sermons, baptisms, and funerals. His fee of 20 or 30 shillings for an adult's funeral was double the scale prevailing in Hackensack" (Federal Writers' Project 1939:449). This assembly has long been considered the first Lutheran Synod meeting in America (Honeyman 1913:163), but more importantly the meeting provided Berkenmeyer with the opportunity to extend his control over the congregants. Upon opening the meeting, Berkenmeyer presented the church constitution he had prepared the year before (1734) for ratification. Wolf immediately signed the document, which led his church's delegates to recoil in fear and anger, denouncing the document as a snare designed to "catch" congregations. Berkenmeyer, the elected president of the assembly, also presented seven "Points for Consideration" (Kreider 1942:95–96). This document essentially provided a full defense and excusal for Wolf's behavior and placed blame for all of the problems squarely on the shoulders of the communicants. The congregation's delegates finally agreed to the provisions of Berkenmeyer's agenda after much deliberation, but they refused to pay any salary past due; Wolf reluctantly agreed but later reneged (Kreider 1942:97,106–107).

Wolf finally sought legal recourse to obtain the back salary due him. He entered pleas before the New Jersey Supreme Court in 1739, which ultimately found in his favor and ordered the Raritan Parish to pay all of his back salary due him, plus costs (Hart and Kreider 1962:198–204). Unfortunately, no legible documents beyond court-issued writs have survived from this case (New Jersey Supreme Court 1739, 1742a, 1742b).

Muhlenberg and the Pietist Reaction

Muhlenberg arrived in Philadelphia during November 1742 and found a situation in Pennsylvania's Lutheran churches remarkably similar to what Berkenmeyer faced upon arriving in New York two decades before. Rather than assume the role of a superintendent, Muhlenberg formed a "Ministerium (Synod) of Pennsylvania" and provided for the laity to gain proper recognition within this assembly (Kreider

1942:104). Leonard Riforgiato (1980:138) describes Muhlenberg as "... an activist, a missionary, and a pastor" who, "[c]ombined with his activism and concern for the pastoral problems of individual souls, not theological systems, was a genius for accommodation and moderate adaptation."

The Raritan Lutherans first called Muhlenberg to assist them with Wolf in 1743, less than a year after he had arrived in America. Conditions had deteriorated rapidly after the 1735 Classical Assembly, and the congregation was desperate to rid themselves of their "minister," once and for all. Initially, Muhlenberg declined their invitation, but he consented after the New Jersey Supreme Court recommended that "a board of arbitration be constituted, embracing two representatives chosen by the parish and two by the pastor, in order to settle the affair permanently" (Kreider 1942:106).

At the end of the arbitration, Wolf received a partial payment for what he sought (£90) with promissory notes for the remainder, and the arbitrating pastors returned to their respective parishes (Kreider 1942:106–107). In the intervening time, social conditions within the Raritan-in-the-Hills community had disintegrated considerably. Muhlenberg (1942:106), writing in 1745 about the previous 10 years, said,

> ... the communion was not administered, the sick not visited; indeed there was such a desolation that it was made among the German a subject of street songs. The congregations were altogether scattered except a few families. ... For eight years there were no confirmations, no sacraments, and everything was in decay.

From this time onward, the Raritan congregations looked to Muhlenberg for oversight of their parish. During the next few years, either he or others of his Pennsylvania pietist pastors returned to provide religious instruction and hold services. In 1748, Muhlenberg reorganized the parish, seeking to place all four congregations into one church, but the Raritan-in-the-Hills communicants refused, reasoning that they were the oldest congregation, they already had their own church and parsonage, and they lived too far from the proposed "centralized" location. Muhlenberg's Pennsylvania Synod assumed official supervision of the Raritan Parish in June 1750—a repudiation of Berkenmeyer and his orthodoxy (Kreider 1942:108–109).

Dissolution of Raritan-in-the-Hills

In 1748, Muhlenberg assigned pietist pastor John Albert Weygand to serve the Raritan church. Similar to Wolf, however, the congregation considered Weygand's behavior unacceptable. He quickly fell from favor with his communicants and ended his service to Raritan-in-the-Hills in 1753 (Honeyman 1913:169–170). In the same year Weygand left, the Reverend Ludolph Heinrich Schrenck, another pietist, became the final pastor assigned to the "Mountain Church." As with the other pastors preceding him, Schrenck proved as unpopular a clergyman as Wolf and Weygand (Honeyman 1913:170). Muhlenberg (1942:364) provides some additional information in his personal journal about the Raritan congregation during this period in his July 1753 entries:

> ... they already had in their possession the gift of a hundred acres of land for a church and parsonage. But in the Wolf controversies, they had lost almost all of it because the English and the Irish had tried to usurp the land for themselves. Now if they held no services at all in their little old church, the land and the so-called parsonage, etc., would be lost altogether and there would be no hope of their ever regaining possession of them.

Schrenck remained in the community for only three years, departing in 1756, at which time the Raritan congregation felt the need to erect a new church. The congregants abandoned their mountaintop churchyard and relocated to the hamlet of Pluckemin, situated about a mile away from the base of Schley Mountain. The Raritan communicants constructed St. Paul's Lutheran Church in the village. The new sanctuary remained in regular use until about 1809, when the congregation drifted away from Pluckemin, as it had from Raritan-in-the-Hills, literally abandoning the building. Within eight years, other people demolished the vacant, decaying edifice and erected a Methodist Episcopal Church in its stead. In 1851, the Methodist house of worship became a Presbyterian church, which it has remained to this day (Honeyman 1913:170–172).

With the construction of St. Paul's Church in the town center of Pluckemin, the congregation apparently abandoned their former burial ground, but it was not completely forgotten. John C. Honeyman visited the site of the church and cemetery in 1902, guided by the landowner's son, writing,

> Mr. Towles lives half a mile or more from the before mentioned main road ["Old Stagecoach Road"]. His son said he would show me all that was left of the old graveyard, viz., two stones, since the burial-ground has now been ploughed over, but could easily be traced by the color of the soil. The boulders were leaning against a tree, and I deciphered as follows: –
>
> 1752   E.L.
> IoF   1755
>
> I found only two stones, although Mr. Towles informed me there are others covered up on the great stone ridge or pile adjoining, as he saw others with dates years ago in this pile. The field and especially the old church site has been ploughed over many times, and the stones carted off to this ridge near by; it is possible they are deep in the stone row (Honeyman 1913:98).

The simple stones described above, consisting of initials or dates, denote rudimentary grave markers that either a family member or church member prepared. No professional grave-marker carvers working in German arrived in New Jersey prior to the 1780s (Veit 2000). It is assumed that cultural and religious differences, together with costs, would have prohibited community members from obtaining carved headstones from neighboring English communities far to the east and south. The presence of these stones with a minimized informational presentation provides some evidence that the congregation embraced the concept of humility in death as in life. If so, the markers merely provided the living with locational information for an individual burial, both for family members and the church sexton who had charge of the graveyard.

Site Excavation

Defining site boundaries was the first problem encountered in excavating Raritan-in-the-Hills. Historical data provided no information on the size of the congregation or the dimensions of the church's graveyard. On the ground, the site and surrounding area had been stripped of its vegetation and partially graded for the new subdivision, making it impossible to use the landscape as a guide towards estimating the limits of the site.

Although the site featured less than ideal conditions, a variety of nonintrusive methods initially provided a means to pinpoint individual graves.

These methods included ground-penetrating radar (GPR) as well as electromagnetic and magnetic sensing devices. Using this equipment, technicians surveyed an area measuring approximately 70 by 100 ft. adjacent to the location of the human remains uncovered by the blasting. The GPR detected a number of subsurface anomalies. Only four appeared to be of a size consistent with human burials, and three of these anomalies extended in a line southeast of the grave shaft uncovered by the blasting. Numerous magnetic anomalies appeared in a seemingly random pattern across the area surveyed.

The field crew subsequently conducted excavations at each of the four most promising soil anomalies, as well as at most of the scattered magnetic anomalies. Removing the densely packed mixture of subsoil and decaying bedrock with hand tools proved extremely arduous, but the excavations produced three burials adjacent to the west side of the blast crater. Feature 1 consisted of remains of a child between 10 to 12 years of age, with only the cranium and arms (right and left humerus, radius, ulna) surviving. Each individual had been placed on their back in an east-west direction, arms fully extended, with the head to the west. Despite the deterioration of all wooden components of the coffin, several in-situ nails accompanied this burial. Their distribution pattern conformed to a coffin shape as identified at other 18th-century cemeteries (LeeDecker 2001). While affixing decorative hardware and placing planks in the burial shaft to prevent the coffin from collapsing could also introduce nails into an interment, these artifacts were consistent in their placement and orientation within the individual burial to represent a specific coffin type. This was observed to be true in all burials excavated at this cemetery. Consequently, these artifacts are referred to as coffin nails throughout this paper.

Feature 2, encountered approximately 4 ft. to the north of Feature 1, had been heavily impacted from the blast, which had lifted the bedrock, causing the feature to become fragmented and slumped. The field notes delineate a 2.5 ft. variation in the elevation between the cranium and the feet. As with Feature 1, cranial and postcranial elements exhibited a generally poor state of preservation. The supine individual was oriented east-west. Postexcavation analysis identified the individual as an adult female between 35 to 40 years of age. The fragmented state of the feature, compounded by recent disturbance, did not allow for recording of arm and hand placement.

Blasting had also impacted Feature 3, encountered 10 ft. to the northwest of Feature 2. Excavation revealed a supine individual with fragmented cranial and postcranial elements, as with the previously mentioned features. The right arm was flexed and lying across the mid-section of the individual. The fragmented state of the feature, compounded by recent disturbance, did not allow for recording of arm and hand placement. Postexcavation analysis identified the individual as an adult male between 30 to 35 years of age.

Although these initial excavations produced positive results, the location of the three burials did not match the four principal soil anomalies defined by GPR. The location of these burials was most closely associated with positive magnetic readings produced by coffin nails found with each burial, rather than GPR anomalies. Many of the other magnetic anomalies, however, failed to produce human remains. Regardless, a second survey using an electromagnetic sensing device produced a large number of "hits." Testing occurred at all of these hits, and all failed to produce positive results, leading to the conclusion that the assumed correlation between magnetic hits and burials was spurious and that remote sensing did not prove to be an effective tool at this site. Rugged ground surface conditions, combined with shallow, ferruginous bedrock, made the equipment ineffective.

From this point onward, the problem of defining the site boundaries was solved methodically by systematic trenching across the site. Observing that the initial interments had been oriented in an east-west alignment, the field crew laid out trenches measuring 3 to 4 ft. wide at intervals of every 5 to 6 ft. on a north-south grid that was perpendicular to the known remains. Once the trench revealed bone or coffin nails (most frequently the upper course of nails used to seal the lid on the coffin), the archaeologists extended excavation to the east and west to discover the complete outline of the grave shaft. In many cases, this could only be reconstructed by the outline of nails in the soil. In some areas of the site, however, the grave shaft had been cut a foot or two into bedrock,

evidently by cleaving through fractures and seams in the basalt to form a narrow shaft to fit the interment. In these cases, the grave shaft could be isolated by cleaning off the bedrock. As planned, each trench extended to the north and south approximately 20 ft. beyond the last grave, at which point the trench terminated, and the outermost grave marked the limits of the cemetery. In some areas of the site, the field crew opened large block excavations to expose a group of burials found close together.

The field crew employed a standardized methodology, dictated by the demands of a salvage operation to record and remove the individual burials. All osseous material is heavily weathered and highly fragmented, with only minimal analytical value. After producing scale drawings and photographing the remains, the field technicians removed all skeletal material for later reburial, and only the crania (where they existed) underwent examination for age and sex determination in the laboratory.

Results of the Salvage Excavation

By the time excavation ended on the mountaintop, some 5,200 sq. ft. had been examined, and the remains of 68 individuals were recovered and removed. Excavations revealed that the cemetery straddled two very different soil environments. The topography in and around the cemetery undulated slightly, with slight rises to the northwest and southeast, separated by a broad, shallow swale area bisecting the cemetery from the northeast downhill to the southwest. Outside the swale area, soil identification matched the Mount Lucas-Watchung very stony silt loam as mapped in the *Somerset County Soil Survey* (Kirkham 1989). Formed on hillsides, slopes and ridges from dark igneous diabase and basalt bedrock, these soils may contain a large percent of decayed bedrock such as the cemetery site exhibited. In contrast, the swale area contained fine, hard-packed silty subsoil with little to no stone. Other than the absence of fractured basalt, the swale's subsoil was virtually indistinguishable from adjacent Mount Lucas series soils, and the crew recorded it as a yellowish-red (2.5YR 4/6) silt loam with clay.

Because the cemetery suffered erosion through repeated agricultural plowing during the 19th and 20th centuries, and construction activities prior to the salvage operation further disturbed the site, it is impossible to gauge the original depth of the grave shafts. Grave shafts in the swale area, however, appeared clearly as slightly darker soil stains. Individual shafts were excavated in this area to a depth between 1.3 and 2.4 ft. below the current ground surface. In contrast to the easy-to-dig silt of the swale area, grave shafts over the remainder of the site not only penetrated the stony subsoil but in many cases also cut into the underlying bedrock to attain the culturally prescribed depth. These grave shafts averaged 1.95 ft. below the current ground surface.

Cemetery Structure and Organization

Archaeologists at Raritan-in-the-Hills successfully exposed two sides of the burial ground. Based on the dimensions of those two sides, the cemetery is believed to have covered a square to slightly rectangular area measuring 70 by 75 ft., or slightly more than one-tenth of an acre. Blasting disturbed approximately one-quarter of this area, so the precise limits of the burial ground must remain speculative. The entire perimeter of the blast crater, however, yielded human remains exhibiting various levels of disruption, leaving no doubt that the explosion had destroyed more than just a few individuals. The population density of the undisturbed portion of the cemetery equaled 0.017 individuals per square foot. Applying this density figure to the total area that the cemetery is believed to have encompassed, it is likely to have originally contained some 90 individuals. Based on documentary evidence, the cemetery would have been in use for approximately 50 years, from sometime in the early-18th century to about 1756, when the community of Raritan-in-the-Hills disintegrated. The remaining congregants relocated to the village of Pluckemin, abandoning their burial ground to the elements. No data point to the possibility that anyone used the cemetery either before or after these dates. The community had moved from its hilltop location to the town of Pluckemin, at the foot of the mountain; the churchyard there contains abundant gravestones dating to the second half of the 18th century.

To the untrained eye, Raritan-in-the-Hills exhibits little spatial organization (Figure 3).

This is deceptive, however, for the fact that grave shafts were sunk through dense, stony soil and cut from bedrock when an area of soft, silty soil could be found nearby speaks to the fact that cultural norms dictated the design and use of this sacred ground. The apparent lack of organization appears to reflect the fact that these norms changed significantly during the brief period of time (ca. 1714 to 1756) that the historical record indicates that the congregants used the cemetery. In order to approach the issue of how the Raritan-in-the-Hills cemetery may have been organized and how that organization changed through time, this paper examines the structure of the burial ground from four separate physical attributes: (1) overall spatial organization of the individual graves, (2) organization by age/sex groups, (3) distribution of coffin types, and (4) distribution of grave goods.

As can be readily seen in Figure 3, there is complete similarity in all graves in that they are aligned east-west with the head placed in the west, consistent with Christian practice generally and not particularly surprising or informative. The most striking organizational aspect of the cemetery is the clearly organized row of graves that form the western edge of the burial ground (Figure 3, row 1), with parts of a second row to the east (Figure 3, row 2). Elements of the second row are most visible at the southern and northern limits of the site and less visible near the center. Beyond that to the east, this pattern becomes less distinct, although the precise point where it terminates is not totally clear.

A second organizational pattern to the site is the location of infant/newborn burials at the outside limits of the subadult and adult burials. This pattern is most clearly observed at the southwestern corner of the site where the archaeologists found four infant burials in a segregated area. There is a corresponding area of infants and small children at the northeastern corner of the site, although some adolescents or adults are also present in this area.

The western portion of the site shows relatively consistent patterning, with adult burials in rows and columns and infants segregated into a reserved area of hallowed ground. Interestingly, this patterning appears to break down toward the center and eastern half of the cemetery. The row and column pattern observed in the western portion of the site is not visible in the eastern half

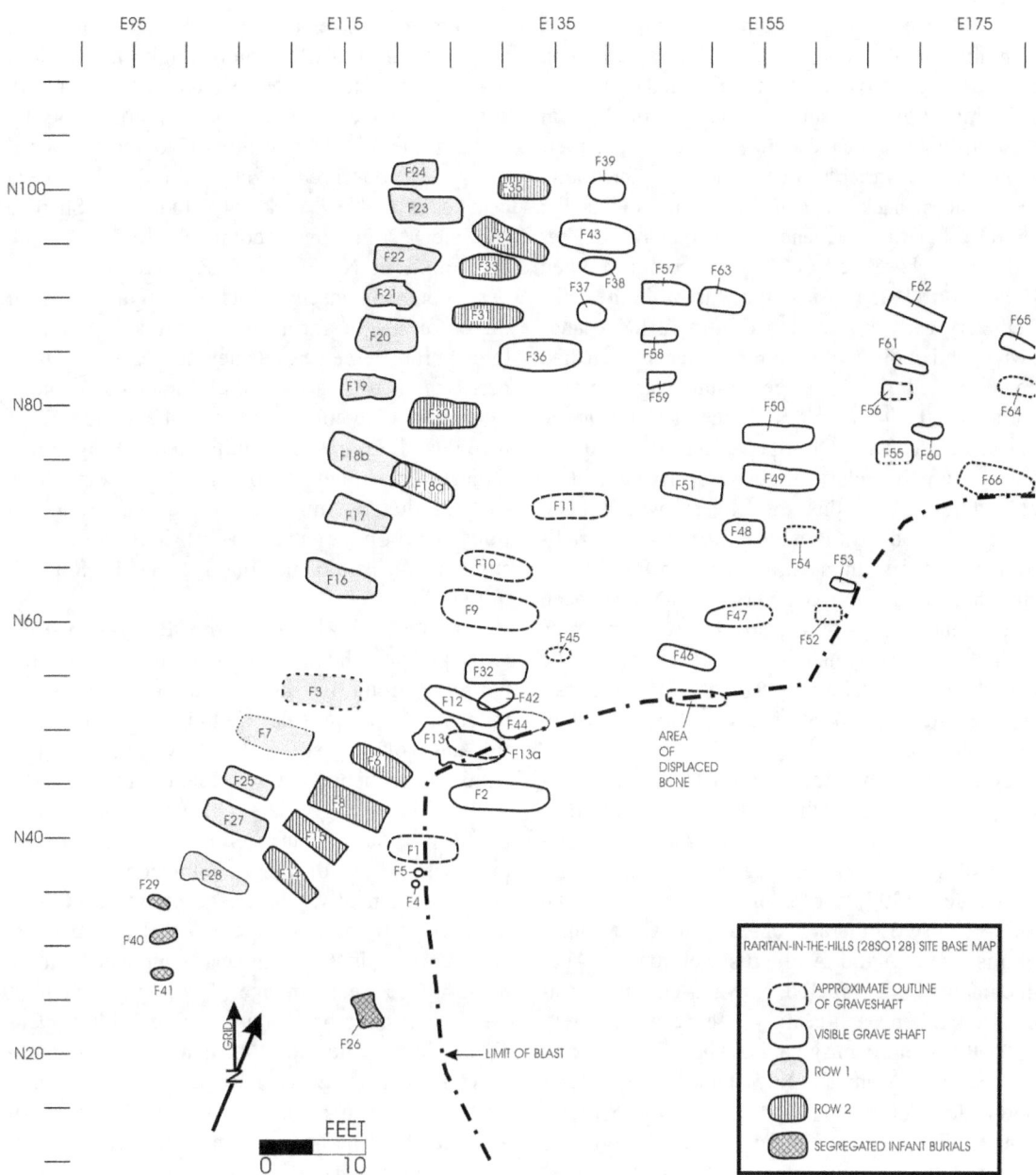

FIGURE 3. Raritan-in-the-Hills (28So128) site base map. (Drawing by Patty McEachen and Laura D. Cushman, 1999.)

of the site. In its place, relatively large areas in the center of the cemetery are vacant, and small groups of 5 to 10 burials, more or less aligned with each other, are found across the eastern portion of the site. Clearly, the practice of burying the deceased in relatively orderly rows was not being observed in the eastern half of the cemetery. As a further indication that burial customs changed, a number of infant/newborn burials were found dispersed across the eastern portion of the

site and in proximity with a variety of other age and sex groups. Apparently, the normative stricture to segregate infants from the remainder of the burial population did not persist for the entire time that the cemetery remained in use.

Although it is not possible to establish an absolute chronology of individual interments, evidence suggests that the western end of the cemetery with its orderly rows and columns represents the earliest period of cemetery use.

The premise of this argument is based on a combination of historical research, oral tradition, and the archeological data generated from the field investigations. In New Jersey, the spatial relationship between colonial churches and their cemeteries is variable (cemeteries may be found to the sides, back, or completely surrounding the church), but they do tend to be found on higher ground (Richard Veit 2006, pers. comm.). When Honeyman (1913) visited the Raritan-in-the-Hills Cemetery early in the 20th century, a local land-owner had indicated to him that the church had been located on the ridge in the southwestern corner of the property, on higher ground above the cemetery. The "Old Stagecoach Road" forms the western boundary of the property, and it is considered likely that the church would have faced the roadway. Provided that the oral tradition represents an accurate description of the church location, the cemetery would have been to the rear of the church, and the western limits of the cemetery would have been closest to the church and, therefore, presumably the earliest, as was the case at St. Mary's City (Riordan, this volume).

Comparative analysis demonstrates that contemporaneous churchyards were frequently, although not exclusively, organized by a row-and-column structure. Suzanne Sanders and colleagues (1997) documented this pattern at an 18th-century Lutheran cemetery at Gettysburg, Pennsylvania, and Augustus Schultze (1912) documented the ordered row-and-column organization of an 18th-century Moravian cemetery in Bethlehem, Pennsylvania. The Old Lutheran Cemetery in Mahwah, New Jersey, shares temporal and cultural similarities with the Raritan-in-the-Hills Cemetery. The earliest individuals interred at this cemetery were part of the Palatine migration that settled the area in 1713, where they established a congregation under the ministry of Pastor Justus Falckner, the same pastor who oversaw early ministerial duties at Raritan-in-the-Hills and elsewhere in the region. A visual inspection of the Old Lutheran Cemetery by the junior author of this article revealed that the location of the 18th-century church at Mahwah is unknown. Nevertheless, the extant cemetery provides a comparative framework to interpret order of interments based on cultural mandates. The earliest interments in this cemetery follow a west to east orientation and conform to the row-and-column pattern observed at Raritan-in-the-Hills. Interestingly, this pattern remains consistent at Mahwah into the mid-19th century, despite the presence of family plots by at least the late-18th century. No family burial plots were observed in any of the colonial-era cemeteries in New York City studied by Sherene Baugher (2006, pers. comm.), although some are found in New Jersey (Richard Veit 2006, pers. comm.). Family plots are regularly found on colonial-era farms and estates but not in the church cemeteries (Sherene Baugher 2007, pers. comm.). Clearly, cultural mandates dictated interment placement, even if the congregants recognized formal and individual family plots. Orderly interments throughout the cemeteries suggest that a church sexton or an organized body of congregants maintained cemetery structure—a pattern not observed at the Raritan-in-the-Hills Cemetery.

Archaeological data from Raritan-in-the-Hills provide the most solid evidence that the temporal trend for interments was from west to east, with the earliest burials placed in a row-and-column pattern. The evidence for this temporal sequence for interments comes in the form of intrusive burials. In two instances, one burial intrudes on another and, in both cases, the easternmost of the two intrudes upon the western. Logically, the westernmost burial was the earlier of the two. Feature 18B in the westernmost row in the cemetery contained a male of 15 to 35 years of age. The eastern edge of the burial shaft of Feature 18B exhibited clear signs of postinterment intrusion from Feature 18A, a female between 20 to 25 years of age. A postexcavation analysis of coffin nail orientation and skeletal remains confirmed the superimposition of these burials. Furthermore, Feature 18B may represent a significantly earlier interment than 18A, as excavation of the 18A burial shaft would have impacted the base of the coffin and skeletal remains in 18B. Presumably, the coffin in Feature 18B had already deteriorated and did not impede the gravediggers' excavation of the later burial shaft. Feature 13 and 13A exhibit similar patterns of disturbance; however, data from these burials are not as conclusive due to disturbance associated with dynamiting the bedrock. Nevertheless, coffin nail orientation in Feature 13 suggests that the burial was not disturbed prior to construction activities. Blasting caused the bottom half of these burials to slump to approximately 2 to 3 ft. below the current ground surface. Coffin nails from the lower half of Feature 13 were sporadic and did not conform to the patterns observed in other interments, suggesting that Feature 13A probably impacted the burial shaft of Feature 13.

Collectively, these data indicate that orderly interments within rows and columns did not characterize the whole period of occupation. The norm during this early phase called for the orderly placement of the deceased in rows, irrespective of age (excepting infants), gender, or kinship. Use of the cemetery proceeded eastward as time progressed, and norms appear to have shifted to the placement of the deceased either at random locations or in small groups. Other physical evidence from the cemetery may be analyzed in an attempt to interpret this change in the spatial patterning of interment.

The Raritan-in-the-Hills Population

In an effort to interpret the meaning of this change in the placement of the deceased in the cemetery, the burial population was analyzed by age and sex groups. Where members of different age/sex groups are interred in the cemetery may reflect structural elements in the social organizational system of the society that created the cemetery. Seven groups were defined anthropometrically from the sample: infants (<1 yr.), infants (>1–<2 yrs.), children and adolescents of undetermined sex (2–16 yrs.), adult males and adult females (16–70+ yrs.), and indeterminate adults (16–70+). The distribution of these age and sex groups for the burial population is presented in Table 1.

Plotting the location of the age and sex groups provides some clues as to what changes occurred

within the Raritan-in-the-Hills congregation (Figure 4). It might be anticipated that the clearest pattern of age/sex differentiation would be observed in that portion of the cemetery where there is the most obvious evidence of order—in the two rows of burials along the western edge of the site. Other than the above-described segregation of infants, there is no clear ordering of the bodies by age/sex group in this area of the site. Male and female adults, adolescents, and children are found together, randomly buried in these rows. Possibly marriage partners or family group members are buried together in this part of the cemetery, a pattern that is more fully observed elsewhere on the site. Within the westernmost row of burials, a single set of burials proximate to each other may represent a married couple, Feature 16 (female, 40–50 yrs.) and Feature 17 (male, 35–45 yrs.).

Turning to the eastern portion of the cemetery, there are greater instances where adult marriage partners or other family members may have been buried next to each other. Feature 9 (male, 40–50 yrs.) and Feature 10 (female, 45–55 yrs.) lay slightly apart from other burials in the east-central part of the site and, thereby, are the most likely candidates for this type of interpretation. A consort may be present among the four adult females (Feature 13, 13a, 32, and 44) clustered around the one adult, a 30 to 35 year-old male represented by Feature 12. Two other family groups suggest themselves. First is a single adult female (Feature 43) at the northern limits of the cemetery with a cluster of three infants (Feature 37, 38, 39) on either side. Second is a group consisting of one adult male (Feature 51), two adult females (Feature 49, 50) aged 16 to 18 years and 25 to 30 years, respectively, one child (Feature 48), and one infant (Feature 54).

TABLE 1
DISTRIBUTION OF AGE AND SEX GROUPS: RARITAN-IN-THE-HILLS CEMETERY

Demographic	Indeterminate Sex	Females	Males
Infants <1 yr.	5		
Infants (>1–< 2 yrs.)	2		
Children and Adolescents (2–< 16 yrs.)	22		
Adults (16–70+ yrs.)	2	15	13

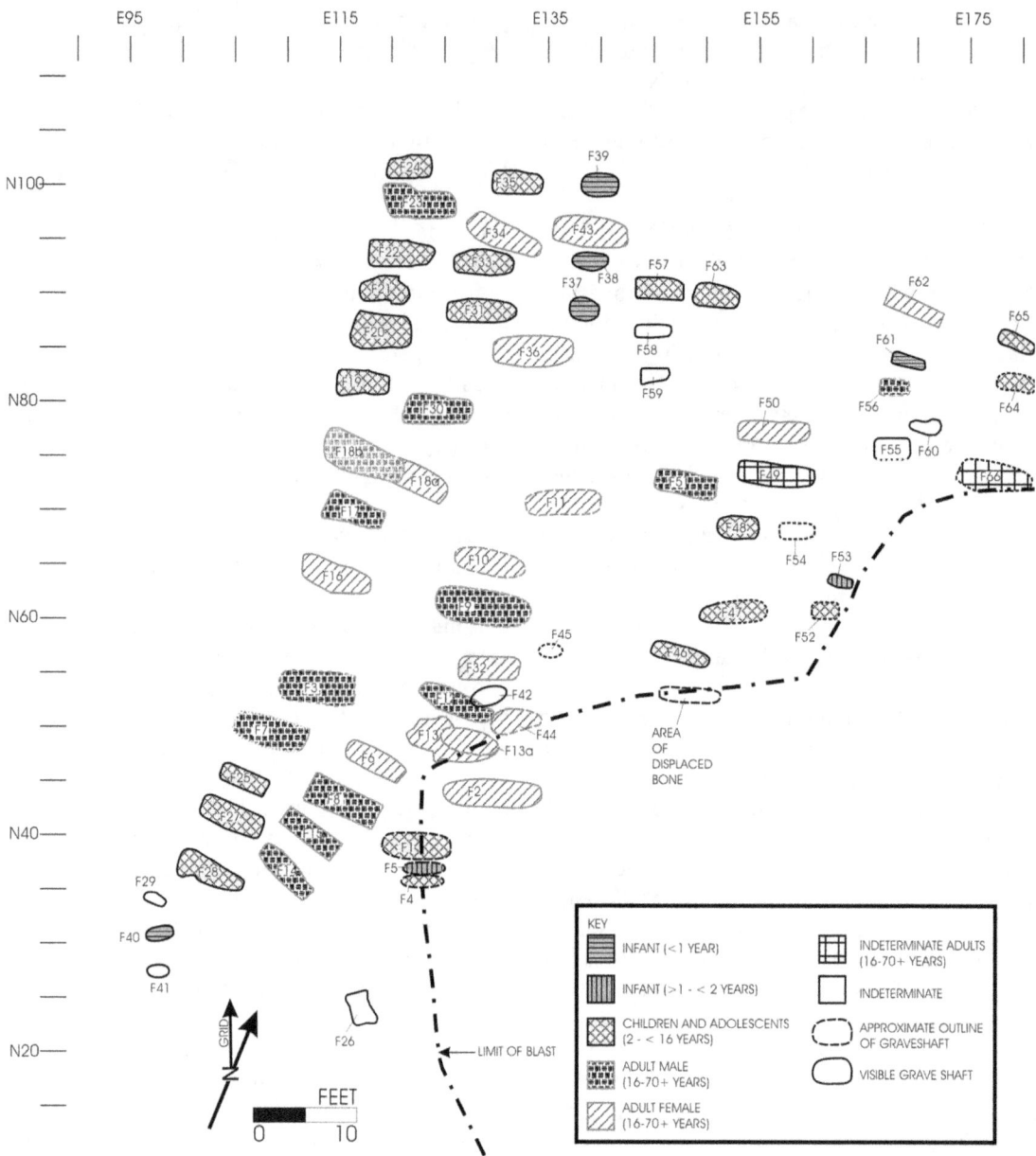

FIGURE 4. Population distribution by age and sex, Raritan-in-the-Hills (28So128). (Drawing by Patty McEachen and Laura D. Cushman, 1999.)

The distribution of identifiable age and sex groups within the cemetery gives weight to the idea that norms for interment changed during the 50-odd years the Raritan-in-the-Hills cemetery remained in use. As discussed above, the western end of the cemetery with its orderly rows and columns is interpreted as representing the earliest phase of interments. The norm during this early phase called for the orderly placement of the deceased in rows, irrespective of age (excepting infants), gender, or kinship. Use of the cemetery proceeded eastward as time progressed, and norms appear to have shifted to the placement of the deceased either at random locations or in proximity to other family members (Figure 5). No physical evidence survives that "family plots" were formally maintained within the graveyard, but they may have been informally recognized by

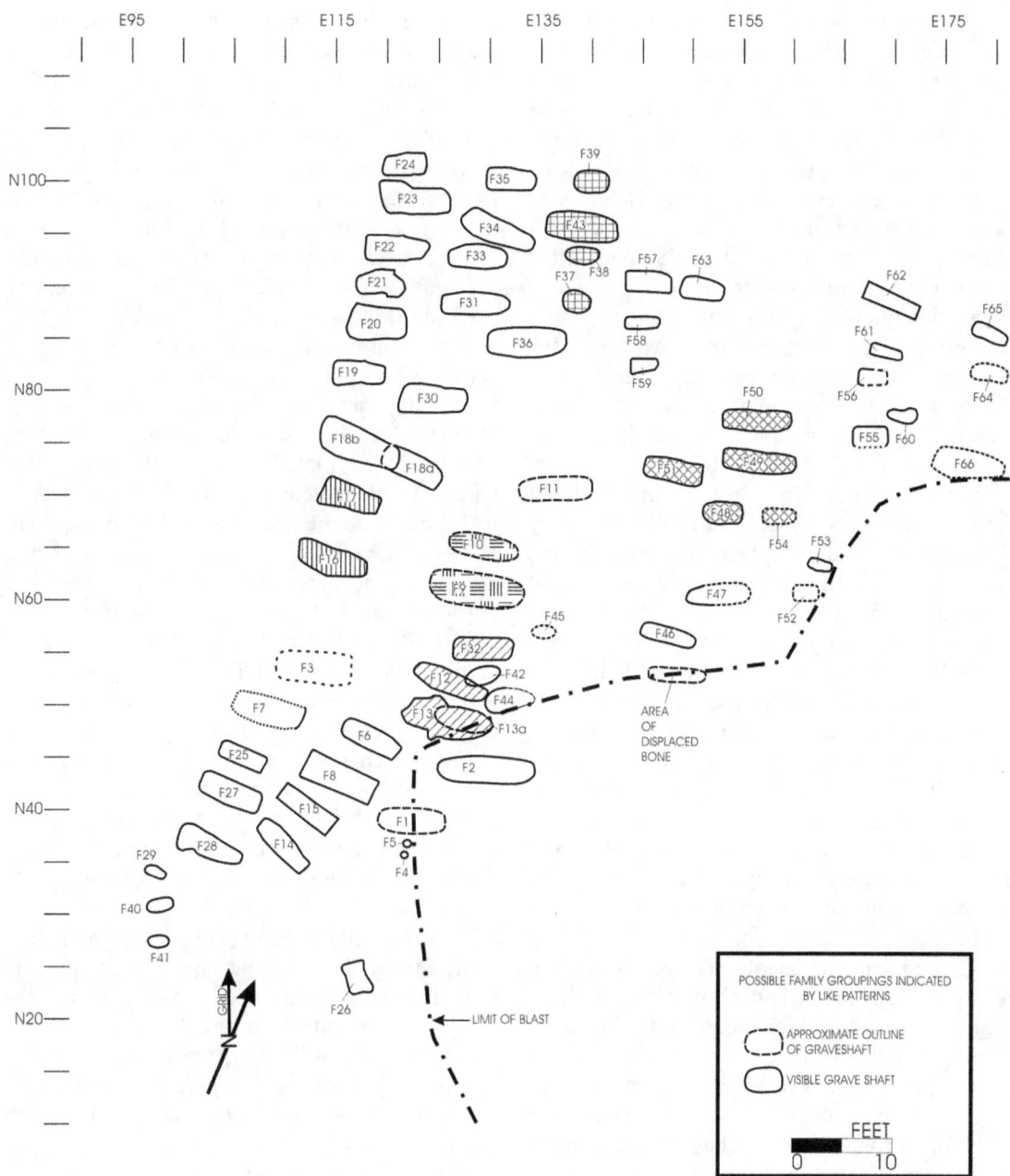

FIGURE 5. Distribution of possible family groups, Raritan-in-the-Hills (28So128). (Drawing by Laura D. Cushman, 1999.)

the congregants. Other physical evidence from the cemetery, however, may be analyzed in an attempt to understand the context in which this change in norms guiding interment of the dead occurred.

Coffin Construction

Formation of Raritan-in-the-Hills occurred at a time prior to the elaboration of decorative coffin hardware, which has figured prominently in the archaeological analysis of later cemeteries (Bell 1990). In this context, preparation of the body, small differences in coffin construction, and the performance of funerary ritual would have become social discriminators, the media through which social status was presented and reaffirmed for the benefit of the living.

Lutherans in early modern Germany certainly used funerary ritual to display social position (Koslofsky 2000:99–100). Tangible indicators show that the Lutherans at Raritan invested a great deal of expense in time, labor, and (probably) specie in the proper disposal of the dead. First are the graves themselves, which in many cases were hewn from bedrock. The level of effort involved speaks for itself. Second is the investment in coffin construction. Every grave excavation yielded coffin nails (but no other hardware), indicating that a coffin encased each individual interred in the cemetery, regardless of age or sex. Clearly, a great deal of effort went into the ritual preparation of the dead. This ritual concern reflects the Christian promise of a physical rebirth after death, particularly in the case of infants (Taylor 2001:112). The body would be cleaned, wrapped in a shroud, and laid out on a cooling board until completion of a coffin (Coffin 1976:79).

During the early-18th century, coffins were generally constructed to fit the individual, so one would expect to find a correlation between body size and coffin dimensions. Craftsmen employed in cabinetry often provided the ancillary service of coffin construction, although it is quite plausible that friends and relatives of the deceased manufactured some as well. Cabinetmakers, however, likely had better access to the supplies needed for construction.

The steps in coffin production remain poorly understood, and archaeological reconstruction remains a viable method to elucidate technological and cultural changes. A basic coffin would typically consist of six boards making up the head, foot, two sides, bottom, and the lid. As has been observed elsewhere (LeeDecker 2001:6), the makers used the greatest number of nails, regardless of coffin shape, at the head and foot of the coffin. They appear to have offered substantial interior bracing to fasten the end boards at the head and foot. This bracing manifests itself in the occurrence of pairs of nails found lying parallel and next to each other with the heads facing in opposite directions. Not all coffins at Raritan-in-the-Hills exhibited the expense of this additional bracing, although many (n=26) coffins throughout the cemetery included at least one of these pairs of nails. Gabled coffins required the same structural support and the use of two boards to create the gabled lid. Although the gabled lid would require more sophisticated carpentry, there is little reason to doubt that the Raritan-in-the-Hills inhabitants would not have possessed this skill. The increasing use of gabled lids and the variety of shapes all support this hypothesis. Current research has also demonstrated that the methods employed in joining the boards of coffins can vary significantly (Riordan, this volume). While research examining the joinery used at Raritan-in-the-Hills is ongoing, significant new information on the subtleties of coffin construction should be uncovered.

The alignment of nails in the Raritan-in-the-Hills features is indicative of several styles of coffins. These include hexagonal, rectangular, tapered, and gabled; however, the vast majority appears to be flat-lidded and hexagonal. Hexagonal coffins are characterized as being narrow at the head and foot, with the widest portion located at the shoulder (Sanders et al. 1997:117). Tapered coffins are defined as narrow at the foot and gradually increasing in width to accommodate the shoulders. A line of nails down the center indicates a possible gabled coffin, which may have been constructed in a variety of forms (i.e., tapered rectangular, hexagonal). Gabled coffins have been observed in a small number of cases in cemeteries (Noël Hume 1982; Basalik et al. 1987; Parrington et al. 1987).

Timothy Riordan (this volume) has demonstrated how the hexagonal form became the standard coffin shape over the course of the 17th century at the English Catholic colony at St. Mary's City; the hexagonal coffin predominated in the early-18th century, and it remained generally popular into the 19th century (Coffin 1976:101; Bell 1990). As one examines the distribution of coffin types within Raritan-in-the-Hills, differences between the western and eastern halves of the cemetery become apparent (Figure 6). In the western segment, coffin shape shows limited variability, while there is a tendency towards greater diversity in form in the eastern portion of the cemetery. Consistent with Riordan's findings, the hexagonal form dominates in what is interpreted to be the earliest (i.e., western) segment of the cemetery. The two exceptions include one gabled coffin (Feature 8) and one coffin tentatively identified as rectangular (Feature

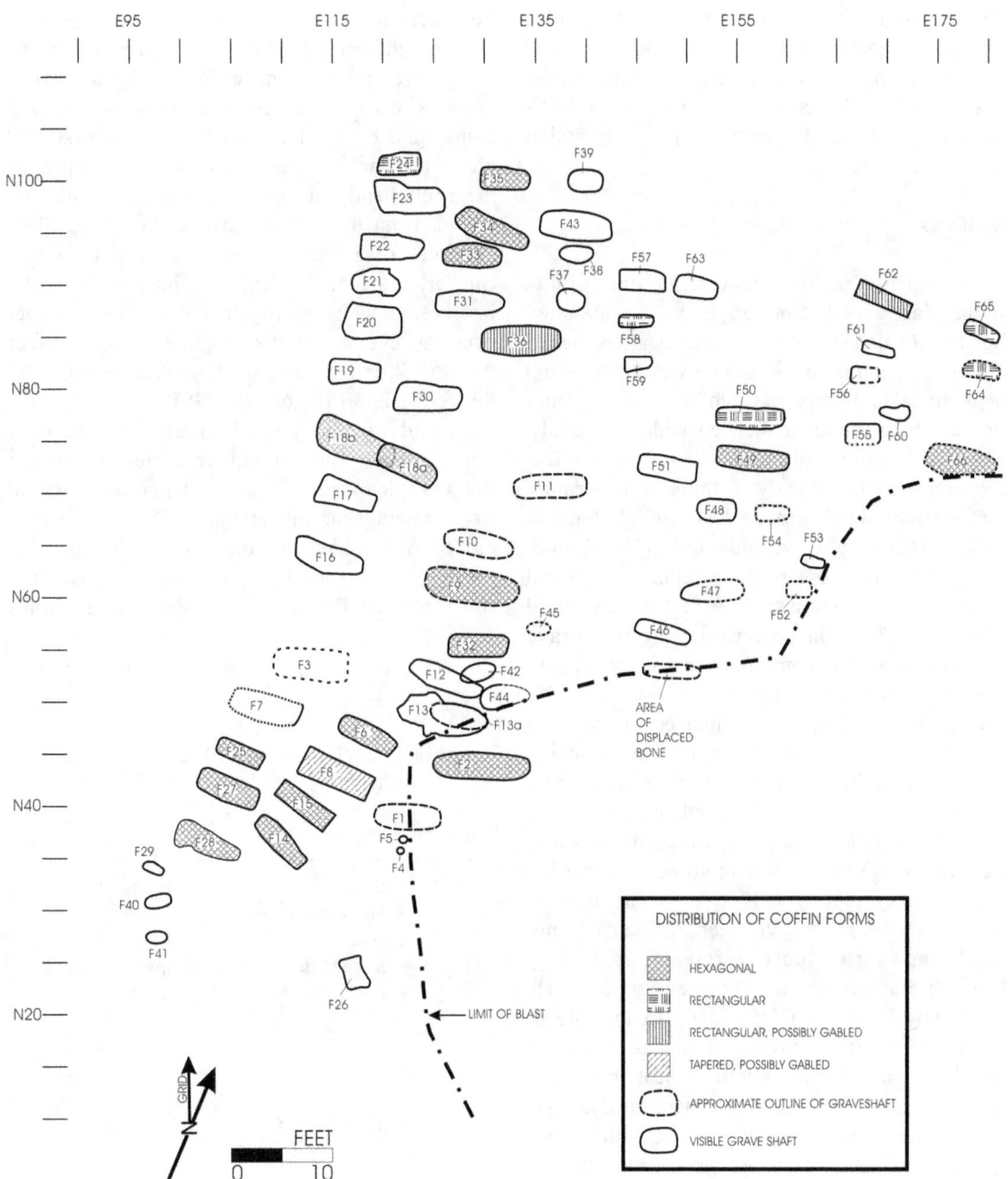

FIGURE 6. Distribution of coffin forms, Raritan-in-the-Hills (28So128). (Drawing by Laura D. Cushman, 1999.)

24). These two exceptions notwithstanding, the predominant use of hexagonal coffins by the earliest inhabitants of Raritan-in-the-Hills was in keeping with generally accepted practices of the early-18th century.

In contrast to the west, the eastern segment of the cemetery is characterized by a greater diversity in coffin shape. While hexagonal coffins remain the predominant shape—rectangular, tapered, and gabled forms are also found. The congregants of Raritan-in-the-Hills maintained a strict adherence to cultural norms associated with mortuary practices, even though there is a subtle change in how it was expressed. The eastern segment of the cemetery may represent a period of reduced community cohesion engendered by strife and a time when family units were gaining prominence over the community. It appears that during the later period of occupation, the coffins reveal more sophisticated carpentry skills, perhaps as an expression of individuality.

Artifacts

As a group of first-generation immigrants to the East Jersey frontier, it can be assumed that the Raritan-in-the-Hills congregation lacked affluence in terms of disposable wealth. It would be a mistake, however, to infer this fact from the paucity of goods associated with the burials, except for coffin nails, shroud pins, and a few prehistoric artifacts. Only in the case of Feature 2 at Raritan was there evidence of clothing (a button) that might preclude use of a shroud. The paucity of these remains reflects a general adherence (with one notable exception, discussed below) to Christian proscription against grave offerings and the common use of shrouds to wrap the body for burial.

Very few artifacts other than coffin nails or shroud pins were found during the salvage excavations (Table 2). Because of their paucity, these artifacts do not figure in further analysis of cemetery remains. In certain cases, the artifacts are not interpreted to be in direct association with an interment. The pipe stem encountered in Feature 19 may have been introduced into the burial during postinterment backfilling. The nondiagnostic olive-colored glass bottle sherd may have been introduced to the site at any time. Artifacts directly associated with an individual burial were found at scattered locations across the cemetery. As mentioned above, Feature 2 contained a brass button with a wire eye (3/4-in. diameter), which appears to be from the pants or coat of the deceased, based on its location in the pelvic region. This highly corroded button did not exhibit any recognizable decorative attributes. In Feature 34, a highly corroded piece of iron has been identified as a knife. The artifact measures 5.5 in. long with a maximum width of 2 in., tapering to 1/4 in. One side has an acute edge, while the opposing side is relatively blunt.

Perhaps the most striking find is two circular lead discs (ca. 3 cm diameter) associated with Feature 28, burial of a child (15–16 yrs.).

Postexcavation analysis of the well-preserved cranium indicates that the individual within the feature was probably male. Precluding a detailed analysis, each round, unmarked disc is currently being held by the land developer. The first lead piece (artifact 1) was found in situ, lying on the right hand side of the body, approximately 0.5 in. from the clavicle. The second lead piece (artifact 2) was encountered lying near the cervical vertebrae of the feature. These artifacts are interpreted to be surrogate coins, placed either over the eyes or in the mouth as a survival of the pre-Christian custom of leaving a coin "for the ferryman" (Taylor 2001:88).

Shroud pins and coffin nails are the only other artifact type found consistently enough for analytical consideration, which were in all cases found near the cranium. Only 10 burials out of 68 yielded shroud pins, indicating that one or more social factors strongly affected who received these. Table 3 lists those burials

TABLE 2
MISCELLANEOUS HISTORIC ARTIFACTS:
RARITAN-IN-THE-HILLS CEMETERY

Feature	Object	Material	Count
2	Button	Brass	1
19	Pipe stem fragment	Kaolin	1
28	Disc	Lead	2
34	Knife blade	Iron	1
64	Bottle glass sherd	Glass	1

TABLE 3
INCIDENCE OF SHROUD PINS:
RARITAN-IN-THE-HILLS CEMETERY

Feature	Sex	Age Estimates	No. Shroud Pins
3	Male	30–35	1
18b	Male	15–35	7
33	Child	5–6	4
37	Infant	≤ 1	6
38	Infant	≤ 1	3
39	Infant	≤ 1	3
40	Infant	≤ 1	4
44	Female	20–25	1
48	Child	2–2.5	3
59	Infant	≤ 1	3

associated with shroud pins. Half of this group is comprised of infants, and 70% of the group includes children less than 6 years of age. These represent 33.3% of all infants and 18.1% of all children less than 6 years of age. The remaining members of this group are two adult males and one adult female, or only 10.7% of all males and females. The average number of pins per infant or child burial is 3.7, with a low standard deviation of 1.1. Clearly, little variability exists in the number of shroud pins that infants and children received. The most extraordinary individual in the group is Feature 18, an adult male (15–35 yrs.) who received the most shroud pins (7) of any individual.

Looking at the spatial distribution of individuals receiving shroud pins, for the most part they are found at scattered locations throughout the site. These include one of the individuals among the segregated infants at the southwest corner of the cemetery (Feature 40), and two children (Feature 3 and 33) and one adult (Feature 18b) in the western half of the cemetery. Infants and children scattered throughout the eastern half of the cemetery also received shroud pins. A cluster of three of the infant burials, however, were found with shroud pins (Feature 37, 38, 39) in the eastern half of the cemetery in what may be a family grouping of four burials (Feature 37, 38, 39, 43).

When reviewing the limited number of variables available for examining the social dimensions of funerary treatment at Raritan-in-the-Hills, coffin construction and the use of shroud pins in the preparation of the body, there is a tendency toward greater diversity in coffin form across the west-east axis of the cemetery, but no strong distributional patterns emerge for the use of shroud pins. The same may be said for the use of nails. Although the number of different coffin forms changes from the west to the eastern sides of the cemetery, the average number of nails used in coffin construction (controlling for age and sex) does not change appreciably (Table 4). A two-tailed nonparametric (Chi-square) test failed to reveal statistically significant difference in the average number of nails used per coffin within the cemetery. The statistic produced a value of 3.98, which with three degrees of freedom has an 80% to 90% chance of occurrence (Blalock 1979). Inasmuch as the use of these items may have signaled

TABLE 4
DISTRIBUTION OF AVERAGE NUMBER
OF COFFIN NAILS:
RARITAN-IN-THE-HILLS CEMETERY

Demographic	East	West	Totals
Adult female	32.9	25.5	58.4
Adult male	27.8	33.8	61.6
Adolescent/Child	20.0	30.1	50.1
Infant	12.5	17.7	30.2
Totals	93.3	107.1	200.4

status, this does not seem to have been the case with the Raritan-in-the-Hills community. This finding echoes that for the incidence of shroud pins.

Whatever conflicts the community might have been experiencing, a common vocabulary relating to funeral custom appears to have been maintained. There is no clear archaeological evidence for social differentiation, except for children who in the nearly exclusive association with shroud pins were the obvious focus of great care. This is observable in both the eastern and western sections of the cemetery. Only two out of seven burials with shroud pins were located in the western portion of the cemetery (Feature 18b and 40). As noted above, three of the burials with shroud pins in the eastern portion belonged to one possible family group. This cluster of infants with shroud pins may be tentatively interpreted as a status display by a single family, although in the context of the entire cemetery, a fairly subtle one. This single cluster of burials with shroud pins at most represents what could have been an emerging trend towards individual family expression of wealth or status.

Conclusions

By and large, the picture that emerges from the Raritan-in-the-Hills is one of increasing diversity in minor details of coffin construction and treatment of the body as one moves across the cemetery from west to east. This increase in diversity is associated with a secular and spatial trend toward what is interpreted to be the formation of family plots. What is the relationship between the archaeological record showing a diachronic change in burial practices and the documentary record, replete with conflict and strife? A basic assumption here is that the two phenomena are associated; how they are associated is a matter of interpretation. Several possible factors are presented here as contributing to the observed change in burial custom at Raritan-in-the-Hills.

The origin and perseverance of conflicts and contradictions in the organization of the community at Raritan-in-the-Hills remain incompletely understood. Conflicts of land ownership between squatters, small freeholders, and the East Jersey Proprietors undoubtedly played a part (Purvis 1986; McConville 1999). Nonetheless, economic disparities do not appear to have provided a motive for the jealousy and anger so evident in the historical documents; at least there is no archaeological evidence to that effect. Judging from the limited ritual vocabulary that included shrouds and coffins and accepted only minor variations (use of shroud pins, shape of the coffin), there is no convincing evidence for diachronic trends in wealth displays within Raritan-in-the-Hills.

Religious factionalism and discord fills the documentary record left by members of the Raritan-in-the-Hills community. It is suggested that this struggle contributed to the change in burial practices employed. The locals participated in a larger game being played out between different Lutheran movements and their proponents in the New World, namely the Hamburg Orthodoxy and the pietist movement centered at Halle University (Kreider 1942). Pietism, in the ascendant at Raritan-in-the-Hills under the influence of Muhlenberg, emphasized personal faith and the individual's search for salvation. It is suggested that the pietist emphasis on the individual may have influenced a shift away from a corporate pattern and toward familial or individual burials by the pietists within the community (the majority), a pattern observed at other Lutheran cemeteries such as Mahwah.

The lack of a respected or effective spiritual leader at Raritan-in-the-Hills would certainly have provided the immediate social context in which congregants may have taken matters into their own hands as to where and how their loved ones were to be buried. More to the point, the lack of a sexton, responsible for organizing church burials, could have led to a situation where individuals or families assumed the responsibility, and a different organizational structure for the cemetery ensued. Unfortunately, the documentary record does not explain whether or when the position of sexton was left vacant at Raritan-in-the-Hills.

Whatever the root causes of community conflict, it is instructive to juxtapose two of the responses by members of Raritan-in-the-Hills: witchcraft accusations and lawsuits. The accusations of witchcraft lodged against Daniel Falckner's wife, Ana Marie, in the late 1720s and early 1730s revealed a continuation of a belief system from late mediaeval Europe that, although at times sanctioned by state and ecclesiastical authority, is in essence a communal sanction against proscribed behavior. In comparison, Wolf's extended litigation in the later 1730s was an attempt at redress through government bureaucracy, not community ethos. Neither method proved successful, but more important is the fact that these radically different forms of conflict resolution were attempted within such a brief period. They are indicative of the degree to which the Raritan-in-the-Hills congregation ultimately proved to be incapable of defining itself as a community and subsequently disintegrated.

What is the significance of the change in interment observed at Raritan-in-the-Hills just prior to the American Revolution? Common themes in the anthropological or historical studies of immigrant groups, regardless of ethnicity, include questions of what makes the immigrant group different from the parent population and why; and, secondly, what mechanisms did the immigrant group employ to adapt to their new social and natural environment. For 18th-century German immigrants to New Jersey, available options for survival have been characterized as *Gemeinschaft* or *Geschellschaft*— the social strategy of survival based on corporate unity and corporate action (*Gemeinschaft*) versus adaptation taken at the level of the individual or individual family (*Geschellschaft*). Rosalind Beiler (1989:41–42) has suggested that both modes of survival were open to German immigrants in New Jersey. The history of Raritan-in-the-Hills and the physical evidence from the cemetery suggest less that these were options to choose from but more that *Geschellschaft* resulted from communal conflicts and the contemporary currents of pietistic religious revival that stressed individual attainment of salvation. The Raritan-in-the-Hills cemetery, where the *Gemeinschaft* of order and structure in the placement of the dead was replaced by the *Geschellschaft* of placing congregants individually or in family groups, is compelling evidence for the strains and ultimate dissolution of this pioneer immigrant community on the eve of the Revolutionary War.

Acknowledgments

The authors thank the entire staff of Richard Grubb and Associates who conducted the archaeological excavations and assisted in production of this report, with particular thanks to Paul George, Laura Cushman, and Patty McEachen. Thomas Crist and Arthur Washburn examined all human remains recovered from the site over the course of this project (1998). We gratefully acknowledge their assistance.

References

BANTA, THEODORE M.
1903   *Yearbook of the Holland Society of New York.* Holland Society of New York, New York, NY.

BASALIK, KENNETH J., A. R. BROWN, C. DORE, AND T. LEWIS
1987   South Christina Relief: Location and Identification/ Evaluation Survey of the South Christina Interceptor, New Castle County, Delaware. Manuscript, Delaware State Historic Preservation Office, Newark.

BEILER, ROSALIND
1989   "Gemeinschaft" or "Geschellschaft"? Germans in Colonial New Jersey. Manuscript [with permission, in author's possession, Burlington, NJ].

BELL, EDWARD L.
1990   The Historical Archaeology of Mortuary Behavior: Coffin Hardware from Uxbridge, Massachusetts. *Historical Archaeology* 24(3):54–78.

BLALOCK, HUBERT M.
1979   *Social Statistics,* 2nd edition. McGraw-Hill, New York, NY.

COFFIN, MARGARET M.
1976   *Death in Early America.* Thomas Nelson, New York, NY.

CRIST, THOMAS A. J., AND ARTHUR WASHBURN
1998   Pluckemin Burial Ground, Pluckemin, New Jersey: Physical Anthropology Methods. Manuscript, Richard Grubb & Associates, Cranbury, NJ.

FAUST, ALBERT BERNHARDT
1909   *The German Element in the United States.* Houghton Mifflin Company, Boston, MA.

FEDERAL WRITERS' PROJECT
1939   *New Jersey: A Guide to Its Present and Past.* The Viking Press, New York, NY.

FEUERHAHN, RONALD R.
1998   Pieper Lectures 1998: The Roots and Fruits of Pietism. Issues, Etc., Concordia Lutheran Laity, St. Louis, MO <http://www.issuesetc.org/resource/archives/feuerhhn.htm>.

GORDON, RONALD J.
1998   Rise of Pietism in Seventeenth-Century Germany. Church of the Brethren Network, Elgin, IL <http://www.cob-net.org/pietism.htm>.

HART, SIMON, AND HARRY J. KREIDER
1962   *Lutheran Church in New York and New Jersey 1722–1760.* United Lutheran Synod of New York and New England, New York, NY.

HONEYMAN, A. VAN DOREN
1913a   The Lutheran Church of "Raritan In The Hills." *Somerset County Historical Quarterly* 2(2) 1913:87–98. Somerset County Historical Society, Somerville, NJ.
1913b   The Lutheran Church of "Raritan In The Hills." *Somerset County Historical Quarterly* 2(3):161–172. Somerset County Historical Society, Somerville, NJ.
1914   The Lutheran Church of "Raritan In The Hills." *Somerset County Historical Quarterly* 3(1):77–78. Somerset County Historical Society, Somerville, NJ.

KIRKHAM, W. C.
1989   *Soil Survey of Somerset County, New Jersey.* U.S. Department of Agriculture, Soil Conservation Service, Washington, DC.

KOSLOFSKY, CRAIG M.
2000   *Reformation of the Dead: Death and Ritual in Early Modern Germany, 1450–1700.* Macmillan Press, London, England, UK.

KREIDER, HARRY J.
1942   *Lutheranism in Colonial New York.* Doctoral dissertation, Columbia University, New York, NY. Harry J. Kreider, Edwards Brothers, Ann Arbor, MI.

LeeDECKER, CHARLES H.
2001   The Coffin Makers Craft: Treatment of the Dead in Rural Eighteenth-Century Delaware. *Journal of Mid-Atlantic Archaeology* 17:1–14.

McCONVILLE, BRENDAN
1999   *These Daring Disturbers of the Public Peace: The Struggle for Property and Power in Early New Jersey.* Cornell University Press, Ithaca, NY.

MUHLENBERG, HENRY MELCHIOR
  1942 *The Journals of Henry Melchior Muhlenberg in Three Volumes,* Theodore G. Tappert and John W. Doberstein, translators. Vol. 1. Philadelphia Muhlenberg Press, Philadelphia, PA.

NEW JERSEY SUPREME COURT
  1739 Supreme Court Case File 45137. Microform edition, New Jersey Supreme Court, New Jersey State Archives, Trenton, NJ.
  1742a Supreme Court Case File 46296. Microform edition, New Jersey State Archives, New Jersey Supreme Court, Trenton, NJ.
  1742b Supreme Court Case File 49297. Microform edition, New Jersey Supreme Court, New Jersey State Archives, Trenton, NJ.

NOËL HUME, IVOR
  1982 *Martin's Hundred: The Discovery of a Lost Colonial Virginia Settlement.* Dell Publishing, New York, NY.

OTTERNESS, PHILIP
  1999 The 1709 Palatine Migration and the Formation of German Immigrant Identity in London and New York. *Pennsylvania History: A Journal of Mid-Atlantic Studies* 66:8–23.

PARRINGTON, MICHAEL, D. G. ROBERTS, S. A. PRINTER, J. C. WIDEMAN, D. DASHIELL, G. FRACE, AND R. BALDWIN
  1987 The First African Baptist Church Cemetery: Bioarchaeology, Demography, and Acculturation of Early-Nineteenth-Century Philadelphia Blacks. Report to the Redevelopment Authority of the City of Philadelphia, from John Milner Associates, Inc., Philadelphia, PA.

PURVIS, THOMAS L.
  1986 *Proprietors, Patronage, and Paper Money: Legislative Politics in New Jersey, 1703–1776.* Rutgers University Press, New Brunswick, NJ.

RIFORGIATO, LEONARD R.
  1980 *Missionary of Moderation: Henry Melchior Muhlenberg and the Lutheran Church in English America.* Bucknell University Press, Lewisburg, PA.

SANDERS, SUZANNE, M. T. MORAN, H. B. McALOON, AND D. CANNAN
  1997 Intensive Archaeological and Architectural Investigations of Portion of Ice House Square, Gettysburg, Adams County, Pennsylvania. Report to Gettysburg College, Gettysburg, PA, from R. Christopher Goodwin Associates, Frederick, MD.

SCHULTZE, AUGUSTUS
  1912 The Old Moravian Cemetery of Bethlehem, Pennsylvania 1742–1910. *Proceedings of the Pennsylvania-German Society* 21:3–218. Pennsylvania-German Society, Lancaster, PA.

TAYLOR, ALISON
  2001 *Burial Practice in Early England.* Tempus, Gloucestershire, England, UK.

VEIT, RICHARD
  2000 John Solomon Teetzel and the Anglo-German Gravestone Carving Tradition of Eighteenth-Century Northwestern New Jersey. *Markers* 17:124–161. Journal of the Association for Gravestone Studies.

JOHN W. LAWRENCE
344 EAST UNION STREET
BURLINGTON, NJ 08016

PAUL W. SCHOPP
P.O. BOX 648
PALMYRA, NJ 08605-0648

ROBERT J. LORE
RICHARD GRUBB & ASSOCIATES
30 NORTH MAIN STREET
CRANBURY, NJ 08512-3241

Shannon A. Novak
Derinna Kopp

To Feed a Tree in Zion: Osteological Analysis of the 1857 Mountain Meadows Massacre

ABSTRACT

In September 1857, some 120 men, women, and children on a wagon train bound for California were massacred in southwestern Utah. Who was responsible for the Mountain Meadows Massacre is a question that still sparks considerable debate. According to traditional historical accounts, the adult males of the company were shot by local Mormon militiamen, while the women and children were killed by Paiutes or other Native Americans. An unexpected opportunity to assess the skeletal evidence in the case arose in summer 1999, when a mass grave containing 28 of the victims was accidentally unearthed. Bullet wounds were found to affect primarily young men, although one subadult and possibly a female also exhibited gunshot trauma. The crania of three children, two subadult males, and one adult female were fractured by blunt force trauma. No wounds were identified that would corroborate historical accounts of the victims being scalped, having their throats cut, or being shot by arrows.

Introduction

In August 1857, Apostle George A. Smith gave a sermon in the small town of Parowan in southern Utah. The fiery lecture took aim at some local boys who had been caught stealing fruit and were publicly whipped. Smith's resolution of the matter was to have the town square planted in fruit so that children would not have to steal. He went on to tell the audience that "bones make good fertilizer; a few bones at the roots of a tree would nourish it a long time." He then made pointed reference to the U.S. Army, which was threatening to invade the Utah Territory: "As for the cursed mobocrats, I can think of nothing better that they could do than to feed a fruit tree in Zion" (Brooks 1962:35).

While the U.S. Army was recalled before a confrontation could occur, Apostle Smith's words were prophetic for one group of emigrants on a California-bound wagon train. Less than a month after Smith's visit, approximately 120 men, women, and children of the Baker-Fancher company were murdered in the southern Utah valley of Mountain Meadows. The only survivors were 17 very young children whose lives were spared because they were deemed not "old enough to talk" (Brooks 1962:81). While Apostle Smith's sermon might not be blamed for inciting the massacre, his words illustrate the xenophobia that had come to permeate the culture of Utah Mormons, many of whom considered their territory to be a new Zion, distinct from the "Babylon" that was the United States.

Just prior to the arrival in Utah Territory of the wagon train led by John T. Baker and Alexander Fancher, a series of events had set the stage for a violent confrontation. In 1856, Territorial Governor Brigham Young called on the Latter-day Saints, popularly known as Mormons, to reaffirm their loyalty to the faith. As part of his so-called great reformation, all church members were required to repent, undergo a new baptism, and renew their covenants, which included avenging the death of their prophet, Joseph Smith (Bigler 1998). As Utah Mormons closed ranks, there was increasing friction with outsiders, especially with federally appointed judges in what was then known as Great Salt Lake City. In July 1857, word reached Utah that President James Buchanan had dispatched the U.S. Army to replace Brigham Young with a non-Mormon governor and to quell any further resistance (Brooks 1962; Arrington and Bitton 1992; Bigler 1998; Bagley 2002).

As the Baker-Fancher wagon train entered Great Salt Lake City on 3 August 1857, the local residents were preparing for war. Goods and ammunition were cached in the foothills; plans had been made to demolish settlements and make the land barren for the invading army; and military organizations were established in every settlement in the territory (Arrington and Bitton 1992:166). Orders made it mandatory that grain be stored and that "no supplies shall be furnished emigrants or others bound for California" (Brooks 1962:21). In fact, the raiding of wagon trains may have been encouraged by Mormon officials to bolster lagging supplies. Commanding Mormon Brigadier General Franklin D. Richards (1857) wrote in orders to his officers, "The

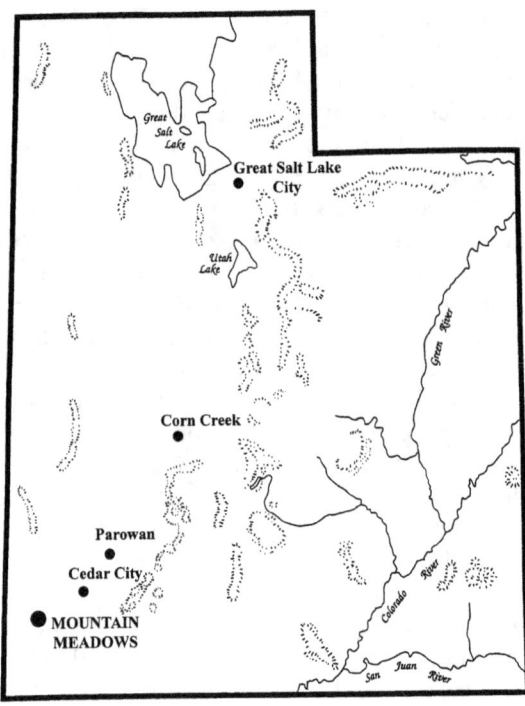

FIGURE 1. Map of Utah showing key locations along the route taken by the Baker-Fancher Company.

opportunities that occur of obtaining arms & ammunition from passing emigrants should not escape your carefull [sic] attention."

After acquiring a few supplies in Great Salt Lake City, the Baker-Fancher company selected the southern route to California as opposed to the northern California Trail, which would have taken them into Idaho. The southern route required that they travel through Mormon settlements until reaching the Spanish Trail just south of Parowan, Utah (Figure 1). As the wagon train proceeded to the southwest, confrontations with local communities became increasingly tense. Mistrust in the Mormon settlements was exacerbated by their extreme isolation. Knowledge of current events was limited to readings from the Mormon-owned *Deseret News*—readings often containing inflammatory speeches or reminders of the persecution of Mormons in Illinois and Missouri (Brooks 1962:31). Because Mormons from these states had been sent by Brigham Young to establish settlements in southern Utah, such persecution was still fresh in the minds of many colonists. In addition, rumors of volatile rela-

tions with Native Americans and anticipation of the approaching U.S. Army had the rural communities highly agitated (Arrington and Bitton 1992:167). Compounding the situation were reports of belligerent behavior by members of the wagon train. This conduct is reported to have included cursing at draft animals that had been named after Mormon authorities, killing chickens from local farms, grazing livestock on lands where provisioning had been refused, and boasting of participation in the attacks on Mormons in the Midwest. Finally, the emigrants were erroneously accused of poisoning a spring near Corn Creek in central Utah (Bigler 1998:175).

Two days southwest of Cedar City, where the emigrants again had been refused supplies, the wagon train came to rest in a grassy valley along the Spanish Trail. Here in Mountain Meadows, the emigrants planned an extended rest to graze their cattle and prepare for the long desert crossing to California. Just before daybreak, on Monday, 7 September, the emigrants were attacked by a combined force of Mormons and their Native American (Paiute) allies (Bigler 1998:169). The first assault killed or wounded approximately 10 men, and the siege continued for another four days. With many emigrants injured or dead and ammunition running low, local militiamen John D. Lee and William Bateman entered the wagon train compound on 11 September to negotiate a surrender. Lee and Bateman convinced the emigrants to sacrifice their cattle and wagons to the Paiutes, and, in return, the militia would provide safe passage back to Cedar City. Agreeing to these terms, the company was segregated by age and sex. Children under the age of six were place in a wagon that led the procession out of the compound. A second wagon carried two or three wounded men and a woman, while at some distance, the other women and older children followed on foot. Approximately one-quarter of a mile behind, each adult male emigrant was escorted by a militiaman. After marching the men to an open space in the meadows, the order was given by Major John Higbee to "Do your duty" (Lee 1877:243; Bigler 1998:172). Each militiaman shot the emigrant he was escorting, and the Paiutes are reported to have rushed from the bushes and beaten the women and older children to death. The surviving children were transported by wagon to a nearby farmhouse and adopted out to local Mormon families until they were retrieved by federal officials a year and a half later.

Many questions remain, however, as to the details of what became known as the Mountain Meadows Massacre (MMM), especially in regard to the individuals who planned and carried out the killings. Lee was the only person brought to trial, and it would be 20 years after the massacre before he was convicted and executed by firing squad. Traditionally, Utah history texts portray the massacre as the work of local Native Americans assisted by a few Mormon zealots (Bancroft 1889; Smith 1928). Many scholars and Native Americans question this version of events (Brooks 1962; Quinn 1997; Bigler 1998; Tom and Holt 2000; Bagley 2002) and suggest that the murders were planned and executed by the local Mormon militia with only limited, if any, Native American participation.

Because many Utah residents, including a number of officials in state government and in the Church of Jesus Christ of Latter-day Saints (LDS), are descendents of the assailants, the reasons for the massacre have long generated acrimonious debate. When the topic of Mountain Meadows is raised, discussion can quickly polarize along pro- or anti-LDS lines (Novak and Rodseth 2001). From the time of the massacre to the present, its history has been tainted by anti-Mormon propaganda on one side (Wise 1976) and the sometimes sanitized accounts by LDS church apologists on the other (Alexander 1996:130–134).

In this emotionally charged context, a number of attempts have been made to establish a memorial at the massacre site. The original memorial was a simple cairn erected in 1859 by U.S. Army troops after they had gathered human remains from the surrounding meadow and buried them in a mass grave. This marker was destroyed by local residents after a visit to the site by Brigham Young in 1861 (Brooks 1962:183). In the early 1930s, a Utah historical society, with the help and approval of the LDS church, erected a second cairn to mark the burial location and commemorate the event.

Decades passed before the massacre site again became the focus of public attention. In September 1990, on a hillside overlooking the grave site, a large granite monument was unveiled that lists the names of those believed to have been on the wagon train. While this monument identifies some of the victims, it fails to provide any explanation of why they were murdered.

In 1999, the grave site itself became a focal point for an attempted reconciliation between the victims' descendants and the LDS church. Plans were made to stabilize and expand the existing cairn, which was believed to mark the place where 34 victims had been buried (Carleton 1859). Brigham Young University archaeologists were commissioned to survey the site, monitor excavation, and prevent any disturbance of the suspected graves below. Despite these precautions, on 3 August 1999, a construction backhoe penetrated a mass grave and disinterred numerous human bones. During the construction of previous monuments, the grave had remained intact, and, in fact, no one had been certain that human remains were actually located beneath the cairn. Once the grave had been disturbed, however, state law required the excavation of the site and analysis of its contents. By 6 August, the Office of Public Archaeology at Brigham Young University had completed excavation of the entire grave. In addition to the commingled human remains, a few artifacts were recovered, including glass and metal buttons, fragments of ceramics, and a nut from a wagon chassis (Smith 2000a). The BYU report on the excavation and artifact analysis is pending.

A word of explanation is required at the outset about the conditions under which the skeletal analysis was conducted. Reinterment was originally scheduled for 10 September 1999 in conjunction with the rededication of the grave site memorial. Sorting, reconstruction, and documentation of the cranial material proved to be extremely time-consuming. To allow more time for the analysis, the Utah State Archaeologist, Kevin Jones, proposed a compromise, according to which only the postcranial material would be buried at the rededication, while the cranial material would remain in the lab until the following spring. On 8 September, however, this agreement was nullified. At the request of Governor Mike Leavitt, the archaeological permit was rewritten by Max Evans, Director of the Division of State History, so that all remains from the massacre would be reburied at once (Smith 2000b). This allowed just 24 hours for further skeletal analysis. On the morning of

10 September, the remains were turned over to Brigham Young University and were buried later that day under the restored monument. As a result, not all individuals had been sorted, and cranial reconstruction was incomplete. The findings are presented here for the elements and fragments, followed by the results for the partially completed crania.

Although incomplete, the study of the Mountain Meadows mass grave provides a unique opportunity to assess skeletal and taphonomic evidence that might clarify the historical events surrounding the massacre. While the human remains reveal much about the victims' lives prior to their deaths (Novak and Kopp 2002), the following will focus on evidence of the assault and its immediate aftermath. In particular, the skeletal study will be used to examine three facets of the massacre. First, the demographic profile of the wagon train will be compared to the mass grave skeletal remains to specify the age and sex distribution of those killed in the massacre. Second, accounts of the killings will be reviewed in relation to the evidence for skeletal trauma associated with the victims' deaths. And finally, the treatment of the victims' bodies in the immediate aftermath of the massacre will be assessed through taphonomic indicators of burial environment and postmortem alteration.

Who Was Buried in the Grave at Mountain Meadows?

In April 1857, members of the Baker and Fancher families assembled their caravan in Carroll County, northwest Arkansas. These two large, relatively affluent kin groups were joined by approximately 30 other families as they prepared to travel to central California, where they planned to raise cattle and wash for gold. There are no logs recording the number or names of the individuals on the Baker-Fancher wagon train, but analysis of diaries and family histories suggests that at departure there were an estimated 135 travelers—at least 15 women, perhaps 60 men, and more than 60 dependent children (Bigler 1998:159). Other accounts lower (Brooks 1962:xx) or raise (Gibbs 1910; Bagley 2002:66) this count by a few individuals, and the company almost certainly gained and lost members along the way to Utah. Uncertainty as to the number of travelers arriving at the

Mountain Meadows is due in part to the fluidity of wagon train composition. At times, members would leave to join another faster or slower moving company, and some companies would join forces to protect against raids and banditry. It is clear that a number of other families, independent travelers, and laborers joined and left the Baker-Fancher company along the route. Approximately 140 people, in any case, seem to have been on the wagon train when it camped at Mountain Meadows.

Based on historical accounts, the grave at Mountain Meadows should contain men, women, and children. Not all individuals who had been on the wagon train would be present in this grave, since Brevet Major James H. Carleton (1859) reported gathering and burying remains of only 34 individuals. According to historical records, the grave should have a higher frequency of males to females, and the distribution by age should include a high frequency of subadults (10–19 years), followed by young adults (20–34 years), and a few older adults (34+ years). Recall that 17 children below the age of eight survived the massacre. If the assailants' accounts are accurate, no children younger than eight should be found in the grave. The one exception was an infant, approximately six months old, who was reportedly killed that day. Lee (1877:249) recalls that this child was being carried by his father when the infant died from a gunshot wound to the head.

Inventory of the Grave

Because the remains from the mass grave were fragmentary and commingled, two levels of analysis were necessary. First, each element or fragment was identified and tracked using ossuary codes (Owsley et al. 1995; Novak and Kollmann 2000). Each element or fragment was then assessed for demographic variables, trauma, and taphonomic indicators. The second level of analysis involved the reconstruction of elements and sorting of individuals. Because trauma was evident in the cranial elements, emphasis was placed on reconstruction of skulls. The cranial remains were unique in morphology, bone color, and soil staining, which aided in the initial sorting of elements. The fragments, however, were only associated with a specific cranium when a common fracture margin was

TABLE 1
ELEMENT AND FRAGMENT COUNTS

Element	1 N	1 %	2 N	2 %	3 N	3 %
CRANIAL						
Frontal	6	0%	66	5%	—	—
Parietal	16	1%	168	12%	—	—
Occipital	4	0%	109	7%	—	—
Temporal	7	0%	113	8%	—	—
Sphenoid	—	—	65	4%	—	—
Vault	—	—	—	—	747	51%
Maxilla	7	0%	56	4%	—	—
Nasal	3	0%	5	0%	—	—
Zygomatic	13	1%	17	1%	—	—
Mandible	4	0%	53	4%	—	—
Subtotal	60	4%	652	45%	747	51%
POSTCRANIAL						
Cervical Vertebra	2	0%	45	4%	—	—
Thoracic Vertebra	3	0%	51	4%	—	—
Lumbar Vertebra	—	—	9	1%	—	—
Vertebra Fragments	—	—	—	—	25	2%
Clavicle	6	1%	22	2%	—	—
Scapula	—	—	73	6%	—	—
Ribs	10	1%	82	7%	168	15%
Humerus	30	3%	45	4%	—	—
Radius	16	1%	24	2%	—	—
Ulna	8	1%	31	3%	—	—
Femur	49	4%	27	2%	—	—
Tibia	28	2%	29	3%	—	—
Fibula	12	1%	28	2%	—	—
Long Bone Fragments	—	—	—	—	246	21%
Innominate	—	—	51	4%	—	—
Sacrum	—	—	1	0%	—	—
Metacarpals, Metatarsals, Phalanges	22	2%	—	—	—	—
Subtotal	186	16%	518	45%	439	38%
TOTAL	246	9%	1,170	45%	1,186	46%
Cranial Grand Total	1,459	56%				
Postcranial Grand Total	1,143	44%				
GRAND TOTAL	**2,602**					

1 = 75% or more of element
2 = 33% to 75% of element
3 = less than 33% of element

identified. Each reconstructed cranium was given an identifying number, and all fragments matched to this individual were subsumed under this new individual number.

The skeletal remains from the Mountain Meadows mass grave consisted of 2,602 cranial and postcranial elements/fragments from adults, subadults, and children (Table 1). The majority of bones from the grave were cranial (56%), but very few of these elements were complete (4%). The postcranial remains were in a similar state of preservation, with only 9% of the elements complete. A minimum number of individuals (MNI) calculated from the commingled material was 28 from postcranial remains and was 21 from cranial elements (Table 2). From these cranial fragments, 18 distinct individuals were reconstructed (Table 3).

If this is the grave dug by Carleton's troops in 1859, only 34 individuals are expected to be present. Even using the maximum count of 28 from left femurs, approximately 100 individuals who are reported to have been on the wagon train are not included in this grave. In addition, if Carleton's counts were correct, then six individuals who were buried in the grave are unaccounted for in this analysis. The discrepancy could be explained by miscounting, incomplete excavation and recovery, or erosion of the grave. Local residents have reported bone eroding from one side of the site for years, and it is likely that this process has altered the make-up of the

TABLE 2
MINIMUM NUMBER OF INDIVIUALS

Element	R	L	MNI	Number Observed	Number Expected
Postcranial					
Humerus	25	20	25	45	56*
Radius	14	14	14	28	56*
Ulna	14	15	15	29	56*
Femur	**23**	**28**	**28**	**51**	**56***
Tibia	17	19	19	36	56*
Fibula	14	19	19	33	56*
Cranial					
Zygomatic	**9**	**21**	**21**	**30**	**42****
Temporal-TMJ	7	16	16	23	42**

* Based on MNI of 28 from left femurs.
** Based on MNI of 21 from left zygomatics.

TABLE 3
SUMMARY INFORMATION FOR THE RECONSTRUCTED CRANIA

Individual	Sex	Age	Perimortem Trauma
1	Male	20–34	Gunshot entrance wound in occipital
2	Male	16–22	Blunt force trauma to frontal and occipital
3	Male	16–22	Radiating fractures
4	Male	25–34	Gunshot entrance wound in occipital
5	Male	16–22	Blunt force trauma to frontal
6	Indeterminate	10–15	Gunshot entrance wound in right parietal
7	Male	30–39	Radiating fractures (probable gunshot wound)
8	Prob. Male	20–34	Gunshot exit wound in frontal
9	Male	29–34	Gunshot entrance wound in frontal and gunshot exit wound in right temporal
10	Male	45–54	No trauma
11	Female	35–44	Radiating fractures
12	Male	18–24	Gunshot entrance wound in left parietal
13	Prob. Male	18–22	Radiating fractures
14	Indeterminate	3.5–4.5	Blunt force cranial trauma
15	Indeterminate	6.5–7.5	Blunt force cranial trauma
16	Indeterminate	8.5–9.5	Blunt force cranial trauma
17	Male	20–34	Gunshot entrance wound in occipital
18	Female	48–54	Blunt force trauma in frontal

element counts. In any case, analysis of this grave reflects only a fraction of those known to have been killed.

Age and Sex Profile

The commingled and fragmentary elements could be assigned only to broad age categories and tentatively classified by sex. A more specific age and sex assessment was possible for the complete elements and the reconstructed crania. Standard procedures were employed to determine the demographic profile of the remains. Methods of sex determination rely primarily on the pelvis (Phenice 1969; Krogman and Iscan 1986; Bass 1995; Suchey and Katz 1998), but very few of these elements were present in the MMM series and none were matched to individuals. Consequently, in a large skeletal sample such as this, intrasite seriation of muscle attachments and sexual dimorphism of the remains are more useful for identifying sex. Because sexual dimorphism was pronounced in these remains, as in many other frontier skeletal populations (Walker and Lambert 1991; Gill 1994; Novak et al. 2002), the long bones were seriated by side and element for sex classification. Sexual dimorphism was also apparent in the cranial and dental morphology of the victims, so seriation was applied to these elements as well (Stewart 1979; Bass 1995; France 1998). In the absence of secondary sex characteristics, it is difficult to determine sex. Unless obvious indicators were present in the pelvis, cranium, or teeth, no sex determination was made for individuals under the age of 15.

Each element/fragment or reconstructed cranium was assigned to a broad age category: infant (<1 year), child (1–9 years), subadult (10–19 years), young adult (20–34 years), or old adult (>34 years). If the element had morphological indicators corresponding to growth standards, then a more narrow midpoint age category was assigned. Dental calcification standards (Moorrees et al. 1963a, 1963b; Deutsch et al. 1984; Ubelaker 1989) were used to determine these more narrow subadult ages in the MMM series. The use of long-bone growth standards (McKern and Stewart 1957; Merchant and Ubelaker 1977; Stewart 1979; Krogman and Iscan 1986) was hampered by extensive postmortem damage. As a result,

these techniques were employed in only a few cases. Adult age assessment relied on morphological and degenerative changes in the skeletal and dental tissues. Again, postmortem damage was present on most of the surfaces for which aging standards have been developed (e.g., pubic symphysis, auricular surface, and fourth rib). Analysis of the adults required secondary methods, including fusion of cranial and palatal sutures, dental attrition, degenerative joint disease, and overall bone density (Lovejoy et al. 1985; Meindl and Lovejoy 1985; Walker and Lovejoy 1985; Krogman and Iscan 1986; Mann et al. 1987; Ubelaker 1989).

Consistent with the sex profile of the Baker-Fancher wagon train, the majority of elements and reconstructed crania were those of males. The long-bone diaphyses, in particular, were predominantly classified as male. Only a few females and even fewer children were represented among these elements. For example, of 53 measurable femurs, 71% were classified as male/probable male, 10% as female/probable female, and 19% were indeterminate for sex. A reliable sex assessment was impossible for most of the cranial fragments, due to their small size. When a classification could be made for the more complete cranial elements, the majority was also determined to be male. Reconstruction of the crania allowed for a more accurate assessment of sex for the 18 individuals identified during the sorting process. Twelve of the crania were determined to be male/probable male, two female, and four were indeterminate for sex (Table 3).

The skeletal age profile of the mass grave was also in agreement with the demographics of the wagon train. The preponderance of postcranial and cranial elements and fragments as well as the reconstructed crania were those of young adults. To take the femurs again as an example, 72% were classified as young adult, 15% subadult, and 9% as old adult. Most cranial material was indeterminate for age, but those elements that could be classified were primarily from young adults. Thus, 37% of the maxillae were determined to be from young adults, 8% from old adults, and 6% from subadults. The reconstructed crania provided a more accurate age estimate of the individuals in the grave, and, here again, younger and older adults are predominant in the sample (Table 3).

No infant remains were identified in the mass grave sample, but three children were present (Crania 14, 15, and 16). Cranium 16 could be any number of juveniles killed in the massacre who were eight or nine years of age. As for Cranium 15, there were only two children, Mary Lovina Baker and America Jane Dunlap, reported to be seven years of age at the time of the massacre (Bagley 2002:385, 386). Finally, Cranium 14, a child approximately four years in age, was identified from the grave. There is no mention of a child this age being killed, and all three-to-five year olds whose names were recorded in historical records are known to have survived. There were, however, a number of juvenile victims without recorded ages. Lee's (1877:248) account of a six-month old infant being killed cannot be confirmed by this skeletal series.

Racial Ancestry

Although the members of the wagon train were assumed to be of European descent, some accounts of the massacre suggest that Native Americans were killed by emigrants during the initial siege of the wagon train (Bigler 1998:169; Bagley 2002:130). If so, there was a possibility that some Native American remains could be present in the grave. The fragmentary nature of the facial elements precluded use of the preferred metric assessment of race in the MMM series. The morphology of the skull, teeth, and femora were used instead as indicators of racial ancestry (Stewart 1979; Gill and Rhine 1986; Krogman and Iscan 1986; Gill 1998).

While the preponderance of skeletal and dental traits indicated, as expected, European descent for most of the victims, two traits more commonly found in Native American populations were observed. Both shovel-shaped incisors and platymeria of the femur shaft were present in the Mountain Meadows remains. Three maxillary incisors, representing two individuals, had "shoveling" or an enamel buildup on the occlusal-lingual surface of the tooth. The highest frequencies of this trait (>90%) are observed in Native American and East Asian populations, while the lowest frequencies are found in people of European descent (Carbonell 1963; Hillson 1996). Platymeria, or the medial-lateral elongation of the proximal femur shaft, was observed in 11 elements. This measurement

classified femurs with an index less than 84.9 as platymeric. Native Americans are characterized by platymeric indices of approximately 74, while individuals with Caucasian ancestry tend to exhibit a rounder diaphysis and have an index in the mid-80s (Bass 1995). A large degree of intrapopulation variation has been found, however, in the expression of platymeria, and the shape of the femur can be influenced by both mobility and activity patterns (Ruff 1992).

While no single morphological trait should be used to classify an individual's racial ancestry, a closer examination of the Fancher family's history suggests why some Native American characteristics may be present. Historical documents indicate Native American admixture for a number of individuals on the wagon train (Bagley 2002). The Missouri-Arkansas area from which the wagon train departed was a center for settlement by many Cherokee and mixed-blood families that had relocated to escape political conflict in the East. Family histories of Captain John T. Baker indicate that he was one-quarter Cherokee and the grandson of Chief William. Garrick Bailey, professor of anthropology at the University of Tulsa, further notes that "many of the family names of the Arkansas victims were common names among the Cherokee mixed-bloods, so that it is likely the many of the victims, in addition to the Baker family, were mixed-bloods as well" (Garrick Bailey 2000, elec. comm.).

What Happened during the Massacre?

After the emigrants agreed to be escorted out of the meadows, they began a walk to their deaths. As the two wagons containing the smallest children and the injured men led the procession, the women and older children walked a short distance behind. Approximately one-quarter mile to the rear, the unarmed men of the Baker-Fancher party were escorted single file by armed Mormon militiamen to their right. When the wagons with the women and children had reached a decline bordered by brush, the order was given to attack. Each Mormon militiaman turned to his left and shot the emigrant man beside him, while the Paiutes, according to standard historical accounts (Brooks 1962; Arrington and Bitton 1992; Bigler 1998), rushed out of the brush, killing the women and children.

Perspectives from *Historical Archaeology*

Reports vary as to the types of weapons used, especially by the Native Americans. While most of the militiamen were armed with guns, the Paiutes were reportedly equipped with various weapons, including guns, knives, hatchets, tomahawks, bows and arrows, poison darts, and rocks (Brooks 1962:74–75; Bigler 1998:172). For example, George A. Smith wrote in 1857 that "a large number of the dead were killed with arrows; the residue with bullets, the Indians being armed with guns and bows" (Brooks 1962:244). Such accounts are highly suspect. Not only were the Paiutes at this time known to "possess few firearms and little skill at using them" (Bigler 1998:169), but the use of tomahawks is typical of tribes in the woodlands rather than the Great Basin.

The osteological study attempted to determine both weapon type and the differential use of each type according to age and sex of the victims. Based on most historical accounts, each adult male victim is expected to exhibit a single gunshot wound, probably in the head, and the attack should have originated from the victim's right side. A single wound is likely for most of the emigrant men, since it was reported by Major Higbee that "they took good aim, and all of the d- -d [sic] Gentiles but two or three fell at the first fire" (Lee 1877:250–251). The women and older children, by contrast, should have evidence of bludgeoning, blade wounds, and projectile wounds from arrows. Only a single infant, as reported by Lee, is expected to have gunshot trauma to the head.

Perimortem Trauma

Distinguishing various forms of trauma from postmortem damage was central to this analysis. Antemortem trauma, as indicated by bone remodeling and healing (Sauer 1998), was identified in this series, but such trauma is reported elsewhere (Novak and Kopp 2002). The focus here will be on perimortem trauma, which by definition has occurred near or at the time of death and is distinguished by an absence of healing or remodeling. Such trauma affects fresh bone and can be discerned by fracture margins that are clean, sharp, and generally similar in color to the adjacent bone (Sauer 1998). Fresh or "green" bone contains moisture and collagen fibers that make it more pliable than dry bone. As a result, the fractur-

ing of fresh bone will produce concentric circular and radiating patterns as the energy is transmitted through the bone (Galloway 1999:16).

The patterns and locations of perimortem fractures are useful in determining the weapon and force that was used in an assault. When the weapon's force is great enough to exceed both the elastic and plastic properties of deformation, the bone will fail and fracture in a predictable manner. As fractures form to release energy, they will often follow a path of least resistance along sutures, sinuses, and toward the foramen magnum in the base of the cranium (Moritz 1954; Berryman and Haun 1996; Berryman and Symes 1998; Galloway 1999).

Perimortem fractures of this kind were evident in the MMM fragments and elements. As in the inventory and demographic analysis, trauma was assessed at two levels. First, each fragment was examined for radiating fractures and other readily identifiable forms of trauma. This was followed by cranial reconstruction to allow a more detailed analysis of the number and kinds of traumatic impacts received by each individual. Results of the first phase of study identified no obvious human-induced perimortem trauma in the postcranial elements or fragments. Two ulnae, two radii, and a humerus fragment had suspicious spiral and jagged fracture margins consistent with perimortem trauma (Figure 2). Closer examina-

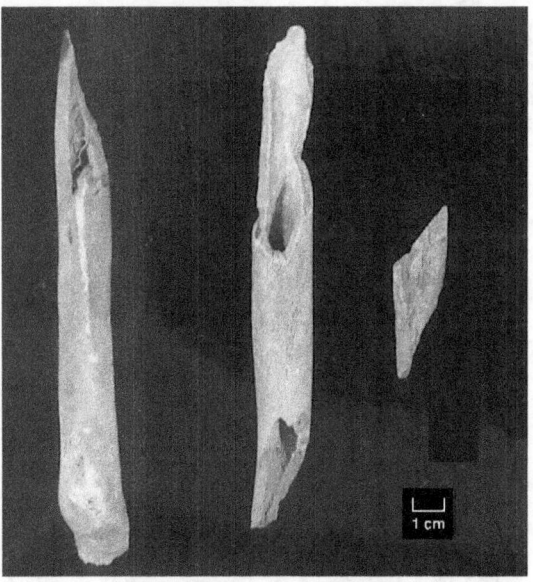

FIGURE 2. Perimortem fractures in ulna and radius fragments. (Photo by Laurel Casjens.)

tion of the fragments indicated pitting from carnivore teeth, suggesting that canids were likely responsible for these fractures. Human-induced perimortem fractures were apparent, however, in the fragments of crania.

The pattern of such cranial fractures can often indicate whether sharp, blunt, or projectile force was used and thus suggest the type of weapon involved (Merbs 1989; Knight 1997; Berryman and Symes 1998; Houck 1998; Symes, et al. 1998). *Sharp force trauma* results from contact with a bladed instrument, producing a distinct polished lesion in bone. The polished surface is often surrounded by fraying and splitting of the bone due to retraction of the blade at an angle that differs from that of entry. No evidence for sharp force trauma was identified in the remains from Mountain Meadows. *Blunt force trauma* is produced during falls or from contact with a blunt instrument such as a rock, fist, or rifle butt. The wounds vary from crushing, which provides little evidence of the weapon used, to lesions with distinct shapes, providing a clear outline of the weapon margin. Both forms of blunt force wounds were observed in this mass grave. *Projectile trauma* is distinguished by the velocity with which the weapon has contacted the body. In this analysis, following Patricia Lambert (1997:90), arrows as well as bullets are considered projectiles because their physical effects on bone are similar at high velocity. The bone flaking, or beveling, around the margins of the wound indicates distinct entrance and exit points, and the pattern of fractures can be used to infer

the speed with which the projectile entered the body. Although high-velocity weapons usually produce extensive fracturing, reconstruction of the bone fragments can often reveal the profile of the weapon. Gunshot entrance and exit wounds were the most common traumatic lesions observed in the Mountain Meadows cranial remains.

The cranial elements in the grave included more than 1,400 fragments, of which 25% had radiating fractures, indicating perimortem trauma (Table 4). The sphenoid and temporal bones had the highest frequency of fracture, 56% and 53% respectively, followed closely by fractures in the frontal and occipital bones. Facial injuries were indicated by perimortem tooth crown and root fractures. These fractures were distinct from antemortem trauma in that the surface of the fracture was similar in color to the surrounding crown or root, and no wear or bone reaction was apparent. In contrast to perimortem trauma, postmortem damage produced a difference in color between the fracture and surrounding tooth, and these fracture margins were more crumbled in appearance. The anterior teeth, especially incisors, were the most commonly affected by perimortem damage. Twenty-six percent of all mandibular teeth and 24% of the maxillary incisors had perimortem fractures or chipping.

Direct blunt force impact to the face could result in the dental damage seen in the Mountain Meadows remains, as could impact from a projectile entering or exiting the lower facial region. Time did not allow matching teeth with reconstructed crania. Thus, in some cases, the

TABLE 4
CRANIAL TRAUMA BY ELEMENT

Element	N	Complete	%	Fragmentary	%	Radiating Fractures	%	Projectile Trauma	%	Blunt Force	%
Frontal	72	6	8%	66	92%	36	50%	2	3%	3	4%
Occipital	113	4	4%	109	96%	48	42%	6	5%	—	—
Parietal	184	16	9%	168	91%	74	40%	3	2%	5	3%
Maxilla	63	7	11%	56	89%	18	29%	—	—	—	—
Mandible	57	4	7%	53	93%	—	—	—	—	1	2%
Nasal	8	3	38%	5	63%	1	13%	—	—	—	—
Sphenoid	65	—	—	65	100%	42	65%	—	—	—	—
Temporal	120	7	6%	113	94%	63	53%	1	1%	—	—
Zygomatic	30	13	43%	17	57%	9	30%	—	—	—	—
Vault	747	—	—	747	100%	76	10%	—	—	—	—
Total	1,459	60	4%	1,399	96%	367	25%	12	1%	9	1%

weapon involved could not be identified. This was not the case for many cranial fragments, in which gunshot entrance and exit wounds were apparent prior to reconstruction.

To determine the trauma patterns in each individual, it was necessary to reconstruct the crania. Matching and refitting cranial fragments to an individual often clarified trauma classifications and further facilitated identification of wounds that were not apparent in each fragment alone. In the course of reconstruction, each wound was drawn, measured, and described in detail (see Novak 2000 for examples). Techniques developed in forensic pathology and anthropology (Maples 1986; Spitz 1992; Reichs 1998) were used to interpret the timing of the injury, the force and velocity of the weapon used, and the number and sequence of impacts.

Of the 18 reconstructed crania, 17 had evidence of perimortem trauma (Table 5). In 13 cases, the injuries could be classified as either blunt force or projectile trauma. Four individuals exhibited perimortem radiating fractures, but the type of trauma had yet to be identified when the crania were reinterred. Only a single individual (Cranium 10) was found to have no sign of perimortem trauma.

Sharp Force Trauma

A number of accounts indicate that knives were used during the massacre to cut the throats of victims (Carleton 1859:6; Lee 1877:251; Brooks 1962:75; Bagley 2002:147–148). In this study, however, no evidence of sharp force trauma was identified in the vertebrae or inferior margin of

TABLE 5
PERIMORTEM TRAUMA IN THE RECONSTRUCTED CRANIA

| Individual | Sex | Age | Perimortem Trauma | | | |
			Radiating Fractures	GSW Entrance	GSW Exit	Blunt Force
1	Male	20–34	1	1		
2	Male	16–22	1			1
3	Male	16–22	1			
4	Male	25–34	1	1		
5	Male	16–22	1			1
6	Indeterminate	10–15	1	1		
7	Male	30–39	1			
8	Prob. Male	20–34	1		1	
9	Male	29–34	1	1	1	
10	Male	45–54				
11	Female	35–44	1			
12	Male	18–24	1	1		
13	Prob. Male	18–22	1			
14	Indeterminate	3.5–4.5	1			1
15	Indeterminate	6.5–7.5	1			1
16	Indeterminate	8.5–9.5	1			1
17	Male	20–34	1	1		
18	Female	48–54	1			1
			N (%)	N (%)	N (%)	N (%)
Total Number of Individuals = 18			17 (94)	6 (33)	2 (11)	6 (33)

Fragments with Identifiable Trauma

Occ03R	Indeterminate	Indeterminate	1		1	
Occ04R	Indeterminate	Indeterminate	1		1	
Occ05R	Indeterminate	Indeterminate	1		1	
Par08L	Indeterminate	Indeterminate	1		1	
Man04C	Male	18–22				1

the mandibular corpus where this type of injury would most likely be found. More extensive sharp force trauma in the form of scalping and beheading was reported in one account (Drewer 1859). Yet there were no cutmarks on the cranial vaults that would be characteristic of scalping (Owlsey 1994), and blade wounds in the base of the crania that would indicate beheading were also lacking in the MMM series. There could be several reasons for the absence of sharp force trauma. First, knives may not have been used in the massacre or simply not used to attack any of the individuals in this grave. Second, knives may have been used but did not penetrate to the bone. Finally, carnivore activity and other postmortem factors may have resulted in the loss of cervical vertebrae—elements of the neck where deep cuts might have been recorded in the bone. In any case, the use of bladed instruments during the massacre cannot be corroborated by these skeletal remains.

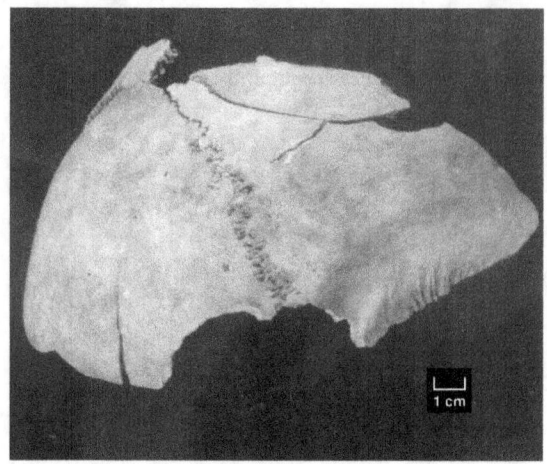

FIGURE 3. Concentric and radiating fractures in the vault of a child (Cranium 16). Left lateral profile of the vault with the frontal bone facing left. (Photo by Laurel Casjens.)

Blunt Force Trauma

Of the 18 reconstructed crania, six displayed lesions consistent with blunt force trauma (Table 6). Three of these cases were children; two were young adult males; and one was an old adult female. The children, in particular, had extensive crushing damage to the vaults (Figure 3)—trauma that is characteristic of blows delivered with great force (Gurdjian 1975; Galloway 1999). Again, cranial reconstruction was interrupted by the expedited reinterment, and the exact locations of impact were not delineated in these children. The pattern of concentric and linear radiating fractures was useful, however, in determining general impact locations. The two young adult males both had blunt force impact sites on the frontal bone. Although the impact on Cranium 5 was rather nondescript, the impact on Cranium 2 was more clearly defined. A blunt linear object created a lesion in the left frontal of Cranium 2 that caused a rectangular section of bone to be removed (Figure 4). Another blow from this same type of weapon resulted in a smaller linear wound on the back of this same individual's head. Lee describes the case of a boy, approximately 14 years old, who was assaulted in a way that would produce linear blunt lesions of this kind. The boy was running to a wagon when Knight, one of the wagon drivers, "struck him on the head with the butt end of his gun, and crushed his skull" (Lee 1877:249).

A mandibular corpus (Man04C) that was not matched to a reconstructed cranium, also had evidence of a blunt force impact site (Table 5).

TABLE 6
BLUNT FORCE TRAUMA ANGLE OF ATTACK

Element/Individual	Age	Sex	Angle of Attack
2	16–22	Male	Anterior and Posterior
5	16–22	Male	Anterior
14	3.5–4.5	Indeterminate	Posterior-Superior
15	6.5–7.5	Indeterminate	Posterior-Superior
16	8.5–9.5	Indeterminate	Superior-Left Lateral
17	18–22	Male	Anterior
18	48–54	Female	Anterior

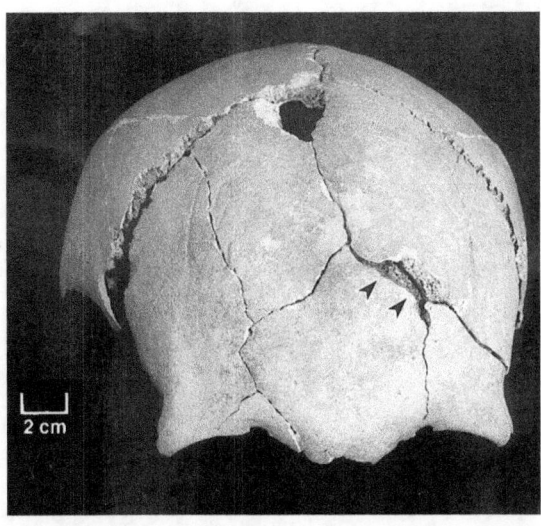

FIGURE 4. Linear blunt force trauma in the frontal of a young adult male (Cranium 2). Note that the hole near bregma is the result of postmortem damage, and during reconstruction, glue has changed the color of the fracture margin along the coronal suture. (Photo by Laurel Casjens.)

This element from a young adult male had a large radiating fracture that ran through the corpus along the midline, and the crowns of the anterior teeth were fractured and missing. Such a wound could have resulted from a direct blow to the face or from the impact of the ground during a fall.

In the cases of blunt force trauma observed here, the direction of attack tended to be from the front of the victim (Table 6). While four of the eight blunt force lesions were produced by an anterior attack, only a single lesion was produced from a posterior position, and this injury occurred in combination with a blow from the front. Three of the blunt force impacts were delivered by the assailants from positions above the victims. This pattern is probably explained by the fact that all three of these victims were children.

The evidence for blunt force trauma in the MMM remains is consistent with the historical accounts. Only children, subadults, and women exhibit lesions that indicate blunt force impacts. Because most of these lesions are nondescript in shape, the kind of weapon involved cannot be specified. The two linear blunt depression fractures found in a young male may have been caused by a rifle butt as described in Lee's account.

Projectile Trauma

Many skeletal lesions characteristic of projectile trauma were found in the MMM series. Some of the historical accounts report that the Paiutes used bows and arrows during the assault. Memoirs of a number of the surviving children tell of arrows piercing or protruding from bodies (Smith and McKnight 1858; Evans 1897). John Calvin Miller, who survived the massacre at age six, later recalled pulling arrows from his mother's body until she was dead (Carleton 1859). In the remains from this grave, however, there was no evidence of arrow wounds, and all projectile trauma was determined to be the result of gunshots.

The reconstructed cranial material exhibited eight unambiguous gunshot injuries. Six of these were entrance wounds and two were exit wounds. An additional four partial exit wounds were identified in the cranial fragments (Table 5). Entrance wounds were located in the frontal, parietal, and occipital bones, indicating that the victims were shot by their assailants from different directions (Figure 5, Table 7). The position of some of these posterior entrance wounds (Figure 6) indicates a bullet trajectory that would have resulted in a facial exit. This trajectory would explain much of the perimortem trauma observed in the facial and dental elements. Early reburial precluded radiographic

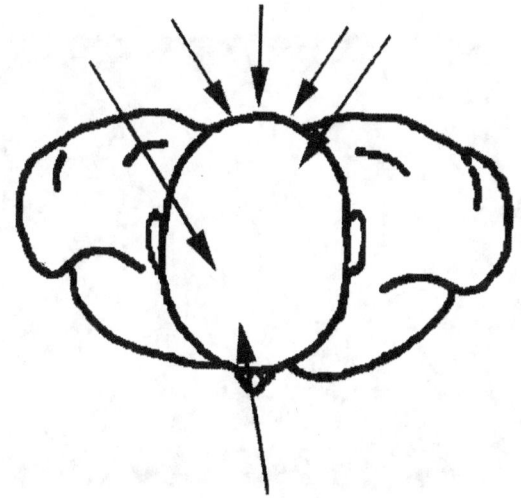

FIGURE 5. Location of gunshot entrance wounds and trajectory of bullets in the Mountain Meadows crania. (Drawing by Jennifer Graves.)

TABLE 7
GUNSHOT ENTRANCE AND EXIT WOUNDS

Individual/ Element	Age	Sex	Entrance Element	Entrance Measurement	Exit Element	Exit Measurement
1	Young Adult	Male	Occipital	13 mm	-	-
4	Young Adult	Male	Occipital	13 mm	-	-
6	Subadult	Indeterminate	Right Parietal	15 mm(A-P) X 12.5 mm (S-I)	-	-
8	Young Adult	Prob. Male	-	-	Frontal	Indeterminate
9	Young Adult	Male	Frontal	14.3 mm (A-P) X 17 mm (S-I)	Right Temporal	Indeterminate
12	Young Adult	Male	Left Parietal	11 mm	-	-
Occ02	Young Adult	Male	Occipital	11 mm	-	-
Occ03R	Indeterminate	Indeterminate	-	-	Occipital	Indeterminate
Occ04R	Indeterminate	Indeterminate	-	-	Occipital	Indeterminate
Occ05R	Indeterminate	Indeterminate	-	-	Occipital	Indeterminate
Par08L	Indeterminate	Indeterminate	-	-	Left Parietal	Indeterminate

analysis to identify trace metal fragments on the facial bones or along other ambiguous perimortem fractures.

While there were equal numbers of entrance and exit wounds in the series, only one entrance wound was clearly associated with an exit wound in the same individual. A young adult male (Cranium 9) had an entrance wound in the left frontal bone and an exit wound in the right temporal bone. The remaining gunshot wounds must be considered the result of separate shootings, indicating that as many as 11 bullets were fired. When the trajectories of the exit wounds are considered (Figure 7), six of the shots were administered from a position posterior to the victims, while the remaining five shots were delivered facing the victims. In the case of one subadult (Cranium 6), 10–15 years in age, the angle of attack was unusual because the entrance wound was located in the top of the right side of the head (Figure 8). The wound was elongated and had beveling on the anterior external margin, creating a distinctive "keyhole" shape. Such a wound indicates that the gun was held by the perpetrator above and behind the right side of the victim.

With the exception of the wound in this subadult, whose sex could not be determined, all

FIGURE 6. Gunshot entrance wound in the occipital of a young adult male (Cranium 17). (Photo by Laurel Casjens.)

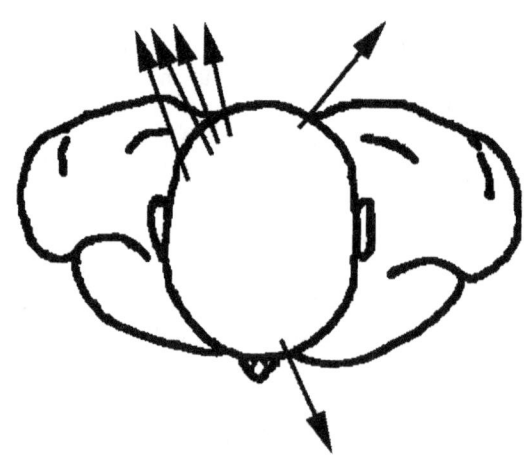

FIGURE 7. Location of gunshot exit wounds and trajectory of bullets in the Mountain Meadows crania. (Drawing by Jennifer Graves.)

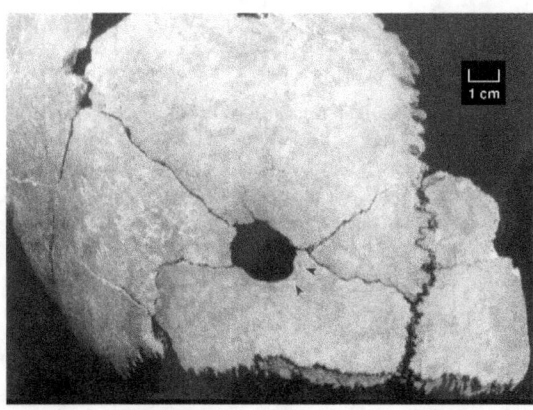

FIGURE 8. Gunshot entrance wound in the superior right parietal of a subadult (Cranium 6). Anterior is toward the bottom of the page. Note a slight rim of external beveling is located along the anterior-superior margin of the wound. (Photo by Laurel Casjens.)

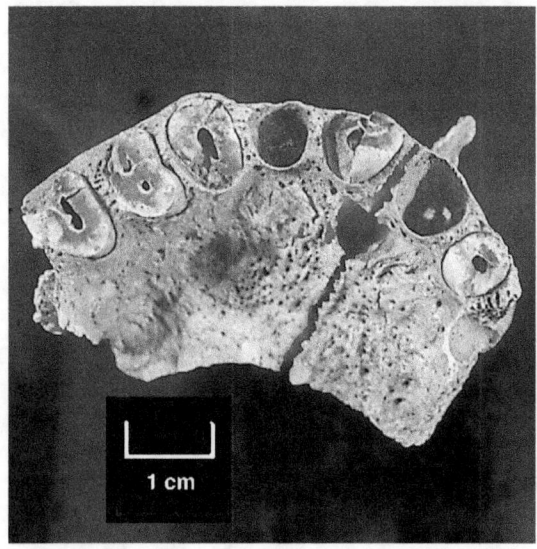

FIGURE 9. Perimortem fractures in the maxillae and dentition of a young adult female (Max06R/L). (Photo by Laurel Casjens.)

gunshot wounds in the reconstructed crania were found in young adult males. The fragments with identifiable exit wounds were too small to assign age or sex with any confidence, although density and thickness of the vault suggested that these were most likely adult males.

While only clearly delineated projectile wounds were scored, a number of elements had fracture patterns that were characteristic of gunshot trauma. This pattern was particularly evident in the maxil-

lae of a young adult female (Max06R/L). These elements had large radiating fractures running through the palate, and the crowns of the anterior teeth were broken and had a blackened, polished appearance (Figure 9). This kind of trauma is consistent with the extensive damage created by projectiles entering or exiting the facial region.

In some respects, the pattern of gunshot wounds found in the human remains corroborates the historical accounts. As predicted, the majority of such wounds were identified in males and only a single lesion perforated each cranium. At the same time, the skeletal evidence suggests that some details of the massacre have been oversimplified. If the militiamen were located to the right of the emigrants, most of the entrance wounds should be located on the victims' right sides. In these remains, however, the shots were fired from the front and from the rear. Lee's account of the massacre has at least one man shot in the forehead: "I saw an Indian from Cedar City, called Joe, ran up to the wagon and catch a man by the hair, and raise his head up and look into his face; the man shut his eyes, and Joe shot him in the head" (Lee 1877:249). The identification of one subadult (Cranium 6) who was shot through the top of the head and another case of a young woman (Max06R/L) who was likely shot in the head are also inconsistent with the traditional accounts of the women and children being beaten to death. A closer study of the primary sources indicates that women and children were not always spared in the firing. Lee's account describes the shooting of "a girl, some ten or eleven years old" (1877:249), approximately the age of the subadult (Cranium 6) who was shot through the top of the head. The account does not indicate, however, in what part of the body she was shot.

What Happened to the Bodies?

Immediately following the massacre, the bodies were searched for valuables (Lee 1877:251). After what Lee described as a good night's sleep, he and his accomplices returned to the site to bury the dead. Upon his arrival, he reported, "the bodies of men, women and children had been stripped entirely naked, making the scene one of the most...loathsome and ghastly that can be imagined" (Lee 1877:252). As he continued to survey the site, he found the "brethren" attempting to cover up the corpses. "They piled the dead bodies up in heaps in little gullies, and threw dirt over them. The bodies were only lightly covered, for the ground was hard, and the brethren did not have sufficient tools to dig with" (Lee 1877:253).

Although other wagon trains passed near the massacre site over the next few days, Mormon escorts either diverted the caravans around Mountain Meadows or led them through the area under cover of darkness. One of the first outside reports of the massacre scene was made by John Aiken approximately one week after the event. In an affidavit filed in San Bernardino, California, Aiken reported seeing "about twenty wolves feasting upon the carcasses of the murdered," and went on to note that "women and children were more generally eaten by the wild beasts than were the men" (Aiken 1857).

It was not until 18 months after the massacre that Brevet Major Carleton was dispatched from Los Angeles with orders to bury the victims. In May 1859, Carleton arrived at Mountain Meadows to find Captain Rueben P. Campbell of the United States Second Dragoons encamped there with his troops. Campbell had supervised the interment of some victims prior to Carleton's arrival. According to Dr. Charles Brewer, the U.S. Army Surgeon on the scene, 18 individuals had been buried in one grave, 12 in another, and 6 in a third (Carleton 1859). Carleton and his troops searched the site for more human bones.

The remains of approximately 34 individuals were widely scattered across the meadows:

> Women's hair, in detached locks and masses, hung to the sage brushes and was strewn over the ground in many places. Parts of little children's dresses and of female costume dangled from the shrubbery or lay scattered about; and among these, here and there, on every hand, for at least a mile in the direction of the road, by two miles east and west, there gleamed, bleached white by the weather, the skulls and other bones of those who had suffered (Carleton 1859).

Carleton's troops buried the remains in a mass grave on the north side of a ditch that had been dug by the emigrants during the initial standoff. A cairn was then raised to mark the grave, upon which a cross was placed with the inscription, "Vengeance is mine: I will repay, saith the Lord."

Postmortem Damage

The remains analyzed here indicate several types of postmortem damage, which can usually be distinguished from perimortem trauma. Dry bone, in particular, is more likely to shatter and produce small irregular pieces of bone (Maples 1986; Sauer 1998:325; Galloway 1999:16). As the collagen degrades, the bone becomes less flexible, and the fracture margins are ragged and often differ in color from the surrounding bone. In the present case, postmortem damage resulted from carnivore activity, weathering, and excavation (Table 8).

TABLE 8
TAPHONOMIC INDICATORS ON POSTCRANIAL ELEMENTS

Element	N	Complete	%	Partial	%	Carnivore	%	Weathering	%	Excavation	%
Clavicle	28	6	21%	22	79%	12	43%	—	—	26	93%
Innominate	51	—	—	51	100%	34	67%	—	—	48	94%
Metacarpals/ Metatarsals	11	11	100%	—	—	11	100%	—	—	6	55%
Phalanges	11	11	100%	8	73%	4	36%	1	9%	—	—
Ribs	260	10	4%	250	96%	85	33%	2	1%	250	96%
Sacrum	1	—	—	1	100%	—	—	—	—	1	100%
Scapula	73	—	—	73	100%	55	75%	3	4%	72	99%
Cervical Verts	47	2	4%	45	96%	14	30%	—	—	39	83%
Thoracic Verts	44	3	7%	41	93%	10	23%	—	—	42	95%
Lumbar Verts	9	—	—	9	100%	1	11%	—	—	9	100%
Vertebrae Frags	25	—	—	25	100%	—	—	—	—	25	100%
Humerus	75	30	40%	45	60%	70	93%	9	12%	55	73%
Radius	40	16	40%	24	60%	31	78%	7	18%	20	50%
Ulna	39	8	21%	31	79%	25	64%	8	21%	24	62%
Femur	76	49	64%	27	36%	68	89%	32	42%	48	63%
Tibia	57	28	49%	29	51%	52	91%	20	35%	36	63%
Fibula	33	12	36%	28	85%	26	79%	5	15%	22	67%

Perspectives from *Historical Archaeology*

Carnivore activity appears to be responsible for the under-representation of certain elements in the grave and for the damage to a number of surfaces on the bones. The alteration of the victims' remains after the massacre is consistent with experimental studies of scavenging by carnivores (Lyman 1994; Fisher 1995). These studies indicate that carnivores, especially coyotes and other dogs, will alter the human body in a predictable manner. With human bodies, feeding usually begins around the neck and moves to the ventral thorax, until the arms become disarticulated from the body (Haglund 1996:368). After a few months, the legs are removed, leaving only the vertebral column, the cranium, and assorted elements and fragments. Depending on the time of exposure, as little as 20% of a body may be recovered due to carnivore feeding and transport. Carleton's (1859) description of skeletal remains widely dispersed across the Meadows is consistent with the experimental studies.

Also consistent with these studies is the under-representation of certain skeletal elements in the grave. Axial elements are particularly susceptible to damage as a result of early abdominal feeding and easy consumption of the small spongy vertebral bones. In the MMM series, there were fewer axial bones, especially vertebrae and innominates, than would be expected with an MNI count of 28. Only a single sacrum was recovered, and the lumbar vertebrae were few and fragmentary. Although a number of innominates were present in the sample, 67% were affected by carnivores, and the pubic bone and ilium were susceptible to alteration. Discrepancies were also present in the expected number of appendicular elements (Table 2). Few bones of the hands and feet were recovered from the mass grave, and long-bone joint surfaces were extremely under-represented. Again, carnivore activity appears to be the primary factor affecting the joint counts, as these spongy bone centers are preferred chewing surfaces for canids.

In addition to the altered element counts, tooth marks of carnivores were clearly evident on the Mountain Meadows remains. A carnivore's dental arcade creates four types of signatures on bone: punctures, furrows, pits, and scoring (Haynes 1980; Binford 1981). Of these, punctures, furrows, and pits were the most common carnivore marks on the victims' remains. Punctures were observed in the blades of the scapulae, the ilium of the innominates, and along the ends of the diaphyses. The proximal and distal articular surfaces of the long bones were consistently removed by carnivore gnawing, leaving scalloped surfaces. Furrows were identified along the centers of the long bone shaft, and pits were numerous in ribs and in the few epiphyses recovered (Figure 10).

Many of the canid tooth marks were bisected by splits in the diaphyses caused by weathering. The breakage and weathering patterns indicate that the bodies were subject to heavy carnivore feeding and that the disarticulated elements were exposed to extremes in temperature and humidity on the surface. Stripping the bodies would have facilitated canid scavenging, especially in the abdominal region. Once the bodies were disarticulated, elements are likely to have been transported over varying distances, creating differential patterns in weathering. The long bone shafts were particularly affected by exposure (Table 8). Weathering signatures were most prevalent on the elements of the legs. Longitudinal splitting was exhibited in 62% of the femurs and 56% of the tibiae. None of the elements were bleached a stark white, although longitudinal splitting of the shafts and the woody appearance of the bone suggest an extended period on the surface (Behrensmeyer 1978; Lyman and Fox 1997).

Finally, both the weathering damage and carnivore marks were often bisected by the more recent excavation damage. Such damage was extensive, especially in the crania, which were

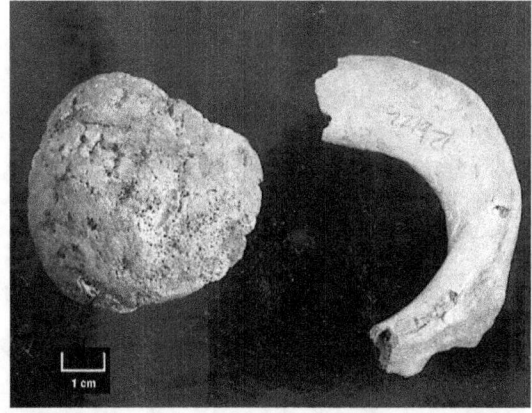

FIGURE 10. Pits from carnivore activity in the proximal epiphysis of a femur and left rib. (Photo by Laurel Casjens.)

broken in irregular patterns with light-colored margins. The degree of excavation damage is clearly related to the positioning of elements in the grave. Carleton (1859) reports arranging the bones by element type in roughly anatomical position. Given the extensive damage to the cranial remains, it appears that the backhoe penetrated at the end of the grave where Carleton had placed the victims' heads.

Summary and Discussion

> No more arresting emblems of the modern culture of nationalism exist than the cenotaphs and tombs of Unknown Soldiers. The public ceremonial reverence accorded these monuments precisely *because* they are either deliberately empty or no one knows who lies inside them, has no true precedents in earlier times. To feel the force of this modernity one has only to imagine the general reaction to the busybody who "discovered" the Unknown Soldier's name or insisted on filling the cenotaph with some real bones (Anderson 1991:9).

This study analyzed more than 2,600 bone fragments representing at least 28 of the victims of the Mountain Meadows Massacre. While these 28 victims make up less than one-quarter of the number reported killed, the demographic profile of the grave appears to be a representative sample of the Baker-Fancher company. On a number of key points, historical accounts of the massacre were corroborated by this analysis. The findings indicate that men, women, and children were killed in the assault and that most of the victims were young adult males. The majority of these men had been shot once in the head, while most of the women and children were bludgeoned to death. The results, however, could not confirm some of the historical details. In particular, there was no evidence for the use of knives to scalp, behead, or cut the throats of these victims. Evidence was also lacking for projectile trauma from arrows. With regard to the postmortem fate of the bodies, there is no apparent conflict between the historical accounts and the findings of this study. Clearly, the bodies were subject to feeding and disarticulation by canids, after which the scattered bones remained exposed on the surface until they were buried in 1859.

Human remains of this kind, as Benedict Anderson reminds us, can be powerful symbols of ethnic and national identity. In a modern Western context, the living tend to have little or no contact with the remains of the dead, but they often invest heavily in funerals, tombs, and other memorials. Such investments serve to eulogize ancestors or other kin and tend to provide a sense of solidarity among the living members of a family, ethnic group, or nation. In traditional societies, ancestral remains are often venerated and ritually protected from desecration. Even in the absence of modern nationalism, these customs again provide a sense of collective identity and continuity along genealogical lines. Yet collective identity of this kind is obviously based on shared sentiment more than scientific fact. Neither the modern nationalist nor the tribal authority welcomes an empirical investigation of bones whose symbolic value might be compromised as a result.

These are familiar facts, but they have difficult implications for scientists who would seek to learn about the past from human remains. Investigation of war crimes in Rwanda or Kosovo, repatriation of museum collections to Native American tribes, even the case of Kennewick Man, all illustrate the potentially explosive political consequences of studying human remains. Perhaps the social and ethical concerns are so deep that such remains should simply not be studied. After all, artifacts and written records document behavior in the past and can provide insight without disturbing the dead.

Yet artifacts and written records cannot always provide a basis for political consensus about past events, especially those involving collective violence by members of one population against those of another. In such cases, an enduring struggle may ensue over the question of historical culpability, with each faction attempting to control the narration of the original historical event. One of the most effective ways of monopolizing the telling of history is to establish permanent or "official" memorials at key historical sites (Clifford 1997:338–339). In controversial cases, such memorials usually serve the interests of some living individuals or factions at the expense of others (Shackel 2001). By building tombs or otherwise caring for the remains, some position themselves closer to the dead and, thereby, lay claim to the charisma of the past. In this way, they may even come to control the way the past is narrated (Verdery 1999).

Such a bid for narrative control was clearly evident in the 1999 rededication ceremony of the Mountain Meadows memorial. This event was sponsored by the LDS church in cooperation with the Mountain Meadows Association, which represents one faction of the victims' descendants. These and other parties have attempted to control the narration of the event since it took place more than 140 years ago. In spite of the new skeletal evidence that had just come to light, the ceremony was enveloped by an atmosphere of "forgive and forget." Gordon B. Hinkley, president of the LDS church, declared, "Let the book of the past be closed" (Hinkley quoted in Smith 2000b). Ron Loving, then president of the Mountain Meadows Association, remarked that the site of the massacre "is hallowed ground. It is neutral ground. It is a place where only love and tolerance and understanding should be brought. Leave everything else behind" (Wadley 1999).

Indeed, what seems to have been left behind is any reference to the events of 11 September 1857. Two engravings in the wall of the newly dedicated monument appear to venerate the monument and its benefactors more than the victims of the massacre. Upon entering the gate to the memorial, the engraving in the north wall reads:

MOUNTAIN MEADOWS MASSACRE
GRAVE SITE MEMORIAL
Built and maintained by
The Church of Jesus Christ of Latter-day Saints
Out of respect for those who died and were
buried here and in the surrounding area
Following the massacre of 1857.
Dedicated 11 September 1999

On the southern wall of the monument, the second engraving commemorates memorials that have been established in both Utah and Arkansas. Six markers are listed, beginning with the original monument established by the U.S. Army in 1859 and concluding with the 1999 memorial. This final entry reads: "1999. Under the direction of President Gordon B. Hinckley and with the cooperation of the Mountain Meadows Association and others, The Church of Jesus Christ of Latter-day Saints replaced the 1932 wall and installed the present Grave Site Memorial. President Hinckley dedicated the memorial on 11 September 1999." Again, in this and the other five entries, the emphasis is placed on the groups or

individuals associated with the establishment and maintenance of the various memorials.

Given the complexity of the Mountain Meadows Massacre, varying historical accounts should be expected, depending on whether the story is told by LDS church officials, descendants of the victims, or descendants of the accused participants. Not all accounts have had an equal hearing. Conspicuously absent from the 1999 rededication ceremony were representatives of the Native American tribes that have long been charged with some responsibility for the massacre. While many accounts continue to implicate Paiutes and other local Indian groups, a great deal of evidence contradicts this assertion (Quinn 1997:252; Bagley 2002). Even within the testimony of a single eyewitness, the evidence for Native American involvement is often ambiguous. Lee, for example, claimed that one emigrant was shot in the head by Joe, "an Indian from Cedar City." At the same time, however, Lee reported that the attack on women and children was led not by Native Americans but by Mormon interpreters—missionaries to the local Paiute population (Lee 1877:237, 243). Militiaman Nephi Johnson later admitted that "white men did most of the killing" (Quinn 1997:252; Bagley 2002:307). Furthermore, in the planning of the attack, there was a systematic attempt to redirect blame onto Native Americans. According to numerous accounts, some of the militiamen disguised themselves as Indians before carrying out the massacre (Carleton 1859; Prince 1859; Rogers 1860; Higbee 1894; Bagley 2002). Oral histories collected among Utah Paiutes contend that their involvement was limited to observing the massacre at a distance and robbing wagon train possessions after the fact (Tom and Holt 2000:133–136).

Even in the face of such evidence, the grave site plaque that was erected in 1932 claimed that the emigrants had been "attacked by white men and Indians" (Brooks 1962:221). This marker was removed prior to the 1999 rededication. On the hill overlooking the site, the Mountain Meadows Association erected two new signposts that provide some details of the event. For the first time at the site, Mormon settlers and militiamen are clearly identified as participants in the attack. The new signs, however, continue to implicate "Indians" as well. One interpretive marker reads, "a party of local Mormon settlers and Indians attacked and laid siege to the encampment ... The local Indians joined in the slaughter, and in a matter of minutes fourteen adult male emigrants, twelve women, and thirty-five children were struck down." While the sign suggests that the Mormon participants had complex motives involving "animosities and political issues intertwined with religious beliefs," no such nuanced explanation is given to account for the purported involvement of Native Americans.

There are obvious limits to what human remains can reveal about the past, and skeletal analysis may never determine who was responsible for the Mountain Meadows Massacre. In particular, the question of the racial or ethnic identities of the killers is left unresolved. Yet it is worth reiterating that the remains analyzed here contained no evidence of scalping or arrow wounds, and this study lends no support to the claim that specifically Native American weaponry was used in the massacre.

As scientists, we are compelled to seek multiple kinds of evidence and to cross-check data using independent sources, especially when controversy surrounds the interpretation of an event. The human remains from Mountain Meadows are a new source of evidence that should be "read" along with the many other historical sources that have accumulated. Until the summer of 1999, diaries, affidavits, newspaper articles, and government documents were the only sources available with which to reconstruct the event—sources that were based in many cases on the coached testimony of killers, hearsay of second parties, or the depositions of young children. More importantly, the skeletal evidence is qualitatively different from the oral accounts because the bones of the victims have not been affected by self-interested rhetoric or shifting political winds. As a result, what was supposed to be a symbolic memorial that contained, like the Tomb of the Unknown Soldier, only vaguely conceptualized remains, has indeed been filled with real bones. By themselves, these bones cannot resolve what happened at Mountain Meadows, but they do force us to question tacit assumptions, reevaluate longstanding "facts," and reconsider evidence of every kind, in the service of all who have a stake in the outcome.

ACKNOWLEDGMENTS

This material is based upon work supported by the office of Research and Development Medical Research Service, Department of Veterans Affairs, SLC Health Care System; Department of Orthopedics, University of Utah School of Medicine; Department of Anthropology, University of Utah; and the Office of Public Archaeology, Brigham Young University. Thanks are due to Shane Baker and students at the BYU Museum of Peoples and Cultures for washing and sorting the remains, Kevin Jones for fighting a good fight, Laurel Casjens for brilliant photography under pressure, Garrick Bailey for solving the mystery, Will Bagley for sharing his manuscript and thoughtful insights, James O'Connell for comments on the manuscript, and Jennifer Graves for preparation of the gunshot trajectory figures. We are grateful to Douglas Scott, Melissa Connor, and an anonymous reviewer for their useful comments on the manuscript. A special thanks to Lars Rodseth for the lengthy discussions and astute editing that allowed this paper to take form.

REFERENCES

AIKEN, JOHN
  1857 Affidavit made before Marcus Kate, Notary Public, 24 November. San Bernardino, CA.

ALEXANDER, THOMAS G.
  1996 *Utah, the Right Place: The Official Centennial History.* Gibbs Smith, Salt Lake City.

ANDERSON, BENEDICT
  1991 *Imagined Communities: Reflections on the Origin and Spread of Nationalism,* revised edition. Verso, London.

ARRINGTON, LEONARD J., AND DAVIS BITTON
  1992 *The Mormon Experience: A History of the Latter-day Saints.* University of Illinois Press, Chicago.

BAGLEY, WILL
  2002 *Blood of the Prophets: Brigham Young and the Massacre at Mountain Meadows.* University of Oklahoma Press, Norman.

BANCROFT, HUBERT H.
  1889 *History of Utah.* The History Company, San Francisco, CA.

BASS, WILLIAM M.
  1995 *Human Osteology: A Laboratory and Field Manual,* 4th edition. Missouri Archaeological Society, Columbia.

BEHRENSMEYER, ANNA K.
  1978 Taphonomic and Ecological Information from Bone Weathering. *Paleobiology,* 4:150–162.

BERRYMAN, HUGH E., AND JONES S. HAUN
  1996 Applying Forensic Techniques to Interpret Cranial Fracture Patterns in an Archaeological Specimen. *International Journal of Osteoarchaeology*, 6:2–9.

BERRYMAN, HUGH E., AND STEVEN A. SYMES
  1998 Recognizing Gunshot and Blunt Cranial Trauma through Fracture Interpretation. In *Forensic Osteology: Advances in the Identification of Human Remains*, 2nd edition, Kathleen J. Reichs, editor, pp. 333–352. Charles C. Thomas, Springfield, IL.

BIGLER, DAVID L.
  1998 *Forgotten Kingdom: The Mormon Theocracy in the American West 1847–1896*. Utah State University Press, Logan.

BINFORD, LEWIS R.
  1981 *Bones: Ancient Men and Modern Myths*. Academic Press, San Francisco, CA.

BROOKS, JUANITA
  1962 *The Mountain Meadows Massacre*, 2nd edition. University of Oklahoma Press, Norman.

CARBONELL, V. M.
  1963 Variations in the Frequency of Shovel-Shaped Incisors in Different Populations. In *Dental Anthropology*, Don R. Brothwell, editor, pp. 211–234. Pergamon Press, London.

CARLETON, JAMES H.
  1859 Report on the Mountain Meadows Massacre. 57th Congress, I Session, House Document 605, Washington, DC.

CLIFFORD, JAMES
  1997 Fort Ross Meditation. In *Routes: Travel and Translation in the Late-Twentieth Century*, pp. 299–347. Harvard University Press, Cambridge, MA.

DEUTSCH, D., E. PEÍER, AND I. GEDALIA
  1984 Changes in Size, Morphology, and Weight of Human Anterior Teeth during the Fetal Period. *Growth*, 48:74–85.

DREWER, THOMAS
  1859 Thomas to Dr. Abram Clauds, Camp Floyd, 31 March. Partial transcription "of the Contents of a Letter from Camp Floyd Utah Territory" in the Paul C. Rohloff Mormon Collection. Copy in Caroline Parry Woolley Collection. Special Collections, Gerald R. Sherratt Library, Southern Utah University, Cedar City.

EVANS, REBECCA DUNLAP
  1897 Mountain Meadows Massacre ... Related by One of the Survivors. *Fort Smith Elevator*, 20 August, 2:1–3. Fort Smith, AR.

FISHER, J.
  1995 Bone Surface Modification in Zooarchaeology. *Journal of Archaeological Method and Theory*, 2:7–68.

FRANCE, DIANE L.
  1998 Observational and Metric Analysis of Sex in the Skeleton. In *Forensic Osteology: Advances in the Identification of Human Remains*, 2nd edition, Kathleen J. Reichs, editor, pp. 163–186. Charles C. Thomas, Springfield, IL.

GALLOWAY, ALLISON (EDITOR)
  1999 *Broken Bones: Anthropological Analysis of Blunt Force Trauma*. Charles C. Thomas, Springfield, IL

GIBBS, JOSIAH F.
  1910 *The Mountain Meadows Massacre*, 2nd edition. Salt Lake Tribune Publishing Company, Salt Lake City, UT.

GILL, GEORGE W.
  1994 Skeletal Injuries of Pioneers. In *Skeletal Biology in the Great Plains: Migration, Warfare, Health, and Subsistence*, Douglas W. Owsley and Richard L. Jantz, editors, pp. 159–172. Smithsonian Institution Press, Washington, DC.
  1998 Craniofacial Criteria in the Skeletal Attribution of Race. In *Forensic Osteology: Advances in the Identification of Human Remains*, 2nd edition, Kathleen J. Reichs, editor, pp. 293–317. Charles C. Thomas, Springfield, IL.

GILL, GEORGE W., AND J. STANLEY RHINE (EDITORS)
  1986 *Skeletal Race Identification: New Approaches in Forensic Anthropology*. Maxwell Museum, Albuquerque, NM.

GURDJIAN, E. S.
  1975 *Impact Head Injury, Mechanistic, Clinical, and Preventive Correlations*. Charles C Thomas, Springfield, NM.

HAGLUND, WILLIAM D.
  1996 Dogs and Coyotes: Postmortem Involvement with Human Remains. In *Forensic Taphonomy: The Postmortem Fate of Human Remains*, William D. Haglund and Marcella H. Sorg, editors, pp. 367–381. CRC Press, Boca Raton, FL.

HAYNES, G.
  1980 Prey Bones and Predators: Potential Ecological Information from Analysis of Bone Sites. *Ossa*, 7:75–97.

HIGBEE, JOHN M.
  1894 Higbee statements, in Mountain Meadows File, LDS Archives. Salt Lake City, UT.

HILLSON, SIMON
  1996 *Dental Anthropology*. Cambridge University Press, Cambridge, UK.

HOUCK, MAX M.
  1998 Skeletal Trauma and the Individualization of Knife Marks in Bones. In *Forensic Osteology: Advances in the Identification of Human Remains*, 2nd edition, Kathleen J. Reichs, editor, pp. 410–424. Charles C. Thomas, Springfield, IL.

KNIGHT, BERNARD
1997   *Simpson's Forensic Medicine*. Oxford University Press, New York, NY.

KROGMAN, WILTON M., AND M. YASAR ISCAN
1986   *The Human Skeleton in Forensic Medicine*. Charles C. Thomas, Springfield, IL.

LAMBERT, PATRICIA M.
1997   Patterns of Violence in Prehistoric Hunter-Gatherer Societies of Coastal Southern California. In *Troubled Times: Violence and Warfare in the Past*, Debra L. Martin and David W. Frayer, editors, pp. 77–109. Alan R. Liss, Inc., New York, NY.

LEE, JOHN D.
1877   *Mormonism Unveiled: The Life and Confessions of John D. Lee*. Reprinted in 2001 by Fierra Blanca Publications, Albuquerque, NM.

LOVEJOY, C. OWEN, RICHARD S. MEINDL, T. R. PRYZBECK, AND ROBERT MENSFORTH
1985   Chronological Metamorphosis of the Auricular Surface of the Ilium: A New Method for the Determination of Adult Skeletal Age at Death. *American Journal of Physical Anthropology*, 68:15–28.

LYMAN, R. LEE
1994   *Vertebrate Taphonomy*. Cambridge University Press, New York, NY.

LYMAN, R. LEE, AND GREGORY L. FOX
1997   A Critical Evaluation of Bone Weathering as an Indication of Bone Assemblage Formation. In *Forensic Taphonomy: The Postmortem Fate of Human Remains*, William D. Haglund and Marcella H. Sorg, editors, pp. 223–247. CRC Press, Boca Raton, FL.

MANN, ROBERT W., STEVEN A. SYMES, AND WILLIAM M. BASS
1987   Maxillary Suture Obliteration: Aging the Human Skeleton Based on Intact or Fragmentary Maxilla. *Journal of Forensic Sciences*, 32:148–157.

MAPLES, WILLIAM R.
1986   Trauma Analysis by the Forensic Anthropologist. In *Forensic Osteology: Advances in the Identification of Human Remains*, Kathleen J. Reichs, editor, pp. 218–228. Alan R. Liss, New York, NY.

McKERN THOMAS W., AND T. DALE STEWART
1957   Skeletal Age Changes in Young American Males. Technical Report EP-45. Headquarters, Quartermaster Research and Development Command. Natick, MA.

MEINDL, RICHARD S., AND C. OWEN LOVEJOY
1985   Ectocranial Suture Closure: A Revised Method for the Determination of Skeletal Age at Death Based on the Lateral-Anterior Sutures. *American Journal of Physical Anthropology*, 68:57–66.

MERBS, CHARLES F.
1989   Trauma. In *Reconstruction of Life from the Skeleton*, M. Yasar Iscan and Kenneth A. R. Kennedy, editors, pp. 161–189. Alan R. Liss, New York, NY.

MERCHANT, VIRGINIA L., AND DOUGLAS H. UBELAKER
1977   Skeletal Growth of the Protohistoric Arikara. *American Journal of Physical Anthropology*, 46:61–72.

MOORREES, COENRAAD F. A., ELIZABETH A. FANNING, AND EDWARD E. HUNT, JR.
1963a   Formation and Resorption of Three Deciduous Teeth in Children. *American Journal of Physical Anthropology*, 21:205–213.
1963b   Age Variation of Formation Stages for Ten Permanent Teeth. *Journal of Dental Research*, 42:1490–1502.

MORITZ, ALAN RICHARDS
1954   *The Pathology of Trauma*, 2nd edition. Lea and Febiger, Philadelphia, PA.

NOVAK, SHANNON A.
2000   Case Studies. In *Blood Red Roses: The Archaeology of a Mass Grave from the Battle of Towton AD 1461*, Veronica Fiorato, Anthea Boylston, and Christopher Knüsel, editors, pp. 240–268. Oxbow Books, Oxford, England.

NOVAK, SHANNON A., EVERETT BASSETT, AND DERINNA KOPP
2002   Osteological Analysis of Human Remains from the Historic Tooele Cemetery, Tooele, Utah. Report to the Utah Division of Transportation, Salt Lake City, from URS, Salt Lake City.

NOVAK, SHANNON A., AND DANA D. KOLLMANN
2000   Perimortem Processing of Human Remains among the Great Basin Fremont. *International Journal of Osteoarchaeology*, 10:65–75.

NOVAK, SHANNON A., AND DERINNA KOPP
2002   Osteological Analysis of Human Remains from the Mountain Meadows Massacre, 42WS2504. Report to the Division of State History, Salt Lake City, UT, from Laboratory of Biological Anthropology, University of Utah, Salt Lake City.

NOVAK, SHANNON A., AND LARS RODSETH
2001   Politics of the Dead: The History and Histrionics of the Mountain Meadows Massacre. Paper presented at the 100th Annual Meeting of the American Anthropological Association, Washington, DC.

OWSLEY, DOUGLAS W.
1994   Warfare in Coalescent Tradition Populations of the Northern Plains. In *Skeletal Biology in the Great Plains: Migration, Warfare, Health, and Subsistence*, Douglas W. and Richard L. Jantz, editors, pp. 333–343. Smithsonian Institution Press, Washington, DC.

Owsley, Douglas W., Douglas H. Ubelaker, M. M. Houck, Kari L. Sandness, W. E. Grant, E. A. Craig, T. J. Woltanski, and M. Peerwani
  1995 The Role of Forensic Anthropology in the Recovery and Analysis of Branch Davidian Compound Victims: Techniques of Analysis. *Journal of Forensic Sciences*, 40(3):341–348.

Phenice, T. W.
  1969 A Newly Developed Visual Method of Sexing the Os Pubis. *American Journal of Physical Anthropology*, 30:297–30.

Prince, Major Henry
  1859 Ground of the Mountain Meadow Massacre, Mountain Meadows, 17th May 1859. National Archives, Washington, DC.

Quinn, Michael D.
  1997 *The Mormon Hierarchy: Extensions of Power*. Signature Books, Salt Lake City, UT.

Reichs, Kathleen J. (editor)
  1998 *Forensic Osteology: Advances in the Identification of Human Remains*, 2nd edition. Charles C. Thomas, Springfield, IL.

Richards, Franklin D.
  1857 Military Records of the Second Brigade, First Division, Nauvoo Legion. Brigham Young University. Provo, UT.

Rogers, William H.
  1860 Statement of Mr. Wm. H. Rogers. *The Valley Tan*, 29 February, 2(16). Salt Lake City, UT.

Ruff, Christopher
  1992 Biomechanical Analyses of Archaeological Human Skeletal Samples. In *Skeletal Biology of Past Peoples: Research Methods*, S. R. Saunders and M. A. Katzenberg, editors, pp. 37–58. Wiley-Liss, Inc, New York, NY.

Sauer, Norm J.
  1998 The Timing of Injuries and Manner of Death: Distinguishing among Antemortem, Perimortem, and Postmortem Trauma. In *Forensic Osteology: Advances in the Identification of Human Remains*, 2nd edition, Kathleen J. Reichs, editor, pp. 333–352. Charles C. Thomas, Springfield, IL.

Shackel, Paul A.
  2001 Public Memory and the Search for Power in American Historical Archaeology. *American Anthropologist*, 103(3):655–670.

Smith, Christopher
  2000a State Wants Mountain Meadows Artifacts Returned to the Grave. *Salt Lake Tribune*, 31 August:A1. Salt Lake City, UT.
  2000b The Dilemma of Blame. *Salt Lake Tribune*, 14 March: A1. Salt Lake City, UT.

Smith, George A., and James McKnight
  1858 Account written at Cedar City, Aug 6, 1858. Journal History of the Church, 1830–1900. Archives of the LDS church historian. Salt Lake City, UT.

Smith, Joseph Fielding
  1928 *Essentials in Church History*. Reprinted in 1945 by Deseret News Press, Salt Lake City, UT.

Spitz, Werner U.
  1992 *Spitz and Fisher's Medicolegal Investigation of Death: Guidelines for the Application of Pathology to Crime Investigation*. Charles C. Thomas, Springfield, IL.

Stewart, T. Dale
  1979 *Essentials of Forensic Anthropology: Especially As Developed in the United States*. Charles C. Thomas, Springfield, IL.

Suchey, Judy Myers, and Daryl Katz
  1998 Applications of Pubic Age Determination in a Forensic Setting. In *Forensic Osteology: Advances in the Identification of Human Remains*, 2nd edition, Kathleen J. Reichs, editor, pp. 204–236. Charles C. Thomas, Springfield, IL.

Symes, Steven A., Hugh E. Berryman, and O. C. Smith
  1998 Saw Marks in Bone: Introduction and Examination of Residual Kerf Contour. In *Forensic Osteology: Advances in the Identification of Human Remains*, 2nd edition, Kathleen J. Reichs, editor, pp. 389–409. Charles C. Thomas, Springfield, IL.

Tom, Gary, and Ronald Holt
  2000 The Paiute Tribe of Utah. In *A History of Utah's American Indians*, Forrest S. Cuch, editor, pp. 123–165. Utah State Division of Indian Affairs/Utah State Division of History, Salt Lake City, UT.

Ubelaker, Douglas H.
  1989 *Human Skeletal Remains: Excavation, Analysis, Interpretation*, 2nd edition. Taraxacum, Washington, DC.

Verdery, Katherine
  1999 *The Political Lives of Dead Bodies: Reburial and Postsocialist Change*. Columbia University Press, New York, NY.

Wadley, Carma
  1999 Monument Instills Healing. *Deseret News*, 12 September:1. Salt Lake City, UT.

Walker, Phillip L., and Patricia M. Lambert
  1991 Human Skeletal Remains from the Historic Cemetery at Seccombe Lake Park, San Bernardino, California. Report to City of San Bernardino Parks, Recreation, and Community Services Department. San Bernardino, CA.

Walker, Robert A., and C. Owen Lovejoy
  1985 Radiographic Changes in the Clavicle and Proximal Femur and Their Use in the Determination of Skeletal Age at Death. *American Journal of Physical Anthropology*, 68:67–78.

Wise, William
1976 *Massacre at Mountain Meadows: An American Legend and a Monumental Crime*, 2nd edition. Thomas Y. Crowell, New York, NY.

Shannon A. Novak
Bone and Joint Research Laboratory (151F)
VA Salt Lake City Health Care System
500 Foothill Drive
Salt Lake City, UT 84148-9998

Derinna Kopp
Department of Anthropology
University of Utah
Salt Lake City, UT

ROSS W. JAMIESON

Material Culture and Social Death: African-American Burial Practices

ABSTRACT

Orlando Patterson has proposed that the institution of slavery caused the "social death" of slaves, in that the inherited meanings of their ancestors were denied to them through control of their cultural practices by slave owners and overseers. A survey of archaeological evidence for mortuary practices in African-American society, however, shows that this was not the case, as such inherited meanings were present throughout the early historical period, and in some communities are still present. The careful identification of such occurrences can only be made through comparison to African archaeological and ethnographic evidence. Such occurrences do not negate the horrors of the dominance of slaveholders over slaves in the New World, but do give an opportunity to celebrate the unique nature of African-Atlantic culture.

Introduction

In a recent review, Parker Potter (1991:95) has warned plantation archaeologists about the "inseparability of knowledge and human interests." For Potter, and I am in basic agreement with him, plantation archaeologists must struggle to celebrate the unique African-American heritage forged while under the dominance of Euroamerican society (Potter 1991:99). Archaeologists of the African-American past have a social responsibility constantly to remind themselves of "*who controlled* the quality of life," and also a responsibility to ask African Americans what interests they have in their cultural heritage, and how these can be related to archaeological research (Potter 1991:98–100).

The recent excavation of a portion of the colonial African Burial Ground in New York City (Harrington 1993) has brought the study of African-American mortuary remains into the public and archaeological spotlight. The wholesale excavation

of cemeteries merely to answer the research questions of archaeologists can validly be classified as desecration, and thus a certain reticence on the part of archaeologists to include discussion of African-American burials when outlining archaeological research potential (cf. Singleton 1990) is understandable. The developments in New York City (Harrington 1993), however, have demonstrated that contract archaeologists are required to deal with such remains, and that a solid understanding of the historical and anthropological aspects of African-American mortuary practices is necessary before interpreting them.

Funerals in plantation slavery contexts in particular appear to have afforded African Americans an opportunity to develop African-American cultural practices in the New World based at least partially on African practices (Genovese 1972:194–202; Thornton 1992:228). Several archaeological excavations of African-American burials have now been carried out (Thomas et al. 1977; Parrington and Wideman 1986; Owsley et al. 1987), although large New World cemeteries from before emancipation are restricted to Handler and Lange's (1978) Barbados sample and the recent New York City excavations (Harrington 1993).

In order to understand fully the cultural implications of such burials, there is a need for historical archaeologists to consider the work of historians of slavery, art historians, Africanist ethnographers, and Africanist archaeologists. Only with such a wide-ranging, "ethnohistorical" approach can historical archaeologists begin fully to put the burial practices of African Americans in context. The interpretation of mortuary rituals and material culture is contingent on the wide-ranging chronological, geographical, and social contexts which characterize the long history of African descendants in the New World.

Burials, Social Death, and Africanisms in the New World

The excavation of burials has always been central to archaeology, and up until the mid-20th century, the emphasis was usually on the "flow of traits" visible in mortuary remains that defined culture areas and cultural diffusion (Chapman and Randsborg 1981:2–3). Since the 1960s archaeological interest in mortuary patterns has grown to include individual status, modes of death, rites of passage, group affiliations, and many other types of specific cultural information. By the early 1970s it became clear that the relationship of mortuary practices to status, group membership, and other societal factors was not a simple one. A debate began as to whether mortuary variability could really prove much about societal structures (Chapman and Randsborg 1981: 4–8). Mortuary data have now been used extensively by archaeologists, ethnographers, and ethnohistorians to study many anthropological and historical issues (Ucko 1969; Brown 1971; Tainter 1978; Chapman et al. 1981; Humphreys and King 1981; Parker Pearson 1982; Johnson et al. 1994).

The study of African-American heritage has broadly paralleled that of the discipline of anthropological archaeology. An emphasis on the "flow of traits" is clear in the anthropological work of Melville Herskovits, whose 1920s scholarship concentrated on African "culture areas." Herskovits (1958[1941]) created the first full formulation of the concept of "African retentions" in the New World with his 1941 book *The Myth of the Negro Past*. Herskovits' affirmation of the existence of an African heritage in the New World was the basis for much of the "black studies" scholarship in the United States, Cuba, Haiti, and other countries from the 1960s onward (Cole 1985:120–124).

During the 1970s anthropologists and historians studying African-American culture began to shift their emphasis from Herskovitsian "survivals," and instead began to concentrate on certain "basic values" and "phenomenology" as defining African-American relationships to Africa (Cole 1985: 120–124). Sidney Mintz and Richard Price in 1976 called for the definition of a "generalized West African heritage" for African Americans, defined by emphasizing cognitive orientations rather than the more formal elements concentrated on by Herskovits. Mechal Sobel (1979:xvii) proposed that in the New World "African worldviews coalesced over time into one neo-African consciousness." For Sobel, West African peoples did not have one Sacred Cosmos, but they did share enough of a world-view to create one worldview in America (Sobel 1979:21).

It is clear that the institution of slavery severely restricted the ability of African Americans to maintain cohesive cultural identities from Africa. Orlando Patterson has attempted to show that the cultural practices of slaves were greatly influenced by the definition of slavery "as a substitute for death, usually violent death":

> Slaves differed from other human beings in that they were not allowed freely to integrate the experience of their ancestors into their lives, to inform their understanding of social reality with the inherited meanings of their natural forebears, or to anchor the living present in any conscious community of memory. That they reached back for the past, as they reached out for the related living, there can be no doubt. Unlike other persons, doing so meant struggling with and penetrating the iron curtain of the master, his community, his laws, his policemen, or patrollers, and his heritage (Patterson 1982:5).

Slaves had to resist this desocialization in countless ways (Patterson 1982:337). The lack of ability to import material culture from their homeland, and prohibitions on many cultural practices, created great difficulties in undertaking such resistance (Genovese 1972). Despite these difficulties, historians of the African-American diaspora have now clearly shown that African culture, and particularly religion, have made important contributions to the African-American experience (Raboteau 1978; Sobel 1987; Creel 1988).

Neither a search for "survivals," nor an anthropological emphasis on "phenomenology" seems suited to the study of African-American mortuary practices. Jean Howson (1990:79–80) has pointed out that the search for formal elements, or "survivals," of African practices in the Americas was and is naive. Attention to specific material traits and their disappearance over time as a way to construct a universal sequence of acculturation is a dangerous oversimplification. James Garman (1994:90) calls for a holistic picture "that does not reduce African Americans to a collection of material traits with links to Africa."

The key that is missing from sterile studies of "Africanisms" and "survivals" is cultural context. The historian John Thornton (1992:211) emphasizes that the dynamics of cultural change in African-American society worked very differently on different elements of culture, such as political systems, language, aesthetics, and religion. Howson (1990:84) advocates the careful interpretation of material culture in all its contexts, a position that is important for research on African-American burials.

The mortuary context was a place within slave culture where in some cases some "freedoms" were allowed by the slave owners. For Parker Potter, the ability of slaves to hunt game or to purchase their own ceramics—or, to bury their own dead—were not really "freedoms"; they were traded off against "the more powerful unfreedoms" of the institution of slavery (Potter 1991:98). Potter goes so far as to suggest that "placing too much emphasis on . . . the ability of slaves to create certain aspects of their own world could do a disservice to contemporary African Americans in the attempt to identify and challenge the racial discrimination that still exists in contemporary American society" (Potter 1991:101). His point is valid; the existence of a burial that shows African religious practices in the New World should not and cannot be used to argue that slavery was a benign institution—and yet African influences cannot be ignored, and should be celebrated. As the art historian Robert Farris Thompson (in Cosentino 1992:59) put it, "Yes, I *am* political if it is a political statement to say that African-Atlantic culture is fully self-possessed, an alternative classical tradition; that one studies Mbanza Kongo, Ile-Ife, and Kángaba as one might study Carthage, Jerusalem, Rome, and Athens."

Historic Burial Studies in Africa
and the Americas

The lack of a well-researched ethnohistorical approach has been a serious limitation of many studies of African-American material culture. Douglas Armstrong (1990:7) has rightly pointed out the seriousness of the "problem encountered in the study of cultural transformations among Africans in the New World . . . the tendency to over generalize West African cultures." In his studies of 18th-century slave houses he felt "forced to rely on vague comparisons and incidental observation to establish elements of African continuity" (Armstrong 1990:8), a problem which seriously compromises the validity of the undertaking. He points out the need for more interaction between historians and archaeologists of West Africa and the Americas, and also the paucity of archaeological work on West African sites contemporary with the period of slaving for the Americas (Armstrong 1990:8).

This is in part due to the lack of focus on the colonial period by governments of independent African countries and Africanist archaeologists. Most Africanist archaeologists are concerned with concentrating on the prehistoric cultural heritage of Africa. The archaeology of the colonial period in Africa is a very new, and still very limited, field of study (DeCorse 1987, 1991, 1993). A major new contribution to the study of African historical mortuary archaeology is the work of Christopher DeCorse at ElMina, Ghana (Figure 1c). His excavations of urban domestic contexts adjacent to the Dutch fort at ElMina, dating to the 17th through late 19th centuries, has recently revealed 200 burials in sub-floor domestic contexts (DeCorse 1992:184). Analysis of this material was still in progress in 1992, but when published it will be an important comparative sample for New World archaeologists. This is just one excavation location, however, and if African-American practices are to be traced to Africa, the historical period must be fully studied on both sides of the Atlantic.

Archaeological excavation of African-American mortuary remains has been undertaken in North America and the Caribbean since the early 1970s, but the pressures of salvage situations have meant that in many cases little attention has been paid to the historical context of burials. Salvage excavation of a slave cemetery by a prehistorian on Montserrat, West Indies, and the discovery of two slave burials on St. Catherine's Island, Georgia, were not accompanied by any historical research other than to find that early maps showed the cemeteries to have been part of a plantation (Thomas et al. 1977:401; Watters 1987:312, 1994:56). David Watters (1994:56) validly points out that, in the case of the Eastern Caribbean, severe funding problems, the lack of

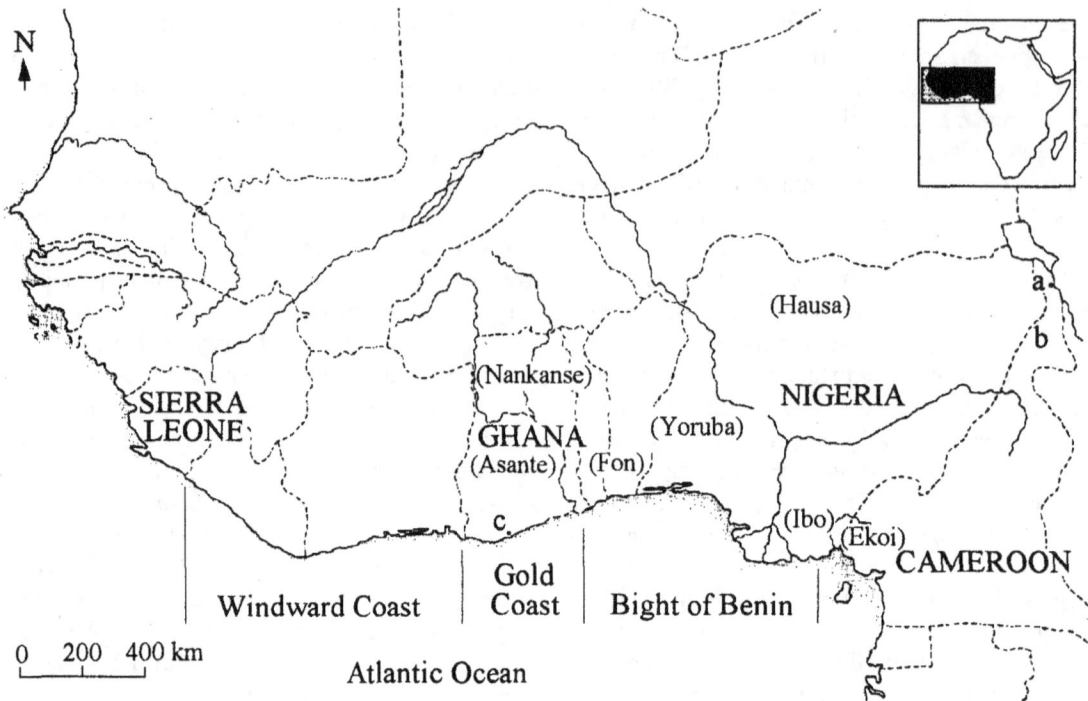

FIGURE 1. Map of West Africa: a, Holouf Cemetery site, Cameroon; b, Mandara Highlands of Cameroon; c, ElMina site, Ghana.

professional archaeologists, and the rapid development of tourist sites have made short salvage projects by avocational archaeologists an unfortunate reality.

Handler and Lange's (1978) work on Barbados is the only major published archaeological case explicitly using an ethnohistorical approach to the study of New World slave mortuary practices. Their research, based on excavation and historical documents, is by far the best archaeological study of mortuary practices of Africans and their descendants in the Americas. They found the excavation of a slave cemetery on Barbados to be of limited use in reconstructing mortuary ideology, with documents as a more useful source. The documents had their own limitations, however, in being very anecdotal and heavily affected by a European bias. The time span and extent of particular mortuary practices were often difficult to define, but the doc-

uments were in the end an extremely useful addition to the archaeological data (Handler and Lange 1978:171). Handler's later attempt deliberately to locate other slave cemeteries in Barbados was unsuccessful; the invisibility of many slave cemeteries may thus be a factor in their preservation, or a factor in their untimely destruction at the hands of developers who are not even aware of their existence (Handler 1989).

The excavation of African-American burials has so far been limited, which has created great limitations on interpretation. Up until the excavation of the African Burial Ground in New York City (Harrington 1993), Handler and Lange's (1978:21, 171) Barbados excavation was the largest group of slave burials (N = 104) excavated in the New World, and also—dating between 1660–1820—the earliest group. Handler and Lange (1978:28) state that with such a small database generalization is premature,

Perspectives from *Historical Archaeology*

but the ongoing research on the African Burial Ground in New York City (Harrington 1993) will soon give archaeologists a large 18th-century sample for comparison to Handler and Lange's excavation. Other published excavation reports (Combes 1972; Thomas et al. 1977; Parrington and Wideman 1986; Bell 1990; Cheek and Friedlander 1990) have been rescue excavations of 19th-century burials, and thus largely post-emancipation, although one salvage exavation of a pre-1800 cemetery on Montserrat has been carried out (Watters 1987, 1994). This gives a good chronological range of data, but more data for the period of slavery in the United States would be desirable.

The limited use of comparative data from Africa on burial practices is perhaps the most serious shortcoming of New World studies to date. Inadequate ethnographic research is notorious for resulting in underestimation of variability in mortuary practices (Chapman and Randsborg 1981:14). Handler and Lange (1978:317) saw great difficulty in using African ethnographic sources because they are often "directly contradictory of each other," but this may be due more to Handler and Lange's attempt to simplify the huge range of African cultural practices than to any real contradictions. Slaves came from wide geographical regions of Africa which changed over time. Thus the wide variation in ethnographic practices, rather than being contradictory, are, in fact, of great relevance to the study of American practices.

Handler and Lange (1978:210) validly point out that the comparison of modern African ethnographic studies to New World burials from the 18th century is in itself not ideal and, in addition, points to a great need for data on West African burial practices from the European colonial period. An even greater problem is outlined by Merrick Posnansky (1989:4), in that in West Africa "it was not major states like Benin, Asante, or the Hausa city-states which contributed the major numbers of slaves but rather the weaker societies, societies which lost out in the process of state formation." This creates a problem in comparative archaeological data, as such societies are very rarely studied by Africanist archaeologists, and by the time ethnographers began to record details about such societies

in the early 20th century they had been displaced, marginalized, and ravaged by the slave trade (Posnansky 1989:4).

For the Kongo region, where huge numbers of slaves originated, the problem is even worse, as the pre- and protohistory of the modern nations of Zaire and Angola remains largely unexplored (Posnansky 1989:6). The first scientific archaeology in the entire Lualaba River basin, for example, began only in 1957 (Hiernaux et al. 1972:148).

The lack of such data has created many false generalizations. David Roediger (1982:170) has claimed that the common burial practice on both continents of orienting the body in an east–west direction is a West African practice "against burying a corpse crossways to the world," something which may well be true but which ignores both the great variation in West African burial orientations and the Christian tradition of east–west body orientation. Handler and Lange (1978:214) concur with this attempt to define broad West African and even Sub-Saharan African beliefs which would override specific differences in mortuary patterns in African-American practices, a type of syncretism built from the varying backgrounds of slaves. Merrick Posnansky (1989:1), however, calls it a naive assumption "that there is a commonality of African traditional culture spread over a wide geographical area and over a long time period."

It is clear that ethnoarchaeological, ethnographic, and historical literature on African burial practices must be used to create valid comparisons. It is also evident that research must focus on the range of areas that slaves came from, and not just be limited to the Yoruba, a single West African culture, and the Kongo, a huge geographic region made up of many groups, two areas which are usually emphasized in the comparative American literature. Nicholas David's (1992:181) caution that ethnoarchaeologists in West Africa have given little attention to mortuary practices is well taken, and brings forward once again the problem of adequate African published data. The influences of Muslim, and perhaps even Christian, religion on African mortuary practices further complicate the African templates from which American practices were drawn.

Cultures of Origin

The mixing of ethnic groups brought about by the slave trade must have caused great changes in African-American burial practices in the New World. The African origin of first-generation slaves in a particular location is a very important factor to consider in research.

The origins of slaves in the British colonies changed over the period of the slave trade, and are of central concern in any future use of African burial data to compare to American practice. Philip Curtin's (1969) data on the ports from which slaves were taken on the African coast (Figure 1) shows that for the 1680s approximately 27 percent of slaves came from the "Windward Coast," or modern Liberia and the Ivory Coast, with another 21 percent from the Gold Coast, modern Ghana, and 15 percent from the Bight of Benin region, Togo, Dahomey, and Nigeria. By the 1750s this had shifted to only 32 percent of slaves coming from Sierra Leone, the Windward and Gold Coasts, combined, and a full 40 percent from the "Bight of Biafra," Cameroon and Nigeria. In 1800 the trade had shifted southward (Figure 2), with 45 percent of slaves coming from the Bight of Biafra, and 34 percent from the Central Africa/Angola region (Curtin 1969:129). A point of origin on the coast does not reveal the ethnicity of the slaves, however, and this "mystery of the ultimate origin of slaves in the African interior" (Handler and Lange 1978: 28) is a very complex topic (cf. Lovejoy 1983; Thornton 1992).

Curtin's (1969) publication of an 1850 census of Freetown, Sierra Leone, taken by ethnic group, is a good indication of the diversity of peoples enslaved at that time. The sample was 54 percent Yoruba, 9 percent Ibo, 8 percent Fon, and apart from that was made up of 160 additional, different ethnic groups—defined by their languages—from mainly West and Central Africa, but also from East Africa and other regions. What ethnic groups are we to use for comparison of burial traits? In the end this question seems to address a moot point. Kongo and Yoruba groups, with high populations enslaved in the American trade, have commonly been compared to African-American examples (Vlach 1978;

Thompson and Cornet 1981; Thompson 1983), but vast numbers of other peoples from many parts of Africa were enslaved as well (Curtin 1969; Lovejoy 1983).

Thornton (1992:192–195) emphasizes that in most cases a single slave ship would pick up its entire cargo from one port, thus increasing the chances of cultural homogeneity. In the common case that slaves were war captives they all could have been from one cultural group. It is in the New World that the separation of African slaves from others of their own ethnic group would more commonly have occurred. The purchasing policies of plantation owners varied greatly. Some felt that deliberate mixing of Africans of different ethnicities prevented rebellions, whereas others preferred having slaves from a particular ethnic group in order to form a stable plantation community (Thornton 1992:195–196). More focused research at the local or plantation level, emphasizing the trade and purchase records for a particular place and time, is one of the few ways to get closer to the ethnic origins in Africa of particular first-generation slave populations.

The Bioarchaeology of African Ancestry

Before African-American burials can be studied, they must be identified as African-American. This identification can be done using cultural material associated with the deceased, using historical evidence for an African-American cemetery in the location, or, finally, by identifying the physical remains themselves as of African descent, using osteological techniques.

Physical identification would seem to be the most objective initial step, and yet it is problematic in itself. The identification of "race" in physical anthropology has a long and infamous history in America, exemplified by the racist work of Samuel George Morton in the 1820s to 1850s (Gould 1981: 51–62), and the 18th- and 19th-century practice of using African-American dead as scientific specimens (Humphrey 1973). In 1962 Frank Livingstone published his now classic 1-page argument in *Current Anthropology*. It urged anthropologists to re-

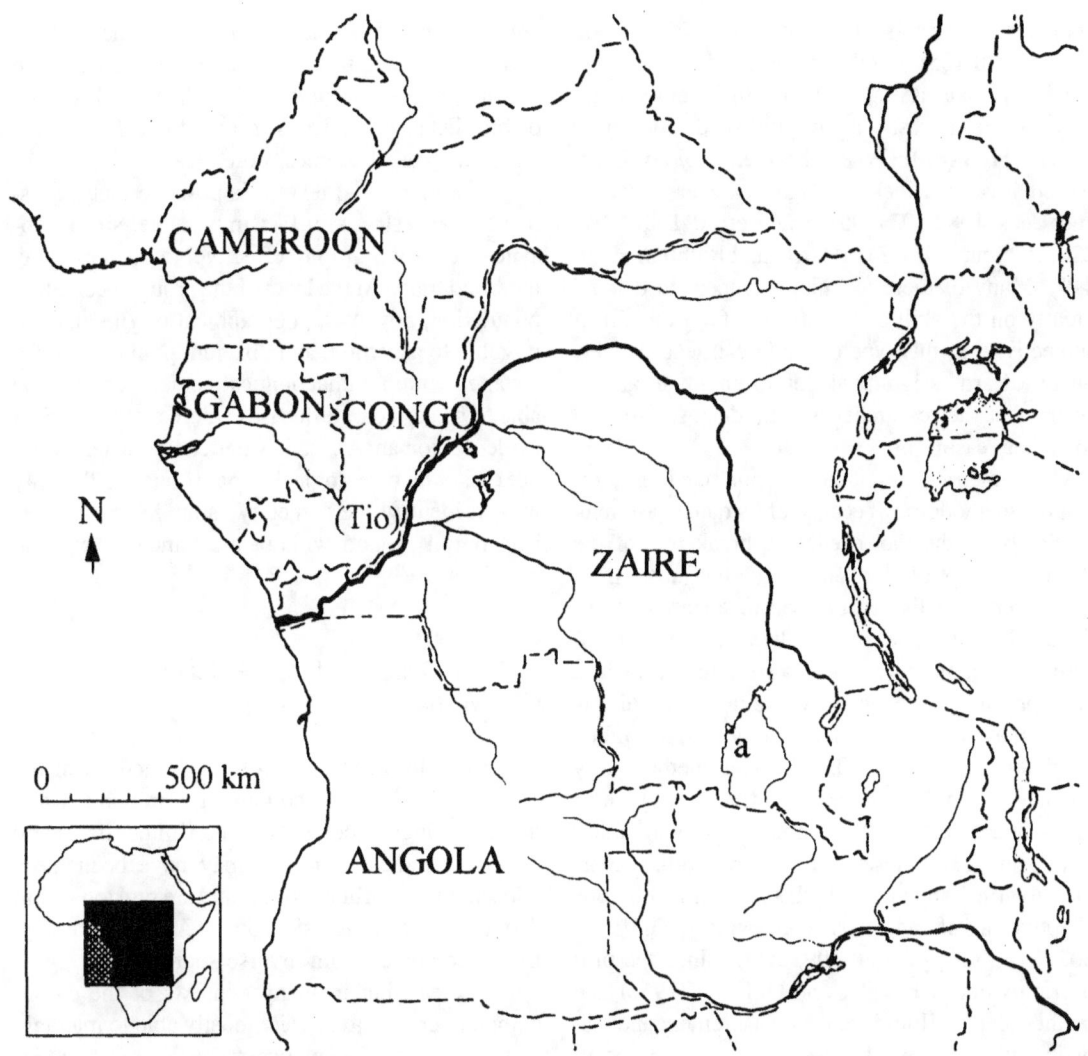

FIGURE 2. Map of Central Africa: *a*, Katoto Cemetery site, Zaire.

ject the concept of ''race,'' because within *Homo sapiens* ''variability does not conform to the discrete packages labelled races'' (Livingstone 1962: 279).

Within modern forensic anthropology, however, the race concept is still in use (Krogman and Işcan 1986:270; Işcan 1988:209), in order to ''categorize the skeletal remains of unknowns in terms that reflect racial reality as locally understood'' (Stewart 1979:227). The tacit acceptance of such fuzzy categorizations has led to a schizophrenic response by physical anthropologists, denying the validity of racial categorization while simultaneously trying to describe its morphology.

Some researchers working with African-American burials have made no attempt to identify the ancestry of their sample through the physical remains, since the historical documentation of the cemetery is taken as sufficient proof (Handler and Lange 1978:105). In other research the ancestry of the individuals is reported, but the methodology used to infer ancestry is not published (Owsley et al. 1987:188–190). When the methodology is reported, it varies widely among researchers (Blakely and Beck 1982:193–195; Angel et al. 1987:216–226; Rathbun 1987:241; Harris and Rathbun 1989:411). Many of these techniques appear to depend greatly on the skill of the analyst; the problem of subjectivity in this type of study can lead dangerously toward assigning skeletal remains to an ancestry that the researcher was predisposed toward for other reasons.

Craniometrics, despite a common reaction to reject the methodology because of its racist past, may ironically be the tool needed to break free of the flawed concept of race, and create the most effective criteria for the assignation of ancestry. T. L. Woo in the 1930s began to realize that cranial measurements commonly in use were often an invalid attempt "to give quantitative value to the differences that were obvious to them at first sight" (Hershkovitz et al. 1990:307). This methodology emphasized measures heavily influenced by environmental selection. The emphasis should rather have been put on those regions of the skull, such as the calvarium and base, which show "little obvious adaptive significance" (Hershkovitz et al. 1990:307, 318; Yongyi et al. 1991:274). Since the pioneering work of E. Giles and O. Elliot (1962), the methodology of bio-distance measurement and statistics on cranial remains has been steadily improving (Gill 1984; Krogman and Işcan 1986:275–280; Brace and Hunt 1990; Hershkovitz et al. 1990; Pietrusewsky 1990). Such modern bio-distance studies look at the polygenic traits of bone or tooth shape, data which include both a genetic and environmental component, and attempt to define patterns in the data thought to reflect degrees of genetic relatedness (Buikstra et al. 1990:1–6).

The almost complete lack of data on the range of variation within most skeletal populations is the first major stumbling block to such cranial studies (St. Hoyme and Işcan 1989:54). This limitation has begun to be remedied in recent research, although a need still exists for data from Africa before a true

comparison can be made to African-American remains. A need also exists for further research on worldwide craniometrics before the complex issue of bio-distance measures in the ethnically diverse American case becomes more clear.

At the individual level it is possible that assessment of ancestry is in fact impossible, since idiosyncratic variation may effectively counteract any inherited traits. At the level of the group or cemetery population, however, geographical origins may be possible to ascertain, and different populations, for instance within archaeological cemeteries, may be able to be sorted out. In cases where clear historical evidence for an African-American cemetery does not exist, the osteological remains may be the only way to identify the cemetery as an African-American burial ground without a reliance on cultural practices.

Material Culture: African Practices in the New World

African influence on mortuary practices in the Americas is evident in both living communities and in archaeological contexts in the United States and the West Indies. Practices may have been more widespread in earlier periods, and are rare today, but they were not extinguished by the Atlantic crossing. Evidence comes from diverse sources.

It is clear that in many contexts of the earlier colonial period slaves were mostly able to maintain control over burial practices. Thornton (1992:206) specifically rejects Mintz and Price's (1976) idea that barriers to cultural transmission from Africa were overwhelming. This cultural transmission appears to have been strongest in the practice of funerary rituals. In Barbados from the 1600s up until the 1780s slaves were usually responsible for burying their own dead, in their own cemetery. Slaves were often not baptized Christians, and whites considered slaves "idolatrous"; thus, slave control over funeral rites seems to have been fairly complete (Handler and Lange 1978:173, 209). In Jamaica in 1688 Hans Sloane noted that slaves from the same ethnic group in Africa would gather at a plantation for the funeral of one of their members

(Sloane 1707:xlviii; cf. Thornton 1992:200). In 1712 in New York the Reverend John Sharpe (in Raboteau 1978:66) complained that slaves "are buried in the common by those of their country and complexion without the office; on the contrary the Heathenish rites are performed at the grave by their countrymen."

Sharpe may have been referring specifically to the African Burial Ground now being investigated (cf. Harrington 1993). This cemetery was founded around 1712 just outside the New York city limits, as church burial had been denied slaves in New York since 1697. Church authorities did not dedicate the burial ground, and control of the funerals, mortuary, and burial practices at the cemetery seems to have rested mostly within the African-American community (Harrington 1993:30). Funerals were in fact the only time slaves in 18th-century New York were permitted to gather in groups larger than three people (Harrington 1993: 30), and thus little doubt remains that such events were of key importance in maintaining many cultural ties.

Up until the late 18th century in English-speaking North America and the Caribbean a general feeling prevailed among slave owners that teaching Christian doctrine to slaves would undermine the authority of the masters (Patterson 1982:73); thus, Christian practice was not at first forced upon slaves in the Protestant New World. In North America from the 16th to the 19th centuries slaveholders were always concerned about the "conspiratorial" or "heathenish" aspects of slaves holding funerals for fellow slaves, but did not forbid the practice. In some cases they felt it callous to do so; in other cases they felt that such a prohibition could cause embitterment leading to slave rebellions (Genovese 1972:194–195).

On some plantations, special groups of slaves appear to have prepared the corpse, with taboos against others touching it, a practice similar to many African cases (Roediger 1981:169). This practice is reflected in David's (1992:187) Mandara Highlands data from Cameroon (Figure 1b), which show that in some societies male "transformers" are responsible for carrying out the funeral, but in others the funeral is carried out by the family of the deceased.

Among the Yoruba the blacksmiths are called upon to put the body in the coffin and seal it (Ojo 1976: 105). A cemetery dating to A.D. 1500–1600 excavated by Augustin Holl at Houlouf in Cameroon (Figure 1a) was within a separate area of the walled house compound of a blacksmith, which Holl (1994:164–165) relates to the modern "recurrent feature in the ethnography of Chadic-speakers of the Mandara Mountains" of having blacksmiths as undertakers and gravediggers.

The age and gender of slaves brought from Africa thus may have been of critical importance in the transmission of burial practices between the cultures of the two continents. As an example, the 18th-century British trade into Jamaica was predominantly in adult males "in the prime of life," with around 58 percent males, 35 percent females, and 7 percent children as fairly standard (Klein 1986:254). The age and gender of the slaves would have influenced their cultural knowledge. Age-grade systems and secret societies in some African groups may have limited the knowledge of burial practices to within certain groups of older, often male, individuals. Thus, transmission of cultural practices to the Americas would have been highly dependent on whether such specialists were present. It can be fairly safely assumed, however, that in most situations at least some of the males would have been old enough to have been versed in the burial practices of their culture.

The physical location of the burials may be another clue to African practices. Separate burial practices for different social groups is a common occurrence in many African societies, with the location of burials often tied to the symbolism of a group's cosmology (Chapman and Randsborg 1981:15, 17). In DeCorse's (1992:183) excavations at ElMina in Ghana, 200 burials were found under the house floors, at least one in each house excavated.

In some African societies those who died a "natural death" were distinguished from those who died in childbirth, from infectious disease, from being struck by lightning, from committing suicide, and as victims of murder or drowning. Among the Yoruba, burial of the dead generally occurred within the town boundary, under a room in their house, whereas those who died "unnaturally" were relegated to outside the town for burial (Ojo 1976:99). Drowning victims specifically were interred at the riverbank where they had died (Ojo 1976:100).

"Natural deaths" in the Mandara Mountains of Cameroon are buried in the clan cemetery, whereas a list of "others" similar to the Yoruba case are often buried at the cemetery margins. Infants are generally interred behind the mother's hut, and clan chiefs may be buried within their house or compound. An emphasis on "belonging" is clear in some groups in the Mandara Highlands, where chiefly and other land-holding clans have separate cemeteries, and "strangers" are buried on the side of the road leading back to their village, explicitly denying their descendants land rights (David 1992: 188). In the Houlouf cemetery in Cameroon the 25 burials were all interred in an upright or seated position, and from ethnographic analogy Holl (1994:139, 168) proposes that these were members of the elite, while other members of the society were buried in other locations. Four empty marked graves may be symbolic burials of those who died away from the town and could not be brought back for burial (Holl 1994:136). Among several Ghanaian tribes burial of children occurred separately, at a crossroads. Among the Asante, children under eight days old were buried in pots in the town (Ucko 1969:271).

Placing multiple individuals in one grave is also an important trait. A cemetery consisting of 47 tombs and dated to ca. A.D. 1100 was excavated at Katoto in Zaire in the 1960s (Figure 2a; Hiernaux et al. 1972). The cemetery contained 32 single burials, and also 14 multiple burials, usually with a woman and infant, or a man, woman, and children together (Hiernaux et al. 1972:148). Two burials in the Barbados cemetery appear to have been of two individuals each, although the reason for this may have been expediency in time of disease rather than any cultural preference (Handler and Lange 1978: 193).

Subfloor burials within the house, as in the El-Mina sample from Ghana, was clearly carried to the Caribbean by slaves. Slaves in Jamaica in the late 18th century were said "sometimes" to bury family members under the bed in their house (Moreton 1790:162; cf. McDonald 1993:110). Handler and Lange have historical evidence of subfloor graves in Barbados slave houses, although the burial plot was a more common place. In the Newton Plantation cemetery child/infant burials are underrepresented. This may mean that they were buried elsewhere, or may simply be a reflection of differential bone preservation (Handler and Lange 1978:124, 174). One male adult at the Drummond Plantation near Jamestown, Virginia, dated to the 1680–1720 period, was buried away from the others and "very near a servants' quarter." This occurrence is interesting, although the ancestry of the individual is not clearly stated as African (Aufderheide et al. 1985: 357–358). In South Carolina in the 1970s the most important aspect of burial for African Americans was to be buried with other family members. Late 19th- and early 20th-century burials were not in church cemeteries in coastal South Carolina, and when church burial became commonplace the power of the clergy in being able to refuse burial in the family plot was much resented (Combes 1972: 56).

Burial in mounds seems to have been desired by many African-American groups. The slave cemetery at Newton Plantation has three mounds, each ½–1 m high, and 4½–7½ m wide, presumably built by the slaves, with burials in and around the mounds (Handler and Lange 1978:107). David Hurst Thomas and other excavators were surprised to come upon two 19th-century plantation slave burials in a native mound group on Saint Catherine's Island, Georgia. Only one mound was partially excavated, but an 1890 map had a cemetery marked in the vicinity, so presumably the mound group was used extensively by the slaves as a burial ground. Slave burials were also found in the Mississippian period temple mounds in Moundville, Alabama, but apparently have not been published (Thomas et al. 1977:412, 417). The reuse of prehistoric mounds was not an exclusively African-American practice, however, as evidenced by the Euroamerican family cemetery located in the Irene Mound near Savannah, Georgia (Aufderheide et al. 1985:358).

Grave goods placed with the body afford the most obvious evidence in an archaeological context of African influences on the burial. The type and placement of grave goods with the corpse varies widely in African practice. In the Mandara Highlands grave goods placed with the body are limited in nature: "The overall concern . . . is to provide the departed with items either of sentimental value to them or that will serve them in good stead in the land of the dead, where they will live a life that is, it would seem, perceived as being on the whole pretty similar to the one they are leaving" (David 1992: 197). At the Houlouf cemetery Holl (1994:140) reports the inclusion of a smoking pipe, lots of stone tools, copper artifacts, and a large number of imported carnelian beads, with a maximum of 174 beads in one tomb. At ElMina the grave goods included ceramic vessels, beads, and tobacco pipes. A 1602 document from ElMina claimed that the Africans would bury all of the deceased's belongings in the grave (DeCorse 1992:183).

High-status chiefs among the Tio were reported in the late 19th century as being buried with plates, guns, and lots of other European items, but low-status burials did not emphasize grave goods (Vansina 1973:211–212). The 13th-century Katoto cemetery in Zaire had multiple ceramic vessels, iron tools, and iron jewelry in the graves (Hiernaux et al. 1972:150–153).

Peter Ucko (1969:265) provides the cautionary note that among the Nankanse of Ghana the grave goods are actually objects owned by a living person which are placed with the dead to get their soul out if it is trapped by the grave, and thus have little to do with the role of the deceased in life. Yoruba grave goods may include items of personal equipment, but do not include valuables, as these are displayed at the funeral but not placed in the grave (Ucko 1969:267). It should also be noted that funerary items, and in particular ceramics associated with the deceased in African practice, may be permanently positioned in an area of spiritual significance other than the burial site, such as the sites for clan spirit pots in Akan funerary customs (Vivian 1992). No reports have been made of such separate areas for "spirit pots" in African-American practice, but perhaps that is because they have gone unrecognized by researchers.

Documentary evidence from the New World gives an interesting example of the belief that death would mean a return to Africa, and of the need for grave goods for the journey. A slave in the southern United States in the 1830s reported on a funeral of the son of African-born slaves, into the grave of whom they placed

> a small bow and arrows; a little bag of parched meal; a miniature canoe and a little paddle (with which he said it would cross the ocean to his own country) . . . and a piece of white muslin with several curious figures painted on it . . . , by which . . . his countrymen would know the infant to be his son (Charles Ball, quoted in Roediger 1981:178).

The clearest New World archaeological example of African influence on grave goods is the "old" adult male from the Newton Plantation buried wearing three copper bracelets; one copper and two white metal finger rings, with a metal knife in the left hand; and a necklace of cowrie shells, dog canines, glass beads, fish vertebrae, and an agate bead; plus an earthenware pipe at the pelvis that was identified as a 17th-century pipe from Ghana (Handler and Lange 1978:129–131; Handler 1981).

The cowries are Indo-Pacific in origin, and served as a West African form of currency (Hogendorn and Johnson 1986). They are also present as grave goods at the Katoto cemetery in Zaire (Hiernaux et al. 1972:154).

The burial thus seems to be an example of slave access to goods from Africa, perhaps brought over by the deceased. The social role of the deceased is unknown, but some sort of special position in the slave community is certainly implied (Handler and Lange 1978:129–131). The other burials at Newton Plantation showed European clay pipes as the most common grave item, in 17 of the 92 burials (Handler and Lange 1978:123). One burial had a large fragment of a shallow red earthenware bowl located under the pelvis (Handler and Lange 1978:136). European-made glass beads, dating mostly to the first half of the 18th century, were found in eight of the burials, with two particular burials containing over 200 beads each (Handler and Lange 1978: 145). Placing a relatively large number of grave goods with the deceased was thus a practice which was present in the New World, but one which is so far only recorded for pre-1820 contexts.

The earth put into the grave, and human relationships to it, may also have had significance to

African Americans. A presumably 19th-century practice of each funeral attendant tossing a handful of earth into the grave is purported to be "in conformity with [unspecified] West African traditions" (Roediger 1981:173), although this also conforms to European Christian traditions. In courts of law in Barbados the practice of drinking grave dirt mixed with water was a form of oath taken by slave witnesses. This practice is not known from Africa, but was certainly not European in origin (Handler and Lange 1978:207). The sacredness of earth from a grave is also evident in Kongo practice, in which it is a part of "nkisi" medicine bags, and is said to embody the spirit of the deceased which can come back to serve the owner of the charm (Thompson 1983:117).

The surface material placed above the grave appears to be the most enduring material marker of African influences in the New World. In the Mandara Highlands pots are usually placed on the graves of adults, with a "variety of pots that are used by different groups to signal a limited range of statuses." The most common and obvious distinction is by gender, as certain pots are only associated with males or females (David 1992:197).

In North America the surface decoration of graves with ceramics and other objects is the most commonly recognized African-American material culture indicator of cemetery sites. William Faulkner, in *Go Down, Moses,* described a black cemetery with "shards of pottery and broken bottles and old brick and other objects insignificant to sight but actually of a profound meaning and fatal to touch, which no white man could have read" (Faulkner 1942:135; cf. Vlach 1978:139).

The 20th-century manifestations of this practice have appeared to some researchers to be miscellaneous piles of "junk" (Combes 1972:54), and include arrangements of a vast array of articles including ceramics, glassware, clocks, lamps, seashells, spoons, doll heads, lightbulbs, flashlights, false teeth, eyeglasses, cigar boxes, piggy banks, gun locks, razors, knives, tin cans, marbles, pebbles, and at least one example of a ceramic toilet tank (Vlach 1978:139). The material is still not always clearly reported and published, as with the Charleston County, South Carolina, cemetery, 38

CH 778, which had unspecified "surface materials" present (Rathbun 1987:240–241).

The earliest published example of material evidence of the practice in the New World appears to be a blue shell-edged plate, dated 1800–1818, found in the surface humus directly above the head of an excavated burial in South Carolina (Thomas et al. 1977:406). This of course does not preclude the use of artifacts as grave markers from the first arrival of Africans in the New World, as such surface remains would be particularly susceptible to disturbance by many processes including reuse of the land for purposes other than as a cemetery. Handler and Lange (1978:205–206) report documentary evidence that post-interment ceremonies in which food and drink were placed on the grave for the dead were common among Barbadian plantation slaves until the 1820s, when a major Christianization period ended them. The practice of placing the last article used by the deceased on the grave was recorded in Georgia in 1850 (Thompson 1983:134).

Early recognition of the relationship of this practice to African customs is related in correspondence in the *Journal of American Folklore* of 1891 and 1892, in which South Carolina graves with oyster shells, white pebbles, ceramics, glass bottles, and other "nondescript bric-a-brac" were described, all "broken and useless," and were compared to such items illustrated in *Century Magazine* from the Congo (Bolton 1891; Ingersoll 1892; Vlach 1978: 142). It is interesting that in this African instance locally made grave goods had by this time been replaced by European trade items, perhaps reflecting high-status associations with such goods in Africa.

What materials were placed on graves, and ethnographic testimony on the meaning of such materials, varies widely. Vansina (1973:217) describes Tio late 19th-century practice, in which a little house was often built over the grave to protect the crockery or jugs left on the mound. John Vlach records several African and American instances of surface grave decoration. A variation on the practice was noted among the Ekoi of Nigeria in 1912, with a low mud mound built over the grave and plates pressed into it all along the edges. Testimony from Alabama in the 1920s and Georgia in the

1930s stated the surface grave goods were what the person owned or used, and were to satisfy the spirit and keep it from wandering. Other 1930s Georgia testimony stated that it was important ritually to break the containers, in order to break the chain of death in the community. Graves in Gabon in the 1970s were noted to be similarly covered with diverse objects. In the United States such surface grave markers are much more common in the South, but Vlach (1978:140–147) points out that they have been recorded as far north as Staten Island, New York.

Particular categories of material have been favored in surface assemblages. The color white, evident in ceramics, shells, and pebbles, is of importance. Association with water is also evident, which took the form of water jugs, marine shells, or mirrors which served as a metaphor for water. Clocks are a 20th-century addition, and may be set either at 12 o'clock to wake the dead on Judgment Day, or at the time of the deceased's death (Vlach 1978: 140–147). White marine shells are reported on graves as wide-ranging as the Kongo, the southern United States, Haiti, and Guadeloupe. A 1912 burial in South Carolina had a large number of pressed glass hens arranged on the surface, a South Carolina grave of a child from 1967 includes a single white rooster statue, and white chicken images are known to have been placed on tombs in the Kongo. These images are perhaps related to the sacrifice of a live white chicken over the grave, a practice reported in the Caribbean in 1816 on each Christmas morning, in the Kongo in the 1880s, and at a wake in Georgia in 1939 where it was claimed to "keep the spirits away" (Thompson 1983:134–135).

Pots that had been deliberately pierced and turned upside down to symbolize the realm of the ancestors or death were reported in the Kongo in the 1970s. The practice was explained by an informant as the last strength of the dead person contained in the last objects that they used. It was repeated that the items kept the spirit in the grave, and kept it from harming the living. When the informant touched the items on his mother's tomb he later dreamed the things she wanted to tell him (Thompson 1983:134, 142).

An informant in Mississippi in the 1920s stated that the last cup and saucer used by the deceased should be put on the grave, as well as the last medicine bottles used. If medicine is still in the bottles they should be turned upside down so that the medicine goes into the grave. Cups, cut glass, bottles, and lamps were common, and it was explained that something that was "the best in the house" was more important than something used by the deceased. Cut flowers and conch shells were said to be just for "dressing up" the grave. A particularly vivid account from South Carolina in the early 1970s stated that a woman whose daughter had died had had repeated dreams of the daughter asking for her hand lotion, dreams which only stopped bothering her when she took the lotion and placed it on the grave (Combes 1972:56, 58).

If there is a general pattern to such practices, it can perhaps be related to the "liminal state" of the deceased in the belief systems of many African groups, formulated in anthropology by Robert Hertz, a student of Émile Durkheim, and further elaborated by Arnold Van Gennep. In Hertz's model the deceased is removed from the social realm through a primary funeral, but then enters a rite of passage in which the living mourn, and the deceased lingers in an ambiguous state and may intervene in human affairs, particularly if the funeral preparations are not correctly carried out (McCaskie 1989:426). Yoruba informants state that for three years after the funeral the deceased is "on his knees," i.e., only after the three years does the spirit go to heaven (Ojo 1976:108). A belief that the spirit component of the individual had to be "managed back" into the spirit world through burial ritual is stated in Asante mortuary customs as well (McCaskie 1989:428). The Tio in the late 19th century also clearly stated that the dead would often come in dreams to tell their needs or to accuse those who had bewitched them (Vansina 1973:218). African beliefs are thus clearly continued in many aspects of American mortuary practices throughout the historical period. Such practices are, however, very rare today.

The End of African Mortuary Practices

No single period exists in the history of African-American burial practices that marks the end of

African influence in the New World. Differences in community cohesion and/or isolation, the change from plantation to urban life, the influence of Christianity, and attempts to gain power in mainstream economic and political structures in the Americas all no doubt contributed to a growing marginalization and syncretization of African burial practices in the Americas. Only in rural African-American communities have practices related to an African past continued into the modern era.

The case of New Orleans provides an interesting early example of a forced end to African-American practices. As early as 1724 Catholic law required Christian slaves to have Christian burial and all New Orleans slaves to be baptized. Parish priests demanded disinterment and reburial in church cemeteries when non-Christian burials were discovered to have occurred. Thirteen African-American skeletons were excavated from a New Orleans cemetery, dating 1720–1810, with no evidence of any African practices in these church-controlled burials (Owsley et al. 1987:185–188).

The orientation of the burial appears to have been one of the first practices to become standardized. African burial orientation varied widely within and between groups. For instance, in the Mandara Highlands burial orientation ranges through seated corpses in boot-shaped tombs, "sleeping position" flexed burials in bell-shaped tombs, urn burials for some potters, and supine burials in sub-rectangular graves. The most common Mandara burial orientation was the flexed burial with the body on its side. Which side the body is laid on is often dependent on gender, and orientation of the body is related to a general concern with the east–west axis. David (1992:195) concludes that with such a variety of burial styles in the Mandara Mountains, inference of the symbolism of the body orientations solely from archaeological remains would probably be impossible. The A.D. 1500–1600 cemetery at Houlouf consisted entirely of individuals in an upright or seated position, facing to the southwest. This orientation is taken from ethnographic analogy to be a sign of high status (Holl 1994:138). For the Asante of Ghana the orientation is usually lying on the side, with the key being that the deceased must face away from the village (Ucko 1969:273).

Among the Tio of the Kongo the corpse was tied into an "N-shaped," flexed position before burial on its side in a round shaft, with a small mound on top (Vansina 1973:209). The cemetery at Katoto had both supine burials and flexed burials on their sides. Orientation was widely varying, with no single direction prevalent (Hiernaux et al. 1972: 148).

In the Americas the variation in burial orientation seems to be minimal. Fifty-five of the 58 burials at Newton Plantation for which orientation was clear were supine and on an east–west axis, 38 with the head to the west and 17 with the head to the east (Handler and Lange 1978:185). This pattern shows only minor variation from the almost universal Christian orientation of supine burial with the head to the west. In the African Burial Ground in New York City all burials seem to have been supine, with Michael Blakey stating that the majority were head to the west, and some with the head to the east. He suggests the head to the east burials may indicate Muslim practice (Harrington 1993:36). John Vlach (1978:147) sees orientation with head to the west as an African practice, "a shared African concept of the cosmos, that the world is oriented following the sun," but Handler and Lange (1978:317) correctly contradict this interpretation in pointing out the great variety of burial orientations in West Africa, some with orientation to the sea, others differentiated on the basis of gender, et cetera.

A brief description of burials at the Drummond Plantation, near Jamestown, Virginia, dating to the 1650–1720 period, suggests that "servants" of both African and European origin may have been buried together. Three adults buried in the same vicinity all had their heads to the north (Aufderheide et al. 1985:357). All burials in the Montserrat mid-18th-century cemetery that were identifiable were supine, head to the west burials (Watters 1987:301, 1994:60), and the supine, head to the west orientation of burials is universal in excavated African-American burials from the beginning of the 19th century onward in both the United States and the Caribbean (Combes 1972:54; Thomas et al. 1977: 410; Blakely and Beck 1982; Parrington 1986). In general it would seem that supine, head to the west burial was common as slaves became Christianized, but may have been more easily accepted than other Christian concepts as it is syncretic with common African associations of life and death with the path of the sun.

The position of one Newton Plantation cemetery burial is of interest, a solitary interment of a woman in a separate mound, in a prone position, face down. Handler and Lange (1978:198–199) point out that burial face down is a practice used for "Nyongo" witchcraft practitioners in coastal Cameroon, in an effort to confuse the spirit so that if it attempted to leave the grave it would go the wrong way. Ethnographic testimony from African Americans in Georgia in the 1940s stated that if repeated deaths of children in a family occurred, burial face down of the last child to die would ensure that the next child would live to adulthood (Combes 1972:58). It is important to note, however, that prone burial was also practiced historically in Europe, particularly in the burial of suspected witches.

Grave goods in 19th-century African-American burials appear to be, in almost all cases, in line with European and Christian practice. Of 140 burials in the First African Baptist Church cemetery in Philadelphia, all dating between 1824 and 1842, eight had a single coin near the head, six had a single shoe placed on the coffin lid, and in two cases a ceramic plate had been placed on the stomach. The plate, although interestingly similar to the surface material common to many African-American burials, is taken as possibly related to the European practice of placing a plate of salt on the corpse to prevent it from bloating and to keep the devil away (Parrington and Wideman 1986:60–61).

The validity of these interpretations is unfortunately not substantiated with any historical documentation of such practices by local Philadelphians. A burial from South Carolina had a penny placed over each eye, conveniently dating the burial as after the 1882—latest—date on the pennies. Placing pennies over the eyes was a common 19th-century practice in many Christian burials to keep the eyes closed (Combes 1972:54). All 17 late 19th-century burials in Atlanta, Georgia, had no grave goods apart from clothing and some jewelry (Blakely and Beck 1982).

James Garman has recently completed an inter-esting study of the Newport, Rhode Island, "Common Burying Ground," focusing on the headstones in the spatially segregated African-American section of the cemetery that date from the 1720–1830 period. These head and footstones were purchased by Euroamerican masters in the pre-emancipation period, up until the year 1800, and Garman (1994: 80–82) concludes that the headstones are more a representation of the desired virtue of the master to the community than they are a representation of the lives or culture of the slaves. After emancipation there are a series of stones commissioned by African Americans themselves. These are mostly identical to Euroamerican headstones of the same period. This may be either a representation of the desire of African Americans to be admitted into the culture of the new republic or due to fear of calling attention to any cultural differences within an overwhelmingly white society (Garman 1994:87–88).

The use of coffins also became increasingly common, and eventually universal, over time, and apparently was not common practice in African traditions. Until the 17th century in Europe, coffins were considered a high-status item, and the poor were not buried in them (Parker Pearson 1982:110). At ElMina, burial was in a specially prepared shroud up until the introduction of coffins in the late 19th century (DeCorse 1992:183). Historical evidence from Barbados shows that, in the 17th through early 19th centuries, coffins were supplied by plantation owners as a final reward for devoted slaves, and were thus an incentive toward acceptance of the dominant European ideology. They were certainly not always used (Handler and Lange 1978:191–192).

A cemetery identified as mid-18th century from a Montserrat plantation had probable coffin nails in five of nine burials, and copper stains from the pins of burial shrouds in the others (Watters 1987:303, 1994:62–63). Two early 19th-century people from a plantation in Georgia were both buried in coffins, without coffin hardware. Coffin hardware was, however, rare for any ethnic group before 1830 in North America (Thomas et al. 1977:410, 412).

By the late 19th century, African-American burials in the United States included coffins with the elaborate mass-produced hardware common to all ethnic groups. These were essentially "high-status" coffins, but the skeletal remains of these free blacks show high trauma rates and low nutritional status. This may demonstrate an attempt by free blacks to negate the socioeconomic differences between them and other ethnic and higher-status groups. Mortuary ritual thus continued to be an opportunity in the late 19th century for expressing the symbolic ideals of African Americans. The ideals, however, had shifted from more directly African-based ones, to an attempt at the time of death to mask the socioeconomic differences between African Americans and other parts of American society (Combes 1972:54; Genovese 1972:201–202; Blakely and Beck 1982; Bell 1990:67–70).

The rise of "fundamentalist Protestantism" in the 1790–1830 period in the English-speaking Americas created an emphasis on Christian piety and obedience. This change resulted in a desire, or pressure, on slave masters to have all slaves made Christian (Patterson 1982:73). Handler and Lange (1978:213) conclude that by the late 18th century, African influences in Barbados mortuary practices were "fading out." Another important influence began in the 1820s, as both European and North American society began moving toward an emphasis on "sanitation," with new municipal cemeteries set up to replace church burial by the 1850s in most urban areas (Parker Pearson 1982:106; Blakely and Beck 1982:178). This, too, may have resulted in less control over their own burial rites by African Americans. Thus, in many cases African-American burials by the mid-19th century, and in some cases well before that date, had become indistinguishable from the burials of any other ethnic group in America.

The Future

There is a clear need in formulations of African burial practices in the New World to have a much larger database of published excavated material. Handler and Lange's Barbados excavation is the only thoroughly researched and published pre-1800 cemetery of African Americans, and in itself has shown the great difference between such early practices and the 19th-century practices which have

been shown by other excavations. The recent New York City finds (Harrington 1993) have demonstrated the importance of descendant community—in this case African-American—involvement in the excavation and research of African-American burials. Despite any controversy involved, or perhaps in this case because of it, an opportunity is provided for greater community involvement in their own heritage. Both the descendant group itself, and all members of society, are shown the key contributions and role that that group has played in American history.

Most, if not all, future African-American burial excavations will probably be undertaken through salvage archaeology efforts. The negative consequences of this are clear, in the minimization of time and investment involved in properly researching and excavating burials which are threatened by development. It is essential that a coordinated historical, biological, and archaeological research effort be made to recognize African-American burials, to protect them from destruction, to maximize the information gained from them when excavation is inevitable, and to publish the results in an accessible format. It is difficult to place such a heavy burden on contract archaeologists alone, and thus the solution for the future may be a coordinated effort between contract archaeologists and university- or museum-based archaeologists when important finds such as the recent New York City burials are initially discovered.

Conclusions

Mortuary remains are a form of ritual communication in which fundamental social values are expressed (Parker Pearson 1982:100). The control of symbolic instruments such as mortuary practices by slave owners and overseers was an attempt to alienate the slaves from claims of belonging to a legitimate social order, and instead to make the master–slave relationship the dominant cultural force (Patterson 1982:5). Yet, did African Americans really cease to have any control over such symbolism and practice?

A 19th-century master in Georgia objected to, but

did not end, the use of African drums to announce slave funerals (Roediger 1981:168). Handler and Lange have shown significant African-American practices in excavated burials. If any conclusions are valid for the limited data available, they would seem to indicate that African Americans before 1800 had control over their own burial practices in many cases, and with that control they chose to practice much of what their ancestors had emphasized for proper burial. The burial practices of the late 19th-century urban, predominantly Christian, African-American communities in centers such as Philadelphia and Atlanta had very different concerns. These focused more on Christian piety and on the denial of the economic hardships that their communities faced in life, through use of dominant-culture symbols such as elaborate industrially produced coffins.

Funerals may have been one of the few times that antebellum slave communities could assume control of the symbolism around them, and thus create the dignity at death that negated the "social death" of their slave status. In the burial practices of many cultures we see an area in which social groups are afforded the possibility of reviewing the past, and thus both reaffirming cultural consent for particular relationships, and also disputing other traditional power relationships. The end of the liminal state for the deceased can also be seen as the reconciliation of cultural ideals with the new power structure (McCaskie 1989:430). For antebellum African Americans the power structure was, however, further complicated by the slave relationship. We see rapid shifts toward more European practices in various African-American communities at widely varying periods in their history. In other communities, however, African Americans continue practices which are not of Euroamerican origin, despite the immense difficulties of adapting to Euroamerican cultural, religious, and economic domination.

ACKNOWLEDGMENTS

My thanks to Laurie Beckwith, Nicholas David, Brenda Kennedy, Scott MacEachern, and anonymous *Historical Archaeology* reviewers, all of whom read and commented on earlier versions of this paper.

REFERENCES

ANGEL, J. LAWRENCE, JENNIFER O. KELLEY,
MICHAEL PARRINGTON, AND STEPHANIE PINTER
1987   Life Stresses of the Free Black Community as Represented by the First African Baptist Church, Philadelphia, 1823–1841. *American Journal of Physical Anthropology* 74:213–229.

ARMSTRONG, DOUGLAS V.
1990   *The Old Village and the Great House: An Archaeological and Historical Examination of Drax Hall Plantation, St. Ann's Bay, Jamaica*. University of Illinois Press, Urbana.

AUFDERHEIDE, A. C., J. LAWRENCE ANGEL,
JENNIFER O. KELLEY, A. C. OUTLAW,
M. A. OUTLAW, G. RAPP, AND L. E. WITTMERS
1985   Lead in Bone III: Prediction of Social Correlates from Skeletal Lead Content in Four Colonial American Populations (Catoctin Furnace, College Landing, Governor's Land, and Irene Mound). *American Journal of Physical Anthropology* 66:353–361.

BELL, EDWARD L.
1990   The Historical Archaeology of Mortuary Behavior: Coffin Hardware from Uxbridge, Massachusetts. *Historical Archaeology* 24(3):54–78.

BLAKELY, ROBERT L., AND LANE A. BECK
1982   Bioarchaeology in the Urban Context. In *The Archaeology of Urban America: The Search for Pattern and Process*, edited by Roy S. Dickens, Jr., pp. 175–207. Academic Press, Toronto.

BOLTON, H. CARRINGTON
1891   Decoration of Graves of Negroes in South Carolina. *Journal of American Folklore* 4:214.

BRACE, C. LORING, AND KEVIN D. HUNT
1990   A Nonracial Craniofacial Perspective on Human Variation: A(ustralia) to Z(uni). *American Journal of Physical Anthropology* 82:341–360.

BROWN, JAMES A.
1971   Approaches to the Social Dimensions of Mortuary Practices. *Memoir of the Society for American Archaeology* 25. Published as *American Antiquity* 36(3), pt. 2.

BUIKSTRA, JANE E., SUSAN R. FRANKENBERG, AND
LYLE W. KONIGSBERG
1990   Skeletal Biological Distance Studies in American Physical Anthropology: Recent Trends. *American Journal of Physical Anthropology* 82:1–7.

CHAPMAN, ROBERT, I. KINNES, AND KLAUS RANDSBORG (EDITORS)
1981   *The Archaeology of Death.* Cambridge University Press, Cambridge, U.K.

CHAPMAN, ROBERT, AND KLAUS RANDSBORG
1981   Approaches to the Archaeology of Death. In *The Archaeology of Death,* edited by Robert Chapman, I. Kinnes, and Klaus Randsborg, pp. 1–24. Cambridge University Press, Cambridge, U.K.

CHEEK, CHARLES D., AND AMY FRIEDLANDER
1990   Pottery and Pigs' Feet: Space, Ethnicity and Neighborhood in Washington, D.C., 1880–1940. *Historical Archaeology* 24(1):34–60.

COLE, JOHNNETTA B.
1985   Africanisms in the Americas: A Brief History of the Concept. *Anthropology and Humanism Quarterly* 10: 120–126.

COMBES, JOHN D.
1972   Ethnography, Archaeology, and Burial Practices among Coastal South Carolina Blacks. *Conference on Historic Sites Archaeology Papers* 7:52–61.

COSENTINO, DONALD J.
1992   Interview with Robert Farris Thompson. *African Arts* 25(4):53–63.

CREEL, MARGARET WASHINGTON
1988   *"A Peculiar People": Community Life and Religion among the Gullah.* New York University Press, New York.

CURTIN, PHILIP D.
1969   *The Atlantic Slave Trade: A Census.* University of Wisconsin Press, Madison.

DAVID, NICHOLAS
1992   The Archaeology of Ideology: Mortuary Practices in the Central Mandara Highlands, Northern Cameroon. In *An African Commitment: Papers in Honour of Peter Lewis Shinnie,* edited by Judy Sterner and Nicholas David, pp. 181–210. University of Calgary Press, Calgary, Alberta.

DeCORSE, CHRISTOPHER
1987   Historical Archaeological Research in Ghana, 1986–1987. *Nyame Akuma* 29:27–31.
1991   West African Archaeology and the Atlantic Slave Trade. *Slavery and Abolition* 12:92–96.
1992   Culture Contact, Continuity and Change on the Gold Coast, A.D. 1400–1900. *African Archaeological Review* 10:163–196.
1993   The Danes on the Gold Coast: Culture Change and the European Presence. *African Archaeological Review* 11:149–173.

FAULKNER, WILLIAM
1942   *Go Down, Moses.* Random House, New York.

GARMAN, JAMES C.
1994   Viewing the Color Line Through the Material Culture of Death. *Historical Archaeology* 28(3):74–93.

GENOVESE, EUGENE D.
1972   *Roll, Jordan, Roll: The World the Slaves Made.* Vintage Books, New York.

GILES, E., AND O. ELLIOT
1962   Race Identification from Cranial Measurements. *Journal of Forensic Sciences* 7:147–157.

GILL, G. W.
1984   A Forensic Test Case for a New Method of Geographical Race Determination. In *Human Identification: Case Studies in Forensic Anthropology,* edited by Ted E. Rathbun and Jane E. Buikstra, pp. 329–339. C. C. Thomas, Springfield, Illinois.

GOULD, STEPHEN JAY
1981   *The Mismeasure of Man.* W. W. Norton, New York.

HANDLER, JEROME S.
1981   A Ghanaian Pipe from a Slave Cemetery in Barbados, West Indies. *West African Journal of Archaeology* 11:93–99.
1989   *Searching for a Slave Cemetery in Barbados, West Indies: A Bioarchaeological and Ethnohistorical Investigation.* Center for Archaeological Investigations, Southern Illinois University, Carbondale.

HANDLER, JEROME S., AND FREDERICK W. LANGE
1978   *Plantation Slavery in Barbados: An Archaeological and Historical Investigation.* Harvard University Press, Cambridge, Massachusetts.

HARRINGTON, SPENCER P. M.
1993   Bones and Bureaucrats: New York's Great Cemetery Imbroglio. *Archaeology* 46(2):28–38.

HARRIS, EDWARD F., AND TED A. RATHBUN
1989   Small Tooth Sizes in a Nineteenth-Century South Carolina Plantation Slave Series. *American Journal of Physical Anthropology* 78:411–420.

HERSHKOVITZ, I., B. RING, AND E. KOBYLIANSKY
1990   Efficiency of Cranial Measurements in Separating Human Populations. *American Journal of Physical Anthropology* 83:307–319.

HERSKOVITZ, MELVILLE J.
1958   *The Myth of the Negro Past.* Reprint of 1941 edition. Beacon Press, Boston, Massachusetts.

HIERNAUX, J., E. MAQUET, AND J. DE BUYST
1972   Le Cimetière Protohistorique de Katoto (Vallée du Lualaba, Congo-Kinshasa). In *Sixième Congrès Panafricain de Préhistoire, Dakar 1967,* edited by Henri J. Hugot, pp. 148–158. Les Imprimeries Réunies de Chambéry, Chambéry, France.

HOGENDORN, JAN S., AND MARION JOHNSON
1986   *The Shell Money of the Slave Trade.* Cambridge University Press, Cambridge, U.K.

HOLL, AUGUSTIN
1994   The Cemetery of Holouf in Northern Cameroon (A.D. 1500–1600): Fragments of a Past Social System. *African Archaeological Review* 12:133–170.

HOWSON, JEAN E.
1990   Social Relations and Material Culture: A Critique of the Archaeology of Plantation Slavery. *Historical Archaeology* 24(4):78–91.

HUMPHREY, DAVID C.
1973   Dissection and Discrimination: The Social Origins of Cadavers in America, 1760–1915. *Bulletin of the New York Academy of Medicine* 49:819–827.

HUMPHREYS, S. C., AND H. KING (EDITORS)
1981   *Mortality and Immortality: The Anthropology and Archaeology of Death.* Academic Press, New York.

INGERSOLL, ERNEST
1892   Decoration of Negro Graves. *Journal of American Folklore* 5 (Jan.–Mar.):68–69.

IŞCAN, MEHMET Y.
1988   Rise of Forensic Anthropology. *Yearbook of Physical Anthropology* 31:203–230.

JOHNSON, JAY K., JENNY D. YEAROUS, AND NANCY ROSS-STALLINGS
1994   Ethnohistory, Archaeology and Chickasaw Burial Mode during the Eighteenth Century. *Ethnohistory* 41:431–446.

KLEIN, HERBERT S.
1986   *African Slavery in Latin America and the Caribbean.* Oxford University Press, Oxford, U.K.

KROGMAN, WILTON M., AND MEHMET Y, IŞCAN
1986   *The Human Skeleton in Forensic Medicine.* Charles C. Thomas, Springfield, Illinois.

LIVINGSTONE, FRANK B.
1962   On the Non-existence of Human Races. *Current Anthropology* 3(3):279–281.

LOVEJOY, PAUL E.
1983   *Transformations in Slavery: A History of Slavery in Africa.* Cambridge University Press, Cambridge, U.K.

McCASKIE, THOMAS C.
1989   Death and the Asantehene: A Historical Meditation. *Journal of African History* 30:417–444.

McDONALD, RODERICK A.
1993   *The Economy and Material Culture of Slaves: Goods and Chattels on the Sugar Plantations of Jamaica and Louisiana.* Louisiana State University Press, Baton Rouge.

MINTZ, SIDNEY W., AND RICHARD PRICE
1976   *An Anthropological Approach to the Afro-American Past: A Caribbean Perspective.* Institute for the Study of Human Issues, Philadelphia, Pennsylvania.

MORETON, J. B.
1790   *Manners and Customs in the West India Islands.* N.p., London.

OJO, JEROME O.
1976   Yoruba Customs from Ondo. *Acta Ethnologica et Linguistica* 37. Elisabeth Stiglmayr, Wien.

OWSLEY, DOUGLAS W., CHARLES E. ORSER, ROBERT W. MANN, PEER H. MOORE-JANSEN, AND ROBERT L. MONTGOMERY
1987   Demography and Pathology of an Urban Slave Population from New Orleans. *American Journal of Physical Anthropology* 74:185–197.

PARKER PEARSON, MICHAEL
1982   Mortuary Practices, Society and Ideology: An Ethnoarchaeological Study. In *Symbolic and Structural Archaeology,* edited by Ian Hodder, pp. 99–113. Cambridge University Press, Cambridge, U.K.

PARRINGTON, MICHAEL, AND JANET WIDEMAN
1986   Acculturation in an Urban Setting: The Archaeology of a Black Philadelphia Cemetery. *Expedition* 28:55–62. Philadelphia, Pennsylvania.

PATTERSON, ORLANDO
1982   *Slavery and Social Death: A Comparative Study.* Harvard University Press, Cambridge, Massachusetts.

PIETRUSEWSKY, MICHAEL
1990   Craniofacial Variation in Australian and Pacific Populations. *American Journal of Physical Anthropology* 82:319–340.

POSNANSKY, MERRICK
1989   West African Reflections on African-American Archaeology. Paper presented at the Conference "Digging the Afro-American Past: Archaeology and the Black Experience," University of Mississippi, University.

POTTER, PARKER B., JR.
1991   What Is the Use of Plantation Archaeology? *Historical Archaeology* 25(3):94–107.

RABOTEAU, ALBERT J.
1978   *Slave Religion: The Invisible Institution in the American South.* Oxford University Press, Oxford, U.K.

RATHBUN, TED A.
1987   Health and Disease at a South Carolina Plantation: 1840–1870. *American Journal of Physical Anthropology* 74:239–253.

ROEDIGER, DAVID R.
1981   And Die in Dixie: Funerals, Death, and Heaven in the Slave Community, 1700–1865. *Massachusetts Review* 22(1):163–183.

ST. HOYME, LUCILE E., AND MEHMET Y. IŞCAN
1989   Determination of Sex and Race: Accuracy and Assumptions. In *Reconstruction of Life from the Skeleton*, edited by Mehmet Y. Işcan and Kenneth A. R. Kennedy, pp. 53–93. Alan R. Liss, New York.

SINGLETON, THERESA A.
1990   The Archaeology of the Plantation South: A Review of Approaches and Goals. *Historical Archaeology* 24(4):70–77.

SLOANE, HANS
1707   *A Voyage to the Islands of Madeira, Barbados, Neives, S. Christopher and Jamaica*, Vol. 1. N.p., London.

SOBEL, MECHAL
1979   *Trabelin' On: The Slave Journey to an Afro-Baptist Faith.* Greenwood Press, Westport, Connecticut.
1987   *The World They Made Together: Black and White Values in Eighteenth-Century Virginia.* Princeton, New Jersey.

STEWART, T. D.
1979   *Essentials of Forensic Anthropology: Especially as Developed in the United States.* Charles C. Thomas, Springfield, Illinois.

TAINTER, J. A.
1978   Mortuary Practices and the Study of Prehistoric Social Systems. *Advances in Archaeological Method and Theory* 1:104–141. Michael B. Schiffer, editor. Serial Publication Series. Academic Press, New York.

THOMAS, DAVID HURST, STANLEY SOUTH, AND CLARK SPENCER LARSEN
1977   Rich Man, Poor Men: Observations on Three Antebellum Burials from the Georgia Coast. *Anthropological Papers of the American Museum of Natural History* 54(3):393–420.

THOMPSON, ROBERT FARRIS
1983   *Flash of the Spirit: African and Afro-American Art and Philosophy.* Random House, New York.

THOMPSON, ROBERT FARRIS, AND JOSEPH CORNET
1983   *The Four Moments of the Sun: Kongo Art in Two Worlds.* National Gallery of Art, Washington, D.C.

THORNTON, JOHN
1992   *Africa and Africans in the Making of the Atlantic World, 1400–1680.* Cambridge University Press, Cambridge, U.K.

UCKO, PETER J.
1969   Ethnography and Archaeological Interpretation of Funerary Remains. *World Archaeology* 1:262–280.

VANSINA, JAN
1973   *The Tio Kingdom of the Middle Congo, 1880–1892.* Oxford University Press, Oxford, U.K.

VIVIAN, BRIAN C.
1992   Sacred to Secular: Transitions in Akan Funerary Customs. In *An African Commitment: Papers in Honour of Peter Lewis Shinnie*, edited by Judy Sterner and Nicholas David, pp. 157–167. University of Calgary Press, Calgary, Alberta.

VLACH, JOHN M.
1978   *The Afro-American Tradition in Decorative Arts.* Cleveland Museum of Art, Cleveland, Ohio.

WATTERS, DAVID R.
1987   Excavations at the Harney Site Slave Cemetery, Montserrat, West Indies. *Annals of the Carnegie Museum* 56:289–318. Pittsburgh, Pennsylvania.
1994   Mortuary Patterns at the Harney Site Slave Cemetery, Montserrat, in Caribbean Perspective. *Historical Archaeology* 28(3):56–73.

YONGYI, LI, C. LORING BRACE, GAO QIANG, AND DAVID P. TRACER
1991   Dimensions of Face in Asia in the Perspective of Geography and Prehistory. *American Journal of Physical Anthropology* 85:269–279.

ROSS W. JAMIESON
DEPARTMENT OF ARCHAEOLOGY
UNIVERSITY OF CALGARY
CALGARY, ALBERTA, T2N 1N4
CANADA

LESLIE C. STEWART-ABERNATHY
BARBARA L. RUFF

A Good Man in Israel: Zooarchaeology and Assimilation in Antebellum Washington, Washington, Arkansas

ABSTRACT

Recovery of faunal remains in a rich deposit of household trash in Washington, Arkansas, presented an opportunity to examine ethnicity in the archaeological record because the trash was discarded by the early 1840s by the Blocks, a prominent Jewish family. Analysis of the faunal collection suggests that Block foodways did not differ markedly from contemporaneous collections in urban settings. However, the ambiguity of ethnic signatures in this case record may provide clear evidence of cognitive uncertainty and assimilation, particularly since the documentary record suggests continued identification by some family members with Judaism.

Introduction

Archaeological studies of ethnicity in North America offer an opportunity for substantive and theoretical contrast because of the data now in hand about the basic Anglo-American traditions and developments. Identification of ethnicity in the historical archaeological record can be difficult (Horvath 1983; Kelly and Kelly 1980; McGuire 1982), even if one uses as a broad definition of ethnicity that ethnic groups define themselves by their differences from the majority (Aronson 1976; Barth 1969; Keyes 1981).

Aside from usual problems about visibility in the archaeological record, many ethnic groups might be expected to stand out in some way from the basic Anglo background. For example, the Overseas Chinese and Afro-Americans are relatively easy to recognize because they carried non-Western cultural traditions and were visible to their contemporaries by distinctive phenotypic characteristics (Schuyler 1980).

Other peoples, despite a heritage that is clearly part of what is ethnocentrically referred to as Western Civilization can still be prominent: for example, the Spanish/Mexican presence in the Southwest and Southeast (Deagan and Scardaville 1985; McGuire 1983). This group represents ethnicity in which nationality is synonymous with religion, language, foodways, and other components of culture, though strong regional variations existed in the homeland.

Less visible are ethnic groups which are in the mainstream of Western Civilization but which cross the bounds of nation states, and whose members differ from their compatriots most clearly not by phenotype but by religion. The best example in the United States may be the Jews, who represent neither a country, nor a vernacular language, nor a phenotype, but who have nonetheless been stereotyped according to all three categories.

There has recently been an opportunity to examine the nature of Jewish ethnicity as a result of excavations in Washington, Arkansas, directed by Leslie C. Stewart-Abernathy and carried out by the Arkansas Archeological Survey and the Arkansas Archeological Society in 1982 and 1983 (Stewart-Abernathy 1983, 1986a). Work in the back yard of the Block house, built by 1832, revealed a small pit 11 m behind the house that was filled with domestic trash no later than the early 1840s.

This domestic trash was probably generated by the Block household, a prosperous merchant family headed by husband Abraham Block and his wife Fanny Isaiah Isaacs Block. Abraham was a founding member of the first Jewish congregation in the Mississippi Valley, Gates of Mercy (Shaarei Chessed), in New Orleans in 1827 (Korn 1969: 198, 326; Society of Israelites 1971), although by then he was already living in Washington with Fanny and a large and still growing family. When Abraham died in 1857, obituaries were published in New Orleans, in Arkansas, and in a national Jewish newspaper, *The Occident and American Jewish Advocate*. One commented he was "one of the oldest of the house of Israel in America," and that "a good man has fallen in Israel" (*Arkansas*

Gazette, 4 Apr 1857). Abraham Block has since become famous in Arkansas and in American Judaism for being an early Jew on the frontier (American Jewish Archives 1956:67–69; Goodspeed Publishing Company 1890:405; LeMaster 1983:42,82).

The location and date of the Block family trash deposit is well suited for exploring the nature of assimilation. On the one hand, Washington up until the 1840s remained on the far western edge of established settlement, with the nearest Jewish congregations in Cincinnati and New Orleans (American Jewish Archives 1956; Cincinnati Congregation 1971; Jonas 1971; Korn 1969). It was recognized at the time that without group support and control, adherents could easily be lost to the dominant culture, and often were (e.g., Jonas 1971:224). The Blocks were in the middle of a great sea of potential secular and Christian antagonists.

The deposit also coincided with the end of a long, homogeneous period in Jewish practice and belief in North America and the beginning of heterodoxy (Brickman 1977:vii–xiv; Glazer 1957; Handlin 1954:38–58). The Block family at the beginning of the 1840s were the inheritors of a vital orthodox tradition. Just before mid-century, relatively large migrations of Germanic Jews brought the beginnings of the Jewish reform movement in which some Judaic traditions were consciously set aside. This migration overwhelmed the Anglo-Spanish tradition that had been dominant in New World Judaism throughout the colonial period. Moreover, the spatial cohesiveness of the Jewish population was lessened. As late as 1800, organized Judaism had been situated largely in secure, comforting enclaves on the Eastern Seaboard, but the trans-Appalachian movement of the first third of the 1800s isolated many Jews (Libo and Howe 1984). By the 1850s the much-increased Jewish population had established synagogues and communities across the eastern half of the United States. By 1854 there were even ten Jewish groups in California (Leeser 1955:78). Thanks to these demographic and settlement changes, the foundations of the diversity of Orthodox, Reform, and Conservative Judaism in the United States had been laid. A Jewish family might no longer be isolated, but it might find competing ideologies when it turned outward for aid.

Unfortunately, it is difficult to use much of the assemblage in the trash deposit to explore ethnicity through standard comparative techniques. The tight date range and the intensity of deposition of the cellar fill are rare in the archaeological literature of Arkansas. Moreover, comparison between data from this deposit and others is complex and difficult as a result of variables introduced by such factors as the urban locale in a thoroughly rural and near-frontier hinterland, the family occupation as merchant entrepreneurs amidst farmers, and the place of this merchant family near the beginning of the distribution system of imported goods throughout the entire Mississippi Valley.

The cellar fill, however, contained 2600 animal bones. The study of this faunal material in the context of well-known Judaic dietary proscriptions and prescriptions provided an opportunity to measure the extent to which traditional Jewish practice of foodways was being maintained. There was also an opportunity to further track the family's Jewishness through the social artifacts preserved only in the documentary record. One could thus explore in detail the nature of Jewish life in isolation in times of change and the extent to which explicitly defined practices could be carried out under difficult circumstances.

Historical and Archaeological Background

To provide a context for interpretation of the faunal collection and the extent to which the Blocks considered themselves Jewish, some background is necessary on the trash deposit, on the household which created it, and on some relevant points of Jewish tradition.

By 1840 the Block family was large and had considerable influence on the commerce of southwest Arkansas and northwest Louisiana. Washington, Arkansas, was then a commercial center and county seat for a region of cotton plantations and yeoman farms (Gwaltney 1958; Medearis 1976;

Williams 1951). The Block family was an important part of the community (Montgomery 1981). Abraham was already old, at 60, but his wife Fanny was only 37. The total household numbered about 15 and included most of their 12 children and two or three female household slaves. The household was quite prosperous. Total assets held in Abraham's name included 10 lots in Washington, counting the three on which their urban farmstead sat and another about 400 m away on the town's main street where their store was located. Holdings also included 80 acres of rural land, a saw mill, and a tanning yard. There was $20,000 invested in the merchandise for the general store, by then known as Abraham Block and Son. That partnership also owned another 280 acres of land (Montgomery 1981:22–40, 72–76, and 1984; Donald R. Montgomery, personal communication).

The trash deposit, Feature 14, began as a pit 1.5 m wide by 3 m long by 1 m deep, probably a small cellar located either under a kitchen ell or out in the open (Stewart-Abernathy 1985 and 1986b). This pit was dug no earlier than 1832, when the Blocks moved to a previously vacant block and built the house. The cellar was dug into the sandy soil on which the town is built and collapse of the exposed sand sidewalls led to abandonment. The pit was filled with domestic trash containing about 5000 artifacts. Filling took place no later than the early 1840s, based on the recovery of coins dated 1831 and 1839 (with New Orleans mint marks), three different sets of ceramic wares impressed with the Davenport anchor with "36" date mark (including vessels with importers' marks of the New Orleans firms of Henderson and Gaines and Henderson, Walton and Company), and a variety of other manufacturers' marks dating to the 1820s and 1830s. The locale of the feature was protected from further deposition by the kitchen ell, constructed at least by the 1860s, if not the 1830s. This ell was torn down in the late 1950s in cleaning up the property to transform the Block house into an open-air museum exhibit.

Actual filling was accomplished in a variety of ways. Most significant was a primary deposit of separate loads of trash including glass and ceramic tablewares, personal items, and food bones. In some cases the pieces of broken ceramic vessels were stacked during cleanup and simply dropped into the pit, retaining the stack order. Other loads mixed broken vessels with food debris. Fill also included loads of ashes and bits of burned detritus from cleaned-out hearths along with adjacent soil and sheet midden scraped in for sanitary purposes. Slumping of walls during the filling also took place. In addition, building materials including brick, rock, nails, and hardware were found in the deposit, although the circumstances of their discard are unknown.

There is one great but predictable omission in this primary deposit. There are no artifacts specifically Jewish in origin or use. Judaism encourages the application of meaningful symbols to goods of ordinary form when used in private and public rituals (e.g., Raphael 1972:145; Weinstein 1985). It also demands extraordinary forms when such are required by liturgy or practice. For example, a miniature wheelbarrow can be used as a serving dish during the Passover meal to provide a vivid reminder of the construction work done in bondage under the Pharaohs (Raphael 1972:75). However, distinctively Jewish items are special objects subject to extraordinary standards of care. One would not expect a menorah or a *mezuza* to be casually discarded.

Jewish Traditions

Traditional Judaism, as it existed in Europe and the New World prior to the 19th century, derived from two principle sources. The first was a corpus of sacred writings. These works included the holy books of the Torah, the Talmud (the codified oral tradition contained in a long set of rabbinical exegeses fitting scriptural pronouncements to daily life), and several commentaries from the Diaspora such as the *Shulhan Aruk* of the 1500s. (All spellings of Hebrew words follow the *Encyclopedia Judaica*). These writings together form the *Halakhah*, the Jewish Law, with its normative and proscriptive teachings (Bermant 1975; Gaster 1955; Klein 1979). The creation of Jewish tradition did not end here, however. To the sacred writings have been added a second source for practices and beliefs, the effects of 2000 years of contact with non-Jewish cultures. Sacred writings and secular contacts have in turn been subjected to minor variation caused by the congregational base, an often divisive but strategically brilliant mechanism for ethnic survival without a nation state.

Well before 1500 European Judaism split into two wings, the Sephardic or Anglo-Portuguese-Spanish wing strongly influenced by Iberian language and culture; and the Ashkenazic or German-Polish-Russian, primarily reflecting Central and East European traditions and languages (*Encyclopedia Judaica* 1972, 4:719–722; Roth and Wigoder 1972, 14:1164–1178). The Ashkenazic wing is most familiar today because of the huge immigration to the United States of East European Jews after 1875, many of whom came from the *shtetl* or rural villages made famous in the stories by Isaac Bashevis Singer and Shalom Aleichem, whose Tevye stories were the basis of *Fiddler on the Roof*. Sephardic Judaism, however, was dominant throughout the New World until the 1840s, and carried much higher status (Raphael 1983). The Block family apparently belonged to this branch, an interpretation based on knowledge of Fanny's upbringing in the Sephardic community of Richmond, Virginia, and Abraham's association with Sephardic Jews there and, after the mid 1820s, in New Orleans (Berman 1979:20–26; Ezekial and Lichtenstein 1917:14–15; Korn 1969; Carolyn LeMasters 1983, pers. comm; Proctor 1957:119–124; Schappes 1971:179–180, 609–610).

Unfortunately, precise distinctions between Ashkenazic and Sephardic practice in New Orleans and the Mississippi Valley in the early 19th century are not clear. Even where documentation on actual Jewish practice exists, as in New Orleans, it has proven difficult to confirm even synagogic activity as one or the other (Korn 1969; Schappes 1971: 609–610). In this paper no distinction will be made.

Traditional Judaism itself was a complex set of symbolic behaviors that infused daily life and the life cycle with rich meanings. In order to support this deliberate and conscious imposition of the sacred onto the profane, a complete array of enfolding and localized institutions was supplied to guide the community of believers in the performance of private and group activities that linked the ordinary and extraordinary events of life both to a supreme being and to hundreds of generations of fellow believers (Douglas 1975).

These institutions began with the formal congregation, the public persona of the local Jewish community. It consisted of all the adult males, their elected leaders, and their hired rabbi, who as teacher and scholar provided the ultimate authority in doctrinal matters. There were also various associations charged with specific rituals or tasks, such as the burial society. Other important individuals included the *shohet,* who supplied ritually clean meat (often through advising other butchers), and the *mohel,* who conducted the critical rite of circumcision on male infants that ultimately insured qualified male members to keep the congregation going. There was also the physical expression of tradition in the synagogue, the community meeting hall where the copies of the Torah and the Talmud were kept; the cemetery with special mortuary house; the *mikveh* or formal bathing facility in which women purified themselves after the pollution of menstruation; and perhaps even a formal school building.

These institutions and officials provided the public context for Jewish life, but much of that life was lived in the household. There, too, Judaism was present. Said a mid-19th century American Jew, "If the Englishman called his home his castle, the Jew could with justice call his home his religion, his comfort, and his delight" (Mayer 1971:311). The Jewish woman was given primary responsibility for maintaining a home where Jewish practice was observed. Ironically, formal education in Jewish heritage was neglected for women if not actively discouraged in Europe and in the United States prior to the mid 1800s when the German reform efforts took hold as part of the large-scale German Jewish immigration (Baum, Hyman, and Michel 1976:1–16, 21–23; Marcus 1980:56–57). However, in the security of a thriving Jewish community, the details of correct practice of daily life could be instilled in daughters as part of their training in the duties and responsibilities of homemakers. There was always the observing presence of the rest of the community to answer specific questions and to enforce adherence.

Jewish tradition even prescribes some distinctive patterns of wasting behavior. The smashing of the betrothal cup is a spectacular example (Gaster 1955:119–121), but identifying such an event in the archaeological record may be impossible. The deliberate breaking of dishes as the funeral cortege leaves the house can be a part of mourning rituals (Gaster 1955:172). The exhaustive cleanup of the house and the careful collection and burning of remnants of unleavened foods associated with preparations for the Passover *seder* (Bermant 1974: 182–188; Raphael 1972) is also systemic behavior that may not be recoverable from the archaeological contexts.

Immense difficulties could arise when it came time for individuals to plant these traditions to the New World. As an historian of American Judaism has remarked, with its congregational worship, dietary laws, scholarly theology, and ritual language with unique alphabet, Judaism was hardly adapted to frontier life (Schappes 1971: editorial note p. 223; cf. Handlin 1954:13–21). In the 1840s there were apparently problems in maintaining rituals and standards even in the Jewish community in New Orleans (Korn 1969:200–215). Cut off from that institutional base, the Block family faced a prospect common in 19th century America—rapid assimilation with loss of their Jewish heritage.

Kashrut and Faunal Analysis

The Jewish system of *kashrut* represents an especially clear instance of the primacy of symbolic concerns even where basic biological needs are involved, with obvious results visible in material culture. The integration of ideology and foodways in Judaism is deliberately intended to move eating from the profane to the sacred, so that the preparation and consumption of food itself becomes a religious act (Douglas 1966, 1975; Klein 1979:302–303). This impact of symbolism on

dietary practice represents one of the key features by which the traditional Jews are considered and consider themselves separate from the rest of the world.

The entire system of *kashrut* is complex, with a scriptural base, a special section accorded to it in the Talmud commentaries, and consideration in every code thereafter (Dresner and Siegel 1959; Gaster 1955:192–214; Klein 1979:302–379; Rabinowicz 1972; Siegel, Strasfeld, and Strasfeld 1973:18–36). *Kashrut* includes the laws of *shehitah* that indicate the prescribed manner of slaughtering, the laws of *terefah* that identify meat not ritually fit for consumption, and the laws regarding final preparations conducted in the home and the steps taken to cleanse vessels, utensils, and facilities that have become ritually contaminated.

The nature of Judaism in isolation from the Jewish community is thrown into sharp relief by a comment by a modern Conservative authority regarding *kashrut:* "Most of the laws connected with the consumption of food are the concern of the *shohet*, the butcher, and the grocer, all of whom are involved before the food reaches the home" (Klein 1979:360). In their isolation, with no trained and licensed *shohet* for hundreds of miles and no trained rabbi in North America until the 1840s (Blau and Baron 1963, 2:524–528), Abraham and Fanny Block were directly responsible for the entire process. It was possible to serve as one's own *shohet* (e.g., Marcus 1970, 2:936–940) and to keep a *kasher* home, though this could be difficult even within a Jewish community (e.g., New Orleans, Korn 1969:243–244). Adherence (or non-adherence) by the Blocks to the formal requirement to consume only ritually clean meat should be obvious through study of the faunal remains from Feature 14.

Analysis of the faunal material was conducted by Barbara L. Ruff in association with Elizabeth J. Reitz of the University of Georgia Zooarchaeology Laboratory (Ruff 1985). The comparative skeletal collection of that laboratory was utilized in the identification process. Faunal materials were weighed and counted, notations of age, symmetry and degree of epiphyseal fusion recorded, and butchering and other bone modifications noted.

TABLE 1
FAUNAL SPECIES RECOVERED FROM THE FEATURE 14 TRASH DEPOSIT
(3HE236-19), WASHINGTON, ARKANSAS

Category	Bone Count	* M.N.I. Number	* M.N.I. %	Bone Weight (g)	Biomass kg	Biomass %
Unidentified Mammal	597			330.32	4.8645	5.43
Sciurus niger black squirrel	1	1	2.44	9.59	0.0164	0.02
Sciurus carolinensis gray squirrel	2	1	2.44	0.53	0.0149	0.02
Sciurus sp. squirrel	1	0	0.00	0.62	0.0171	0.02
Rattus sp. rat	4	1	2.44	0.31	0.0092	0.01
Unidentified Artiodactyl	370			1259.22	16.2215	18.10
Sus scrofa pig	114	3	7.32	784.72	10.5985	11.83
Odocoileus virginianus white-tailed deer	50	3	7.32	593.35	8.2410	9.20
Bos taurus cow	79	3	7.32	3294.78	38.5517	43.03
Unidentified Bird	897			180.34	2.8215	3.15
Anas platyrhynchos mallard	1	1	2.44	2.30	0.0557	0.06
Anas sp. duck	33	3	7.32	55.46	0.9763	1.09
Gallus gallus chicken	248	12	29.27	227.81	3.4819	3.89
Meleagris gallopavo turkey	46	3	7.32	117.72	2.7846	3.11
Galliformes galliform bird	4	1	2.44	3.05	0.0718	0.08
Corvidae corvid bird	1	1	2.44	0.30	0.0089	0.01
Colaptes auratus yellow-shafted flicker	2	1	2.44	0.39	0.0113	0.01
Unidentified Anura frog/toad	5	1	2.44	0.24	0.0073	0.01
Unidentified Fish	155			11.83	0.2430	0.27
Ictaluridae catfish	11	4	9.76	5.93	0.1305	0.15
Catostomidae catostomid fish	3	1	2.44	2.23	0.0541	0.06
Lepomis sp. sunfish	1	1	2.44	0.10	0.0033	0.00
Unidentified Bone				21.46	0.4154	0.46
TOTALS	2625	41	100	6953.6	89.6003	100

*Minimum Number of Individuals

The minimum number of individuals represented in each taxon was calculated using the principle of paired elements (Casteel 1977; see Grayson 1973); the additional criteria of age, size, and sex were applied when appropriate. These data are summarized in Tables 1–4 and in Figure 1.

The following is a brief discussion of some relevant aspects of the methods used. First, a

TABLE 2
BONE MODIFICATIONS

Category	Sawed or Sliced	Cut	Hacked	Burned	Calcined	Rodent Gnawed	Worked
UD Mammal				24	145		
UD Artiodactyl	18	10	10		58		1
Pig	5	5	2		2		
Deer	7	4	4	3	1	1	1
Cow	14	13	6	1	1	1	
UD Bird				5	20		
Chicken		1		3	3		
Turkey				1			
TOTALS	44	33	22	37	230	2	2

possible bias may have been introduced by the recovery technique. During excavation, select bulk matrix samples were collected from nearly all proveniences for flotation and wet screening but no dry screening was done. This may have resulted in under-representation of smaller food resources (such as freshwater fish) in the Block household diet.

With respect to quantification procedures, it should be noted that the estimated minimum number of individuals is conservative and might have been higher if the entire feature had not been treated as a single analytical unit (see Grayson 1979). Also, in calculating biomass, this study used the allometric principle that proportions of body mass, skeletal mass, and skeletal dimensions change with increasing size according to a formula that has been previously applied by Elizabeth Reitz, Dan Cordier, and others (Reitz and Cordier 1983; Reitz et al. 1987).

Finally, the faunal sample is small and may under-represent either resource diversity or utilization or both (see Grayson 1978). Fortunately, since Feature 14 is quite restricted both spatially and temporally and bone preservation is generally good, it seems reasonable to assume that the sample is adequate for subsistence interpretation of a single household. The presence of unlocated or destroyed contemporaneous deposits of household faunal material associated with the Block household may have provided a more complex view.

Given that reconstruction of subsistence patterns is an inherently inferential process influenced by unavoidable information loss, it is nonetheless possible to form a good idea about Block meat consumption in the late 1830s and early 1840s. The faunal assemblage is characterized by a predominance of domestic species, chiefly large mammals. Forty-one individuals are present. The assemblage represents a total meat weight of 89.6 kg or about 40 lb of biomass. Cows represent the largest contribution of biomass, followed by fowl (including chickens, turkeys, and wild or domestic ducks), pig, and deer. The diet was apparently supplemented from time to time with additional small game including squirrels and fish (such as catfish, suckers, and sunfish).

Butchering data are suggestive of preferred cuts. The distribution of cow and pig elements, presented in Table 2 and Figure 1, indicates that although all sections of the beef and pork carcass are represented in the sample, the largest percentage of bones are from meaty portions. These come primarily from high-value cuts, such as roasts and hams, and from animals in the approximate age range that yields the highest quality of meat. The deer remains also suggest preparation of roasts. The apparent preference for roasts and hams implies that a primary mode of consumption was as a group, not an unexpected finding given the known size of the household. Pigs' feet or knuckles are also present as are occasional bones such as might be used in soups and stew meat, also means of preparation for a group. The discovery of a preference for individual cuts of chops or steaks would

TABLE 3
ELEMENT DISTRIBUTION

Category	Pig	Deer	Cow
Head	24	1	3
Vertebrae	25	4	13
Ribs	7	3	25
Forequarters	9	7	4
Forefeet	7	0	2
Hindquarters	12	25	24
Hindfeet	10	7	11
Feet	16	3	1
Other	4	0	0
TOTALS	114	50	83

TABLE 4
SUGGESTED AGE CATEGORIES BASED ON FUSION OF ELEMENTS

Pig	
Age Group	No. of Elements
Less than 9 months	1
Less than 1.5 years	3
Less than 2 years	6
Less than 3.5 years	7
TOTAL	17

Deer	
Age Group	No. of Elements
At least 12 months	1
Less than 29 months	3
Older than 29 months	3
TOTAL	7

Cow	
Age Group	No. of Elements
Less than 2.5 years	2
Less than 3 years	2
Less than 4 years	5
TOTAL	9

have indicated the contrary mode of viewing the carcass as an assemblage of individual portions.

The butchering data also suggest aspects of acquisition. Element distribution patterns for deer and cow indicate that these animals were usually not slaughtered at the site but elsewhere; otherwise bones representing unusable portions would be more obvious. At least in the case of cows, the meat represented by recovered bones implies purchase of meat cuts in the market place by the Blocks. Remains of pigs, including cranial and feet elements, indicate, in contrast, that they were usually slaughtered on site, raised by the household on their urban farmstead, or at least bought on the hoof.

Two species of avian fauna were butchered and probably raised on site. The chickens were clearly obtained on site as they are represented by eggs, very young birds, medullary deposits indicating hens killed while laying, and elements from all parts of the skeleton. Tarsometatarsal spurs confirm the presence of roosters. Bits of highly abraded whiteware ceramics found in the gizzard area of a complete turkey buried elsewhere in the Block back yard, probably by the 1840s, suggest that turkeys were fattened on site or at least not fully wild. (The laws of *kashrut* forbid eating animals that die without human intervention, *nevelah* [Rabinowicz 1972:39], but so does folk wisdom.)

In summary, the overall pattern that emerges from examination of the element distribution and butchering patterns of Feature 14 is use of high-value cuts of meat that were roasted (or smoked, in the case of pork) or otherwise prepared to serve many individuals at a sitting. As the Blocks were a large and prosperous household, this pattern is not surprising. In many respects the Block household conforms to expectations of foodways in a high-status urban farmstead. At present, an urban pattern seems to consist of dietary staples provided by domestic animals including poultry, with a wild component (and consequently some variety) in the form of deer, fish, and small game (Reitz and Ruff 1982; Reitz 1986; Ruff and Reitz 1984).

There is little in this dietary regime that obviously indicates ethnicity. From their food bones at least, the Blocks appear to be completely assimilated. Certainly the pork was obviously forbidden by Jewish law on the grounds that it was a non-ruminant with cloven feet. Catfish was also proscribed as having no scales visible to the eye (Klein 1979:304; Rabinowicz 1972:35). At least rabbits are not present, which are suspicious and often banned (Klein 1979:305; Rabinowicz 1972: 31). Indeed, the cuts of pork suggest a classic preference for the meat storage strategy of smoking hams (in 1862 Block son David lost "a smoke house and a large amount of meat" in a fire at his

BOS TAURUS

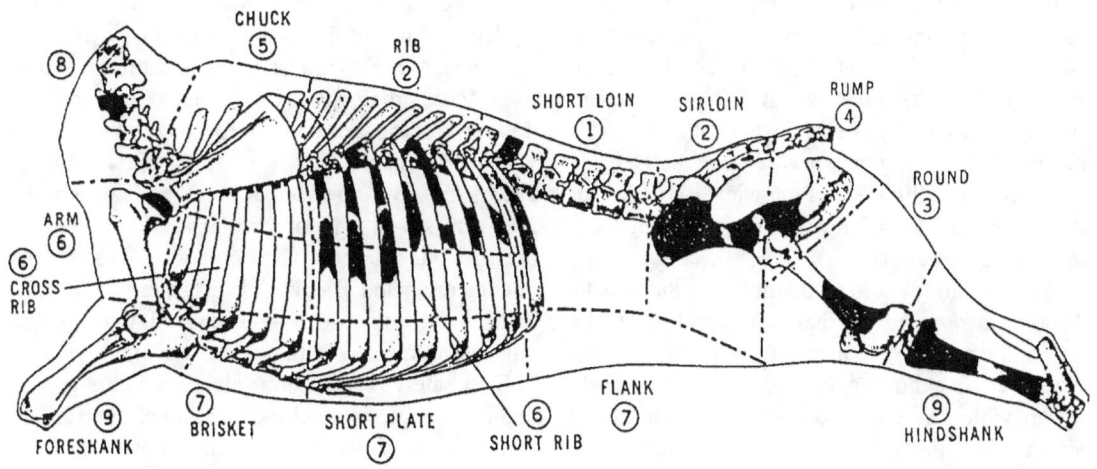

SUS SCROFA

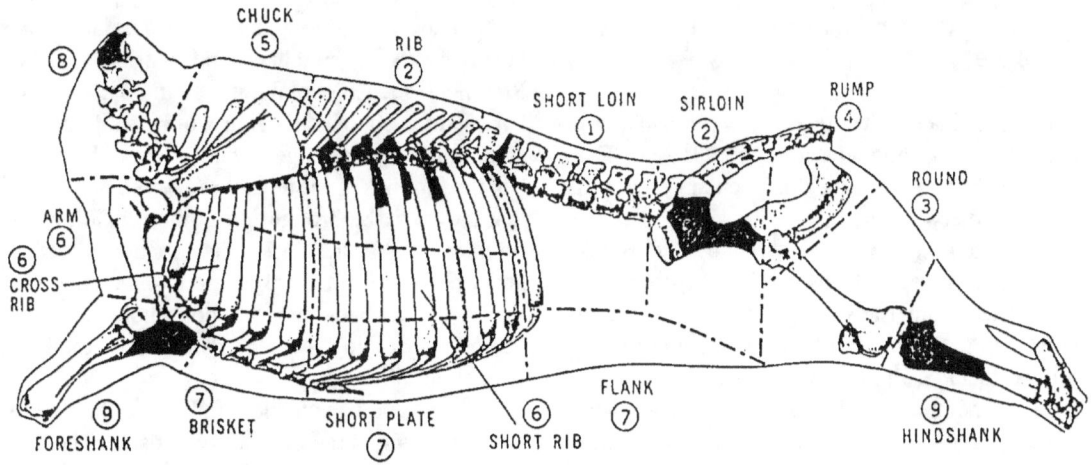

FIGURE 1. Representation of butchering patterns. Bones recovered have been filled in. Numbers in circles indicate ranking of meat cuts by late 19th century retail values (see Gust 1980).

own place elsewhere in town [*Washington Telegraph*, 26 Feb. 1862]). The parallel preference for hindquarter cuts from permitted deer and cows further hint at a non-*kasher* diet. Down the back of the thigh runs the sciatic nerve, the presence of which is repeatedly noted in Jewish law as a special feature that must be carefully removed in spite of the difficulty or else the meat is unclean no matter what the original species was (see Genesis 32:31; Klein 1979:349; Rabinowicz 1979:39). In short, the Blocks seem no different from their prosperous neighbors.

There is little reason to assume that the Blocks observed *kashrut* but fed their household slaves the pork and catfish. Such a policy would be difficult to maintain in a thoroughly pure home, particularly one in which the slaves were closely associated with daily routine and may have done much of the cooking. Without totally separate cooking and eating facilities, not to mention separate cook and wash pots, butchering knives, and all the rest of the equipment necessary, the household's material culture would quickly have become ritually contaminated. Such contamination could have been removed in an homogenous community guided by a rabbi and numerous like-minded neighbors, but in isolation it would be one more argument for abandoning strict adherence.

Identifying Jewish Practice: Documentary Evidence

If the archaeological record were the sole criterion, the Blocks might be considered lapsed. There are, however, hints in the documentary record that suggest otherwise.

The interpretation is hindered by the Blocks' distance from an established Jewish community and hence from the official institutions charged both with maintenance of the literate environment critical to Judaism and with the careful documentation of members' lifelong sacred activities. Many of the diagnostic social artifacts of Jewish religious behavior are precisely those aspects of past life least likely to be documented otherwise. For example, one cannot ascertain the occurrence of circumcisions unless the congregation's or *mohel's* circumcision record book is available. Moreover, given the exclusion of women from the historical record in general, it would be astonishing to find evidence of use of the *mikveh* bath for purification after menstruation unless such a bathing facility was not only maintained by a congregation, but the minutes of the necessary repair committee survived (Bermant 1975:130–133; e.g., Marcus 1955:995). Even the secular archives fail, because Abraham's will and probate inventory have not been found. There are also no surviving accounts documenting the Blocks' observance of the Sabbath, perhaps the most important religious festival but one performed in the privacy of the home.

Fortunately, some minor clues available in secular and congregational records and circumstantial evidence allow estimation of the presence of Judaic observances in the lives of the Blocks. There are two major areas to consider: life cycle ceremonies and the celebration of important group festivals. Both are heavily laden with symbolic behavior. The evidence suggests that although at times the Blocks were lax, at other times at least the senior Blocks remained inwardly Jewish and were not as integrated with their neighbors as the archaeological data might suggest.

Both Abraham and Fanny Block had visible ties to Judaism prior to the 1830s, although the strength of those ties are occasionally problematical. Fanny was the daughter of Isaiah Isaacs (1747–1806), a merchant and patriarch of the Richmond Jewish community. In his will of 1803, Isaacs directed that his four young children, including Fanny (then age seven), were to be placed "in the families of respectable *Jews* (sic) to the end that they may be brought up in the religion of the forefathers" (Isaacs 1971). Isaacs died in 1806, and whether or not the provision was carried out, Fanny established her own household only five years later at age 15 when she married Abraham, then about 30.

Circumstantial evidence indicates that Abraham's training in the faith was extensive. The facts about Abraham's life in his native Bohemia or in the United States following his immigration (around 1795 at about age 12 in company with other

TABLE 5
BLOCKS AND THE MAJOR LIFE CYCLE RITUALS OF JUDAISM

	Extent of Participation	
Rituals	by Abraham and Fanny Block	by Block children 7 males 5 females
Male Circumcision	yes	5 likely 2 problematical
Male Bar Mitzvah	yes	all problematical
Betrothal and Wedding	probably	1 male probably remainder no
Marriage to a Gentile	no	1 male no, 2 males yes 2 females yes 3 died unmarried 2 unknown
Jewish Funeral	yes	1 male yes remainder no
Burial in Jewish Cemetery	yes	1 male yes remainder no

Blocks, probably his kin) are limited. By 1811 he was in central Virginia where he married Fanny in Charlottesville, although he evidently lived in Richmond. That Abraham was listed as a charter member of the New Orleans Gates of Mercy congregation is strong evidence that he was fully qualified through circumcision and *bar mitzvah* (Korn 1969: 198, 326; Society of Israelites 1971).

Life cycle ceremonies in Judaism, as usual important rites of passage, were sometimes the responsibility of parents, sometimes of grown children, and some finally of the survivors (see Bermant 1975). Table 5 shows participation by Blocks in life cycle ceremonies. The first ritual was circumcision of males. Failure of parents to carry this out could mean refusal of burial for their sons in a Jewish cemetery, not to mention forever being separated from synagogue membership and the company of the ancestors. Circumcision was probably possible for most of the first five Block boys because they were born in central Virginia, in reach of a strong Jewish community. At least one son, Augustus (1818–1869), was buried in the Jewish Dispersed of Judah Cemetery in New Orleans (Carolyn LeMasters 1983, pers. comm.), so he was probably circumcised before the family left Virginia. It would have been harder to arrange

circumcision for the last two boys (born 1820 and 1823) because both were born in or near Washington, Arkansas. Still, it may have been possible because it was not uncommon for the ceremony to be delayed months or years until a *mohel* or even a *shohet* could be found, and sometimes fathers performed the operation on their own sons (Marcus 1970:984–988).

Next came the *bar mitzvah*, at age 13, again only for males. This was foremost a public ceremony that required demonstrating some training in Hebrew and basic beliefs in front of the congregation. This milestone may also have been difficult to secure for the children, because not one of the seven sons reached 13 before the family moved to Washington. Acquiring a qualified teacher would have been hard unless Abraham himself was enough of a scholar, and one would have had to obtain the prayer books and shawls. The actual ceremony would have been postponed until one of several regular buying trips by the Blocks to New Orleans.

The betrothal and marriage of Fanny and Abraham could have been conducted within tradition (the wedding took place in Virginia in 1811), but this would have been nearly impossible for their children. The ceremonies would once again have been difficult to arrange since both required the presence of the *minyan* or quorum of ten qualified males. The nearest quorum was in New Orleans.

In fact, only one of the 12 children, Augustus, is known to have married a Jewish woman. He married into the Jonas family of New Orleans about 1856, but only after he moved there and reentered a Jewish community (Carolyn LeMasters 1983, pers. comm.). The other known marriages were with local Washington men and women, generally offspring of prominent Christian families with whom local alliances were both neighborly and useful. Because a rule of Jewish law states that the faith of the mother passes to the children, many of the Block grandchildren of Christian spouses were automatically lost to the faith, and none even of the children of Block daughters is known to have remained Jewish. Within two generations, primarily as a result of intermarriage, nearly all of the Blocks were separated from Judaism.

A final ceremony concerns death and the preparations of the living and the dying for death. As there is a Jewish way of life, there is also a Jewish way of death and mourning (Bermant 1975:236–251; Lamm 1969; Rabinowicz 1964). The importance of this way to the cognitive well-being of transplanted faithful Jews was repeatedly emphasized by contemporaries. For example, one mid-19th century Jewish memoirist of Cincinnati noted, "it is remarkable how anxious the Jews are to provide a resting place for their dead, when as yet they have scarcely a foothold for the living; this is noticeable through all their history" (Mayer 1971:308).

It is difficult to say to what extent Jewish traditions informed the Blocks' thoughts and actions at the death of their first-born son, Simon, in 1833 at age 16 in Washington. His is the first known death of their offspring. There was no burial society at hand to carry out the *taharah*, the ritual washing and wrapping in a plain white shroud, and there was no Jewish cemetery in Washington. Simon was buried in the town's Christian cemetery, permitted by Jewish ritual (Klein 1979:297), and he was later joined there (though not in adjacent graves) by several of the Block children and their Christian spouses.

Did Abraham and Fanny rend their garments on the left side as required, and did they carry out the mourning cycle of *shivah, sheloshim,* and twelve-month? Did the Blocks say the formal memorial prayers of *yahrzeit* on the yearly anniversary of this and other family-related deaths? Such prayers were necessary because they were redemptive and provided one type of immortality for the deceased. Block participation in the annual congregational mourning ritual as part of *Yom Kippur* would once again have been difficult, because that required a full congregation, and thus a trip to New Orleans in September or October. Their observance in private in their home in Washington may have further emphasized their isolation from fellow believers.

At least they could be comforted at the preparations for death made by an apparent nephew named Augustus E. Block who lived in nearby Fulton before his murder in 1855. Although when he died his probate inventory showed 10 hogs, in his will filed in 1848 he made sure to include a requirement consistent with Jewish belief. He asked that "my body be put in a coffin without paint or cover of any sort, but it should be the plain wood" (Hempstead County Will Records, Book C.:76–77; Lamm 1969).

Abraham Block's preparations for his own death are unknown, but when he died of a sudden illness at age 79 in 1857, he was within the community of friends in New Orleans. The obituary in the national *Occident* noted that "he had time to pray to the God of Israel. . . . His remains were followed to the grave by his sorrowing relatives, and numbers of his oldest and most valued friends" (*Occident*, April 1857). His funeral was probably traditional. He was buried in the Dispersed of Judah (*Nefutze Judah*) Cemetery, a Sephardic one, in the city. The grave is marked with a columnar granite tombstone. Without Hebrew lettering or symbols, the stone does not look too different from those of the prosperous dead in cemeteries of other faiths. When his wife Fanny died in 1871, she too was in New Orleans, having moved there to be near two of her children. She was buried beside Abraham though without a tombstone (Carolyn LeMasters 1983, pers. comm.).

The other important visible area of Jewish practice is that of the major annual religious festivals (Gaster 1953; Kitov 1970; Klein 1979). However, even a devout observer in southwest Arkansas would have had difficulty keeping these festivals since they were often public celebrations and required a congregation for their performance. The Blocks had regular commercial contact with New Orleans, and thus may have scheduled buying trips to coincide with occasions for joining with their fellow Jews.

Because the rivers were the interstate highways of the day, the Blocks' mobility may have been limited by water level. Thus, it would have been especially troublesome to reach New Orleans during one of the two major festivals, the High Holy Days, including the Day of Atonement (*Yom Kippur*) and New Year's (*Rosh Hashanah*). This festival occurs in late September and early October before the fall and winter rains would have made the Ouachita and Red Rivers navigable again.

The next primary festival, Passover, occurs at a more opportune time for river travel, in early spring. It may therefore be evidence of religious commitment that when Abraham Block died in late March of 1857, it was in New Orleans rather than in Washington, and that an obituary noted that he was "but recently arrived on his annual visit to his family" (*Arkansas Gazette*, 4 April 1857). Passover particularly celebrates the family since a major part of the celebration is the *seder* meal representing the hurried dinner the night before departure from Egypt (Raphael 1972). This is one important annual event that requires no congregational worship or synagogue to be observed. This festival, along with the High Holy Days, represents major occasion for modern far-flung Jewish families to reunite temporarily. Perhaps in following such a pattern, Abraham Block received a permanent resting place among his fellow Jews from whom he was spatially distant for much of his life.

Conclusion

The recognition of subcultural differences in the archaeological record within polycultural state-level societies in an industrial context has frequently depended on finding distinctive culture-specific items, such as Chinese ceramics and opium pipes (e.g., Garaventa and Pastron 1983), or foodways differences, such as contrasts in patterns of butchering, utilization of meat cuts, and proportions of wild game to domestic animals (Cleland 1970:16–17; Gust 1984; McGuire 1982; McEwan 1985). It may be just as significant for understanding cognitive aspects of ethnicity when a rich archaeological data base is found to be silent on this issue in spite of historically documented differentiation.

That the best antebellum physical clue to Block family retention of Judaism is the placement of Abraham's tombstone in a Jewish cemetery indicates how difficult it is to determine ethnic affiliation from surviving material evidence. That the material evidence for the ethnicity of a merchant family who helped bring the world manufacturing order into Washington and into the archaeological record of the region is not in Washington where the family lived but in New Orleans, the major transshipment point in the Mississippi Valley, where Abraham Block died, reveals the spatial and symbolic complexity of culture even in antebellum southwestern Arkansas.

In Abraham Block's obituary in the *Occident*, it was noted that he was "religious without pretension" (*Occident*, April 1857). Perhaps it is easier to understand better the struggle hidden in that phrase now that he is known to have been head of a family that tried and largely failed to maintain Jewish traditions in isolation. The Block family had its start within the Jewish community of Virginia where most of the customary supporting institutions were available. In the 1820s, however, they chose to move to a situation spatially and spiritually isolated both from Jewish institutions and from other Jews. There they prospered, settling into the Christian and secular community of Washington socially and economically as well as physically.

By the 1840s their success was clear, but so now is the potential ideological cost. When Abraham and Fanny Block set aside the demands of *kashrut* in their Washington home, whether through negligence or through a conscious desire for reform, they were no doubt aware they were transgressing a major principle of Jewish doctrine by which Jews chose to remain separate. They were also no doubt aware that in much of their daily lives they were violating other important provisions of Jewish orthodoxy.

In this they were not alone. Even where some of the elements of institutional Judaism were present, as in New Orleans where sharp criticisms by a German Jewish traveller about 1840 indicated laxity in avoiding forbidden foods, insuring circumcision, and even keeping the Sabbath (Dr. M. Weiner, cited in Korn 1969:243–244). One result for Abraham and Fanny Block was that they also failed in their parental duty to pass on the heritage of Judaism to their children.

However, no matter how much the Blocks might have blended in, the senior Blocks continued to define themselves as members of an ethnic group separate from their neighbors, although that ethnic group had become dispersed and diverse. For the senior Blocks at least, ethnicity was not a false consciousness that confused class distinctions, but a social reality, an ideology based on an ethnic symbol system that tied the now scattered members of the Jewish community to common values of group, identity, and history (Aronson 1976). The complete historical archaeological record thus documents how one family dealt with the deliberate integration of ideology and daily life that is Judaism, an integration not revealed by faunal remains alone.

ACKNOWLEDGMENTS

The field research discussed in this paper would not have been possible without the eager help of members of the Arkansas Archeological Society during the Society Training Program in 1982 and 1983 and without continued support by the Arkansas Archeological Survey directed by Charles R. McGimsey III and State Archeologist Hester A. Davis. The faunal analysis was funded by a research grant from the Survey awarded to Elizabeth J. Reitz and the Zooarchaeology Lab, University of Georgia. Significant research aid was provided by Donald R. Montgomery, Park Historian at Old Washington Historic State Park, and by Carolyn LeMasters, Little Rock, Arkansas. An earlier version of this paper was given at the 1986 annual meeting of the Society for Historical Archaeology in Sacramento, California.

REFERENCES

AMERICAN JEWISH ARCHIVES
1956 Trail Blazers of the Trans-Mississippi West. *American Jewish Archives* 8(2 Oct.):59–130.

ARONSON, DAN R.
1976 Ethnicity as a Cultural System: An Introductory Essay. In *Ethnicity in the Americas*, edited by Frances Henry, pp. 10–29. Mouton Publishers, The Hague.

BARTH, FREDRIK (EDITOR)
1969 *Ethnic Groups and Boundaries*. Little, Brown, Boston.

BAUM, CHARLOTTE, PAULA HYMAN, AND SONYA MICHEL
1976 *The Jewish Woman in America*. The Dial Press, New York.

BERMAN, MYRON
1979 *Richmond's Jewry 1769–1976: Shabbat in Shockoe*. University Press of Richmond, Charlottesville.

BERMANT, CHAIM
1975 *The Walled Garden: The Saga of Jewish Family Life and Tradition*. Macmillan Publishing Co., New York.

BRICKMAN, WILLIAM W.
1977 Introduction: The American Jewish Community in Historical Perspective. In *The Jewish Community in America: an Annotated and Classified Bibliographical Guide*, edited by William H. Brickman, pp. vii–xxvii. Burt Franklin and Co., New York.

BLAU, JOSEPH L., AND SALO W. BARON (EDITORS)
1963 *The Jews of the United States, 1790–1840, a Documentary History*. 3 vols. Columbia University Press, New York.

CASTEEL, R. W.
1977 Characterization of Faunal Assemblages and the Minimum Number of Individuals Determined from Paired Elements: Continuing Problems in Archaeology. *Journal of Archaeological Science* 4:125–134.

CINCINNATI CONGREGATION
1971 Hebrew Congregation in Cincinatti to Elders of the Jewish Congregation at Charleston, July 3, 1825. In *A Documentary History of the Jews in the United States 1654–1875*, edited by Morris U. Schappes, pp. 177–179. 3rd ed. Schocken Books, New York.

CLELAND, CHARLES E.
1970 Comparison of the Faunal Remains from French and British Refuse Pits at Fort Michilimackinac: A Study

in Changing Subsistence Patterns. *Canadian Historic Sites: Occasional Papers in Archaeology and History* No. 3:8–23.

DEAGAN, KATHLEEN AND MICHAEL SCARDAVILLE
1985 Archaeology and History on Historic Hispanic Sites: Impediments and Solutions. *Historical Archaeology* 19(1):32–37.

DOUGLAS, MARY
1966 The Abominations of Leviticus. In *Purity and Danger*, edited by by Mary Douglas, pp. 41–57. Praeger Books, New York.
1975 Deciphering a Meal. In *Implicit Meanings*, edited by Mary Douglas, pp. 249–275. Routledge and Kegan Paul, London.

DRESNER, SAMUEL H. AND SEYMOUR SIEGEL
1959 *The Jewish Dietary Laws*. Burning Bush, New York.

ENCYCLOPEDIA JUDAICA
1972 Ashkenazi. In *Encyclopedia Judaica*, editors in chief Cecil Roth and Geoffrey Wigoder, 4:719–722. Keter Publishing House, Jerusalem.

EZEKIAL, HERBERT T. AND GASTON LICHTENSTEIN
1917 *The History of the Jews of Richmond from 1769–1917*. Richmond privately printed, Richmond, Virginia.

GARAVENTA, DONNA M., AND ALLEN G. PASTRON
1983 Chinese Ceramics from a San Francisco Dump Site. In *Forgotten Places and Things*, edited by Albert A. Ward, pp. 295–320. Center for Anthropological Studies, Contributions to Anthropological Studies No. 3, Albuquerque, New Mexico.

GASTER, THEODOR
1953 *Festivals of the Jewish Year*. William Morrow and Co., New York.
1955 *The Holy and the Profane: Evolution of Jewish Folkways*. William Slone Associates, Publishers, New York.

GLAZER, NATHAN
1957 *American Judaism*. University of Chicago Press, Chicago.

GOODSPEED PUBLISHING COMPANY
1980 *Biographical and Historical Memoirs of Southern Arkansas*. The Goodspeed Publishing Company, Chicago.

GRAYSON, DONALD K.
1973 On the Methodology of Faunal Analysis. *American Antiquity* 38:432–439.
1978 Minimum Numbers and Sample Size in Vertebrate Faunal Analysis. *American Antiquity* 43(1):53–65.
1979 On the Quantification of Vertebrate Archaeofauna. In *Advances in Archaeological Methods and Theory*, vol. 2, edited by M. B. Schiffer, pp. 200–230. Academic Press, New York.

GUST, SHERRI M.
1983 Problems and Prospects in Nineteenth Century California Zooarchaeology. In *Forgotten Places and Things, Archaeological Perspectives on American History*, edited by Albert E. Ward, pp. 341–348. Center for Anthropological Studies, Contributions to Anthropological Studies No. 3, Albuquerque, New Mexico.
1984 Mammalian Fauna from the Woodland Opera House Site. *California Arcaheological Reports* No. 24, pp. 181–192. Sacramento, California.

GWALTNEY, FRANCIS IRBY
1958 A Survey of Historic Washington, Arkansas. *Arkansas Historical Quarterly* 17(4):33–96.

HANDLIN, OSCAR
1954 *Adventure and Freedom: Three Hundred Years of Jewish Life in America*. McGraw-Hill, New York.

HORVATH, STEVEN M., JR.
1983 Ethnic Groups as Subjects of Archaeological Inquiry. In *Forgotten Places and Things*, edited by Albert A. Ward, pp. 23–26. Center for Anthropological Studies, Contributions to Anthropological Studies No. 3, Albuquerque, New Mexico.

ISAACS, ISAIAH
1971 Will of Isaiah Isaacs of Charlottesville, Virginia, Aug. 30, 1803, and Codicil Jan. 8, 1806. In *A Documentary History of the Jews in the United States 1654–1875*, edited by Morris U. Schappes, 3rd ed., pp. 100–101. Schocken Books, New York.

JONAS, JOSEPH
1971 Autobiography, The Jews in Ohio, Dec. 25, 1843. In *A Documentary History of the Jews in the United States 1654–1875*, edited by Morris U. Schappes, 3rd ed., pp. 223–235. Schocken Books, New York.

KELLY, MARSHA C.S., AND ROGER E. KELLY
1980 Approaches to Ethnic Identification in Historical Archaeology. In *Archaeological Perspectives on Ethnicity in America*, edited by Robert L. Schuyler, pp. 133–143. Baywood Publishing Company, Farmingdale, New York.

KEYES, CHARLES F. (EDITOR)
1981 *Ethnic Change*. Publications on Ethnicity and Nationality of the School of International Studies Vol. 2. University of Washington, Seattle.

KITOV, ELIYAHU
1970 *The Book of Our Heritage: The Jewish Year and Its Days of Significance*. 3 vols. Phillip Feldheim, New York.

KLEIN, ISAAC
1979 *A Guide to Jewish Religious Practice*. Jewish Theological Seminary of America and KTAV Publishing House, New York.

KORN, BERTRAM WALLACE
1969 *The Early Jews of New Orleans*. American Jewish Historical Society, Waltham, Massachusetts.

LAMM, MAURICE
1969 *The Jewish Way in Death and Mourning*. Jonathan David, New York.

LEESER, ISAAC
1955 Comments (Excerpts from the *Occident*). In *Memoirs of American Jews 1775–1865*, vol. 2, edited by Jacob R. Marcus, pp. 60–82. Jewish Publishing Society of America, Philadelphia.

LEMASTER, CAROLYN GRAY
1983 The Jews of Arkansas. *Arkansas Times* 10(4):42–45, 82–90.

LIBO, KENNETH AND IRVING HOWE
1984 *We Lived There, Too: in Their Own Words and Pictures—Pioneer Jews and Westward Movement of America 1630–1930*. Marek/St. Martin's Press, New York.

MARCUS, JACOB R.
1970 *The Colonial American Jew 1492–1776*. 3 vols. Wayne State University Press, Detroit.
1980 *The American Jewish Woman 1654–1980*. KTAV Publishing House, New York.

MARCUS, JACOB R. (EDITOR)
1955 *Memoirs of American Jews 1775–1865*. 3 vols. Jewish Publishing Society of America, Philadelphia.

MAYER, LEOPOLD
1971 Recollections in 1850–1851. In *A Documentary History of the Jews in the United States 1654–1875*, edited by Morris U. Schappes, 3rd ed., pp. 306–312. Schocken Books, New York.

McEWAN, BONNIE G.
1985 Appendix B.: Faunal Analysis. In *Beneath the Border City*, edited by Edward Staski, pp. 262–287. University Museum Occasional Papers No. 13, New Mexico State University, University Park, New Mexico.

McGUIRE, RANDALL H.
1982 The Study of Ethnicity in Historical Archaeology. *Journal of Anthropological Archaeology* 1:159–178.
1983 Ethnic Group, Status, and Material Culture at the Rancho Punta de Agua. In *Forgotten Places and Things*, edited by Albert A. Ward, pp. 193–203. Center for Anthropological Studies, Contributions to Anthropological Studies No. 3, Albuquerque, New Mexico.

MEDEARIS, MARY (EDITOR)
1976 *Washington, Arkansas: History on the Southwest Trail*. Etter Printing Company, Hope, Arkansas.

MONTGOMERY, DONALD R.
1981 Documents Summary, Block 19, Washington, Arkansas. In *Block-Catts Historical Structure Report*, com- piled by Charles Witsell, Jr., pp. 1–92. Prepared for the Arkansas Division of Parks and Tourism, Little Rock.
1984 A History of Block 6 in Washington, Arkansas. Unpublished ms. in the Old Washington Research Report series, Old Washington Historic State Park, pp. 1–14. Washington, Arkansas.

PROCTOR, SAMUEL
1957 Jewish Life in New Orleans, 1718–1860. *Louisiana Historical Quarterly* 40(April):110–132.

RABINOWICZ, HARRY
1964 *Guide to Life: Jewish Laws and Customs of Mourning*. Jewish Chronicle Publications, London.
1972 Dietary Laws. In *Encyclopedia Judaica*, vol. 6, editors in chief Cecil Roth and Geoffrey Wigoder, pp. 26–45. Keter Publishing House, Jerusalem.

RAPHAEL, CHAIM
1972 *A Feast of History: Passover Through the Ages as a Key to Jewish Experience*. Simon and Schuster, New York.
1983 Jewish History and the Sephardim. *Commentary* 75(5): 39–44.

REITZ, ELIZABETH J.
1986 Urban/Rural Contrasts in Vertebrate Fauna from the Southern Atlantic Coastal Plain. *Historical Archaeology* 20(2):47–58.

REITZ, ELIZABETH J., AND DAN CORDIER
1983 Use of Allometry in Zooarchaeological Analysis. In *Animals and Archaeology 2: Shell Middens, Fishes, and Birds*, edited by C. Grigson and J. Clutton-Brock, pp. 237–252. British Archaeological Reports International Series 183, London.

REITZ, ELIZABETH J., I.R. QUITMEYER, H.S. HALE, S.J. SCUDDER, AND E.S. WING
1987 Application of Allometry to Zooarchaeology. *American Antiquity* 52(2):304–317.

REITZ, ELIZABETH J., AND BARBARA L. RUFF
1982 Cultural Ecology: Vertebrate Fauna. In *Historic Archeology: Data Recovery at the New Orleans General Hospital Site (160R69)*, pp. 162–179. R. Christopher Goodwin and Associates, New Orleans.

ROTH, CECIL, AND GEOFFREY WIGODER
1972 Sephardim. In *Encyclopedia Judaica*, editors in chief Cecil Roth and Geoffrey Wigoder, pp. 1164–1177. Keter Publishing House, Jerusalem.

RUFF, BARBARA L.
1985 *Analysis of the Vertebrate Fauna from Feature 14 (3HE236-19), Washington, Arkansas*. Report submitted to the Arkansas Archeological Survey, Fayetteville, Arkansas.

RUFF, BARBARA L., AND ELIZABETH J. REITZ
1984 Appendix 1: Vertebrate Fauna from Algier's Point. In

Archaeological Data Recovery from Algier's Point. 2 vols, pp. 207–260. Prepared for the Department of the Army, Corps of Engineers, New Orleans District, by R. Christopher Goodwin and Associates, Inc., New Orleans, Louisiana.

SCHAPPES, MORRIS U. (EDITOR)
1971 *A Documentary History of the Jews in the United States 1654–1875*. 3rd ed. Schocken Books, New York.

SCHUYLER, ROBERT L. (EDITOR)
1980 *Archaeological Perspectives on Ethnicity in America: Afro-American and Asian American Culture History*. Baywood Publishing Company, Farmingdale, New York.

SIEGEL, RICHARD, MICHAEL STRASSFELD, AND SHARON STRASSFELD
1973 *The Jewish Catalog*. Jewish Publishing Society of America, Philadelphia.

SOCIETY OF ISRAELITES
1971 Act to Incorporate a Society of Israelites, New Orleans, March 25, 1828. In *A Documentary History of the Jews in the United States 1654–1875*, edited by Morris U. Schappes, 3rd ed., pp. 179–180. Schocken Books, New York.

STEWART-ABERNATHY, LESLIE C.
1983 Urban Farmsteads in Washington, Arkansas: the Dynamics of Spatial and Chronological Patterning on Two House Lots from the Mid 1800s to the Present. Paper presented at the 16th annual meeting of the Society for Historical Archaeology, Denver, Colorado.
1985 The Block House Cellar. *Arkansas Archeological Society Field Notes* 203:9–11.
1986a Urban Farmsteads: Household Responsibilities in the City. *Historical Archaeology* 20(2):5–15.
1986b The Analysis of the Feature 14 Trash Deposit. Report in preparation, Arkansas Archeological Survey, Pine Bluff Station, Pine Bluff, Arkansas.

WEINSTEIN, JAY
1985 *A Collector's Guide to Judaica*. Thames and Hudson, London.

WILLIAMS, CHARLEAN MOSS
1951 *The Old Town Speaks: Washington, Hempstead County, Arkansas*. Anson Jones Press, Houston, Texas.

LESLIE C. STEWART-ABERNATHY
ARKANSAS ARCHEOLOGICAL SURVEY
UNIVERSITY OF ARKANSAS AT PINE BLUFF
P.O. BOX 136, UAPB
PINE BLUFF, AR 71601

BARBARA L. RUFF
DEPT. OF GEOLOGY
UNIVERSITY OF GEORGIA
ATHENS, GEORGIA 30602

BRIAN W. THOMAS

Inclusion and Exclusion in the Moravian Settlement in North Carolina, 1770–1790

ABSTRACT

The study of the late 18th-century Moravian community in Salem, North Carolina, provides an excellent opportunity to illustrate the value in looking beyond "boundedness" in historical archaeological research. Rather than viewing Salem as an isolated and homogenous community, this article focuses on the ways in which the leaders of this community struggled with conflicting needs. The Moravian leadership needed to balance the maintenance of group cohesion and internal social control with a need to appear as part of the larger Anglo-American world around them. How the Moravians confronted and mediated these conflicting needs is examined through the use of documentary information, the built environment, and archaeological material.

Introduction

Anthropologists have employed the concept of boundedness—implicitly if not explicitly—as an analytic tool in their research since the early part of this century. Recently, critiques of this concept have appeared in the anthropological literature (Southall 1970; Wolf 1982:6; Roseberry 1989:49–54; Steinberg 1989). The alternative view presented by these and other scholars emphasizes the need to examine the complexity of interaction that exists both within and between groups rather than viewing them as isolated entities. Historical archaeologists also can profit from this perspective, one that treats individuals and groups as interactive and engaged in the constant negotiation of internal and external relationships.

Many of the situations encountered by historical archaeologists (e.g., plantations, urban neighborhoods, and multiethnic mining districts) offer excellent opportunities to explore the means by which well-defined groups remained both distinct from, yet a part of, a larger community. Each group faced a unique set of circumstances and developed its own strategies in negotiating a balance between group cohesiveness and inclusion in a larger society. The material evidence of these strategies may be present in various forms, many of which can be recovered by archaeologists.

This article examines a classic example of a bounded society: the 18th-century Moravian community in Salem, North Carolina. Rather than employ the concept of boundedness to understand this group, this paper explores conflicting and contradictory needs faced by the leaders of Salem. For social and political reasons, the leaders needed to maintain control over the distinctive character of the Moravian community. At the same time, the Moravian leadership needed to present their community as part of the larger Anglo-American political structure. The dilemma that arose from these conflicting needs is the focus of this study—a focus that would not be possible by emphasizing the bounded nature of the Moravian community.

The Moravian leaders at Salem adopted a split but balanced approach to address their needs. It emphasized inclusion and exclusion, and was directed both internally and externally. The goal was to maintain internal social cohesion, yet protect the Moravians' special political status as an autonomous religious settlement within the broader social setting. Internally, the Moravian leadership used the social structure of the Church community, the built environment, mortuary practices, language, and the regulation of marriage to maintain social cohesion and exclude outsiders from their community. At times when it was politically beneficial, however, some of these practices were deemphasized to give the appearance of Moravian inclusion in the larger Anglo-American society.

The methods used here to address the Moravian practices of inclusion and exclusion include the examination of several lines of evidence. A combination of historical documents—primarily translations of official diaries, extant and documentary evidence of the built environment, and archaeological material are used to illustrate how the Moravian leaders reinforced group cohesion. This information also is used to examine the relationship between Salem and the Anglo-American town of

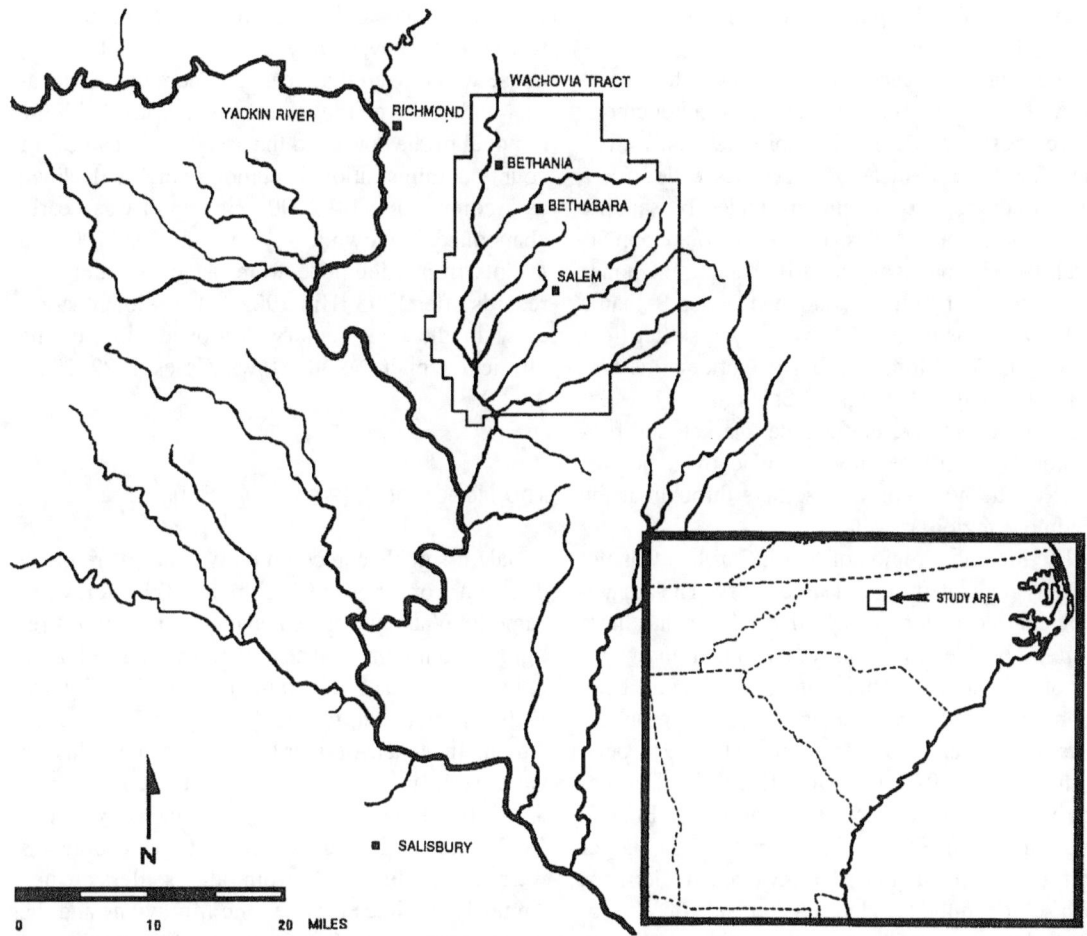

FIGURE 1. Map of study area showing Wachovia Tract (after Thorp 1989:31).

Richmond, the seat of Surry County from 1774 to 1789, to demonstrate how the Moravians balanced inclusion and exclusion externally.

The Moravian Settlement in North Carolina

The Moravians were a German-speaking religious group with a history dating to the early 15th century. In 1734 the Moravian Church obtained a land grant to settle in the Georgia colony; however, conflicts with the British colonists over objections to bearing arms forced the Moravians to abandon

this effort in 1740 (Fries 1905). Meanwhile, the Moravian Church had acquired land in Pennsylvania and began to build a series of towns there in the early 1740s. In 1753 the church purchased approximately 100,000 acres of land in the Piedmont of North Carolina from the Earl of Granville, one of the Lords Proprietors who held title to most of the lands of the North Carolina colony (Figure 1). The following year the Moravians sent a small group to North Carolina to begin the settlement of *Wachau*, or Wachovia, the name given by the Moravians to their tract of land. (For a detailed history of the Moravian Church and its colonial settlements, see

Clewell [1902], Hamilton and Hamilton [1967], Davis [1973], Thorp [1989].)

The Moravians came to Wachovia with one primary goal: to establish a successful, autonomous church-based settlement (Thorp 1986:42). The plan for the settlement of Wachovia called for a central congregation town surrounded by satellite agricultural communities (Hartley 1987). Upon arrival, the Moravians founded Bethabara, the house of passage, and built a second town called Bethania in 1759. It was not until 1767, 14 years after their arrival, that the Moravians began work on this central town, which they named Salem. By 1772, Salem had become the craft, trade, market, and professional center not only for Wachovia, but for most of the non-Moravian settlers throughout the Piedmont region as well.

The Piedmont region of North Carolina was not densely populated in the 18th century. The archaeological and historical records indicate that there were no Native American settlements in the vicinity of Wachovia by this date, most having been abandoned well before the arrival of European settlers to the area (J. Ned Woodall 1991, pers. comm.; Fries 1922–1930:vols.1, 2). The Europeans who settled this area were primarily English speaking, with Scots-Irish making up the larger part of the population. Non-Moravian Germans also settled in the area but lived outside of Wachovia and did not participate in the social or religious structure of the Moravian community.

The Town of Richmond

In 1771 the colonial government formed a new county out of the western lands of North Carolina. After a great deal of political maneuvering over the location of the county courthouse, it eventually was located on land 5 mi. northwest of the Wachovia tract, or approximately 20 mi. northwest of Salem (Figure 1). The settlement that grew up around the courthouse was called Richmond, the seat of Surry County. From its very beginnings in 1774, Richmond depended upon the court and its associated legal business for its existence. Richmond remained a viable community until 1789,

when the state took land from Surry County to form another new county. The Surry County courthouse was moved that year to a more central location within the county's new boundaries. With the removal of the court and the associated business of county administration, Richmond quickly declined as a community. By 1790, Richmond was nearly abandoned. No town lots were sold after 1790, and no lots from Richmond were listed in county tax records after 1793 (Hill 1982:15). A violent storm early in the next century destroyed most of the physical remains of the town (Fries 1922–1930, 2:649).

The Needs of Salem and Richmond

Salem's goals and community needs were much different from those of Richmond. The Moravians came to Wachovia to establish an autonomous religious community. They were recognized as a unique Protestant denomination in 1749 by the British Parliament, giving them special privileges. Among the tenets of their faith protected by this act were exclusions from having to take oaths, bear arms, or serve in any military capacity (Fries 1922–1930, 1:23). The fact that the Moravians were treated differently from other settlers created animosity at times between the Moravians and the Anglo-Americans. The failure of the colonization effort in Savannah, Georgia (1735–1740), in particular, created an awareness among the Moravians that the alienation of non-Moravian neighbors posed a significant impediment to establishing a successful Moravian settlement.

The turbulent political events of the late 18th century threatened the Moravian leadership's efforts to establish and maintain an autonomous community of believers. The threats to the community were both internal and external. Internally, the Moravian leadership faced increasing interaction between its congregation members and non-Moravian settlers. This contact had the potential to erode the tightly structured social order of the community. The Moravians were, since their arrival, an important element of commercial activity in the Piedmont; with the shortages and interruptions in commerce during the Revolutionary War period, this role became even more important. Contacts between Moravians and non-Moravians in the area increased, and hence were more difficult for the Moravian leadership to control. Externally, the Moravians were pressed with growing demands to provide men to fight in the war with Great Britain, a direct threat to Moravian autonomy.

Richmond and Salem played different roles in the Piedmont: Richmond functioned as a political center; Salem, as an economic one. Richmond was isolated from established trade connections due to the artificial, politically driven circumstances of its creation. This situation placed Salem in a position to fill the economic and commercial needs of the county seat. The Moravians relished the role of economic provider because it provided their community with financial resources. It also acted as a means by which Salem could transmit messages about itself to the surrounding communities. The messages sent by the Moravians assisted their leaders in their effort both to maintain the community's autonomy and to project an image of Moravian inclusion in the region.

Maintaining the Community

The Moravians needed to continue to distinguish themselves from the Anglo-American settlers and towns around them as part of the effort to preserve both the integrity of their community and the special privileges they enjoyed. By practicing inclusion—that is, enforcing social norms within the community—and excluding outsiders from these practices, the Moravian leadership continued to set Salem apart.

Methods for the maintenance of group integrity can be seen in several aspects of Moravian life. Perhaps the most important were the social divisions of the Moravian Church, which structured most community interaction in Salem. The congregation was divided into nine groups called choirs. Choirs formed the basic social unit for the church, with divisions based on gender, age, and marital status. Choir categories included Single Brethren, Single Sisters, Married Persons, Widowers, Wid-

ows, Older Boys, Older Girls, Little Boys, and Little Girls. Choirs were important in reinforcing the church's dominance in the personal lives of the congregation, as well as in the maintenance of gender roles in the community.

The Moravian Church also tightly regulated marriages within the community. The congregation's Elders' Conference, a group of senior male church leaders who oversaw the spiritual health of the community, influenced marriages by making recommendations about prospective mates. Marriage to a non-Moravian often resulted in sanctions or expulsion from the community. By overseeing marriages, the leaders attempted to ensure a homogenous and orderly society.

The Use of the Built Environment

The Moravians at Salem also set themselves apart from their neighbors through the use of the built environment. One of the many roles of the built environment is to communicate messages to individuals within and outside of a community (Leone 1977:44, 1978:195; Rapoport 1982; Anderson and Moore 1988:386). Frederick Marshall, the chief administrator of Wachovia during the establishment of Salem, articulated the connection between the physical layout of Salem and the reinforcement of Moravian social structures. In an official diary entry in 1765, he wrote:

> A congregation town differs from other congregations in that it is more like one family, where the religious and material condition of each member is known in detail, where each person receives the appropriate Choir oversight, and also the assistance in consecrating the daily life. This must be considered in deciding the form of the Town Plan (Fries 1922–1930, 1:313).

The size of the town lots, for example, was one of the important considerations in the town planning. If the town lots were too large, and the town too spread out, the residents could "not be so well supervised by the Ministers and other Congregation officers" (Marshall 1765, cited in Fries 1922–1930, 1:314).

Along with the placement and arrangement of domestic dwellings, public buildings were also an important consideration for the Moravians in the planning of Salem. Salem was designed with a central square, dominated by congregation buildings on the opposite sides of the streets facing the square (Figure 2). This town plan followed the Moravian pattern seen in European towns and in Pennsylvania (Murtagh 1967:10). The architectural tradition of these buildings clearly reflected the Germanic heritage of the Moravians, as indicated in Figures 3 and 4. Congregation buildings such as the Single Brothers' House—built in 1769—and the *Gemeinhaus,* or congregation hall—built in 1771, were half-timbered structures, a tradition reaching back into medieval central Europe (Murtagh 1967:113–117). These structures were important, particularly in Salem's early years, in maintaining a sense of community among Moravians by visually reinforcing the organization of the social structure (Anderson and Moore 1988: 386).

An interesting transition, however, began to occur architecturally in Salem as the 19th century approached. While typically Moravian traits continued to be visible, buildings erected in the mid-1780s increasingly displayed architectural elements clearly belonging to the English tradition of the colonies (Murtagh 1967:118, 124–127). The changes in architecture may reflect a conscious suppression of certain visible signs of group identity, acting to minimize differences between Moravians and their Anglo-American neighbors. A similar trend has been noted among Rhenish immigrants in the Shenandoah Valley of Virginia (Chappell 1980), suggesting that other distinct groups in the region also saw some benefit in de-emphasizing their differences from the Anglo-Americans around them.

Salem established a tavern in its early years to accommodate visitors to the town. The fact that it was one of the first buildings planned indicates its importance to the Moravian leaders. The tavern at Salem was removed from the center of town, placed on its southern outskirts. By locating it on the town's periphery, Salem leaders were able to limit communication and interaction between residents and visitors.

Court records indicate that Richmond had four taverns located within its borders, a clear sign of how much more open its social life was in comparison to Salem. As a town that revolved around the court and its associated steady flow of visitors conducting legal, political, and military business, the presence of four taverns is not surprising. However, visitors were also important to the economy of Salem. Both towns benefited significantly from the business brought by outsiders: while Richmond opened itself to them, Salem attempted to keep them at arm's length.

Mortuary practices also participated in the design and implementation of Salem's inclusion/exclusion dichotomy. The Moravian cemetery at Salem, known as God's Acre, played an important role in reinforcing the community's ideology. The location of the burial plot, its physical layout, and the manner in which individuals were interred all reinforced Moravian social structure and excluded non-Moravians.

The location for God's Acre at Salem was chosen very early in the planning process for the town—12 April 1766, the same day that the location for the main square was selected (Fries 1922–1930, 1:326). Following the Moravian tradition, the cemetery was located directly adjacent to the town. Unlike in Anglo-American cemeteries, families were not buried together. Rather, the social structure of the congregation, defined by choir membership, was the social unit for interment.

A second unique characteristic of the cemetery is the gravestones. No distinction is made between individuals through the use of ornate or unique grave markers. All markers are uniform. They consist of rectilinear gravestones with simple, standardized inscriptions bearing the name of the individual, place of birth, date of birth and death, and age (Figure 5). The stones are set flush with the ground at the head of the burial (Figure 6), rather than standing upright as in the British tradition. The graves seem to tell the observer that this is a community of equals, where no distinctions are made. This is clearly the message that the Moravian Church preached to its living members, that they were a community of Christians, equals before God. The mortuary practices of the Moravians reinforced this notion.

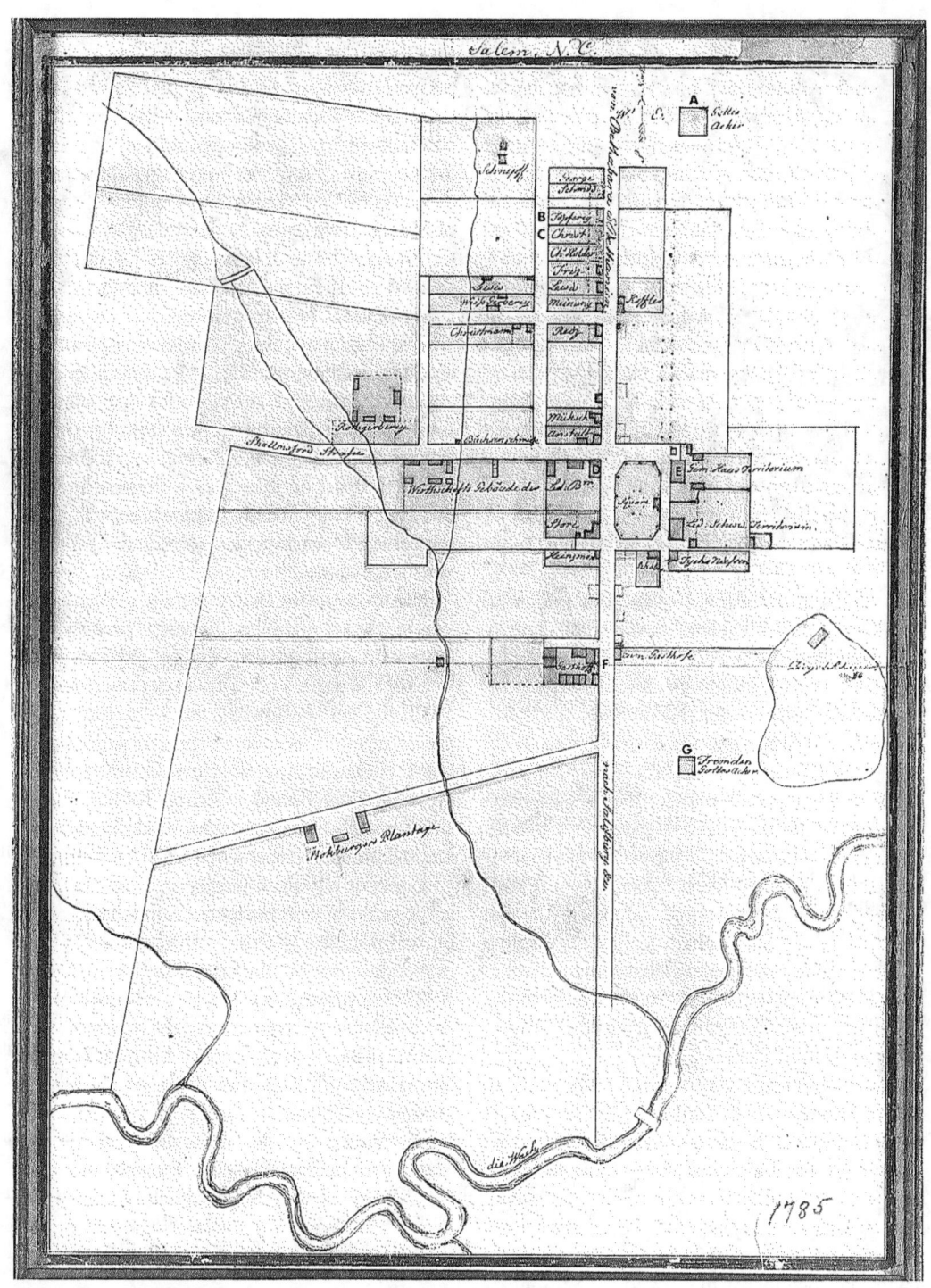

FIGURE 2. Map of Salem in 1785: *A*, God's Acre; *B*, Pottery; *C*, Fifth House; *D*, Single Brothers' House; *E*, *Gemeinhaus*; *F*, Tavern; *G*, Strangers' Graveyard. (Courtesy of Old Salem Inc., Winston-Salem, North Carolina.)

FIGURE 3. Single Brothers' House as it appears restored. (Courtesy of Old Salem Inc., Winston-Salem, North Carolina.)

Outsiders were rarely granted admission into the Moravian community, and this exclusion is reflected in the burial ground as well. In 1773 Salem was faced with the need to bury a visitor who had died while in the town. Rather than open God's Acre to outsiders, they established a separate cemetery for non-Moravians:

> There is no Graveyard near Salem except our God's Acre, so the Vestry has resolved to open a Parish Burying Ground below Salem, which shall be as decently kept as our own God's Acre above Salem. . . . The Parish Graveyard for Salem will be laid out on a hill near the road between the Sisters' House and Tavern meadows. In digging the graves, no difference will be made as to age or sex (Marshall 1773, cited in Fries 1922–1930, 2:771).

As with the location of the Tavern, the Strangers' Graveyard, as it was called, was in a location removed from town. This acted literally and symbolically to reinforce the separation of the Salem community from its non-Moravian neighbors.

Public ritual centered on God's Acre further maintained group cohesion and reinforced differences between the Moravian community and its neighbors. One example is the Easter ritual practiced by Moravians. Early each Easter morning the congregation would be awakened by the sound of horns and trumpets and gather at the *Gemein Saal,* the meetinghouse used for church services. A procession would follow to God's Acre, for an Easter liturgy. This custom was unique in the Piedmont, and from the Moravians' earliest days in Wachovia it attracted the attention of settlers nearby. The Bethabara Diary in 1762 describes this interest:

> An explanation was given in English (at the Easter Service), to the strangers present, telling them the grounds and reason for our procession to the graveyard and our liturgy there; for

Perspectives from *Historical Archaeology*

FIGURE 4. Fourth House, photographed in 1967. (Courtesy of Old Salem Inc., Winston-Salem, North Carolina.)

certain remarkable reports have been spread about it, for instance that we open the graves and wake the dead with our trumpets (Fries 1922–1930, 1:245).

The curiosity of Salem's non-Moravian neighbors about this ritual continued to be strong. According to a Salem Diary entry for 18 April 1778 (in Fries 1922–1930, 3:1228), Salem was besieged by visitors, "so many they camped in the neighboring bush," arriving in the evening on Easter Sabbath to observe the Moravians in their march to the cemetery.

The Easter procession to God's Acre was a public ritual in which only the members of the Moravian community participated. The uniqueness of the ritual, and the fact that it received such attention from non-Moravian settlers in the area, made this a particularly effective means of communicating exclusion from the Moravian community to these visitors.

Language

Another means by which the Moravian leadership balanced inclusion and exclusion was through the use of language. Language set the towns of Richmond and Salem apart. The Moravians were German speakers, and German was the official lan-

FIGURE 5. Moravian headstone at God's Acre, Salem.

FIGURE 6. God's Acre, the Moravian burial ground at Salem.

guage of the Moravian Church. The residents of Richmond, on the other hand, spoke English. To balance the conflicting needs of their community, the Moravian leaders adopted a two-fold strategy: they used language differences to restrict interaction, while at other times they eased communication through bilingual community leaders.

The Moravians consciously used language differences to exclude outsiders and maintain internal control. One method of achieving this goal was to censor views to which their residents were exposed, effectively controlling what opinions might be formed. An entry in the Wachovia Diary illustrates this point. In March 1776, in the midst of the Revolutionary War, "a Presbyterian minister from the Jerseys," who "had been commissioned by the

Continental Congress to explain the causes of the strife with England," asked to speak to the residents of Salem. According to the Salem Diary for 1 March 1776 (in Fries 1922–1930, 3:1054), rather than allow the minister to address their people, the Moravian leaders told him that most of the residents were German and that they would not understand him. Apparently, no offer to translate was made.

The Moravians, however, often made an effort to deemphasize language barriers and encourage communication, particularly when dealing with key individuals. During Governor Tryon's visit to Wachovia in 1767, for example, the Wachovia Diary entry states that one of the Brethren held the service, "speaking in English, with well-chosen words, on the Text for the day" (Fries 1922–1930, 1:354). In the midst of the Revolutionary War, Lord Cornwallis and Governor Josiah Martin, the last royal governor of North Carolina, were received by Moravians Frederick Marshall and Traugott Bagge as the British marched through Wachovia. These Moravian leaders were both fluent in English. In such contexts, both acted as cultural brokers for this encounter; that is, as individuals who translated between the idioms of two segments of society (Wells 1990:181). In this capacity they acted as mediators of a politically valuable commodity: good will. They not only facilitated communication because of their knowledge of English, but also expressed the Moravian character in a way that left a favorable impression in the minds of their visitors. The Moravian leaders were always eager to facilitate intercourse with individuals who were in a position to influence the special privileges that the Moravians enjoyed as a semi-autonomous religious settlement. Historical documents make it clear that these targeted individuals included the leaders of Richmond.

Regional Inclusion and Exclusion

The strategy of inclusion and exclusion was practiced on another level by the Moravian leadership. Along with internal considerations, the Moravians needed to demonstrate Salem's inclusion in the larger society. At the same time, however, they needed to exclude themselves from aspects of that society which conflicted with their goals as a distinct community. Richmond, seat of political power in the region, was the principal target of this inclusion/exclusion strategy. Because the political establishment at Richmond was capable of influencing which special privileges the Moravians could exercise, the Moravians sought to demonstrate inclusiveness with Richmond and the broader Anglo-American society. They accomplished this in two ways: by being the primary market for Anglo-American settlers in the region, and by deemphasizing cultural differences and maintaining positive relations with key Anglo-American leaders.

Ceramics

Salem was the center of trade in the Piedmont region. Its economic status allowed Moravian leaders to transmit messages of inclusion, directed primarily at Richmond. A study of the ceramics recovered archaeologically from Richmond and Salem demonstrates how this signalling of inclusion took place through commerce. It also shows that, despite these inclusive messages, the residents of Salem were not full participants in the larger Anglo-American regional community.

Wake Forest University conducted field work at the Richmond site between 1973 and 1987. This work is partially reported in Robertson (1985). Over 4,900 individual sherds were recovered and examined for this study. Stanley South and Garry Wheeler Stone recovered the material from Salem through excavations at the Fifth House site in 1968 and 1969. While no formal final report was published on the work, Stone prepared a summary of the work which was later appended to South's (1972) "Discovery in Wachovia."

All sherds were initially sorted and categorized by standard types. These types are based on those developed by Noël Hume (1991[1969]) for imported British ceramics and Clauser (1978) for Moravian ceramics. For purposes of this analysis, ceramics were then placed into three categories: (1) Moravian-produced ceramics of Moravian de-

FIGURE 7. Slip-decorated redware plate attributed to Gottfried Aust, circa 1780. Diameter is 12 9/16 in. (Courtesy of the Wachovia Historical Society, Winston-Salem, North Carolina.)

sign (Local); (2) Moravian-produced ceramics of British design (British Copies); and (3) imported British ceramics (Imported).

The Moravians had accomplished potters who produced a wide range of ceramics, from simple utilitarian vessels to highly decorated tablewares (Figure 7). After 1774 their products included copies of certain British ceramic styles, including Whieldon ware, Tortoise-shell ware, and Queensware (Figure 8). Along with these locally produced items, the Moravians continually ordered stocks of British imported ceramics for sale at their town store.

Imported sherds that were not of British origin (e.g., Chinese porcelain) were excluded from the analysis. When a sherd could not be classified by type because of severe degradation of the sherd's surface treatment, it was categorized as unidentifiable. In nearly all cases it was possible to determine, based on an examination of paste and/or morphology, whether a sherd was a local product or an import (Clauser 1978). Overall, 72.8 percent (60.5% of Local and British Copies and 92% of Imported) of the sherds could be identified. Only these sherds were used for the analysis.

Due to the small size and generally poor condition of much of the ceramic material, particularly

FIGURE 8. Potter's mold for Queensware plate. Diameter is 8 ¾ in. (Courtesy of the Wachovia Historical Society, Winston-Salem, North Carolina.)

that from Richmond, sherd counts were used rather than vessel counts. Fragments which were determined to be part of the same larger piece were combined and counted as a single sherd.

The chronology at the Fifth House is separated into four periods (Stone 1974), only the first two of which are of concern in this study. Period I covers the construction of the Fifth House and the subsequent use of the house and lot during Gottfried Aust's tenure as Master Potter, from 1771 until his death in 1788. Period II corresponds with the activities at the Fifth House during Rudolph Christ's occupation of the pottery, 1789–1821. Periods III and IV cover the years 1821–1860 and 1860–1910, respectively.

The Fifth House served a number of roles during periods I and II, many of which were tied to the Salem Pottery next door. A small kiln was built on the back of the Fifth House property in the early 1790s. The yard area also had been used at various times for ceramic storage (1778–1780, 1789–1792) and for the storage of the pottery's wood stocks (1779–1782). The Fifth House itself served as a residence for Ludwig Meiner (1767–1776) and for Rudolph Christ (1780–1786). From 1786 to 1812 the house was used as congregational housing, and from 1812 to 1821 it was used as the residence of John Holland, the senior journeyman.

Because of the site's nearness to the pottery, some of the deposits recovered from the Fifth House represent activity of the pottery operation. During analysis, distinctions were made between deposits representing ceramic production (e.g., waster and other kiln-associated deposits) and those attributed to the occupational phases of the property. Thomas (1991) discusses this process.

The results of the ceramic analysis illuminate clear differences in the distribution of ceramic categories from Richmond and Salem. Table 1 shows the count and relative frequencies of the sherds recovered from the two sites. The identifiable ceramics recovered at Richmond consisted of 58 percent British styles (49% imported British ceramics and 9% British copies). Salem, by comparison, had only 21 percent British styles.

To understand the significance of these differences with respect to Salem's strategy of inclusion, it is helpful to discuss Salem's role in the ceramics trade. It is well documented that Salem was the economic cynosure of the Piedmont region. From their earliest days in Wachovia, prior to the establishment of Salem, the Moravians established an extensive network of trade with their neighbors. The Bethabara Diary recorded in 1768: "people came from Haw River, Orange County, bringing 50 bushels of wheat to exchange for pottery" (Fries 1922–1930, 1:380). An entry from Bethabara, dated May 1770, noted that visitors came from "sixty or eighty miles, to buy milk crocks and pans in our pottery. They bought the entire stock, not one piece was left; many could only get half they wanted, and others, who came too late, could find none" (Fries 1922–1930, 1:412).

Salem was originally designed as a town that provided craft specialization and professional services for the outlying Moravian congregations in return for agricultural and other subsistence products. In practice, Salem also operated in this capacity for non-Moravian settlements well outside of the Wachovia tract. The Moravians participated in an extensive trade network, bringing in imported goods and other hard-to-find commodities from Charleston. These goods often were in demand among their Anglo-American neighbors. To obtain these goods, Moravians paid in cash or traded local

Perspectives from *Historical Archaeology*

TABLE 1
RELATIVE PERCENTAGES OF IDENTIFIABLE
CERAMICS FROM RICHMOND AND SALEM*

Ceramic Type	Richmond N	%	Salem N	%
Moravian Styles	1,475	42	592	79
British Copies	334	9	22	3
Imported	1,736	49	138	18
Total	3,545	100	752	100

*$X^2 = 343.9$, df 2, $p<.001$

products that they acquired from their neighbors (e.g., deer skins and tobacco).

Imported British ceramics were one of the products in demand by Salem's neighbors. The supply of these wares, however, was not reliable. Faced with this problem, the Moravian leadership decided to begin producing copies of certain British ceramics in 1774. The stimulus for making British copies was economic, since these were intended for sale to non-Moravian settlers, rather than a reflection of changing tastes in the Moravian community. Frederick Marshall's report to the Unity's Elders Conference, dated December 1773, discussed disruptions in trade with Charleston and the relatively new trading center of Cross Creek. He described the poor assortment of goods from which to select, and stated, "It looks as though it would soon be necessary to make the English Queensware and Tortoise-shell, that is, a fine pottery resembling porcelain" (Fries 1922–1930, 2:762). The Moravians clearly serviced an established market for these products, and it is evident from the ceramic analysis that Richmond was an important component of that market.

One conclusion of this analysis is that the differences observed in the ceramic distribution reflect a conscious Moravian effort to communicate inclusion with towns such as Richmond. By producing and importing British ceramics, Salem transmitted the message that it ostensibly participated in the symbolic world of the British. They supplied the area with a source for British ceramics. When disruptions in trade threatened the sup-

ply of these products, Salem took steps to fill the demand with locally produced copies of British styles. However, despite the projection of this message outside of its borders, the small percentage of imported ceramics recovered from the Fifth House suggests that the Moravian community did not participate in the British world.

Discussion

The political and economic realities of life during the late 18th century were key factors in the relationship between Richmond and Salem. Salem's success as the market center of the region was in large part due to the tight control that the church exerted over the social and economic life of the community. Throughout the period, Salem remained secure economically, but it also had certain needs that it was unable to provide for itself. The Moravians had one paramount goal: the establishment and preservation of a successful, autonomous Moravian community. This goal is manifested in the internal controls of Moravian society and guided its relationships with non-Moravians. The purchase of Wachovia, the eventual establishment of Salem, and the practices of exclusion were driven by this goal. However, to maintain an autonomous community, the Moravians were dependent on the good will of the colonial, and later state, political structures, dominated by the British or Anglo-Americans. Without the continuing good will of government leaders, the privileges that the Moravians enjoyed as a church could be revoked, making it impossible for their community to function according to its principles and beliefs.

The Revolutionary War had a tremendous impact on the Piedmont region. It disrupted trade at the same time that great demands were being placed upon resources to support military activity. It created an atmosphere of political insecurity, with settlers in the region divided over the conflict. Richmond clearly sided with the forces of independence. As the location of the political and military leadership for the region, Richmond was responsible for mustering and supporting a militia regiment. To accomplish the needed provisioning, they turned to the economic resources of Salem.

The political upheaval associated with the Revolutionary War period was also of great concern to the Moravian community. The Moravian Church had no quarrel with England; yet, it was possible that a change in the political structure of the colony was at hand. As a result, Salem tried to steer a course that was noncommittal. Wanting to avoid the impression of favoring either side, residents were advised to keep their individual opinions to themselves: "Warning was given that in view of the constantly increasing unrest in the land, and the constant coming and going of strangers, bringing all kinds of reports, it was necessary to be very careful in speech, and best to be silent" (Minutes from Salem's Helfer Conferenz, 5 February 1776, in Fries 1922–1930, 3:1082). Furthermore, the potential loss of their exemption from having to bear arms threatened Moravian autonomy. Because the leaders in Richmond were in a position to affect this privilege, Salem's leaders were eager to nurture and maintain a good relationship with the county's political leadership.

As a consequence, a unique relationship developed between Richmond and Salem. Richmond took advantage of Salem's economic strength as the demands for war supplies increased. In return, the Richmond leadership was in favor of granting Moravians exemptions from mustering requirements, either outright or through the payment of substitute fees. They did this at a local level, often without the consent of state authorities.

The Moravian leaders clearly saw the need to keep their community geographically and, more importantly, socially distinct from the Anglo-American settlers around them. They accomplished this by carefully balancing the inward focus of their population against the selective exclusion of outsiders from it. The exclusionary practices of the Moravians had external value as well, for there were practical political reasons to maintain these distinctions. And yet, as they had learned from their experience in Georgia, to demonstrate the separateness of their community too clearly led to the alienation of the non-Moravian settlers and, ultimately, to the failure of their set-

tlement. This was the dilemma that the Moravian leadership faced. Their response was to adopt a strategy of reinforcing internal conformity and values, while masking or obfuscating some of these exclusionary practices from the outside world. This strategy balanced the Moravians' needs as a unique social and cultural group with the realities of their political existence as a distinct segment within a broader homogenous society. Through it, Salem was able to achieve specific social and political goals which were designed to protect the political, economic, and social autonomy they regarded as paramount to the success of their settlement.

Conclusion

This case study has illustrated the value of using an approach that explores the complex web of relationships and needs faced by putatively bounded groups. It has focused on the conflicting needs of Salem's leaders and the strategy of inclusion and exclusion adopted by these leaders to balance these needs. By refusing to view Salem as an isolated community, one is able to discern the contradictory needs with which it was faced. Salem's leaders sought to balance their control over the character of their community with the recognition that they were situated in a larger social, political, and economic context. The actions that these leaders took to control their relationship with Richmond can be seen as part of a larger strategy aimed at the reproduction of their community.

The efforts of Salem's leadership certainly did not end after 1790. However, after the turn of the century an entirely new set of social, political, and economic circumstances was present. There are indications that Moravian leaders were losing the ability to control the changes that were taking place within their community into the 19th century. Official diary entries indicate growing difficulties in maintaining the unique character of the Moravian community. Materially, these changes can be seen in Moravian architecture, which increasingly moved away from its Germanic heritage. By the 1830s, the exterior of buildings in Salem almost completely reflected the English tradition

(Murtagh 1967:127). In 1815 the Moravians lost their exemption from bearing arms during times of war, and in 1831 lost this exemption altogether. It has been observed that by 1856 the Moravians essentially had been "absorbed into the life-style of the Carolina Piedmont" (Hammond 1989:38).

ACKNOWLEDGMENTS

I would like to express my gratitude to Randy McGuire, Larry McKee, and Larissa Thomas for their thoughtful and helpful comments on previous drafts of this paper. I would also like to thank Ned Woodall and Dave Weaver at Wake Forest University and Paula Locklair of Old Salem Inc. for their support and assistance in this research. The material from Richmond is curated by the Archeology Laboratories, Department of Anthropology, Wake Forest University. Field notes from the Fifth House excavations were made available by the Office of State Archaeology, North Carolina Department of Cultural Resources. Old Salem Inc. and the Museum of Early Southern Decorative Arts are curating the material recovered from the Fifth House site and graciously made it available.

REFERENCES

ANDERSON, TEXAS B., AND ROGER G. MOORE
1988 Meaning and the Built Environment: A Symbolic Analysis of a 19th-Century Urban Site. In *The Recovery of Meaning*, edited by Mark P. Leone and Parker B. Potter, Jr., pp. 379–406. Smithsonian Institution Press, Washington, D.C.

CHAPPELL, EDWARD A.
1980 Acculturation in the Shenandoah Valley: Rhenish Houses of the Massanutten Settlement. *Proceedings of the American Philosophical Society* 124(1):55–89.

CLAUSER, JOHN W., JR.
1978 The Excavation of the Bethabara Pottery Kiln: An Analysis of Nineteenth Century Potting Techniques. Unpublished M.A. thesis, Department of Anthropology, University of Florida, Gainesville.

CLEWELL, JOHN HENRY
1902 *History of Wachovia in North Carolina*. Doubleday, New York.

DAVIS, CHESTER S.
1973 *Hidden Seed and Harvest: A History of the Moravians*. Winston Printing Company, Winston-Salem, North Carolina.

FRIES, ADELAIDE L.
1905 *The Moravians in Georgia*. Edwards and Broughton, Raleigh, North Carolina.

FRIES, ADELAIDE L. (EDITOR)
1922– *Records of the Moravians in North Carolina*. Four
1930 volumes. Edwards and Broughton, Raleigh, North Carolina.

HAMILTON, J. TAYLOR, AND KENNETH G. HAMILTON
1967 *History of the Moravian Church: The Renewed Unitas Fratrum, 1722–1957*. Interprovincial Board of Christian Education, Moravian Church of America, Bethlehem, Pennsylvania.

HAMMOND, MICHAEL
1989 New Light on Old Salem. *Archaeology* 42(6):36–41.

HARTLEY, MICHAEL O.
1987 Wachovia in Forsyth. Manuscript on file, Old Salem Inc., Winston-Salem, North Carolina.

HILL, MICHAEL
1982 Historical Research Report: The Old Richmond Courthouse and the Lost Town of Richmond. Manuscript on file, North Carolina Department of Archives and History, Raleigh.

LEONE, MARK P.
1977 The New Mormon Temple in Washington, D.C. In Historical Archaeology and the Importance of Material Things, edited by Leland Ferguson. *Special Publication Series* No. 2:43–61. Society for Historical Archaeology, California, Pennsylvania.
1978 Archaeology as the Science of Technology: Mormon Town Plans and Fences. In *Historical Archaeology: A Guide to Substantive and Theoretical Contributions*, edited by Robert L. Schuyler, pp. 191–200. Baywood, Farmingdale, New York.

MURTAGH, WILLIAM J.
1967 *Moravian Architecture and Town Planning*. University of North Carolina Press, Chapel Hill.

NOËL HUME, IVOR
1991 *A Guide to Artifacts of Colonial America*. Reprint of 1969 edition. Vintage Press, New York.

RAPOPORT, AMOS
1982 *The Meaning of the Built Environment*. Sage, Beverly Hills, California.

ROBERTSON, BEN P.
1985 An Interim Report on the Excavations at Richmond (31FY230). Manuscript on file, Archeology Laboratories, Department of Anthropology, Wake Forest University, Winston-Salem, North Carolina.

ROSEBERRY, WILLIAM
1989 *Anthropologies and Histories: Essays in Culture, History, and Political Economy*. Rutgers University Press, New Brunswick, New Jersey.

SOUTH, STANLEY
1972 Discovery in Wachovia. Manuscript on file, Old Salem Inc., Winston-Salem, North Carolina.

SOUTHALL, AIDAN W.
1970 The Illusion of Tribe. *Journal of Asian and African Studies* 5:28–50.

STEINBERG, STEPHEN
1989 *The Ethnic Myth: Race, Ethnicity, and Class in America.* Beacon Press, Boston, Massachusetts.

STONE, GARRY WHEELER
1974 Excavations at the Fifth House, Lot 49, Old Salem, North Carolina. In Discovery in Wachovia, by Stanley South, pp. 208–241. Manuscript on file, Old Salem Inc., Winston-Salem, North Carolina.

THOMAS, BRIAN W.
1991 Historical Archaeology and Ethnicity in the North Carolina Piedmont: The Role of Ethnic Boundaries in the Towns of Richmond and Salem, circa 1790. Unpublished M.A. thesis, Department of Anthropology, Wake Forest University, Winston-Salem, North Carolina.

THORP, DANIEL B.
1986 Assimilation in North Carolina's Moravian Community. *Journal of Southern History* 52(1):19–42.

1989 *The Moravian Community in Colonial North Carolina: Pluralism on the Southern Frontier.* University of Tennessee Press, Knoxville.

WELLS, MIRIAM J.
1990 Brokerage, Economic Opportunity, and the Growth of Ethnic Movements. In *American Culture: Essays on the Familiar and Unfamiliar,* edited by Leonard Plotnicov, pp. 179–195. University of Pittsburgh Press, Pittsburgh, Pennsylvania.

WOLF, ERIC R.
1982 *Europe and the People without History.* University of California Press, Berkeley.

BRIAN W. THOMAS
DEPARTMENT OF ANTHROPOLOGY
STATE UNIVERSITY OF NEW YORK AT BINGHAMTON
BINGHAMTON, NEW YORK 13902

Jane Lydon

Imagining the Moravian Mission: Space and Surveillance at the Former Ebenezer Mission, Victoria, Southeastern Australia

ABSTRACT

Colonization of Australia was shaped by a culturally specific, imagined geography that entailed a precise conception of what the indigenous landscape and its people were to become. In establishing a system of Aboriginal reserves in the southeastern colony of Victoria around 1860, this European worldview was expressed in the creation of didactic landscapes, designed to teach Aboriginal residents how to live like white people. Archaeological investigation of the former Ebenezer Mission, in northwestern Victoria, demonstrates how Moravian missionaries sought to establish a paternalistic relationship with the indigenous people, expressed through spatio-visual organization and embodied practices. This program was successfully inaugurated, as indicated by evidence for the settlement's landscaping and for the function of the mission-house, especially in its role as hub and contact place, its central and commanding position, its regular extension and rebuilding, and the operation of European systems of domesticity within it. The missionaries' apparent success in controlling aspects of mission-house operation must be viewed, however, in the context of the uncertainties and difficulties their evangelical program encountered as well as of Aboriginal strategies of mobility and evasion that undermined the spatial apparatus of the reserves.

Introduction

Colonization of Australia was shaped by a culturally specific, imagined geography that entailed precise conceptions of what the indigenous landscape and its people were to become. In establishing a system of Aboriginal reserves in the southeastern colony of Victoria around 1860, this European worldview prompted the creation of idealized landscapes that were intended to teach through example and performance, their success measurable through visual inspection. Central to the administration's conception of these settlements, and to its vision for the Aboriginal people of Victoria, was a reformed gender and class order that would appropriately locate the indigenous population within modern settler society. Archaeological investigation of the former Ebenezer Mission, near Dimboola, in Victoria, southeastern Australia (Figure 1), explores the disjunction between missionaries' attempts to create an idealized didactic landscape that would inculcate order among the residents and the actual complexity of Aboriginal-European cultural exchange.

The Moravians in Port Phillip

Beginning in 1835, rapid pastoralist expansion through the Port Phillip District (now the state of Victoria) wreaked havoc upon indigenous society. By the late 1850s, humanitarian concern prompted the colonial government to establish a Central Board for the Protection of the Aborigines that would manage six Aboriginal reserves designed to protect and "civilize" the surviving indigenous population. Moravian missionaries established Ebenezer Mission in 1859 (following the earlier failure of a station at Lake Boga, also in Victoria), and its success in converting the colony's first Aboriginal person (Nathaniel Pepper) to Christianity was widely lauded. The Moravian Church, based in Saxony, had by this period become a global force, influencing the course of English Protestant evangelicalism, and the new British missionary societies of the late-18th century modeled themselves upon its example (Edwards 1999:31; Mason 2001:16). Moravian faith was founded in a tradition of persecution, and to an extent, the members saw themselves as outsiders and believers in unpopular truths, prepared to withstand great hardship to pursue their beliefs. Originating in Moravia, a province of what is now the Czech Republic, in the early-15th century, the faith's founder Jan Hus preached church reform. He consequently suffered excommunication and was burned at the stake in 1415. Hus's followers established the Moravian Church (known as the Unitas Fratrum) in 1457, eventually finding refuge on the estate of Count Nicholas von Zinzendorf in 1722, where they established their headquarters, Herrnhut.

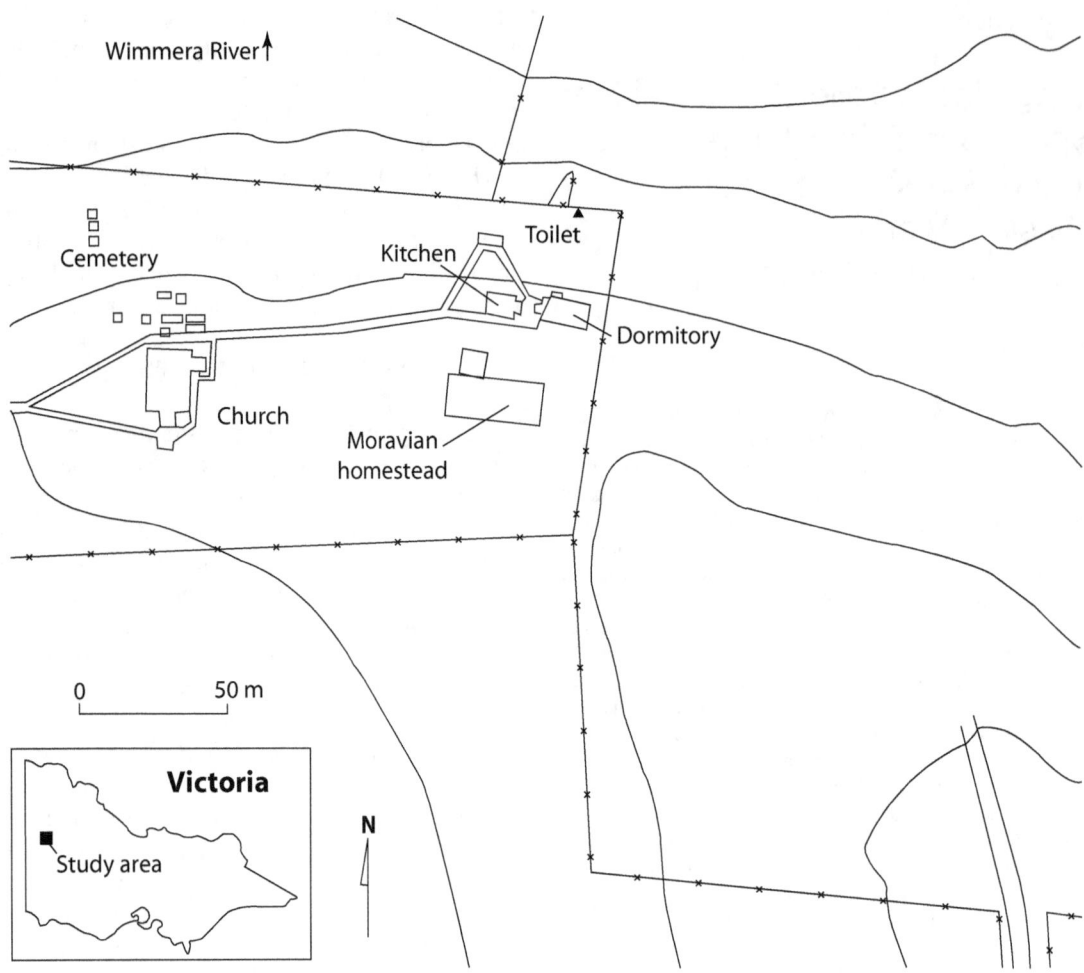

FIGURE 1. Location plan showing Ebenezer Mission, Victoria, Australia. (Drawing by Wei Ming, 2001.)

When an Australian fund was established in 1844 to "go to the most remote, unfavourable, and neglected parts of the surface of the earth," a group of young Moravians was motivated to form an Australian Association to pray for "these poor outcasts of the great human family" (Church of the United Brethren 1849:156). The Moravians were assigned a particularly privileged role in official attempts to protect the Aboriginal people of the Port Phillip District, largely due to the efforts of Governor Charles Joseph La Trobe, a member of the British Moravian Church's most prominent family (Kenny 2003; Mason 2003). In addition, the Moravian Church's long evangelist tradition, its reputation as a useful colonizing tool, and widespread perceptions of its local success at Ebenezer and its other Victorian mission, Ramahyuck, contributed to the considerable influence the church exerted over colonial Aboriginal policy.

Ebenezer

The site of Ebenezer was established on a major ceremonial ground, known to the local Aboriginal people as Bunyo-budnutt. The traditional owners of this area were Wergaia speakers who comprised at least four distinct dialect groups (Clark 1990:20), and the group upon whose land Ebenezer was established was called the Wotjobaluk (Howitt 1904:54; Clark 1990:358). Ebenezer was the first Victorian mission to develop a strong relationship with the indigenous occupants, in part due to the early religious conversion of Nathaniel and Phillip Pepper (Pepper and De Araugo 1980; Mulvaney

1989); however, traditional social customs and language were preserved to a greater extent than at other reserves (Kamminga and Grist 2000:38). The attitude of the Moravians toward the indigenous people with whom they worked was relatively egalitarian, at least at first. Detailed accounts of the Lake Hindmarsh Reserve reservation history and the development of the mission settlement are provided by Marie Fels (1998) and du Cros and Associates (1997).

The settlement fluctuated in size from around 67 in 1876 (Board for the Protection of the Aborigines in the Colony of Victoria [BPA] 1876:2) to 101 in 1882 (BPA 1882:2), as many came and went as they wished. As for all the Victorian stations, the passing of the 1886 Aborigines Protection Law Amendment Act, requiring all Aboriginal people of part-European parentage and their spouses leave the reserves, effectively marked the beginning of the end for Ebenezer (Broome 1994:82). By 1890, only 35 residents remained (Clark 1990:348), and the BPA returned all land along the west side of the Wimmera to the Lands Department in October 1900. The mission was closed in 1904 when the Lake Hindmarsh Act threw open the reserve for license, lease, or perpetual lease, and many residents moved to the nearby Antwerp Aboriginal Reserve (Fels 1998:9–10). Despite a lack of official involvement with the site, many Aboriginal families maintained their connections to the site into the present (Rhodes 1998:30). Moravian descendants such as the Whitehead family also maintain links with the site. Moravians believed that they were helping indigenous peoples by converting them to Christianity, yet despite their good intentions and although Victoria's Aboriginal reserves acted as refuges from the worst effects of invasion, Moravians are sometimes resented today by Aboriginal people who see them as part of the process of colonial dispossession.

The buildings still standing are the oldest-surviving mission buildings in Victoria, and the site is one of the most significant Aboriginal places in southeastern Australia (recorded as Aboriginal Affairs Victoria site no. 7225/179, place no. 6.1-3, Victorian Heritage Register H288, Register of the National Estate 00484). The local non-Aboriginal community has been instrumental in preserving the remains. In 1968 the National Trust was appointed as a Committee of Management, and ownership of the land containing the church and cemetery was transferred to it in 1971. This portion of the site was transferred to Goolum Goolum Aboriginal Cooperative in 1991 under the provisions of the Aboriginal Land Act 1991 (Williamson 1999). In 1968 the National Trust also bought the land on which the other remaining mission buildings were located, including the mission-house. The Aboriginal community has driven a substantial state-funded conservation program that has restored the church and surviving buildings. As of this writing, a Native Title determination is being negotiated between the Wotjobaluk and the federal government.

A rich and well-preserved archaeological record provides evidence for Aboriginal life from before colonization up to the present day, reflecting Aboriginal responses to the mission and potentially explaining the processes of cultural transformation, continuity, and exchange. Several excellent cultural heritage management projects have identified an extensive series of archaeological sites and features within and around the former mission site (du Cros and Associates 1997; Fels 1998; Raworth and Rhodes 1998; Brown 2001; Long and Howell-Meurs 2001; Brown et al. 2002). In 2004, a three-year archaeological investigation of the former mission site was funded by the Australian Research Council through a Discovery Grant made to the author, who is based at the Centre for Australian Indigenous Studies at Monash University. This grant is managed jointly between Monash University, Goolum Goolum Aboriginal Cooperative, and the Wotjobaluk Traditional Land Council. The project goals include reconstruction of the everyday life of different groups within and across the Aboriginal community, exploration of the roles played in the colonial process by social categories (such as gender organization), and investigation of cultural transformation as well as continuity.

A Didactic Landscape

Scholars across several disciplines have drawn attention to the privileged status assigned visual and spatial forms of knowledge in the Western intellectual tradition (Carter 1989; Lefebvre 1991; Blunt and Rose 1994). As Johannes Fabian (1983:116) argues, this "visualism" equated the "knowable with that which can be visualized, and logic with orderly arrangements of pieces of knowledge in space." The geometric perspectivalism of Western modernist vision spatially and temporally distanced the object of vision; the Other, as object of knowledge, was rendered separate, distinct, and preferably distant from the knower. As new media such as photography's transparent realism opened up distant territory to imperial eyes, certain visual conventions such as the perspectival representation of landscape were especially useful in attaining the imperial goal of charting and knowing (S. Ryan 1996; J. Ryan 1997; Snyder 2002). A range of feminist and postcolonialist scholars have now shown that this imagined topography, rather than being universal and homogeneous, has been complicit with colonialism and is implicated in constructing racial, class, and gender hierarchies (Noyes 1992).

The Moravians brought preconceptions with them to the Australian colonies, including ideas about how to create an environment that would teach Aboriginal people to live and behave like Europeans. They sought to confine the indigenous inhabitants on reserves where they could be "civilized" by spatial and visual practices; they created didactic landscapes intended to impose corrective technologies of hierarchical observation and normalizing judgment upon them. Like the panopticon in Michel Foucault's (1991:170–171) celebrated formulation, the mission was intended to be "a mechanism that coerces by means of observation; an apparatus in which the techniques that make it possible to see induce effects of power, and in which, conversely, the means of coercion make those on whom they are applied clearly visible." In a sense, the Aboriginal settlements were intended to be machines, embodying an orderly spatial layout, a division between public and private space, and isolation from wider society. Buildings symbolizing the settlement's core values were constructed along the top of a shallow ridge; the church was built on the highest point with its tower pointing toward the heavens. Moravian social categories, defined according to gender, age, and marital status (the "choir system"), were embodied in distinct living and sleeping spaces and practices within the settlement. Through the material structures of domesticity, including diet, household furnishings, and personal grooming and comportment,

the missionaries sought to impose new ideas of order and time-discipline upon the residents. The visibility of people and landscape was a crucial element of this apparatus: for the managers of the reserves, the importance of being *seen to be* clean, orderly, and industrious was a straightforward index of the residents' progress.

Throughout the reserves' operation, therefore, Moravian missionaries and other officials carefully represented settlements such as Ebenezer in ways that argued for efficient management of settlements as well as adoption of Western culture and, especially, successful conversion to Christianity by Aborigines (Lydon 2005a, 2005b). Such representations centered upon these settlements' orderly and prosperous appearance as expressed both in their spatial arrangement, drawing upon European pictorial conventions of landscape as scenic and cultivated, and in the demeanor of the residents. In 1882, for example, a newspaper engraving (Figure 2) emphasized the settlement's picturesque status and agrarian productivity by exaggerating the slope of the hill, the lushness of the settlement, and the regularity of its arrangement. The pictorial message was accentuated by the accompanying text, informing the reader that

> The mission station ... comprises Mr. Kramer's house and outbuildings, the church, which is also utilized as a school, and other convenient premises. The whole station is kept scrupulously clean, and a visitor, who is always most hospitably entertained, comes away from the station with a high opinion of the worthy pastor's administrative ability, as well as of the kindness of his amiable wife (*Illustrated Australian News* 1882:36).

Some scholars have continued to emphasize the efficacy of Aboriginal stations as carceral institutions, and the capacity of spatial organization and landscape to shape human behavior and legitimate power relationships. In an influential account, historian Bain Attwood (1989:29) argued for successful imposition of European social structures upon the residents of the Victorian station Ramahyuck through the station "machinery"—a material environment configuring "the very souls of its Aboriginal inmates [as the missionaries'] ideas and values actually came to be imbricated in the very fabric of the Aborigines' consciousness and way of being." On the Victorian reserves, however, there is evidence for contestation of BPA policy, despite

FIGURE 2. "Mission Station, Dimboola," *Illustrated Australian News* 1882:36. (Drawing from La Trobe Picture Collection, State Library of Victoria, Melbourne.)

its growing repressiveness over the last decades of the 19th century. In addition, the relationship among institutional structures—such as those that shape contemporary documentary and graphic accounts, produced by white administrators—and actual behavior requires interrogation. A range of anthropological and archaeological studies have cast doubt on the effectiveness of institutional control, showing that certain aspects of traditional culture, such as attachments to place and kin, may in fact strengthen within missions as an oppositional social domain develops (Morris 1988; Read 1988:114; Trigger 1992; Brock 1993; Rowse 1993:34–41; L'Oste-Brown and Godwin 1995). Alternatively, Francesca Merlan (1998) suggests that transformation is intercultural, reflecting settler ambivalence and meeting indigenous objectives.

While the missionaries initially planned to lay Ebenezer's settlement out on the model of the "village green" in order to control the Aborigi-

nal residents' movements and routines, it is by no means clear that their vision was effectively imposed upon the landscape and its people. Despite their intention to erect huts "forming three sides of a square" (Longmire 1985:12), facing inwards to a large central open space overlooked by the church and mission-house, a 1904 surveyor's plan (Figure 3), for example, shows that the west side of the settlement remained open. It has been argued (Lydon 2003) that at other stations, such as Coranderrk, evidence indicates that the "village green" division of the landscape into public and private domains actually facilitated the maintenance of traditional practices.

Rather than assuming any subject's experience to be determined by spatial frameworks, more recent approaches argue for a concept of space "not as a given, but ... as many social spaces negotiated within one geographical place and time" (Mills 2003:693; also Massey 1994; Pratt

Mortuary and Religious Sites 141

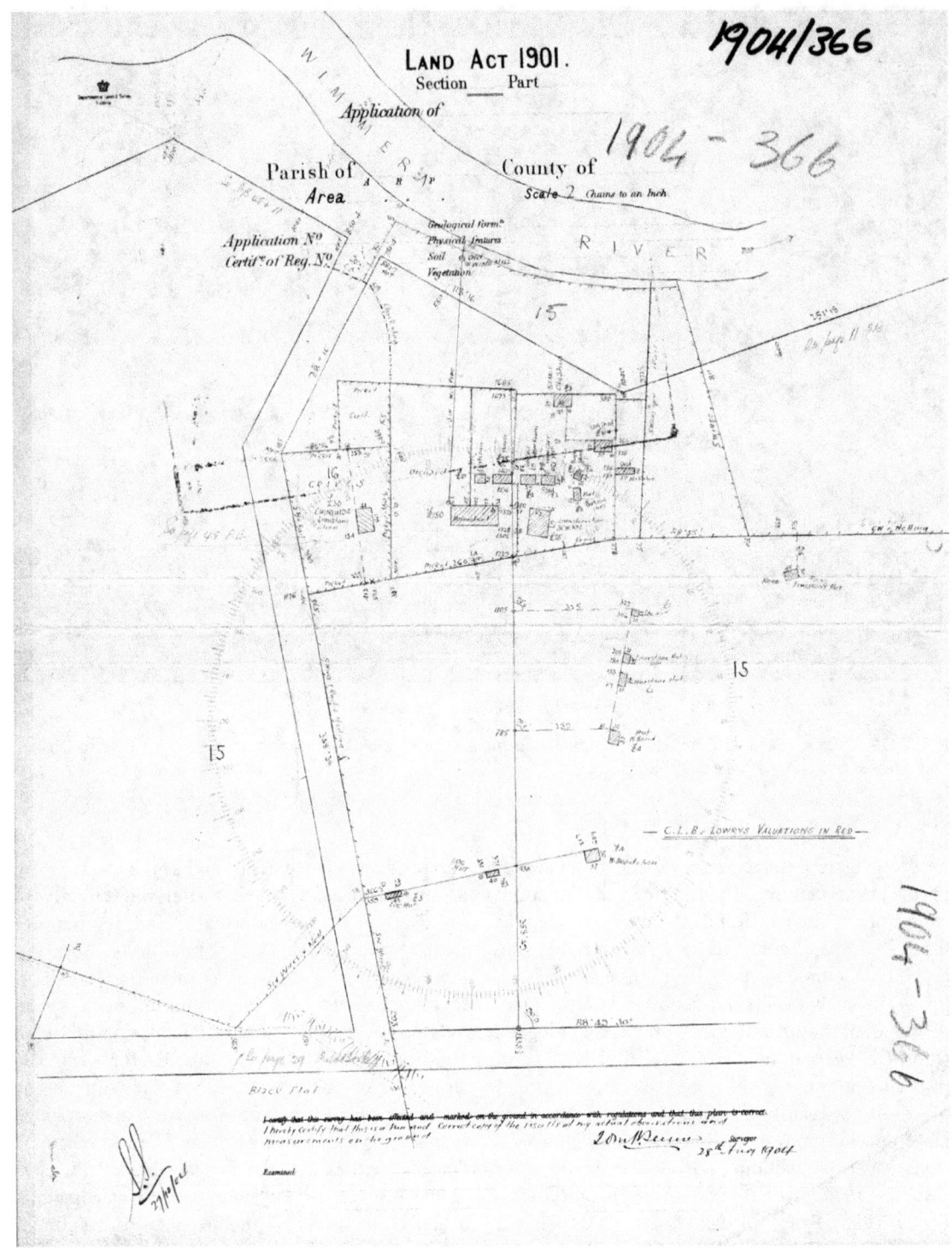

FIGURE 3. Survey plan of Ebenezer, 1904. (Drawing from Yearly Field Notes 1903–366, Plan B762; © Crown [State of Victoria], all rights reserved; reproduced with the permission of the Surveyor General, Victoria, Land Victoria, Department of Sustainability and Environment, Victoria.)

Perspectives from *Historical Archaeology*

and Hansen 1994). Although power is spatialized, shaping gender and racial relations, space is also constituted *within* social relations and therefore assumes dynamic and multiple forms, experienced differently according to perspective. Within the Australian colonies, particularly, the social order was constantly created anew and was always subject to uncertainty, instability, and challenge. While official representations of the reserves indicate the success of the "civilizing" enterprise in transforming indigenous values into those of white administrators, by contrast archaeological investigation of the mission environment aims to reveal both the missionaries' and the Aboriginal experience in a less mediated fashion, exploring the Moravian "civilizing" program as well as the creative ways Aboriginal residents found to evade or disregard European control/surveillance.

The Mission-House

Investigation of the former mission-house forms the first stage of the archaeological program, initially defining the structure of the house and its role within the mission's operation. The mission-house (Figure 4) was the first limestone rubble building constructed on the station in June 1860. The reverends Spieseke and Hagenauer noted that

> We have begun the erection of a dwelling-house of limestone, of which we have plenty at our place. The mason-work is done by a man engaged for the purpose, but all the wood-work we have undertaken to do ourselves. The place of worship we have to finish ourselves too. Our hands are full (Melbourne Association in Aid of the Moravian Mission to the Aborigines of Australia 1861:6).

Prior to excavation, it was known the mission-house was home to the successive missionaries supervising the settlement and their families as well as some Aboriginal people; a married Aboriginal couple, probably Phillip and Rebecca Pepper, occupied two rooms (Melbourne Association in Aid of the Moravian Mission to the Aborigines of Australia 1866:5; Fels 1998:20).

FIGURE 4. "Moravian Mission-House Blacks Station, Dimboola, Feb 19, 1885." (Painting by Samuel Hartley Roberts, La Trobe Picture Collection, State Library of Victoria, Melbourne.)

Some details of the building materials and techniques are also available. The missionaries used limestone from the surface of the low banks above the Wimmera River (Longmire 1985:12) to construct the 10-roomed building, divided into small apartments. The symmetrical house had three chimneys and a large central doorway, two side doors, five large symmetrically placed multipaned windows, and a shingled roof. In 1864, an attached room was used as the girls' sleeping room (BPA 1864:6). At this time, the bailiff described it as 86 by 45 by 9 ft. (26.21 × 13.71 × 2.8 m), made of limestone rubble with a double roof of bark and iron, pine flooring, and a hessian ceiling. It had a double verandah, which was floored and in fair repair, and a cellar measuring 12 by 6 by 8 ft. (3.65 × 1.82 × 2.43 m).

Description of church construction in 1875 offers some indication of how the earlier building may have been built. For the church, all the men were employed in getting the stone for construction; the interior was plastered cement

with a red pine floor, while the ceiling was made of tongue-and-groove boards and painted a lead color. The plastering and other work were done by Aboriginal people (BPA 1875:5). Lime for building and whitewashing the church was burned at the station. A sawpit was constructed, and timber was produced by the Aboriginal men (BPA 1877:9–10). It is not known precisely when the mission-house was dismantled, although Elder Uncle Jack Kennedy remembers it during the 1930s, and an aerial view of 1946 shows it to have been dismantled by that date.

Archaeological Investigations

Two large excavation areas that targeted the northeastern and western portions of the mission-house were opened up, exposing the fullest surviving extent of the mission-house towards northeast and southwest and allowing reconstruction of its basic plan and many specific features (Figure 5). Despite damage to the site caused in part by a National Trust "junior

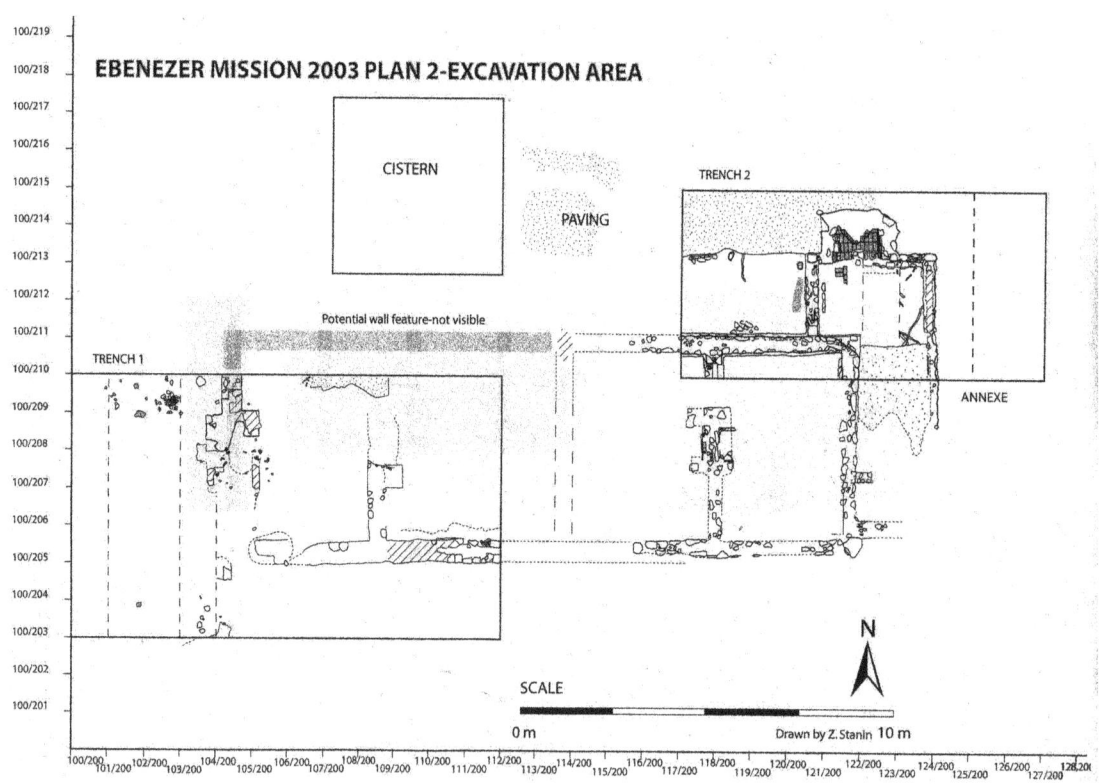

FIGURE 5. Plan of excavation areas. (Drawing by Zvonkica Stanin, 2004.)

Perspectives from *Historical Archaeology*

working bee" in 1972, substantial evidence for the construction and demolition of the building was recovered (Lydon et al. 2004). Five main rooms were defined with evidence for enclosed annexes at each end. A detailed picture of the construction and life of the annex against the east and northeastern sides of the 1860 house was obtained. In 1882 and 1885 images (figures 2 and 4), an annex is shown extending along both eastern and western sides of the mission-house, providing a *terminus ante quem* for the annex of ca.1882. Additions to the annex included modern conveniences such as concrete flooring and a brick base for a copper.

This evidence refutes the suggestion that the annexes formed part of the original construction of the mission-house (du Cros and Associates 1997:79–80). Instead, evidence indicates that the missionaries chose to extend their communal household rather than construct new buildings. Archaeological investigation confirmed the mission-house was the settlement's principal building throughout the mission's operation. The limestone church, constructed in 1874–1875 (BPA 1874:7) and sited on the ridge's highest point to symbolize God's glory, was given greater prominence in representations of the settlement. In 1904, however, it was valued at only £50, whereas the mission-house was assessed at £100. Although the mission-house received least mention in contemporary records of all the settlement's buildings (Fels 1998:20), the archaeological evidence indicates it was the symbolic and functional heart of the settlement, home to both missionaries and some of the Aboriginal residents. It was the mission's public face, to which visitors came and from which they were guided around by missionaries. Its commanding aspect, located along the top of a ridge and facing over the central public space, was intended to allow missionaries to monitor Aboriginal residents and their movements among their dwellings—communal buildings, such as the church and school, that were distributed in a line to the east and south and across the wider landscape.

This carefully chosen site symbolized missionaries' paternalistic relationship with Aboriginal residents, positioning the former as watchful guardians whose benign discipline was sanctioned by God in the apparently natural and nonviolent affiliation between father and children. The trope of the family appeared to naturalize hierarchy within unity, but as Anne McClintock (1995:45) points out, domesticity is both a *space* and a *relationship of power*. For missionaries, Aboriginal people were part of the family of man by virtue of their conformance to civilized practices; as a race, they were regarded as children.

The mission-house was also home to several families, and archaeological evidence reveals their lifestyles. A relative lack of domestic and personal items indicates that nonessential European goods were scarce commodities at Ebenezer in the late-19th century: 80% of the almost 15,000 artifacts are architectural; 14% are charcoal fragments, most probably related to the building's demolition; and only 6% comprise domestic artifacts. An initial research question asked whether occupation was characterized by distinctively Moravian practices, given that several studies have demonstrated the special character of self-contained Moravian settlements around the world, created by the evangelist brethren as the material expression of "Christ's grace operating in the world" (Thorp 1989; Southern 1997:113, 2003). Investigation of the Wachau settlement in North Carolina, for example, revealed highly specific ceramic forms used in "lovefeasts," the Moravian ritual of fellowship (South 1999). The artifacts recovered at Ebenezer, in contrast, point to adaptation to local, predominantly British, markets and practices, rather than a Moravian way of life. Three ceramic fragments, however, appear to depart from the British stoneware tradition. They may be German made or perhaps German-tradition stoneware from South Australia; future research may help to clarify this point (Brooks 2004).

Evidence was recovered for a range of activities and practices, including recreation and diet. Domestic and personal items include slate pencil fragments and clothing-related artifacts such as buttons and beads. Toys, in the form of six porcelain doll fragments, were also recovered. The faunal remains indicate that the settlement's inhabitants relied predominantly upon domestic animals such as chicken and sheep—confirmed by the presence of chicken gizzard stones, or gastroliths (Stanin 2004). As a source of meat and eggs, chickens would have played an important role in this small self-sufficient community. Evidence of onsite meat butchery is also present on sheep and rabbit bones, but evidence for the exploitation of native fauna that may previously have been exploited by the Aboriginal population, such as kangaroo and possum, is noticeably absent. Few other organic remains were recovered, although peach pits were common enough to indicate the presence of a peach tree in the adjacent orchard.

While the ceramic assemblage is relatively small (representing slightly under 0.5% of the artifact total), in character it is unremarkable for a Victorian assemblage dating to the second half of the 19th century (Brooks 2004). Most of the assemblage is whiteware, occurring in plate, cup, and saucer forms and in a typical range of decorations, including banded and transfer-printed decorative schemes, such as the common Asiatic pheasants pattern (Figure 6). Much of the rest of the assemblage consists of porcelain (soft-paste bone china and hard paste), stoneware, and a standard black-glazed buff earthenware teapot fragment. Given the

otherwise standard patterning evident within this assemblage, it is clear that the inhabitants of the mission-house were integrated on some level—whether through choice or necessity—with the tastes of the colony. This conclusion is supported by the range of ceramics recorded elsewhere on the site, which are also typically British (Williamson 1999:23). Overall, the assemblage is typical of colonial Victorian sites of the second half of the 19th century, reflecting systems of European domesticity.

The investigation demonstrates that Moravians were successful in creating key elements of a European landscape and lifestyle within an alien environment. Their seeming achievement of fundamental goals in the colonial program of transforming Aboriginal people was recognized by contemporaries, as measured in the appearance of the settlement and the comportment of its residents. The representation of the mission—even in such concrete and embodied terms as revealed here by the archaeological

FIGURE 6. Ceramics: (from *top center, clockwise*) Asiatic pheasants, unidentified pattern, coarse red earthenware, molded stoneware, bone china, burnt banded porcelain. (Photo by Monash University Photography, 2004.)

investigation—must not, however, be understood solely on the missionaries' own terms. Although the evidence demonstrates that the missionaries successfully controlled aspects of the material and social function of the mission-house, these attainments must be seen in the context of instabilities that discredit their claims to successful governance and delineate the limits of their regime.

Limits of Colonialism

The missionaries were undermined by their own uncertainties as well as by Aboriginal opposition and evasion, which was grounded in a very different cultural orientation. The disciplinary spatio-visual regimes of the reserves established some parameters for the negotiation of social relations but did not fully determine them: they must be understood, rather, in terms of the heterogeneous, multiple experiences of differently positioned indigenous subjects. As Lynn Meskell (1999) argues, inscriptive models of experience emphasizing the processes by which power relations are mapped on the body, as a surface for visible display, may overlook lived experience and corporeality. Personal diaries of the newly arrived German Moravian missionaries at Ebenezer Mission during the early 1860s reveal that their lives were fraught with anxiety and self-doubt, if not despair, as they struggled with putting doctrine into practice. This was exacerbated by their acute awareness of the complete failure of all previous missionary enterprises in southeastern Australia (especially their own at Lake Boga, also in northwestern Victoria, between 1851 and 1856). In the years before white settlement spread to this remote corner of the colony, the traditional owners saw no need to settle on the reserve or adopt European customs. Although Ebenezer did gradually become home to many Aboriginal people, residents mounted a letter campaign against their treatment at the mission during the 1870s and 1880s, protesting the BPA's refusal to grant sufficient land to make the reserve self-supporting and the harshness of the missionaries' regime (Ryan 1999:29–30,33).

Further, the missionaries' Western visual regime overlooked or denied disjunctions with the Aboriginal residents' profoundly different cultural orientation, in which vision was subordinated to aurality and in which collective forms of personhood took precedence over the individual, allowing for the persistence of tradition and the evasion of control in the pursuit of Aboriginal objectives. Aboriginal residents maintained unrecognized forms of collective identity, reflected in forms of sociality such as group regulation or "shaming." Some retained practices such as a camp lifestyle or more covert taboos. In some cases, such persistence was possible because Aboriginal practices were not recognized by whites, their very *invisibility* contributing to survival of practices (Lydon 2003). Beyond idealizing Western visions of Aboriginality, indigenous people evaded scrutiny through movement and concealment, escaping or undermining the spatial apparatus of the reserves. At Ebenezer there is evidence that Aboriginal people deployed strategies of mobility and evasion to pursue their own objectives, played out across different levels and scales of colonial space.

Despite establishment of the six reserves, for example, up to half the colony's indigenous population lived elsewhere or moved in and out of these communities, instead choosing to work for European employers or to receive rations from Honorary Correspondents' depots (Penney 1997). Aboriginal people in Victoria's northwest remained mobile and dispersed, moving on and off Ebenezer for work with relative ease. In this sparsely settled area, their labor was a useful resource for pastoralists. Men worked as shepherds, shearers, stockmen, and casual laborers, while women worked as servants, sometimes establishing long-lasting relationships with particular pastoralist families. Some chose to live in camps in traditional country, utilizing traditional food sources where possible, such as along the Murray and Darling rivers. Some supplemented their income or diet through fishing, shooting, or begging (Penney 1989).

The life of Augusta Robinson exemplifies this negotiation of diverse social spaces, as Dja Dja Wurrung Elder Gary Murray's research has shown. Murray's great-great-great grandmother Augusta (Minnie) Logan-Nicholls, née Robinson, raised her son Herbert with de facto husband Robert (Bobbie) Nicholls until her death in 1886. Augusta took the name Nicholls from 1882, but Augusta and Bobbie were forced to live in separate houses at Ebenezer, despite repeated requests that they be allowed to marry. As a result, while they chose to live on the mission at certain times, they also moved away for periods to achieve freedom from the regime. Around 1879 they went to live on nearby Towanninnie Station where Augusta and Bobbie worked for the Finley family who wrote to the BPA on their behalf, again urging that they be given permission to marry. During this time at Towanninnie Augusta and Bobbie's son was educated with the Finley's own children by their governess (Murray 2003:25). Bobbie worked as a shearer, requiring that he travel great distances away from Augusta and her son. In 1881, she returned to Ebenezer for a while. Good relations with local station owners allowed some freedom from the constraints of reserve surveillance. These people's lives were characterized by mobility and a degree of independence that define some of the parameters of the European reserve system.

The limits of missionary control are also suggested by contextual archaeological evidence for intensive longitudinal occupation of the landscape around the mission settlement. A survey recorded 246 sites within a 6 km radius around the mission, almost all on the Wimmera River and its anabranch Datchak Creek (Raworth and Rhodes 1998:10–12). Most of these sites contain scarred trees, many marked by steel axes, indicating their use during the contact period, a practice that the late Elder Jack Kennedy observed continued throughout the 20th century. Freshwater shell middens with associated surface artifacts, artifact scatters, and isolated artifacts provide evidence for traditional lifestyle, and several sites indicate ongoing land use through prehistoric, early (ca.1840) contact, and mission periods. The high density of postcontact sites around the mission may indicate intensified use following its establishment (Raworth and Rhodes 1998:12). Another desktop survey revealed 302 sites (scarred trees, mounds, surface scatters, isolated artifacts, and burials) in a broader area (Bird 1990:22). Such evidence suggests that, as at other Aboriginal reserves, the bush remained an Aboriginal haven, and the river in particular served as private space (Lydon 2003); it indicates that traditional practices were maintained and transformed alongside newer customs. Future research at Ebenezer will extend this fieldwork and research in a systematic investigation of evidence for non-European activity around the settlement and in specifically Aboriginal spaces such as dwellings.

Conclusion

The Moravians' influence in structuring Aboriginal policy in Victoria has not previously been fully acknowledged. Their long, global, and respected tradition of evangelizing provided them with an influential model for establishing Aboriginal settlements, centered upon embodied and spatial practices and designed to teach residents how to live like Europeans. At Ebenezer, this program was successfully inaugurated, as demonstrated by archaeological evidence for the settlement's landscaping and for the function of the mission-house, especially in its role as hub and contact place, central and commanding position, regular extension and rebuilding, and operation of European systems of domesticity. As a symbol of order and authority, the mission-house constituted a representation of the Moravians' successful construction of a European landscape and way of life. Viewing this household within the wider context of the mission's life, however, suggests the limits of the Moravians' program: documentary records express the missionaries' uncertainties, their ongoing battle to maintain control over the residents, and the relative mobility and freedom of many residents, at least for periods of time. Archaeological survey points toward the maintenance as well as the transformation of traditional culture around the mission and will serve as the basis for further investigation. In sum, without denying the very real constraints imposed upon the Aboriginal people of Victoria and the harsh restriction of Aboriginal peoples' rights entailed by the mission regime, it is important not to view missionaries' and managers' representations—however concrete—with too credulous an eye: the different cultural orientation of Aboriginal visual and spatial regimes, linked to a cultural order grounded in relations to kin and country, persisted in practices unrecognized or "overlooked" by Western settlers.

Acknowledgments

Thanks to project partners Alan Burns at Goolum Goolum Aboriginal Cooperative and

Peter Kennedy at the Wotjobaluk Traditional Land Council, as well as community participants in fieldwork: Leon Burns, Shane Campbell, Brett Harrison, Jenny Beer, Eddie Kennedy, Susie Skurrie, and Noeline Granbeau. Thanks to Dja Dja Wurrung Elder Gary Murray for sharing his research with me. For expert work in the field and lab, thanks go to Alasdair Brooks and Zvonkica Stanin. I also appreciate Alasdair's assistance in presenting preliminary results of the first season at The Society for Historical Archaeology's 2005 Conference at York, England, UK, and his patience as editor. Thanks to many members of the local community for their support, especially Evelyn King and Ray King, the Dimboola and District Historical Society, Eleanor Bourke, and Ivan Werner and Yvonne Werner. Barry Whitehead and John Whitehead, descendants of Reverend Paul and Amalie Bogisch were generous with their assistance. At Aboriginal Affairs, thanks to Mark Dugay-Grist, Harry Webber, Julia Cusack, and Richard Macneil. At Heritage Victoria, thanks to Jeremy Smith, Andrew Jamieson, Jenny Dickens, and Annie Muir. At the National Trust of Australia (Victoria), thanks to Conservation Manager Jim Gard'ner. At Monash University, thanks to Lynette Russell. Thanks for assistance in the field are due to Michael Slack, Sam Wickman, student participants from Monash and La Trobe universities, and particularly our fabulous cook, Enya Gannon!

References

ATTWOOD, BAIN
1989 *The Making of the Aborigines*. Allen and Unwin, Sydney, Australia.

BIRD, CAROLINE
1990 Aboriginal Sites in the Horsham Region. Victoria Archaeological Survey, Melbourne, Australia.

BLUNT, ALISON, AND GILLIAN ROSE
1994 Introduction: Women's Colonial and Postcolonial Geographies. In *Writing Women and Space: Colonial and Postcolonial Geographies*, Alison Blunt and Gillian Rose, editors, pp. 1–25. Guilford Press, New York, NY.

BOARD FOR THE PROTECTION OF THE ABORIGINES IN THE COLONY OF VICTORIA (BPA)
1861–1895 *Report of the Central Board Appointed to Watch Over the Interests of the Aborigines in the Colony of Victoria*. Office of the Central Board, Melbourne, Australia.

BROCK, PEGGY
1993 *Outback Ghettos: Aborigines, Institutionalisation, and Survival*. Cambridge University Press, Cambridge, England, UK.

BROOKS, ALASDAIR
2004 Appendix 1: Ceramics and Glass Report. In Archaeological Investigations at the Mission-House, Ebenezer Mission, by Jane Lydon, Alasdair Brooks and Zvonkica Stanin. Report to Aboriginal Affairs Victoria and Heritage Victoria, Melbourne, from the Centre for Australian Indigenous Studies, Monash University, Melbourne, Australia.

BROOME, RICHARD
1994 *Aboriginal Australians*. Allen and Unwin, Sydney, Australia.

BROWN, ANNE
2001 *Wotjobaluk Dreaming: A Case Study of the Wotjobaluk People and Their Country*. Aboriginal Affairs Victoria, Goolum Goolum Aboriginal Cooperative, Melbourne, Australia.

BROWN, STEVE, STEVEN AVERY, AND MEGAN GOULDING
2002 Recent investigations at the Ebenezer Mission Cemetery. In *After Captain Cook: The Archaeology of the Recent Indigenous Past in Australia*, Rodney Harrison and Christine Williamson, editors, pp. 147–70. Sydney University Archaeological Methods Series, No. 8. Sydney, Australia.

CARTER, PAUL
1989 *The Road to Botany Bay: An Exploration of Landscape and History*. University of Chicago Press, Chicago, IL.

CHURCH OF THE UNITED BRETHREN
1849 *Periodical Accounts Relating to the Missions of the Church of the United Brethren, Established among the Heathen*, vol. 19, p. 156. The Brethren's Society for the Furtherance of the Gospel Among the Heathen, London, England, UK.

CLARK, IAN
1990 *Aboriginal Languages and Clans: An Historical Atlas of Western and Central Victoria, 1800–1900*. Monash Publications in Geography, No. 37. Monash University Press, Melbourne, Australia.

DU CROS AND ASSOCIATES
1997 Former Ebenezer Mission Reserve: Site Conservation and Management Plan. Draft report for Aboriginal Affairs Victoria and Goolum Goolum Aboriginal Cooperative, Melbourne, Australia.

EDWARDS, WILLIAM HOWELL
1999 *Moravian Aboriginal Missions in Australia 1850–1919*. United Church Historical Society (South Australia), Adelaide, Australia.

FABIAN, JOHANNES
    1983   *Time and the Other: How Anthropology Makes Its Object*. Columbia University Press, New York, NY.

FELS, MARIE
    1998   *A History of the Ebenezer Mission.* Occasional Report, No. 51. Aboriginal Affairs Victoria, Melbourne, Australia.

FOUCAULT, MICHEL
    1991   *Discipline and Punish: The Birth of the Prison.* Penguin Books, London, England, UK.

HOWITT, ALFRED WILLIAM
    1904   *The Native Tribes of South-East Australia.* Macmillan, London. Reprinted in 1996 by Aboriginal Studies Press, Canberra, Australia.

ILLUSTRATED AUSTRALIAN NEWS
    1882   Mission Station, Dimboola. *Illustrated Australian News* 22 March:36 [State Library of Victoria].

KAMMINGA, JOHANNES, AND MARK GRIST
    2000   Yarriambiack Creek Aboriginal Heritage Study. Report to Aboriginal Affairs Victoria, Melbourne, from National Heritage Consultants, Canberra, Australia.

KENNY, ROBERT
    2003   La Trobe, Lake Boga, and the "Enemy of Souls": The First Moravian Mission in Australia. *La Trobe Journal* 71:97–113.

LEFEBVRE, HENRI
    1991   *The Production of Space.* Basil Blackwell, Oxford, England, UK.

LONG, ANDREW, AND JONATHAN HOWELL-MEURS
    2001   Archaeological Excavations at Ebenezer Mission (2000). Report to Aboriginal Affairs Victoria, from Andrew Long and Associates, Melbourne, Australia.

LONGMIRE, ANNE
    1985   *Nine Creeks to Albacutya: A History of the Shire of Dimboola.* Hargreen Publishing Company and the Shire of Dimboola, Melbourne, Australia.

L'OSTE-BROWN, SCOTT, AND LUKE GODWIN, WITH GORDON HENRY, TED MITCHELL, AND VERA TYSON
    1995   *Living under the Act: Taroom Aboriginal Reserve 1911–1927.* Queensland Department of Environment and Heritage, Brisbane, Australia.

LYDON, JANE
    2003   Seeing Each Other: Colonial Photography in Nineteenth-Century Victoria. In *Archaeologies of the British: Explorations of Identity in Great Britain and Its Colonies 1600–1945*, Susan Lawrence, editor, pp. 174–190. One World Archaeology Series. Routledge, London, England, UK.
    2005a *Eye Contact: Photographing Indigenous Australians.* Duke University Press, Durham, NC.

    2005b "Watched over by the indefatigable Moravian missionaries": Colonialism and Photography at Ebenezer and Ramahyuck. *La Trobe Journal* 76:27–48.

LYDON, JANE, ALASDAIR BROOKS, AND ZVONKICA STANIN,
    2004   Archaeological Investigations at the Mission-House, Ebenezer Mission. Report to Aboriginal Affairs Victoria and Heritage Victoria, Melbourne, from the Centre for Australian Indigenous Studies, Monash University, Melbourne, Australia.

MASON, J. C. S.
    2001   The Moravian Church and the Missionary Awakening in England 1760–1800. Manuscript, The Royal Historical Society, Rochester, NY.
    2003   Benjamin and Christian Ignatius La Trobe in the Moravian Church. *La Trobe Journal* 71:17–27.

MASSEY, DOREEN B.
    1994   *Space, Place, and Gender.* Polity, Cambridge, England, UK.

McCLINTOCK, ANNE
    1995   *Imperial Leather: Race, Gender, and Sexuality in the Colonial Contest.* Routledge, New York, NY.

MELBOURNE ASSOCIATION IN AID OF THE MORAVIAN MISSION TO THE ABORIGINES OF AUSTRALIA
    1861   *Further Facts Relating to the Moravian Mission in Australia: Second Paper.* Wm. Goodhugh, Melbourne, Australia.
    1866   *Further Facts Relating to the Moravian Mission in Australia: Fifth Paper.* Wm. Goodhugh, Melbourne, Australia.

MERLAN, FRANCESCA
    1998   *Caging the Rainbow: Places, Politics, and Aborigines in a North Australian Town.* University of Hawai'i Press, Honolulu.

MESKELL, LYNN
    1999   *Archaeologies of Social Life: Age, Sex, Class et cetera in Ancient Egypt.* Blackwell Publishers, Oxford, England, UK.

MILLS, SARA
    2003   Gender and Colonial Space. In *Feminist Postcolonial Theory: A Reader*, Reina Lewis and Sara Mills, editors, pp. 692–719. Edinburgh University Press, Edinburgh, England, UK.

MORRIS, BARRY
    1988   Dhan-Gadi Resistance to Assimilation. In *Being Black: Aboriginal Cultures in "Settled" Australia*, Ian Keen, editor, pp. 33–63. Aboriginal Studies Press, Canberra, Australia.

MULVANEY, D. J.
    1989   *Encounters in Place: Outsiders and Aboriginal Australians 1606–1985.* University of Queensland Press, St Lucia, Australia.

MURRAY, GARY (WRYKER MILLOO)
2003 Sacred to the Memory of Augusta: The Lake Hindmarsh Clothing Distribution Book 1882–1903. Manuscript in author's possession.

NOYES, JOHN
1992 *Colonial Space: Spatiality in the Discourse of German South West Africa 1884–1915.* Harwood Academic Publishers, Philadelphia, PA.

PENNEY, JAN
1989 Encounters on the River: Aborigines and Europeans in the Murray Valley 1820–1920. Doctoral dissertation, Department of History, La Trobe University, Melbourne, Australia.
1997 Victorian Honorary Correspondent Supply Depots: Final Report. Manuscript, Aboriginal Affairs Victoria, Melbourne, Australia.

PEPPER, PHILLIP, AND TESS DE ARAUGO
1980 *You Are What You Make Yourself To Be: The Story of a Victorian Aboriginal Family 1842–1980.* Hyland House, Melbourne, Australia.

PRATT, GERALDINE, AND SUSAN HANSON
1994 Geography and the Construction of Difference. *Gender, Place, and Culture* 1:5–29.

RAWORTH, BRYCE, AND DAVID RHODES
1998 An Archaeological and Architectural Report on the Ebenezer Mission Station. Manuscript, Aboriginal Affairs Victoria, Melbourne, Australia.

READ, PETER
1988 *A Hundred Years War: The Wiradjuri People and the State.* Australian National University Press, Sydney, Australia.

RHODES, DAVID
1998 An Archaeological Report on the Ebenezer Mission Station. Manuscript, Aboriginal Affairs Victoria, Melbourne, Australia.

ROWSE, TIM
1993 *After Mabo: Interpreting Indigenous Traditions.* Melbourne University Press, Melbourne, Australia.

RYAN, JAMES R.
1997 *Picturing Empire: Photography and the Visualization of the British Empire.* University of Chicago Press, Chicago, IL.

RYAN, SIMON
1996 *The Cartographic Eye: How Explorers Saw Australia.* Cambridge University Press, Cambridge, England, UK.

RYAN, TED
1999 Wergaia Worlds: A Study of Indigenous/European Cultural Contact in the Mallee Region of North-West Victoria, 1870–1910. Honours thesis, Department of History, La Trobe University, Melbourne, Australia.

SNYDER, JOEL
2002 Territorial Photography. In *Landscape and Power,* W. J. T. Mitchell, editor, pp. 175–201. University of Chicago Press, Chicago, IL.

SOUTH, STANLEY
1999 *Historical Archaeology in Wachovia: Excavating Eighteenth-Century Bethabara and Moravian Pottery.* Kluwer Academic Publishers, New York, NY.

SOUTHERN, RON
1997 Going Home: The Moravian Settlement of Fulneck, 1750–1760. Doctoral dissertation, School of Archaeological and Historical Studies, La Trobe University, Melbourne, Australia.
2003 Strangers Below: An Archaeology of Distinctions in an Eighteenth-Century Religious Community. In *Archaeologies of the British,* Susan Lawrence, editor, pp. 87–101. Routledge, London, England, UK.

STANIN, ZVONKICA
2004 Appendix 2: Faunal Analysis. In Archaeological Investigations at the Mission-House, Ebenezer Mission, by Jane Lydon, Alasdair Brooks and Zvonkica Stanin. Report to Aboriginal Affairs Victoria and Heritage Victoria, Melbourne, from the Centre for Australian Indigenous Studies, Monash University, Melbourne, Australia.

THORP, DANIEL
1989 *The Moravian Community in Colonial North Carolina: Pluralism on the Southern Frontier.* University of Tennessee Press, Knoxville.

TRIGGER, DAVID
1992 *Whitefella Comin': Aboriginal Responses to Colonialism in Northern Australia.* Cambridge University Press, Cambridge, England, UK.

WILLIAMSON, CHRISTINE
1999 An Archaeological Investigation of an Historical Artefact Scatter, Ebenezer Mission, North-West Victoria. Manuscript, Aboriginal Affairs Victoria and Goolum Goolum Aboriginal Cooperative, Melbourne, Australia.

JANE LYDON
CENTRE FOR AUSTRALIAN INDIGENOUS STUDIES
MONASH UNIVERSITY
CLAYTON, VICTORIA 3800, AUSTRALIA

Alberta Zucchi

Churches as Catholic Burial Places: Excavations at the San Francisco Church, Venezuela

ABSTRACT

In Venezuela and in other Latin American countries, little information exists on burial practices at churches used to dispose of the dead. New data has been obtained on burials and underground funerary structures found during limited excavations of the church of the colonial Franciscan convent of Nuestra Señora de la Salceda of Coro, Venezuela, occupied during the period 1620–1920. Some burials within the church could date as early as the first half of the 18th century, and individuals continued to be interred within the church through the early-20th century. Types of burials and their treatment are described.

Introduction

By describing excavations at the San Francisco Church in Coro, colonial burial practices within Venezuela's Catholic churches are examined. Few archaeological excavations of Catholic churches in Venezuela have been conducted, although important information about church construction and use and mortuary patterning can be recovered through such study. Limited excavations conducted by the Instituto Venezolano de Investigaciones Científicas at San Francisco Church has generated a wealth of evidence about burial patterning at this particular site from the 18th through the early-20th centuries and demonstrates the value of the archaeological study of churches and their associated cemeteries.

Background

Christians acquired the right to build their own temples and cemeteries in A.D. 313 when the Emperor Constantin issued his famous Edict of Milan. Before that, Christians were buried in the catacombs (Gómez Salazar 1872:518–525). By the 5th century, the relics of saints and martyrs that had been previously deposited in the catacombs were now transferred into these first temples, and bishops were being buried inside them, with kings and emperors in the porticos and atria. By the 6th century, emperors, kings, abbots, and individuals who had died "with the scent of sanctity" were also being buried in the temples. As more Christians requested burial near the relics of the saints, the custom was slowly extended to the other faithful. By the 9th century, burial inside the temple had been adopted by all of Christendom (Arco Moya 1989: 318–322) and, during the 15th and 16th centuries, the custom passed to Spanish America.

Initially, the deceased were interred only in their parish churches. As the number of churches and convents increased, an individual could select another church or even the courtyard or the cloister of a convent for burial. These selections were often linked to a specific religious interest, membership in a particular confraternity, or devotion to a particular saint. The monarchs and the religious authorities soon came to identify the inconveniences of this practice, since the fear of epidemics and the dreadful smell from the corpses greatly reduced attendance at religious services. Dr. Juan José Díaz de Espada y Fernández de Landa, Bishop of Havana, claimed,

> Many churches cast out an unbearable smell, capable of causing several and dangerous diseases. There is such a multitude of corpses buried in some churches, that their pestilent fermentation produces such a smell, that its waves spread and diffuse to a distance of more than thirty and forty *varas*, and although in another church [the smell] is not so much[,] it is enough to withdraw the assistance of the faithful to the divine services (Peña et al. 1987).

In 1442, the Vaison Council prohibited the practice of burying individuals within churches and declared that burials should be located in the courtyards, vestibules, and exedras of churches. Although the Braga Council (1563) and those that followed reiterated the pronouncement, the practice of interring the deceased within churches continued both in Europe and in America. In 1698, the Synodal Constitutions of the Caracas Episcopate ordered that cemeteries were to be located at the sides of churches. Still, burials inside churches continued. Not until the second half of the 19th century, with laws and decrees promulgated in 1873 by the government of Guzman Blanco, did the secularization of death in the country begin. These laws and decrees established public cemeteries, regulated interments and exhumations, required the scientific determination of death, and the state assumed the official register of deaths and expenses of charity burials.

Convent of Nuestra Señora de la Salceda

The convent of Nuestra Señora de la Salceda, located in Coro, Venezuela, is associated with the San Francisco Church, a World Monument Site. The town of Coro was founded in 1527. Although the precise date when the convent was established is unknown, the Franciscan José Torrubia (1972:449) indicates that it was the ninth convent established in Venezuela. Cayetano Carrocera (1943:139), also a Franciscan historian, argues it was in existence by 1585, since it was mentioned in a Memorial written that year. The governor of Margarita sent a list to the king in 1603 (Archivo General de Indias) stating that the town of Coro had one friar. If indeed there was a Franciscan convent in Coro during the 16th century, the building was probably severely damaged or even destroyed during the English-instigated fire of 1595 (González Batista 1994:25–26).

The first secure dates for the building are 1613–1617, when the convent and its church were constructed through the generosity of Captain Ambrosio Hernandez and his wife, Inés López. Because of their generosity, the couple was given the title of founder in 1620. This one-aisle building may have been damaged during the 1659 English invasion and again by the great storm of 1681, which destroyed much of the city (González Batista 1994:25–26). In 1720, the church was reconstructed, with the contract requiring the building to have walls of "limestone and bricks" and a wooden roof (Archivo Historico de Coro 1720).

Although ample donations were obtained for the rebuilding, the church was ultimately constructed with sun-dried bricks (adobes) (González Batista 1994:27). When Bishop Mariano Martí visited Coro in 1773, he noted that the church had one aisle and was of moderate capacity and strength. By 1796, the church had become a three-aisle building with arches supported by Tuscan columns (Vázquez and Briceño 1989; Gasparini 1994; González Batista 1994:27). The characteristics and dimensions of this enlarged structure are similar to those of the existing church (Gasparini 1994:71).

The building was probably damaged during the Federation War (1859–1863) and was restored in 1867 by Marshal Juan Crisóstomo Falcón (Gasparini 1994:72). Between 1903 and 1906, the church underwent yet another reconstruction. Most of the building's colonial features were eliminated or modified, acquiring a neo-Gothic style popular in Venezuela during that period. The latest remodeling of the church took place between 1987 and 1994, when the floor was lowered some 60 to 65 cm. During this process, most of the burials and other cultural remains from the 19th and early-20th centuries were destroyed without any description or record (Zucchi 2003).

Archaeological Investigations

There are at least 200 colonial churches in Venezuela, but many of them were substantially modified during the 19th and 20th centuries (Gasparini 1969:13). Although architectural descriptions of these buildings have been published (Gasparini 1969, 1976, 1994:43–78), there is little information regarding their remodeling, and no archaeological excavations were carried out before or during these reconstructions and rebuilding efforts. When investigations at San Francisco began, then, there was no information regarding the nature of burials or of other subterranean funerary structures at these types of churches.

Since the church was to remain open during the fieldwork to accommodate religious services, the excavations were necessarily limited in size and scale. Fifteen test pits (50 × 50 cm) were excavated in the northern section of the right-hand aisle and seven other excavation units of varying sizes were located elsewhere in the right-hand and central aisles of the church (Figure 1). To locate other subsurface features,

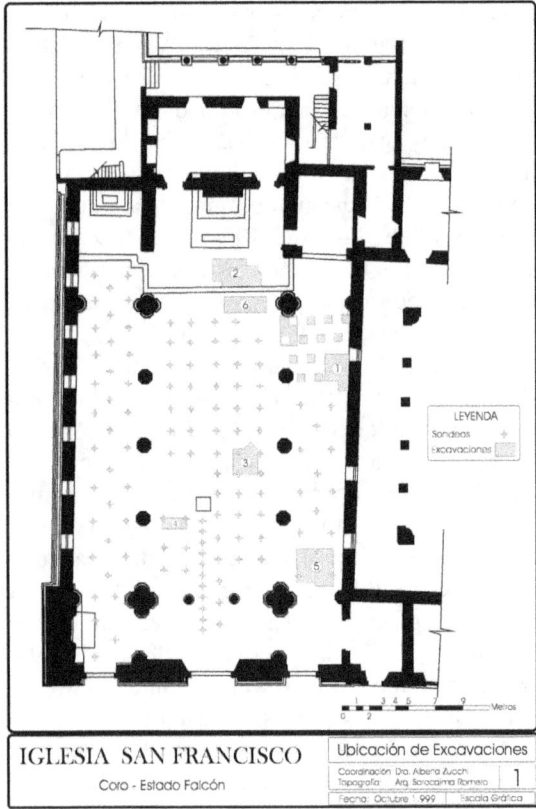

Figure 1. Location of test units and other excavations. (Drawing by Sorocaima Romero.)

broken bricks, sun-dried bricks, and roof tiles, apparently representing construction debris. Layer 1 also contained animal bones, small amounts of Indian pottery, 16th- and 17th-century majolica, and several secondary burials, most of which rested directly on Floor 1.

In Unit 7, at a depth of 45 cm below surface, a group of large foundation stones, three post holes, and a compacted earth surface originally covered with square floor tiles was defined as Floor 2 (Figure 2). Layer 2 rested on top of this second floor, and consisted of a thin layer (15 to 20 cm) of yellowish-brown sandy clay. Layer 2 appears to date from ca. 1796 to 1920. According to information provided by one of the architects involved in the most recent remodeling of the church, a layer of dirt measuring 60 to 65 cm thick was removed in order to lay crushed rock, sand, concrete, and ceramic tiles for the new floor (Amelia González 2000, pers. comm.). Through this process, most of the upper section of Layer 2 was removed, together with cultural materials and human remains. As a result, significant data were lost. This loss included information on the number and general organization

127 holes (2 cm) spaced at 80 cm were drilled through the floor of the three aisles. Two iron rods (1 and 2 m long and 2 cm in diameter) were inserted one after the other into each hole in an effort to detect features.

Two distinct strata and two occupational floors were identified during the excavations. The earliest floor, Floor 1, was found at a depth of 1 m in the sanctuary (Unit 2) and between 60 and 65 cm in Units 3 and 7, located in the main aisle (Figure 1). Floor 1 consisted of compact sandy clay, occasionally covered in Units 2 and 7 by a layer of mortar (3 to 4 cm thick). The test pits (50 × 50 cm) excavated in this floor revealed that Floor 1 overlays compact sterile sandy clay.

Above Floor 1 at a depth of 40 to 60 cm below surface is Layer 1, a slightly moist yellowish-brown, loose sandy clay ranging from 50 to 60 cm thick. In Units 2, 3, and 7, this layer consisted almost completely of

Figure 2. Probable stone foundation of the main arch of the church of 1720 with remnant floor of square ceramic tiles. (Photo by author.)

Perspectives from *Historical Archaeology*

of burials from the second half of the 19th to the beginning of the 20th century; the location, position, and orientation of the bodies; types of shrouds and coffins; building techniques and materials employed in the construction of tombs; typological and spatial similarities and differences between primary and secondary burials of the 19th and 20th centuries; and evidence for modifications of the church occurring during the last two centuries.

Subsurface Elements and Structures

As previously noted, when the excavations began there was little to no information on the characteristics of burials within colonial churches. The limited available data indicated that, for burial purposes, church interiors were divided into sections extending from the sanctuary to the main front door (Figure 1). The first section, located adjacent to the sanctuary, was used exclusively by the clergy. The cost of a burial in other areas decreased in relation to its distance from the main altar. Children were interred in the lateral aisles, while poor people, servants, and slaves were buried in the more distant areas near the vestibule (Zucchi 2001:47). No monuments could be erected above floor level nor could new graves be opened until the previously interred body had "worn out according to the time that others take to be consumed in that church" (Arco Moya 1989:320).

During the excavations, the burials of 34 individuals were identified (12 without coffins and 22 in small wooden coffins) (Table 1) (Figure 3). The skull of the only excavated primary burial was missing (Figure 4), but its impression was still visible in the ground. Bordering this skeleton was a thin dark line apparently left by the decomposition of the shroud, and

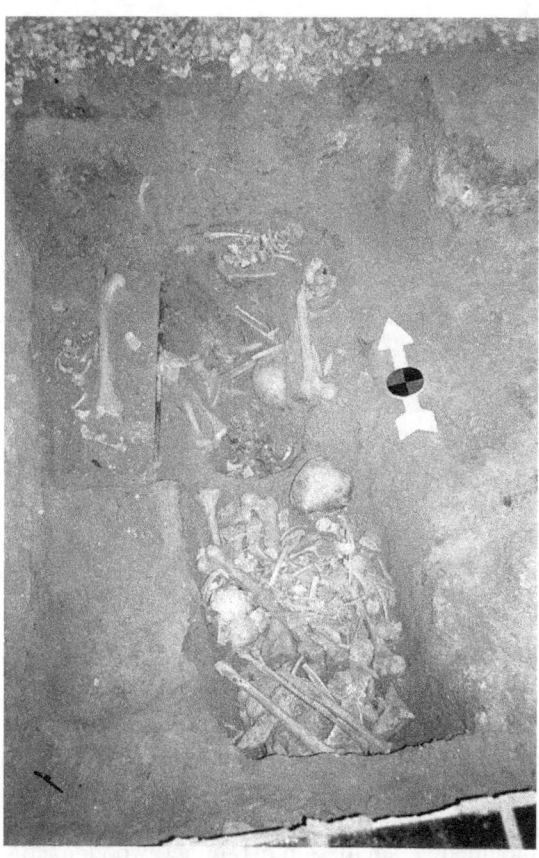

Figure 3. Individual and multiple secondary direct burials found in Pit 3. (Photo by author.)

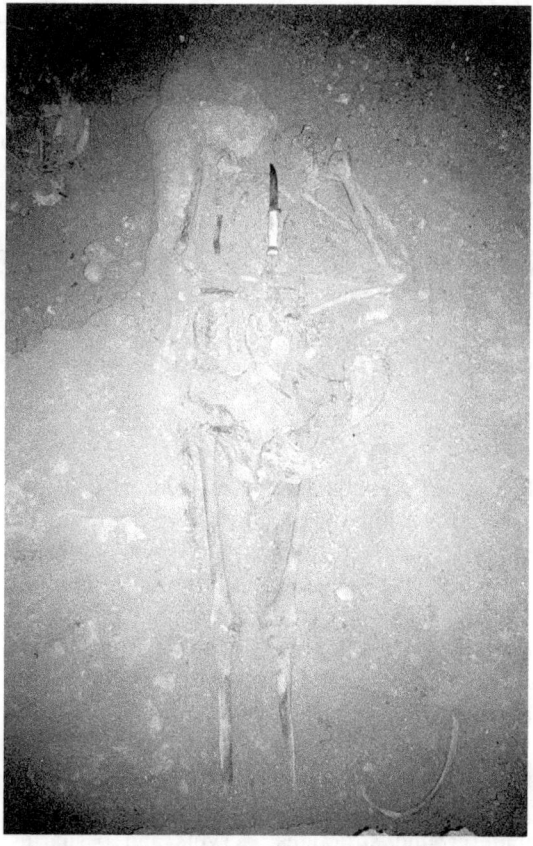

Figure 4. Primary direct burial, probably the remains of a Franciscan friar (Pit 2). (Photo by author.)

TABLE 1
SUMMARY OF BURIAL TYPES AND MORTUARY REMAINS FROM THE SAN FRANCISCO CHURCH

Note: Burial population includes 34 individuals out of an unknown total population.

Type of burial	1 extended, hands crossed over pelvic area, skull missing
Pit/Layer	Pit 2/Layer 2
Period	unknown
Orientation	head to north
Coffin	none
Type of burial	7 individual secondary (6 adults, 1 child)
Pit/Layer	Pits 2/Layer 1, Pit 3/Layer 1, Pit 4/Layer 1
Period	1790–1795
Orientation	variable
Coffin	none
Type of burial	2 multiple secondary (one contained 2 adults and 2 children; the second contained 2 adults; in both cases, bones placed with no visible pattern)
Pit/Layer	Pit 2/Layer 1
Period	1720–1795
Orientation	north to south
Coffin	none
Type of burial	3 individual secondary coffin burials
Pit/Layer	Pit 3/Layer 1, Pit 4/Layer 2, Pit 5/Layer 2
Period	unknown
Orientation	north to south
Coffin:	rectangular wooden coffins and urn (the coffin found in Pit 4 had traces of taffeta inner lining; characteristics of the urn could not be established)
Type of burial	3 secondary individual coffin burials in ossuaries
Pit/Layer	Pit 1/Layer 2
Period	unknown
Orientation	north to south and east to west
Coffin	small rectangular wooden coffins (one interior lined with tin)
Type of burial	16 secondary individual coffin burials; 10 from Crypt 1 and 6 from Crypt 2
Pit/Layer	Crypts 1 and 2 (Pit 5)
Period	unknown
Orientation	north to south
Coffin	Small rectangular wooden coffins

below the skeleton was a fragment of a leather rope. Since this burial was located close to the sanctuary, it is possible that it is the remains of one of the Franciscan friars of the convent. The thin dark line bordering the skeleton could have been left by the decomposition of the Franciscan garment, which would have served as a shroud (Zucchi 2001:65–66). This burial was associated with the earliest part of Layer 2 (dated 1796–1850).

The excavations also revealed two types of underground structures: crypts and ossuaries. Crypt 1, first discovered in the late 1950s, is located in the central aisle. Constructed with layers of bricks placed in alternate rows, Crypt 1 has a north-south orientation and an almost square, box-like shape (3.34 x 327 m) with an arched roof having a maximum height of 1.62 m (Figure 5). Descendants later added a small stairway to the southern wall of the crypt. Unfortunately, the contents of this crypt have been repeatedly disturbed, with the last episode apparently occurring just before these excavations. Crypt 1 was examined some months before this last episode. Observations included 4 small, almost intact wooden coffins; 2 small, broken wooden coffins with their contents still in place; bones from different

Figure 5. Crypt 1. (Drawing by author.)

individuals scattered on the floor and the stairs (apparently thrown inside the crypt during the last remodeling of the church); and 32 marble tombstones removed during remodeling. When the excavations were begun, all the wooden coffins were broken, and the bones were piled in the northern end of the crypt. Because of this disturbance, it was impossible to make a detailed record of the contents.

Crypt 2 also has a north-south orientation and is located in the right aisle of the church (Figure 6). It is smaller than Crypt 1 (1.93

Figure 6. Crypt 2. (Drawing by Carlos Quintero.)

x 1.35 m) and has a roof with three rounded lobes. The central lobe is slightly higher (1.76 m) than the other two (1.56 m). The roof and three of the walls were constructed with bricks and mortar, while the north wall was made of

sun-dried bricks without any type of mortar. This was probably intended to facilitate the removal of the upper adobes of the front wall in order to place new burials. It also explains why the most recent burials found inside this crypt were piled in the central area.

Artifacts were recovered from under two burials (burials 3 and 4) lying directly on the floor of Crypt 2. Artifacts associated with Burial 3 (Figures 7, 8) include a probable iron door knocker, a musket bullet, three iron nails, three unidentified hollow conical iron objects, one blue porcelain English button (corresponding to Stanley South type 23) (Noël Hume 1991: 90), one fragment of Gaudy Dutch ware, three probable iron window latches, and two small unidentified iron objects; two small cannon balls (7.8 cm in diameter), one utilized stone, and one bronze lock plate (Zucchi 2003). The presence of these artifacts under the burial is puzzling. Although the lock plate could have been part of the coffin used for the primary burial, there is no explanation for the presence of the other artifacts.

Two copper alloy one-cent coins were recovered from under Burial 4. The first is Venezuelan and is dated 1858 (Stohr 1965:87–88), while the second is North American and dated 1853 (Noël Hume 1991:170). Five secondary urn burials were found on top of the five burials on the floor of the crypt. All coffins were broken owing to time, humidity, and the collapse of the upper section of the adobe wall, and some of the human remains were very deteriorated. In spite of this, five types of urns were identified, and the typology is shown in Figure 9. Two urns (Type 6) bore the engraved initials A, G, M, H and P, L, C, G.

In addition to the crypts, three ossuaries were found at the base of the wall of the right aisle. These ossuaries are associated with the removed upper levels of Layer 2, which dates from ca. 1850 until 1915. The upper levels of Layer 2 were removed from most of the church during the last reconstruction. Ossuaries and crypts are the only structures belonging to this late time period. The upper surface of these ossuaries was immediately below the present floor of the church. All had rectangular box-like shapes (75 × 41.7 cm and 65 × 46 cm) and were constructed of ceramic tiles (23.7 × 11.5 × 3 cm) and mortar. The first ossuary contained

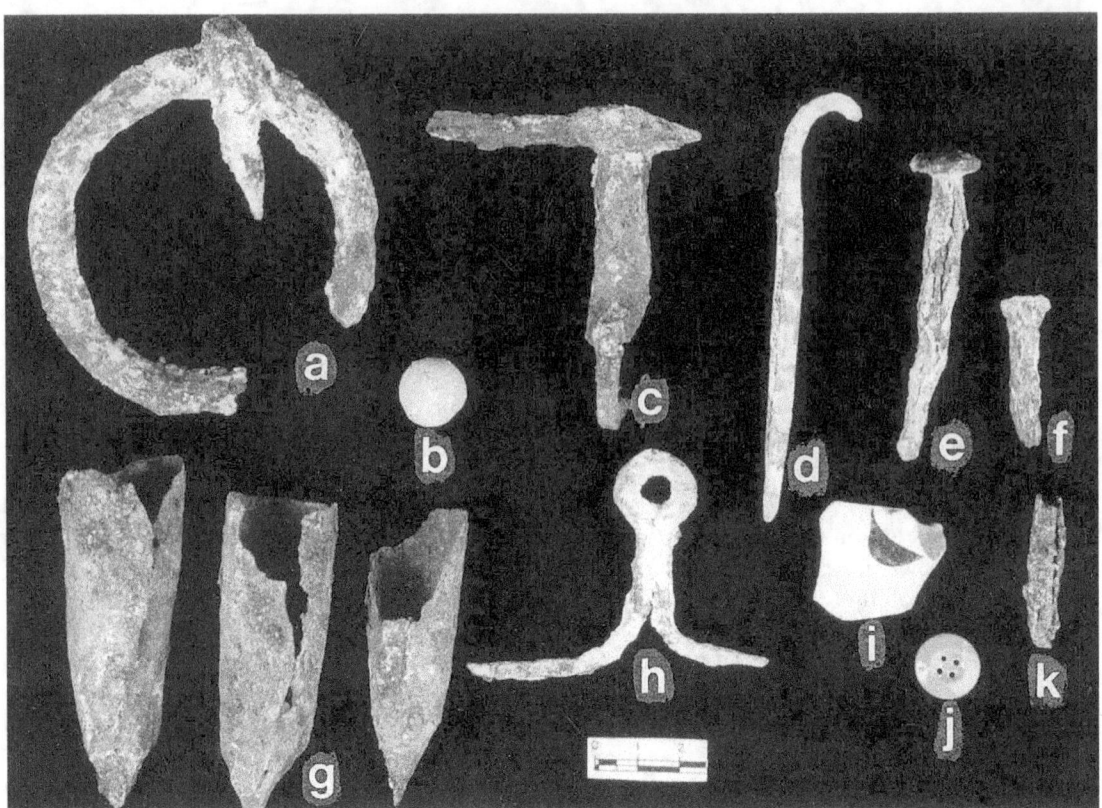

Figure 7. Objects found in Crypt 2 under burial 3: (*a*) a probable iron door knocker, (*b*) a musket bullet, (*e, f, k*) three iron nails, (*g*) three unidentified hollow conical iron objects, (*j*) one blue porcelain English button, (*i*) one fragment of Gaudy Dutch ware, and (*c, d, h*) three probable iron window latches. (Photo by departmento de fotografia del IVIC.)

a small, broken wooden coffin (Type 1) lined with tin attached by small prongs. Inside this ossuary were 80 nails of different sizes, 16 small square clamps, 2 screws with a flat floral adornment, and 1 small dental prosthesis. The second ossuary was located north of the first and had a north-south orientation, but most of it was located outside of Unit 1 and was therefore not extensively tested. The inner surface of the third ossuary was covered with a thick layer of mortar. In addition to human remains and fragments of a small wooden coffin, this ossuary contained a rounded iron handle adhered to a plate. Based on size and other characteristics, the handle could have belonged to the coffin. On top of all three ossuaries numerous broken roof tiles and bricks were found, some of which may have been from the ossuaries. Others could derive from construction debris related to earlier remodeling episodes.

Artifacts recovered during the investigation were not abundant. Most were apparently introduced into the church through redeposited fill used to raise the church floor during the restorations of 1720 and 1791–1795. The materials from Layer 1 include a few fragments of Spanish and Mexican majolica (Columbia Plain and San Luis Blue on White), coarse earthenware, Creole pottery, fragmented bricks, adobes, roof tiles, mortar, and animal and human bones (Zucchi 2003). The archaeological materials from Layer 2 include Spanish and Mexican majolica fragments (Columbia Plain, Puebla Polychrome, and an unidentified type with mottled blue paint over white enamel), brown stoneware, fragments of middle- and late-style olive jars, redware, transfer-printed creamware, English tin-glazed earthenware, Indian and Creole pottery, white and brown glass bottle fragments, pieces of bricks, floor and roof tiles, nails and other unidentified

Perspectives from *Historical Archaeology*

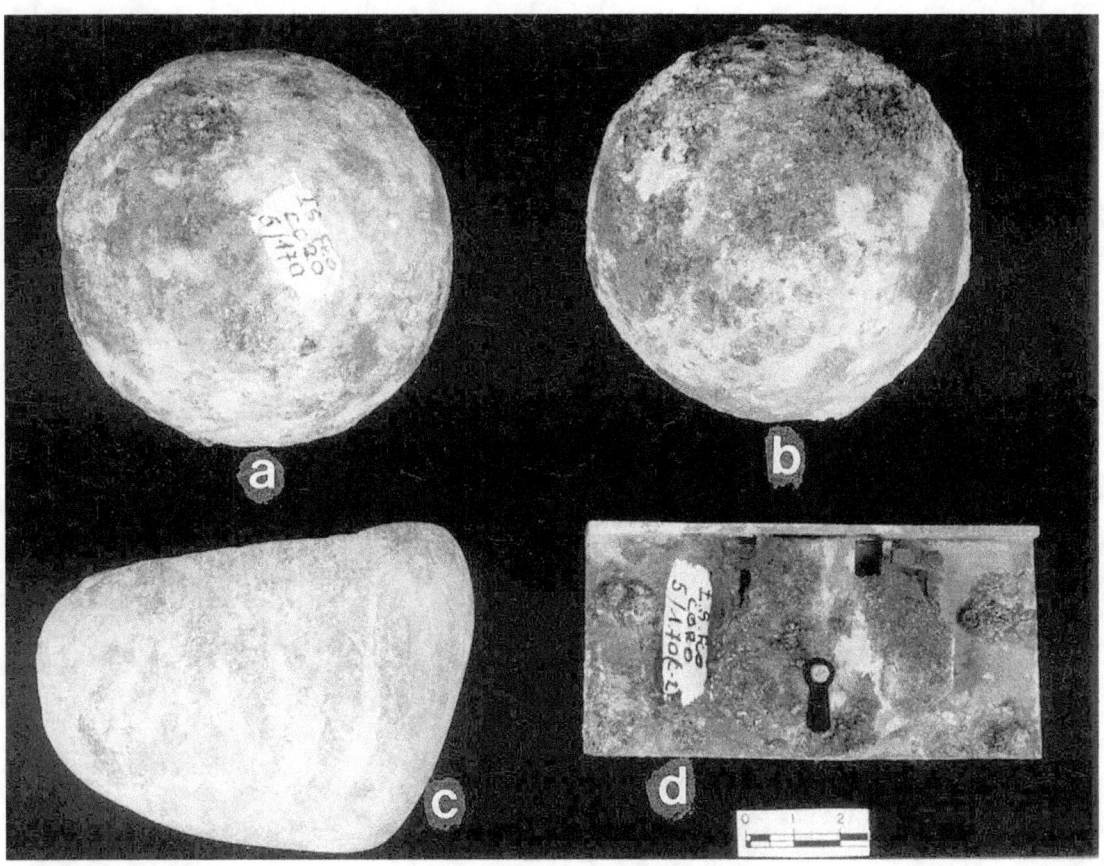

Figure 8. Objects found in Crypt 2 under burial 3: (*a, b*) two small cannon balls (7.8 cm in diameter), (*c*) one utilized stone, and (*d*) one bronze lock plate. (Photo by departmento de fotografia del IVIC.)

iron objects, cattle bones, a small marine shell, and wood fragments.

Chronology

As previously noted, historical documents provide the following dates on the evolution of the San Francisco church:

1613–1619	Construction of the first church
1681–1695	Damage to the building during the great storm of 1681 and the English invasion of 1695
1720	Construction of the second church
1791–1795	Remodeling of the church into a three-aisle building
1887	Reconstruction of the building after the Federation War
1903–1906	Remodeling of the church into a neo-Gothic building; most colonial features are removed
1987–1994	Rebuilding resulting in the destruction of most of the 19th- and 20th-century human and cultural remains

Since Floor 1 was the earliest occupational floor and overlaid compact, sterile clay subsoil, Floor 1 probably represents the church floor constructed between 1613 and 1617. This conclusion seems to be supported by a ^{14}C age determination of 220 +/- 70 years B.P. (Beta 147596), obtained from the surface of Floor 1 in Test Unit 2. This translates into a date range

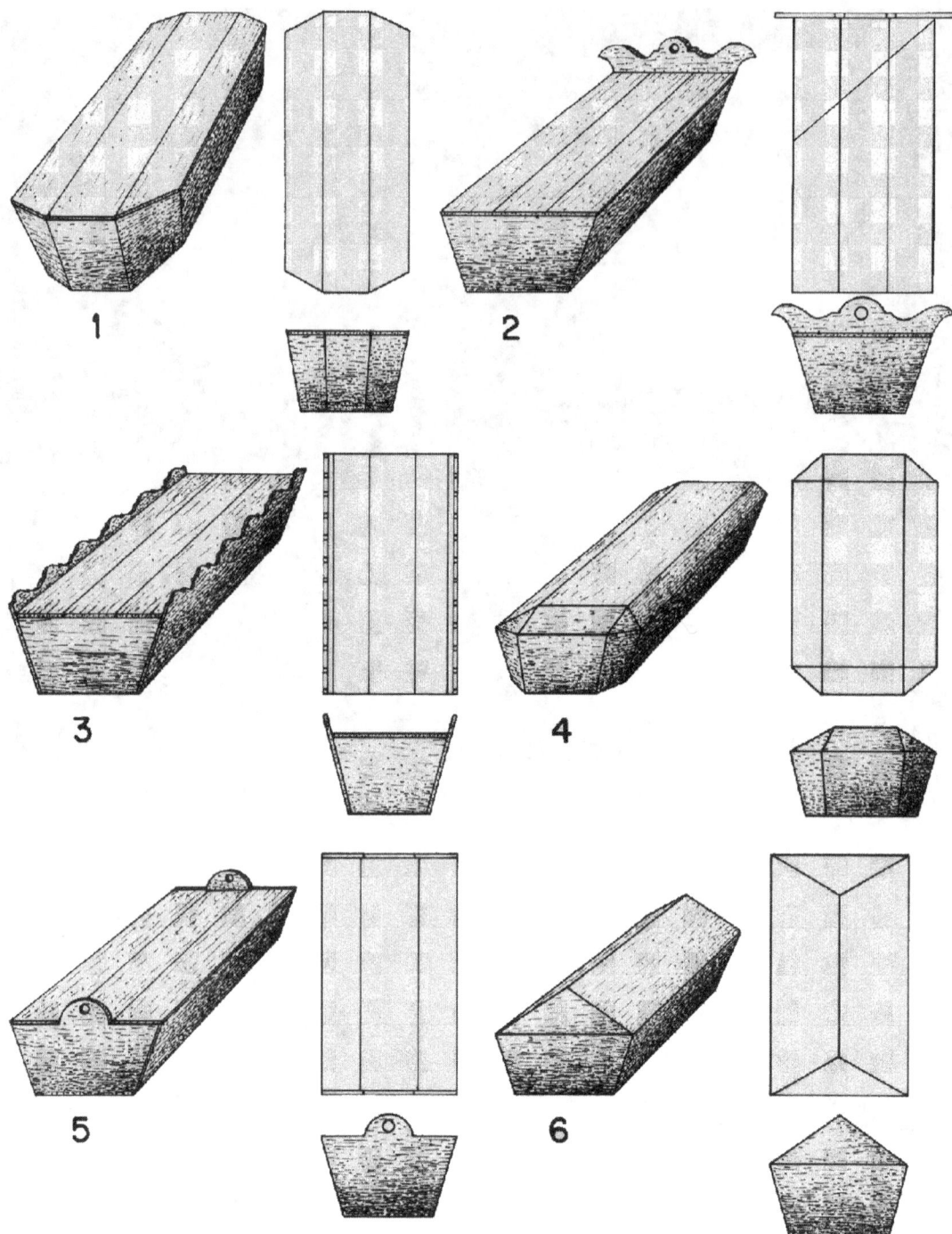

Figure 9. Typology of wooden coffins for secondary burials. (Drawing by author.)

(with 2 sigma or 95% of confidence) extending from 1500 to 1950 (B.P. 450 to 0), with the interception of the radiocarbon age with the calibration curve at A.D. 1660 (Cal B.P. 290).

Floor 2 was originally covered by square ceramic tiles. Since it was found at the same level as the probable foundation stones of an old main arch, it was determined that this floor belonged to the second church constructed in 1720. Furthermore, the presence of Layer 1, located between floors 1 and 2, indicates that Floor 2 was raised with fill obtained from a nearby site, containing cultural remains from different periods. Construction rubble found just above Floor 1 (Units 2, 3, and 7) probably relates to the destruction of the first church (1613–1617) and the construction of the second (1720).

Eleven bone samples were analyzed using X-ray diffraction (Bartioskas and Middleton 1992: 63–72,99). The dates provided by six of these samples were discarded since they were clearly erroneous (three derived from Crypt 2 [No. 9, 10 and 11] provided dates of 37,000, 14,000, and 50,000 years; two [No. 4 and 5] could not be dated; and a sixth [No. 8] yielded 0 years). Of the five remaining samples, No. 7 from Crypt 1 provided a date of A.D. 1890, which fits well with the date of this crypt derived from stratigraphic evidence. Samples 1, 2, and 3 from Unit 1 provided dates that range from the 16th through the beginning of the 20th centuries. These dates are stratigraphically mixed (Level 40–60 cm dated A.D. 1550; 60–80 cm dated A.D. 1910; and 90–100 cm dated A.D. 1730). The same applies to Sample 6, which provided a date of A.D. 1670 for Level 0.37–0.53 cm of Unit 3; the stratigraphy of this unit was also altered through repeated burial processes.

Discussion

The excavations at the San Francisco Church in Coro, Venezuela, yielded important evidence for church construction and mortuary patterning at this particular site. The original church, constructed in 1620, appears to have had an earthen floor located between 80 cm and 1 m below the existing sanctuary floor and between 60 and 80 cm below the floor elsewhere in the church. Although excavations did not yield information about the characteristics and materials used in this first building, historical documents indicate that, in 1632, Coro's cathedral was the only masonry structure in the town. Therefore, it is likely that the first church was of mud or adobe construction, similar to the rest of the buildings of the town. Three postholes found in Floor 1 in Unit 3 may be related to the wattle-and-daub wall of the left aisle. Further, all of the test units excavated in Floor 1 revealed that the underlying soil was sterile sandy clay. No burials were encountered intruding this sterile subsoil. While it is the case that only a small percentage of this subsoil surface was exposed during excavations, the fact that not a single burial shaft or other structure was even partially encountered strongly suggests that the first church was apparently not used as a burial ground.

The characteristics of the stone foundation and its alignment with a half-column visible in the wall of the right-hand aisle suggest that it might have been the base of the main arch of the church constructed in 1720. Furthermore, the foundation's location indicates that this reconstructed building was adjacent to the western corridor of the convent, that its only aisle was 7 to 7.50 m wide, and that it was floored with square ceramic tiles placed over a thin layer of mortar. This type of floor was probably easier to remove and replace during burial.

The presence in Layer 1 of domestic refuse such as ceramics and animal bone from the 16th and 17th centuries suggests that this fill was most likely obtained elsewhere in the town for the purpose of raising the floor some 40 to 60 cm. These cultural materials almost certainly represent off-site domestic occupations. Further, although documents indicate that the second church was constructed with sun-dried bricks (González Batista 1994:27), the presence of broken bricks, tiles, and stones in certain areas of Layer 1 suggests that these materials were also used in the building's construction.

During the reconstruction of the church that occurred between 1791 and 1795, the floor of the new three-aisle building was raised above Layer 1 through the intentional placement of Layer 2. During the last reconstruction, in the 1990s, most of Layer 2 was removed together with many of the post-1795 primary and secondary burials.

The only primary burial was found in the remaining portion of Layer 2. This particular burial was located at the foot of the old sanctuary, and it is likely that these remains belonged to one of the Franciscan friars. On top of the skeleton's pelvis, excavators observed an isolated coccyx, a fragmented pelvis, some vertebrae, and ribs. These bones apparently belonged to a more recent burial that was incompletely removed. This later exhumation may explain the absence of the skull of the underlying primary burial.

No primary burials of children were encountered during the excavations, so it is impossible to establish whether it was customary, as in Spain, to locate children in the lateral aisles of churches. The evidence obtained at San Francisco does indicate that secondary burials of children could be placed in the central aisle of the church.

Although there are no absolute dates for the secondary burials that were found in Layer 1, 18th-century documents indicate that, from the 1720s, at least some people were already requesting burial inside the church. As these burials were excavated, earlier ones could conceivably be disturbed. It is possible that some of the secondary burials could date to the first half of the 18th century. Two individual secondary burials recovered from Layer 2 in Units 4 and 5 were interred in wooden coffins. Although a small sample, these two burials suggest that, by the second half of the 18th century, the practice of reburying exhumed individuals in small wooden coffins had begun among the local population (Zucchi 2001).

The stratigraphic position of the secondary burials and their characteristics, including the lack of a coffin, indicate that the arrangement of the bones inside the graves did not follow an established pattern. In each case, these burials were differentially placed, and several contained the bones of more than one adult or of children and adults. At present, it is impossible to establish if these multiple secondary burials belonged to persons related through kinship.

Between 1720 and 1795, the secondary burial shafts were only 50 to 60 cm deep. If primary burials were interred in equally shallow graves, this would certainly explain the terrible smell that characterized the churches.

During the 19th century, the types of small coffins became more diverse and more modern, as indicated by the appearance of simple carved wooden ornaments placed vertically over the lid. Coffins were also occasionally ornamented by small brass tacks; tin or fabric urn linings; or iron or brass lock plates, handles, and/or other adornments.

The evidence from San Francisco suggests that the construction of underground masonry ossuaries and crypts is a phenomenon of the 19th century. The characteristics, location, depth, materials, and contents of the three masonry ossuaries indicate that the use of these underground structures began in the second half of the 19th century and continued through the second decade of the 20th century. Oral tradition indicates that the crypts were constructed by wealthy families. The available evidence from San Francisco indicates that these underground structures were typically used to deposit secondary urn burials of family members. Given the size of Crypt 1, it is possible that this crypt might have also been used for primary burials.

The dates found on the marble tombstones removed during the last remodeling of the church ranged between 1871 and 1920. The use of tombstones became common in Venezuela during the 19th century. Although the laws of 1873 mandated that the dead could only be buried in public cemeteries, in certain towns and cities people continued to be buried inside churches until the second decade of the 20th century. This is clearly the case at San Francisco (Zucchi 2001).

Conclusion

The excavations at the San Francisco Church in Coro, Venezuela, have yielded important information about changing burial practices at this particular church. Because no other investigations have been undertaken at contemporary churches in the country, this information provides important baseline data that can be compared with new evidence as future excavations are undertaken.

Acknowledgments

Excavations of the San Francisco Church were financed by the Archiepiscopal Diocese of Coro and the Instituto Venezolano de Investigaciones Científicas. Bonnie G. McEwan made invaluable corrections and suggestions for the improvement of this paper. Julia A. King assisted with final revisions. Sorocaima Romero assisted during the excavations and along with Carlos Quintero produced some drawings.

References

ARCHIVO GENERAL DE INDIAS
1630 Manuscript, Santo Domingo, 221, ramo 2, no. 49, letras G y H , Archivo General de Indias, Sevilla, Spain.

ARCHIVO HISTORICO DE CORO
1720 Manuscript, Instrumentos Públicos, T. VIII. F.215 vto, Archivo Historico de Coro, Venezuela.

ARCO MOYA, JUAN
1989 Religiosidad popular en Jaén durante el siglo XVIII. Actitud ante la Muerte. In *La religiosidad Popular. II, Vida y Muerte: La Imaginación Religiosa*, coordinated by C. Alvarez Santaló, Maria Buxó, and S. Rodríguez Becerra, pp. 309–327. Anthropos Editorial del Hombre-Fundación Machado, Barcelona, Spain.

BARTSIOKAS, A., AND A. P. MIDDLETON
1992 Characterization and Dating of Recent and Fossil Bones by X-ray Diffraction. *Journal of Archaeological Science* 19:63–72.

CARROCERA, CAYETANO
1943 Convento de Nuestra Señora de Salceda, de Coro. *Venezuela Misionera* 5(52):138–139.

GASPARINI, GRAZIANO
1969 *Restauración de Templos Coloniales en Venezuela*. Ministerio de Justicia, Dirección de Cultos, Caracas, Venezuela.
1976 *Templos Coloniales Venezolanos*. Ernesto Armitano Editor, Caracas, Venezuela.
1994 *Coro Patrimonio Mundial*. Armitano Editores, Caracas, Venezuela.

GÓMEZ, ZALAZAR, FRANCISCO G.
1872 *Manual Eclesiástico*. Librería de M. Miguel Otamendi, Madrid, Spain.

GONZÁLEZ BATISTA, CARLOS
1994 *CORO donde empieza Venezuela*. Caracas Paper Company (CAPACO)–Fundación Museo de las Ventanas de Hierro. Litografía Radiante, Maracay, Venezuela.

NOËL HUME, IVOR
1991 *A Guide to Artifacts of Colonial America*. Vintage Books, New York, NY.

PEÑA OBREGON, A., J. E. JARDINES, AND M. J. GARIT
1987 La Parroquial de San Isidoro de Holguín. Manifestación de una costumbre funeraria. Paper presented at the Congreso Dominicano de Historia, Santo Domingo, Dominican Republic.

STOHR, TOMAS
1965 *Venezuela numismática*. Universidad del Zulia, Dirección de Cultura, Venezuela.

TORRUBIA, JOSÉ
1972 *Crónica de la Provincia Franciscana de Santa Cruz de la Española y Caracas*. Fuentes para la Historia Colonial de Venezuela. Biblioteca de la Academia Nacional de la Historia 108, Caracas, Venezuela.

VÁZQUEZ, ILEANA, AND ELIZABETH BRICEÑO
1989 Informe Preliminar "Iglesia de San Francisco," Coro, Estado Falcón. Dirección de Arquitectura–Dirección de Patrimonio Cultural. CONAC, Caracas, Venezuela.

ZUCCHI, ALBERTA
2001 Polvo eres y en polvo te convertirás: la muerte y su entorno en Venezuela hasta 1940. *Antropológica* 93–94:3–133.
2003 *Recuperando el Pasado: Arqueología e historia documental de la Iglesia de San Francisco de Coro*. Departamento de Antropología, IVIC-Arquidiócesis de Coro, Venezuela.

ALBERTA ZUCCHI
DEPARTAMENTO DE ANTROPOLOGÍA
INSTITUTO VENEZOLANO DE INVESTIGACIONES CIENTÍFICAS
APARTADO 21827
CARACAS, VENEZUELA

Douglas V. Armstrong and LouAnn Wurst

Clay Faces in an Abolitionist Church: The Wesleyan Methodist Church in Syracuse, New York

ABSTRACT

For many years, a group of sculpted clay faces, in desperate and immediate need of conservation, tenuously clung to the walls of the dug-out space called a "tunnel" beneath the former Wesleyan Methodist Church, the home of a noted abolitionist and social-reform oriented congregation in downtown Syracuse, New York. Archaeological and historical research indicates a 19th-century origin for the faces. The church openly participated in abolition and the Underground Railroad, and housed a national abolitionist press. However, even in a pro-emancipation community such as Syracuse, the dangers for refugees fleeing bondage were real, and the consequences of capture were life threatening. This was particularly true after the passage of the Fugitive Slave Act in 1850. This study presents evidence that the clay faces may have been created by African American refugees from slavery. Moreover, it describes a community's efforts to conserve and protect this resource.

Introduction

A group of enigmatic sculpted clay faces clung tenuously for many years to the wall of the basement of the former Wesleyan Methodist Church in downtown Syracuse, New York (Figure 1). These clay faces are a unique and important historical resource that may be related to the actions of refugees fleeing enslavement in the era preceding emancipation (Armstrong and Wurst 1998). The faces presented researchers with a perplexing dilemma. They were found within a context suggesting that the faces were possibly the work of African American artists, yet they were neither signed nor dated and were created on walls that are difficult to date. Moreover, the clay faces were in desperate need of conservation and restoration.

In 1843, the Wesleyan Methodist Church splintered from the Methodist Episcopal Church since the latter would not take an active stand against slavery. The church in Syracuse was built to provide a place for this group to worship and to facilitate abolition. In addition, the building also facilitated the congregation's activism in temperance, women's rights, and religious reform. The Wesleyan Methodist Church property also housed a publishing concern that produced the *American Wesleyan* and the *True Wesleyan*, significant forums dedicated to the abolition of slavery.

There is also a great deal of information that links many of the Wesleyan Methodist Church members and the Underground Railroad. Research indicates that the church was utilized as a station and that the congregation was actively engaged in assisting refugees in transit to Canada. Moreover, members of this congregation were active and public in their opposition to the Fugitive Slave Act of 1850, indicating that individuals in Syracuse practiced political abolition and were willing to flaunt federal law when they deemed it necessary.

The oral traditions provide a mix of disparate information about the origin of the sculpted clay faces. It was said that they were made by fugitive slaves hiding in this station on the Underground Railroad, and that they were created by the furnace attendant who created the faces to pass his time while in the underground passage. Laura Grover [Phillips], an 83-year-old former church member, tells that as a small child (approximately 6 years old), she and three to four other children skipped church and stole into the basement. They entered through a trap doorway on the north side of the building and proceeded

FIGURE 1. Syracuse Wesleyan Methodist Church. View of the northeast. (Photo by Armstrong.)

single file into the passageway. The area was not very well lit, and she could not really see the art, but she relates that "I could feel them on the wall … we ran our hands across them but we did not know that they were faces. We would have been too scared" (Grover 1998, pers. comm.). This first-hand account places the art on the dug-out wall by 1923.

Jean Galvin, daughter of long-time pastor William Montgomery, recounts being led to the basement single file with flashlights at a Halloween party in the mid-1940s. Her story describes a group of faces in one area. She reports that she was told that the art was made by the janitor, William Gebhardt, to add "a bit of mystique to a Halloween celebration for the youths there" (Brieaddy 1998). Oriette Meloon shares similar impressions, that the faces were made by the custodian to amuse her Sunday School class at Halloween (Meloon 1998, pers. comm.). These stories are compelling in their detail but also indicate a degree of uncertainty. It is clear, that as children, each of these individuals made observations of the art. By the 1940s, memories of the church's involvement with the abolition movement had faded, leaving little basis to explain the presence of these faces.

This paper presents the results of historical and archaeological investigations conducted by Syracuse University at the Wesleyan Methodist Church. The discussion is divided into three sections. The first entails a detailed study of the historic context of the church and the history of the church building. A wide range of published and manuscript accounts establish linkages between the building and the wide range of social reforms that the congregation participated in. The church was part of a complex web of community organizations and individuals that actively participated in the abolition movement.

The second part of this paper presents the results of archaeological investigations centering on the dug-out basement and a thorough description of the cultural features found there. The research provides strong evidence for a mid-19th-century date for the passageway and, thus, supports a 19th-century origin for the art. The third section provides a brief overview of community-based grass-roots efforts that raised more than the $225,000 necessary for the conservation, long-term curation, and initial exhibition of these remains. This discussion

demonstrates the importance of engaging the public in the protection of significant historic resources. Through this process, not only were the specific resources "saved" but the community gained a stake in the future of its past.

Historical Background: Setting the Stage

The central region of New York played a pivotal role in the movement to abolish slavery. African Americans worked alongside growing numbers of people of differing backgrounds to bring about social change. There can be little doubt that the location of this region, along the very open and sparsely populated border with Ontario, played a major part in the attractiveness of the region to those seeking freedom. However, the impact of social and religious reform movements cannot be underestimated.

Central New York played a pivotal role in what has been called the "Second Great Awakening." In *The Burnt-Over District,* Whitney Cross (1950) presents a compelling argument for the linkages between religious reform movements and an awakening to an array of moral issues. These issues initially focused on temperance and slavery but expanded to include the care of the poor and women's rights. Converts to religious reform spearheaded by leaders such as Charles G. Finney became "converted again" to pursue immediate emancipation (Meyers 1962:149–181; Sernett 1989:55).

During the height of the abolition movement, from the 1830's until the outbreak of the Civil War, the city of Syracuse and much of Central New York played a nationally prominent role in efforts to free enslaved African Americans and abolish the institution of slavery (Lee 1882; Fordham 1989). As early as 1839, abolitionists had been involved in the well-known case of Harriet Powell who escaped to Kingston, Canada, while visiting Syracuse with her owner from Mississippi (Sperry 1924:59–66). This event affected the lives of many, including Dr. Silas Bliss, who assisted with abolitionist communications and was later to become a founding member of the Wesleyan Methodist Church (WMC-TR 1843; Sperry 1924:63).

The leadership of the abolition movement in Central New York split from William L. Garrison and his emphasis on moral suasion toward a policy of political abolition. In 1840 Gerrit

Smith, supported by African American leaders Frederick Douglass and religious leaders including Luther Lee, established the Liberty Party, a political party organized around the single issue of abolition. While garnering few votes, the notion of political activism expressed by the Liberty Party laid the groundwork for the establishment of religious groups premised upon the issue of abolition. Throughout the northeast, pastors and church members from many denominations were faced with the ethical dilemma of accepting increasingly clear church policies supporting the institution of slavery or breaking away in support of abolition. In the case of the Methodists, the debate focused on the abolitionist leanings of some pastors who used their pulpits and other public venues to lecture against slavery, even though the official church position did not condemn the institution (Lee 1882). These ministers felt that Methodism should follow the lead of John Wesley who in 1774 had clearly stated his opposition to human bondage. Wesley wrote that slave holding was "not consistent with any degree of natural justice, mercy, and truth" (Wesley 1774).

Lee, who would become the first pastor of the Syracuse Wesleyan Methodist Church, was a leading figure both in the abolition movement and the Wesleyan Methodist Connection. Trained as a Methodist Episcopal minister, Lee followed the Methodist practice of itinerant preaching and served pastorates throughout Central New York and Massachusetts (Lee 1882). Lee held positions in Watertown in 1836 and in Fulton from 1837 to 1838, both towns that became noted as stops on the Underground Railroad (Lee 1882).

Lee began speaking out against slavery (Matlack 1849; Kaufman 1994:87, 97). Based upon a speech on the "sinfulness of slave-holding" at an antislavery conference in Utica, New York, in May 1838 and later travels to Kingston, Ontario, where he continued to preach on the issue, Lee was charged with "contumacy and insubordination" at the Methodist Episcopal New York Conference of 1838 (Kaufman 1994:104). Lee along with fellow pastors James Floy, Paul R. Brown, and David Plumb were all convicted and suspended from the conference. The internal revolt within the church was further fueled by several cases in the late 1830's that involved Methodist ministers from the south who actually owned slaves (Matlack 1849: 34–36). Separated from

his church, Lee became further involved with abolition and traveled a wide circuit lecturing as an agent of the New York Anti-Slavery Society (Kaufman 1994: 107).

Perhaps inspired by his wife Mary's involvement with the Ladies Anti-Slavery Society in Boston, Lee took a stand in support of women's involvement in the abolition effort (Kaufman 1994:123). On another front, and against the strong warning of leaders such as Garrison, Lee strongly supported political action as a means of change. Thus, in this period of forced separation from his church and prior to the formation of the Wesleyan Methodist Connection, Lee joined with other reformers in the Utica area to form the Liberty Party, which was dedicated to the abolition of slavery (Kaufman 1994:124–129). This merger of religious reform with political action and social reform, including abolition, temperance, and women's rights, would embed itself in the future Wesleyan Methodist Church and publishing house in Syracuse. It would also be part of a fusion of ideals that would lead to Syracuse and Central New York being a leader in the advocacy for a diverse array of mid-19th-century social and political reform.

By the early 1840's, secessions had already begun in the Methodist Episcopal Church (Matlack 1849:320). Encouraged by this trend, a group of pastors met in February 1843 in Andover, Massachusetts, where they agreed to withdraw their membership from the Methodist Episcopal Church due to the church's policy governing the issue of slavery. They decided to organize a convention in Utica, New York, on 31 May 1843 (Matlack 1849: 212). Among the organizing ministers were Lee and Cyrus Prindle, both prominent in the Syracuse church and publishing house. In anticipation of this meeting, dissident members of Syracuse's Methodist Episcopal Church held an organizational meeting in the basement of the Methodist Episcopal Church on 2 May 1843 (WMC-TR 1843). Their preliminary resolutions show that opposition to slavery was clearly the foundation of this organization (WMC-TR 1843). Membership records for the church show that once established, the congregation quickly grew to more than 60 individuals by year's end (WMC-MR 1843).

The Wesleyan Methodist Connection assigned Lee as the pastor of the recently formed Syracuse Church (Lee 1843). Since the Syracuse church had no building of its own, the members met in the basement of the Congregational Church, and later the congregation bought the old Unitarian Church after that denomination built a new house of worship (Lee 1882:252; Kaufman 1994:180). The Wesleyan Methodist Church of Syracuse elected its first trustees on 9 August 1845. While building up the Syracuse Church, Lee utilized his experience as a traveling lecturer for the abolition cause and recruited new preachers. As the pastor of the Syracuse church, Lee spent much of his time organizing other congregations in the region. Among the many churches started at this time was the Wesleyan Chapel at Seneca Falls at which Lee gave the dedication sermon on 14 October 1843 (Lee 1843). This church would host the Women's Rights Convention in 1848.

The Wesleyan Methodist Connection, with its dedication to the cause of abolition, quickly grew from 6,000 members in 1843 to 15,000 in fall 1844. After helping found the Syracuse Church and preaching to its congregation for a year, Lee was elected president of the Wesleyan Methodist Connection at its first conference in Cleveland, Ohio. This represents a departure from the Methodist tradition of using the religious title bishop towards the political title of president. In addition to his role of president of the Connection, Lee was appointed editor of the *True Wesleyan*, an abolitionist newspaper that was later renamed the *American Wesleyan*. Assuming organizational responsibilities, Lee moved to New York City. Pastorage of the Syracuse church was assumed by P. R. Sawyer, the second in a series of pastors who rotated annually until Lee resumed his post in Syracuse in the early 1850s (WM-ACM 1843, 1853–1855; Lee 1882).

Wesleyan Methodist Church and the Underground Railroad

The connection between the Wesleyan Methodist Church of Syracuse and the abolition movement is obvious from the above description. However, there is also good evidence that the church members actively participated in the Underground Railroad. The *True Wesleyan*, edited by Lee, was a public forum not only for the Wesleyans but also for others who supported abolition and participated in the Underground Railroad. Many of the published letters are explicit and take no pains to hide the names of those assisting fugitive slaves to Canada. Lee's assessment of his personal involvement in the Underground Railroad points to Syracuse as the place where he had the most success: "In the spring of 1852 I removed from the city of New York to the city of Syracuse, where, during a three years' pastorate, I did the largest work of my life on the Under-ground Rail-road. I passed as many as thirty slaves through my hands in a month" (Lee 1882:331).

Lee praised the efforts of the Syracuse community in helping fugitive slaves and noted that money was always forthcoming to assist the Underground Railroad efforts (Lee 1882:339). An example of this support was noted in the church's Trustee Report in 1854, which records a gift of money to Lee and his Wesleyan church by a group of nonmembers, including several influential local abolitionists (WMC-TR 1854). One of the names on the list was Horace White, a local railroad magnate who was remembered for allowing fugitive slaves to ride in his trains (Sperry 1924:34–35).

If refugees made it to Syracuse, their prospects for freedom were great, but they were travel-weary, often hungry, fearful, and uncertain of their future. Into this uncertainty, runaway slaves streamed with the hope for freedom, and it is against hope, fear, and uncertainty that the record of the abolition movement in Syracuse stands out. While freedom was not obtained until the northern border was crossed, history shows that arrival in Syracuse meant freedom.

The active defiance represented by the Underground Railroad did not go unchallenged. However, attempts to counter the movement, including the Fugitive Slave Act of 1850, were largely unsuccessful and may have served to galvanize broader support for the abolition cause. In 1850, Lee wrote a series of articles opposing the Fugitive Slave Law. In the third article of this series, he wrote, "the law is unconstitutional because it deprives persons of liberty, without due process of law, and seeks to secure the results of a solemn adjudication, without the intervention of a court, or the action of a judge" (*True Wesleyan* 1850). In May 1851, supporters of the Fugitive Slave Act invited Daniel Webster to Syracuse. He gave a speech in which he strongly condemned any that violated the law. He threatened that they "bring upon themselves the penalty of the law ... Depend upon it, the law will be executed in its spirit and to its letter. It will be executed in all the great cities—here in Syracuse—in the midst of the next anti-slavery convention, if the occasion shall arise" (cited in Sperry 1924:22–23).

In fact, an attempt was made to execute the Fugitive Slave Law in Syracuse on 1 October 1851 and as per Webster's threat, this action was taken during a convention of the abolitionist Liberty Party (Sperry 1924:22). Organized resistance came to a head with the dramatic "Jerry Rescue," when William "Jerry" Henry was arrested under the Fugitive Slave Law. Henry was a refugee from slavery who had lived and worked in Syracuse for more than a year. He was arrested while at work and taken into custody. Upon news of Henry's arrest, the Liberty Party convention was adjourned, and Gerrit Smith and Rev. Samuel May went to the arraignment. On the evening of his capture, a group met at Dr. Hoyt's office and planned an escape. Among those present were Charles and Montgomery Merrick, George Carter, and Edward K. Hunt (Wesleyan Methodist members), along with such notables as Jermain Loguen and Gerrit Smith (WMC-MR 1851; Chase 1924:164; Sperry 1924:24). Ultimately, the rescue involved packing the police office with people. By sheer numbers, the mob of abolitionists overwhelmed the police and was successful in freeing Henry from custody. Henry was hidden in town for four days at the home of the "pro-slavery Democrat" Caleb Davis and reached Kingston, Ontario, via a schooner departing from Oswego (Sperry 1924). The only fugitive ever captured in Syracuse, Henry was freed by a group that included activists from the Wesleyan Methodist Church (Sperry 1924:26–33). This action became a political rallying point and a focal point for abolition efforts in Syracuse.

The church served not only as a station on the Underground Railroad but also as a meeting place that allowed both men and women to express themselves. This is evident from events that occurred during the New York State Men's Temperance Conference in Syracuse in 1852 when Susan B. Anthony of Rochester was not allowed to address the floor. When she was not permitted to address the convention, Rev. May made an announcement that Elizabeth Cady Stanton would speak that evening at the

Wesleyan Methodist Church. A reporter went to the Wesleyan Methodist gathering and noted "a large number of ladies were in attendance among whom we noticed Miss Susan B. Anthony of Rochester and Mrs. Stanton and Mrs. Bloomer of Seneca Falls" (*Syracuse Standard* 1852). The reporter noted that considerable dissatisfaction was expressed at the unceremonious manner in which the lady delegates to the convention had been treated during the earlier proceedings.

In addition to abolition, the Underground Railroad, temperance, and women's rights, the church played an important role as the facilitator of the Wesleyan Methodist press. While the press initially operated out of New York City, the Wesleyan Methodist Connection's publishing house was founded in Syracuse following Lee's return in 1852. By this time, Syracuse was firmly established as a city that would resist the Fugitive Slave Law, and the Wesleyan publications utilized freedom of the press in direct defiance of that law. A friendly environment was required to publish this material.

The historical summary presented here has demonstrated the importance of the Wesleyan Methodist Church (both the physical structure and the congregation) to the abolition movement in general and to the Underground Railroad in particular. The church members, not content with moral suasion approaches to slavery, took matters into their own hands through political activism and the defiance of federal laws to further the cause of emancipation.

Wesleyan Methodist Church Building

The Wesleyan Methodist Church building stands on Lot 4 of Block 114 in Syracuse, on the corner of Onondaga and Jefferson Streets. The lot upon which the church was built was purchased by Freeborn G. and Fanny Jewett on 17 December 1845 from Moses D. Burnet for $400. The Jewetts, prominent citizens of Skaneateles, sold the lot to the Wesleyan Methodist Church of Syracuse on 10 January 1846 for the original amount of purchase.

Wesleyan Methodist Trustees formally recorded plans to build a church on 16 September 1845. The trustees resolved to build a meetinghouse 35 × 45 ft. in size; the walls were to be 18 ft. high. Before the end of the meeting, this proposal was amended to allow adjustments to the specifications as needed. A building committee was appointed to supervise construction and make modifications to the plans as necessary (WMC-TR 1845). Church drawings by E. W. Levensworth were approved, and construction of the church was completed at its current site in 1847 (WMC-TR 1847). The church was built of brick in a typical meetinghouse style.

The initial Wesleyan Methodist Church structure was modified on several occasions over the next few decades (Figure 2). In the early 1850s, with the return of Rev. Lee as pastor, the church became the site of the Wesleyan Methodist publishing house. Modifications to the church building were initiated in 1857 in response to additional space requirements. Changes included the expansion of the audience room by 20 ft., the construction of a brick tower at the entry to the church, and the addition of a gallery with stairs (*Syracuse Journal* 1858; *Syracuse Standard* 1858). Newspaper articles also describe the construction of an addition to the east end

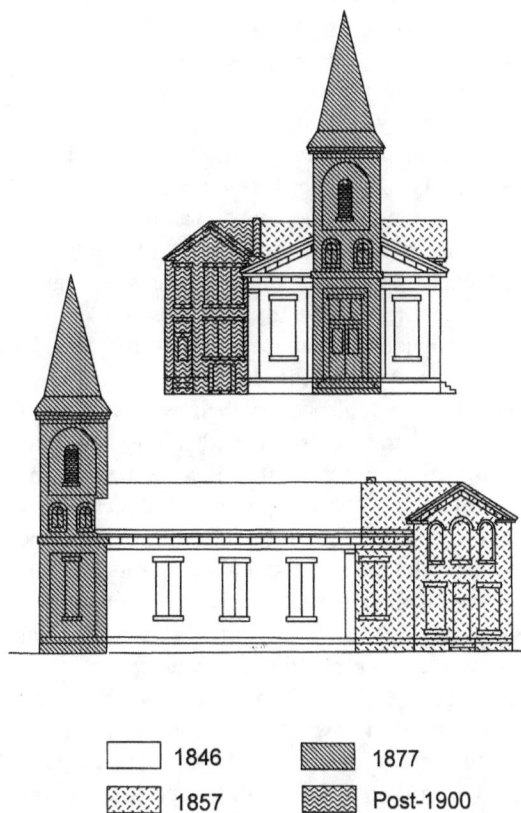

	1846		1877
	1857		Post-1900

FIGURE 2. The four periods of construction of the Wesleyan Methodist Church.

of the building. The ground floor was used as a book room and publishing office for the *True Wesleyan* (a nationally circulated abolitionist newsletter), while the second floor served as a Sabbath School (*Syracuse Journal* 1858; *Syracuse Standard* 1858). This addition measured 36 × 19 ft. and had a roofline running perpendicular to the auditorium. The cost of these improvements and the addition was $1,400 (*Syracuse Standard* 1858).

Structurally, the addition is observable by the junction in the sill stone, and a portion of the foundation stone from the original wall is still present in the basement. The original wall had been demolished to ground level; however, subsurface foundation stones were left intact and can be seen in the dug-out path that cuts through it.

The next major renovation to the church building was reported by Rev. N. E. Norton in 1877 (*American Wesleyan* 1877). In addition to a new roof and a cement walkway, the exterior of the church was adorned with a spire and a set of eve brackets. Inside, the gallery was removed and a frescoed painting added behind the pulpit. Auditorium windows with 70 panes of glass were replaced with "handsome mullion-post windows of stained glass." Pulpit furniture was replaced and a "step-up" added as a choir loft. The total cost of these renovations was approximately $1,150 (*Syracuse Journal* 1879).

In 1898, the church was burned by a fire that caused significant damage to the interior of the church building. This fire is reported to have begun in the wood-burning furnace in the basement (located immediately adjacent to the faces). It scorched the varnish off the pews and blew out most of the stained-glass windows in the auditorium (*Syracuse Standard* 1898). One of the few windows to survive the fire had been dedicated to Charles and Lanfear Merrick and is still in place on the south side of the auditorium. The newspaper reported "no wood or inflammable substance was left around the furnace after the fire was started in the morning" (*Syracuse Standard* 1898).

The 1898 fire is significant in that it definitively establishes a 19th-century date for the art on the dug-out walls of the church beneath the auditorium. The faces closest to the furnace, along with a support beam immediately adjacent to them, show clear indications of having been burned. As a result of this fire, two of the faces were actually fired and show traces of scorching. Ironically, the fire can probably be credited for the good state of preservation of these two faces.

After the 1898 fire, the wood-burning furnace was replaced by the coal-burning model that is still in the basement. This furnace was subsequently altered to use natural gas. Photographs of the building after the fire indicate that the duel chimneys were replaced with a single chimney at the northwest corner of the auditorium. A photograph (ca. 1861) (Figure 3) shows the same chimney pattern present in photographs dating to the 1890s. This suggests that the wood-burning furnace, blamed for the 1898 fire, was probably in place when the 1857 construction was completed.

A second fire swept the Wesleyan Methodist Church block in 1957. This fire destroyed the Methodist Episcopal Church building located next door and the Wesleyan Publishing House. While the fire raged, the Wesleyan Methodist Church building was encased in a sheet of ice created by the spray of the fire hoses and managed to survive with only water and smoke damage (Gunderson n.d.). The water caused extensive damage to the northeast end of the building, and the north wall of the later addition was replaced. Because of water damage in the basement, the west and north walls of the Sunday School building were replaced with a cinder block wall. This altered the entryway between the Sunday School basement and the area beneath

FIGURE 3. Wesleyan Methodist Church, ca. 1861 (Onondaga Historical Association).

the auditorium, limiting ability to evaluate the entry to the dug-out basement.

The most recent modifications to the building were carried out between 1994 and 1997. In 1989 the congregation, by then associated with the First Gospel Baptist Church, sold the property to Vaughn Lang. Over the past several years, Lang has stabilized the property with a new roof and exterior paint and trim work. The stained-glass windows were repaired, and extensive modification was done to the interior auditorium and former meeting rooms. The church is now the site of a restaurant and the offices of a property title company.

Archaeological Investigations

Archaeological investigations entailed a study of the dug-out passageway under the Wesleyan Methodist Church. This included compiling a detailed description of all cultural features by extensively photo-documenting and locating them on a scale drawing of the basement. In addition, archaeological testing was performed in an attempt to determine whether there was any direct physical evidence that refugees from slavery made use of the basement, and whether there was any evidence for the construction date of the tunnel passageway (Armstrong and Wurst 1998). The evidence obtained through excavation suggests that the tunnel passageway was in existence by the time of the 1857 renovations. The existence of the tunnel passageway at this time supports its use by refugees and provides indirect evidence that the faces were created by those who passed through this station on the Underground Railroad on their way to freedom.

None of the descriptions detailing the church modifications refer to the dug-out tunnel under the structure. The only reference directly related to the basement was by Rev. J. B. Knappenburger, who began his tenure at the church in 1889. In a newspaper article written in 1933, Knappenburger relates stories of the building's use during the period before emancipation (Knappenburger 1933). He reported that there were many stories known to the congregation relating to the use of the church building as part of the Underground Railroad. According to these stories, the "slaves were usually secreted in the church auditorium during the daylight hours." He also recounts that "sometimes the slaves were hidden beneath the church" and that "the hollow places in the earth below the floor are believed to be the original hiding places" (Knappenburger 1933). It was hoped that investigations would clarify the role the basement played as a fugitive hiding place.

The first task was to document the clay faces and the dug-out basement. Each of the faces was photographed and plotted on a map. Initial recordings were followed up with excavations to further define the context of the tunnel passageway and the art. Archaeological investigations were carried out in 1994 as part of Syracuse University's summer archaeological field training program.

Inspection of the passageway walls clearly indicated that the basement was dug with hand tools, including pick and shovel. These tools, however, are not diagnostic of a particular period and do not help to date the tunnel, which opens up at the west end of the building to a complex of features (Figure 4). Most obvious is the large 3-m diameter area to the south in which both

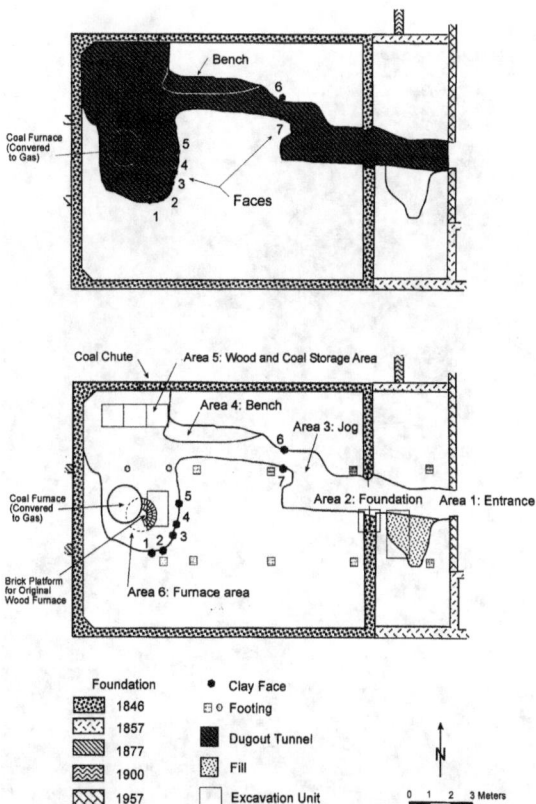

FIGURE 4. Archaeological plan of basement passageway.

the furnace and five faces are located. Other features include a long "bench" cut out of the earth on the north side of the dug-out path and a coal chute located immediately to the north side of the dug-out area adjacent to the furnace. The coal storage area was located beneath a small opening that served as a coal, and earlier wood, chute. This fuel storage area was on the north side of the dug-out path but still in close proximity to the furnace.

The area of the furnace was excavated to a depth lower (by 25–35 cm) than the passageway leading to it. This area was divided from the rest of the tunnel by a wooden beam or sill. In 1994 the furnace was still in use but had been modified to use gas. This area was relatively free of debris. However, when the basement was first inspected, a considerable amount of wood and other recent construction material had to be removed in order to inspect the remainder of the dug-out area. The surface of the basement on either side of the dug-out passageway was littered with artifacts. Large sections of old stained glass attached to lead were located near the entrance. A nearly complete slate shingle found in the same area relates to roofing material that was replaced by asphalt shingles some time after 1940.

In all, six areas or cultural features were defined by preliminary analysis. These areas were numbered beginning from the eastern origin of the passageway. Each of these six areas was investigated using some combination of surface observations, shovel testing, and excavation. These areas are described separately below, followed by individual descriptions of the clay faces.

Area 1 refers to the basement entrance. It was immediately apparent that the construction of the cinder block wall at the east end of the auditorium (a post-1957 reconstruction) destroyed any 19th-century evidence in that area. A small dug-out area is located to the south of the passageway, just west of the cinder block wall. This dug-out area is currently filled with rubble. Partial clearing of this area demonstrated that the west wall had originally been excavated in the same manner as the remainder of the passageway. This area may represent an original ramp from an external opening to the pre-1857 structure.

Area 2 designates the foundation footing to the east wall of the original 1846 structure. All above-ground brick had been cleared away and may have been reused in the 1857 construction. Mortared subsurface stones were laid in a relatively shallow builder's trench that measured approximately 40 cm deep. This trench and foundation footing were subsequently crosscut by the dug-out passageway, indicating that the passageway postdates the initial construction of the building. It was only possible to clear debris and fully expose the foundation wall to the south side of the passageway since a support pier had been placed on the wall immediately north of the dug-out area.

A jog in the tunnel passageway is referred to as Area 3. When one looks into the tunnel beneath the church from the entrance at the east end, it appears to stop abruptly about halfway into the building. Hence, any quick inspection would have revealed the appearance of a short, dead-end tunnel. The jog begins about 50 cm back, or east of the dead end, and cuts sharply to the north (left) around a foundation pier and support beam. The tunnel then continues on a straight course to the west end of the building.

The reason for this jog is not obvious from the structural remains. Since the entire basement was cut through clay subsoil, there was no apparent obstacle to the original path. The first section of the passageway runs parallel with and on the south side of a set of structural supports. The second section continues parallel with the first but is on the north side of the supports. Even though the tunnel seems to have been dug after the building's initial construction, there is no reason why it could not have continued in the original trajectory. The jog may represent a purposeful effort to deceive people entering the passageway with bad intentions; thus, it may be a mechanism to protect refugees. It may also have simply resulted from two parties digging from either end and missing in the middle. Finally, if one allows for the faces having been produced serially, over time, it is possible that the art on the west wall of the furnace area was already created and the construction simply avoided its destruction. While there is no evidence to support any of these possibilities, the area of the jog in the passage contributes to the argument that it was constructed after the initial 1846 construction.

A fourth cultural feature is an earthen bench located on the north side of the tunnel passageway immediately adjacent to the coal/wood chute (Figure 5). This bench was identified after removing considerable surface debris (wood and wallboard) in 1994. It has suffered considerable decay over the past two years. While other cultural features such as the furnace and coal/wood chute can be tied directly to the function of heating the building, this flat, 300 × 65 cm (12 × 1.75 ft.) platform cannot. Moreover, the platform is longer than necessary for a person simply tending to the fire. This bench may have served as a resting place for refugees; the raised area would have allowed them to avoid the moist or wet floor and could accommodate sleeping, while the proximity of the bench to the furnace would have insured their warmth.

Area 5 was used as a coal/wood storage area, a function obvious from the residual coal located directly beneath the coal chute. Three 1 × 1 m units were excavated here in the hope of finding artifacts from the mid-19th century in the lower levels. Excavation revealed 90 cm representing three distinct cultural periods that yielded a small

FIGURE 5. Bench on the north side of the basement passageway. (Photo by Armstrong.)

Perspectives from *Historical Archaeology*

sample but a wide variety of 20th-century debris and fill, including several kilograms of coal. A second level represents the period of the 1898 fire that caused significant damage to the building and resulted in a change from wood-burning to coal-burning furnaces. Soils beneath the burned levels contained almost no coal, and the ash shifted from coal to wood. The wood ash varied in color from white to gray. This soil layer is represented by only a few centimeters of ash-rich deposits. No diagnostic artifacts were recovered from these levels, although the artifacts do indicate a possible mid-century date. In addition to the absence of coal, the materials present included wood ash, clear window glass, and iron fragments. While not definitive, the archaeological investigation of the coal/wood storage area does not rule out a 19th-century origin for the dug-out passageway.

The furnace area (Area 6) provided the most significant new information from the archaeological investigations. Three excavation units were dug in this area. The surface levels of these units contained a mix of materials dating from recent trash to the late-19th century, including clear and painted window glass and cut nails. Unlike the coal/wood storage area, excavation of the furnace area provided no direct evidence of the 1898 fire. However, the artifacts recovered from this area do provide testimony to the use of this building as a meeting place and as a church. Among the artifacts recovered from the upper level were an ivory piano key and about two-thirds of a glass communion cup.

The discrete and stratified nature of the deposits provides important information about the early history of the tunnel passageway. A discrete series of stratigraphic layers were defined that predate the 1898 fire. From 10 to 35 cm below surface, a series of five distinct cultural levels were encountered. These levels contained lenses of white to gray wood ash. The upper-most levels were composed primarily of burnt and hardened clay. The soils in these levels shifted from clay at the top to thin lenses of sand and clay containing a few glass and ceramic artifacts and ash. At 13 cm below surface, a round brick feature (Figure 6) was encountered. The bricks had been laid to form a platform to support the original wood-burning furnace. This circular brick feature was offset to the south and east

of the existing furnace but extended under the existing furnace to the west.

The brick feature provides definitive evidence that a furnace existed in the basement prior to the 1898 fire. The ash lenses adjacent to the brick collar indicate that this early furnace was fueled by wood. This evidence, combined with the photographic record, indicates that the basement passageway area was constructed before the Civil War. The artifacts recovered from this early context, though relatively sparse, all point to a mid-century date and include three clear window glass fragments of the type described for the 1846–1877 era and a fragment of black transfer-print ceramics popular in the 1840s and 1850s. The other two artifacts present are a thick black graphite pencil and a fragment of a glass bead. The glass bead was of a black, opaque, and faceted variety and measures 8 × 8 mm.

Description of the Sculpted Faces

At least seven sculpted faces were identified lining the dug-out wall of the Wesleyan Methodist Church basement. Five of the faces (numbered 1–5, Figure 7) were located on the walls of the circular area that housed the furnace at the west end of the building. The remaining two faces (numbered 6–7) were located on either side of the tunnel just beyond the jog. The origin of these sculptures was unclear when the project began and remained uncertain as it concluded. Archaeological evidence provided only indirect support for their creation in the 19th century, and oral history indicated their presence by at least the early-20th century.

FIGURE 6. Brickwork base beneath former wood-burning heater. (Photo by Armstrong.)

FIGURE 7. Sculpted Faces No. 1–5. (Photo by Armstrong.)

The faces were constructed at a height varying from 1.35 to 1.5 m (4 to 4.5 ft) from the floor of the respective dug-out areas. They range in size from approximately 46×37 cm to 11×16 cm. The faces exhibit a great deal of variation in design, shape, and form, although they all appear to have been created using a similar style of construction. Reconstructing the steps taken by the artists to create the faces has been assisted by the severe decomposition of most of them. The artists prepared the wall surface by gouging out oval support forms on the wall. The resulting channels not only helped to form the face but also provided the means to adhere layers of clay. Moist clay was then applied to the surface building up the final form. The moisture necessary to form the clay would probably have been available from the damp floor of the dug-out passageway.

For at least two of the faces, black ash was used to darken the natural clay color; this darker clay was inserted to effect a different eye color. The final clay surface was molded, sculpted, and smoothed to form facial detail. Upon close inspection, the clay features appear to suggest tight curl patterns found in African American hair. Thus, even where the hair appears to be parted and slicked back, characteristics of African American hair were incorporated into the face by the artist. In addition, Warren Barbour lifted fingerprint impressions from the three most intact faces. While this analysis cannot reveal who actually constructed these faces, the fingerprints

were all different, suggesting that they represent the work of several artists.

Sculpted Face 1 is the best preserved of the surviving faces in the Wesleyan Methodist Church basement (Figure 8). This face was located furthest to the west on the south wall of the circular dug-out area adjacent to the furnace. Face 1 includes both the face and a background platform. These features measure approximately 46 cm wide by 37 cm high, and the face itself is much smaller than life size (14 cm wide × 18 cm high). The lower end of the face was 140 cm from the current floor surface and extended to within 5–7 cm of the top of the wall. The face was built up with sharp features including chin, eyes, nose, and hairline. Of note on the otherwise smoothed down and parted hair are a series of small 1.5 cm knobs that suggest the curls characteristic of hair of persons of African descent.

The date "1817" was scratched into the clay surface below Face 1. It is not clear if the date was incised by the artist or by a later visitor. The significance of the date can only be guessed

FIGURE 8. Sculpted Face No. 1. (Photo by Armstrong.)

at; however, it has been noted by many observers that the face resembles Frederick Douglass, who was born in 1817. This would imply a relationship between the art and an influential African American in the local and national abolition movement.

The forehead of Face 1 was streaked with several drops of wax. It is not clear if the wax was the result of a candle used for illumination, either for the artist or other visitors to the tunnel, or if it resulted from some kind of ritual application.

The good state of preservation of Face 1 was probably the indirect result of the 1898 fire that baked the clay. The fire left traces of irregular black and red patterns linked with oxidation associated with the firing of clay. Though Face 1 is in relatively good condition, the clay is more densely packed and hardened than the wall upon which it was applied. This face was barely adhering to the wall.

FIGURE 9. Close-up of Sculpted Face No. 2. (Photo by Armstrong.)

Sculpted Face 2 was located immediately to the east of Face 1; its built-up background began 10 cm from the first face (Figure 9). Face 2 was divided from its neighbor to the west by a small trough that may have been the result of surface erosion. When first encountered in 1994, a significant portion of the surface of face had already been lost. The entire outline of the face is clearly visible, but only the area below the nose remains intact. A section of the chin had been lost sometime between 1994 and 1997. This damage was the result of general deterioration that had been accelerated by environmental changes due to the building's renovations. The base of the platform for Sculpted Face 2 began at a height of 146 cm from the floor and, thus, lay slightly higher on the wall than Face 1 and extends to the top of the tunnel wall. The surface of the face has crumbled despite the fact that it was also baked by the 1898 fire.

While much of the upper portion of Face 2 is gone, its dimensions are easily discernable. The face measures 22 × 29 cm. The hair portrayed on Face 2 projects from the main body of the face and forms clear clusters of circular knobs. The resulting hair suggests a natural Afro style that contrasts with the smoothed down and parted style of Face 1. Like Face 1, the area surrounding Face 2 also exhibited evidence of candle wax. In addition, a cut nail protrudes from the surface of this face. It is not clear whether this nail represents an inadvertent inclusion in the clay or the material remains of ritual activity (Brown and Cooper 1990:18).

The third face was located on the east wall of the circular area in which the furnace is located (Figure 10). This face was positioned slightly lower on the wall than Faces 1 and 2, with the top more than 20 cm below the top of the wall. With the exception of the forehead and residual eye and mouth openings, the surface of this face is almost entirely eroded. Unlike the first two faces, Face 3 has a relatively small border of built-up background. Face 3 is the largest identified, measuring 24 × 31 cm, and its background extends only a few centimeters from the face. The upper forehead of Face 3 survives, but no trace of hair is evident.

Despite its relatively eroded condition, the deep contours of the face project a haunting mask-like image. Just as the erosion of the face makes it an abstraction of the artist's

FIGURE 10. Sculpted Face No. 3. (Photo by Armstrong.)

Face 6 is represented only by the carved platform to which the molded clay was originally applied. This area measures 11 × 16 cm (Figure 11), and the actual face may have originally been much larger. Sculpted Face 7 yields few details (Figure 12). It is relatively small, measuring only 16 × 24 cm. No fingerprints from Face 7 were preserved even though a segment of the surrounding background area survives. This area exhibits smoothing of the surface, similar to all of the other faces.

All of the faces show similarities in both construction and design. Basic construction involved preparing surface areas on which various layers of clay were applied, modeled, and smoothed. The faces show differences in size and shape, and the rendering of facial features and hairstyles. Along with the differing fingerprints, this variability would suggest that the faces were created by at least several different people rather than an individual. This

original work, so the anonymous nature of the art compels one to look beyond its creation to the people and events of the mid-19th century. Sculpted Face 3 also yielded traces of wax, presumably from candles used to illuminate the basement area.

Faces 4 and 5 are the least visible of all identified. Face 4 was represented only by a small patch of background platform, while Face 5 survived only as a residual oval that was difficult to see in most light. These fragmentary remains do not yield the full dimensions of the faces. Both of these faces were located on the east wall of the circular furnace area to the north of Sculpted Face 3.

Faces 6 and 7 were located on either side of the tunnel just to the northwest of the jog in the passage. Little of these faces remained except for the etched pattern of surface preparation and a few scant traces of the surface of Face 7. Their location, immediately beyond the false dead end of the passage, suggested a possible symbolic positioning at the entry to the inner passage.

FIGURE 11. Sculpted Face No. 6. (Photo by Armstrong.)

Perspectives from *Historical Archaeology*

FIGURE 12. Sculpted Face No. 7. (Photo by Armstrong.)

explanation fits nicely with the expectations that they were made by refugees from slavery who occupied the basement while they awaited transport.

Historical and Archaeological Conclusions

The historical review of the Wesleyan Methodist Church indicates that it was founded as a direct challenge to the support that the Methodist Episcopal mother church gave to the institution of slavery. The pastors and congregation of the Wesleyan Methodist Church were engaged in the abolition cause, exemplified by political actions ranging from the Liberty Party to the "Jerry Rescue." Evidence clearly establishes that this congregation was involved in the Underground Railroad. The archaeological investigation of the dug-out basement indicates that the tunnel passageway was probably in existence by 1857 and, thus, would have been available as a hiding place for African Ameri-

cans seeking refuge. With the surfaces of the tunnel available, it is possible that refugees sculpted the faces to help pass the time before their final journey to Canada. However, like cave art, the faces on the tunnel walls cannot be directly linked to artifacts recovered from archaeological investigations.

Two of the faces show clear evidence of firing, which can be associated with the fire of 1898. While it cannot be known when the faces were created, a 19th-century context is certain. The presence of stratigraphic deposits and a brick support base for an early wood-burning and later coal-burning furnace in the immediate area of the faces also support a pre-Civil War date for the tunnel and, thus, the art. The only ceramic fragment from the deposits associated with the early wood-burning furnace is a mid-19th century ware.

The presence of the jog in the passageway also supports the use of the basement area by refugees. The configuration of the jog indicates an attempt to mask the fact that the passage continues. Even today, viewed from the entrance, the passageway appears to be a dead end. Traces of two faces bracket either side of the tunnel just past this jog in the passage, perhaps symbolically delimiting safe territory. Finally, the role of the passage as a temporary shelter is supported by the presence of a long bench on the north wall of the passage. While the passage itself could simply exist to provide access to the furnace, there is no other logical explanation for this long dirt bench.

Research shows that there is strong archaeological and historical evidence supporting the use of the basement passageway and for the creation of the sculpted faces in the 19th century by African Americans seeking freedom. Stories of the use of the basement date to the 19th century and have continued to persist to the present. Folklore explaining the faces are of two opinions: either they were made in the 20th century, perhaps by the custodian and keeper of the furnace or by unknown African American artists seeking refuge before emancipation. Former members of the church identify the presence of the features on the wall by 1923. In the 1940s, the basement was used as an excursion for a Halloween party, and the faces were understood as being created by the church's janitor for their entertainment. In contrast, research provides strong support for a 19th-century origin, and the historic context make African American artists plausible. Even with strong inference, however, no proof can be presented as to who actually made the faces.

The key question remains: Are these faces the artwork of refugees of enslavement? Given the historic context of the era, one may never have an absolute answer. Yet, the art is both significant and provocative. The faces provide a tangible link to a silent past. As such, they represent a legacy and monument to the hope and faith of countless journeyers and a community that at a point in time in the 19th century acted in direct defiance to the law to facilitate social and political change.

Local Initiative to Protect the Sculpted Faces

Preservation of the faces was a difficult task both technically and financially. However, after a four-year struggle and with strong community support, they have now been conserved and are on public display at the Onondaga Historical Association located about a block away from the Wesleyan Methodist Church in downtown Syracuse. The story of the effort to save the faces illustrates problems in protecting privately owned resources, even if they are associated with National Register sites. It also highlights the importance of developing a wide range of community support to facilitate the protection of archaeological resources.

The former Wesleyan Methodist Church building has been listed on the National Register of Historic Places since the 1970s. It was grouped within the Columbus Circle/Montgomery Street National Register District as part of a sweeping effort to recognize the significance of the city's 19th-century architecture before the integrity of the area was lost through demolition. The brief one paragraph statement of significance for this property simply notes that the structure was an old building and the oldest church in the city. This "curbside" nomination made only casual reference to the role of this site in the abolition movement and does not mention the sculpted clay faces in the basement (Syracuse Planning Department 1979). Hence, the site was not included in general surveys of Freedom Trail sites conducted by the National Park Service

(1995) or the New York State Office of Parks Recreation and Historic Preservation (1997).

In order to enhance local protective measures, the National Register District was nominated for local Landmark status in 1981 (Syracuse Planning Department 1981; Hardin and Crispin 1993). The initial application included the Wesleyan Methodist Church, but at the request of the Board of Deacons of the First Gospel Church, the congregation in residence at that time, the property was eliminated from the district and, thus, not afforded the protection of the city's local preservation ordinance. Based on formal correspondence with the city planning department, it appears that the Gospel Baptist Church was concerned about the church having to respond to political and secular authority, even though the property was already listed on the National Register. In retrospect, it is ironic that the building of a Wesleyan Methodist congregation that so boldly embraced political activism in the 19th century was ultimately omitted from local recognition on the basis of modern perceptions of the separation between religion and polity.

The church was sold to Vaughn Lang in 1989 who had the objective of rehabilitating the structure to create law offices. Lang's initial architectural plans called for digging out the basement in order to create a more secure foundation for the structure above and storage space in the basement. However, Lang was aware of the faces in the basement and wanted to determine their context before proceeding. In fact, Lang was within his rights as a property owner to simply destroy the art and go about his business. Syracuse University archaeologists volunteered to research the building and ultimately carried out excavations that confirmed the 19th-century context of the tunnel passageway and the art and the strong role that this church had played in Underground Railroad and mid-19th-century social movements. When this information was conveyed to Lang, he was unusually accommodating, changed his architectural plans to avoid destroying the faces, and began to seek ways in which the art could be conserved.

Over a period of four years, the authors attempted to obtain the funding necessary to conserve the art and develop their interpretive potential. But the expensive price tag for conservation, the fact that the property was privately owned, and the lack of direct proof identifying the artists all combined to limit financial support from government or community sources. Meanwhile, when the building's restoration was complete and the heat went on, the faces began to deteriorate at an even more rapid rate. Fortunately, a poster exhibit displayed at the 1996 Society for Historical Archaeology meetings in Cincinnati caught the attention of New York-based conservators Cheryl LaRoche and Gary McGowan who were impressed by the significance of the art and the urgent need for conservation. They not only came to Syracuse to provide *probono* assessment and conservation but also invited the senior author to present an appeal to a group of New York City conservators.

A representative of the new National Underground Railroad Freedom Center in Cincinnati was present at this lecture and heard the appeal. The National Underground Railroad Freedom Center responded positively by arranging for that museum to secure ownership of the art. As long as the faces were in private hands, they were not eligible for conservation grants. Once the title of ownership passed to Cincinnati, the group planned to begin fund-raising for the badly needed conservation work. Their plan included the removal of the faces from the wall, their conservation, and their eventual display at their museum in Cincinnati. With the financial assistance of Mr. Lang, the Cincinnati group immediately initiated measures to insure the stabilization and temporary protection of the faces. The stabilization was performed by LaRoche and McGowan in August 1997.

While thankful for the generous intervention of the National Underground Railroad Freedom Center in Cincinnati, many in the Syracuse community remained convinced that this art represented a legacy of Central New York's historical past that should not leave the city. At the city's annual celebration of the "Jerry Rescue" on 1 October 1997, a copy of the pending New York State Freedom Trail Act was circulated, and the community was informed that the plans to conserve the art would involve the faces leaving Syracuse. The response among community activists and political leaders was clear and definitive—an effort should be made to retain the faces. A group adjourned to the newly opened restaurant in the former sanctuary of the Wesleyan Methodist Church (at a table immediately over the art) and made plans to rally support to

keep the faces in Syracuse. When Governor Pataki signed the Freedom Trail Act into law in Buffalo later that month, a delegation was present to communicate the need to protect the art. New York State Assembly Deputy Speaker Arthur Eve, an author of the state Freedom Trail legislation heard of the problems surrounding the preservation of the sculpted faces and immediately threw in his support. What followed was an outpouring of support for a local effort to conserve and protect the art in Central New York.

After four years with little progress, support built rapidly. The Preservation Association of Central New York (PACNY) stepped forward to lead a community effort to protect the art in Syracuse. As president of that organization, the senior author was able to quickly organize a proposal for the protection of the art. A task force was organized through the cooperative action of the Central New York Urban League, Bethany Baptist Church, and PACNY. On 20 October 1997, a public forum was held to define the problem and pursue the local protection of the art. This meeting filled an assembly hall and was attended by a cross-section from the Syracuse community as well as a representative of the National Underground Railroad Freedom Center in Cincinnati. At the meeting and in correspondence after it, the representatives of the Cincinnati museum expressed a willingness to work cooperatively with the Syracuse community to protect this resource.

With extensive media attention and the community now squarely in support of conserving the art, proposals for funding were fast-tracked through local foundations and corporations. The Central New York Community Foundation responded to the "Save the Faces" campaign almost immediately with a challenge grant and established a dedicated fund. Corporate and foundation donations, including $100,000 from the Rosamond Gifford Charitable Trust, combined with donations from the general public, including local school children, raised more than $225,000 for the conservation effort in three months (Figure 13).

As the fund-raising phase of the local effort proceeded, efforts to ensure the protection of the faces resulted in a number of positive community-based actions. First, the organization of the grassroots Save the Faces task force brought the community together on an informal common-cause basis. The task force was open to all and

Underground Railroad "Faces" Conservation Project Task Force
149 Beattie Street, Syracuse, New York 13224 (315) 446-5080, fax (315) 446-6490

HELP SAVE THE FACES !!!

Contributions should be made payable to the CNY Community Foundation and sent to:

Underground Railroad Conservation Project
C/O CNY COMMUNITY FOUNDATION
500 S. Salina Street – Suite 428
Syracuse, New York 13202

FIGURE 13. "Save the Faces" fund-raising flyer.

engaged a significant level of participation from a cross-section of the African American community, educators, preservationists, and supporters of the arts. Second, an effort was made to deal with broader issues of the Underground Railroad and the range of social movements associated with pre-Civil War activism in the region. In order to insure continuity of efforts in this area, the Save the Faces task force asked for the creation of a county Freedom Trail Commission. This commission was chartered in Spring 1998 and adopted the faces project as its first task.

Third, the support from the community led a number of organizations, including the Onondaga Historical Association, the Syracuse Community Folk Art Gallery, and Syracuse University to come forward to offer short- and long-term support for curation, exhibition, and maintenance of the faces once they were conserved. The desire of these facilities to take an active part in the protection of these significant resources was viewed as a strong indicator that the community would be able to maintain the art once it was conserved.

Fourth, the involvement of a broad cross-section of the community in the project and, in particular, the involvement of the African American community allowed for the successful campaign to raise conservation and curatorial

traveling exhibition:

The carved faces
of the
Wesleyan Methodist Church

ONONDAGA
HISTORICAL
ASSOCIATION

321 Montgomery St. Syracuse, NY 315-428-1864

FIGURE 14. "Symbol of a Journey" traveling exhibit of the Onondaga Historical Association.

funds. Community involvement also was instrumental in returning ownership of the faces to Syracuse. In light of this, the title to the faces was transferred from the museum in Cincinnati to Bethany Baptist Church, a local African American congregation that rallied to support the conservation effort. They held title while the conservation effort proceeded.

Conservation, including the removal of the art from the basement wall in order to stabilize the art, was completed over a period of 18 months by a team led by conservators McGowan and LaRoche (details concerning the process of conserving the faces are reported elsewhere). Once completed, a public ceremony was held and the faces were turned over to the Onondaga Historical Society for public display, ultimately to become a centerpiece for a permanent exhibit dedicated to the Freedom Trail. A traveling exhibit was also put together using the carved faces as the beginning point of the discussion of the journey to freedom (Figure 14).

The archaeological component of this project is minimal yet pivotal. By documenting the faces and the importance of the Wesleyan Methodist building in relation to mid-19th century social movements, an important component of the region's past was highlighted. The effort to save the faces brought the Syracuse community together in a common cause. In this way, the preservation and interpretation of the past has become a vital living element of the community's life and future.

ACKNOWLEDGMENTS

We would like to thank Vaughn Lang for his efforts to protect the clay faces in the basement of his property. The project relied heavily on the resources of the Onondaga Historical Association and the Wesleyan Archives housed at the archives of the United Methodist Church. The successful effort to raise funds to save the faces was a community effort that would not have been possible without the contributions of Rev. Ronald Dewberry of Bethany Baptist Church, the Honorable Samuel Roberts of the Onondaga County Legislature, the Honorable Arthur Eve, deputy speaker of the New York State Assembly, the Central New York Community Foundation, the Rosamond Gifford Charitable Trust, the Preservation Association of Central New York, the Onondaga County Freedom Trail Commission, the Save the Faces task force, the National Underground Railroad Freedom Center in Cincinnati, Ohio, and the students and teachers of Dr. King Elementary School (along with Alan and Amanda Armstrong). Daniel Roberts provided useful and insightful editorial comments on a draft of this article. We are appreciative of Warren Barbour for his examination of the surface of the art for possible fingerprints. The stabilization and conservation of these fragile resources has been carried out by Gary McGowan and Cheryl LaRoche.

REFERENCES

AMERICAN WESLEYAN
    1877   American Wesleyan, 8 November 1877.

ARMSTRONG, DOUGLAS V., AND LOUANN WURST
    1998   Faces of the Past: Archaeology of an Underground Railroad Site in Syracuse, New York. Syracuse University Archaeological Research Center Report, Volume 10 (1).

BRIEADDY, FRANK
    1998   The Post Standard, 7 January 1998:Sec B2.

BROWN, KENNETH L., AND DOREEN C. COOPER
    1990   Structural Continuity in an African American Slave and Tenant Community. Historical Archaeology, 24(4): 7–19.

CHASE, FRANKLIN H.
    1924   Syracuse and Its Environs: A History. Lewis Historical Pub, New York, NY.

CROSS, WHITNEY R.
    1950   The Burned Out District: Social and Intellectual History of Enthusiastic Religion in Western New York, 1800–1850. Cornell University Press, New York.

FORDHAM, MONROE (EDITOR)
    1989   The African American Presence in New York State History: Four Regional History Surveys. New York African American Institute, SUNY Albany, NY.

GUNDERSON, REV. GUNNAR A.
    n.d.   A history of the congregation. Typed letter, The First Gospel Church. Syracuse, NY.

HARDIN, EVAMARIA, AND JON CRISPIN
    1993   Syracuse Landmarks: An AIA Guide to Downtown Historical Districts. Syracuse University Press, Syracuse, NY.

KAUFMAN, PAUL LESLIE
    1994   Logical Luther Lee and the Methodist War against Slavery. Doctoral dissertation, Department of History, Kent State University, OH.

KNAPPENBURGER, REV. J. B.
    1933   Reflections of a Minister. Newspaper file 1933, Onondaga Historical Association, Syracuse, NY.

LEE, REV. LUTHER
    1843   No title. True Wesleyan, 28 October. Wesleyan Archives, Indianapolis, IN.
    1850   Editorial. True Wesleyan, 9 November. Wesleyan Archives, Indianapolis, IN.

1882. *Autobiography of the Rev. Luther Lee D. D.* Phillips and Hunt, New York, NY.

MATLACK, LUCIUS C.
   1849 *The History of American Slavery and Methodism, from 1780–1849.* Wesleyan Book Concern, New York, NY.

MEYERS, JOHN L.
   1962 The Beginning of the Anti-Slavery Agencies in New York State, 1833–1836. *New York History,* 43: 149–181.

NATIONAL PARK SERVICE
   1995 *Underground Railroad: Special Resources Study.* National Parks Service, Denver Service Center, CO.

NEW YORK STATE OFFICE OF PARKS RECREATION AND HISTORIC PRESERVATION
   1997 *Guide to the Survey of Historic Resources Associated with African Americans in New York State.* New York State Department of Parks Recreation and Historic Preservation, Albany, NY.

SERNETT, MILTON
   1989 On Freedom's Threshold: The African American Presence in Central New York, 1760–1940. In *The African American Presence in New York State History: Four Regional History Surveys,* Monroe Fordham, editor. New York African American Institute, SUNY, Albany, NY.

SPERRY, EARL E.
   1924 *The Jerry Rescue.* Onondaga Historical Association, Syracuse, NY.

SYRACUSE JOURNAL
   1858 *Syracuse Journal,* 3 July 1858.
   1879 *Syracuse Journal,* 14 March 1879.

SYRACUSE PLANNING DEPARTMENT
   1979 National Register Nomination Form for the Columbus Circle/Montgomery Street National Register District. Manuscript, Community Planning, Syracuse, NY.
   1981 Local Columbus Circle/Montgomery Street Preservation District, Case File PD-80-1. Manuscript, Community Planning, Syracuse, NY.

SYRACUSE STANDARD
   1852 *Syracuse Standard,* 18 June 1852.

   1858 *Syracuse Standard,* 10 July 1858.
   1898 *Syracuse Standard,* 10 January 1898.

WESLEY, JOHN
   1774 Thoughts on Slavery. In *The Works of John Wesley.* Zondervan Publishing House, Grand Rapids, MI.

WM-ACM (WESLEYAN METHODIST, ANNUAL CONFERENCE MINUTES)
   1843 Annual Conference Minutes. Wesleyan Archive, Indianapolis, IN.
   1854–1855 Annual Conference Minutes. Wesleyan Archive, Indianapolis, IN

WMC-MR (WESLEYAN METHODIST CHURCH, MEMBERSHIP RECORD)
   1843 Membership Record of the Wesleyan Methodist Church of Syracuse (1843–1846). Onondaga Historical Association, Syracuse, NY.
   1851 Membership Record of the Wesleyan Methodist Church of Syracuse (1847–1858). Onondaga Historical Association, Syracuse, NY.

WMC-TR (WESLEYAN METHODIST CHURCH, TRUSTEE RECORDS)
   1843 Founding of the Wesleyan Methodist Church. Onondaga Historical Association, Syracuse, NY.
   1845 Electing Trustees and Planning for the Construction of a Building. Onondaga Historical Association, Syracuse, NY.
   1847 Note on Payment of Loan on Building. Onondaga Historical Association, Syracuse, NY.
   1854 Note on Gift for Abolition Cause to Luther Lee. Handwritten manuscript, Onondaga Historical Association, Syracuse, NY.

DOUGLAS V. ARMSTRONG
ANTHROPOLOGY DEPARTMENT
209 MAXWELL HALL
SYRACUSE UNIVERSITY
SYRACUSE, NY 13244

LOUANN WURST
DEPARTMENT OF ANTHROPOLOGY
SUNY COLLEGE AT BROCKPORT
BROCKPORT, NY 14420

Stacy C. Kozakavich

Doukhobor Identity and Communalism at Kirilovka Village Site

ABSTRACT

In early 1899, a migration of more than 7,000 Russian immigrants belonging to the Christian sect known as the Doukhobors arrived in western Canada and established three colonies in the districts of Saskatchewan and Assiniboia in the Northwest Territories. Due to internal tensions in the sect and conflicts with the Government of Canada's Department of the Interior, most of these villages were abandoned by 1920. Previous historical characterizations of the Doukhobors in Saskatchewan are inconsistent in their portrayal of the Doukhobors as an ethnic group and/or religious sect, and of the degree of internal cohesion and homogeneity at the community level. Combined archaeological and historical investigations suggest that the Doukhobor identity in Saskatchewan involves multiple levels of practice and belief. Further, Doukhobor identity is characterized by constant change brought about by repeated migrations through two centuries.

Introduction

The Doukhobors' place in the collective memory of western Canadians represents both the industriousness and communal spirit of this Christian sect, and the seclusion and fanaticism characteristic of its fundamentalist subsects. Whether regarded as brave and hearty pioneers, god-fearing Christian ascetics, or rebellious zealots, the Doukhobors of popular understanding are often only a caricature of these Russian-Canadian immigrants. Historical archaeology can help to unravel common myths while weaving a more complex and interesting story about Doukhobor identity. Investigation of the material text, in conjunction with written and oral works, helps to unfold multiplicities and tensions that were present in Doukhobor society on the Canadian prairies in the first years of the 20th century.

Doukhobor History and Religion

Doukhobors are members of a Christian sect whose philosophy is based on the core beliefs of guidance of the inner spirit, rejection of externalities (including worldly government), the equality of all life, and the attainment of salvation through the daily practice of faith (Gale 1973:24). Doukhobor historian and anthropologist Koozma Tarasoff (1972:1) describes them as a "Russian-derived ethnic group" who arose in the southern part of the Russian Empire in the late-18th century, loosely tied to a schism in the Russian church known as the Raskol (Tracie 1996:1). The Union of Doukhobors as a social and economic group depended on the migration of many individuals and families from different parts of Russia, coalescing in 1801 at a settlement called Milky Waters, or Molochnaya, near Crimea. Subsequent relocation to colonies in the Transcaucasus failed to protect the Doukhobors from persecution by Tsarist forces. An internal schism based on issues of leadership and spiritual practice split the followers into factions, including the "Large Party" under the spiritual guidance of Peter Verigin.

Verigin formulated the tenets of his "new Doukhoborism" while exiled in Siberia in 1893, inspired by the work of and his correspondence with contemporary writer Lev Tolstoy. These spiritual guidelines encouraged the faithful to adopt a vegetarian diet, avoid intoxicants, abstain from sexual relations, develop a system of economic communalism derived from the Russian mir system and the influences of contact with Russian Mennonites in the Transcaucasus, and, most controversially, refuse to participate in any military organization. While Verigin's zeal as a leader lent to the sense of newness of the new Doukhoborism, the reformation was really more of "a return to an original and pure sectarian asceticism" (Fry 1976:390–391).

Doukhobor Migration to Canada

Early in 1899, four voyages took approximately 7,400 Doukhobors across the Atlantic ocean into Halifax Harbour on the SS *Lake Superior* and the SS *Lake Huron*. Lured by free homestead land, and encouraged by Tolstoy's followers in Europe and by Canadian immigration officials such as Clifford Sifton, the Doukhobors settled in the Northwest Territories. Sixty-one Doukhobor villages were established in three separate colonies. Within these settlements, members of each Doukhobor community established varying degrees of communal farming practice. Each village accommodated approximately 200 people, or 40 families, in individual houses arranged according to a *strassendorf* plan, in which two identical rows of houses faced each other across a wide main avenue (Figure 1). This pattern of settlement reflects, to an extent, the egalitarian principles on which Doukhobor society and economy were thought to be based.

The Doukhobors who first congregated at Milky Waters came from varied geographical, economic, and social backgrounds; however, the shared lifeway of most Russian Doukhobors who migrated to Canada was that of the agricultural peasant. These Doukhobor families shared similar modes of daily practice, or *habiti* (Bourdieu 1977), and strong similarities with the activities of non-Doukhobor rural agrarian Russians. For example, the steam bath, or *bania*, was part of all Canadian Doukhobor villages but was also traditional to many rural Russians (Fry 1976:371). Further, Gary Fry (1976:350) and Nicholas Breyfogle (1995:27) attribute the Doukhobors' ability to recognize Verigin as a nearly divine leader (a concept that seems irreconcilable with the egalitarian nature of the sect's beliefs) to an adaptation of belief in the all-powerful tsar. An internal propensity for schism and the external pressures placed on Doukhobors by the Canadian government led to the eventual depopulation of almost all Doukhobor villages in Saskatchewan within the first two decades of the 20th century.

Archaeological Investigation of Kirilovka

The village of Kirilovka was located near the south bank of the North Saskatchewan River valley, 6 km from the present-day town of Langham (Figure 2). The former main street

FIGURE 1. Doukhobor village near Langham, Saskatchewan (after McKeand and Kozakavich 1997). (Original in private collection of Jack Dear, Langham, Saskatchewan, photographer unknown.)

Perspectives from *Historical Archaeology*

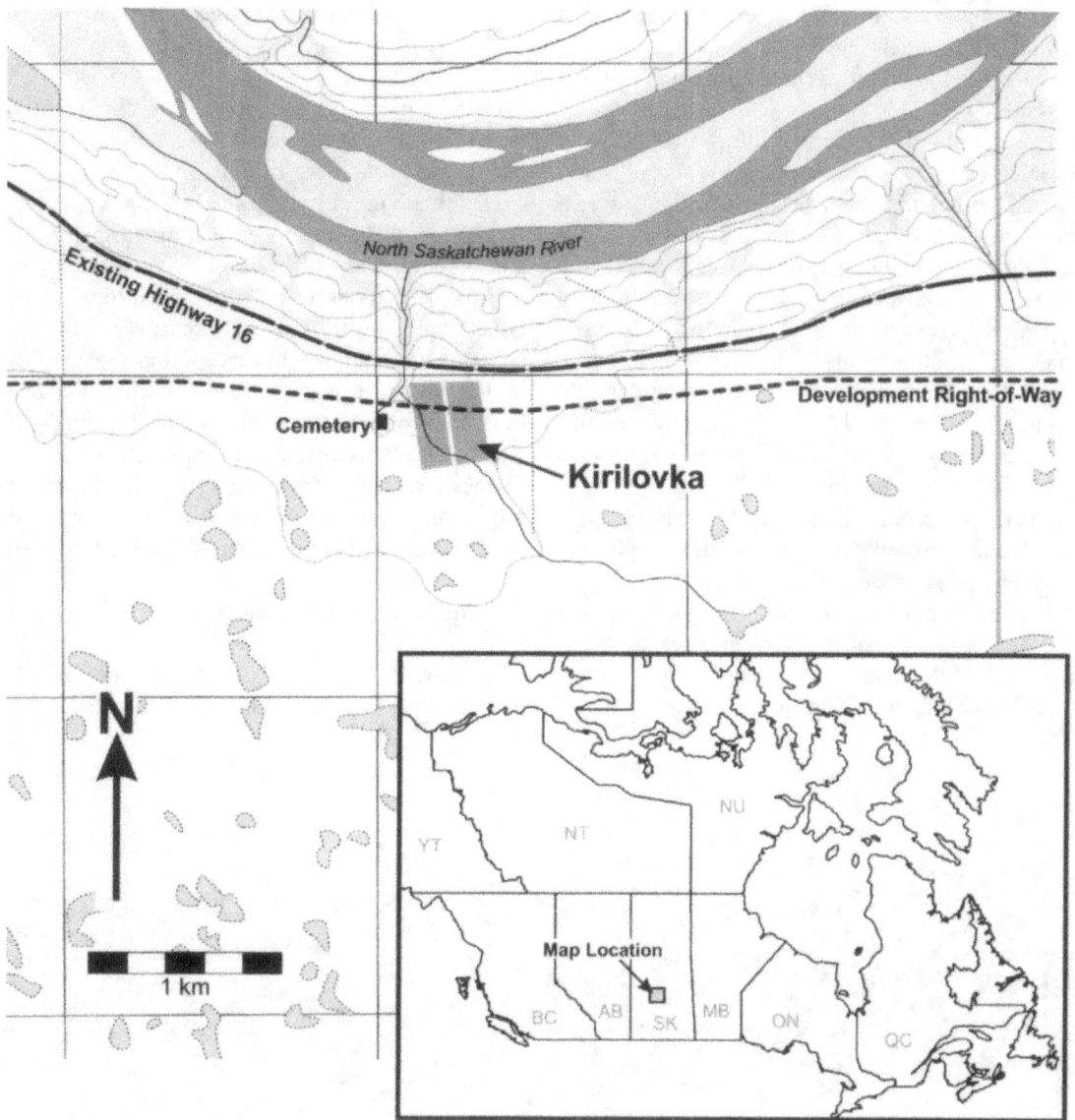

FIGURE 2. Location of Kirilovka (after Fairchild 1909; Natural Resources Canada 1986).

of the village was aligned roughly north-south and was used until recent decades as the access road to a private family farm.

Archaeological investigations at the Kirilovka Village site (FcNs-1) commenced as a cultural resource management project associated with a Saskatchewan Department of Highways and Transportation road twinning development. At the time of site discovery, it was believed that 7,800 m² of the site had already been disturbed by right-of-way clearing activity, and that in 30% of this area (2,300 m²), the

site was virtually destroyed. What remained consisted only of subsurface features such as cellars, privies, and buried middens, as all surface debris and architectural remains were destroyed by decades of cultivation and highway construction activity.

The features present at Kirilovka were divided into four groupings based on spatial proximity and location in relation to C. C. Fairchild's (1909) Canadian Department of the Interior survey map. Each feature cluster is interpreted to represent the remains of one family house lot, in which there is at least one cellar, one trench or midden feature, one or more privies, and other miscellaneous features (Figure 3).

Excavation of 37.75 m² within 19 surficially visible features was conducted by shovel shaving (scraping) in 20-cm levels according to 1-m provenience. Following hand excavation of 19 features, 14 remaining features were tested by a backhoe. Bulk matrix samples were taken from organic deposits in privies (Figure 4) to be used later for flotation analysis.

Artifacts recovered from Kirilovka, which include a total of 15,952 pieces, were subdivided into six function-based categories (Table 1). A sample of 3,777 conclusively identifiable pieces from the household, personal, and miscellaneous categories (including commercial packaging) was used in the analysis and interpretation presented here. The following discussion considers archaeological findings from Kirilovka within the historical context of Doukhobor belief and custom.

Doukhobor Belief and Practice: Archaeological Correlates

Certain behaviors are considered, both within and outside of the Doukhobor community, to be an essential part of the historical practice of Doukhobor faith in Canada. These include pacifism, vegetarianism, abstention from tobacco and alcohol, and village-level economic communalism. Variations in practice and differences of belief regarding these tenets are apparent in episodes throughout the history of the Doukhobors in Russia and Canada and in the archaeological evidence from the Canadian Doukhobor village of Kirilovka. This discussion addresses these differences within a framework that considers the migration history and predisposition for variability among the individual families of Kirilovka.

Abstinence from Intoxicants

As part of his memoirs of life in the village of Petrofka, Alex Bayoff (1985:10) recalls

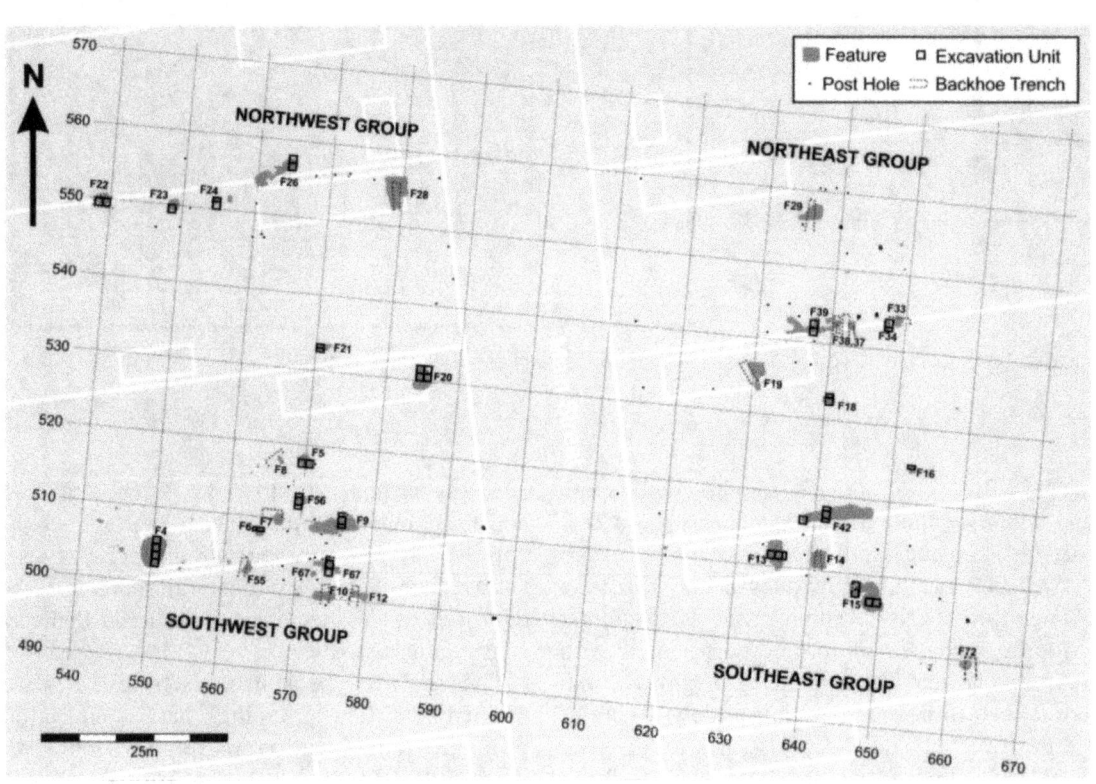

FIGURE 3. Features, feature groups, and excavation units at Kirilovka. Approximate location of 1909 buildings, lot divisions, and main street shown in white (after Fairchild 1909 and McKeand and Kozakavich 1997).

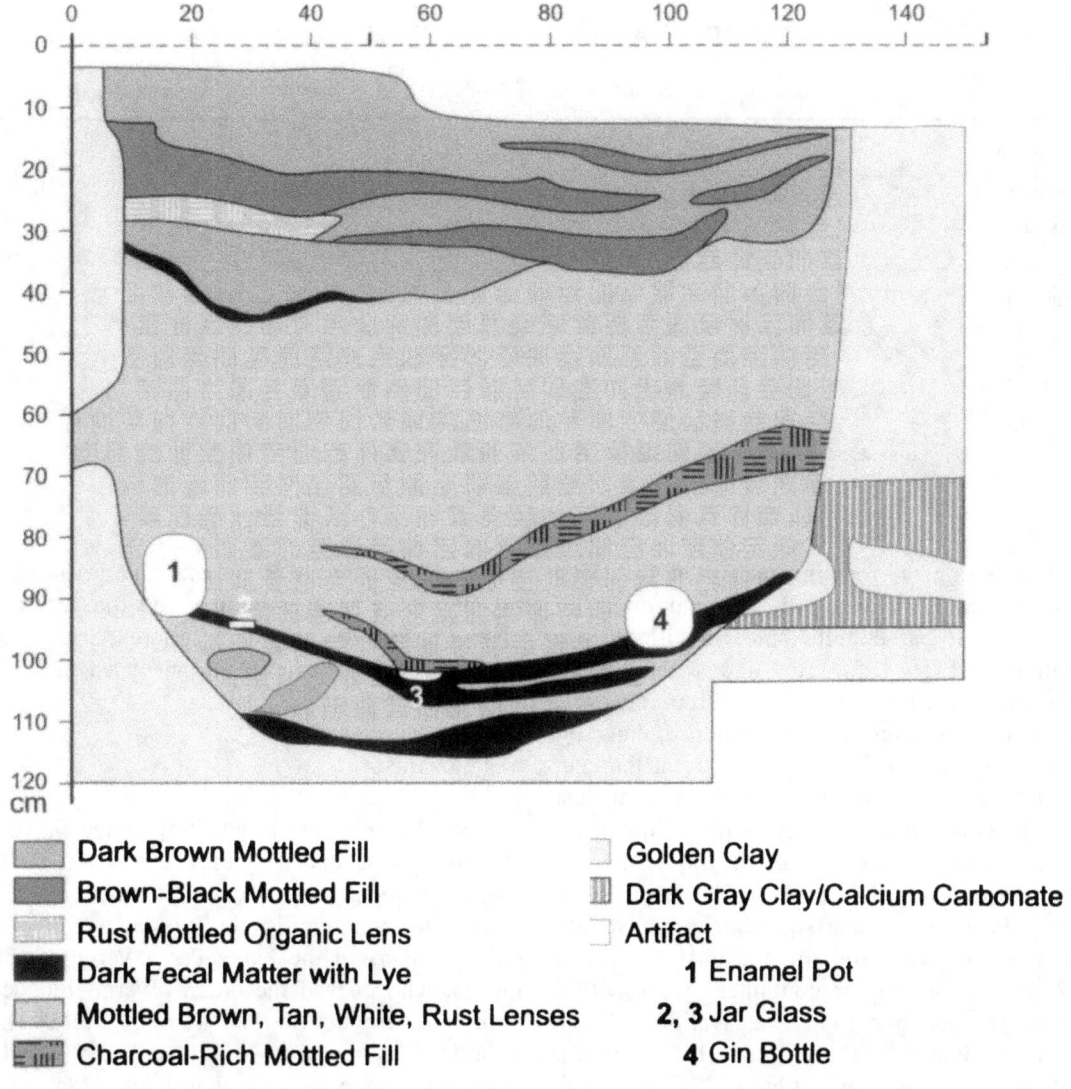

FIGURE 4. Profile of Feature 24, privy, from Kirilovka; view north (after McKeand and Kozakavich 1997).

Dark Brown Mottled Fill
Brown-Black Mottled Fill
Rust Mottled Organic Lens
Dark Fecal Matter with Lye
Mottled Brown, Tan, White, Rust Lenses
Charcoal-Rich Mottled Fill

Golden Clay
Dark Gray Clay/Calcium Carbonate
Artifact
1 Enamel Pot
2, 3 Jar Glass
4 Gin Bottle

an evening of recreation on which "a load of supplies, etc., came in from Rosthern. Naturally wine was one of the items brought in." Throughout the text of his short memoir, there is no sense that Bayoff's family and neighbors were not "true Doukhobors," nor is there any indication that the consumption of some alcohol was considered to be wrong. Non-Doukhobor neighbors in Canada also noticed and reacted to inconsistency in local Doukhobor attitudes toward well-known behavioral restrictions. In 1907, Yorkton resident J. K. Johnson (1907) wrote to Minister of the Interior Frank Oliver:

[Y]ou were aware they had 100 years of [military] exemptions and privileges in that country [Russia] and that about twelve (12) years ago those privileges being nearly ended they stopped chewing or smoking tobacco, stopped liquor drinking (a custom till that time general with them) and also stopped eating meat. . . . It is well understood that this rapid change was in great part due to a cunning desire to still escape military duties by assuming great religious aversion to eating meat and bloodshed in general—Those who leave the company now in many cases drink (in all cases of course, excess depending on the person), also eat meat & c. Company men also will drink on the sly, and smoke and chew in a great number of cases.

TABLE 1
SUMMARY OF ARTIFACT CLASSES BY SITE AREA

	Northeast	Northwest	Southeast	Southwest	Unassigned	Total
Household	175	77	518	278	213	1,261
Miscellaneous activities[a]	1,004	1,099	4,064	3,474	992	10,633
Personal	344	97	297	188	286	1,212
Structural	166	226	1,092	1,081	186	2,751
Transport	12	11	21	12	15	71
Work	5	1	6	3	9	24
Total	1,706	1,511	5,998	5,036	1,701	15,952

[a]Includes unlabeled commercial packaging and unidentified fragments such as sheet-metal scrap.

Archaeological remains recovered from the features at Kirilovka indicate that drinking had a small but definite place in village life. Whiskey (Figure 5), gin, and wine bottles are represented in three of the four clusters; the southwest cluster also contained the only cognac bottle identified conclusively at the site, while the small collection from the northwest cluster contains only beer bottles (Table 2). Whereas low concentrations of liquor bottles are present in other privies at the site, the privy Feature 72, unassigned to a household cluster, is anomalous because it produced 22 identifiable liquor containers from within its single backhoe trench excavation. These were dominated by beer bottles (55%, n=12), followed by gin case bottles (27%, n=6), and also included small numbers of identifiable whiskey and wine bottles. The unusual predominance of beer bottles, and the presence of many bottles, suggests a different pattern of alcohol consumption than is evidenced in other features at the site.

Vegetarianism

When Verigin introduced the practice of vegetarianism less than a decade before the 1899 migration to Canada, factionalization occurred within the communities in Russia, and it was only members of the Large Party, Verigin's followers, who obeyed the order. Warm-blooded animals were not to be eaten by followers, although fish eating was allowed and widely practiced. There is suggestion that the "fasting," or vegetarian, Doukhobors of the Large Party

TABLE 2
LIQUOR BOTTLES BY SITE AREA

	Northeast	Northwest	Southeast	Southwest	Feature 72	Total
Cognac	0	0	0	1	0	1
Whiskey	1	0	3	3	1	8
Gin	4	0	1	1	6	11
Wine	1	0	2	1	3	7
Beer	2	2	1	0	12	17
Unidentified	1	1	0	2	0	4
Total	9	3	7	8	22	48

Perspectives from *Historical Archaeology*

FIGURE 5. Whiskey bottle from Saskatoon liquor manufacturer. (Photo by author.)

of the Interior's 1907 Doukhobor Commission (McDougall 1907), indicate that vegetarian and meat-eating Doukhobors occupied the same communities on the Canadian prairies.

Many families who were vegetarian at the time of their arrival in Canada abandoned the practice shortly after they settled in Saskatchewan (Tarasoff 1977:129), while other families began to eat meat after they left the village community (Tarasoff 1977:122). Some individuals also lapsed from vegetarianism while on threshing or railway work crews away from their village.

Contemporary Doukhobors, many of whom lived in the Saskatchewan villages as children, discuss the significance of vegetarianism to their understanding of Canadian Doukhoborism in Tarasoff's 1977 oral history compilation. As an example, one respondent stated on 22 October 1975,

> I'm not anti-vegetarian nor am I pro but I feel that it has nothing to do with Doukhoborism; that you could be a Doukhobor whether you eat meat or not and the thing is if you arrive at those convictions whether from your own belief or just because somebody said it's so. There's the big thing. Unfortunately, Peter V. Verigin commanded his followers not to eat meat, so everybody in the Community had to quit. If you were caught eating meat, you were excluded from the Community. Naturally, there were weaker members, members that were more or less forced to quit eating meat not from conviction but by order. This is why forced adoption of vegetarianism also contributed to communal disintegration, and has been one of the big problems (Tarasoff 1977:127).

Most compelling in this passage is the link between forced behavioral restraints and the disintegration of communalism in the Doukhobors' otherwise egalitarian society. Similar views regarding the practice of vegetarianism are expressed by Tarasoff's other informants.

Archaeological material from Kirilovka also indicates an inconsistency in or abandonment of vegetarian practice. Skeletal remains from a variety of domesticated and wild animals, many with butchering or cut marks from preparation and consumption, were found in site deposits related to the period of village occupation. It is evident that residents consumed beef, poultry, and rabbit in addition to fish. Isolated elements also indicate the possibility that pork and sheep were also consumed.

continued to raise cattle for butchering and sale even though they would not consume the meat (Gale 1973). Further, notes in the Voskrisennie Village File, made under the Department

The estimated meat weights are relatively low, as the northeast and southeast clusters contain remains from less than 10 lbs of small animal meat, while the northwest cluster weight is skewed to almost 20 lbs by the presence of one lake sturgeon (Table 3). Larger animals, whose meat was likely shared, account for the majority of the meat weight from Kirilovka. Beef remains represent the highest estimated weight of consumed meat, followed by fewer butchered sheep remains in the southwest, northwest, and northeast clusters and a single pig element in the northwest cluster. The density of *Bos taurus* remains (elements/m²) by site area was 0.15 in the northeast cluster, 1.5 in the northwest cluster, 0.08 in the southeast cluster, and 3.65 in the southwest cluster.

Communalism and Consumerism

The *strassendorf* village plan provided a model of equality and uniformity within the Doukhobor village and an appearance of group cohesiveness to the outside observer. Despite such appearances, true economic communalism at the village level was not a consistent feature of Doukhobor settlement. It is suggested here that different levels of communal behavior existed within the village of Kirilovka: those behaviors closer to the household level tended to have roots in a Russian-based habitus, deeper than the enforced ideals of new Doukhoborism, and were maintained when the larger economic communism of the village was not.

Family dining serves as an excellent example of a communal behavior with an origin separate from the tenets of new Doukhoborism. Group eating practices originated among the Doukhobors in Russia and also dominated in their households on the Canadian Prairies (Figure 6), as remembered by Mary Sookerokoff (n.d.: 10) of Petrofka: "[a]s a child I remember sitting at the table and eating soup which was in a large home carved wooden bowl. I was (and everyone else) eating with a red carved spoon as well. There were no other kinds of spoons around. Just a few families had them, the richer ones, Fausts and Grandpa Makaroff to name a few." This practice was carried to and expanded at the Doukhobor settlements in British Columbia, where Doukhobor women would "cook for the whole village, and four

FIGURE 6. Russian-made iron pot recovered from Kirilovka. (Photo by author.)

TABLE 3
ESTIMATED SMALL MAMMAL, FISH, AND BIRD MEAT WEIGHTS (LBS) BY SITE AREA

	Northeast	Northwest	Southeast	Southwest
Chicken	5.0	5.0	5.0	22.5
Goose	0	0	0	5.0
Turkey	0	0	0	17.0
Rabbit	1.75	1.75	1.75	5.25
Fish	0	12.5	3.0	1.5
Total	6.75	19.25	9.75	51.25
Meat weight/m²	0.5	2.41	0.81	2.2

Perspectives from *Historical Archaeology*

people would eat from one bowl" (Tarasoff 1977:123).

While oral history supports the maintenance of vessel sharing in family dining, material remains from Kirilovka indicate that family dining behavior incorporated mass-produced, purchased tableware into everyday meals (Figure 7). Clearly, however, the communal family eating practices of the Doukhobors contrast sharply with the late-Victorian dining etiquette that informed production of late-19th- and early-20th-century ceramic tablewares. As different spoken languages interfered with communications between Doukhobor immigrants and their neighbors, different languages of material acquisition structured the consumer choices of immigrants and disrupted the transmission of meanings regularly associated with certain objects in the Anglo-Canadian market. While the association of separation of individuals and food products using the material culture of dining was entrenched in Anglo-Victorian dinner practice, the material culture itself held little specific, inherent meaning and could be separated from the structured ideal while being incorporated into other dining behaviors. The collection of different ceramic tableware decorative patterns from Kirilovka, nearly as many different patterns as vessels, suggests that pieces were not acquired as parts of formal sets but as individual items. Also, a paucity of flatware items in the archaeological record (Figure 8) suggests that metal forks, knives, and spoons were not common in the kitchens and on dining tables of the Kirilovka Doukhobors.

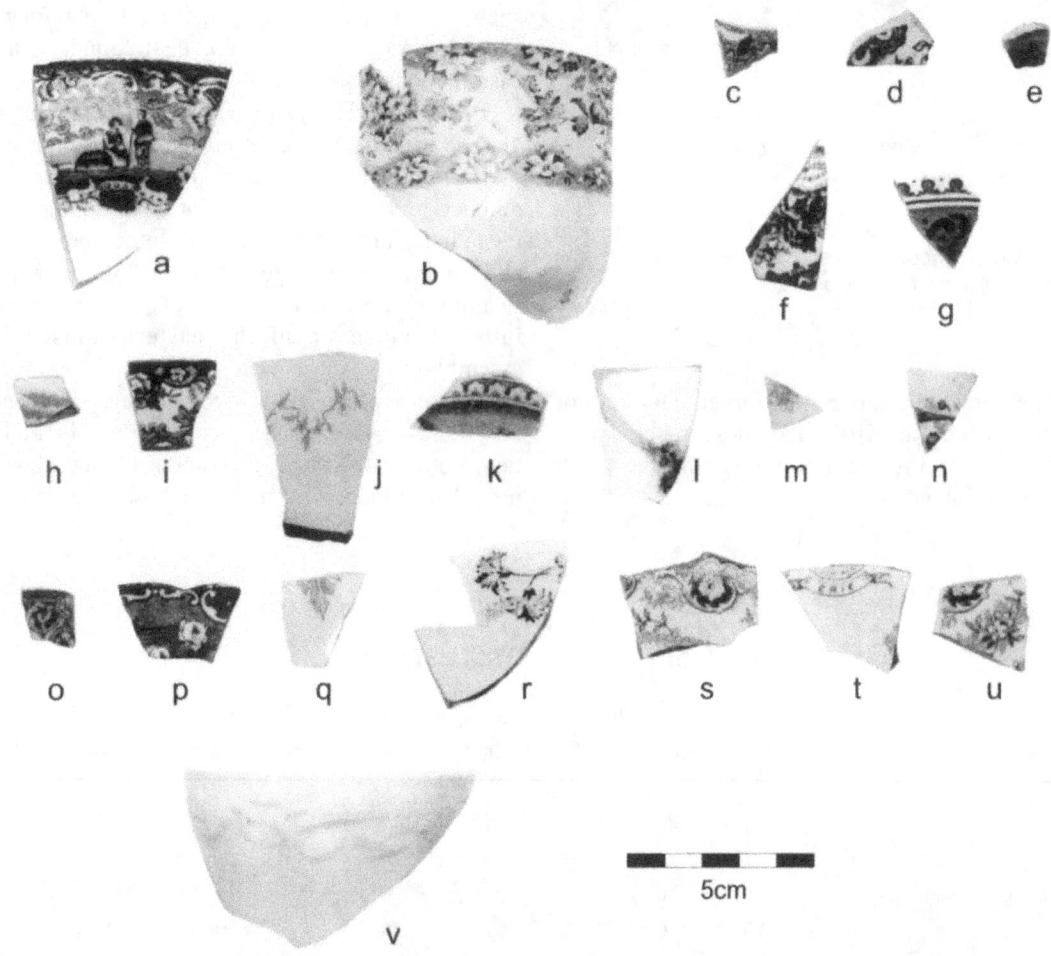

FIGURE 7. Examples of variety in ceramic decorative patterns represented at Kirilovka: (*a–b*) relief-molded, transfer-printed tableware fragments; (*c–u*) transfer-printed tableware fragments; (*v*) relief-molded teacup fragment. (Photo by author.)

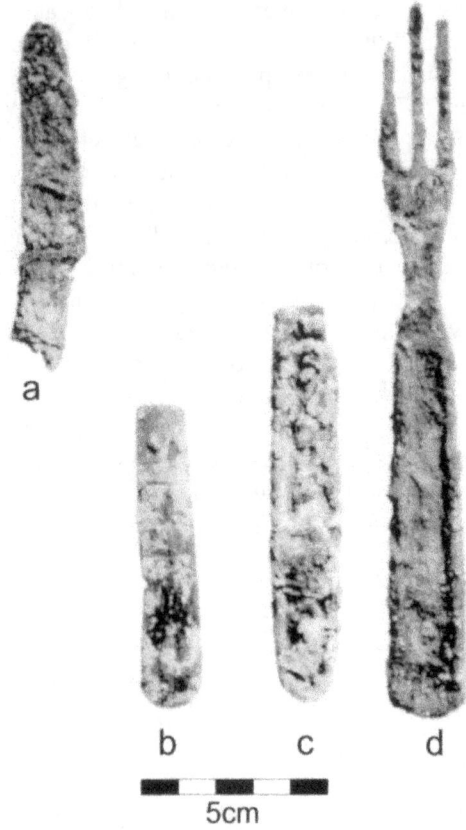

FIGURE 8. Entire cutlery collection from Kirilovka: (*a*) iron knife blade, (*b*) wood-and-metal knife handle, (*c*) iron utensil handle, (*d*) iron fork. (Photo by author.)

While store-bought goods joined Doukhobor table settings at Kirilovka, these pieces were not matched into individual settings as their designers intended.

Archaeological remnants of purchased goods from Kirilovka may also be studied to address questions of group behavior at a scale larger than the individual household. A weakness of communalism at the village level in Kirilovka is suggested not by any individual artifact class but, rather, by the differences in variety and amount of goods found among the households at the site.

For example, textile samples from the southwest and northwest households contain higher frequencies of wool than cotton or silk fibers, suggesting that most of the corresponding households' textiles could have been produced on site (Table 4). The eastern households show a different pattern, however, in that they contain higher frequencies of cotton and silk textile remains, indicating purchased yarns and/or finished textiles. Higher frequencies of shoes and of shoes produced by mechanical means such as turning, machine nailing (metal peg), and standard screwing were also found in the eastern households (Table 5).

Further, the density of commercially produced glass containers is higher in the eastern than the western households. This includes a greater number and greater variety of both liquor and medicinal containers as well as other beverage- and toiletry-related glass. Small numbers of seemingly incidental artifacts also offer insight into the make up of the eastern household assemblages. Three watch or clock gears and two battery parts recovered from the site were all found in the eastern households. In addition, both the northeast and southeast households provided evidence of such purchased household

TABLE 4
TEXTILE TYPES BY CLUSTER

Textile	Northeast		Northwest		Southeast		Southwest		Total	
	no.	%	no.	%	no.	%	no.	%	no.	%
Wool	4	13.3	20	49	15	17	35	61.0	74	34.0
Cotton	11	36.7	21	51	47	53	1	1.8	80	37.0
Wool & cotton yarn	3	10.0	0	0	0	0	1	1.8	4	1.8
Silk	4	13.3	0	0	17	19	0	0	21	9.7
Unidentified	8	26.7	0	0	10	11	20	35.0	38	18.0
Total	30	100.0	41	100	89	100	57	100.0	217	100.0

TABLE 5
SHOE MANUFACTURE TYPE BY CLUSTER

	Northeast	Northwest	Southeast	Southwest
Nail	3	3	5	0
Wood peg	1	0	5	3
Metal peg	0	0	1	0
Nail & peg	3	0	1	0
Stitch	1	0	2	0
Turn	1	0	1	0
Screw	1	0	0	0
Welt	0	0	0	1
Turn/welt	0	0	0	0
Unidentified	0	1	0	0
Total	10	4	15	4

improvements as cast-iron stoves and linoleum flooring. Purchased toys, including doll heads and marbles, were almost exclusively recovered from the eastern features. The most remarkable purchased toy, recovered from the northeast household, is part of a cast-iron pistol, which not only suggests commercial acquisition of goods but also a departure from the deeply held Doukhobor tenet of pacifism.

When several artifact types recovered from Kirilovka are considered together, there appears to be a broad difference in material remains between the eastern and western households of the site. This is taken to suggest that the consumer activities of the households that correspond to each feature cluster were not uniform across the village. Individual families engaged in their own consumer pursuits, motivated by different priorities than their neighbors across the street. These varied consumer activities are believed to reflect variations in interpretation of the tenets of Doukhoborism and the practice of basic activities of rural, agrarian Russians among Kirilovka's families.

Discussion

In a 1911 magazine article, journalist John A. Cormie attributed the abandonment of communalism by some families to the materialism of the prevailing consumer society.

Cormie blames what he sees as the failure of Doukhobor communities on the irresistible allure of the kinds of commercially produced goods that were recovered archaeologically from several features at Kirilovka. Cormie (1911:596) remarked "[t]hose three houses with the stained walls, are they a pathetic tribute to the brutal power of a material age, which has proved too strong for a Utopian dream? At least one whole village has abandoned the community life, unable to stand against the insistent lure of private wealth, and every village has its house with the stained wall."

His position oversimplified the situation of the Doukhobors in the first two decades of the century. While store-bought, Anglo-Canadian-made items entered the daily lives of Doukhobor families at the same time that the tenets of new Doukhoborism appeared to lose hold, the objects themselves were integrated into an already changing social milieu.

Religion was part of the conscious identity of Doukhobors both in Russia and in North America. The tenets of Doukhoborism were adopted deliberately by those who joined the sect and were taught as part of the practice of faith to succeeding generations. Even though the tenets of new Doukhoborism were encouraged and enforced as part of the practice of Doukhobor faith by Verigin's spiritual leadership, there is a sense among some members of later Canadian communities that the restrictions were peripheral to the religious beliefs of Doukhobors in Canada. For example,

> [e]ating meat, all those things, drinking alcohol and not smoking, were all part of a self-disciplining process at a certain period in the Doukhobor history; particularly to make them strong, to say "no" to the military forces in Tsarist Russia, by refusing to participate in bearing arms. This is where it started and it's something that's perhaps important towards one's health and so on. But it should not have the religious significance that some people attach to it. It's just purely a disciplinary technique and a cleansing process which is very admirable (Tarasoff 1977:128).

Evidently, Verigin prescribed restrictions to behavior more as social-control mechanisms than as spiritual necessities to core beliefs of the faith. Further, they were situationally applicable to a specific period in Doukhobor history when group organization and boundary maintenance were required. Those Doukhobors who did not accept Verigin's supreme leadership, such as members of the "Small Party" that stayed in Russia and the "Independent Doukhobors" in Canada, had different concepts of what it meant to practice Doukhoborism.

The very nature of oral transmission and documentation in the Doukhobor faith led to the potential for constant reinterpretation of the meaning of practice in daily religious life. As stated by John Friesen and Michael Verigin (1996:7): "Theoretically, on the basis of the Divine spark, every believer becomes his own priest . . . the individual is directly led by the Spirit of God." Schisms within the faith were frequent, usually based on variations in practice among different groups of Doukhobors, splitting factions on the grounds of such issues as vegetarianism and communal land tenure. Resulting changes in group belief and structure were not always unidirectional. Those who followed Peter Verigin to Canada did so, for the most part, because of their conviction to live according to the tenets of their religion. The period of village settlement in Saskatchewan saw the dispersion of many families who had strayed from these tenets and abandoned their communal villages, while the following decades were ones of communal rejuvenation for those who moved on to British Columbia.

During their many migrations, Doukhobors carried visions of a perfect society attainable through the daily practice of their religion. They maintained this ideal more in mind and philosophy than in reality, as specific circumstances rarely fostered the realization of such Utopian aspirations. Archaeological traces of the material world in which the Saskatchewan Doukhobors lived bear witness to this struggle between real and ideal. In the 20 years following Kirilovka's settlement, residents did not consistently practice vegetarianism or abstinence from intoxicants as Verigin wished, and most eventually left community life to farm independently. At the same time, as material remains indicate, the Russian immigrants acquired and incorporated commercially mass-produced Anglo-Canadian goods into their daily lives. None of these changes, however, marked the death or failure of the Doukhobor religion. Today, local descendants of the families who left Kirilovka to farm independently identify themselves as Doukhobor and participate actively in the church.

Multiple levels of identity informed Doukhobor practice in the Saskatchewan colonies. First, the uniting common background of Russian agricultural peasantry incorporated group eating behaviors, the individual house plan, the *bania*, and craft traditions that are still valued in the modern day. Such practices, while not maintained for many years after the migration to Canada, live on in oral history as points that separate the Doukhobor settlers from their contemporaries and demonstrate a pride in tradition and heritage. These generations-old activities drew from the habitus brought by the Russian settlers to Saskatchewan.

The behavior-structuring ideals of the new Doukhoborism, conversely, were restraints created by the sect's leadership in order to rejuvenate a spiritual ideal that was inconsistent through the group's history. Vegetarianism, abstinence from intoxicants, and economic communalism were instrumentalist objectives that, in some circumstances, actually conflicted with the habitus to which Doukhobors were accustomed. Whether by necessity or opportunity for choice, Doukhobor settlers tended to favor the older habits and customs over those imposed by a sometimes overzealous religious leadership.

While the tenets of new Doukhoborism were reworked over time, other fundamental religious tenets form threads that maintain the continuity of Doukhobor spiritual identity from its founders in 18th-century Russia to their descendants in 21st-century North America. These include the idea of the spirit of God in each person and the equality of all, rejection of structured religious institutions or icons, and the oral transmission of prayers and psalms through song. The internalizing and individualizing traits that allowed for change and factionalization among North American Doukhobors were also the ones that gave the faith its flexibility to perpetuate through generations of geographical, political, and cultural change.

What may at first appear in the archaeological record to indicate abandonment of tradition, an acculturation or assimilation from traditional Doukhobor to Anglo-Canadian behaviors, actually represents a state of flux characteristic of Doukhoborism from Milky Waters, to Transcauasia, to the different Canadian settlements. From the beginning of the sect, Doukhobor identity and practice were dynamic and complex. Coexisting dimensions of ethnicity, ideology, and economics shaped the daily practices of these people, a situation that was reflected in and resulted from their material choices.

Acknowledgments

Mitigative excavation of the Kirilovka Village Site (FcNs-1) was undertaken in August and September 1996 by Western Heritage Services, Inc., of Saskatoon, Saskatchewan. Thanks to Shelley McConnell for her work on maps and to Peggy McKeand for faunal analysis. Funding for analysis and reporting was generously provided by the Saskatchewan Heritage Foundation and the Saskatchewan Archaeological Society. Special thanks to Mary Sookerokoff and the Popoff family of Saskatoon. This paper is dedicated to the memory of George Stushnoff.

References

BAYOFF, ALEX
  1985 Petrofka. Manuscript memoir in collection of Mary Sookerokoff, Saskatoon, Canada.

BOURDIEU, PIERRE
  1977 *Outline of a Theory of Practice*. Cambridge University Press, Cambridge, MA.

BREYFOGLE, NICHOLAS B.
  1995 Building Doukhoboriia: Religious Culture, Social Identity, and Russian Colonization in Transcaucasia, 1845–1895. *Canadian Ethnic Studies* 27(3):24–51.

CORMIE, JOHN A.
  1911 Untitled. *The University Magazine* 10:589–596.

FAIRCHILD, C. C.
  1909 Map of the Doukhobor Village of Kirilovka. Saskatchewan Archives Board, Saskatoon, Canada.

FRIESEN, JOHN W., AND MICHAEL M. VERIGIN
  1996 *The Community Doukhobors: A People in Transition*. Borealis Press, Ottawa, Canada.

FRY, GARY DEAN
  1976 The Doukhobors, 1801–1851: The Origin of a Successful Dissident Sect. Doctoral dissertation, Department of History, American University, Washington, DC.

GALE, DONALD T.
  1973 Belief and the Landscape of Religion: The Case of the Doukhobors. Master's thesis, Department of Geography, Simon Fraser University, Burnaby, British Columbia, Canada.

JOHNSON, J. K.
  1907 Letter to Frank Oliver, 11 March. Department of the Interior RG15, D-II-1, Volume 755, File 494483, Part 6, National Archives of Canada, Ottawa.

McDOUGALL, JOHN
  1907 General Report: Doukhobor Commission. Department of the Interior RG15, D-II-1, Volume 755, File 494483, Part 6, National Archives of Canada.

McKEAND, PEGGY, AND STACY KOZAKAVICH
  1997 Heritage Resources Impact Assessment of Karilowa, A Doukhobor Village near Langham, Saskatchewan, HRIA Permit No. 96–64. Report to Saskatchewan Highways and Transportation from Western Heritage Services, Saskatoon, Canada.

NATURAL RESOURCES CANADA
  1986 Map, 73B6 Borden, National Topographic System 1: 50 000 series. Centre for Topographic Information, Ottawa, Canada.

SOOKEROKOFF, MARY
  [n.d.] Untitled. Personal memoirs in collection of Mary Sookerokoff, Saskatoon, Canada.

TARASOFF, KOOZMA J.
  1972 Doukhobors—Their Migration Experience. *Canadian Ethnic Studies* 4(1–2):1–12.
  1977 *Traditional Doukhobor Folkways: An Ethnographic and Biographic Record of Prescribed Behavior*. Ottawa, National Museums of Canada.

TRACIE, CARL J.

1996 *Toil and Peaceful Life: Doukhobor Village Settlement in Saskatchewan 1899–1918.* Canadian Plains Research Centre, Regina, Canada.

STACY C. KOZAKAVICH
DEPARTMENT OF ANTHROPOLOGY
UNIVERSITY OF CALIFORNIA, BERKELEY
232 KROEBER HALL
BERKELEY, CA 94720-3710

Stephen R. Van Wormer
G. Timothy Gross

Archaeological Identification of an Idiosyncratic Lifestyle: Excavation and Analysis of the Theosophical Society Dump, San Diego, California

ABSTRACT

Refuse deposited by members of the Theosophical Institute in San Diego, California, ca. 1900–1920 provides a basis for defining patterns that reflect the idiosyncratic lifeways of the people who lived there. Comparisons with assemblages from urban and rural sites of the same period allow isolation of the areas of divergence. The Theosophical Society assemblage has low proportions of consumer items and bottled products along with lower values for ceramic tableware price scaling. Dietary differences were noted, as well, and the refuse has a large number of homeopathic medicine vials, reflecting specialized health practices. The patterns noted indicate less than full participation in the consumer society of the time and deviations in diet and healing practices from those of the mainstream society, and may have served as boundary markers, reinforcing the sense of group membership and cohesiveness.

Introduction

The results of archaeological test excavations are presented, which were undertaken at a refuse dump (California site CA–SDI–10,531H) used by the Theosophical Institute on Point Loma in the City of San Diego, California, from ca. 1900 to 1920. The site is located in a small natural gully within Sunset Cliffs Park on the west side of Point Loma (Figure 1). One of the main objectives was to determine if quantified artifact analysis could identify patterns that represented the idiosyncratic lifestyle of the institute's residents. The deposit consisted of randomly dumped homogeneous refuse. Approximately 310 kg of material were analyzed, resulting in the identification of an estimated minimum number of 4,284 items.

The site was tested by Affinis of El Cajon, California, in March 1990 as part of a program to determine the impact to cultural resources of the proposed construction of a 12-inch sewage pipeline designed by the City of San Diego Water Utilities Department (Gross et al. 1991). The Theosophical Society dump lies adjacent to and partially in the pipeline corridor.

As a homogeneous deposit representing the Theosophical Society commune, data from the assemblage can be compared to other sites in order to define unique patterns reflective of the idiosyncratic lifestyle of the residents. Data analysis consisted of comparing artifact profiles, socioeconomic data, and consumption patterns from the Theosophical Society refuse assemblage to mainstream urban and rural assemblages dating between 1900 and 1920. The analysis resulted in identification of distinctive patterns reflective of the lifestyle at the Theosophical Society during those decades.

Historical Background of the Theosophical Institute

Founded and run by Madame Katherine Tingley (Figure 2) until her death in 1929, the Theosophical Institute on Point Loma served as the headquarters of the American Theosophical Society from 1897 to 1942 and consisted of an

FIGURE 1. Location of the Theosophical Society dump site. (Drawing by G. Timothy Gross, 2001.)

agricultural commune, boarding school, and art colony (Wright 1974; Kamerling 1980). Tingley had been born in Massachusetts on 6 June 1847. She dedicated her life to philanthropic enterprises and had a strong interest in spiritualism and the occult. In 1892, she joined the Theosophical Society (Wright 1974).

FIGURE 2. Katherine Tingley in 1892. (Courtesy of the San Diego Historical Society, San Diego, CA.)

Madame Helena Petrovna Blavatsky, a Russian seeress, and Henry Olcott, an American attorney, formed the society in 1875. The purpose of theosophy was to achieve a universal brotherhood of man established through an ever-increasing awareness of the relationship between the spirit of man and the universe. Theosophy was defined as speculative thought about God and the universe that arises through the study of the universal truths of various religious schools including Judaism, Christianity, Hinduism, and Buddhism. The movement became worldwide, and societies were established in England, India, the United States, and several Asiatic countries (Wright 1974; Kamerling 1980).

The death of Madame Blavatsky in 1891 caused a power struggle within the society's leadership that resulted in the establishment of the Theosophical Society of America in 1895. In 1896, Katherine Tingley became head of the newly established organization (Wright 1974; Kamerling 1980). Under Tingley's leadership, the society purchased land on Point Loma in 1897 for a Theosophical School for the Revival of the Lost Mysteries of Antiquity (Wright 1974). Known as the Raja Yoga School, the aim of the educational program was to create free men and women: "free intellectually, free mentally, unprejudiced in all respects, and, above all, things, unselfish" (Aryan Theosophical Press 1922). Tingley believed that children should be taught self-reliance, love for all people, altruism, mutual clarity, and, more than anything else, to think and reason for themselves. In addition, they should reject love of money, worldly position, social advancement, success, personal stature, selfish aggrandizement, and worldly pleasures (Aryan Theosophical Press 1922). A pupil's success in life depended primarily on physical health, followed by mental vigor, and finally upon moral purity. The goal of the Raja Yoga curriculum was to achieve a perfect balance of these three (Aryan Theosophical Press 1922). Coursework ranged from the elementary through the university level, and classes emphasized the study of literature, ancient and modern languages, mathematics, philosophy, law, the fine arts, practical forestry, horticulture, and domestic economy (Figure 3) (Wright 1974).

By 1913, the school and commune had become well established and home for more than 500 individuals, of which half were students. The grounds resembled, on first impression, "a great farm lined with cypress trees" (Koch 1913:340). Hill slopes were planted in oats and barley. Groves of citrus, avocado, and other fruit trees, as well as vegetable gardens, were planted throughout the property (Koch 1913; Wright 1974). The grounds also included living quarters, a refectory (kitchen and dining room), bakery, stables, carpenter shop, smithy, machine shop, print shop, bindery, and facilities for the production of textiles and clothing (Wright 1974). The architectural style of the buildings was a blend of Eastern, ancient Egyptian, and Moorish styles resulting in an effect that led one observer to describe it as "a bit

FIGURE 3. The grounds of the Theosophical Society on Point Loma ca. 1900. (Courtesy of the San Diego Historical Society, San Diego, CA.)

of old India here in the United States" (Koch 1913:342). Purple, green, and red glass domes crowned several of the more prominent structures (Figure 4) (Koch 1913; Wright 1974).

Madam Tingley believed that most adults were incapable of raising their own offspring. Children lived apart from their parents in sexually segregated dormitories under the supervision of their teacher. Parents could visit for a few hours on Sundays once or twice a month. The pupils followed an extremely rigorous and active daily routine. They rose at a quarter to five, attended physical training, then ate breakfast, did house chores, changed into school clothes, and attended an hour of formal classroom instruction. Lunch was served in the refectory at 12 o'clock, then came cleanup and playtime. The day finished with an hour of garden work, another hour of lessons, a light dinner, and then music lessons. Supervision remained so strict throughout the day that it was extremely difficult for the pupils to do anything wrong. The

refectory served a vegetarian diet that avoided red meat and emphasized fruits, cereals, soup, bread, and fish. Milk, eggs, and butter were seldom served, although margarine was used (Figure 5) (Shepherd 1995:11,87,114).

The Theosophical commune thrived from the turn of the century through the 1920s. The death of Katherine Tingley in 1929, combined with financial problems resulting from the depression of the 1930s, brought a decade of steady decline. The Raja Yoga School closed in 1940, and in 1942 the property was sold when the society's headquarters moved to Covina, California (Wright 1974).

Field Methods

The site is located on the edge of a terrace at the base of the western slope of the Point Loma peninsula. The Theosophical Institute campus was just a few hundred meters east of and upslope from the refuse deposit on the

FIGURE 4. The Egyptian gate was one of the main entrances to the Theosophical Society Compound. (Courtesy of the San Diego Historical Society, San Diego, CA.)

FIGURE 5. Children eating a meal at the Theosophical Society. (Courtesy of the San Diego Historical Society, San Diego, CA.)

Perspectives from *Historical Archaeology*

present site of Point Loma Nazarine College. The dump covers an area of approximately 30 by 15 m. It had been badly disturbed by relic hunters and was covered with a dense scatter of recently disturbed artifacts. It was believed that in spite of relic hunting the artifact assemblage still accurately represented lifestyles of the Theosophical Society population. This assumption was based on the large quantity of cultural material the site contained and the fact that relic hunters had taken only whole bottles, ignoring faunal remains, ceramic and metal items, and broken bottle fragments, which represented the majority of glass containers discarded at the site. Artifact recovery was designed to collect the largest possible sample within the time and budget constraints of the project. Recovery consisted of an intensive surface collection and stratigraphic excavation of five units (1 x 1 m). The surface collection produced 1,275 items that constituted 29% of the artifact assemblage. Unit excavation produced 3,009 items, making up 71% of the artifacts identified.

Research Objectives, Artifact Analysis, and Data Synthesis

Analysis of datable artifact attributes indicated the refuse had been deposited during the first three decades of the 20th century (Van Wormer 1991b). Refuse deposited by members of the Theosophical Institute in San Diego, California, ca. 1900–1920, provides a basis for defining patterns that reflect the idiosyncratic lifeways of the people who lived there. Comparisons with assemblages from urban and rural sites of the same period allow isolation of areas of divergence. The patterns noted indicate less than full participation in the consumer society of the time and deviations in diet and healing practices from those of the mainstream society. These deviations may have served as boundary markers, reinforcing the sense of group membership and cohesiveness.

The research objectives and artifact analysis were framed and conducted within a theoretical context of functional pattern definition and consumerism studies. Studies in consumer behavior indicate people buy things for what they mean culturally, as well as for their functional purpose. Consumption is one of the important ways of signifying membership in a group, particularly in

class, status, and ethnic groups, and is therefore an important reflection of lifestyle. Some groups, known as reference groups, exert a greater influence on individuals. Since individuals are influenced by the groups to which they belong, people can follow a group lifestyle. There will be variability in the group lifestyle as practiced by its individual members; however, there will be more similarity among individuals within the group than between groups (Henry 1991).

The primary cultural unit of historical archaeology has traditionally been the household, which is defined as a domestic residential group consisting of the inhabitants of a dwelling or set of dwellings and appears as a discrete group in historical documents (Henry 1987a, 1987b). It includes all the residents in the group that could have contributed to primary artifact deposits within the premises' yard or other defined boundary during a single time period (Spencer-Wood 1987:2). The household can generally be seen as a member of the social group to which its members belong. Households are members of two powerful reference groups: social class and ethnic affiliation. This commonality of group membership allows comparison of large numbers of households on a consistent measure. If a sufficient database has been developed, research can focus on analytical units larger than the single site, making comparisons within and between social groups possible (Henry 1987a, 1987b). The refuse in the Theosophical Society Dump site represents members of a specific reference group—the Theosophical Society.

Several procedures have been developed to study consumerism and the relative value different reference groups placed on certain artifact classes. These include economic indexing, consumption pattern analysis, and dietary studies. George L. Miller (1980) first developed economic indexing for ceramic tableware, based on indexes derived from cost relationships of tableware form and decoration during specific time periods. Indexes have been developed by Susan Henry (1982, 1987a) for late-19th- and early-20th-century ceramic assemblages. Bottled products consumption patterns have proven useful to help define site function and social group affiliation by revealing beverage, dietary, and medicinal preferences. Relative frequencies of bottled products differ between domestic households and commercial establishments as well as between social groups (Van Wormer 1983a; Blanford 1987).

Based on the theoretical framework of functional profile definition and consumerism studies discussed above, five basic areas of inquiry were identified for investigation through various means of data synthesis. These are as follows:

1. To compare the artifact pattern profile of the Theosophical Society dump with those from urban and rural sites of the same period (1900–1920), in order to determine how the Theosophical Society pattern differs from those representing mainstream populations.
2. To conduct socioeconomic analysis of the assemblage using ceramic price scaling in order to compare the economic status of Theosophical Society residents with those of the population at large.
3. To conduct consumption pattern analysis by comparing relative frequencies of bottled products from the Theosophical Society to other sites in order to detect significant differences from defined pattern norms.
4. To identify dietary preferences based on quantitative analysis of culinary bottled products patterns and faunal analysis.
5. To assess the patterns represented by the above data to determine if the Theosophical Society refuse represents an idiosyncratic pattern reflective of the inhabitants' unique lifestyle.

Cross-Site Artifact Patterns

In order to determine the types of activities represented, artifacts were divided into functional categories or groups. The purpose of this classification is to allow detection of relationships between functionally defined artifact groups at a generalized level of analysis in order to define broad patterned regularities. The need for analysis at this level is to define patterned regularities so variations in the norm can be detected through cross-site comparisons (South 1977:10). The analysis of the Theosophical Society dump artifacts used a broader classification system with 20 artifact groups (Figure 6), rather than the 8 developed for Stanley South's models.

South's original eight groups are appropriate for sites dating prior to the Civil War. The quantity and availability of manufactured goods as well as consumer purchasing increased greatly after 1870 (Thomas 1982; Gordon and McArthur 1985; Schlereth 1991). Relationships among the resulting wide variety of artifacts often found on late-19th- and early-20th-century sites are more easily understood with a broader classification system. Artifacts in each group were quantified by estimated minimum number, and the amount converted into a percent of the total number of artifacts from the deposit. It could thus be determined to what degree different activities were represented, resulting in a functional pattern or profile of the artifact assemblage.

Table 1 shows relative frequencies for functional artifact groups by quantity for the Theosophical Society dump assemblage, and Figure 7 graphically presents the activity profile. The assemblage is dominated by kitchen items at 42%, followed by garment items at 16%, and personal items at 14%. Consumer items constitute 11% of the assemblage. The remaining activity groups represented less than 10% each of the items identified.

The pattern was compared to other assemblages from the same period (1900–1920). Data from three urban sites were used: the 1908–1913 San Diego City dump (Van Wormer 1991a, 1996a, 1996b); the Orange County Transit District Terminal Site (OCTD) project in Santa Ana, California (Brock 1985); and refuse deposits from Phoenix, Arizona (Henry and Garrow 1982). San Diego and Santa Ana represented upper-middle-class urban populations (Elliott 1985; Van Wormer 1991a; 1996a, 1996b). The assemblage from Phoenix represented a mixed neighborhood of working- and middle-class residents, many with Hispanic surnames (Henry and Garrow 1982). In addition, the Theosophical Society pattern was compared to assemblages from Ventura, California, and a pattern generated from the combined assemblages of five rural San Diego County farmsteads. The artifacts from Ventura represented a small-town, working-class population (Benté 1975, 1976). The farm sites included Rancho Guajome (Fink 1980), Rancho Peñasquitos (Van Wormer 1986), the Hubert Ranch near Oceanside (Van Wormer 1984), the Root farmstead near Chula Vista (Kupel 1986), and a farmstead site in Rainbow Valley north of

Consumer Item Group: Items containing products purchased and consumed on a regular basis

Bottles
Jars
Tin cans and other tins
Bottle caps, can lids, and related items

Kitchen Group: Food preparation and serving

Stove parts
Flatware
Canning jars
Canning jar lids and related items
Jelly tumblers
Glass tableware
Ceramic kitchen and tableware
Cooking items
Butchered bone
Shellfish
Seeds

Household Items Group: Daily household maintenance

Household ceramics
   Toiletry items, decorative dishes, vases & other bric-a-brac
Household glassware
   Toiletry items, decorative dishes, vases & other bric-a-brac
Lamp parts
Light bulbs
Medical items
Batteries
Miscellaneous household items

Garment Items Group: All clothing items

Shoe parts
Collar stays
Strap slides
Buttons
Garter clasps
Hook and eyes
Suspender clasps
Straight pins
Snaps
Buckles
Clothing rivets
Corset Hardware

Personal Items Group: Belonging to a single individual

Watches
Jewelry
Toys and gaming items
Musical instruments
Eye glasses
Toiletry items (toothbrush, razor, comb, hairbrush, etc.)
Smoking pipes

Furniture Parts Group: All furniture parts

Upholstery tacks
Springs
Cabinet hinges
Drawer pulls
Scroll trim
Trunk parts
Bed and other furniture frames and springs

Hardware Group: Miscellaneous hardware not included in a specific group

Bolts and nuts
Screws
Washers
Chain links
Metal bands and strapping
Cotter pins
Rivets
Bailing wire
Wire fencing

Tools Group: All hand tools

Gardener's tools
Carpenter's tools
Mason's tools
Mechanic's tools
Jeweler's tools
Artist's tools
Other miscellaneous hand tools

FIGURE 6. Activity groups used in the artifact pattern analysis.

Livery Items Group: Horse and horse-drawn vehicle items

Bridle parts
Saddle parts
Harness parts
Horse shoes and nails
Wagon parts
Buggy parts

Munitions Items Group: All firearms and related items

Bullets
Cartridges
Musket balls
Shotshells
Gun parts

Coins Group: All coinage and tokens

Building Materials and Architecture Group: Construction materials

Nails and spikes
Window glass
Construction hardware
Door locks and parts
Electrical hardware
Counter glass
Asphalt
Plaster
Concrete
Ceramic drain pipe
Ceramic flue lining

Machinery Items Group: All machine parts except agricultural implements

Forge Materials Group: All forge, furnace, and stove wastes

Coal, clinkers, and slag

Agricultural Implements Group: All farm machinery

Plow parts
Harrow parts
Chain belting
Cultivator parts

Mower parts
Hay rake parts
Threshing machine parts
Manure spreader parts
Tractor parts

Other Occupations Group: Specialized occupation items

Farmstead items
Mining items
Factory items

Unique Items Group: Items not included in other groups

Unidentified Items Group: Items that cannot be identified

Intrusive Items Group: Items intrusive to a discrete dated deposit

FIGURE 6. Activity groups used in the artifact pattern analysis. (CONTINUED)

TABLE 1
THEOSOPHICAL SOCIETY ACTIVITY PATTERN

Activity	No.[a]	%
Consumer	396	11
Kitchen	1,463	42
Household	448	13
Personal	490	14
Garment	574	16
Other	156	4
Total	3,527	100

[a]Estimated minimum number of individual items.

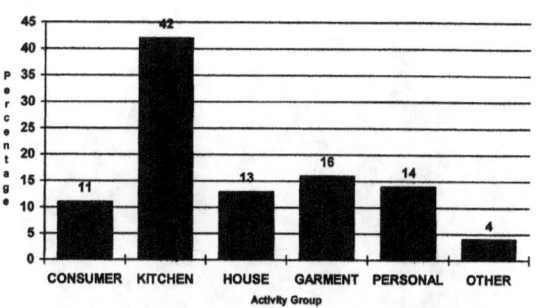

FIGURE 7. Theosophical Society dump activity profile. (Drawing by Stephen R. Van Wormer.)

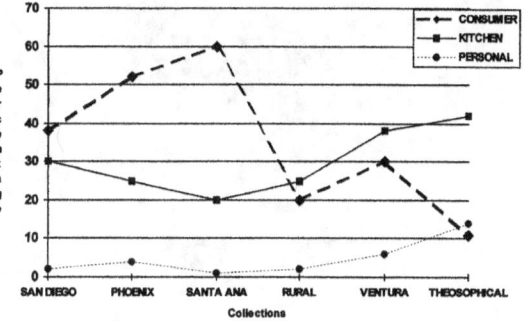

FIGURE 8. Cross-site activity profiles. (Drawing by Stephen R. Van Wormer.)

Escondido (Van Wormer 1985). Data from the rural sites were combined and averaged. Building materials dominated most of the assemblages used for comparison. So that the relative value of the other activity groups could be more easily assessed, building materials were eliminated from the assemblage, and the percentages of the remaining activity groups recalculated.

Figure 8 shows some interesting patterns. The Theosophical Society is lowest in relative quantities of consumer items—largely bottled products—which make up only 11% of the artifacts recovered, while constituting 20%–60% of the other assemblages. The Theosophical assemblage, on the other hand, is one of the highest in kitchen items at 42% and is the highest ranking assemblage for personal items at 14%. In the other assemblages, personal items made up 2%–6% of the totals. Personal artifacts from the Theosophical Society assemblage appear to largely reflect activities associated with the students at the Raja Yoga School. The most numerous were 254 glass beads, 75 toys, 53 bone toothbrushes, and 15 artists supplies (Figures 9–14). Toys included marbles, animal figurines and dolls, gaming pieces, and china dishes. Artists supplies consisted of watercolor paint cups, paint brush ferrules, a palette knife, blue paint pigments, and a brush holder. Large quantities of beads were recovered from all units. Two activities of the school probably account for the high number. The school had a very active drama program and also emphasized studies in fine arts (Kamerling 1980). Costumes

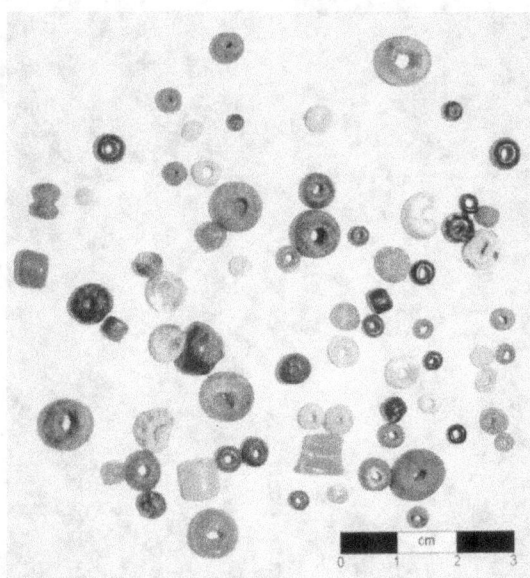

FIGURE 9. Beads recovered from the Theosophical Society dump. (Photo by the authors; courtesy of the San Diego Historical Society, San Diego, CA.)

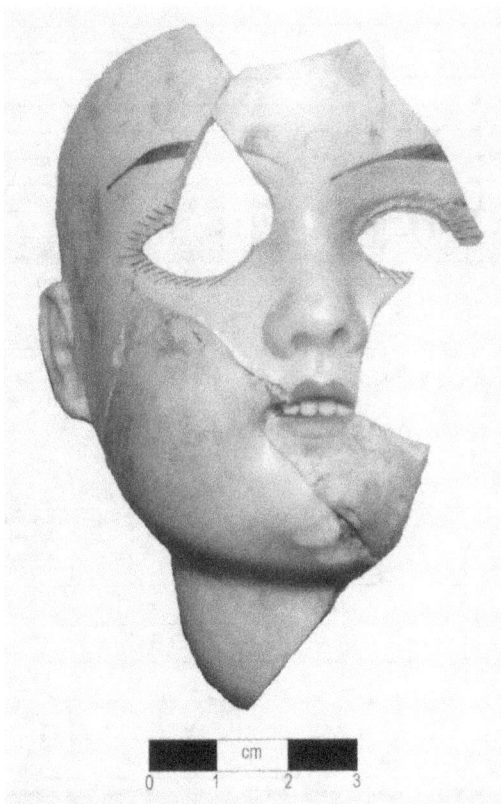

FIGURE 10. Doll's head recovered from the Theosophical Society dump. (Photo by the authors; courtesy of the San Diego Historical Society, San Diego, CA.)

for theatrical productions may have required decorative beadwork, and they may also have been used in art projects.

Ceramic Price Scaling

For ceramic price scaling, this analysis used the index developed by Henry for ceramic tableware manufactured between 1900 and 1909 (Henry 1982). Decorative ware types used in the index included undecorated, molded, gilt, color, color and gilt, and porcelain. The index value calculations for the Theosophical Society assemblage resulted in a mean index value of 1.6. In Figure 15, the Theosophical Society's value is compared to that of the urban and rural sites. Data for the Ventura assemblage were not presented in a manner so that an index value could be calculated. The economic index value of the Theosophical Society assemblage is low when compared to urban sites, corresponding more to the value of the rural households assemblage. It may also reflect the institutional nature of the ceramic assemblage.

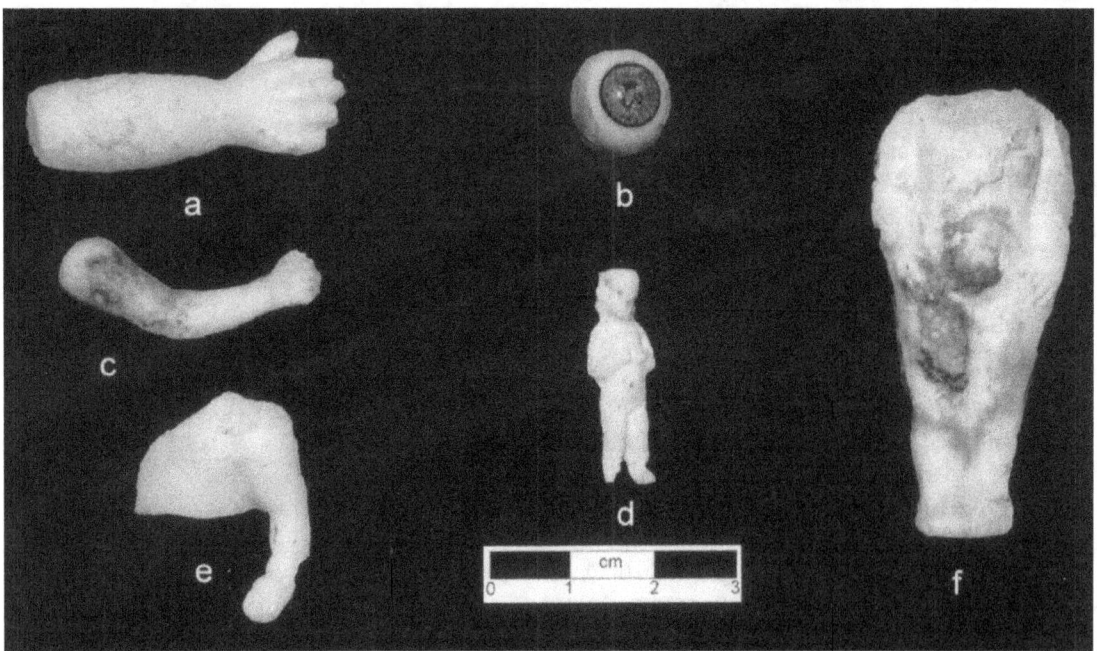

FIGURE 11. Ceramic doll parts from the Theosophical Society dump: (*a*) arm, (*b*) glass eye, (*c*) arm, (*d*) small frozen Charlotte, (*e*) arm and shoulder, (*f*) large frozen Charlotte. (Photo by the authors; courtesy of the San Diego Historical Society, San Diego, CA.)

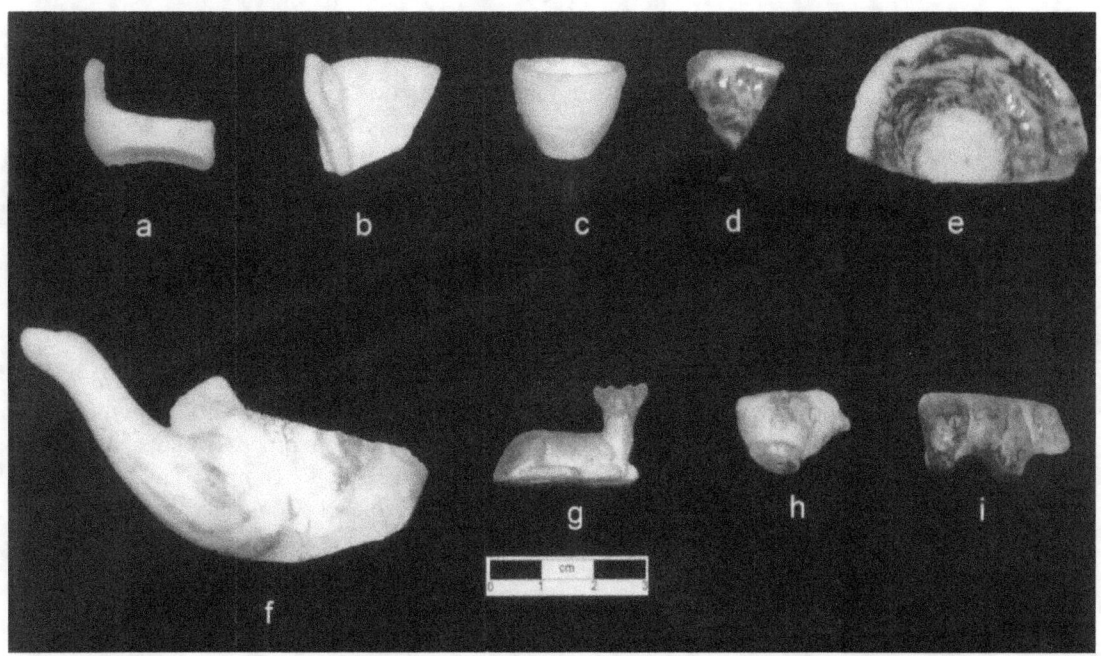

FIGURE 12. Ceramic toys from the Theosophical Society dump: (*a–d*) tea cups, (*e*) saucer, (*f*) teapot spout, (*g–i*) animal figurines, possibly from a Noah's Ark set. (Photo by the authors; courtesy of the San Diego Historical Society, San Diego, CA.)

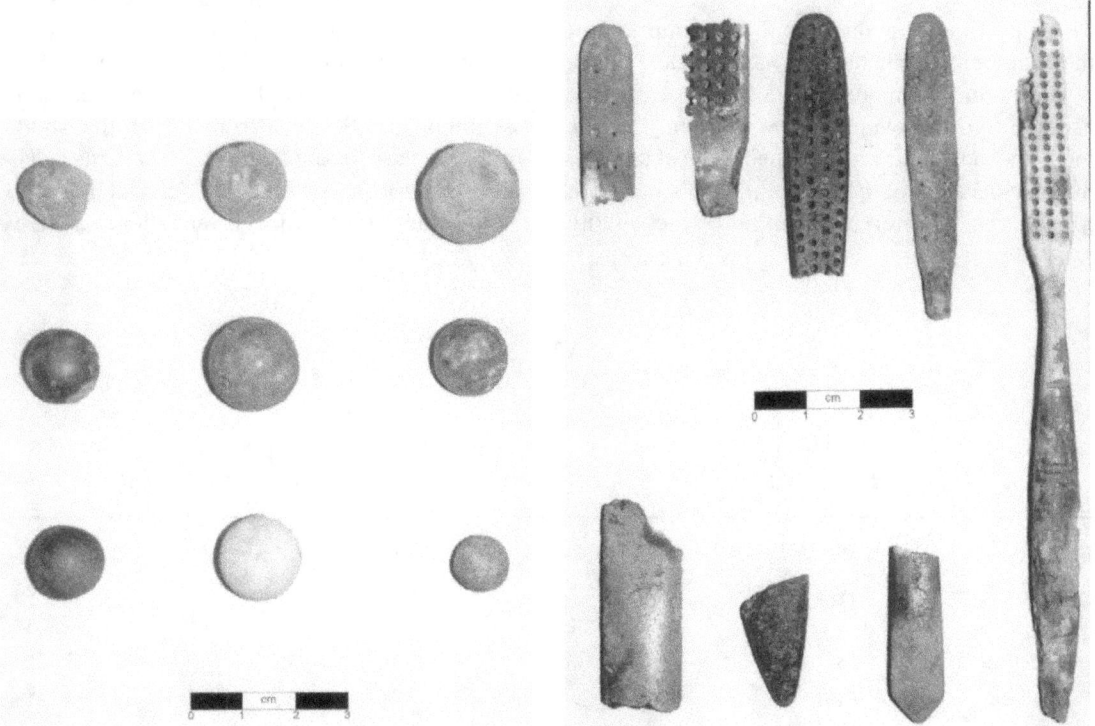

FIGURE 13. A variety of different marbles from the Theosophical Society dump. (Photo by the authors; courtesy of the San Diego Historical Society, San Diego, CA.)

FIGURE 14. Examples of bone toothbrushes from the Theosophical Society dump. (Photo by the authors; courtesy of the San Diego Historical Society, San Diego, CA.)

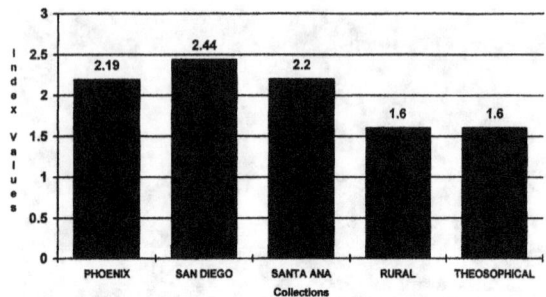

FIGURE 15. Cross-site ceramic index values. (Drawing by Stephen R. Van Wormer.)

Bottled Products Consumption Patterns

Table 2 and Figure 16 compare relative frequencies of different bottled products to those from the Theosophical Society. Beverage frequencies for the Theosophical assemblage are extremely low, constituting 6% of the total, while making up 38%–49% of the other collections. Household and toiletry items at 22%, on the other hand, are higher than in any of the other assemblages, where they range between 6% and 13%.

In addition, the medicinal consumption of the commune's inhabitants was unique. Table 3 shows medicine bottle quantities from the assemblage. Seventy-three percent of the medicine bottles from the Theosophical Society dump consisted of homeopathic vials. Small, glass-cork-stoppered cylinders, measuring

approximately 2 cm in diameter and 6 cm in length, these vials made up only 14% of the medicine bottles recovered from the San Diego City dump. Each originally held a large number of small pills prescribed for a specific ailment.

Dietary Preferences

Culinary bottled product consumption patterns indicate that members of the Theosophical Society had dietary preferences that differed significantly from other populations. Very little fresh meat was consumed, although there was a heavy reliance on processed meat products. Table 4 and Figure 17 compare culinary bottled product assemblages from sites of well-defined ethnic identities to the Theosophical Society assemblage. Sites used included refuse from the foundation units of the Encino Roadhouse, Santa Ana, San Diego, Features 1 and 3 of the Encino Roadhouse, the Pio Pico Adobe in Whittier, and the Diaz Adobe in Monterey. San Diego, the Encino foundation units, and Santa Ana represent Anglo-American culinary traditions (Van Wormer 1983a, 1991a, 1996a, 1996b; Elliott 1985). The other sites represent southern European and Hispanic populations (Felton and Schulz 1983; Van Wormer 1983a, 1983b). The Theosophical Society culinary assemblage is different from either the southern European-Hispanic or Anglo patterns. The Anglo-American patterns are characterized by a wide variety of products and dominated by

TABLE 2
CROSS-SITE BOTTLED PRODUCTS

Product	San Diego No.[a]	San Diego %	Santa Ana No.[a]	Santa Ana %	Ventura No.[a]	Ventura %	Rural No.[a]	Rural %	Theosophical No.[a]	Theosophical %
Beverage	1,169	38	213	48	104	41	105	24	22	6
Culinary	520	17	41	9	35	14	64	15	75	20
Medicinal	679	22	148	32	80	31	146	34	133	34
Household/toiletry	245	8	13	3	17	7	25	6	81	22
Unidentified	491	15	39	8	18	7	53	12	72	18
Other	0	0	0	0	0	0	37	9	0	0
Total	3,104	100	472	100	254	100	430	100	383	100

[a]Estimated minimum number of individual items.

Perspectives from *Historical Archaeology*

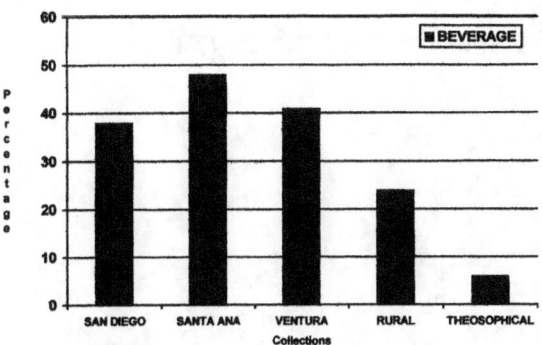

FIGURE 16. Cross-site beverage bottles. (Drawing by Stephen R. Van Wormer.)

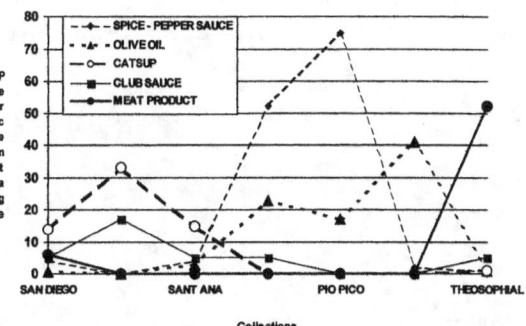

FIGURE 17. Comparative culinary product consumption patterns. (Drawing by Stephen R. Van Wormer.)

TABLE 3
THEOSOPHICAL SOCIETY
MEDICINAL PRODUCTS

Type	No.[a]	%
Antiseptic	5	5.5
Homeopathic	58	73.0
Tonic	5	5.5
Stomach	4	5.0
Liniment	6	8.0
Coughs and Colds	2	3.0
Total	80	100.0

[a]Estimated minimum number of individual items.

packer lip, club sauce, and catsup bottles. The southern European-Hispanic assemblages exhibit far fewer products and are dominated by pepper sauce and olive oil containers. The Theosophical Society pattern shows a wide variety but is dominated by meat products (potted beef and albumenized food), which make up 52% of the culinary assemblage.

Lynne E. Christenson analyzed faunal material. Bone was recovered from three units. Seven identified large mammal specimens consisted of burned distal axial skeletal remains from either goats or sheep. Fifteen bird bones included *Gallus gallus* (chicken) and an unidentified species of duck. Twenty-six fish bones, primarily vertebrae, were recovered. All represented large locally available ocean fish that may have been purchased commercially. Overall the faunal assemblage was too small to compare with other sites. The amount of bone indicates some residents of the Theosophical Institute were eating fresh meat; however, they constituted a very small part of the more than 500 people living at the compound (Christenson 1991:10).

Idiosyncratic Pattern

Overall, the artifact assemblage from SDI–10,531H exhibits a unique pattern representative of the lifestyle and values of the Theosophical Society inhabitants. Several aspects appear to reflect a reduced participation by the society in the dominant consumer culture prevalent at the turn of the century. Madam Tingley's dictate that members deny love of money, worldly possessions, social advancement, success, self-aggrandizement, and worldly pleasure certainly provided a mandate to reject consumerism. This is revealed in the low percentage of consumer items and beverage bottles in the assemblage and lower economic index value of the ceramic assemblage when compared to urban sites. The lower ceramic index value may also, in part, reflect the institutional nature of the society's lifestyle.

The lower number of consumer items is largely a result of the extremely low quantity of beverage bottles in the assemblage. Liquor containers made up more than 90% of the beverage bottles from all the sites used for comparison. The low consumption of alcoholic drinks by the society members was undoubtedly one of the means of complying with Madam Tingley's mandate

TABLE 4
CROSS-SITE PERCENTAGES OF CULINARY PRODUCTS CONSUMPTION

Product	San Diego	Encino Foundations	Santa Ana	Encino Features	Pio Pico	Diaz	Theosophical
Albumenized food	0.5	0	0	0	0	0	20
Catsup	14	33	15	0	0	0	1
Cheese	2	0	0	0	0	0	1
Condiment	36	25	47	10	8	0	0
Flavoring extract	5	0	2	0	0	17	3
Juice	0.5	0	0	0	0	0	0
Lemon juice	0.2	0	0	0	0	0	1
Malted milk	4	8	7	0	0	0	3
Marmalade-jam- preserves	2	0	0	0	0	0	5
Milk	5	0	7	0	0	0	0
Mustard	2	0	0	10	0	0	3
Olive oil	0.5	0	3	23	17	41	1
Olives	2	8	0	0	0	0	7
Pepper sauce	2	0	2	52	75	2	0
Potted-chipped beef	6	0	0	0	0	0	32
Preserved fruit	0	0	0	0	0	34	0
Salad dressing	5	9	7	0	0	0	0
Spice	2	0	2	0	0	0	1
Vinegar	0.5	0	3	0	0	4	0
Wide-mouth jar	1	0	0	0	0	0	0
Unidentified	5	0	0	0	0	0	17
Worcestershire sauce	5	17	5	5	0	0	5
Total	100	100	100	100	100	100	100

to reject worldly pleasures. Articles advising against strong drink and advocating temperance appeared regularly in the society's magazine *The New Century*, which was edited by Tingley (1903, 1904a, 1904b, 1904e).

The similarity between the ceramic index values of the Theosophical Society and rural assemblages is probably the result of a similar nonparticipation in contemporary middle- and upper middle-class urban cultural consumption by Theosophical Society members and rural agrarian residents, although this may have occurred within each group for different reasons.

The Victorian cult of domesticity developed as a major component of urban middle-class values during the last half of the 19th century (Howe 1975:529). Rising levels of family income allowed middle-class women to remain at home, specializing in the maintenance of a higher standard of living (Brownlee 1979). Within the cult of domesticity, therefore, a woman's status was revealed in her success as a homemaker. Success was reflected materially in well-kept, stylish homes with neat yards, nice furnishings, decorated wallpaper, and tables properly set with attractive tableware, which led to an urban culture of conspicuous consumption, dominated by middle-class wives, that was well established by the 1870s (Hill 1880:151; Howe 1975:523; Gordon and McArthur 1985:35–46).

Neither farmers nor Theosophists were trying to establish or maintain middle-class households based on conspicuous consumption. Agrarian consumption priorities were focused toward the establishment and preservation of a stable way of life as opposed to urban Victorian consumption patterns designed to express the wife's success as homemaker and the appearance of upward mobility (Howe 1975:515; Gordon and McArthur 1985:3). Economic gain was important to farm families. However, it did not dominate their spending priorities. Two other goals—yearly subsistence and the long-term financial security of the family unit—dominated economic priorities so that maximization of profit was less important than meeting household needs and maintaining established social relationships (Henretta 1978:7).

Although their own value system that rejected worldly possessions and self-aggrandizement may have been a motivation to avoid purchasing expensive ceramics, the Theosophist main objective for acquiring tableware was to meet the needs of their communal meals, where large numbers of young students undoubtedly resulted in high levels of breakage and a reluctance to invest in costly table settings. The fact that for very distinct reasons farm families and Theosophists did not attempt to maintain traditional mainstream middle-class households resulted in similar ceramic index values for rural agrarian sites and the Theosophical Society dump assemblage.

Other unique aspects of the Theosophical Society assemblage appear to reflect the adoption of idiosyncratic behavior in diet and health practices, represented by the high percentage of homeopathic vials and dominance of processed meat products in the culinary products assemblage (Figure 18). Tingley believed that the success of the lives of her pupils depended primarily upon physical health (Aryan Theosophical Press 1922). Consequently, the diet of the students and commune members was based on her own views of what constituted a healthy lifestyle and eating habits.

Tingley's philosophy of health consisted of elements drawn from several different schools of medical thought popular at the end of the 19th century. Commonly practiced medical science during the 19th century was a tragic failure (Jones 1967:23). Doctors had no idea what caused disease and were helpless to prevent or cure it. Not until the 1870s did the works of

Louis Pasteur and Robert Koch prove the existence of bacilli, thereby laying the foundation for the development of germ theory. At the end of the century, however, some doctors still doubted that germs caused disease. Numerous theories existed, each resulting in its own school of practice. A partial list of different 19th-century practitioners included homeopaths, hydropaths, herbalists, chrono-thermalists, Thompsonians, Mesmerists, Indian doctors, clairvoyants, and spiritualists (Jones 1967:28).

Tingley apparently picked aspects from several different schools, especially hydropathy, homeopathy, and the ideas of the German chemist

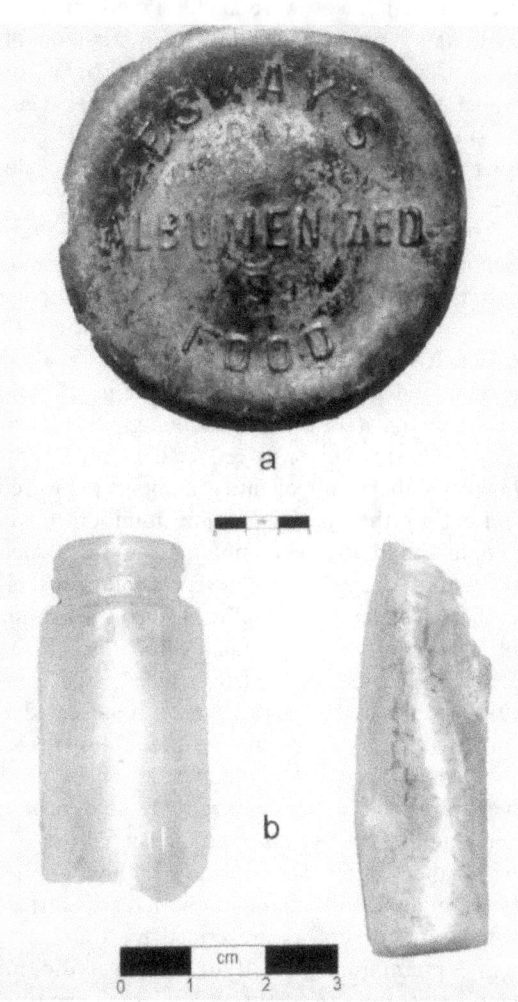

FIGURE 18. (a) albumenized food bottle base and (b) homeopathic vials from the Theosophical Society dump. (Photo by the authors; courtesy of the San Diego Historical Society, San Diego, CA.)

Justus von Liebig. Von Liebig developed the theory that all living tissues (including food) were composed of carbohydrates, fats, and albuminoids or proteins. Body heat was produced by the oxidation of fats and carbohydrates, and the oxidation of proteins was necessary for muscle movement and tissue replacement. Von Liebig concluded that protein or albumin was the muscle-building substance and absolutely necessary for human strength. It was felt, therefore, that an individual's protein consumption should be proportional to the amount of physical work required. Meat was identified as the best source of protein (Tannahill 1973:375; Whorton 1982:227; Levenstein 1988:90).

Other schools of medical thought felt that diets rich in meat were bad. Practitioners of hydropathy prescribed a diet consisting mainly of fruits, vegetables, and brown or whole wheat bread, rather than meat (Kuepper 1905: 42–44). Medical reformers such as J. H. Kellogg (1885) and E. B. Foote (1892) advocated the same fare.

The diet of the students at the Raja Yoga School consisted of very little fresh red meat and emphasized cereals, nuts, fruits, fish, and soups (Atherton 1982). "A Prescription for Long Life," published by Madam Tingley emphasized eating slowly a minimum of food, of which meat is a very small ingredient (Tingley 1904d). This was reflected in the assemblage by the small quantity of bone recovered, indicating that a very minor number of the people living in the compound ate fresh meat (Christenson 1991:10). By prescribing this bill of fare, Tingley was conforming to the writings of Foote, Kellogg, and the hydropaths. Meals at the school, however, also included large quantities of processed meat products represented in the artifact assemblage by the albumenized food and potted beef containers. These products provided a high source of meat protein and could have been served in soup broths or with other dishes. Katherine Tingley supplied her students and residents with concentrated sources of protein as prescribed by von Liebig while maintaining a bill of fare that did not emphasize the consumption of large quantities of fresh red meat.

Tingley also drew ideas from the homeopathic school of thought and discouraged use of the numerous fraudulent patent medicines popular during the period (Tingley 1904d). Her mentor in theosophy, William Avan Judge (1892), professed a faith in homeopathy and its medicines. Homeopathy was a method of treatment founded on the assumption that if a drug given to a healthy person produced a certain symptom, the same drug would cure someone suffering from an ailment that produced those symptoms. This belief was summed up in their motto "like cures like" (Pierce 1895:294). Homeopathy was compatible, and perhaps even responsible for, Tingley's overall philosophy on health since the homeopathic school associated hydropathy with its practice as well as rigid dietetic and hygienic regulations. Madame Tingley's philosophy of health, hygiene, and diet, therefore, are also reflected by the numerous homeopathic vials (73% of the 80 patent medicine bottles identified) in the artifact assemblage.

Conclusions

Overall the artifact assemblage from the Theosophical Society dump exhibits a unique pattern indicative of the lifestyle and values of the Theosophical Society inhabitants. Several aspects appear to reflect the rejection by the society of the dominant urban consumer culture prevalent at the end of the 19th and beginning of the 20th centuries. These include the assemblage's low percentages of consumer items and beverage bottles and lower economic index value of the ceramic tableware. Other aspects of the artifact assemblage's unique pattern reveal the adoption of idiosyncratic behavior in diet and health practices reflected in the high percentage of homeopathic vials and dominance of meat products in the culinary products assemblage and low quantities of faunal material.

As discussed above, these dietary and health practices were derived from the philosophy of the group, but they probably also served as boundary markers, setting the members apart from the larger society at the time and reinforcing group cohesiveness. Cults often impose dietary restrictions on their members, so it would appear that dietary anomalies may be important archaeological indicators of the existence of cults. Cults often include special beliefs about healing and medicine so that deviations in medical practice may also be archaeological clues to cults. The low percentage of consumer items and the low value of the economic index for ceramic tableware is consistent with the eschewing of material wealth professed by the tenets of Theosophy and is a common element of cults in general (Galanter 1989). Having observed these patterns in the Theosophical Society dump assemblage, it would be worthwhile to explore the refuse of other communes to see if similar patterns are found. Ethnoarchaeological studies of existing cults would also help to test the applicability of these patterns to cults in general.

Acknowledgments

The authors would like to thank Rebecca Allen, Judy Tordoff, Lynn Christensen, and Susan Hector for reviewing the original manuscript; Susan Walter for additional editing; and Mary Robbins-Wade for overseeing the original project.

References

ARYAN THEOSOPHICAL PRESS
1922 *Katherine Tingley's Raja-Yoga System of Education: Its Aims and Achievements*. The Aryan Theosophical Press, Point Loma, CA.

ATHERTON, MAY DAVIDSON
1982 Oral interview with Sylvia Arden, 11 September. Transcript on file, San Diego County Historical Society Research Archives, San Diego, CA.

BENTÉ, VANCE G.
1975 Trash Pits, Privies, and Promises. In 3,500 Years on One City Block, Roberta S. Greenwood, editor, pp. 209–294. Report to Redevelopment Agency, San Buenaventura, CA, from Greenwood and Associates, Pacific Palisades, CA.
1976 Well, a Borrow Pit, and Six Privies. In The Changing Faces of Main Street, Roberta S. Greenwood, editor, pp. 299–350. Report to Redevelopment Agency, San Buenaventura, CA, from Greenwood and Associates, Pacific Palisades, CA.

BLANFORD, JOHN
1987 Overseas Chinese Ethnicity and Euroamerican Glass Bottles at the Wong Ho Leun Site. In *Wong Ho Leun: An American Chinatown*, Vol. 2, Clark W. Brott, ed., 189–232. Great Basin Foundation, San Diego, CA.

BROCK, JAMES
1985 Excavations in Early Santa Ana: The OCTD Terminal Site [CA–ORA–103H]. Report to Orange County Transit District, Garden Grove, CA, from ECOS Management Criteria, Cypress, CA.

BROWNLEE, W. ELLIOTT
1979 Household Values, Women's Work, and Economic Growth, 1800–1930. *The Journal of Economic History* 39(1):199–209.

CHRISTENSON, LYNNE E.
1991 Ethnobiology of the Theosophist Society San Diego, California (SDI–10,531H). In The Sludge Management Facility Twelve Inch Force Main Accelerated Phase, San Diego Water Utilities, San Diego, California, Part II, Non Navy Property, Sunset Cliffs Shoreline Park to the San Diego River, by Timothy Gross, Stephen R. Van Wormer, and Mary Robbins-Wade, Attachment 2, pp. 1–11. Report to the City of San Diego Clean Water Program, San Diego, CA, from Affinis, El Cajon, CA.

ELLIOTT, JOHN F.
1985 History. In Excavations in Early Santa Ana: The OCTD Terminal Site [CA–ORA–103H], James Brock, editor, pp. 12–65. Report to Orange County Transit District, Garden Grove, CA, from ECOS Management Criteria, Cypress, CA.

FELTON, DAVID L., AND PETER D. SCHULZ
1983 The Diaz Collection: Material Culture and Social Change in Mid-Nineteenth-Century Monterey. *California Archaeological Reports*, No. 23. Department of Parks and Recreation, Sacramento, CA.

FINK, GARY R.
1980 *Rancho Guajome: Window on the Past, a Test of the Historic Resources at the Casa de Rancho Guajome*. San Diego County Department of Parks and Recreation, San Diego, CA.

FOOTE, EDWARD B.
1892 *Plain Home Talk Embracing Medical Common Sense*. Murray Hill Publishing Company, New York, NY.

GALANTER, MARC
1989 Cults and New Religious Movements. In *Cults and New Religious Movements: A Report of the American Psychiatric Association*, Marc Galanter, editor, pp. 25–40. American Psychiatric Association, Washington, DC.

GORDON, JEAN, AND JAN MCARTHUR
1985 American Women and Domestic Consumption, 1800–1920: Four Interpretive Themes. *Journal of American Culture* 8(3):35–46.

GROSS, TIMOTHY, STEPHEN R. VAN WORMER, AND MARY ROBBINS-WADE
1991 The Sludge Management Facility Twelve Inch Force Main Accelerated Phase, San Diego Water Utilities, San Diego, California, Part II, Non Navy Property, Sunset Cliffs Shoreline Park to the San Diego River. Report to the City of San Diego Clean Water Program, San Diego, CA, from Affinis, El Cajon, CA.

HENRETTA, JAMES A.
　1978　Families and Farms in Pre-Industrial America. *William and Mary Quarterly* 35(1):3–32.

HENRY, SUSAN L.
　1982　Economic Scaling of Ceramics. In City of Phoenix, Archaeology of the Original Town Site, Blocks 1 and 2, pp. 322–335. Report to Central Phoenix Redevelopment Agency, Phoenix, AZ, from Soil Systems, Phoenix, AZ.
　1987a　A Chicken in Every Pot: The Urban Subsistence Pattern in Turn-of-the-Century Phoenix, Arizona. In Living in Cities: Current Research in Urban Archaeology, Edward Staski, editor, pp. 19–28. The Society for Historical Archaeology, *Special Publication Series*, No. 5, California, PA.
　1987b　Factors Influencing Consumer Behavior in Turn of the Century Phoenix, Arizona. In *Consumer Choice in Historical Archaeology*, Suzanne M. Spencer-Wood, editor, pp. 359–379. Plenum Press, New York, NY.
　1991　Consumers, Commodities, and Choices: A General Model of Consumer Behavior. *Historical Archaeology* 25(2):3–14.

HENRY, SUSAN L., AND PATRICK GARROW
　1982　City of Phoenix Archaeology of the Original Town Site, Blocks 1 and 2: Part II—The Historic Component. Report to Central Phoenix Redevelopment Agency, Phoenix, AZ, from Soil Systems, Phoenix, AZ.

HILL, THOMAS
　1880　*Hill's Manual of Social and Business Forms*. Moses Warren and Co., Chicago, IL.

HOWE, DANIEL WALKER
　1975　American Victorians as a Culture. *American Quarterly* 27(4):507–532.

JONES, BILLY M.
　1967　*Health-Seekers in the Southwest, 1817–1900*. University of Oklahoma Press, Norman.

JUDGE, WILLIAM AVAN
　1892　The Cure of Diseases. *The Path*. 8 September:187–190. Reprinted 1975 in *Echoes of the Orient: The Writings of William Avan Judge* by Point Loma Publications, San Diego, CA.

KAMERLING, BRUCE
　1980　Theosophy and Symbolist Art: The Point Loma Art School. *Journal of San Diego History* 36(4):231–255.

KELLOGG, J. H.
　1885　*Man, the Masterpiece: Or Plain Truths Plainly Told*. Health Publishing Company, Battle Creek, MI.

KOCH, FELIX J.
　1913　With the Theosophists at Point Loma. *Overland Monthly* 62(4):340–344.

KUEPPER, WILHELMINE
　1905　*Nature Cure (Formerly Called Water Cure) or Home Treatment Without Medicine*. John C. Wirsten Company, Philadelphia, PA.

KUPEL, DOUGLAS
　1986　Part Two—Historical Analysis. In Bonita-Miguel Substation: Archaeological Investigations into the History and Prehistory of the Substation Area, pp. 128–196. Report to San Diego Gas and Electric Company, San Diego, CA, from Wirth Environmental Services, Division of Dames and Moore, San Diego, CA.

LEVENSTEIN, HARVY A.
　1988　*Revelation at the Table*. Oxford University Press, New York, NY.

MILLER, GEORGE L.
　1980　Classification and Economic Scaling of Nineteenth-Century Ceramics. *Historical Archaeology* 14:1–40.

PIERCE, R. V.
　1895　*The Peoples Common Sense Medical Adviser*. World's Dispensary Medical Association, Buffalo, NY.

SCHLERETH, THOMAS J.
　1991　*Victorian America: Transformations in Everyday Life, 1876–1915*. Harper Collins, New York, NY.

SHEPHERD, DON F.
　1995　Education, Culture, and the Performing Arts in the Point Loma Theosophical Society: From Helena Blavatsky to Katherine Tingley. Master's Thesis, Department of History, California State University, Fullerton.

SOUTH, STANLEY
　1977　*Method and Theory in Historical Archaeology*. Academic Press, New York, NY.

SPENCER-WOOD, SUZANNE M. (EDITOR)
　1987　*Consumer Choice in Historical Archaeology*. Plenum Press, New York, NY.

TANNAHILL, RAY
　1973　*Food in History*. Stein and Day, New York, NY.

THOMAS, SAMUEL J.
　1982　Nostrum Advertising and the Image of Women as Invalid in Late Victorian America. *Journal of American Culture* 5(3):104–112.

TINGLEY, KATHERINE (EDITOR)
　1903　Temperance Reform. *The New Century* 6(14):2. San Diego (San Diego Historical Society Research Archives), CA.
　1904a　English and American Stimulants. *The New Century* 7(39):4. San Diego (San Diego Historical Society Research Archives), CA.
　1904b　Ice, Alcohol, Health, and Longevity. *The New Century* 7(44):4. San Diego (San Diego Historical Society Research Archives), CA.

1904c A Prescription for Long Life. *The New Century* 7(10): 3. San Diego (San Diego Historical Society Research Archives), CA.

1904d The Secret of Patent Medicine Testimonials. *The New Century* 7(51):3. San Diego (San Diego Historical Society Research Archives), CA.

1904e Substitutes for Alcoholic Beverages. *The New Century* 7(44):4. San Diego (San Diego Historical Society Research Archives), CA.

VAN WORMER, STEPHEN R.

1983a Beer, Wine, and Sardines with a Dash of Pepper Sauce: An Analysis of the Glass and Tin Cans of the Encino Roadhouse. *Pacific Coast Archaeological Society Quarterly* 19(1):47–66.

1983b Pio Pico Bottles, Tableware, and Domestic Glass. In Archaeological Report, Volume II, Data Report, Pio Pico Research Project, by Michael A. Hood, pp. 68–76. Report to State of California Department of Parks and Recreation Resource Protection Division, Sacramento, from Scientific Resource Surveys, Huntington Beach, CA.

1984 Analysis of Refuse Recovered from Two Privies at the Hubert Ranch, Oceanside, California. Manuscript, Ogden Environmental (formerly WESTEC Services), San Diego, CA.

1985 An Analysis of a Historic Trash Deposit at W–1696. *Pacific Coast Archaeological Society Quarterly* 21(4): 39–50.

1986 Historic Cultural Remains. In Archaeological Excavations at Los Peñasquitos Ranch House Resource Area, San Diego, Vol. 1, by Susan Hector and Stephen R. Van Wormer, pp. 90–136. Report to County of San Diego Department of Parks and Recreation, San Diego, CA, from RECON, San Diego, CA.

1991a Even the Kitchen Sink: Archaeological Investigations of SDI–10258: The 1908 to 1913 San Diego City Dump. Report to the City of San Diego Development and Environmental Planning Division, San Diego, CA, from RECON, San Diego, CA.

1991b The Theosophical Society Dump. In The Sludge Management Facility Twelve Inch Force Main Accelerated Phase, San Diego Water Utilities, San Diego, California, Part II, Non Navy Property, Sunset Cliffs Shoreline Park to the San Diego River, by Timothy Gross, Stephen R. Van Wormer and Mary Robbins-Wade, pp. 51–104. Report to the City of San Diego Clean Water Program, San Diego, CA, from Affinis, El Cajon, CA.

1996a Cultural Resource Mitigation for the Home Avenue Trunk Sewer: Archaeological Data Recovery of a Portion of SDI–10,528H the 1908 to 1913 City of San Diego Dump. Report to the City of San Diego Water Utilities/Engineering Departments, San Diego, CA, from RECON, San Diego, CA.

1996b Revealing Cultural, Status, and Ethnic Differences through Historic Artifact Analysis. *Proceedings of the Society for California Archaeology* 9:310–323.

WHORTON, JAMES C.

1982 *Crusaders for Fitness: The History of American Health Reformers.* Princeton University Press, Princeton, NJ.

WRIGHT, ROBERT

1974 Reminiscences of Lomaland by Iverson L. Harris, in an interview with Robert Wright. *Journal of San Diego History* 20(3):1–32.

STEPHEN R. VAN WORMER
238 SECOND AVENUE
CHULA VISTA, CA 91910

G. TIMOTHY GROSS
AFFINIS
847 JAMACHA ROAD
EL CAJON, CA 92019

LAURIE A. WILKIE

Secret and Sacred: Contextualizing the Artifacts of African-American Magic and Religion

ABSTRACT

Although historical archaeologists have accumulated a large amount of data regarding African-American magical and religious systems, researchers still underestimate the importance of magical and religious systems within African-American communities. In addition, archaeologists seem reluctant to interpret these data in a diachronic manner. Spiritual beliefs affected all arenas of the African-American experience including medicine, childcare, gender, family, and community relations. To properly understand African-American daily life, attention must be paid to spiritual traditions. This paper addresses the role of magical practices within African-American society and the importance of recognizing the role of gender ideologies within magical and religious practice, and proposes a diachronic model for understanding the changing relationship between magic and religion. The model, consisting of three stages of cultural change, Formative, Persisting, and Transformative, provides a means of linking the archaeological and documentary databases. Application of the model to three archaeologically well-studied regions demonstrates that, despite growing interest in the archaeological study of African-American spiritual traditions, archaeological evidence for these traditions is sparse when analyzed diachronically.

Introduction

In the last 10 years, archaeologists have made important strides in recognizing material culture associated with African-American magical and religious practices from the earliest time of enslavement through the early 20th century (e.g., Adams 1987; Klingelhofer 1987; Ferguson 1992; Patten 1992; Orser 1994; Santorio 1994; Wilkie 1994, 1995; Yakubik and Mendéz [1995]; Yakubik et al. 1994; Leone 1995; Handler 1996; Stine et al. 1996). The abundance and breadth of material leaves no doubt that enslaved African, then African-American, families and communities created secret and sacred landscapes, separated and internally constructed, but still sometimes influenced by the spiritual lives of European and Native Americans.

Archaeologists continue to accumulate a broad array of material evidence associated with this spiritual and magical realm of African-American life, drawing upon oral histories, ethnographies, and documentary evidence to shed light on the meanings of specific types of artifacts (e.g., Patten 1992; Pearce 1993; Santorio 1994; Wilkie 1994a, 1994b, 1995; Samford 1996; Stine et al. 1996; Young 1996, 1997). While we may successfully identify uses and meanings of individual artifacts, we have been hesitant to understand the broader cultural tapestry in which these artifacts derived meaning. Unless archaeologists begin to study magical-religious artifacts in their broader cultural, geographic, and temporal context, we will not contribute any greater knowledge about African-American spiritual life to the social sciences.

In this article, a summary of the ways that magical and religious practice shaped and influenced African-American life, and how we as archaeologists can strive to more fully recognize and interpret material cultural reflections of this facet of the African-American experience, both during and after enslavement, will be provided. The discussion will focus on the following issues:

1) the role of magical practice within African-American society, magical practitioners, and the uses of magic; 2) the importance of recognizing the role of gender ideologies within magical and religious practice; 3) the changing relationship between magic and religion through time, and how we might employ a diachronic approach in our interpretations which recognizes the cultural processes of syncretism and creolization.

While archaeologists have begun to discuss African-American religious practices, we have not attempted, in any clear way, to understand the changing relationship between the broad range of magical and religious practice in any diachronic way. To this end, I propose the adoption of a three-stage model of religious change employed by George Brandon (1993) in his study of

Santeria. Brandon's model recognizes three stages of religious transformation: Formative, Persisting, and Transformative. The Formative period represents the initial changes that take place in a religion or belief system as a result of contact or internal culture change, and is represented by the development of numerous religious alternatives. As one alternative becomes the norm, the religion has entered a stage of religious Persistence. The Transformative stage represents a new series of innovation that affects a religion, as seen in the Formative period. I will be discussing this model and its potential applications in the diaspora, below.

While always linked, magic and religion represent and fulfill different needs within African and African-American society through time. Religion is a set of rituals, symbols, and sacred histories that explain a culture's origin and regulate the interaction between humans and culturally postulated extra-humans. Magical practices represent a means of manipulating supernatural forces, be they deities, ancestral spirits, witches, or ghosts. Magical practices can be a means of manipulating or interacting with deities, and therefore are inherently entwined in religious practice (Marwick 1970; Mbiti 1970).

In this article, a summary of the ways that magical and religious practice shaped and influenced African-American everyday life will be provided. Further, the potential for recognizing artifacts that represent African continuities in organized religious practice versus syncretised magical-medical practices, the range of magical practice recorded historically and ethnographically, the gender constructs that shape African-American magical practice, and the importance of archaeological provenience in the recognition of magical and religious artifacts will be discussed.

The Societal Role of African-American Magic and Religion

Magical practices within the African-American community do not represent merely a single facet of the African-American experience. Magic, ideas about divinity, spirituality, the nature of life and death, and control of natural and supernatural elements are all intertwined to create an African-American worldview that is distinct and unique from that of Chinese Americans, Hispanic Americans, Euroamericans, and Native Americans. Just as archaeologists studying overseas Chinese populations have come to recognize that Chinese Taoist, Confuscionist, and Buddhist philosophies shape every facet of overseas Chinese culture (e.g., Langenwalter 1987; Mueller 1987; Wegars 1993), so African Americanists must recognize that African-American philosophies shaped gender relations, family life, food preparation, medicinal practice, religion, and work.

Scholars have been tempted to dismiss magic as an important element of African-American life. In ex-slave narratives, many African Americans deny knowledge of hoodoo or magic. Likewise, anthropologists working in the American South during the 1920s and 1930s also portray magical beliefs as declining (e.g., Puckett 1968[1926]; Powdermaker 1993[1937]). Before dismissing the importance of magic within African-American communities, it is important to consider the following experience of Zora Neale Hurston:

> I was once talking to Mrs. Rachel Silas of Sanford, Florida, so I asked her where I could find a good hoodoo doctor. "Do you believe in dat ole fogeyism, chile? Ah don't see how nobody could do none of dat work, do you?" She laughed unnecessarily. "Ah been hearin' about dat mess ever since Ah been big enough tuh know mahself, but shucks! Ah don't believe nobody kin do me harm lessen they git somethin' in mah mouth."
>
> "Don't fool yourself," I answered with assurance. "People can do things to you. I done seen things happen."
>
> "Sho nuff? Well, well, well! Maybe thing *kin* be done tuh harm yuh, cause Ah done heard *good* folks—folks dat ought to know—say dat it sho is a fact. Anyhow, Ah figger it pays tuh be keerful" (Hurston 1990b[1935]:185–186).

By the end of her conversation with Mrs. Silas and another neighbor, Hurston established not only that both women believed in hoodoo, but actively sought magical protection from specialists, and were able to direct Hurston where to find a "two-headed doctor." Hurston's experience illustrates not only the prevalence of magical practice but the secret nature of these beliefs.

That African-influenced magical religious traditions exist in the New World is now clear from archaeological, ethnographic, and documentary evidence (e.g., Ferguson 1992; Wilkie 1995; Stine et al. 1996). The question that must be more clearly addressed is why these continuities persist and how their meanings may change through time. Dollard, writing in 1937, had the following observations to make about the role of African-American supernatural beliefs:

> There is another means of accommodating to life when it is not arranged according to one's wishes. This is the use of magic. Of course, one can think of magical practices among the Negroes as lagging culture patterns, which they are, but one can also think of them as forms of action in reference to current social life. Magic accepts the *status quo* [original emphasis]; it takes the place of political activity, agitation, organization, solidarity, or any real moves to change status. It is interesting and harmless from the standpoint of the caste system and it probably has great private value for those who practice it. These psychological satisfactions are important, even if they do not alter the social structure and are mere substitutes for more effective efforts to alter it (Dollard 1957[1937]:263).

Although written over 60 years ago, Dollard's argument that the use of magic had psychological merits for the African-American community is relevant for contemporary consideration. Although rarely discussed in a forthright manner by historical archaeologists, violence and the threat of violence, in both physical and psychological forms, were an ongoing aspect of the African-American experience during the period of enslavement and beyond (Farnsworth 1996).

Magic, particularly magic to harm, provided African Americans with a means of retaliating against Euroamerican violence with a supernatural violence of their own. In the 19th century, African Cubans were reported to have used magic to attack slaveholders (Thompson 1983:125). Likewise, Young (1997) has explored the role of magic as a means of combatting planter violence. Just as planters threatened and used violence to attempt to control enslaved, and

later freed, African Americans, magic provided a potential threat wielded by African Americans.

While early historians and anthropologists of the American South often portray European culture as "advanced" or based in "reason," whereas the African-American population was "primitive," "superstitious," or "heathen" (e.g., Dollard 1957[1937]; Puckett 1968[1926]; Saxon et al. 1989[1945]; Powdermaker 1993[1937]), such descriptions are not only racist but also misrepresentative of both groups' cultural beliefs. The European-descended population of the American South had its own complex cosmology regarding the use of magic and the existence of supernatural beings (e.g., Hand 1980). The magical/supernatural beliefs of Europeans and Africans were complementary, and undoubtedly influenced one another. The use of fetishes, for instance, was common to each group, as were beliefs in witches and ghosts. Ethnohistorical data clearly demonstrate that many Euroamericans consulted African-American conjurers for magical assistance (e.g., Hurston 1990a[1938], 1990b[1935]; Powdermaker 1993[1937]).

Likewise, Euroamericans were known to have peddled magical charms. One African American interviewed by the North Carolina Federal Writer's Project in the 1930s stated:

> White folks comes round sometimes, not much now as dey use to, tryin' to sell stones and roots and one thing after another, to keep off bad luck, dey claims. I always told 'em I didn't mind buyin' nothin' dat would bring me good luck, but wa'nt (worth) while to talk to me' dey wa'n't no money for good luck at our place. I don't worry much about dey bad lucks (Terrill and Hirsch 1978:93).

Puckett (1968[1926]) demonstrated that many magical practices among the African-American populations he studied in Mississippi were similar to magical beliefs he found in Europe. While Puckett interpreted these similarities as evidence that black folk traditions only represented holdovers of extinct European beliefs, it seems more likely that the similarities represent a form of syncretism or creolization on both ethnic groups' part. As new magical tools were encountered, they were added to the magical tool kit. Just as people of European descent came to consult African and African-American magical practitioners, European magic was incorporated into the African-based magical and religious arsenal. That there are similarities between the coexisting magical systems is potentially significant and meaningful when considering race relations. If a common magical language was shared between the black and white populations of the diaspora, then the implied threat of magical use would be understood as such by both parties.

The idea that continuities of African-based belief systems served as a means of resistance is often advanced in historical archaeological arguments attempt to explain its existence (e.g., Orser 1994; Leone 1995; Wilkie 1995). As yet, however, archaeologists have been slow to recognize magical systems as more elemental expressions of an African-American cultural reality. The secret maintenance of magical practices was not merely a means of exerting control over circumstances of life or of resisting planter authority, beliefs in magic and magical practices also persisted because they were intrinsic to the ways in which enslaved Africans defined themselves, their families, and their relationship to life, death, and the world around them (Herskovits 1962[1941]; Thompson 1981, 1983). Magical and religious beliefs within enslaved African and, then, African-American cultures served as an explanatory system for the workings of the world. Magic and religion provided not only information regarding the inhabitants of the natural and supernatural worlds, but also how these players related to and impacted one another. To completely abandon one's cosmology would be to completely abandon one's original image of oneself.

Magical and Medical Practitioners of the African-American Community

Three predominant types of professional practitioners offered magical and magico-medical services to the African-American community: midwives, root doctors, and conjurers. While these types of practitioners will be discussed as independent and distinct from one another, it is important to note that in some communities, a midwife may act as a root doctor, or a root doctor may also serve as a conjurer. Root doctors and midwives used a combination of spiritual and physical techniques to treat illness or attend a delivery (Campbell 1946; Laguerre 1978), while conjurers (often referred to as Hoodoos or Hoodoo Doctors in the American South or Obeahs in the Caribbean) provided a range of magical services that typically were related to social control of some kind, be it a love charm or a spell to kill or sicken. Each of these practitioners came to their trade as a result of a vocation. While the infamous Marie Laveau received her vocation to conjuring from a rattlesnake (Hurston 1990b[1935]:193), many later conjurers attributed their vocation to God. Powdermaker described one conjurer who gave the following account of his calling:

> His first experience came to him when he was a young man, walking along a country road after church. The moon was full, and looking up he saw in it a face he had never seen before. Then he heard a voice telling him how to cure his ailing wife. He followed instructions, and his wife became better. Ever since then he sees spirits and hears voices. He knows the past and can foretell the future (Powdermaker 1993[1937]:293).

Another conjurer gave an account of his calling:

> Chile, I could always see things. God Almighty fixed me so I could. No, chile, I didn't study no books to learn, that is a gift just handed down from my forefathers. You know even before we was brought here from Africa by the white folks, and heathens as they say we was, there was that gift shown in many ways. I'se still traveling 'cause I got faith in God (Terrill and Hirsch 1978:23).

African-American healers often attributed their strength and skill not only to God and the training they received, but often credited their forebears in a spiritual way. For instance, a midwife recounts her experiences while attending a difficult birth:

My feelings were all mixed up with praying and wishing Aunt Jeanie [the woman who trained her to be a midwife] was there to help. Then, like a sudden swift witness, a new strength and wisdom came into me and steadied my heart and mind and holded my hands to do the right thing. And after that Ludy birthed her baby . . . .Then I knew what had happened to me. Aunt Jeanie had been there in the spirit to lend me her help and strength. Not no ghost nor no vision from heaven . . . . And knowing that, my mind picked up the last words Aunt Jeanie said to me, 'After a little rest, I'll be right back there to take hold and help out with sick folks and babies' (Campbell 1946:244–245).

After receiving their vocation, a person would become an apprentice to an expert in the field of their calling. Often, the person training them would be a close relative or friend, who would pass along their practice to the younger person once the training was complete.

Magical specialists did not seem to be gender-exclusive roles, although midwives were likely to be women who had already raised their own children, and were beyond their childbearing years. I have found one instance of a male African-American midwife (Logan as told to Clark 1989). There is some debate concerning whether or not conjurers are more likely to be men than women, and whether women are more likely than men to be root doctors. While claims have been made on both accounts (e.g., Herskovits 1962[1941]; Puckett 1968[1926]; Powdermaker 1993[1937]), my survey has found no clear correlation between gender and the form of magical practice.

Root doctors, while also employing a range of magical techniques, mainly specialized in the production and use of herbal and animal product pharmaceuticals to combat diseases that were perceived as being caused by natural agents of illness (Wilkie 1996a, 1996b). Teas, brewed from medicinal herbs or substances, salves, or whiskey-based "home-made bitters" were made and found in the medical kits of midwives, root doctors, and sometimes, conjurers (Campbell 1946; Logan as told to Clark 1989; Clayton 1990; Mathews 1992). Conjurers were more likely to use magical means to treat diseases that were perceived as being caused by supernatural

agents or to create magical means of control—be it in matters of love, hate, or luck—and used a combination of charms and spells to exert magical influence. As Powdermaker (1993[1937]) observed, conjurers were varied in their chosen magical styles. Four conjurers provided magical services to the community studied by Powdermaker. "Reverend" D. used the state pharmaceutical regulation to write legal prescriptions. He also created medicines after going into a trance and wrote charms on pieces of paper. "Reverend" R., another conjurer, used a steel rod he called an "electreat" on his patients and consulted with spirits. He did not use charms. Mr. T., of mixed Cherokee and African descent, used herbal potions that can attract luck and repel danger. Finally, Dr. A. wrote charms on papers, but relied upon published magical volumes for his inspirations (Powdermaker 1993[1937]:292–294).

Archaeologically, the distinctive magical specialists of the African diaspora should be identifiable to some degree. I have analyzed artifacts associated with an African-American midwife's housesite in Mobile, Alabama (Wilkie and Shorter [1997]) and found a range of artifacts that seem to be associated with midwifery, including large numbers of medicine bottles once containing patent medicines sold broadly throughout the United States to treat illnesses related to children and infants; large numbers of whiskey containers, likely to be related to the preparation of home-made bitters; zooarchaeological remains related to the preparation of calf's foot jelly (a medicine-food for invalids, children, and mothers recovering from childbirth); and objects of potential magical significance, including yellow sulfur, a glass crystal, and flaked stones.

Kenneth Brown (Brown and Cooper 1990), in his excavations at Levi-Jordan plantation, discovered an assemblage of artifacts that he has interpreted as representing a "traditional healer/magician." This assemblage included "five cast iron kettle bases, pieces of utilized chalk, fragments of a small scale, bird skulls, and animal's paw, medicine bottles, bullet casings put together to form a sealed tube, ocean shells, small doll parts, a high frequency of nails and spikes, several tablespoons, metal knives—both real and 'fake,' a chert projectile point, and two chert scrapers" (Brown and Cooper 1990:16–17). This assemblage dates between 1848, when the plantation was founded, and 1891, when the plantation was abandoned, probably favoring the later date range (Brown and Cooper 1990). As will be discussed later, the assemblage is intriguing because it contains artifact materials that could be related to the creation of Kongo-influenced *mniski* charms, or magical medicine.

Handler and Lange (1978) identified a possible Obeah man in the burials of Newton plantation, Barbados. Burial 72 contained an old male, who was buried with his head facing the east. This individual wore two copper bracelets on his left arm, and was buried wearing two white metal rings, a copper ring, and a necklace of seven cowrie shells, 21 drilled dog canines, 14 glass beads, five drilled vertebrae from a bony fish, and one large agate bead. Accompanying the burial were a pipe, possibly of African origin, and an iron knife blade (Handler and Lange 1978:125–132). The wealth of the burial goods associated with this individual led to the interpretation that he had been an Obeah man (conjurer). The prone position of another burial, and its isolation from other burial features, has more recently led Handler (1996) to argue that an "African-witch or other negatively viewed person" may be present in the cemetery. It is important to recognize, however, that witches were commonly seen in African society as individuals who, by their own nature rather than spells, could cause harm to others, and is not necessarily an example of a magical practitioner.

Magical Uses in African-American Society

Ethnographic, documentary, and oral historical sources suggest that African Americans exercised magical control over many aspects of their lives, including healthcare, protection from spirits, to maintain family relationships, to attract or dispel love, to gain a job, to attract money, or even harm one's enemies or rivals (Puckett 1968[1926]; Tallant 1983[1946]; Saxon et al. 1989[1945]; Botkin 1989[1945]; Clayton 1990; Hurston 1990a[1938], 1990b[1935]; Powdermaker 1993[1937]). Magic could be performed through ritual action or through the use of potions or charms. While some charms, potions, and magical ritual could be performed within the home, for many magical tasks and needs, a magical specialist had to be employed.

Medicinal Magic

Magical as well as pharmaceutical means were used to treat diseases that were perceived to be of either natural or unnatural agents. Illnesses in many African-American communities were, and often still are, perceived to be caused by human interference (witchcraft), natural illnesses, or through the interference of spirits or ghosts (Wilkie 1995, 1996a). Magical cures could be used individually, or in conjunction with herbal pharmaceutical remedies. Both sympathetic (i.e., the idea that an object can influence others that have an identity with it) and contagious magic (i.e., the belief that associated objects can have influence on each other) could be found within medicinal magic (Lehmann and Myers 1985). Many magical cures for naturally-caused illnesses or conditions did not require a professional practitioner to be implemented but rather were part of a family's own magico-medical repertoire.

Naturally-occurring medical conditions of a serious nature such as childbirth and changes in child development often received magical aid. For instance, during childbirth, a knife would be placed under the expectant mother's bed in hopes that it would "cut" the pain (Logan as told to Clark 1989:54). Likewise, burning chicken feathers under the mother's bed or having her wear a hat belonging to the father during birth were also believed to ease the pain of contractions (Campbell 1946:114). Once born, a child was not to have its umbilical cord removed until the seventh day (Campbell 1946:35). A pierced penny worn around the neck of an infant was believed to ease the difficulty, pain, and potential danger of teething; a necklace of six plain buttons, or a necklace of rattlesnake rattles, hog teeth, or alligator teeth, would serve the same purpose (Puckett 1968[1926]:346). Each of these magico-medical charms would leave an archaeological trace, although in the context of a midden assemblage, their exact use may not be readily apparent. For instance, researchers (e.g., Wilkie 1994b; Yakubik and Méndez [1995]) have noticed the relatively high proportion of buttons recovered from African-American archaeological sites. In addition to their importance as pieces of adornment, buttons have many recorded magical uses.

The ethnohistorical literature contains numerous examples of charms relating to easing the pain and danger of teething. The fear of an infant's teething period should not be underestimated for throughout the American South both African and Euroamerican populations believed that the condition of teething and the process of weaning made a child more prone to life-threatening diseases (McMillen 1990:151). Physical anthropological investigations of enslaved African-American cemeteries in the American South and Caribbean (e.g., Corruccini et al. 1985; Kelley and Angel 1987; Harris and Rathbun 1989) have demonstrated that African-American skeletal materials exhibit evidence of nutritional stress during childhood. Corruccini et al. (1985:701–702) were able to link the development of hypoplastic conditions in Afro-Barbadian teeth to the period of weaning (approxiately three years of age) in a 1660–1820 skeletal population. Excavations of African-American skeletal material from the Cedar Grove Baptist Church, in Lincoln County, Arkansas, included the remains of 32 children (total excavated skeletal population numbered 79), aged between zero to two years. Of this number, 16 of the children were believed to be newborns (Rose and Santeford 1985). This high incidence of mortality for infants (40.5% of the Cedar Grove skeletal population) during the late 19th and early 20th centuries clearly illustrates

why magical means of ensuring children's health were so important.

The loss of teeth also had magical significance. Human teeth are commonly recovered archaeologically, often representing deciduous teeth, teeth pulled or dropped due to decay, or pulled for aesthetic or cultural reasons (Handler and Lange 1978). Recovered near a house roofline, however, human teeth can have magical meanings. Herskovits described the following ritual:

> In Trinidad, Haiti, and Dahomey appropriate rituals mark the appearance of the permanent teeth; the essence of one such rite is to throw the first deciduous tooth to fall out on the roof of the mother's house or into some near-by place, asking that the new teeth be strong and beautiful. Parsons reports from the Seas Islands that: "When a chil sheddin teet', take an' put 'em in a corncob, an' fling it right over de house." This practice was referred to as "callin' de new teeth back" (Herskovits 1962[1941]:195).

In my research in Louisiana and the Bahamas, I have twice encountered teeth that were recovered just along the roof-drip line, and may represent evidence of magical practice. Turner (1993:116) reports that "in Bahamian folk tradition teeth are not merely discarded but are thrown onto the rooftop, over the shoulder, to bring good luck." The loss of teeth was not an unusual event. Harris and Rathbun (1989:411–412), in their analysis of 36 skeletal individuals from a 19th-century slave cemetery from a South Carolina plantation, found that women in the population lost a mean of 11.6 teeth prior to death, whereas men, who lived a shorter time, lost a mean of 6.5 teeth.

While this discussion has focused upon childbirth and child development, many magical cures are associated with commonly occurring natural illnesses. For instance, in Louisiana, swallowing a gold bead was believed to relieve a sore throat (Saxon et al. 1989[1945]:534). More commonly, however, a wide range of magical treatments is used to cure magically caused illnesses. The treatment of illness in the African diaspora needed to consider not only natural agents of disease but magical causes of disease. Magical cures were often employed, sometimes in conjunction with pharmaceutical cures. Magic intended to harm, which caused illnesses, possession, bodily infestation by reptiles or small animals, and even death, required magical treatments and will be discussed below.

Magic to Harm

Magic to harm, if oral histories and ethnographies are a fair basis for evaluation, is by far the form of magic most feared, although probably the least employed as well. Although archaeologists have recovered little evidence of artifacts intended to cause harm, abundant evidence exists of artifacts apparently used as apotropaics, or devices to turn away evil.

Magic to harm can be performed through the creation of charms—also known as goofers, tobis, hands, gris-gris—or through the performance of elaborate ritual. Hurston (1990b[1935]), once initiated into a New Orleans Voodoo sect, participated in a long and complicated death ritual. The ritual lasted 90 days and involved the sacrifice of chickens, the building and maintaining of an altar, and the burning of black candles (Hurston 1990b[1935]:210–211). Death, however, was not often the result of magic to harm. Often, a person would exhibit an illness commonly associated with magical interference, such as being infested with snakes (the snakes could be seen crawling under the skin). The physical withdrawal of the snakes by a conjurer, the breaking of the original "trick," or a counter "trick" aimed against one's enemy were common cures for magically caused illnesses.

The great majority of magic to harm involves the use of exuvia (body fluids and substances). Dirt removed from footsteps, clothing items, body fluids, skin, hair or finger/toenail clippings, are all commonly involved in magic to cause harm. Puckett (1968[1926]) describes "conjure balls, bottles and bags" in his ethnographic research.

Bottles, used in a variety of ways to conjure or to protect from conjure, are often mentioned in the literature of magic to harm. Bottles or preserve jars are filled with magically meaningful ingredients and buried near doorsteps or houses, or in paths and crossroads. The intended victim, upon passing over the conjure bottle, will be tricked. Puckett (1968[1926]:231) describes "in one case where there was reason to suspect conjuring, a bottle filled with roots, stones, and reddish powder was found under the doorstop, and in the yard more bottles with beans, iron nails and the same powder. The man burned them up and got well again."

Iron nails, needles, bags of red flannel, roots, snakes, snakeskins, insects, keys, and hairballs are just a few of the ingredients described as components of conjure bottles (Puckett 1968[1926]; Hyatt 1978). Preserve jars containing a snake and several insects in addition to something else wrapped up in cloth; vials containing nails, red flannel, and whiskey; and snuff bottles containing vinegar and other liquid ingredients are all discussed as conjure bottles that were employed in the 1920s (Puckett 1968[1926]:231). In addition to bottles and jars, teacups and tin cups were also described as vessels containing conjures (Puckett 1968[1926]; Hyatt 1978).

Conjure bottles, due to their location and contents, should be recognizable archaeologically. Whole bottles, jars, teacups, or tin cups buried near doorways, steps, pathways, or house walls would leave an unmistakable archaeological signature. A review of ethnographic evidence indicates that such vessels were commonly used in the American South and Caribbean. In the Bahamas, bottles containing needles, herbs, and urine would be buried near houses to cause harm (Grace Turner 1996, pers. comm.).

Conjure bottles have been recovered from at least one archaeological setting in the Caribbean, and two in the United States. Excavating at Juan de Bolas plantation in Jamaica, Reeves (1996) recovered two nearly intact bottles that were located upright and adjacent to a former slave house mound. The tops of the bottles had been sheared off during post-depositional horticultural activities, but the bottles were otherwise intact and appeared to contain charcoal and a thin white residue. Samford (1996:107–109) reported the recovery of conjure bottles from the walls of slave cabin sites in North Carolina and Virginia, and has suggested that intact bottles recovered from beneath the floors of slave cabins at the Hermitage plantation, Tennessee, may have also been *minkisi* containers. It is likely that other conjure bottles have been excavated archaeologically but not recognized.

Despite the common practice throughout the diaspora of burying conjure bottles, it is not necessarily likely that these artifacts will be abundant archaeologically. To break the "trick" (misfortune caused by the buried bottle) required that the bottle be found and broken or discarded so that the spell could be ended. Because the bottles were hidden in well-known, archetypal places, part of the intention of the conjure was surely that it be known to the victim. By casting a spell to harm another person through this means, an individual was publicly stating a grievance against another. By actively looking for and finding a conjure bottle, a potential victim was recognizing and acknowledging that they were involved in a serious dispute with another person that could jeopardize their safety. The catalyst that served to ignite the search for conjure would be a spell of bad luck or unexplained ill health, or concern that a particular individual had reason to fear becoming the object of conjure.

Charms to divert evil are commonly mentioned in the oral historical and ethnographic literature. Apotropaics are often worn on the individual. One very common charm for turning away evil is a pierced coin worn on a string around the ankle or neck:

> A silver dime worn about the ankle or neck or placed in the shoe will prevent any trick from exerting its influence against you—this being one of the common charms given by Marie Laveau. Some Negroes openly say that such a coin keeps off evil spirits . . . . Frank

Dickerson says only silver ball will do the work, while others suggest a copper coin in toe of shoe, a silver ring about the finger, or a goose quill filled with quicksilver worn below the knee (Puckett 1968[1926]:288).

Archaeologically, silver coins with holes pierced through them have been recovered from archaeological sites in Virginia, Georgia, Louisiana, and Arkansas (Rose 1985; Adams 1987; Patten 1992; Wilkie 1995; Yakubik and Méndez [1995]). A pierced silver dime and a silver half dollar were found in a late 19th- to early 20th-century African-American cemetery positioned at the necks of two burials (Rose and Santeford 1985:73–75, 115–116).

Red flannel charm bags, commonly made by Kongo peoples (Thompson 1983:129–131), are still popularly used in Louisiana (Fontenot 1994). The flannel bags can contain any number of potentially magical ingredients. The bags can be used either as "fixes" to cause harm or as apotropaics but seem to be most commonly used in the latter capacity. An African-American midwife described one such bag that she obtained to rid herself of a ghost: "After a time I went to a conjure woman to get help to drive off the friendly pirate (the ghost). She made up a strong conjure bag with hog bristles and black cats' hair and a rabbit's foot and dirt from the graves of seven murderers and seven little stones from south-running water all tied up in a red flannel rag greased with snake oil and tied with dead woman's hair" (Campbell 1946:181). It is important to remember that ghosts are not merely a frightening problem, but can be bearers of disease and death. Once in possession of the conjure bag, the midwife was rid of her ghostly visitor.

Animals could also provide magical protection: "If a frizzled hen is kept in the yard she will scratch and destroy all conjuration which will cause discomfort to the family" (Herskovits 1962[1941]:237). This belief is prevalent in West Africa, the Caribbean, and the American South. It is intriguing to wonder if the small guinea fowl charm recovered from the orangery of the Calvert family plantation in Maryland

Perspectives from *Historical Archaeology*

(Yentsch 1994:214) had any meaning to its holder as a protective device. The importance of plant and animal materials and imagery within African-American magic indicates that archaeologists need to carefully consider the religious and magical implications of floral and faunal materials from African-American sites.

Magic and the Dead

Magical practice relates as well, and not surprisingly, to the treatment and care of the dead. As previously discussed, the dead, as ghosts, have the ability to harm the living, and they must be treated properly to ensure that a loved one completes the journey to the next realm, and to ensure that no malignant spirits remain to harm the living. While it is possible to drive off ghosts with other magical means, as in the case of the midwife and the pirate, it is often easier to anticipate the problem with preventative measures.

The material culture of African-American magic for the dead is found in and above graves, as well as can be seen in the way that the living areas of the deceased are treated. A number of practices are related to the disposal of the deceased's belongings. The understanding that the improper treatment of the dead and their belongings may lead to hauntings is common throughout the American South and Caribbean. In Alabama, Puckett recorded the belief that "unless you bury a person's things with him he will come back after them"(Puckett 1968[1926]:103). In Mississippi, "to keep the deceased from coming back again, the cup and saucer used in the last illness should be placed on the grave. The medicine bottles placed there are also turned upside down with the corks loosened so that the medicine may soak into the grave" (Puckett 1968[1926]:105). Examples of the latter practice have been discovered archaeologically during the excavation of an Arkansas African-American cemetery (Rose and Santeford 1985). Personal belongings from life may decorate the grave: "In South Carolina, bleached sea-shells, broken crockery and glassware, broken pitchers, soap-dishes, lamp chimneys, tureens, coffee-cups, syrup jugs, all sorts of ornamental vases, cigar boxes, gun locks, tomato cans, teapots, flower pots, bits of stucco, plaster images, pieces of carved stonework from one of the public buildings during the war, glass lamps and tumblers in great number, and forty other kitchen articles are used. On the children's graves were dolls' heads, little china tea-bowls and pitchers, toy images of animals, china vases, pewter dishes and other things which would interest a child" (Puckett 1968[1926]:105).

In many parts of the Caribbean, disturbing a grave can provoke retaliation by *duppies* (ghosts). On Crooked Island, Bahamas, an entire village of houses stands empty, with household belongings intact. The village had been inhabited by old people whose children had moved to other islands. According to older residents of the island, as people died and were buried, the houses were left as they had been so no spirits would be disturbed (June MacMillan 1995, pers. comm.).

Magic and Gender Tensions

If archaeologists are to understand the importance and role of magical and magic-related artifacts recovered from African-American settings, we must remember to situate these artifacts in the places where they are found: households. The overwhelming majority of artifacts recovered that are related to African-American spiritual beliefs have been recovered from households. The spiritual and magical beliefs studied archaeologically are within the context of family life. Be they hidden in root cellars, stored behind hearths, dropped through floorboards, or accidentally dropped or buried in a yard, these artifacts must be understood in the context of the family.

Inherent in the magical practices of Africa and African America is a tension and duality in power between men and women. Men and women, due to their intimate access to one another and their opposing magical makeup, are potentially healing or potentially harmful to one another. As already mentioned, the hat of the father worn during childbirth can ease a woman's labor pains. Likewise, many of the magical charms and spells to harm require access to the victim's exuvia, with sperm, urine, menstrual blood, or excrement being the most powerful magical substances. These substances are protected and disposed of carefully, to avoid their falling into potentially dangerous hands. Powdermaker (1993[1937]:288–289) reported one African-American woman who kept all the hair that she lost in her comb and carefully destroyed it. However, the individuals with greatest access to these substances are other family members.

A man and woman engaged in a sexual relationship and cohabiting in a house without plumbing have a great deal of access to those bodily substances which are most potentially harmful to their mate, and are themselves vulnerable to magical attack from loved ones. Likewise, children, parents, and any extended family living within a house are potentially vulnerable to attack. This circumstance creates a tension within the family. The family must trust its members not to harm each other either directly or indirectly.

In times of marital strife, there is always the potential threat of magical attack and retaliation. Magical attacks that involve substances as strong as urine, semen, menstrual blood, or night soil, can be fatal. Philandering spouses not only endanger themselves by allowing persons outside of the family to gain access to potentially dangerous substances but also threaten the safety and coherence of the family.

Magical spells abound that are intended to destroy marriages, lead another woman's husband away, or bind a man's or woman's affections to another, and so forth (e.g., Puckett 1968[1926]; Hyatt 1978). For instance, in the Bahamas, it is a common Obeah belief that if a woman puts her urine in the bathwater of her husband or sons, they will never abandon her (Grace Turner 1996, pers. comm.). Likewise, African-American women throughout North America have believed that if they put some of their menstrual blood in a man's meal, he will be bound to them forever. Powdermaker (1993[1937]:289) reported hearing that "a woman can hold a man by putting some-

thing in his food," but had not learned what that something was. The intent of the users of love potions was not always sincere: "a young woman has been mentioned who uses love charms to hold men whom she wants only for their money, but who depends solely upon affection to keep the men she really cares for" (Powdermaker 1993[1937]:287). Men were aware of these attempts at magical control and would try to defeat them.

A Bahamian woman told me of a battle over bathwater between her brothers and mother. Her mother had long urinated in their bathwater, unbeknownst to her sons. As the sons neared adulthood, one caught her "fixing" the bathwater, and the sons began to demand that they draw their own baths. While the mother complied, she would create diversions while the baths were being drawn and continued the magical practice whenever possible. Through her actions, she tried to ensure that even when grown and with families of their own, her sons would not fully abandon her. Her sons, by attempting to avoid this binding, were not so much stating a lack of love for their mother, but a desire to become independent of her. Marriage and family life is not just a contract of love and commitment, but also a magical battleground for control.

Given this state of magical combat, and potential issues of control, the division of tasks and activities within the household by gender and age rank can be very important, depending upon the level of stress or strife within a relationship. If a woman suspects her husband of cavorting with another woman, or the husband is thinking of leaving, the act of allowing your mate to prepare a meal versus preparing the meal oneself has new meaning and implications.

Conjurers understood the importance of magic as a means of protecting and healing relationships, and were quick to dispense advice with their medicine. Puckett describes a particularly insightful charm,

A "conjure-woman" in Algiers, La., was given $5 for a bottle of medicine (lemonade) to break a husband of quarreling. Her directions were for the unhappy wife to fill her mouth with the medicine whenever her good man began to quarrel and not to swallow it until he had ceased. Then she was to swallow the medicine and kiss him. So successful was this treatment that several wives came to the doctor upon recommendation for the same prescription (Puckett 1968[1926]:209).

While it may appear that this "magical remedy" is nothing more than dressed-up advice, in the emotional heat of a marital spat, the dictates of a magical recipe are more likely to be heeded than the advice to "just keep quiet until he calms down." While this particular story is sweetly amusing, it also clearly demonstrates that magical solutions to dispute resolution were important.

Outside the realm of marriage, men and women remain potentially dangerous to one another, particularly when lovers. Hyatt (1973, 1974, 1978), when gathering his inventory of magical charms and potions, recorded a wide range of spells related to the prevention of venereal disease. For instance, a woman who rubs earwax on a man's genitals and holds a coin to the roof of her mouth during intercourse could give a man venereal disease (Hyatt 1978:2376). A man could defend himself by holding a penny in his mouth during intercourse (Hyatt 1978:2369). Likewise, a man could test a woman for venereal disease, unbeknownst to the woman, by rubbing the woman's genitals with a bit of his earwax. If the woman complained of a burning sensation, she was "positive" for the disease. In rural Louisiana, African-American men still joke about their lovers passing the "earwax test."

That oral traditions suggested that venereal disease could be acquired through the malicious action of a sexual partner illustrates not only the intrinsic danger of members of the opposite sex to one another, but also demonstrates another way in which a strong marriage bond could eliminate the threat of magical harm. Long-term partners would not be well served to inflict venereal disease on a life partner. Sex, outside of the realm of marriage, was a magically dangerous pursuit.

If we are to successfully study gender within African-American households, we must consider the magical dimension of gender relationships, and, likewise, if we are to consider magical practices, then we must consider gender.

Magical and Religious Systems: A Diachronic Approach

While this review of African-American magical uses is by no means exhaustive, it should be evident that magical practices were a pervasive influence on most arenas of daily life. Acts as simple as leaving a footprint or using another person's comb could have profound magical impacts upon one's life. Family relations, child care, personal hygiene habits, the preparation of food, relations with neighbors, were all aspects of everyday life that had magical implications. Threat of magical harm or retaliation for one's actions profoundly shaped important personal and social relations within the African community.

The ways in which magical practice and religion are articulated in African-American society have changed through time. Within traditional West African religions, magical and religious practices were often completely entwined within the belief system. For instance, within Kongo belief systems, the creation of medicine is a magical process that involves the use of a *nkisi*, or charm, which is believed to contain a captured soul of a spirit from the religious pantheon. On some plantations, enslaved Africans and African Americans were discouraged from engaging in religious worship. Organized, African-based religions did continue to be practiced in the New World in the form of Obeahism, Myalism, and Vodun in the Caribbean, Santeria in Cuba, Shango in Trinidad and Brazil, and Voodoo in Louisiana (Herskovits 1962[1941]; Raboteau 1978; Tallant 1983[1946]; Murphy 1988; Brandon 1993).

The extent to which West African religious structures survived the Middle Passage has been a focus of scholarly debate (e.g., Raboteau 1978).

Demographic, political, social, cultural, and geographical factors have all impacted the extent to which enslaved Africans could recreate their religious values throughout the diaspora. As Raboteau summarized:

> The historical circumstances, then, in which religious traditions from Africa have been transmitted to New World societies have varied from society to society. Some traditions extend relatively far into the past of colonial slavery; others have died out with the passage of time; and still others have developed out of more recent contact with Africa. Moreover, Afro-American cults have modified traditions and added new ones. Yet, despite discontinuity and innovation, the fundamental religious perspectives of Africa have continued to orient the lives of the descendants of slaves in the New World (Raboteau 1978:42).

Understanding the myriad of cultural and contextual factors that have contributed to the historical transformations of African religions in the New World is confusing and daunting. Add to the complexity of the situation the secret nature of African-American religious systems during enslavement and beyond, and the task is impossible from documentary sources. Given the temporal nature of the archaeological database, archaeologists are in the best position to contribute to the broader understanding of religions and religious change within the diaspora.

Mechanisms of Religious/Magical Change: Creolization and Syncretism

The processes of culture change that shape the religious and magical developments in the diaspora are creolization and syncretism. Creolization (cf. Joyner 1984; Ferguson 1992) is the process through which a group's "cultural grammar" absorbs a new lexicon. In other words, the ideas that shape cultural action remain the same, but the material way in which they are expressed changes. For example, Ferguson (1992) argues that, while enslaved Africans may have adopted some European foods and products into their diet, the continuity in vessel shapes for

their Colono Ware, and continuities in the ways these vessels were used, suggest that enslaved people continued to use these pots and prepare their meals in an African way.

In later African-American archaeological assemblages, the process of creolization can be seen as African-American ethnic values are increasingly expressed through the selection of mass-produced consumer goods. For instance, Wilkie (1996a) has argued that African-American consumer choices in over-the-counter medicines are influenced by the "grammar" of traditional ethnomedical systems. Likewise, Stine et al. (1996) have argued that the relatively high proportions of the color blue among glass beads recovered archaeologically from African-American sites are reflective of active consumer choice. Creolization, as a process, represents retentions in cultural values that become expressed in new ways due to cultural contact and relocation.

Syncretism, most commonly discussed in terms of religious transformations, is the process through which two formally distinct cultural values or icons become fused into a third, new reality (e.g., Thompson 1983). The fusion of the African spirits and Catholic saints within Haitian vodun or Cuban Santeria represents the process of syncretism. The aspects of the respective saint and African deity become merged and inseparable, yet unique and distinct from each original.

In addition to the growth of the North-American born enslaved population, by the beginning of the 19th century, greater numbers of planters were allowing their enslaved peoples to be baptized and practice Christianity. It is clear from ex-slave narratives and accounts from abolitionists that some enslaved people embraced the philosophy and faith of Christianity with great sincerity. With greater access to the theology and rituals of Christianity, enslaved Africans found fertile ground for the expression and elaboration of African religious and magical systems. The syncretic religious and magical practices that arose as a result of the merging of Christian and African theologies remain a largely unrecognized component in archaeological interpretations.

Through time, as more enslaved people adopted Christianity, African traditions became increasingly merged with Christian sacred histories and pantheons. The form in which syncretisms developed was dependent upon a number of factors, including what branch of Christianity was practiced by the enslaved people (Raboteau 1978). For instance, Catholicism includes a broad and diverse pantheon of saints, angels, martyrs, and so on, and incorporates a certain level of mysticism within its theology. As such, Catholicism provided a medium for African Americans to identify, recognize, and continue to worship African deities within the Catholic context, such as in the syncretistic religions of Shango and Santeria. In contrast, the majority of Protestant religions condemn the recognition of other supernatural forces or powers as deviltry, leaving less opportunity to recognize specific African deities. However, the Baptist faith, with its emphasis on water immersion baptism and camp revival meetings—a context in which "shouting" as a religious expression developed— provided a means for continuities in beliefs about water spirits and the religious expression of possession, so important in Yoruban religion (Thompson 1983; Pitts 1993).

As descendants of African populations increasingly embraced different forms of Christianity, traditional magical and magico-medical beliefs diverged in the ways that they were expressed. While attending church services became one means of expressing and experiencing religious worship, magical expressions of belief were increasingly likely to occur outside of the church context. These two facets of religious activity, however, remained linked by a single cosmology. Hortense Powdermaker, working among a rural southern African-American community in the 1930s observed:

> Among the Negroes of Cottonville, many who are deeply religious are not especially superstitious, and

some heartily disapprove of voodoo doctors. Often, however, those who are devoutly religious are also devout believers in current folk superstitions and do not look upon Christianity and Voodoo as conflicting in any way. Some of the "doctors" themselves insist that they work their miracles by the grace of God, and feel that their effectiveness bear witness to their piety (Powdermaker 1993[1937]:286).

Within Catholicism, Africans and African Americans found a spiritual medium that could provide coverage for their own, resulting in the development of syncretic religions such as Santeria, Voodoo, and Vodun. Within these contexts, magical traditions from Catholicism and African-based belief systems were incorporated and merged together. Magic remained an aspect of group, structured religion. In Protestant Christian traditions, while some aspects of worship were compatible, most magical beliefs, while not eliminated, were separated from the realm of organized religion.

Within African-Catholic syncretised religions, apparently traditional Catholic iconography and relics are imbued with new meanings and roles. For instance, Puckett (1968[1926]) reports the importance of "Lucky St. Joseph" in New Orleans. A small gilt figurine of Joseph and the Christ child, kept in a small case, was carried as a good luck charm or for getting a husband by the European-Catholic community. Puckett wrote, "Negroes also carry this Lucky Saint Joseph, but in their case, lacking the spiritual background, they look upon it in much the same fashion as a rabbit's foot, horseshoe, or any other less sacred charm" (Puckett 1968[1926]:564).

However, an interaction between an African-American man, Robert, and his Saint Joseph figurine, as reported by Lyle Saxon, adds another dimension to this interpretation:

> "Yah! Yah! See dat, Saint Joseph!" he (Robert) cried in glee, "I sho' fixed o' dat time!" He addressed a small statue of a saint which stood upside down on the wash-stand, propped in this uncomfortable position between tooth mug and soap dish. And to my further amazement, he reached out his hand, righted the out-

raged saint, and placing him upon the altar beside the Statue of the Virgin, he fell upon his knees and began to pray, rapidly . . . . In response to my questions he told a remarkable story. He had prayed to Saint Joseph that he might have the day off from his work, for he loved the Mardi Gras festivities more than anything else. But it appeared that Saint Joseph did not heed his prayer and he was not chosen as the lucky one that would accompany the children on their all-day wandering . . . he had learned his fate last night and had decided to take desperate measures. This very morning he had quarreled with the saint, "stomped" his foot at him, and turned him upside down against the soap dish for punishment. And now, did I not see that Saint Joseph had come to his senses? Robert had known, the very moment that I came walking into the courtyard . . . St. Joseph sent me in answer to his prayer (Saxon 1988:18).

Saint Joseph is not merely a charm to be carried, like a rabbit's foot; instead, he represents a spiritual power with whom to negotiate and even to bully when not performing satisfactorily. Saxon provides an additional description of Robert's room:

> The walls were covered with pictures of saints in various agonies of torture; Saint Lucy carrying her eyes on a plate, Saint Roch with his sores, followed by a collie that held a cake in its mouth; Saint Somebody else being burned at the stake. I thought them all magnificent. A crucifix hung on the wall, and beneath it was a sort of altar draped in a white lace scarf and bearing three black candles in small candlesticks. A bunch of artificial flowers stood at the foot of a statue of the Virgin Mary (Saxon 1988:17).

It is evident from Saxon's description that Robert was involved to some degree in voodooism. Saxon later describes Robert stopping in the French Quarter to gaze in the window of a voodoo shop. Saxon's work must be viewed with a cautious critical eye, for he was writing memoirs of his childhood, and is known to have confused some dates and events, either accidentally or intentionally. However, Saxon also had a lifelong interest in the supernatural beliefs of African-American Louisiana, and later directed the Federal Writer's Ex-Slave Narratives project in that state, ensuring that interviewers spent a concerted effort in interviews asking about Marie Laveau and Voodoo (Clayton 1990). In any case, Saxon's description does provide some insight into the possible interaction between saint relics and their users.

Throughout Louisiana "Candle Shops," which cater to practitioners of hoodoo and Santeria, stock a wide range of candles decorated with different saints as well as a range of saint medals. "Seven Powers of Africa" candles depict seven saints with the name of their recognized equivalent Yoruban *Orisha*. While the "Seven African Powers" candles are manufactured specifically for practitioners of Santeria, they are bought and used by Louisiana African-American families who do not consider themselves Santerians. Yet, the imagery and the powers of the Santeria deities are familiar and meaningful to these users. In addition to artifacts related to saint iconography that can archaeologically signal continuities in African magical and religious practice, each of the *Orisha* have additional material cultural symbols associated with them (González-Wippler 1992[1973]:15).

Due to the complexity of the relationship between Catholic icons and practice, such as the burning of candles in association with prayer, and syncretised African religions, artifacts that bear Catholic iconography cannot be assumed to represent evidence of strictly Roman Catholic beliefs. Discussing a rosary recovered from an 18th-century African/African-American burial in New Orleans, Orser (1994:38) wrote of the buried individual: "Tooth mutilation is well known in Africa, and it is tempting to suppose that this individual had spent a portion of his life there. The presence of the rosary, however, implies that he had accepted Christianity at some point in his life. We will never know if his conversion occurred in Africa or in his New World home." Orser's attribution of the rosary to a strictly Christian conversion is an oversimplification of a potentially complex situation. The rosary recovered from the burial context in New Orleans is as likely to represent a participation in African syncretic religious belief (of geographic origin in Africa or the New World) as to represent Catholicism.

Likewise, a handmade St. Christopher's medal and rosary recovered from the free-black settlement of Fort Mose in Florida may also represent syncretic religious beliefs rather than pure Spanish Catholicism (Deagan and MacMahon 1995:23, 35). From the Hermitage plantation, Tennessee, three copper-alloy clenched-fist charms, showing the wrist and back of hand, have been recovered from early 19th-century African-American contexts (McKee 1992, 1995). McKee reports that these charms are similar to *figas* and *milagras* used in Brazil and Latin America as votive items, for fertility, good luck, and defense from witchcraft. McKee also recognizes that these artifacts could have Islamic meanings, and could represent the "Hand of Fatima," which was also used to ward off the "evil eye" (McKee 1995:40). A similar charm has been recovered from another planter/slave context in Maryland, from the Calvert site (Yentsch 1994:33, Figure 2.2).

The absorption of Christian iconography by African Americans is visible archaeologically from at least the 18th century to the present, and represents an important direction for further archaeological study. In addition, once a diachronic approach is employed, it is clear that syncretism of African and Christian belief systems was taking place simultaneously as the creolization of African beliefs in other regions. While the processes of creolization and syncretism have been discussed to some extent within the archaeological literature (e.g., Ferguson 1992; Wilkie 1995), as yet, there has been little attempt to situate these processes, and the archaeological evidence of these cultural processes, within a temporal landscape.

A Model for Understanding Religious/Magical Change

Archaeologists have tended to treat African-American magical and religious practices as if they occur synchronically, and have paid little attention to these practices across time and space. In order for researchers to approach African-American magical and religious systems from a diachronic perspective, however, it is necessary for archaeologists to adopt a framework in which to organize and interpret material evidence of African-American religious continuities and transformations. George Brandon (1993), in studying ethnographically the development of Santeria as it spread from its Yoruban origins to Cuba, and eventually to New York City, employed a three-stage framework for understanding the religious transformations he encountered and documented. This three-step framework may likewise prove useful for historical archaeologists studying magical-religious transformations. The three stages, the Formative, Persisting, and Transfomative, were defined by Brandon as follows:

> In terms of religion, a Formative period is when a religion is beginning to assume a different physiognomy than previously, through exposure to other religions, internal developments, economic or political catastrophe, and so forth. What marks this period is exposure, innovation, recoil, or seeking, and these are seen in a number of processes which do not necessarily eventuate in a coherent direction of change. Eventually, though, these developments eventuate in a period of conflict over a small number of alternatives, followed by a taking of positions and the working out of these alternatives until one of more of them becomes a major direction of change. Those alternatives that survive assume a form which is recognizable and whose recognizability can be successfully and consistently reproduced. When this happens it constitutes a period of persistence, and the new form is repeatedly reproduced within a range of variation that assures its uniqueness and coherence. The Transformative stage is simply another version of the Formative stage, with the form that exists during the Persisting stage as its point of departure (Brandon 1993:3).

Brandon is quick to point out that his framework should be seen as one of multilinear, not unilinear, progression. Within the African diaspora, each geographic region will have its own distinctive Formative period, depending upon its political, historical, and social-cultural context.

As the geographic and temporal breadth of African-American archaeology continues to expand, we should be able to evaluate the development of African-American magical and religious systems within their distinct social, cultural, and temporal contexts.

The cultural influences that shape the Formative period are not just the mixing of different West African cultures in the New World setting of enslavement, but also contact with Native American and European cultures. As archaeologists continue to collect archaeological data and interpret them within a contextual framework (Hodder 1986), we will be able to clarify which recurring magical assemblages represent Persisting belief structures and practices, and finally, as we begin to consider our data in a diachronic manner, we can begin to recognize and understand succeeding Transformative and Persisting stages.

Archaeological Expectations of the Model

To effectively employ this model, archaeological assemblages related to African-American magical and religious practices have to be studied across time and space. The development and expression of African-American magical-religious systems will be different in every area of the diaspora. For instance, as will be discussed below, while cosmogram-marked Colono Ware bowls were important to the creation of sacred medicines in 17th- and 18th-century South Carolina (Ferguson 1992), no similar uses of Jamaican African-produced pottery (*yabba* wares) have been reported (Armstrong 1990).

Population dynamics and social and political factors influenced and shaped the processes of creolization and syncretism in different areas. Enslaved populations in different colonies may have been relatively isolated from one another during the 17th and 18th centuries, perhaps leading to the development of distinctive regional religious and magical traditions. Movements of slaves between states became more common during the early 19th century, as growing demand for slaves in the deep south increased, and as abolitionist movements attempted to eliminate and restrict enslavement on a state-by-state basis (Davis and Donaldson 1975; Genovese 1975, 1989; Gutman 1976). By the period of Reconstruction, African-American populations that had been previously isolated from one another mingled throughout the American South as well as in new, large urban centers such as Chicago, New York, and Philadelphia (Davis and Donaldson 1975). For this later period, regional differences in magical-religious traditions would be expected to lessen, if not disappear.

As defined by Brandon, the Formative period for African-American religions in any part of the diaspora should be archaeologically indicated by a variety of syncretic and creolization events. These events would not necessarily be widespread within a geographic region nor be of particular time depth, since a Formative period would be marked by a variety of competing options. Archaeologically, both Formative and Transformative stages will be difficult to recognize, since these are stages that are characterized by flux and change. The periods of Formative and Transformative stages within a region will have short-lived material correlates. Artifact types or assemblages of limited duration, or single examples of artifacts may be the only material indicators of these stages. The low archaeological profile of these periods, however, does not diminish their importance. The Formative and Transformative periods are the periods of culture change, when the mechanisms of syncretism and creolization are at work. Through documentary evidence it should be possible to understand what contextual influences and events trigger periods of change.

Once a pattern is established within a region, the tradition represents one of Persistence. Periods of Persistence represent phases of stability and are likely to be of greatest visibility in the archaeological record. The repeated recovery of an artifact type, or assemblage of artifact types within a given temporal and spatial context would represent evidence of a persisting magical-religious tradition.

The application of a model such as Brandon's (1993) that explicitly recognizes syncretism and creolization as mechanisms of change to the archaeological study of African-American magical and religious systems is severalfold. First, the stages defined by Brandon have explicit material/artifactual signatures, even if these artifactual signatures may be of short duration or limited distribution. Second, by adopting such a model, magical and religious practices would be placed within a diachronic interpretive framework which acknowledges these practices are not stagnant. Third, the model is intrinsically tied to the sociohistorical cultural context. The model cannot be employed without the researcher considering the cultural landscape in which the artifacts derived meaning. Therefore, the researcher is encouraged to articulate the material with the documentary record, and to maintain a dialectic between these two databases.

Archaeological Examples of the Model Applied

Below, I will provide a brief overview of the published archaeological evidence of African-American spiritual traditions from three geographical regions: South Carolina, the Chesapeake, and Louisiana, and how the application of a diachronic model in these areas could enlighten our understanding of African-American belief systems in these areas. As will be clearly seen, despite the sense within historical archaeology that we have a better understanding of New World African-American religions than ever before, there is no area for which a complete archaeological timeline is available.

South Carolina

South Carolina was home to a large enslaved African population early in its history. The relatively high proportion of Africans to Europeans in South Carolina allowed enslaved populations greater ability to retain African traditions and limit contact with European belief systems and practices (Joyner 1984; Ferguson 1992; Deetz

1993). South Carolina, due to this historical circumstance, is an intriguing area in which to study African and African-American religious traditions.

In South Carolina, Leland Ferguson (1992:110–116) has found evidence of Bakongo-influenced water cults. African-American-produced Colono Ware pottery bowls bear crosses and crosses contained in circles on the interior and exterior bases. Ferguson (1992) has argued, most convincingly, that these symbols bear close resemblance to the Bakongo sign of the cosmos. The cosmogram represents the cycle of life and death, continuity and change, the division between this world and the afterworld, land and sea, sky and earth (Thompson 1981:27–28). Complete bowls bearing these symbols and sherds with these marks have been recovered from rivers and riversides. These bowls may be related to the creation of traditional Kongo sacred medicines, or *minkisi* (*nkisi* = singular), that served to control power emanating from supernatural powers (Ferguson 1992:114). As containers for sacred medicines, the bowls could have once contained any number of magical materials, including stones, white clay, animal remains, shells, broken glass, beads, and so forth.

Ferguson does not propose a date range for the incidence of this cultural manifestation; however, Colono Wares associated with African-American sites date from the 1670s to the early 1800s, after which time they become rare, then disappear all together. The disappearance of Colono Wares does not necessarily mean that the practice of using clay bowls for the preparation of sacred medicine disappeared as well. There is no reason to suppose that American- or European-produced ceramics could not have been used as containers for sacred medicines. Likewise, new containers of organic materials such as wood, gourd, or cloth could have been employed. However, the disappearance of these vessels from the archaeological record does suggest the transition from one Persisting stage to a Transformative stage in the development of African-American religious magical practices in South Carolina.

In South Carolina, it would appear that excavators of 19th- and early 20th-century African-American sites should consider, when evaluating artifacts from these sites, how the magical-religious practices documented archaeologically by Ferguson may have transformed into new cultural and material expressions during this later period.

The Chesapeake

The Chesapeake remains one of the best-studied areas of Colonial America. Unlike South Carolina, where enslaved African people outnumbered Europeans early in the colony's history, in the Chesapeake, the growth of the enslaved population was slower. Africans and African Americans lived in closer contact with Europeans, and the impact of this continued contact is evident in the material culture of enslaved people of the Chesapeake. For instance, unlike the South Carolinian Colono Wares which retain African vessel form shapes, Chesapeake Colono Wares are more likely to take European-influenced forms (Deetz 1993). This difference in historical context should be apparent in the development of African-Chesapeake religious expression.

In the Chesapeake, terra-cotta tobacco pipes have been found with regularity on sites dating between 1640 and 1720 (Deetz 1993:91). Several of these pipes have been found to bear the Nigerian *Kwardata* motif. According to Emerson (1994:43), when placed on a ritual beer vessel the *Kwardata* symbol represents "the transition from youth to adulthood in contemporary Ga'anda society." Emerson states that pipes bearing the *Kwardata* motif have been recovered from sites in Maryland and Virginia, including St. Mary's City, Jamestown, Governor's Land, and Martin's Hundred (Emerson 1994:43). The recovery of these pipes from a number of sites may represent a material expression of a persisting religious tradition within the enslaved population of the Chesapeake.

The placement of a symbol of obvious ritual and religious importance on a new form, a tobacco pipe, reflects some Native American cultural influence as well as a transformation in the original presentation of this symbol. Whether the pipe, and the presumed associated use of tobacco, serves as a substitute for the ritual(s) associated with the traditional beer vessels, or reflects a new, syncretised version of the ritual(s) cannot be determined from the available evidence. These potentially African-American-made pipes disappear early in the 18th century, around the same time that Colono Ware pottery is first found in this region (Deetz 1993). Whether the construction of Colono Ware vessels allowed for a new religious expression is not known. Again, the disappearance of one form of artifactual material expression of religious belief suggests a Transformative process.

Further to the north, in 18th-century Maryland, another set of archaeological finds may represent another manifestation of either Kongo sacred medicines or continuities in the creation of family sacred altars honoring ancestors. Leone (1995; Wilford 1996) has reported the discovery of caches of potentially sacred artifacts associated with hearths and the northeast corners of rooms in two 18th-century houses in Annapolis, Maryland. Curated and hidden artifacts include buttons, doll parts, rings, rock crystals, and pierced disks. Unlike the instances of the cosmogram-inscribed Colono Ware, or the *Kwardata*-adorned tobacco pipes, these artifact assemblages cannot be tied directly to the material cultural expressions of Africa. Instead, the processes of creolization have led to the development of a religious expression which has endowed non-African forms and artifacts with new spiritual meanings. By the date of these caches, the majority of the enslaved population of North America were not Africans themselves, but the descendants of Africans.

Again, the widespread use of these artifacts is suggestive of a Persisting stage of religious expression. The components of Leone's artifact caches include objects that have been recovered from potentially magical contexts at other late 18th- and 19th-century African-American sites in

Virginia and Maryland, such as pierced disks/ coins, crystals and doll parts (Klingelhofer 1987; Patten 1992). The recovery of similar artifact caches and similar artifact types suggests the Persistence of a magical-religious tradition dating from the 18th to mid-19th centuries.

Louisiana

Louisiana stands as a distinct region of the deep south for several reasons particular to its history. Settled as a colony by the French and Spanish before becoming acquired by the United States, Louisiana had a strong Catholic religious heritage. After the Haitian Revolution, formerly enslaved Africans from that island migrated to Louisiana, settling in New Orleans during the late 18th century. This immigrant population has often been credited with bringing Voodoo to the city (Tallant 1983[1946]).

Syncretic African-Catholic rituals represent a Persisting component of African-American religious practice in Louisiana from the earliest periods of occupation to the present. The earliest dated African-American religious-magical artifacts recovered from Louisiana are the previously discussed rosary recovered by Charles Orser and Douglas Owsley from a burial dated before 1788 (Orser 1994:38). No other Catholic artifacts are reported from African-American sites until the late 1800s.

By the 1840s, the growth of the sugar industry in Louisiana brought increasing numbers of enslaved people to the state. Contact between previously isolated African-American populations led to a Transformative stage with African Americans in Louisiana adopting artifacts similar to those used by enslaved people in Virginia and Maryland for magical uses. The ensuing Persisting stage appears to bear other similarities to the Chesapeake traditions; at one site, religiously significant artifacts have been found in caches associated with hearths. A pierced 1793 Spanish real, associated with two black barrel glass beads, was recovered from a mid-19th-century slave cabin at Ashland Belle-Helene plantation (Yakubik et al. 1994:10–94). In addition, re-

searchers reported that hearth areas of the slave cabins at this plantation may have served as ceremonial centers: "The coin, beads, shells, buttons and smoothed stones were found more frequently near hearths than in other parts of the cabins or in the yards. This may reflect ritual activity occurred within the house, where it could be hidden" (Yakubik and Méndez [1995]:27).

Excavations of hearth areas of slave cabins at Riverlake plantation, which was occupied from the mid-19th century through the mid-20th century, failed to recover evidence of any similar caches of artifacts. The longer duration of occupation at this site may have eliminated any archaeological trace of earlier religious activities around the hearths, suggesting the development of a different Transformative and Persisting tradition. Other religiously and magically important artifacts, such as crystals and projectile points, were recovered from this site, but were recovered from underneath houses and from yard areas. A Catholic St. Anne medal was recovered from a late 19th-century African-American household at Riverlake. While Riverlake plantation was located in the French Catholic parish of Pointe Coupee, the African Americans of the plantation were self-identified Baptists.

Located across the Mississippi River from Pointe Coupee is the predominately Protestant parish of West Feliciana. A rosary medal and a Christ's head relic were recovered from a late 19th- to early 20th-century African-American household in this parish. The occupants were known, through both oral and documentary history, to have been practicing Baptists (Wilkie 1995). Again, the presence of these artifacts in a seemingly contradictory setting—Baptists do not condone the Catholic use of idols—suggests the presence of African nuanced practices. The adoption of Catholic iconography for magical use by Baptists in Pointe Coupee and West Feliciana parish may represent Transformative processes within a very localized area. Pointe Coupe and West Feliciana parish were economically tied during the 19th and 20th centuries. Enslaved, and later freed, African Americans moved across the river between these two parishes seasonally, to work cotton or sugar fields in turn. It seems likely that contact between these Catholic and Baptist populations led to the adoption of each other's magical-religious toolbox during the Persisting stage.

Also recovered from this housesite was an 1855 Britannia pierced penny. The coin has been interpreted as the birth coin of Silvia Freeman, who was born in 1855 and lived in the house (Wilkie 1995). Interestingly enough, Freeman's birthplace is identified from census records as "Virginia." In her case, the magical practice of using coins as protective devices was quite literally brought by her from Virginia. In the example of Silvia Freeman, one can see how religious innovation is ultimately instituted by individuals and their families through time, as they maintain and adapt the magical-religious practices of the proceeding generations.

Summary

The purpose of applying Brandon's (1993) model is not merely to provide a descriptive analysis of where and when different manifestations of African-American spiritual practices can be found. Instead, the model provides an interpretive framework for understanding how African Americans altered their expressions of religious and magical beliefs as their magical-religious needs changed to meet new demands within their communities, and against a changing cultural, social, economic, and political backdrop. As argued above, magical and religious practice is of overarching importance within African-American culture, and influences community relationships, family life, as well as the way individual families view and respond to the world around them. As stated eloquently by Edwards (1995:5), "analyses that treat slave culture as responses only to plantation society in the New World subvert aesthetics, beliefs, craftsmanship, and other issues relevant to African-American research."

The model discussed above offers several benefits for the archaeological study of African-American magical-religious practice. The model provides a vocabulary for describing stages of magical-religious change, and offers a diachronic framework in which to understand data. The intent of the model is not to ignore or simplify the very complex cultural negotiations in which Africans and African Americans participated during the construction of religious expressions. The model provides a means of organizing the limited evidence now available regarding African-American magical-religious tradition and highlights time periods and regions that require further research. It is evident, through the application of a diachronic model, that the archaeological evidence of African-American magical-religious practices from any given area is very incomplete and patchy. While scholars have been able to identify some very important manifestations of African-American spiritual beliefs during and beyond the period of enslavement, we have not directed our investigations in a way that allows us to understand the dynamics of the cultural and social transformations in African-American spiritual traditions, and ultimately, family life. The adoption of an interpretive framework that attempts to contextualize religious change and link the archaeological and documentary records is necessary at this time in the development of the field of study.

Conclusions

A review of ethnographic, oral historical, and documentary evidence indicates that African-American religious and magical beliefs, although geographically and diachronically varied, were pervasive and of great importance to the African-American community. Magical-religious practice influenced every aspect of life, including health care, relationships within the household, gender ideologies, matters of love and marriage, community dispute resolution, and the afterlife. In interpretations of African-American material culture, archaeologists must be careful to recognize the potential magical meaning artifacts may have carried.

Some of the magical-religious artifacts recovered from household middens are distinctive and can be argued to be of religious significance wherever they are found, such as amulets, pierced coins, curated crystals, curated projectile points, and so on, since ethnographic and oral historical evidence identifies them as such. Other artifacts, which are well known to hold multiple functions within African-American households, such as bottles, straight pins, cups and saucers, glass beads, unpierced coins, and buttons, also have, among their other uses, possible magical functions. For many of these artifacts, we can never know if they had magical functions or not but should acknowledge the possibility, although not as an exclusive interpretation.

It is important that archaeologists do not become overly enthusiastic in their attributions of common household materials to magical uses. Doll parts found as part of a cache of religious materials, such as those recovered from Annapolis, may have possessed magical-religious meanings similar to the *figeras* recovered from the Hermitage plantation, or may be distantly culturally related to the meaning behind the "Hand of Power" candles still popular in Voodoo and Santeria shops. However, a doll's hand or foot recovered from mixed household garbage may be merely a broken children's toy. The challenge that archaeologists must face is recognizing contexts in which seemingly mundane artifacts may have had magical and religious meanings. As examples from Levi-Jordan plantation and Annapolis clearly demonstrate, considerations of archaeological and cultural context are necessary if we are to identify distinct African-American traditions.

It is also necessary that archaeologists add a diachronic dimension to their study of African and African-American spiritual traditions. To understand African-American magical-religious practice, archaeologists must also remember that these practices were not static but changed and evolved as African Americans found new ways to express their spiritual values. To understand these transformations, archaeologists must consider the cultural processes of creolization and syncretism: The use of a magical charm does not necessarily represent a continuity in other aspects of African religions, and the embracing of Chris-

tian values does not necessarily dictate an abandonment of African religious practices.

An interpretive model, or framework, has been proposed to structure and organize the available and growing body of archaeological evidence related to magical and religious systems in the African diaspora. The model recognizes three stages of religious process: Formative, Persisting, and Transformative. Archaeologically most visible is the Persisting stage, which represents periods of limited flux in religious processes. As discussed above, archaeologists have identified a number of Persisting magical-religious systems within the diaspora. When particular artifacts or artifact assemblages disappear from the archaeological record, it represents evidence of a Transformative development in religious practice. The documentary record can provide contextual insight into what social, political, demographic, cultural, communal, and so on, influences may have led African Americans to negotiate different magical and religious expressions through time and space.

The model presented was derived from one successfully used to study the development of Santeria in the Americas (Brandon 1993). Like Brandon, I would argue that this model should not be seen as supporting a unilinear evolutionary scheme. Further, I would argue that the purpose of applying a model such as this is not to adopt an evolutionary framework of any sort, but to provide a means of conceptualizing religious changes through time. The use of this model requires archaeologists to articulate the documentary and archaeological records to lead to a better understanding of religious and spiritual change in the diaspora.

The application of this model, provided above, demonstrates that archaeologists still know and understand very little about African-American magical and religious expressions through material culture. To better understand the magical-religious artifacts that we are finding archaeologically, we must better understand the ways in which magic was used in the African-American community. Only then can archaeologists recognize magically meaningful artifacts, representing a general worldview, versus continuities in African religions and the development of syncretic New World religions. Our interpretations of African-American magical-religious artifacts will remain limited and constrained until we attempt to understand the broader worldview that these artifacts represent.

ACKNOWLEDGMENTS

I would like to thank the Louisiana State Division of Archaeology and the National Park Service for funding the archaeological research at Oakley plantation. The recovery of magical-religious items from that site prompted my initial explorations of this topic. I would like especially to thank reviewers Leland Ferguson, Patricia Samford, Daniel G. Roberts, and an anonymous reviewer for their comments on this manuscript. So much material has recently become available on this topic that it is difficult for any individual to stay abreast of the developments. Not only did these reviewers provide thoughtful comments but they were generous in providing offprints and references to additional works. I greatly appreciate their contribution to this manuscript, but take all responsibility for any remaining weaknesses. Finally, I would like to thank Paul Farnsworth, who remains my most challenging reviewer and tireless editor, and Stealth, who has ensured that I completed this research in a timely manner.

REFERENCES

ADAMS, WILLIAM HAMPTON (EDITOR)
1987 Historical Archaeology of Plantations at Kings Bay, Camden County, Georgia. *Reports of Investigation* 5. Department of Anthropology, University of Florida, Gainesville.

ARMSTRONG, DOUGLAS V.
1990 *The Old Village and the Great House.* University of Illinois Press, Urbana.

BOTKIN, B. A. (EDITOR)
1989 *Lay My Burden Down.* Reprint of 1945 edition. University of Georgia Press, Athens.

BRANDON, GEORGE
1993 *Santeria from Africa to the New World: The Dead Sell Memories.* Indiana University Press, Bloomington.

BROWN, KENNETH L., AND DOREEN C. COOPER
1990 Structural Continuity in an African-American Slave and Tenant Community. *Historical Archaeology* 24(4):7–19.

CAMPBELL, MARIE
1946 *Folks Do Get Born.* Rinehart, New York.

CLAYTON, RONNIE W.
1990 Mother Wit: The Ex-Slave Narratives of the Louisiana's Federal Writers' Project. *University of Kansas Humanistic Studies* 57. Peter Land, New York.

CORRUCCINI, ROBERT S., JEROME S. HANDLER, AND KEITH JACOBI
1985 Chronological Distribution of Enamel Hypoplasias and Weaning in a Caribbean Slave Population. *Human Biology* 57(4):699–711.

DAVIS, GEORGE A., AND O. FRED DONALDSON
1975 *Blacks in the United States: A Geographic Perspective.* Houghton Mifflin, Boston, MA.

DEAGAN, KATHLEEN, AND DARCIE MACMAHON
1995 *Fort Mose: Colonial America's Black Fortress of Freedom.* University of Florida Press, Gainesville.

DEETZ, JAMES
1993 *Flowerdew Hundred: The Archaeology of a Virginia Plantation, 1619–1864.* University of Virginia Press, Charlottesville.

DOLLARD, JOHN
1957 *Caste and Class in a Southern Town.* Reprint of 1937 edition. Doubleday/Anchor, New York.

EDWARDS, YWONE DECARLO
1995 "Primitive" and "Folk" in African American Archaeology. Paper presented at the Annual Meeting of The Society for Historical Archaeology Conference on Historical and Underwater Archaeology, Washington, DC.

EMERSON, MATTHEW C.
1994 Decorated Clay Tobacco Pipes from the Chesapeake: An African Connection. In *Historical Archaeology of the Chesapeake*, edited by Paul A. Shackel and Barbara J. Little, pp. 35–49. Smithsonian Institution Press, Washington, DC.

FARNSWORTH, PAUL
1996 Brutality or Benevolence in Plantation Archaeology. Paper presented at the Annual Meeting of the American Anthropological Association, San Francisco, CA.

FERGUSON, LELAND
1992 *Uncommon Ground: Archaeology and Early African America, 1650–1800.* Smithsonian Institution Press, Washington, DC.

FONTENOT, WONDA L.
1994 *Secret Doctors: Ethnomedicine of African Americans.* Bergin and Garvey, Westport, CT.

GENOVESE, EUGENE D.
1975 *Roll, Jordan, Roll.* Reprint of 1972 edition. Vintage, New York.
1989 *The Political Economy of Slavery.* Wesleyan University Press, Wesleyan, CT.

GONZÁLEZ-WHIPPLER, MIGENE
1992 *Santeria: African Magic in Latin America.* Reprint of 1973 edition. Original Publications, New York.

GUTMAN, HERBERT
1976 *The Black Family in Slavery and Freedom: 1750–1925.* Vintage, New York.

HAND, WAYLAND D.
1980 *Magical Medicine: The Folkloric Component of Medicine in the Folk Belief Custom, and Ritual of the Peoples of Europe and America.* University of California Press, Berkeley.

HANDLER, JEROME S.
1996 A Prone Burial from a Plantation Slave Cemetery in Barbados, West Indies: Possible Evidence for an African-Type Witch or Other Negatively Viewed Person. *Historical Archaeology* 30(3):76–86.

HANDLER, JEROME S., AND FREDERICK W. LANGE
1978 *Plantation Slavery in Barbados: An Archaeological and Historical Investigation.* Harvard University Press, Cambridge, MA.

HARRIS, EDWARD F., AND TED A. RATHBUN
1989 Small Tooth Sizes in a Nineteenth Century South Carolina Slave Series. *American Hournal of Physical Anthropology* 78:411–420.

HERSKOVITS, MELVILLE
1962 *Myth of the Negro Past.* Reprint of 1941 edition. Beacon Press, Boston, MA.

HODDER, IAN
1986 *Reading the Past: Current Approaches to Interpretation in Archaeology.* Cambridge University, Cambridge, UK.

HURSTON, ZORA NEALE
1990a *Tell My Horse: Voodoo and Life in Haiti and Jamaica.* Reprint of 1938 edition. Harper and Row, New York.
1990b *Mules and Men.* Reprint of 1935 edition. Harper and Row, New York.

HYATT, HARRY MIDDLETON
1973 *Hoodoo-Conjuration-Witchcraft-Rootwork,* Vol. 3. Western Publishing, St. Louis, MO.
1974 *Hoodoo-Conjuration-Witchcraft-Rootwork,* Vol. 4. Western Publishing, St. Louis, MO.
1978 *Hoodoo-Conjuration-Witchcraft-Rootwork,* Vol. 5. Western Publishing, St. Louis, MO.

JOYNER, CHARLES
1984 *Down by the Riverside: A South Carolina Slave Community.* University of Illinois Press, Urbana.

KELLEY, JENNIFER OLSEN, AND J. LAWRENCE ANGEL
1987 Life Stresses of Slavery. *American Journal of Physical Anthropology* 74:199–211.

KLINGELHOFER, ERIC
1987 Aspects of Early Afro-American Material Culture: Artifacts from the Slave Quarters at Garrison Plantation, Maryland. *Historical Archaeology* 21(2):112–119.

LAGUERRE, MICHEL S.
1978 *Afro-Caribbean Folk Medicine.* Bergin and Garvey, Amherst, MA.

LANGENWALTER, PAUL E. II
1987 Mammals and Reptiles as Food and Medicines in Riverside Chinatown. In *Wong Ho Leun: An American Chinatown,* Vol. 2, pp. 53–106. The Great Basin Foundation, San Diego.

LEHMANN, ARTHUR C., AND JAMES E. MYERS (EDITORS)
1985 *Magic, Witchcraft, and Religion: An Anthropological Study of the Supernatural.* Mayfield, Palo Alto, CA.

LEONE, MARK
1995 A Historical Archaeology of Capitalism. *American Anthropologist* 97(2):251–268.

LOGAN, ANNIE LEE, AS TOLD TO KATHERINE CLARK
1989 *Motherwit: An Alabama Midwife's Story.* E. P. Dutton, New York.

MARWICK, MAX (EDITOR)
1970 *Witchcraft and Sorcery.* Penguin, New York.

MATHEWS HOLLY F.
1992 Doctors and Root Doctors: Patients Who Use Both. In *Herbal and Magical Medicine: Traditional Healing Today,* edited by James Kirkland, Holly F. Mathews, C. W. Sullivan III, and Karen Baldwin, pp. 68–97. Duke University Press, Durham, NC.

MBITI, JOHN S.
1970 *African Religions and Philosophies.* Doubleday, Garden City, NY.

McKEE, LARRY
1992 Summary Report on the 1991 Field Quarter Excavation.

Report submitted to The Hermitage, TN.

1995 The Earth Is Their Witness: Archaeology Is Shedding New Light on the Secret Lives of American Slaves. *The Sciences*, March/April:36–41.

McMILLEN, SALLY G.
1990 *Motherhood in the Old South: Pregnancy, Childbirth and Infant Rearing.* Louisiana State University Press, Baton Rouge.

MUELLER, FRED W., JR.
1987 Feng-Shui: Archaeological Evidence for Geomancy in Overseas Chinese Settlements. In *Wong Ho Leun: An American Chinatown*, Vol. 2, pp. 1–24. The Great Basin Foundation, San Diego, CA.

MURPHY, JOSEPH M.
1988 *Santeria: African Spirits in America.* Beacon Press, New York.

ORSER, CHARLES E., JR.
1994 The Archaeology of African-American Slave Religion in the Antebellum South. *Cambridge Archaeological Review Journal* 4(1):33–45.

PATTEN, M. DRAKE
1992 Mankala and Minkisi: Possible Evidence of African-American Folk Beliefs and Practices. *African-American Archaeology* 6:5–7.

PEARCE, LAURIE
1993 To Whom Do They Belong?: Cowrie Shells in Historical Archaeology. *African-American Archaeology* 9:1–3.

PITTS, WALTER F., JR.
1993 *Old Ship of Zion: The Afro-Baptist Ritual in the African Diaspora.* Oxford University Press, Oxford, UK.

POWDERMAKER, HORTENSE
1993 *After Freedom: A Cultural Study in the Deep South.* Reprint of 1937 edition. The University of Wisconsin Press, Madison.

PUCKETT, NEWBELL NILES
1968 *Folk Beliefs of the Southern Negro.* Reprint of 1926 edition. Negro Universities Press, New York.

RABOTEAU, ALBERT J.
1978 *Slave Religion: The Invisible Institution in the Antebellum South.* Oxford University Press, Oxford, UK.

REEVES, MATTHEW
1996 "To Vex a Teif": An African-Jamaican Ritual Feature. Poster and text presented at The Society for American Archaeology Conference on Historical and Underwater Archaeology, New Orleans, LA.

ROSE, JEROME C. (EDITOR)
1985 Gone to a Better Land. *Arkansas Archeological Research Series* 25. Arkansas Archeological Survey, Fayetteville.

ROSE, JEROME C., AND LAWRENCE GENE SANTEFORD
1985 Burial Descriptions. In Gone to a Better Land, edited by Jerome C. Rose. *Arkansas Archeological Research Series* 25:39–129. Arkansas Archeological Survey, Fayetteville.

SAMFORD, PATRICIA
1996 The Archaeology of African-American Slavery and Material Culture. *The William and Mary Quarterly*, third series, 53(1):87–114.

SANTORIO, ALESSIA ANNE
1994 The Path Least Traveled: Religion and Ritual as Interpretive Frameworks in African-American Archaeology. Unpublished M.A. thesis, Department of Anthropology, University of South Carolina, Columbia.

SAXON, LYLE
1988 *Fabulous New Orleans.* Reprint of 1928 edition. Pelican, New York.

SAXON, LYLE, EDWARD DREYER, AND ROBERT TALLANT
1989 *Gumbo Ya Ya.* Reprint of 1945 edition. Pelican, New York.

STINE, LINDA FRANCE, MELANIE A. CABAK, AND MARK D. GROOVER
1996 Blue Beads as African-American Cultural Symbols. *Historical Archaeology* 30(3):49–75.

TALLANT, ROBERT
1983 *Voodoo in New Orleans.* Reprint of 1946 edition. Pelican, New York.

TERRILL, TOM E., AND JERROLD HIRSCH
1978 *Such as Us: Southern Voices of the Thirties.* University of North Carolina Press, Chapel Hill.

THOMPSON, ROBERT FARRIS
1981 *Four Moments of the Sun.* National Art Gallery, Washington, DC.
1983 *Flash of the Spirit.* Vintage, New York.

TURNER, GRACE
1993 An Archaeological Record of Plantation Life in the Bahamas. In *Amerindians, Africans, Americans: Three Papers in Caribbean History*, by Gerard Lafleur, Susan Branson, and Grace Turner, pp. 107–125. Department of History, University of West Indies, Mona, Jamaica.

WEGARS, PRISCILLA (EDITOR)
1993 *Hidden Heritage: Historical Archaeology of the Overseas Chinese*. Baywood Monographs in Archaeology Series. Baywood, Amityville, NY.

WILFORD, JOHN NOBLE
1996 Slave Artifacts Under the Hearth. *New York Times*, 27 August:C1-1.

WILKIE, LAURIE A.
1994a *"Never Leave Me Alone": An Archaeological Study of African-American Ethnicity, Race Relations and Community at Oakley Plantation*. Ph.D. Dissertation, Archaeology Program, University of California, Los Angeles. University Microfilms International, Ann Arbor, MI.
1994b Archaeological Evidence of an African-American Aesthetic. *African-American Archaeology*10:1, 4.
1995 Magic and Empowerment on the Plantation: An Archaeological Consideration of African-American Worldview. *Southeastern Archaeology* 14(2):136–148.
1996a Medicinal Teas and Patent Medicines: African-American Women's Consumer Choices and Ethnomedical Traditions at a Louisiana Plantation. *Southeastern Archaeology* 15(2):119–131.
1996b Transforming African-American Ethnomedical Practices: A Case Study from West Feliciana. *Louisiana History* 37(4):457–471.

WILKIE, LAURIE A., AND GEORGE SHORTER
[1997] An Archaeological Glimpse of an African-American Midwife's Life: Excavations at 1MB99. Monograph, in preparation for publication.

YAKUBIK, JILL-KARIN, CARRIE A. LEVEN, KENNETH R. JONES, BENJAMIN MAYGARDEN, SHANNON DAWDY, DONNA K. STONE, JAMES CUSICK, CATHEREN JONES, ROSALINDA MENDÉZ, HERSCHEL A. FRANKS, AND TARA BOND
1994 Archaeological Data Recovery at Ashland-Belle Helene Plantation (16AN26), Ascension Parish, Louisiana. Vol. 1, Investigations in the Quarters and Archaeological Monitoring. Submitted to Division of Archaeology, Louisiana Department of Culture, Recreation and Tourism, Baton Rouge, LA.

YAKUBIK, JILL-KARIN, AND ROSALINDA MÉNDEZ
[1995] *Beyond the Great House: Archaeology at Ashland-Belle Helene Plantation*. Discovering Louisiana Archaeology One. Louisiana Department of Culture, Recreation and Tourism, Baton Rouge, LA.

YENTSCH, ANNE
1994 *A Chesapeake Family and Their Slaves*. Cambridge University Press, Cambridge, UK.

YOUNG, AMY
1996 Archaeological Evidence of African-Style Ritual and Healing Practices in the Upland South. *Tennessee Anthropologist* 21(2):139–155.
1997 Risk Management Strategies Among African-American Slaves at Locust Grove Plantation. *International Journal of Historical Archaeology* 1(1).

LAURIE A. WILKIE
DEPARTMENT OF ANTHROPOLOGY
UNIVERSITY OF CALIFORNIA
BERKELEY, CA 94720-3710

Marcel Moussette

An Encounter in the Baroque Age: French and Amerindians in North America

ABSTRACT

European colonization of North America had its origins in the expansion of European capitalism. But, on the ground, what occurred during the 16th and 17th centuries was the encountering of certain European nations by certain native peoples. Our present field of interest is the particular nature of the encounter between Amerindians and the French, expressed in cultural *métissage* (mixture or hybridity) and political alliances, since this interaction contains all the ingredients that would lend distinctive colors to the new colonial societies. Exploration of European-Amerindian contacts on the part of archaeologists has already resulted in numerous studies focused on the economy, particularly with respect to the fur trade, or on the newcomers' adaptations to a different environment. For the past few years, however, the author has attempted to approach the issue from another angle, that of representations. It is hoped that this approach will lead to a better understanding of the encounter and shed light on the elusive perceptions of that encounter deep in the minds of the actors involved. The thesis presented here is that a true compatibility existed between representations of the world by the French and by the Amerindians, that this compatibility explains the special nature of the relation between the two groups, and, finally, that the archaeological remains left behind by the two groups lend support to the argument for compatibility, enabling the author to make an original contribution to the comprehension of this encounter. The problem of colonial origins in New France may be approached within a dynamic framework whose main stages are linked one to another in time and space, from Europe to North America: the departure, the passage, the encounter, the contact, the exchange, and the *métissage*.

Departure and Passage

Departure from the homeland and trans-Atlantic passage took place mainly in the second half of the 17th century at a time when, following the Spaniards, greater numbers of the French became involved in far-away travels. "Modernity is the first unity of the world, the terrestrial globe caught up in a common adventure, however fragile that community life might be ... a world that tends towards unity," writes Fernand Braudel (1997:301). For the great French historian, this period was marked by the expansion of European capitalism on other continents: Africa, Asia, and America. Initially this incipient capitalism was mercantile and distant, and used bills of exchange (Braudel 1997:328). However, this definition of capitalism is not accepted unanimously. Eric Wolf (1982:78–87) has contrasted the capitalist mode of production, which he linked mainly to the Industrial Revolution of the 18th and 19th centuries, to a tributary mode of production "in which the primary producer, whether cultivator or herdsman, is allowed access to the means of production, while tribute is exacted from him by political or military means" (Wolf 1982: 79–80). For Wolf, the tributary mode of production includes Braudel's incipient capitalism with merchants conducting their business within a feudal system. Yet, regarding an activity such as the fur trade, in which Amerindians indebted to traders had to pledge the results of their future trapping, Wolf (1982:87) agreed that what was happening was close to capitalism, though not yet governed by capitalistic types of relations. Immanuel Wallerstein best reconciles the diverse authors' ideas on the nature of what he calls the capitalist "rupture." He sees it as a three-step phenomenon marked by three important dates—

around 1500, 1650, and 1800; three (or more) theories of history: 1800, with an emphasis on industrialism as the crucial change; 1650, with an emphasis either on the moment when the first "capitalist" states (Britain and the Netherlands) emerged or on the emergence of the presumably key "modern" ideas of Descartes, Leibnitz, Spinoza, Newton, and Locke; and 1500, with an emphasis on the creation of a capitalist *world*-system, as distinct from other forms of economies. It follows that the answer one gives to the query, "crisis of the seventeenth century?" is a function of one's presuppositions about the modern world. The term *crisis* ought not to be debased into a mere synonym for *cyclical shift*. It should be reserved for times of dramatic tension that are more than a conjuncture and that indicate a turning point in structures of *longue durée* (Wallerstein 1980:7).

For the topic under study, it is the earliest and particularly the second epochs of capitalism that are most interesting. In the 17th century, France was still feudal, and Braudel has presented it as a large country kept on the sidelines of the world economy by its economic backwardness. In fact, Braudel (1979:287) distinguished two Frances; one that is Atlantic, the "France of the margins," rich and trading; and the other, the "France of the interior," agrarian and underdeveloped. In this he agreed with Edward Fox who drew a distinction between a maritime France and a landowning France, thus contrasting a more modern France, open to the sea and commerce, with a backward France, tangled in its old ways (Fox 1971; Braudel 1979:292). It is from the ports of the Atlantic France that ships set off westward on their way to the "pays de Canada," the "Terres Neuves," "Labrador," the "Grand Baye," and "Norembègue," following the maritime route already traced by cod fishermen and whale hunters by the end of the 15th century. The motivations—or pretexts—underlying these expeditions were numerous: the search for a passage to China, the lure of precious metals or diamonds, the wish to add new territories to the Kingdom of France, the mission of converting the indigenous peoples, etc. But, aside from fish, it was the furs taken back from this part of the New World that generated the most profit and continued to dominate the economy of New France and then Canada during the 17th and 18th centuries.

The Encounter, Contact, Exchange, and *Métissage*

This sequence is unidirectional and necessarily progresses towards a deepening of the relationships among the peoples involved in its trajectory. An encounter often has the meaning of a fortuitous or unplanned event between two or more persons. The first glance (at the Other) exchanged between Europeans and the Amerindians of the Northeast has been very well described by James Axtell (1988) in his book, *After Columbus: Essays in the Ethnohistory of Colonial North America*. As for *contact*, it may be defined literally as being the state of things or peoples touching each other. Being "in contact," for the purposes of this study, thus signifies that the encountering parties have a certain interest in each other and that they are ready to spend some time communicating. From a thorough encounter, contact results. From sustained contact, the exchange that leads to *métissages* results. The final stage of

the sequence, characterized by *métissages* (the mixture or hybridity) (Davis 2001) occurring among the actors of this encounter (that is to say, the French and the Amerindians of the Northeast during the 17th and 18th centuries), interests us since this outcome marks one of the most important aspects of colonialism.

Wolf (1982:286–387) has written, "the encounter of different modes (of production) spells contradictions and conflicts for the populations they encompass." In the 17th and 18th centuries, precisely this type of encounter took place between the French and the Amerindians, with the French participating in a tributary or feudal mode of production and the Amerindians engaged in a mode of production based on kinship relations. Denys Delâge (1985:126) has studied the exchange between the French and Dutch on the one hand and the Amerindian horticulturalists on the other. According to Delâge, modes of production played a crucial role in establishing the dynamics of relations among these different groups. It was because of this that France, still bogged down in its feudal system and economically disadvantaged, was to base its action in good part on the missionaries' evangelization, while Holland with Amsterdam at the center of the world economy would favor capitalist-type relationships. In any case, these encounters between European modes of production, capitalist or tributary (according to the point of view of different authors), and Amerindian modes of production (based on blood ties) were bound to end in conflict, which Delâge has called the unequal exchange—a situation that has endured with all its negative effects to this day.

> The more deeply the Amerindian societies became involved in the exchange, the more they increased their working time, in spite of the acquisition of more efficient tools. Since the development of the forces of production did not enable the Amerindians to reproduce the European goods on their own, subordination to the Europeans constituted the framework on which commercial relations were woven (Delâge 1985:339).

An interpretation of the relations between Europeans and Amerindians in terms of exchange, that is, in economic terms, concurs with the model of capitalism proposed by Immanuel Wallerstein (1980), based on the subjection of the periphery by the center. This explains the tragic destiny experienced by the Amerindian population of North America. However, the strong polarization posited by this recognition of the inequality of the exchange between the French and the Amerindians may color interpretations of the protagonists' behaviors. For example, whereas Delâge (1985:177–178) simply saw in the display and magnificence of church decorations and religious offices a means for missionaries to persuade Amerindians to convert (which was no doubt to a great degree the case), Victor Tapié (1957: 134–136) regarded the opulent European Baroque churches as places where common peoples were admitted to admire the richness of the sanctuaries and to participate in the joy of the Roman Catholic Church's celebrations. These sumptuous architectural and religious productions belong to the Counter-Reformation in the Baroque age, and they cannot be entirely explained in terms of inferiority and superiority.

Beyond the exchange stage comes the stage corresponding to *métissages*; for only after intensive, diversified, and well-assimilated exchanges can there arise conditions propitious to the mixing of cultures. In this line of thought, how the pomp and ceremony of Baroque religious art gave birth to a hybrid peculiar to the autochthonous societies of Iberian America should be recalled, where native art

> blended into the ocean of Mannerist and Baroque forms that eventually inundated town and countryside, contributing its prodigious inventivity and exuberance to a style that very soon became a civilization. The magnification of the image by the Catholic Church and the indigenous tradition, the shared taste for spectacle, recourse to sensual pleasure, and triumph of the senses, of color, of light gave an impulse to Baroque America, the mirror of all the *métissages*, past and present (Gruzinski 1991:222).

Inferiority of the Amerindians? Superiority of the Europeans? The issue cannot be approached in these terms; new identities had been negotiated and were expressed through new mixed forms, both among the natives and among the *métis* and Creoles of the colony. To go back to the initial question, that of the colonial origins of New France, it is clear that *métissages* offer a very important lead since it is through them that the deep effects of mutual connections can be identified but also understood better with respect to mental universes.

The Baroque

Most basic anthropology textbooks discuss the mechanisms of rejection or acceptance of cultural elements from one cultural system to another. One condition for the acceptance of a cultural element is that the host system must be able to integrate the element into its functioning or its structure by making a place for it—a place that does not necessarily correspond to what it was intended for at its conception. This is equally true for cultural elements invented inside a cultural system and for those transferred from one system to another. When we consider a cultural complex, for example, a system of beliefs, a mode of exploiting the environment, or even representations of the world through decorative arts, the same principles still apply but with an incomparably higher degree of complexity. Thus, for a transfer of cultural elements or complexes to be effected from a transmitting group to a receiving group (and in the case of North America where the roles of transmitter and receiver were shared by each of the groups), there must exist favorable conditions for such cultural transfers and the changes that necessarily come with them. These conditions are three in number. First, each group must have a motive or a basic motivation that colors its undertakings. For the French, this motivation can be summed up in three words: commerce, evangelization, and power. For the Amerindians, it is clear that such motives included commerce and power linked to the acquisition of European goods and technologies. Second, the encounters, contacts, and exchanges must create a certain instability, indeed even a state of crisis, between the two groups involved so that the cultural systems become more flexible and more open to change. And third, the two communicating cultural systems must show a certain compatibility with one another, a compatibility expressed less in the content than in the structure of mental universes, with all the ensuing consequences this may have for the world vision of each, the relation to the Other, and the negotiation of each one's own identity.

It is the third condition, the compatibility of the mental universes of the actors involved, that is favored here as a research path. In order to evaluate this compatibility or noncompatibility, it is first necessary to describe mentalities, define their main characteristics, and establish their general outlines.

At the end of the 15th century and during the first half of the 16th century, the Indians of the Caribbean and Mexico met and were conquered by the Spaniards who were, in fact, men of the Renaissance, still caught up in the spirit of their combats against the Moors. One hundred years later, the Amerindians of northeastern North America had to deal with French people who were experiencing the jolts of capitalist expansion and the tensions accompanying the Protestant Reformation and the Catholic Counter-Reformation. The French-Amerindian meeting took place at the height of the Baroque age, described by historian Johan Huizinga as a vast complex of ideas that, while not necessarily well defined, cumulatively expressed the essence of civilization in the 17th century.

> Now painting, poetry, literature, even politics and theology, in short, every field of skill and learning in the 17th century, have to measure up to some preconceived idea of "the Baroque." Some apply the term to the beginning of the epoch, when men delighted in colourful and exuberant imagination; others to a later period of sombre stateliness and solemn dignity. But, taken by and large, it evokes visions of conscious exaggeration, of something imposing, overawing, colossal, avowedly unreal. Baroque forms are, in the fullest sense of the word, art-forms (Huizinga 1971:208).

The Baroque paradigm, born in reaction to the Protestant Reformation, had at its center an obsession with reconciling the human with the divine. For Roman Catholics, God was present on Earth in a perceptible way, while for Protestants he could be reached only through his Word. Consequently, the spirit of Roman Catholicism was strongly characterized by the reconciliation of contraries, the absorption of difference, and the resolution of the tensions between reality and appearance. To express this fundamental tension between two poles, the Baroque offered a performance of the world, often exuberant and sometimes outrageous, in which theatricality and rhetorical figures sought to persuade the spectator through a sensation of being engulfed or of stupefaction. As expressed by Claude-Gilbert Dubois (1995:15), the "fundamental principle of Baroque imagination is the search for unity through the irrepressible duality related to the human condition."

In France the Baroque evolved in opposition to Classicism. However, the two art styles were so intertwined that, at the level of stylistic typology, modern authors no longer agree on what was Baroque and what was Classical, to the point that Tapié (1957:238) has spoken of "Classicism on a Baroque background," and Robert Muchembled (1995) of the "Baroque temptation." C-G Dubois's proposal on this subject appears most valuable to the line of thought pursued here, since he brings together under the Baroque label both baroquism and classicism, considering them "as internal movements, oscillatory and indissociable, which are nourished by one another, through conjunction or reaction, depending on the period and the country" (Dubois 1995:15). This debate need not concern us since it was the segments of society nearest to the Baroque spirit, according to Muchembled (1995:145–147), who formed substantial ingredients of the colonial society that emerged in New France—the Jesuits, the military, and the hired hands among the lower classes. In fact, a migrant stream emanated largely from the "France of the margins," open to the Atlantic space, trading and adventurous, described by Braudel.

The Baroque in New France

With respect to the history of New France, the term "Baroque" has been used almost exclusively by art historians and then only sparingly until recently; the expression "French Classical style" is much more prevalent. Although hesitant yet to talk about a "Baroque New France," the few studies carried out so far on some of the material stored in the basement of the King's Stores in Québec City during the first half of the 18th century seem to lead towards such an interpretation. The study of a collection of 21 brass religious medallions of three different types from that site (Figure 1), along with those already studied by Charles Rinehart (1990) for the Great Lakes region and the Mississippi Valley and some others from the St. Lawrence Valley, has revealed unequivocal affinities between Counter-Reformation spirituality, Baroque representations, and the Amerindian world view (Moussette 2002). The result is a collection of 84 medallions dug from more than 15 different sites, most of them made of coppery metals much appreciated by the Amerindians. The nature of these sites and

TYPE I

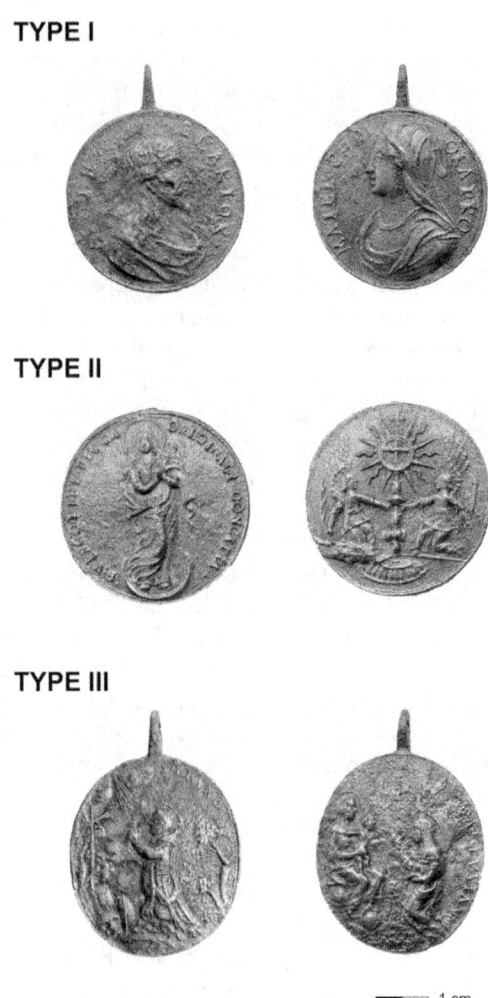

TYPE II

TYPE III

■——— 1 cm

FIGURE 1. The three types of religious medallions found on the site of the Intendant's Palace in Québec City. (*A*) Type I: obverse, Christ; reverse, the Virgin Mary. (*B*) Type II: obverse, Immaculate Conception; reverse, two angels holding a monstrance. (*C*) Type III: obverse, St. Bruno; reverse, St. Rosalina offering a rose to the Virgin Mary and the Christ child. (Photo by Lise Jodoin; computer graphics by Andrée Héroux.)

FIGURE 2. Sites of the French Regime where religious medallions and trade gun parts have been excavated. (Drawing by Andrée Héroux.)

their very wide distribution (Figure 2) demonstrate that from the medallions' point of arrival in New France (at the site of the Intendant's Palace in Québec City), they were transported, in some cases via a portage trail (Pointe-du-Buisson), towards French settlements (Ouiatenon), Amerindian villages (Guebert), and some fur trade posts (Frontenac, St. Joseph, Michilimackinac) as well as missions (St. Marie I, La Prairie, Marquette). The medallions might accompany deceased Amerindians on their final journey, since some

of the medallions have been found in burials (Rock Island, Lasanen).

Counter-Reformation spirituality is shown in three main ways through the motifs molded on the obverse and reverse of these medallions. First, there is the fundamental theme of Christ's incarnation and his true presence on Earth, which is represented by the adoration of the Holy Sacrament (Figure 1*B*, two angels holding a Monstrance); the head and shoulder of Christ viewed in profile, often accompanied on the reverse by his mother shown in the same way (Figure 1*A*); and by certain aspects of Jesus Christ's life or by persons of his entourage (the Holy Family, Mary Magdalen, the apostles, etc.). A second set of representations is mostly characterized by Baroque theatricality, either related to the rapture of ecstasy (Figure 1*C*, St. Bruno; Figure 3, St. Theresa of Avila) or to physical pain (the descent from the Cross and the martyrs Venantius, Agatha, Barbara, and Lucia). Third, certain obverse and reverse images represent to the Amerindian, whether baptized or about to be converted, the devotions

Perspectives from *Historical Archaeology*

FIGURE 3. The ecstasy of St. Theresa of Avila: (A) medallion from Michilimackinac (drawing by Marcel Moussette); (B) sculpture by Bernini (Santa Maria della Vittoria, Rome).

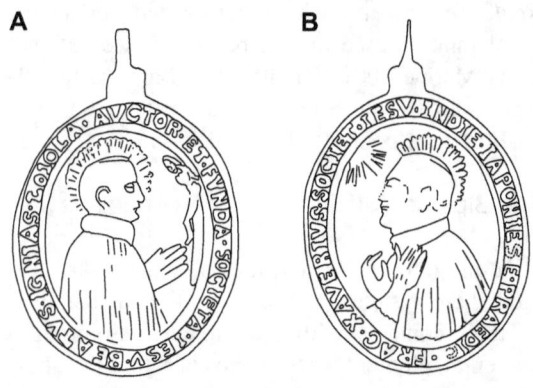

FIGURE 4. New saints of the Counter-Reformation: (A) Ignatius of Loyola; (B) Francis Xavier. Obverse and reverse of a medallion found on the site of St. Marie among the Hurons. (Drawing by Marcel Moussette.)

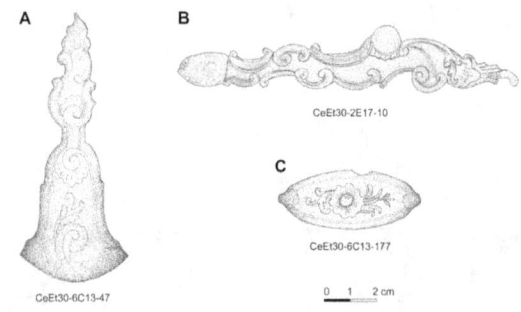

CeEt30-2E17-10

CeEt30-6C13-177

CeEt30-6C13-47

0 1 2 cm

FIGURE 5. Brass trade gun parts from the site of the Intendant's Palace in Québec City decorated in the Rococo style: (A) buttplate finial (CeEt-30-6C13-47); (B) sideplate (CeEt-30-2E17-10); (C) trigger guard (CeEt-30-6C13-177). (Drawing by Alain Delisle; computer graphics by Andrée Héroux.)

of the Counter-Reformation (the Sacred Hearts and, Figure 1B, the Immaculate Conception); and the new saints of the Church, many of them linked to the Jesuit order: Bruno, Ignatius of Loyola, Francis of Sales, John Capistrano, John of the Cross, Francis Xavier, John Francis Regis, Theresa of Avila, and Rosa of Lima (Figure 4).

Comparable results have been obtained from a collection of more than 2,000 iron and brass trade gun parts—trigger guards, butt plates, side plates, and ramrod holders (Figure 5) with incised decorations in the purest Rococo style. These gun parts were uncovered in Québec City from the rubble of the King's Stores, destroyed during the battle of the spring of 1760 (Moussette 2001). The Rococo style was used to decorate firearms made between 1735 and 1790 (Gusler and Lavin 1977:2) and may be considered the ultimate stage of the Baroque style. It is characterized by a subtle and lively grace that materializes in the asymmetry of flowing scrolls and the interlacing of vegetal and shell motifs, producing forms in constant metamorphosis. Generally, this ornamental style is found on the very fine guns of European aristocrats, on "the most beautiful firearms of that period" (Venner 1979:72–73; Gaier and Sabatti 1998). In regard to the collection from the site of the Intendant's Palace, the decorations are incised in brass or iron instead of being embossed or embellished with gold or silver damascening, so these are certainly more common objects, acquired for a cheaper price. But the fact remains that the work of the gunsmiths is of good quality; firearms that bore such parts could very well be considered "fine guns." An important fact revealed by the study of this collection is the vast distribution of gun parts decorated in the Rococo style on sites occupied by Amerindians and the French, from the North Shore of the Gulf of St. Lawrence to the Great Lakes to the Mississippi Valley (Figure 2). Apart from Québec City, most of the sites where such gun parts have been recovered are Amerindian sites (Old Kaskaskia, Angola Farm, Malta Bend, Nevada, and Trudeau), or fur trade posts (Michilimackinac, St. Joseph, Pontchartrain, Sept-Îles), as well as one undetermined site, Bay City (Moussette 2001:69–70). Consequently, it is plausible to think that these objects were intended for exchange in the fur trade, as ornaments on the "trade guns" used by the Amerindians that are mentioned in archival documents,

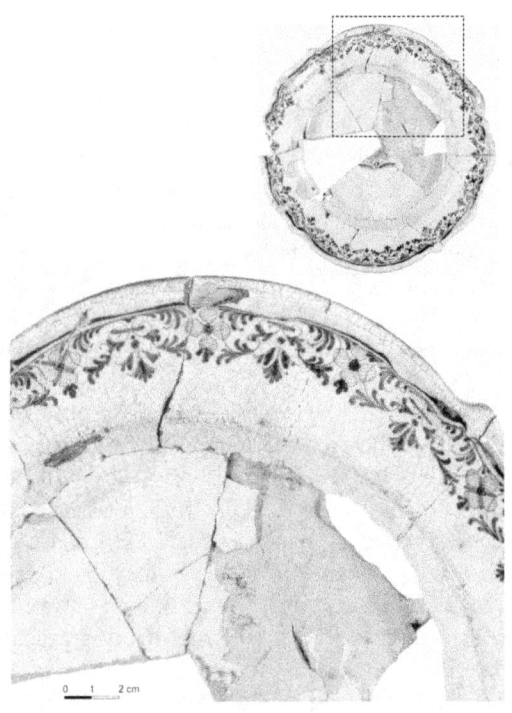

FIGURE 6. Moustiers style faïence platter (CeEt-30-27D82-1) from the site of the Intendant's Palace, Québec City. (Photo by Lise Jodoin; computer graphics by Andrée Héroux.)

without ever being described precisely by French merchants or administrators.

The presence of the Baroque has been attested to in many other cultural elements of New France. Music had an important place in the work of evangelization by the missionaries, and Baroque music was certainly known to the Amerindians of New France, as demonstrated by the recent discovery of a manuscript score of Baroque inspiration to which words in the Abnaki language were added (Pacquier 1996; P-A Dubois 1997). Religious paintings and prints were part of the propaganda used by Counter-Reformation agents seeking to "civilize" the Amerindians and persuade them to convert to the Catholic faith. Different categories of pottery decorated in the Baroque and Rococo styles, especially the faïence of Moustiers and Rouen (Figure 6) as well as the gray German stonewares, have been unearthed on Amerindian sites and French advanced posts (Neitzel 1965; Brain 1979; Walthall 1991; Genêt 1996; Gaimster 1997). Carved wooden statues and altar screens were often gilded with gold leaf in the workshops of the Ursuline and Augustine

nuns in Québec City and Montréal (Porter 1975). The nuns, who embroidered altar cloths and sacerdotal vestments with silk, silver, and gold threads in the Baroque style, also taught their craft to Indian girls (as well as taking care of sick Amerindians). Wrought-iron work in this style is best exemplified by Lozeau's crosses (Figure 7) with the double-curve motif, one of which stood above the chapel of the Chicoutimi Indian mission. In fact, this artistic and decorative production was used as an instrument of Baroque theatricality, laid out before the eyes of the Amerindians to impress them and convince them of the superiority of French civilization. All these elements were demonstrations of power, albeit on a smaller scale but not all that different from the fantastic gilded Baroque decorations of tall galleys (such as the *Grande Reale de France*), which transported persons of royal rank (Musée du Québec et Musée national de la Marine 2001), or the great Baroque festivities given by the Sun King and other monarchs of European courts (Alewyn 1964).

The Bipartite Ideology of the Amerindians

Turning to the Amerindians, what characterized their systems of representation at the time of their contacts with the French? Some fundamental elements in the answer to this question are found in one of Claude Lévi-Strauss's (1991) most recent books, *Histoire de Lynx*. In this general study of Amerindian myths of the Pacific Northwest Coast, Lévi-Strauss recounted a myth concerning the origin of wind and mist, the first represented by Coyote and the second by Lynx. Through the intrigues of this mis-

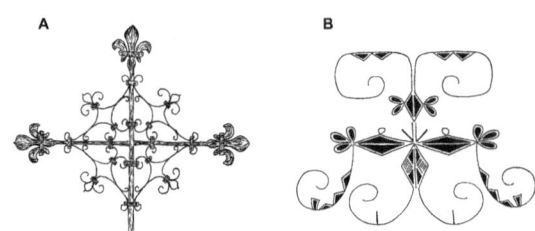

FIGURE 7. (*A*) Iron cross at the Ursuline convent in Québec City made by Jean-Baptiste Lozeau (drawing by Marcel Moussette); (*B*) Penobscot double-curve design (Speck 1914: figure 5a). (Computer graphics by Andrée Héroux.)

matched couple or pair, Lévi-Strauss recognizes, as he has elsewhere as well, the impossible or paradoxical twinness that serves as a basis for the bipartite ideology of the Amerindians. Indeed, from the imbalance and the disparity that govern the pair's relationship, there arise dynamics of difference, of opening up to the Other and to the World, which characterize the mental universe of the Amerindians. It is thus, according to the author, an unstable dualism, one from which there "always results another unstable dualism" (Lévi-Strauss 1991:306) or "a dualism in perpetual imbalance, the successive states of which fit into each other" (Lévi-Strauss 1991:316).

But the structures generated by the bipartite ideology are not only found in mythology. They also have been recognized in an ancient ornamental tradition of bilateral symmetry, which Franz Boas (1955:32, 223–244) identified among the Amerindians of the Northwest Coast of Canada and which, according to Rémi Savard (1969), is spread all over America and in many other regions of the world. From this ornamental tradition of bilateral symmetry, the botanist-ethnologist Jacques Rousseau (1956) derived the double-curve motif (Figure 8) that had been studied by Franck G. Speck (1914). This motif, based on the principle that "one half maintains with the other a mirrored relation" (Savard 1977:29–30), has its main expression among the Algonkians of the Northeast. In spite of the fact that no example of this

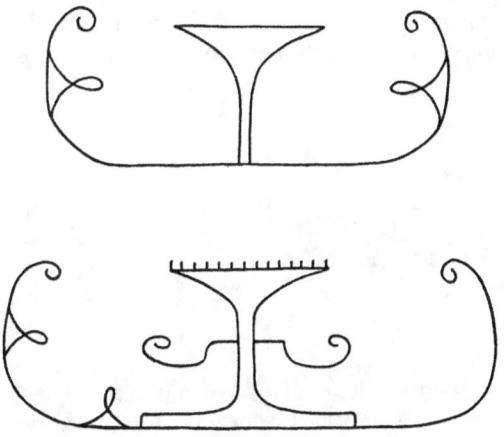

FIGURE 8. Micmac double-curve motif (Speck 1914: figure 9).

style has been found so far on objects dating from the prehistoric period, some historians and anthropologists (Guy 1969; Savard 1969, 1977; Dickason 1974; Phillips 1987:61; Whitehead 1987:42) have seen in it an ancient indigenous ornamental tradition. In this, they were no doubt influenced by Speck (1914) who established the vast distribution of this motif, which spread from the Northeast to the Iroquoians of the East, to the nations of the Northwest, as well to the Algonkians of the central and upper Mississippi Valley regions. In fact, Camil Guy (1969:18) and Olive Dickason (1974:38) thought that the double-curve style, because of its formal polyvalence, could have constituted a link between the ancient geometric style and the vegetal style introduced by the Europeans. Actually, it cannot be concluded with certainty that the double-curve ornamentation existed before the arrival of the Europeans. It is known that this motif was used on European-made objects in the 17th and 18th centuries in conjunction with floral ornamentation. However, for our purposes, what is important is not to determine if the double-curve motif is of Amerindian or European origin but, rather, what its use by both peoples tells us about their bipartite representation of the world.

To return to the original question, it could, at this stage in our reflection, be proposed that the duality characterizing the mental universes of both the French and the Amerindians of the Northeast created a fertile middle ground for cultural *métissages* and transfers between the two groups. In this way the French and Amerindians, caught in the meshes of the net set by the capitalist world system, had to adapt to the conditions created by unequal exchange and accommodate their cultural systems, one to the other. These processes of accommodation and of adaptation, so well analyzed by Richard White (1991:10), of mixing and blending, are at the origin of all cultural *métissages*.

Conclusion

In conclusion, a few cases of such *métissages* will be outlined. The double-curve motif and the vegetal ornamentation that replaced it were ornamental motifs appropriated by Amerindians who reproduced them in paintings and as embroideries made with glass beads or porcupine quills on clothes or other ordinary objects. But they are also found in the repertory of Baroque decoration, on embroidered altar screens, faïence plates and stoneware containers, gun parts, and even wrought-iron crosses. This should not come as too much of a surprise, since Euro-American and European folk art traditions also show a binary structure very much akin to the Amerindian bilateral symmetry.

> Through the utilization of different patterns in a single artifact, a complex, over-all design can be accomplished, but the thinking in the design of folk ornamentation (or in the performance of folksong or tale) does not often go beyond repetition, with bilateral symmetry being a special case of repetition. And it does not often go beyond variation in terms of the number two, with three being a special case of two, when two of the three elements form a pair (Glassie 1972:272).

For example, it is interesting to compare the complex execution of the double-curve motif in two different objects—the cross that surmounted the Québec Ursulines chapel in 1724 (Dupont 1979:90) and the collar-cape worn by a Penobscot chief during a funerary ceremony (Figure 7). While the iron cross shows a perfect symmetry in all directions, the Penobscot motif, also cruciform, is symmetrical only bilaterally, showing a clear asymmetry from top to bottom. From a symbolic viewpoint, the Ursulines' cross with its stylized fleur-de-lys proclaims the Gallic character of the institution, while the motif on the Penobscot collar-cape signifies the central place for mourning the deceased chief. Finally, in spite of their strong geometrical compositions, the two motifs show vegetal elements: the fleur-de-lys in the case of the Ursulines' cross, and leaves and boughs in the case of the Penobscot collar-cape. The mingling of these elements clearly exemplifies how the morphology of the double-curve ornamentation fitted very naturally between the geometrical and the floral or vegetal stylistic traditions. Another example of the same sort is a Pottawatomi glass-bead and porcupine-quill embroidery decoration, whose central motif is a flower flanked by symmetrical boughs bearing flowers and leaves (Figure 9). A similar composition is found engraved on a brass trigger guard from the 1760 destruction context of the King's Stores in Québec City (Moussette 2001), with a central motif consisting of a Rococo shell with one leafy bough on each side (Figure 9). Could this not be seen

as expressing the construction of a renewed identity resulting from exchanges and alliances with the Europeans? The same question might be asked about Amerindian stories and myths incorporating traditional French-Canadian tales in which the hero "Ti-Jean" (Little John), the famous trickster, is associated with Coyote, another great trickster, paired with Lynx (Lévi-Strauss 1991; Jacquin 1996). In the same vein, a recent article by the ethnologist Jean-Pierre Pichette (1995) demonstrates how the tale entitled "Le Lynx et le Renard" (The Lynx and the Fox), now incorporated in the oral tradition of the Ojibways of northern Ontario, is in fact a French-Canadian tale coming from a more ancient French oral tradition.

The French of New France also had to rethink and renegotiate their identity. By the end of the 17th century, they were already referring to themselves as *Canadiens*. The study of French colonial sites in light of this question of construction of identity and of *métissages* has barely begun. However, Hélène Côté (2001), who has done such a study for one of the sites dug under the author's supervision on Île aux Oies, has already been able to point out a few identity markers, such as stone pipes decorated in the Amerindian fashion but made locally by *Canadien* settlers as well as a preference for game over the meat of domestic animals. Also, very recently, on the site of the Jesuit's mission of La Prairie de la Magdeleine, some archaeological contexts have been discovered that are culturally so mixed that so far it can not be decided if they were French or Amerindian. The hunch is that they are hybrid.

These avenues of research seem promising enough and certainly deserve to be pursued using

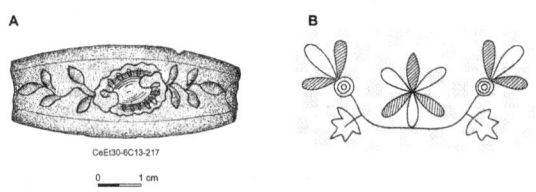

FIGURE 9. (*A*) Brass trigger guard (CeEt-30-6C13-217) found on the site of the Intendant's Palace in Québec City (drawing by Alain Delisle); (*B*) Pottawatomi double-curve design (Speck 1914: figure 23). (Computer graphics by Andrée Héroux.)

the conceptual framework just outlined. However, it must be confessed that the scope and complexity of such a research project present quite an overwhelming challenge. For any success in reaching a solution to the problem will depend on an eclectic marshalling of extremely diverse resources from the history of art, social history, the history of mentalities, anthropology, and refined archaeometric analyses, in addition to classic archaeological approaches linked to spatial, chronological, and typological analysis.

ACKNOWLEDGMENTS

I am very grateful to the persons who were involved in one way or another in the production of this article: Bonnie G. McEwan and Gregory A. Waselkov, who invited me to participate in the plenary session at the 2002 Society for Historical Archaeology Conference in Mobile, where a first version of this article was read; Jane Macaulay, who revised my sometime laborious English; Lise Jodoin, who photographed some of the artifacts; Alain Delisle, who drew the gun parts; Andrée Héroux, who created the computer graphics; and Clara Marceau, who typed the text. This research was financed in part by the City of Québec and Laval University through an agreement with the Ministère de la Culture et des Communications du Québec. I should also mention the important role played by Célat (Centre d'études sur la langue, les arts et la tradition), which provided me with a favorable and creative intellectual environment.

REFERENCES

ALEWYN, RICHARD
1964 *L'univers du baroque.* Éditions Gonthier, Geneva, Switzerland.

AXTELL, JAMES
1988 *After Columbus: Essays in the Ethnohistory of Colonial North America.* Oxford University Press, New York.

BOAS, FRANZ
1955 *Primitive Art.* Dover Publications, New York.

BRAIN, JEFFREY P.
1979 Tunica Treasure. *Papers of the Peabody Museum of Archaeology and Ethnology, 71.* Harvard University, Cambridge, MA.

BRAUDEL, FERNAND
1979 *Le temps du monde: Civilisation matérielle, économie et capitalisme, vol. 3.* Armand Collin, Paris, France.
1997 Expansion européenne et capitalisme (1450–1650). In *Les ambitions de l'histoire: Les écrits de Fernand Braudel, vol. 2,* Roselyne de Ayala and Paule Braudel, editors, pp. 299–345. Éditions de Fallois, Paris, France.

CÔTÉ, HÉLÈNE
2001 Le site de la Nouvelle Ferme à l'Île aux Oies. Doctoral dissertation (Archéologie), Département d'histoire, Université Laval, Québec, PQ.

DAVIS, NATALIE ZEMON
2001 Polarities, Hybridities: What Strategies for Decentering? In *Decentering the Renaissance: Canada and Europe in Multidisciplinary Perspective, 1500–1700,* G. Warkentin and C. Podruchny, editors, pp. 19–32. University of Toronto Press, Toronto, ON.

DELÂGE, DENYS
1985 *Le pays renversé.* Boréal Express, Montréal, PQ.

DICKASON, OLIVE P.
1974 *Indian Arts in Canada.* Indian and Northern Affairs, Ottawa, ON.

DUBOIS, CLAUDE-GILBERT
1995 *Le baroque en Europe et en France.* Presses universitaires de France, Paris, France.

DUBOIS, PAUL-ANDRÉ
1997 Naissance du cantique en langue vernaculaire dans les missions de la Nouvelle-France et conquête des langues amérindiennes. *Recherches amérindiennes au Québec,* 27 (2):19–31.

DUPONT, JEAN-CLAUDE
1979 *L'artisan forgeron.* Les Presses de l'Université Laval, Québec, PQ.

FOX, EDWARD WHITING
1971 *History in a Geographic Perspective: The Other France.* Norton, New York.

GAIER, CLAUDE, AND DE PIETRO SABATTI
1998 *Les plus belles gravures d'armes de chasse.* Hatier, Paris, France.

GAIMSTER, DAVID
1997 *German Stoneware, 1200–1900.* British Museum Press, London, UK.

GENÊT, NICOLE
1996 La faïence de Place Royale. *Collection patrimoine, dossier 45.* Ministère de la Culture et des Communications, Québec, PQ.

GLASSIE, HENRY
1972 Folk Art. In *Folklore and Folklife: An Introduction,* Richard M. Dordson, editor, pp. 253–280. University of Chicago Press, Chicago, IL.

GRUZINSKI, SERGE
1991 *L'Amérique de la conquête peinte par les Indiens du Mexique.* Flammarion, Paris, France.

GUSLER, WALLACE B., AND JAMES D. LAVIN
1977 *Decorated Fire Arms, 1540–1870, from the Collections of Clay P. Bedford.* Colonial Williamsburg Foundation, Williamsburg, VA.

GUY, CAMIL
1969 L'Art décoratif des Indiens de l'Est. *Culture vivante,* 14:9–18.

HUIZINGA, JOHAN
1971 *Homo Ludens.* Paladin, London, UK.

JACQUIN, PHILIPPE
1996 *Les Indiens blancs.* Libre Expression, Montréal, PQ.

LÉVI-STRAUSS, CLAUDE
1991 *Histoire de Lynx.* Plon, Paris, France.

MOUSSETTE, MARCEL
2001 Les garnitures de fusils de traite des magasins du roi à Québec: un autre chemin de l'univers baroque en Amérique du Nord. *Archéologiques,* 14:50–78.
2002 Les médailles religieuses, une forme de l'imagerie baroque en Nouvelle-France. *Les Cahiers des Dix,* 55:295–329.

MUCHEMBLED, ROBERT
1995 *Culture et société en France du début du XVIe siècle au milieu du XVIIe siècle.* Sedes, Paris, France.

MUSÉE DU QUÉBEC ET MUSÉE NATIONAL DE LA MARINE
2001 *Les génies de la mer.* Musée du Québec, Québec, PQ, and Musée National de la Marine, Paris, France.

NEITZEL, ROBERT S.
1965 Archaeology of the Fatherland Site: The Grand Village of the Natchez. *Anthropological Papers of the American Museum of Natural History,* 51(1).

PACQUIER, ALAIN
1996 *Les chemins du baroque dans le Nouveau Monde.* Fayard, Paris, France.

PHILLIPS, RUTH B.
1987 Like a Star I Shine: Northern Woodland Artistic Traditions. In *The Spirit Sings,* Glenbow-Alberta Institute, editor, pp. 51–92. McCelland and Stewart, Toronto, ON.

PICHETTE, JEAN-PIERRE
1995 Le Lynx et le Renard: Un relais déroutant dans la transmission du conte populaire français en Ontario. *Cahiers Charlevoix,* 6:169–240.

PORTER, JOHN A.
1975 *L'art de la dorure au Québec du XVIIe siècle à nos jours.* Éditions Garneau, Québec, PQ.

RINEHART, CHARLES J.
1990 Crucifixes and Medallions: Their Role at Fort Michilimackinac. *Volumes in Historical Archaeology,* 11. South Carolina Institute of Archaeology and Anthropology, University of South Carolina, Columbia.

ROUSSEAU, JACQUES
1956 L'origine du motif de la double courbe dans l'art algonkin. *Anthropologica,* (2):218–221.

SAVARD, RÉMI
1969 Les Indiens de l'Est du Canada et leur art. In *Chefs-d'oeuvre des arts indiens et esquimaux du Canada,* n.p. Société des amis du Musée de l'Homme, Paris, France.
1977 *Destins d'Amérique, les autochtones et nous.* L'hexagone, Montréal, PQ.

SPECK, FRANK G.
1914 The Double-Curve Motive in Northeastern Algonkian Art. In *Geological Survey of Canada, Memoir 42 (No. 1 of the Anthropological Series).* Department of Mines, Ottawa, ON.

TAPIÉ, VICTOR L.
1957 *Baroque et classicisme.* Plon, Paris, France.

VENNER, DOMINIQUE
1979 *Les armes à feu françaises.* Jacques Grancher, Paris, France.

WALLERSTEIN, IMMANUEL
1980 *The Modern World-System II: Mercantilism and the Consolidation of the European World-Economy, 1600–1750.* Academic Press, New York.

WALTHALL, JOHN A.
1991 French Colonial Fort Massac: Architecture and Ceramic Patterning. In *French Colonial Archaeology: The Illinois Country and the Western Great Lakes.* John A. Walthall, editor, pp. 42–64. University of Illinois Press, Urbana.

WHITE, RICHARD
1991 *The Middle Ground: Indians, Empires, and Republics in the Great Lakes Region, 1650–1815.* Cambridge University Press, Cambridge, UK.

WHITEHEAD, RUTH H.
1987 I Have Lived Here Since the World Began: Atlantic Coast Artistic Traditions. In *The Spirit Sings,* Glenbow-Alberta Institute editor, p. 17–49. McClelland and Stewart, Toronto, ON.

WOLF, ERIC
1982 *Europe and the People without History.* University of California Press, Berkeley.

MARCEL MOUSSETTE
CÉLAT, DÉPARTEMENT D'HISTOIRE
UNIVERSITÉ LAVAL
QUÉBEC, QUÉBEC, CANADA
G1K 7P4

Gaynell Stone

Sacred Landscapes: Material Evidence of Ideological and Ethnic Choice in Long Island, New York, Gravestones, 1680–1800

ABSTRACT

Long Island grave markers from the 17th and 18th centuries are examined and analyzed. Due to its strategic location, between the English culture sphere of New England and the "Dutch" culture sphere of New Amsterdam/New York, Long Island is an excellent laboratory for studying cultural recombination in various forms of material culture. Long Island has no quarryable stone, so all colonial gravestones, except fieldstone markers, were imported from New England, New Jersey, or New York City. This study found a different pattern of motifs for Long Island compared to New England, but memorialization by status was more like that of New England than Virginia. Ideological, social, and ethnic boundaries are demonstrated. Location or proximity to a culture sphere also played a role in choice of grave marker, as did customary trade networks. More than 4,300 stones were photographed and statistically analyzed; the data are of use to scholars in many fields.

Introduction

Long Island is one of the earliest settlement centers of northeastern North America and one of the least studied scientifically. It is geographically located between the New England and Mid-Atlantic culture hearths. Politically, it was originally part of New Netherland, which was the most ethnically diverse early settlement in the New World. Long Island occupies a strategic area at the confluence of numerous waterways—the Hudson River of New York, the Connecticut and other rivers of Connecticut, the eastern rivers of New Jersey—and it is just above the Mid-Atlantic waterways, all prime trade routes (Figure 1). As a morainal deposit, Long Island contained no quarryable stone; as such, it is a transition zone, a laboratory of cultural recombination whose gravestones were imported from numerous sources in New England and several areas of New Netherland/New York.

Because of its location on the Atlantic coastal plain, its siting that fostered trade networks throughout the region, its position between competing polities and culture spheres, and its polyethnic social composition, Long Island contains the largest number of different types of gravestones—materials, designs, sources—in the Northeast, if not the country. For this study, 164 cemeteries were located, and data from more than 4,300 stones were recorded and analyzed. This fortuitous circumstance provides a sizable material culture database to examine for colonial ethnic, ideological, and cultural choices.

Historical Background

Long Island is one of the earliest colonized areas of the Northeast, shortly after the early "Dutch" colonists (actually Flemish Walloons) settled in Manhattan in the early 1600s. The west end Brooklyn/Kings County colonists, primarily from the Lowlands of Europe, were there in the 1620s and spilled eastward into Queens County by the 1640s. The east end (Suffolk County) was settled by the English coming from New England in 1640 and later; there was an interface of these varying cultural forces in mid-Long Island (eastern Queens, now Nassau County, and western Suffolk). Long Island's settlement history stems from the political and social complexion of the founding colonists—their ethnicity or national origin, religious beliefs or ideology, and time of settlement, which was often related to the political arena in Europe. The gravestone record of this settlement history will be discussed below.

Politically, Long Island was a major geographical portion of early New Netherland, which stretched north from the Delaware River, through New Jersey, up both sides of the Hudson River to Fort Orange (now Albany), and west along the Mohawk River (Figure 1). Eastern Long Island was peopled by the third wave of Puritan emigration to America and was the outpost of Puritan and Pilgrim territorial ambitions. New Netherland was polycultural from the beginning, with 18 languages spoken in New Amsterdam (Jameson 1909:259), making

FIGURE 1. New Netherland. (from Blackburn and Piwonka 1988.)

it the earliest, most ethnically diverse colony. After the English takeover in 1664, brief Dutch rule in 1673, then final English control in 1674 through English/Dutch negotiation in Europe, all non-English were subsumed under the category "Dutch." That included Flemish, Belgian Walloons, French Huguenots, Scandinavians, Irish, Scots (who inscribed on stones their natal land so as not to be confused with the English), Germans, as well as those from various Lowland provinces, later known as Holland. There were some Turks and Polish

Perspectives from *Historical Archaeology*

(who left no material record), Italians (who did), Jews (only in Manhattan), and enslaved Africans, freedmen, and Native Americans, for whom an extremely sparse mortuary record exists.

The Study Area

Long Island, 120 mi. long by about 20 mi. wide, occupies a strategic spot at the confluence of the Hudson and other rivers between New England and the Mid-Atlantic. This location facilitated easy access to prime trade routes and, thus, cultural influences. The island became a repository for various forms of material culture, such as architecture, gravestones, place names, and surnames. With no quarryable stone, all colonial gravestones, except those of local fieldstone, were imported from stone cutters in Boston and Plymouth, Massachusetts; Newport, Rhode Island; New Haven, the river towns, and eastern Connecticut in the English sphere of cultural influence. From the "Dutch" sphere, stones were obtained from Newark and Elizabeth, New Jersey and New Amsterdam/New York City, whose stone came from the New Jersey quarries (Figure 2).

Material Culture Research

A material culture artifact, which is original and little modified, composes a sizable universe and is easily quantified for systematic analysis. It has the potential to amplify the documentary record (indeed, gravestones *are* original documents) and provide further insights into a region or a society. As such, cemeteries are museums without walls, harboring a collection of artifacts that are related by their social matrix. Edwin Dethlefsen (1981:137) noted, "the graveyard is a microcosmic material history of the systemic evolution of the living community." He demonstrates this with several Florida cemeteries of varying configurations that are related to their origin and evolution (Dethlefsen and Jensen 1977). Thus, in a family cemetery the gravestones yield the evolution of the family on a micro scale; on the macro scale, the totality of cemeteries reveals regional patterns of human choice affected by social, economic, political, and cultural factors—as on Long Island.

Mortuary material evidence will also be affected by spatial and temporal constraints; all variables change through time. On Long Island, both of these factors affect the cemetery and gravestone record, which also co-varies with the composition of the social group creating it. A study of all cemeteries in an area can indicate patterns that may not be revealed in the study of a few cemeteries or in the documentary record. On this regional scale, culture hearths or spheres of influence may be delineated,

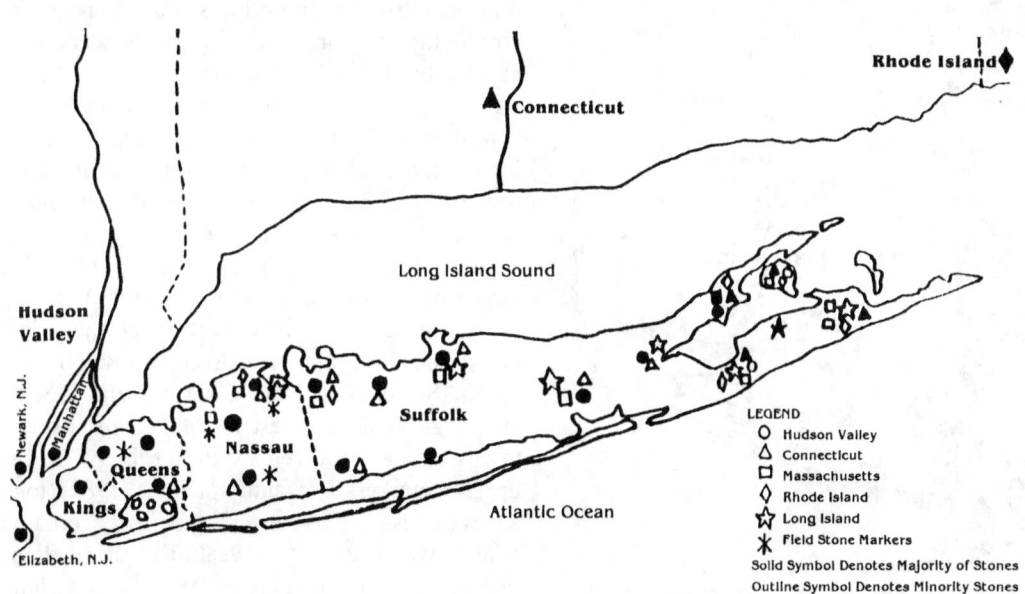

FIGURE 2. Sources of gravestones on Long Island. (from Stone 1991.)

perhaps more finely than by the usual artifact used for this—architecture. An example of this is the evidence of German ethnicity found on gravestones, but not in architecture, in highland North Carolina, the study area of Ruth Little-Stokes (1984).

Analyzing an area's cemeteries and stones will also show the distribution of ethnically and ideologically bounded groups on the landscape, a record that is usually invisible today. For example, historian Patricia Bonomi's map (1971:21) of 17th-century settlement flow in New York shows most cultural influence to the island from New England but truncates the Dutch influence to a small part of Kings County (Figure 3). This division does not reveal the complexity shown by the gravestone evidence. (See author's dissertation (Stone 1987) for the detailed distribution pattern through gravestones of ethnic peoples and ideological groups on Long Island.)

Within an area that appears homogeneous, such as all British-settled New England, antecedent

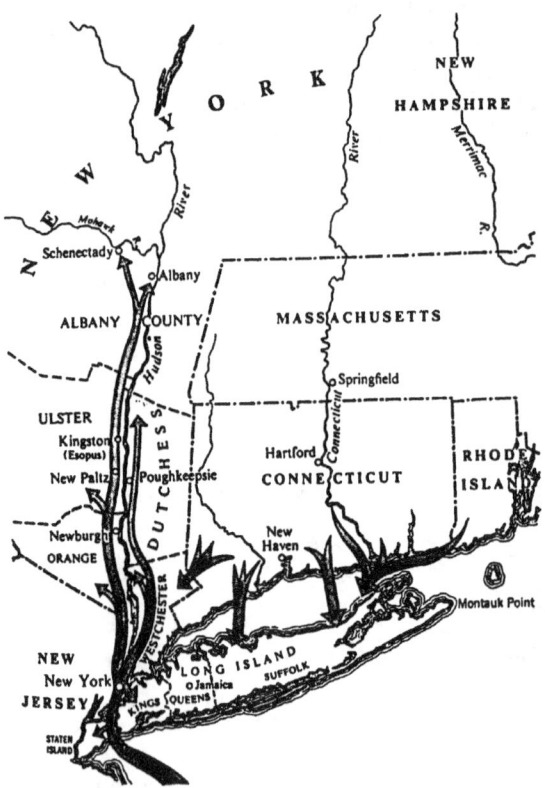

FIGURE 3. Settlement flow in 17th-century New York. (from Bonomi 1971.)

regionality, rather than ethnicity, will surface if looked for. Historians David G. Allen (1981) and Peter Benes (1977) provide the documentary and genealogical evidence of New England's varied regional composition, Benes using the Kentish mortuary designs transplanted to their new Plymouth home. Archaeologists Peter S. Allen (1968) and Anne Yentsch (1981) demonstrate the regionality evidence illustrated by gravestones and fence types as related to surnames on Cape Cod, showing the transplantation of English regional subsistence practices to New England settlement siting.

Two contemporaneous cemeteries in an area can graphically illustrate a social or ideological schism, while two others may exist because of temporal or spatial factors. Leslie Abernathy's (1981) analysis of settling a river system at Rehoboth, Massachusetts, reveals an ideological, and thus social, schism in the cemeteries. Elizabeth Crowell (1981) found that Quaker ideology in Philadelphia allowed the popular culture marker to be used, but it was plain, without a design. The author (Stone 1987:265,310–321) also found this choice for some Long Island Quakers. Her research indicates Long Island cemeteries whose establishment was determined by temporal and spatial factors as well. Either of these occurrences can provide insight into local social dynamics for which the documentary record may be silent. The popular culture stone is defined as the basic types produced in large numbers by the sometimes-multigenerational stone-cutting workshops. Markers were often carved by formula and sometimes stockpiled, with only the inscription carved to order.

Mortuary evidence also illustrates the differing attitudes among regions (and within them) toward wealth, status, power, and occupation. Norman Mackie (1987), upon examining Virginia gravestones, found status distinctly related to gravestone types, such as box or table tombs for the wealthy, the upright marker for the middle class, and none for the classes below. Historian Kevin Sweeney (1985) describes the wealthiest citizens of the western Massachusetts river towns as memorialized by the ordinary regional upright marker. The author (Stone 1987) found an even less status-conscious situation on Long Island, where even the wealthiest original proprietors of manors had cedar posts or simple upright markers. At times memorialization was carried out much later, if at all—sometimes on a monumental scale by descendants, a form of ancestor worship?

Cemeteries and gravestones reveal choice that is culturally, ideologically, and geographically shaped. When all stones are systematically recorded and statistically analyzed—the home-carved "folk" fieldstones as well as the popular culture workshop-produced stones—patterns of differing ethnic and ideological choice may be revealed.

These patterns vary through time both nationally and regionally. (See many issues of the Association for Gravestone Study's journal, *Markers* [1994–2007], for varied national gravestone choices.) While James Deetz's pioneering quantitative gravestone analysis (much of it distilled in *In Small Things Forgotten*, 1977) described one pattern of design motifs for one portion of New England, the regional studies of Dethlefsen and Jensen (1977) in Florida; Crowell in Philadelphia (1981) and in Cape May, New Jersey (1983); Mackie (1987) in Virginia; Sweeney (1985) in Western Massachusetts; Frederick Gorman and Michael DiBlasi (1976) in South Carolina; Little-Stokes (1984) in highland North Carolina; Sophia Hinshalwood (1981) in the Mid-Hudson Valley; Richard Veit (2000, and this volume) in Middlesex County, New Jersey; the author (Stone 1978, 1987, 1990, 1991) in Long Island; Sherene Baugher and Frederick Winter (1983) in New York City; and many others describe the regional variations of gravestone choice and use.

Gorman and DiBlasi's study of two Charleston, South Carolina, cemeteries was the first to include the ethnic gravestone choices in the southeast and northeast. This study is the second to do so, on a larger scale in one region. Other studies of ethnicity reflected in gravestones are Eva Eckert's (1998, 2002) analyses of Moravian acculturation in Texas and ethnic maintenance through the Czech language; Roberta Halporn's (1997a, 1997b) history of American Jewish cemeteries; Thomas Graves's (1998) introduction to Pennsylvania German gravestones; and Gary Collison's (1999) German American gravestones of trans-Susquehanna, Pennsylvania. These studies are all primarily descriptive studies rather than statistical analytical studies.

Those who followed Deetz and Deethlefsen's normative statistical approach are Darrel Norris's

(1988) analysis of Ontario, Canada, gravestones for ethnicity and status as well as other variables; Crowell and Mackie's (1990) study of burial patterns and social status in Tidewater, Virginia, stones; Tadashi Nakagawa's (1994) meta analysis of a sampling of all of Louisiana's cemeteries for regional and ideological variables; Gregory Jeane's (1987) study of "sacred artifacts" in upland south folk cemeteries; and Gary Foster and Richard Hummel's examination (1995) of one cemetery for sociological data. Others have recorded specific aspects of cemeteries and stones, such as Marcy Frampton's (1995) study of North Louisiana grave houses; Richard Welch's (1987) identification of Hudson Valley carvers; Robin Nigh's (1997) search for meaning in motifs in North Florida African American cemeteries; and Scott Baird's (1996) structural linguistic analysis of a cemetery "community" in Texas. These are a scant number of examples of the hundreds of gravestone studies that have been done, both internationally and nationally, and that have enhanced the growing interest in the database of systematic material culture analysis for comparative study in historical archaeology, American studies, cultural geography, history, and other fields.

An early theorist in analyzing material culture, Jules Prown (1982) reviewed the multiple and interrelated elements one must elicit from a material culture object. Material culture research is instructive in this regard; it is a rigorous task. Further cautions on carrying out material culture research, including gravestone, have been outlined by Thomas Schlereth (1985:107–114). Systematic, statistical gravestone research appears to fulfill his requirements of

1. adequate survival of data (stones survive in far larger number than houses or other forms of material culture, thus providing a more normative database);

2. adequate techniques of analysis (provided by complete recording and statistical handling);

3. avoidance of the exaggeration of human efficacy (systematic gravestone studies avoid the usual art history approach of studying the elite or the unusual);

4. avoiding the scholarly tendency toward progressive determinism in American history

(the ubiquity of surviving gravestones when studied normatively can eliminate that bias, although the poor and social subgroups are generally underrepresented in all historical materials); and

5. avoiding the proclivity toward synchronic method (complete recording of an area with stones from a wide time span will provide as much of a diachronic method as possible and thus allow more broadly based interpretation).

Archaeologists who analyze gravestone material culture usually use the approaches outlined above, Deetz and Dethlefsen (1966, 1967; also Dethlefsen and Deetz 1966) being the first to do so. They postulated the three major colonial stone motifs—death's head, cherub, urn and willow—as correlating to changes in Puritan theology and the rise of other religions, a structuralist ideological perspective. Veit (this volume) provides a useful overview of the conflicting theoretical approaches to gravestone choice and change by historians such as David Hall (1977) who denies any connection between style of gravestone and Puritanism, while Cary Carson (1994) sees cultural change fueled by a consumer revolution. As Veit notes, other archaeologists and historians see the cultural shifts as reflecting the growth of mercantile capitalism (Leone 1982), with many theories falling between these poles.

The Long Island Study

Geographically delimited, Long Island offers a naturally circumscribed area in which the universe of stones may be studied holistically, as opposed to study areas based on later geo-political boundaries, which may or may not reflect past settlement. The current four counties—Kings, Queens, Nassau, and Suffolk—were delineated in 1683 by New York's English Governor Andros as Kings, Queens, and Suffolk. Nassau split off from eastern Queens in 1898; for this study, Nassau is noted separately but considered as eastern Queens in the data.

Each of the counties contained townships; each township had a nuclear settlement from which subsequent villages hived off. This settlement pattern produced the chronological dimension of design choice in the cemeteries.

Previously, the author (Stone 1987:310–321) revealed the hierarchy of settlement of each town; this chronological factor is also reflected in gravestone choice. Since the island is a morainal deposit of field boulders from New England, this lack of quarryable stone precipitated the procurement of all stones (in rounded numbers) from Massachusetts at 12% (Figure 4), from Rhode Island at 8% (Figure 5), from Connecticut at 20% (Figure 6), from New Jersey at 27% (Figure 7), and from New Amsterdam/New York City at 2% (Figure 8; also, the category labeled "unknown" is listed at 2%. The stones made from local boulders were usually picked for a gravestone-like shape and lettered with initials and death date; a few were carved to resemble the popular stones (Figure 9b). Some Quakers used popular stones but left the tympanum undecorated, relating to their belief in simplicity (Figure 9a).

The 164 located cemeteries holding 17th- to early-19th-century slate, sandstone, schist, and early marble stones were photographed and

FIGURE 4. Rhode Island grave marker carved by John Stevens II for John Sands (d. 1712), Sands Cemetery, Sands Point, Nassau County. (Photo by author, 1987.)

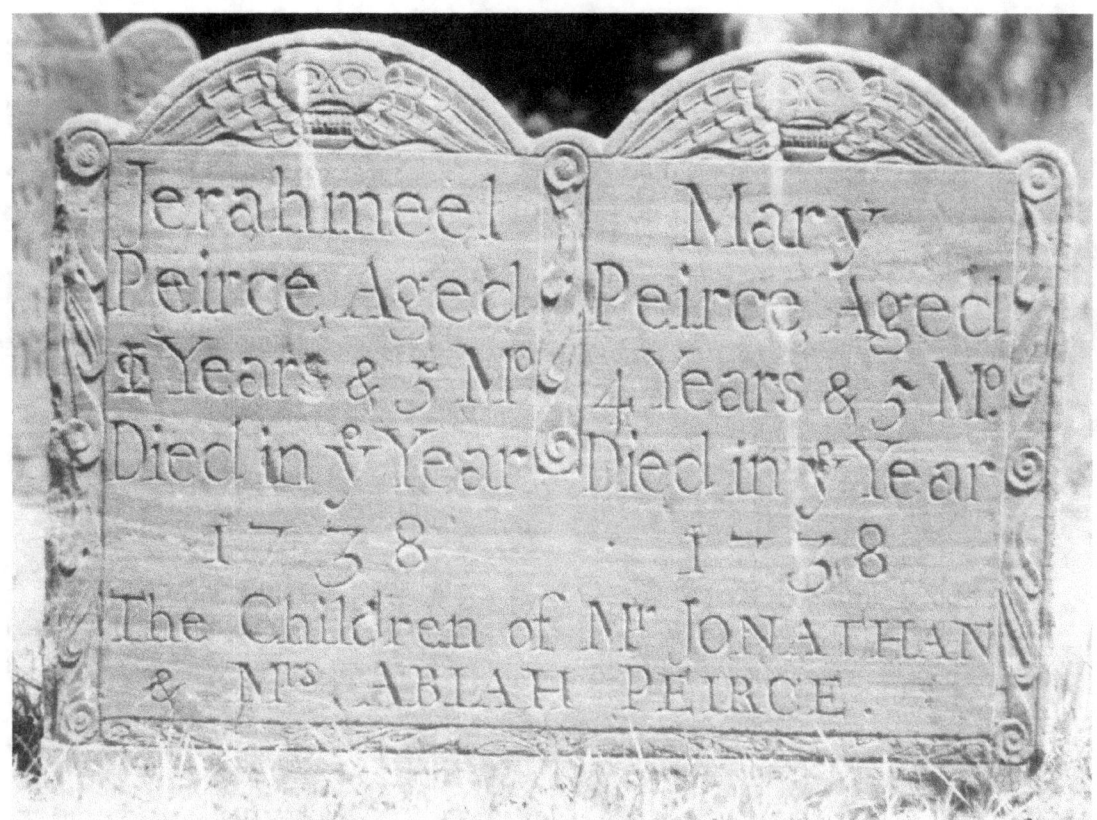

FIGURE 5. Lamson workshop Boston grave marker for Jerahmeel and Mary Peirce (d. 1738), North End Cemetery, Southampton, Suffolk County. (Photo by author, 1987.)

analyzed for 44 variables. They encompassed nine denominations, nondenominational cemeteries, and "unknown." Most of the ideologies continue from their colonial beginnings: the Puritan (Congregational or Presbyterian since 1717) with 62% of the gravestone population; the Anglicans at 6%; Quakers at roughly 3% (greatly underrepresented, as they did not believe in memorialization); and Methodists (including Baptists and Anabaptists) at 2.5%. "Unknown" accounts for about 7%, and "nondenominational" accounts for almost 10% of the stones. Only the early Anabaptist, Lutheran, and Baptist churches no longer exist; while some former Dutch-Reformed congregations (12% of the stones) are now represented only by their cemeteries.

Not only is the ideology of Long Island settlers expressed in the material record but also their ethnicity, which creates cultural boundaries. The gravestone surnames show that of the purportedly "English" towns, half of Newtown and Hempstead villages (partitioned into North Hemp-

stead after the end of the Revolutionary War) were "Dutch," including about one-third of North Hempstead, one-quarter of Oyster Bay Town, and one-fifth of Jamaica; of course, the five towns of Kings County were solidly "Dutch."

Research Methods

More than 4,300 gravestones in the 164 cemeteries located were photographed and computer coded for 44 variables on optical scan forms. (See Stone 1987:267–302 for the codebook, gravestone and cemetery recording forms, and recording procedures.) The systematic photography of all possible traditional slate, sandstone, schist, and early marble stones (even stumps, which could later be identified from recorded cemetery inscriptions) in a cemetery and landscape views from the four sides of a cemetery (useful in case future restoration is needed) were done. Today, recording can be completed using many facets of GIS, GPS, video, etc., techniques

FIGURE 6. Connecticut grave marker carved by Thomas Johnson III for Hannah Peirson (d. 1777), Sagaponack Cemetery, Sagaponack, Suffolk County. (Photo by author, 1987.)

FIGURE 7. Grave marker carved by Uzal Ward of Newark, New Jersey for Nehemiah Smith (d. 1750), Prospect Presbyterian Cemetery, Jamaica, Queens County. (Photo by author, 1987.)

(Foster and Hummel 2000:111–123). The codebook for the variables discerned as recording progressed was amplified from that of Deetz and Dethlefsen to deal with the greater number of variables: ethnicity, ideology, cemetery hierarchy, epitaphs, siting, etc. The universe of stones was not sampled but recorded as completely as possible. This was necessary to retrieve the data of the more difficult-to-locate small Quaker and Dutch family cemeteries. Sampling would largely have missed this aspect of the region. A universal, open-ended coding system was devised to allow the inclusion of whatever was found. Data were entered into the university mainframe computer, using SAS, and runs were made for the variables of space (location by county, town, and cemetery), chronology (decade, quarter-century, half-century, and century), design, ethnic group, religion, etc. Some results were so diffuse at the finest levels of analysis (decade, for example), it was necessary

to cluster them into quarter-century or higher periods to make sense of the data. Of the more than 4,300 stones, no date could be ascertained for 6%, and 3% were after 1820. The largest number of deaths recorded on stones was in the 1800 decade, followed by the 1790, 1810, 1780, 1750, and 1770 decades. The further rise in gravestone population after 1810 was largely recorded on marble stones (not part of this study), which are mostly illegible today.

Ethnicity and Race in the Long Island Gravestone Record

Some groups are poorly represented in the gravestone record. Enslaved Africans were quite numerous in colonial New Netherland; for example, the early east end Southampton Town population was around 20% enslaved people. None of the colonial African mortuary record has survived on west end Long Island, but

Perspectives from *Historical Archaeology*

FIGURE 8. Grave marker carved by John Zuricher of New York City for Sara Martenese (d. 1763), Flatbush Dutch Reformed Cemetery, Flatbush, Kings County. (Photo by author, 1987.)

there are a few stones in several east end cemeteries and some wooden crosses in mid-Long Island outside family grounds, usually in estate cemeteries. The only community cemetery with wood markers for Africans is one in Oyster Bay Town (Nassau County), which contained many Quakers and free thinkers having close trading ties with nonconformist Newport, Rhode Island. The exceptionally tolerant atmosphere there and enslaved African carvers working for the John Stevens shop may account for the notable body of slate gravestones for Africans in Newport's main burying ground.

Also, the Native Americans of colonial Long Island, many of them servants and some slaves, have no carved markers of stone, although there is a wood post in one cemetery said to mark Native graves and some cobble mounds in others said to be Native/African burials within settler cemeteries. There are a small number of 19th-century marble markers (outside the scope

of this study) memorializing African American and Montaukett Civil War soldiers in East Hampton's North End Cemetery and in the AME Zion churchyard in Sag Harbor, as well as in the Shinnecock and Poosepatuck Reservation burying grounds.

Ethnic and Ideological Choices in Gravestones

There are somewhat better records for other groups. The "Dutch" represent about 15% of the extant gravestone record of 1680 to about 1800; yet, according to census records, in 1698 about one-half of the New Netherland population was Dutch (Cohen 1981:13). As late as the 1790 first census of the United States (five generations after the influx of the English), the Dutch represented 16% of the New York population, 2% nationally, and were five times as numerous as the Scots (Rossiter 1909). These figures appear conservative, as David Fischer (1989:817) notes higher figures. These "Dutch" ethnic groups are represented in the Long Island gravestone record roughly as 0.5% Flemish-Belgian, 10.1% Hollanders, 1.7% German, 2.7% French, 0.9% Scandinavian, and 0.9% Scots and Irish (Figure 10).

The Dutch and the English Quakers are also underrepresented in the gravestone record, for several reasons. The earliest "Dutch" entrepreneurs established waterside plantations, and their fieldstone and carved markers did not survive the urbanization of the sites. This destruction was repeated later for the homesteads of Kings and Queens counties. As the extant gravestone record shows, the "Dutch" were twice as likely to use fieldstone memorials as the English, except for the Quakers, who were about 50% more likely to use fieldstone markers than their fellow English. Most of these boulder markers were carved with initials and death date. Many were purposely chosen for a pointed or gravestone-like shape (Figure 9b). Some had simple designs carved on them, but many are illegible now. Since the Dutch and Quakers were solid farmers and craftsmen, this evidently was not a choice dictated by economic necessity. Early Quaker settlers present another problem in assessing memorialization. The Society of Friends' Meetings on Long Island became distressed about the increasing

a

use of commercial grave markers by their members, so the Westbury Meeting in 1776 ordered that all carved markers be removed from their meetinghouse grounds. In keeping with their philosophy of simplicity and equality, meetinghouse grounds that contain many burials from the 1600s on are mostly unmarked and thus invisible today. Because of this, the Quakers are greatly underrepresented in the gravestone record.

Since markers frequently mirror cultural choices, ideological beliefs are reflected in the larger number of fieldstone markers and plain (no design) stones in this Dutch and Quaker-influenced the mid-Long Island hinterland Oyster Bay and Hempstead towns. Fieldstone markers account for about 6% of all Long Island stones; their currently visible use peaked between 1750 and 1775, but about a 20% use continued through the early 1800s. Another expression of ideology by the Quakers or nonconformist families was an adaptation of the traditional gravestone; the usual tripartite colonial shape was used, but the tympanum was left blank (Figure 9a).

b

FIGURE 9 (*a*) Quaker grave marker for Hannah Seaman (d. 1759), Townsend Cemetery, Jericho, Nassau County; (*b*) fieldstone marker for JosiphiF Worden, MacCoun Cemetery, Oyster Bay, Nassau County. (Photo by author, 1987.)

Perspectives from *Historical Archaeology*

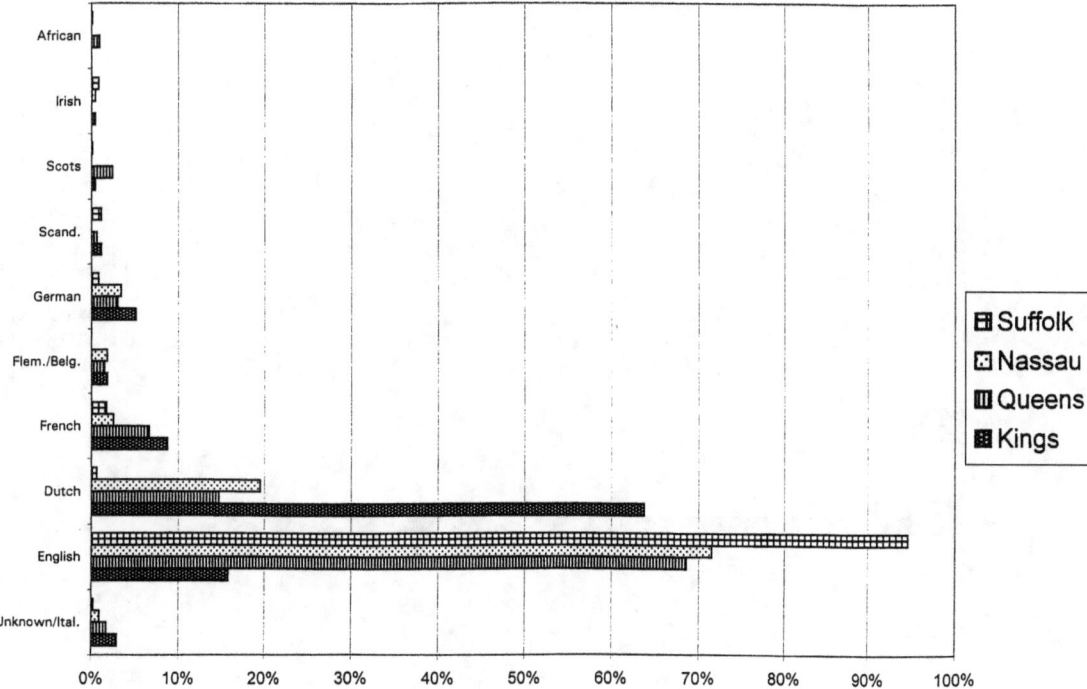

FIGURE 10. Ethnicity of gravestones by county. (Graph by author.)

The importance of this Quaker population has been overlooked in traditional American history. The American tradition of religious pluralism and freedom of belief stems from the Flushing Remonstrance and other precedents established by these freethinking individuals in Queens County. Governor Peter Stuyvesant of New Amsterdam imprisoned John Bowne, an English nonconformist and later Quaker of Flushing, for refusing to pay taxes for the established (Dutch Reformed) church. He demanded a hearing before the Dutch West India Company and pleaded his case in Amsterdam. The company subsequently ordered Stuyvesant to free Bowne and to allow freedom of conscience in the colony, which became the basis of the American separation of church and state, along with the general Dutch practice of toleration of belief.

These gravestones also demonstrate the persistence of the Dutch language in an English polity. The stones were analyzed for ethnic group by the surname on the stone, by inscribed biographical information, by the language used, and the burial location. Inscriptions in Dutch on stones in the Kings County Dutch Reformed churchyards comprise 2% of the total stones of the island but comprise 90% of the Kings County

subset (Figure 8). The use of this language was maintained for 200 years after takeover by the English; Dutch was used on stones until 1817, in church even later, and at table (by the Roosevelts, for example) until the late-19th century (Hammond 1990, pers. comm.). This is the most clear-cut ethnic distinction in Long Island cemeteries. Another strong ethnic division is shown in the orientation of headstone inscriptions (Figure 11). The Dutch and English both sprang from a common Calvinist heritage, yet 54% of the earliest Dutch stone inscriptions face east (91% in Dutch Reformed churchyards), while 87% of English inscriptions face west. Is this an ethnic boundary, a cultural practice? Is it a superstition of "do not step on the grave" (not likely when reading the west-facing stones)? With the passage of time and as the descendants of the early Dutch colonists moved east to the mid-Island area, their headstones conformed to the English practice, leading to a 37% east-facing use overall.

Besides surname and language, ethnicity is also expressed in the gravestone inscription format. Dutch women in most early Dutch Reformed burying grounds were denoted by their natal name first (not losing their lineage)

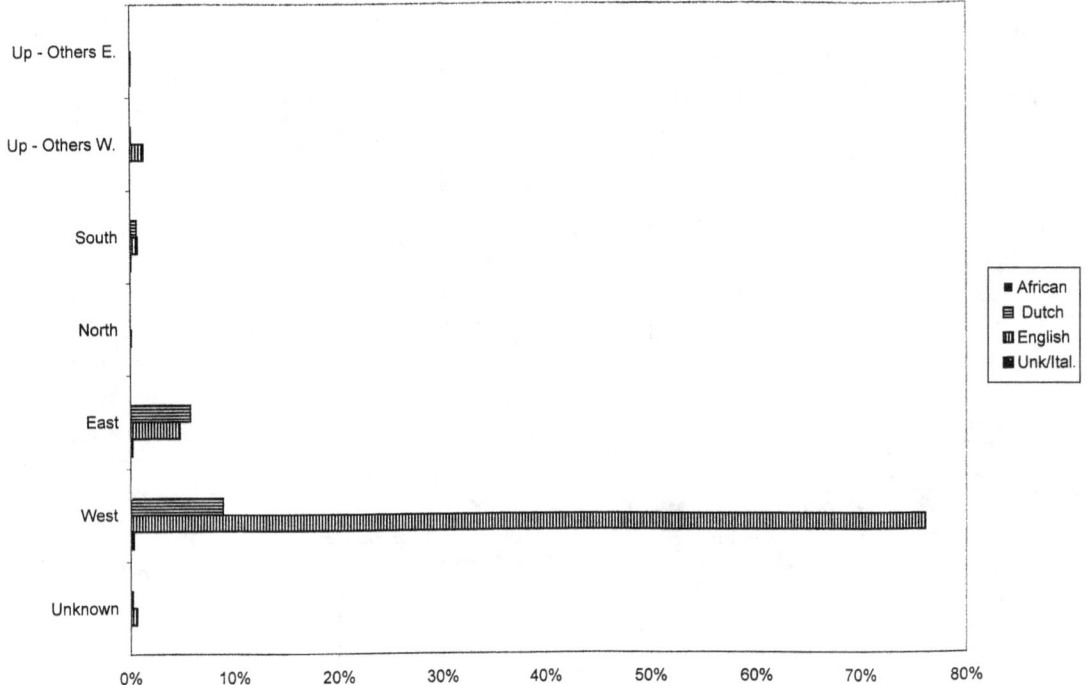

FIGURE 11. Orientation of gravestones by ethnic group. (Graph by author.)

and then by the name of their husband; English women almost never were. Only English women of status were further identified, for example, as "Hannah, wife of Herrick Rogers and daughter of Capt. David and Mrs. Mary Rose." This identification was evident in only a minuscule fraction of the English female population; overwhelmingly, English women were anonymous wives. From accounts of the time, Dutch women apparently also had more freedom to engage in business, be executrices of wills, and be educated (Quaker women also) than Puritan women, which may relate to this form of gravestone identity.

In the choice of design motif on stones, ethnic or ideological differences were also displayed (Figures 12, 13). Puritan and Dutch Reformed choices differed strongly. Only 12% of all Long Island stones have a death's head; of these, less than 1% occurred in the Dutch-influenced west end, whereas 89% are in the Puritan churchyards that later became Congregational or Presbyterian. There was never similarity in design choice between the two culture area groups, except to a limited extent in the 1750–1775 period. There was also variation in gravestone design choice through time. (Stone

1987 contains the overall Long Island record by decade.) The graph (Figure 14) shows that Long Island had plain stones contemporaneously with death's heads, differing from Deetz and Dethlefsen's New England pattern.

The secularization of motif (through consumer revolution? more ideological choice?), which Veit (this volume) finds for central New Jersey, also occurred on Long Island. There appears to be more choice of motifs, however: no design (10.1 % English to 03.2% Dutch); floral and vegetal designs (1.0% English to 0.01% Dutch); decorative "In ..." (20.4% English to 6.5% Dutch); and lettering (3.7% English to 3.0% Dutch); as well as urn and willow stones (subsumed under the category "Other," 2.1% English to 0.3% Dutch). The late-18th century, which accounts for 25% of all stones by time, is represented by many plain stones, which were 40% of the total.

Carvers and Availability of Stones

Instructive here is the record of the Hill family of carvers who left Connecticut in 1783 and moved to Sag Harbor, Long Island, when they deduced they could secure the east

Perspectives from *Historical Archaeology*

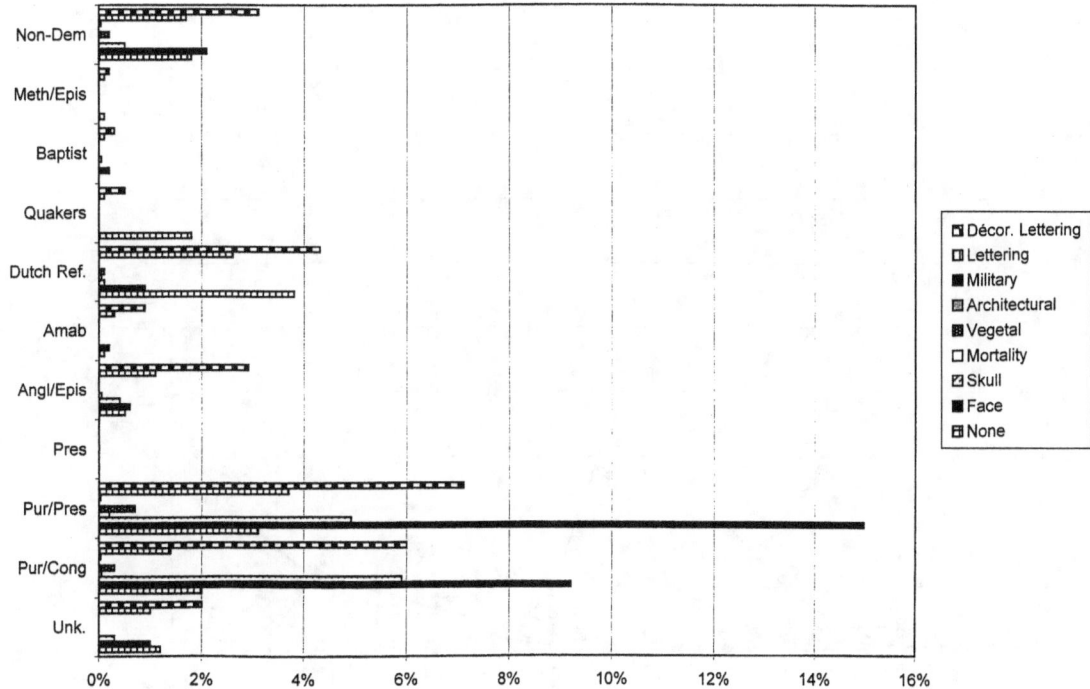

FIGURE 12. Gravestone design choice by religion. (Graph by author.)

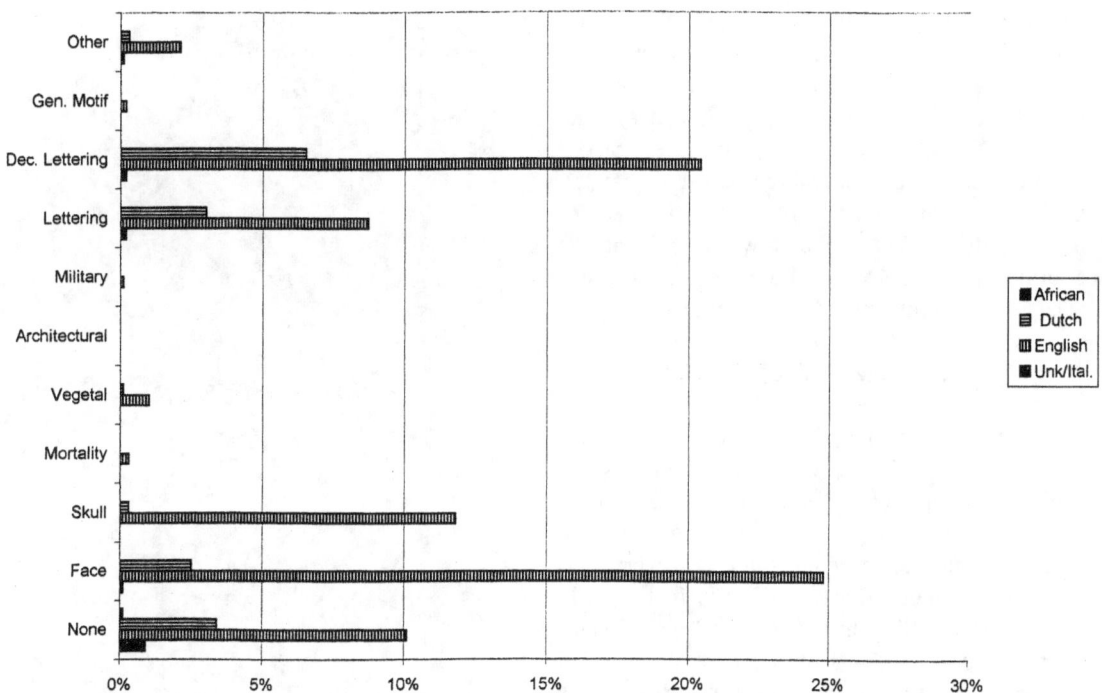

FIGURE 13. Gravestone design choice by ethnic group. (Graph by author.)

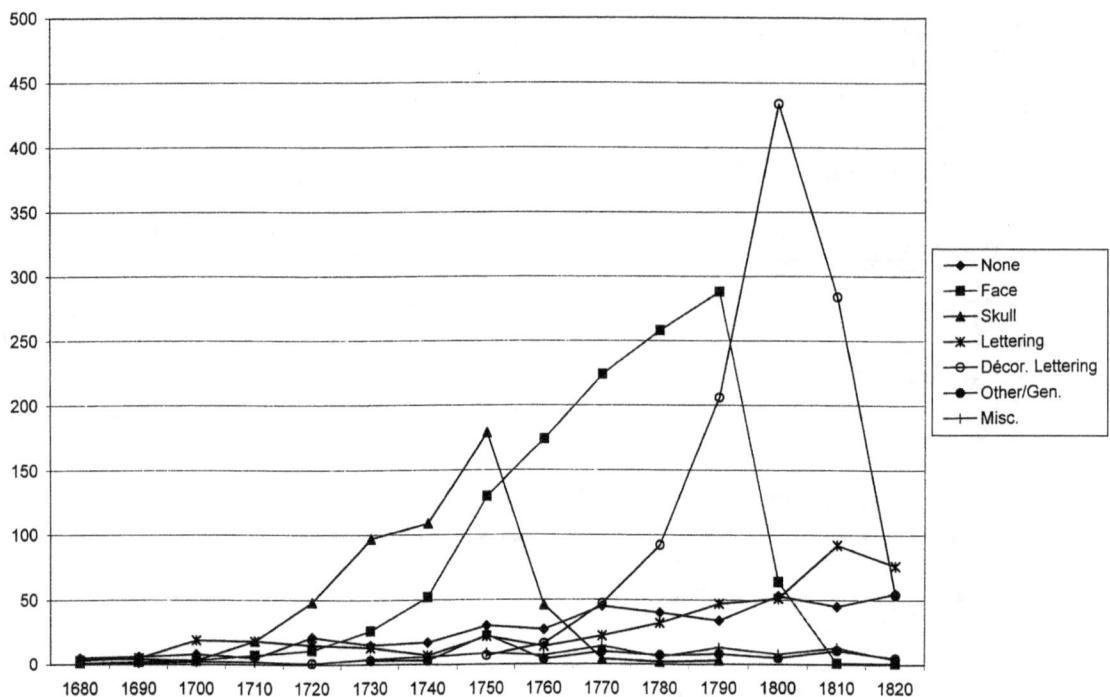

FIGURE 14. Long Island gravestone designs by decade. (Graph by author.)

end business from the New England carvers. While in Connecticut, they mostly carved for Long Islanders the "cookie cutter" (they all looked the same) cherub (face with wings) style (Figure 15). While on Long Island they carved almost every type of motif (consumer demand?): the cherub, plain, ornate "In …" (as "in memory of …"), floral, and urn and willow in various combinations. They continued most of these except the cherub into the early-19th century.

Gravestone Choice Variables

It appears that location as well as ethnicity had some effect in Long Island gravestone choice. Overall, 57% of east end Suffolk County stones came from nearby New England. The proportion changed through time, however: 70% in the late 1600s, averages of 85% in the early 1700s, 64% in the third quarter (Revolutionary War disruption?), 34% at the end of the 18th century, and only 3% in the early 1800s. This drop was influenced by an increase in stones from the New York City stone-cutting center as it came to dominate trade and by the establishment of the Hill family workshop in Sag Harbor

FIGURE 15. The Hill family carvers produced the marker for Hannah Platt (d. 1811). It is the most numerous design they produced. Manhasset Episcopal Cemetery, Manhasset, Nassau County. (Photo by author, 1987.)

in 1783, which took over the former share of the New England carvers.

Proximity, or shipping distance, also appears to be a factor: 94% of Kings County stones and 89% of those in Queens came from the New Netherland stone-cutting centers in New Jersey and New York City, regardless of the ethnicity or ideology of the deceased. Mid-Long Island (Nassau County) inhabitants imported more than 50% of their stones from the closer New Netherland/New York carvers, with the balance being locally crafted fieldstones and examples from New England. This area was a hotbed of religious dissension from Puritan orthodoxy, harboring Quakers, the radical Quaker offshoot Gortonists, Baptists, Methodists, and others. This dissent is reflected in the larger number of plain stones (50%) and home-carved boulders (6% of all stones) used there.

Conclusions

In the 164 cemeteries studied, the cultural choice of gravestones appears to be affected by proximity, but ethnic and ideological differences between the two culture area groups are clearly expressed through variations in language used on the stone, expressions of gender, orientation of headstones, use of fieldstones as markers, and choice of design motifs. The small English Quaker subgroup gives evidence of its ideological tenacity through the differential use of gravestones (or lack of them), a higher usage of fieldstone markers (also the Dutch), and the later choice of stones with no design.

The Long Island gravestone record relates to Deetz's tripartite New England model but varies in that the oldest stones are not death's heads but are plain stones, followed by death's heads, then "cherubs" (faces in many styles, with and without wings), then contemporaneously a few urn and willow stones with a much larger number of plain stones (44%) or with an ornate "In ..." motif. Besides varying chronologically, the choice and use of stones on Long Island also varied by cultural sphere (ethnic group?) and ideology. This normative database provides previously unknown information for scholars in many fields.

These data refine Bonomi's (1971:22) statement, based on 1698 population records, that there were no "Dutch" in Suffolk County;

Huguenot refugees were assigned to each county after the Edict of Nantes in 1683. There were a number of "Dutch" in many of the towns of the county almost from the beginning—Schellingers and Lopers in East Hampton; Pelletreau and others in Southampton; Genin, L'Hommedieu, and others in Southold; many others in Huntington, Smithtown, and Islip towns—still reflected in building practices, surnames, and gravestones. This information also provides a finer grained picture of the settlement influences and ethnic composition of Long Island than is depicted in the maps of Bonomi (Figure 2) and Donald Meinig (1975:133).

This gravestone material record provides further support for Allen Noble's (1984) designation of New Netherland as the Hudson Valley culture hearth and exemplifies the multicultural nature of the Dutch hearth, more closely aligned to the mid-Atlantic culture area than that of New England. A culture hearth is a seedbed in which a culture displays most strongly its essential features that remain primary, whatever the subsequent development (Zelinsky 1973:89). Geographer Meinig (1986:124) believes that a distinctly new American people were formed largely of the "Dutch" and English, laced with many other ethnic elements (recorded in this study) and self-consciously different from New England. Current scholars (Goodfriend 1991, and others) believe that the English were engulfed in a "Dutch" world for generations before they became the most populous; because of this and the Dutch cultural tenacity, American society became more like the "Dutch" than the English.

The "Dutch" subgroup, eventually submerged by 200 years of pervasive English culture, demonstrates in this material record the strength of ethnic inheritance. People died and were memorialized as they lived, bounded by their cultural roots. English rule began only 30 years after "Dutch" settlement on Long Island, so the majority of the later "Dutch" gravestones represent, more than the founding settlers, the succeeding generations who were becoming the new Americans, making the evidence of these continuing early ethnic and ideological boundaries all the more remarkable. Gravestones are an enduring and traditional part of a people's culture, and the cemetery is a nodal point of the social landscape. Both represent choices illustrating their beliefs; their presence provides a fuller record of an area's history. On Long Island, that record was shaped by the 10 ethnic groups and 9 (plus "unknown") religious denominations functioning within a unique situation of competing culture spheres and multiple sources of grave markers. On the national scale, the Dutch presence, as shown here, has contributed to U.S. English vocabulary (almost all ship terms, "Yankee," and more are Dutch), enriched our cuisine (doughnuts, crullers, cookies, pancakes, salads, "kol sla" [cole slaw], and more). They also introduced the idea of caucus and political representation, and, with the Quakers, enabled the concept of freedom of belief—the underpinnings of American society.

Acknowledgments

This extensive project would not have been accomplished without the interest and support of Phil C. Weigand, for which I am very grateful. Also helpful was Ralph Solecki, a long-time Long Island archaeologist, and material culture specialist Dolores Newton. Sherene Baugher greatly aided the organization of the project and continues to give good counsel in this publication. The editorial assistance of Richard Veit is also appreciated. The National Science Foundation provided partial support for the fieldwork, and the New York Council for the Humanities partially supported the work in the boroughs of New York City under then City Archaeologist Baugher. Without the germinal work of Jim Deetz and Ted Dethlefsen—who knows if any of the many gravestone scholars would have been inspired to contribute this important new information that enhances U.S. history?

References

ABERNATHY, LESLIE C.
1981 *Landscape, Communities, and the Community at Palmers River: Settling a River System, 1665–1737, Rehoboth, MA.* Doctoral dissertation, Department of Anthropology, Brown University, Providence, RI. University Microfilms, Ann Arbor, MI.

ALLEN, DAVID GRAYSON
1981 *In English Ways: The Movement of Societies and the Transferal of English Local Law and Custom to Massachusetts Bay in the Seventeenth Century.* University of North Carolina Press, Chapel Hill.

ALLEN, PETER SUTTON
1968 An Investigation into the Validity of a Fundamental Assumption of Archaeology Utilizing Data from New England Gravestones. Master's thesis, Department of Anthropology Brown University, Providence, RI.

BAIRD, SCOTT
1996 The Taylor, Texas Cemetery: A Language Community. *Markers 13*:113–141. Journal of the Association for Gravestone Studies.

BAUGHER, SHERENE, AND FREDERICK WINTER
1983 Early American Gravestones: Archaeological Perspectives on Three Cemeteries of Old New York. *Archaeology* 36(5):46–53.

BENES, PETER
1977 *The Masks of Orthodoxy: Folk Gravestone Carving in Plymouth County, Massachusetts, 1689–1805.* University of Massachusetts Press, Amherst.

BLACKBURN, RODERICK, AND RUTH PIWONKA
1988 *Remembrance of Patria: Dutch Arts and Culture in Colonial America, 1609–1776.* Albany Institute of History and Art, Albany, NY.

BONOMI, PATRICIA U.
1971 *A Factious People: Politics and Society in Colonial New York.* Columbia University Press, New York, NY.

CARSON, CARY
1994 The Consumer Revolution in Colonial British America: Why Demand? In *Of Consuming Interests: The Style of Life in the Eighteenth Century*, Cary Carson, Ronald Hoffman, and Peter Albert, editors, pp. 483–697. University Press of Virginia, Charlottesville.

COHEN, DAVID S.
1992 *The Dutch American Farm.* New York University Press, New York, NY.

COLLISON, GARY L.
1999 German-American Gravestones in Trans-Susquehanna, Pennsylvania, 1750–1850. Paper presented at the Annual Meeting of the American Culture Association, San Antonio, TX, 23–29 March 1997.

CROWELL, ELIZABETH
1981 Philadelphia Gravestones, 1760–1820. *Northeast Historical Archaeology* 10:23–26.
1983 *Migratory Monuments and Missing Motifs: Archaeological Analysis of Mortuary Art in Cape May County, New Jersey, 1740–1810.* Doctoral dissertation, Program in American Civilization, University of Pennsylvania, Philadelphia. University Microfilms, Ann Arbor, MI.

CROWELL, ELIZABETH A., AND NORMAN V. MACKIE III
1990 The Funeral Monuments and Burial Patterns of Colonial Tidewater Virginia, 1607–1776. *Markers* 7:103–138. Journal of the Association for Gravestone Studies.

DEETZ, JAMES
  1977 *In Small Things Forgotten.* Doubleday Anchor Books, Garden City, NY.

DEETZ, JAMES, AND EDWIN S. DETHLEFSEN
  1971 Some Social Aspects of New England Colonial Mortuary Art. *American Antiquity* 36(3):30–38.

DETHLEFSEN, EDWIN S.
  1981 The Cemetery and Culture Change: Archaeological Focus and Ethnographic Perspective. In *Modern Material Culture: The Archaeology of Us*, Richard Gould and Michael Schiffer, editors, pp. 137–159. Academic Press, New York, NY.

DETHLEFSEN, EDWIN S., AND JAMES DEETZ
  1966 Death's Heads, Cherubs, and Willow Trees: Experimental Archaeology in Colonial Cemeteries. *American Antiquity* 31(4):502–510.

DETHLEFSEN, EDWIN S., AND KENNETH JENSEN
  1977 Social Commentary from the Cemetery. *Natural History* 86(6):32–38.

ECKERT, EVA
  1998 Language and Ethnicity Maintenance: Evidence of Czech Tombstone Inscriptions. *Markers 15:*205–233. Journal for the Association for Gravestone Studies.
  2002 From Moravia to Texas: Immigrant Acculturation at the Cemetery. *Markers 19:*175–211. Journal of the Association for Gravestone Studies.

FISCHER, DAVID HACKETT
  1989 *Albion's Seed: Four British Folkways in America.* Oxford University Press, New York, NY.

FOSTER, GARY S., AND RICHARD L. HUMMEL
  1995 The Adkins-Woodson Cemetery: A Sociological Examination of Cemeteries as Communities. *Markers 12:*93–117. Journal of the Association for Gravestone Studies.
  2000 Applications of Developing Technologies to Cemetery Studies. *Markers 17:*111–123. Journal of the Association for Gravestone Studies.

FRAMPTON, MARCY
  1995 Gravehouses of North Louisiana: Culture History and Typology. *Material Culture* 27(2):21–48.

GOODFRIEND, JOYCE
  1991 *Before the Melting Pot: Society and Culture in Colonial New York City, 1664–1730.* Princeton University Press, Lawrenceville, NJ.

GORMAN, FREDERICK, AND MICHAEL DIBLASI
  1976 Nonchronological Sources of Variation in the Seriation of Gravestone Motifs in the Northeast and Southeast Colonies. In *Puritan Gravestone Art: The Dublin Seminar for New England Folklife Annual Proceedings,* Peter Benes, editor, pp. 79–87. Boston University, Boston, MA.

GRAVES, THOMAS E.
  1988 Pennsylvania German Gravestones: An Introduction. *Markers 5:*61–95. Journal of the Association for Gravestone Studies.

HALL, DAVID
  1976 The Gravestone Image as a Puritan Cultural Code. In *Puritan Gravestone Art: Dublin Seminar for New England Folklife Annual Proceedings,* Peter Benes, editor, pp. 23–32. Boston University, Boston, MA.

HALPORN, ROBERTA
  1997a African-American Gravestones in the Northeastern United States. Paper presented at the Annual Conference of the Association for Gravestone Studies, West Long Branch, NJ, 25–28 June.
  1997b *Only Yesterday We Drained the Cup of Sorrow: American Jewish Cemeteries and History.* Center for Thanatology Research and Education, Brooklyn, NY.

HINSHALWOOD, SOPHIA GRUYS
  1981 *The Dutch Culture Area of the Mid-Hudson Valley.* Doctoral dissertation, Department of Geography, Rutgers University, New Brunswick, NJ. University Microfilms, Ann Arbor, MI.

JAMESON, JAMES FRANKLIN
  1909 *Narratives of New Netherlands, 1609–1664.* Random House, New York, NY. Reprinted in 1976 by Random House, New York, NY.

JEANE, GREGORY
  1987 Rural Southern Gravestones: Sacred Artifacts in the Upland South Folk Cemetery. *Markers 4:*55–86. Journal of the Association for Gravestone Studies.

LEONE, MARK P.
  1982 Some Opinions about Recovering Mind. *American Antiquity* 47(4):742–760.

LITTLE-STOKES, RUTH
  1984 *Sticks and Stones: A Profile of North Carolina Grave Markers through Three Centuries.* Doctoral dissertation, Department of History, University of North Carolina, Durham. University Microfilms, Ann Arbor, MI.

MACKIE, NORMAN V. III
  1987 Social Structure Reflected in Virginia Gravestones. Paper presented at The Society for Historical Archaeology, 6–9 January.

MEINIG, DONALD H.
  1975 The Colonial Period, 1609–1775. In *The Geography of New York State,* J.R. Thompson, editor, pp. 121–129. Syracuse University Press, Syracuse, NY.
  1986 *The Shaping of America: A Geographical Perspective on 500 Years of History,* Vol. I, *Atlantic America, 1492–1800.* Yale University Press, New Haven, CT.

NAKAGAWA, TADASHI
    1994 Louisiana Cemeteries: Manifestations of Regional
          and Denominational Identity. In *Markers 11*:28–51.
          Journal of the Association for Gravestone Studies.

NIGH, ROBIN FRANKLIN
    1997 Under Grave Conditions: African American Signs of
          Life and Death in North Florida. *Markers 14:*158–189.
          Journal of the Association for Gravestone Studies.

NOBLE, ALLEN
    1984 *Wood, Brick, and Stone: The North American
          Settlement Landscape,* Vol. 1, *Houses.* University of
          Massachusetts Press, Amherst.

NORRIS, DARRELL A.
    1988 Ontario Gravestones. *Markers 5:*123–149. Journal of
          the Association for Gravestone Studies.

PROWN, JULES
    1982 Mind in Matter: An Introduction to Material Culture
          Theory and Method. *WinterthurPortfolio* 17(1):19.

ROSSITER, W. S.
    1909 *A Century of Population Growth from the First to the
          Twelfth Census of the United States:1700–1900.* Bureau
          of the Census, Washington, DC. Reprinted in 1989 by
          the Genealogical Printing Co., Baltimore, MD.

SCHLERETH, THOMAS J.
    1985 Material Culture Studies: A Symposium. In *Material
          Culture* 17(23):7–114.

STONE, GAYNELL
    1978 Colonial Long Island Gravestones: Trade Network
          Indicators, 1670–1799. In *Puritan Gravestone Art
          2: The Dublin Seminar for New England Folklife,
          Annual Proceedings*, Peter Benes, editor, pp. 46–57.
          Boston University, Boston, MA.
    1987 *Spatial and Material Aspects of Culture: Ethnicity and
          Ideology in Long Island Gravestones, 1670–1820.*
          Doctoral dissertation, Department of Anthropology,
          State University at Stony Brook, NY. University
          Microfilms, Ann Arbor, MI.
    1990 Spatial and Material Aspects of Culture: Ethnicity and
          Ideology in Long Island Gravestones, 1680–1800.
          Paper presented at the Symposium, Religion, Popular
          Culture, and Material Life in the Middle Colonies and
          Upper South, 1650–1800, University of Maryland-
          College Park, 17 November.
    1991 Material Evidence of Ideological and Ethnic Choice
          in Long Island Gravestones, 1670–1800. *Material
          Culture* 23(3):1–29.

SWEENEY, KEVIN
    1985 Where the Bay Meets the River: Gravestones
          and Stone Cutters in the River Towns of Western
          Massachusetts, 1690–1810. *Markers 3:*1–46. Journal
          of the Association for Gravestone Studies.

VEIT, RICHARD
    2000 John Solomon Teetzel and the Anglo-German
          Gravestone Carving Tradition of Eighteenth Century,
          Northwestern New Jersey. *Markers 17:*124–161.
          Journal of the Association for Gravestone Studies.

WELCH, RICHARD F.
    1987 The New York and New Jersey Gravestone Carving
          Tradition. *Markers 4:*1–54. Journal of the Association
          for Gravestone Studies.

YENTSCH, ANNE
    1981 *Expressions of Cultural Diversity and Social Reality
          in Seventeenth-Century New England.* Doctoral
          dissertation, Department of Anthropology, Brown
          University, Providence, RI. University Microfilms,
          Ann Arbor, MI.

ZELINSKY, WILBUR
    1973 *The Cultural Geography of the United States.*
          PrenticeHall, Englewood Cliffs, NJ.

GAYNELL STONE
2332 N. WADING RIVER RD.
WADING RIVER, NY 11792

JAMES C. GARMAN

Viewing the Color Line Through the Material Culture of Death

ABSTRACT

Historical archaeologists have recently begun to explore the intersections of race, class, gender, and death in American society. This paper uses an approach to the material culture of death grounded in the reception theory of Wolfgang Iser (1978). Grave markers from the African-American cemetery at Newport, Rhode Island, are considered as intersubjective texts with ranges of different meanings for different viewers. Understanding the ranges of possible meanings is crucial for determining the extent to which the color line dividing African Americans and Euroamericans has been set, negotiated, and reset through time and space. The reception theory framework is used to interpret three time periods in Newport's history ranging from 1720 to 1830; interpretations of textual similarities and differences in cross-cultural mortuary activities revolve around white paternalism, conspicuous consumption, and African-American strategies of resistance and assimilation.

Introduction

On a dark winter afternoon, when the southwesterly winds blow snow clouds in from the Atlantic Ocean, H. P. Lovecraft's (1983[1939]:94) description of Newport, Rhode Island, as "climbing wraithlike from its dreaming breakwater" acquires a certain resonance for visitors to the city's Common Burying Ground. Within the overgrown confines of this place, which served as the secular municipal cemetery for three centuries, a deeply-rutted dirt road divides the main burial ground from its northernmost corner (Figure 1). The monuments north of the road are smaller than those in the other parts of the burying ground, and the arrangement less linear than the neat rows stretching to the south. Even the names of the dead—Pompey, Subiner, Nero—are strikingly different from the English names surrounding them, for this northern corner has been the burying place of Newport's African-American community since the

18th century, when the slave ships of Lopez and Rivera moored along Bannister's Wharf, and when Africans in chains were considered merchandise at the city's Brick Market.

In *The Souls of Black Folk,* W. E. B. Du Bois (1990[1903]:8) wrote that "the problem of the twentieth century is the problem of the color-line,—the relation of the darker to the lighter races of men in Asia and Africa, in America and the islands of the sea. . . ." Du Bois contended that to live with this color line was to experience a dual consciousness:

> the Negro is a sort of seventh son, born with a veil and gifted with second-sight in this American world,—a world which yields him no true self-consciousness, but only lets him see himself through the revelation of the other world (Du Bois 1990[1903]:8).

Scholars have quoted and requoted these passages to the point where they have come to symbolize all of Du Bois's work. Yet while archaeologists have studied African-American sites in the Northeast for almost 20 years (Deetz 1977; Baker 1978; Schuyler 1980), they have only recently turned their attention to Du Bois's problem of the color line, and the extent to which it has been negotiated and contested through time and space (Paynter 1990; Bower 1991; Hauteniemi 1992; Muller 1992). This paper explores the color line's relevance for historical archaeologists, particularly for those working on what are loosely termed "African-American" sites. From such a perspective, questions of what particular characteristics constitute "Euroamerican" or "African-American" identities assume less significance than questions concerning the dialectical relationship between these two groups. This dialectic, which has material as well as social, political, and economic correlates, is what Du Bois meant by the color line.

The objects studied here are part of the material culture of death—that is, the visible, above-ground artifacts associated with mortuary activities, like funerary monuments and cemetery landscapes. Artifacts usually recovered through excavation, like coffin hardware (Bell 1990; Little et al. 1992), are not part of this study. Building on a previous analysis of the Common Burying Ground (Tashijan

FIGURE 1. View northeast of the African-American section of the Common Burying Ground. Note the road in the foreground dividing the Euroamerican cemetery from the wedge-shaped corner in which African Americans and others perceived as "outsiders" were interred.

and Tashijan 1988), three related questions about race and death are raised in this paper. First, what do the form and narrative content of gravestones for African Americans indicate about racial and racist attitudes in 18th- and 19th-century Newport? Second, how is an interpretive framework that emphasizes the readers of artifacts useful for viewing ranges of symbolic meaning in the material culture of death? Finally, how does reception theory enable historical archaeologists to link African-American pasts with the sociopolitics of practicing historical archaeology in the present?

Material Culture, Reception Theory, and Hermeneutics

Post-processual attempts to interpret material culture as texts have become increasingly visible in archaeology within the last five years (e.g., Shanks and Tilley 1987, 1992; Tilley 1990; Beaudry et al. 1991; Little 1992a). Most efforts have aimed at understanding the writers of material culture texts and their cultural-historical contexts. In a recent analysis of Ian Hodder's theoretical positionings,

Johnsen and Olsen (1992) note that one of Hodder's professed aims has been to understand the decision-making processes of people who actively create material culture. Conversely, historical archaeologists have paid relatively little attention to the readers of material culture texts, and the diversity of messages readers take away from their encounters with objects or landscapes in the visible world.

Social theorists have long argued that people view the world from a range of subject positions—wealthy and poor, female and male, African-American and Euroamerican, to cite just a few examples. Sometimes the same individual experiences life from several different subject positions, depending on the situation. Determining the range of these subject positions offers insight into the past, especially when the archaeologist also incorporates the social and historical conditions of material culture production into the interpretation. Reception theory, a form of hermeneutics articulated by Wolfgang Iser (1978), offers a way to attempt this project.

From Hermeneutic Theory to Iser's "Aesthetic Response"

While a comprehensive review of the origins and development of hermeneutic theory is outside the scope of this paper, it is necessary to trace briefly its origins to provide a context for understanding Iser's ideas. Derived from the Greek verb *hermeneuein,* "to interpret," hermeneutic theory is used in many disciplines ranging from literary criticism to anthropology (cf. Crapanzano 1992). In tracing the theory's development, Johnsen and Olsen (1992:421) point to the significance of Johann Gustav Droysen, a 19th-century German philosopher. Droysen delineated the difference between approaches of *Verstehen,* understanding, and *Erklärung,* explanation, ascribing them to the social and natural sciences, respectively. In its boldest Romantic manifestation, hermeneutic theory represented the empathy of the humanist historian with the thoughts of people in the past. By putting one's self in the position of historical figures, one could project back to learn why people responded as they did to specific circumstances. Such an approach is not without some rather obvious limitations. As others have pointed out (Barret 1987), attempting to recover intentionality is idealistic, especially because life rarely unfolds in the way humans intend it to unfold.

In the mid-20th century Hans-Georg Gadamer developed a more explicitly self-reflexive brand of hermeneutics, one in which the dialectic between the past and the present provides the stimulus for understanding (Gadamer 1975): "enriched self-knowledge," writes Terry Eagleton (1983:79), "springs from an encounter with the unfamiliar." The relevance of Gadamer's hermeneutics for archaeology is seen as threefold (Johnsen and Olsen 1992): first, hermeneutics moves the act of interpretation explicitly into the present; second, archaeologists can therefore learn something about themselves by interpreting the past; and finally, this critical perspective develops theoretical debate in archaeology.

Writing from a perspective grounded in the work of Gadamer and Anthony Giddens, Shanks and Tilley (1992:110) have argued that archaeology *is* hermeneutics, based on "a dialectical approach to the past." They are especially adamant about opening up dialogues between the past and the present, noting that "the task of a philosophy of archaeology should be to offer potentialities rather than to foreclose them" (Shanks and Tilley 1992:114).

Although descended from trends in literary theory, rather than philosophy, reception theory is similarly concerned with the "interplay between text and reader" (Iser 1978:107), an interesting parallel with the reflexive interplay between the interpreter and interpreted. Eagleton describes the theory's relatively late appearance as ironic, compared with previous movements aimed at the author and the text itself, respectively:

> The reader has always been the most underprivileged of this trio—strangely, since without him or her there would be no literary texts at all. Literary texts do not exist on bookshelves: they are processes of signification materialized only in the practice of reading. For literature to happen, the reader is quite as vital as the author (Eagleton 1983:74).

Iser describes a "reading process" in which a reader encounters a text, an event that generates recall and reassessment of one's surroundings:

> This feature of the reading process is of great significance for the compilation of the aesthetic object. As the reader's conscious mind is activated by the textual stimulus . . . the unit of meaning is linked to the new reading moment in which the wandering viewpoint is now situated (Iser 1978: 117).

The "new reading moment"—the encounter between the reader and the text—is the focus of this paper, although elements of Gadamer's hermeneutics will be used to develop a reflexive perspective on the practice of archaeology. Understanding the ranges of subject positions from which readers experience texts—conscious or unconscious, intentional or not—is the first step in understanding the dialectical nature of the color line in the material world. And understanding the color line in the past entails understanding its manifestations in the present. The ultimate positioning of the historical archaeologist in a dialectic with the past, an approach advocated by Shanks and Tilley (1992), is seen as a necessary further step, particularly in the charged sociopolitical context of African-American archaeology.

Pre-Revolutionary Newport (1720–1770): Euroamerican Paternalism and African-American Markers

African-American slavery in New England is a topic that has been downplayed or sanitized in most secondary histories of the region. "The New Englanders, at the worst, were not hard task-masters," writes Mason (1884:104) in his *Reminiscences of Newport,* "and it is well known that, as a general thing, they took a lively interest in the welfare of their dependents."

Newport, favored with a deep, protected harbor and its situation on Narragansett Bay, was settled as a trading port in 1639–1640. Surprisingly, the city's complex history as an imperial entrepôt has attracted relatively little attention from historical archaeologists (Mrozowski 1981; Schmidt and Mrozowski 1989). Throughout the 18th century

Newport's merchants extended their trade networks toward first the West Indies and then Africa, a phenomenon well-chronicled by social and maritime historians (Chyet 1970). The success of Newport's mercantile efforts would ultimately lead to increased attention from British authorities, and an eventual crackdown on smuggling in the decade prior to the outbreak of the American Revolution (Schmidt and Mrozowski 1989).

Newport's first slaving expedition took place in 1649, when William Withington hired the vessel *Beginnings* for a West Indian venture, although debate exists as to whether the ship returned to Newport with slaves (Bridenbaugh 1976[1974]: 24–25). Crane (1985:17) cites 1723 as "the year in which [Newport's merchants] became irrevocably committed to the slave trade," since that was the year Rhode Island traders began shipping their home-distilled rum directly to the west coast of Africa.

The social characteristics of slavery in a northern entrepôt like Newport have yet to be adequately resolved. The census of 1774 lists 1,084 African slaves (some of whom actually may have been Native Americans) out of a total city population of 9,209 (Rhode Island State Archives [RISA] 1774). The same document lists 311 white families with one or more slaves co-residing; relatively few white families (n=32) are shown as co-residing with more than five slaves. With the additional presence of free African Americans and Native Americans in various degrees of freedom and enslavement, urban Newport must have been a place where the color line was a part of daily life.

What were the attitudes of white Newporters toward African Americans in the context of their daily life, where material constraints forced a sharing of physical space? On her 1704 journey through New England, Madam Sarah Kemble Knight recorded her disgust at finding African Americans and Euroamericans sharing the same dinner table in nearby eastern Connecticut:

> But too Indulgent (especially ye farmers) to their slaves: suffering too great familiarity from them, permitting them to sit at Table and eat with them, (as they say to save time,) and into the dish goes the black hoof as freely as the white hand (Knight 1935[1825]:37–38).

A recent study of room-by-room probate inventories from nearby Portsmouth, Rhode Island, from 1640 through 1762 reveals that both African-American and Native American slaves lived within the houses of their masters, usually in a garret or a cellar (Garman [1994]). Unlike Southern masters, whose slaves dwelt in cabins as autonomous family units, Rhode Island masters forced slaves inside the main house. While some writers have taken this circumstance as a symbol of a kinder, gentler Northern slavery (Mason 1884:104), the degree of surveillance, supervision, and spatial control by masters probably actually increased when slaves were brought together with Euroamerican families, resulting in heightened tensions over the use of domestic space.

An important aspect of surveillance was religious instruction, although Newport's clergy rarely admitted that even their most earnest efforts to gain African-American converts were of any success. An exception was the Reverend Ezra Stiles who, bemoaning the lack of African Americans in his congregation, enthusiastically held meetings at his own home on Sabbath evenings:

> 24 February 1772 . . . In the Evening a very full and serious Meeting of Negroes in my House, perhaps 80 or 90. I discoursed to them on Luke XIV, 16, 17, 18. . . . They sang well. They appeared attentive and much affected; and after I had done, many of them came up to me and thanked me, as they said for taking so much care of their souls, and hoped they should remember my Counsel (Dexter 1901: 213–214).

As far as Stiles and other white Newporters were concerned, African Americans needed to be watched over constantly during their coerced acculturation to Euroamerican life. This supervision took place in all arenas of life: in homes, in workplaces, and especially, as Piersen (1988) has shown, in Euroamerican churches.

The cultural landscape of the city's Common Burying Ground was a visible material reminder of Euroamerican control of ritual space. The graves of African Americans lie scattered north of the main burying ground, an arrangement not without precedent in 18th-century New England; Greene (1966[1942]:284) notes that a 1714 petition by Boston's grave diggers asked the government to

FIGURE 2. Grave marker for Hector, "late Servant to Mrs. Ann Butcher of Barbadoes," 1720, Newport, Rhode Island. This marker was probably cut by John Stevens I, and is distinguished from other gravestones by its comparative lack of detail.

appoint a place to bury "strangers and Negroes." The earliest surviving marker for an African-American in Newport, the monument for Hector (Figure 2), lies so far to the north and west of Euroamerican graves that it represented a remote and isolated point when it was placed in 1720 (Connelly 1973). Although Euroamericans shared living space with African Americans, they seem to have objected strongly to sharing the space of death, perhaps because of the permanent nature of the latter state (Piersen 1988; Garman 1992).

The marker for Hector is worth examining in greater detail (Figure 3). John Stevens I, the patriarch of a well-documented family of stone cutters, apparently carved the gravestone in the year 1720

shown on the epitaph. The text relates Hector directly to his mistress "Mrs. Ann Butcher of Barbadoes." What is immediately striking about the stone is its blankness, its utter lack of detail within both the lunette and the finials. Possibly the stone represents a limited or tentative economic commitment to memorializing a slave; alternatively, the blankness may also imply an absent soul, or as an anonymous reviewer of an early draft of this article wrote, "doubt about the slave's fate after death." Since no other stones for African Americans are as undecorated as this one, an argument about limited investment seems more appropriate than one concerning general attitudes of Euroamericans toward slaves.

FIGURE 3. Detail of marker for Hector, showing lunette and finial areas delineated but left blank, either by a decision of the stonecutter or, more likely, the client purchasing the headstone.

Certainly other white New Englanders thought that slaves were capable of attaining Christian salvation, expressing this belief by commemorating African Americans with gravestones (Bell 1991). Mann and Greene (1962:26) list several epitaphs memorializing "good and faithful servants," including this 1780 example from North Attleboro, Massachusetts:

> Here lies the best of slaves
> Now turning into dust
> Caesar the Ethiopian craves
> A place among the Just.
> His faithful soul is fled
> To realms of heavenly light,
> And by the blood that Jesus shed
> Is changed from Black to White.

Mann and Greene (1962:37) also cite the epitaph of Amos Fortune, found in Jaffrey, New Hampshire:

> Sacred to the Memory of Amos Fortune
> who was born free in Africa
> a slave in America, he purchased
> liberty, professed Christianity,
> lived reputably, died hopefully.
> Nov. 17 1801 AEt. 91

Both the form and narrative content of the African-American material culture of death in Newport are strikingly different from forms and contents documented in other areas of the United States. In *Texas Graveyards,* for example, Jordan (1982) includes a photograph of wooden grave markers shaped into stylized human figures by African-American artisans. "The human effigy shape may be of African origin," he writes, "since it appears, generally in wood, among blacks in Texas, Georgia, and perhaps elsewhere in the South" (Jordan 1982:45). Jordan (1982:17) and Vlach (1978, 1991) cite other African-derived forms of Southern burial ritual, including shell decoration of graves, scraped earth in burying grounds, and broken pottery scattered on burial mounds.

Archaeological studies of African-American cemeteries in the Northeast have found similar evidence of burial practices derived from Africa. In a discussion of the burials from the 10th and Vine Street First African Baptist Church (FABC) cemetery in Philadelphia, McCarthy (1990:4) ascribes the placement of shoes on coffin lids as a material representation of the journey home to Africa. Interestingly, excavations by John Milner Associates at the two FABC cemeteries did not recover any evidence of headstones or footstones; Parrington and Wideman (1986) note that any burial practices described as African at the Eighth and Vine Street FABC were within the graves, not at the surface of the grave sites; the same was true at the 10th and Vine Street FABC cemetery (McCarthy 1990).

In Newport, where no African-American burials have actually been excavated, one is struck by the dominance of Euroamerican form and narrative content in the headstones and footstones that have survived. The tendency is not surprising when one considers who was doing the actual ordering and purchasing of the grave markers. Possibly Newport's African-American community practiced rituals of commemoration, such as outlining grave mounds with shells, that would only be recoverable through archaeological excavation of the burying ground.

The actions of the masters in staking out and monitoring the landscape of death rendered these rituals invisible to the viewer. Euroamericans interred African Americans in plots generally arranged by masters, while their own burying

FIGURE 4. For Euroamericans, African Americans' most significant relationships were with their masters. This 1762 marker for Mille and Katharine was commissioned by Henry Bull, Esq., a prominent Newport merchant who listed his name in both epitaphs on the stone.

grounds remained arranged in family plots. An example is the double marker for Mille and Katharine, two slaves of Henry Bull, Esq. (Figure 4). Although the two women died a year apart, Bull chose to commemorate them thriftily on a single stone, mentioning his own name on both epitaphs. Husbands and wives lie in separate plots established by their different masters, underscoring that, in the eyes of Euroamericans, an African American's most important connection was to the master, not to any blood relations. The stone commemorating Cato, for example, lists not only Cato's current master in the epitaph text but also the one who preceded him (Figure 5), and that for Dinah Tweedy includes her husband's master as well as her own (Figure 6).

The contradiction between Madam Knight's observations about shared space at the table and the archaeological evidence of segregation in the burying ground can be resolved by considering white paternalism (Kruger-Kahloula 1989). This paternalism is the logical extension of the Christianizing rationalization offered by white elites for enslaving Africans. Mason, for example, cites an unidentified Newport minister who

> always returned thanks on the Sunday following the arrival of a slaver in Newport 'that an overwhelming Providence has been brought to this land of freedom another cargo of benighted heathen to enjoy a gospel dispensation' (Mason 1884:104).

The gravestones support the notion of whites treating African Americans as naive beings requir-

FIGURE 5. The marker for Cato (1763) lists not one but two of his masters, underscoring the point that for white Newporters, Cato and other African Americans existed only in relation to their owners.

FIGURE 6. An unusual variant on the epitaph is that for Dinah Tweedy (1762), listing the names of her own master, her husband, and her husband's master.

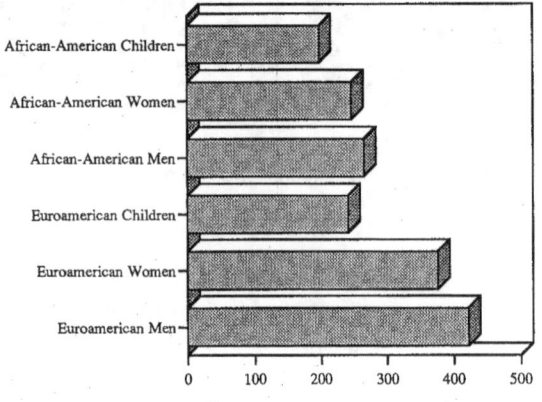

Average Surface Area (sq. in.)

FIGURE 7. Cross-cultural comparison of gravestone surface area during the pre-Revolutionary period, 1720–1770, reveals overlap between markers for African Americans and markers for white children, a tendency reflecting Euroamerican paternalism.

ing instruction in the ways of Euroamerican culture. A comparison of markers for African Americans with markers for whites reveals overlap in the surface area for African-American gravestones and the surface area of those cut for Euroamerican children (Figure 7). To term this finding the conscious artifact of planned activities by crafts workers would be problematic. One may argue that the size hierarchy is clear, whether or not direct comparison to children is intended.

Other evidence for paternalism comes directly from the epitaph texts of African-American gravestones. Epitaphs containing both testaments to the virtues of deceased slaves and the identities of their masters are seen most often in the period 1720–1770. These expressions, exemplified in the marker for Edward Collins (Figures 8, 9), border on the formulaic: "Faithful and loyal servant,"

"Well-beloved of his Master," and "A Faithful servant for more than Forty years." Furthermore, they echo ironically the words of Jesus Christ in the parable of the talents (Matthew XXV:21): "His lord said unto him, Well done, thou good and faith-

FIGURE 8. Formulaic expressions of masterly affection abound in the pre-Revolutionary period. This marker, cut by John Stevens II of Newport, was commissioned by merchant Henry Collins of Newport.

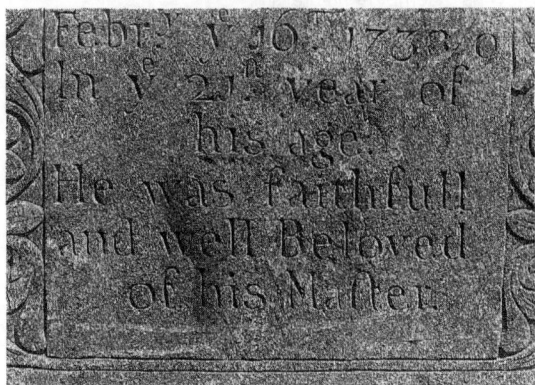

FIGURE 9. Detail of epitaph for Edward Collins (1738/9).

ful servant . . . enter thou into the joy of thy lord.'' Whether or not the masters viewed themselves in a god-like relationship with their slaves, the voiced

sentiments are perhaps not as significant as the more subtle function of visually linking the bodies of slaves in the burying ground with the masters who survived them.

Who would have read these messages of ownership? And what ranges of understanding, or *Verstehen,* would have resulted from those acts of reading? Kruger-Kahloula (1989) has argued that masters selected epitaphs that projected ideals of how slaves ought to behave. Her argument can be carried further, with emphasis on the others who would have read the texts. Newport's elite, who controlled both the creation of material culture and the surrounding landscape, were struggling to justify their power over at least three different communities: over living African Americans (Kruger-Kahloula 1989); over whites of lower economic and social standing; and over each other, in a material dialogue similar to that seen in the formal gardens of Maryland's elite families (Leone 1984).

These three different levels of experience are worth examining in detail. One would have spoken to an audience of living African Americans, who may have read the epitaphs as warnings from their masters. White elites controlled the boundaries of space in death as they did in life; furthermore, those slaves who were faithful and virtuous, and who served virtuous masters, would be reunited with their masters in death, a sentiment many African Americans may have found somewhat less than reassuring (Piersen 1988; Kruger-Kahloula 1989). A second communication may have been experienced by white Newporters of lower status than the masters: not only could elite families afford slaves, they could also commemorate them with expensive and permanent gravestones. This reading would have forced whites to grasp the material extent of the elites' social and economic power.

The final communication is one of shared prestige among masters. One of the ways that elite families maintain their standing within their communities is through patterns of conspicuous material consumption (St. George 1985; Sweeney 1985). Given the relatively small number of surviving gravestones for Newport's large African-American population, burial in temporarily-marked or unmarked graves was certainly more common than commemoration with permanent stone markers. The act of placing a gravestone from the John Stevens Shop may have been read by other masters with approval. Alternatively, masters may have made the implied connection that loyal and virtuous slaves can only belong to a master who is himself loyal and virtuous; these monuments, then, attest to that masterly "virtue" in the visible world.

Revolution and Emancipation (1770–1800): Expressions of Crisis in the Common Burying Ground

Changes in the pre-Revolutionary meanings of Newport's material culture of death were engendered by twin crises in the city's social structure: the erosion of slavery as a mode of production, and the occupation of Newport by British and Hessian troops from 1776 until 1779. Among the numerous effects of these crises was an alteration in the relationships between gravestone carvers and their clientele, an alteration that is perhaps most usefully studied through a group of three markers carved by John Stevens III.

The marker for Dinah Wanton Wigneron is representative of this group of three, which includes monuments for Violet Hammond and Pompey Brenton. The high-quality slate used in Wigneron's marker is indicative of significant investment on the part of the consumer, while the use of modillion blocks as a visual frame for the epitaph evokes the changing architectural order of the day (Figure 10). The bold signature "Cut by John Stevens, junior" across the bottom of this frame (Figure 11) reflects both pleased self-appraisal and a shrewd sense of promotion on the part of the artist (Tashijan and Tashijan 1974). Unlike most of the ready-made stones of the pre-Revolutionary period, all three of the 1772 markers were expensive and specific to the individuals they commemorate, especially the well-known "portrait" of Pompey Brenton (Figure 12).

One reading for the group of stones is that other consumers of gravestones would have realized the

FIGURE 10. Grave marker for Dinah Wanton Wigneron (1772), carved by John Stevens III of Newport. The modillion blocks around the epitaph evoke the changing architectural order of the time, while the portrait may represent Stevens' attempt at naturalism.

cost of these markers and made the correlation that the masters of Dinah, Pompey, and Violet held them in particular esteem (Franklin 1913; Battle 1932; Howe 1959). Yet 18th-century readers would only have experienced a similar message if they too equated expenditure with esteem, a problematic assumption when considering the mortuary activities of any time period (Parker Pearson 1982).

A second interpretation sees the 1772 markers as objects of conspicuous consumption by elites demonstrating their wealth, rather than their affection for their slaves. Such expenditures would have been significant during the period prior to the Revolution because of Newport's uneasy economic status in the world system. Tariffs imposed by Brit-

FIGURE 11. Detail of marker for Dinah Wanton Wigneron, showing the signature of "John Stevens, Junr.," i.e., John Stevens III, across the bottom of the epitaph.

ish authorities, including the Molasses, Sugar, and Hovering Acts, had interfered with the city's trade, resulting in a dramatic increase in smuggling and rebellion:

> Tensions grew between 1763 and 1776, reaching their peak with the burning of H.M.S. *Gaspee* on June 10, 1773 [*sic*], in Narragansett Bay. The *Gaspee,* significantly, had been harassing the smugglers of Narragansett Bay; in the group that burned her were prominent merchants (Schmidt and Mrozowski 1989:36).

If Doctor Wigneron, Captain Hammond, or former Governor Brenton had surplus resources on which to draw, it seems unlikely that they would have chosen to spend them in a flagrant display of wealth, unless there were conscious motivations to the act of display. These motivations did exist, and are found in the maintenance of power, which often underlies conspicuous consumption by elites during crisis periods (St. George 1985; Sweeney 1985). The three 1772 markers could represent an effort by the elite to assert their control of the city's strategic resources in the face of a faltering economy.

No active conspiracy to manipulate the material culture of death existed during this period, but after the arrival of the 1772 markers in the Common Burying Ground, several other, similarly-expensive gravestones appeared beside them in the burying ground. The marker for Portsmouth is interesting in this regard because it was cut in 1772 by John Bull, rival of John Stevens III (Figure 13). That Bull was also carving equally elaborate, and costly, stones for African Americans at this time

argues that the statements of power originated with the consumers of material culture, and not the carvers who executed the work. Free African Americans, slaves, and Euroamericans of lower status would all have read the 1772 markers as texts delineating the elites' emphatic claim as the controllers of secular and sacred landscapes.

A final point worthy of consideration in the Revolutionary War era is the increasing separation of material culture by gender, rather than ethnicity. As Figure 14 shows clearly, the tendency is for the surface area of gravestones for white adult males to form a category unto themselves. This tendency foreshadows later analyses of patriarchy in the cemeteries of upstate New York (Roveland 1983; McGuire 1988), and continues in the final period considered in this study.

Post-Revolutionary Newport (1800–1830): The Triumph of Industrial Capital Over Artisanry

The disruption of Newport's commerce and the occupation of the city by foreign troops had a devastating effect on the local maritime economy. In a speech made on the eve of the American Centennial, a local antiquarian described these depredations from the perspective of 100 years:

> Hundreds of buildings had been destroyed, the vessels and wharves had gone to decay altogether. . . . The forests and groves of native trees had been cut down, the farm fences had been wasted, farm stock had been consumed . . . schools

FIGURE 12. Detail of marker for Pompey Brenton (1772) by John Stevens III, indicating the individual nature of the cluster of 1772 monuments.

broken up, churches scattered, houses deserted, buildings out of repair, and ruin was stamped on everything which eight years before was alive with prosperity (Sheffield 1876:45).

After peace had been established, Newport's merchants attempted to rebuild the city's maritime economy through trade with Asian ports, but the leveling of the infrastructure rendered them unable to compete with their Massachusetts counterparts in Salem or Boston. By 1800 most efforts to recover from the vicissitudes of revolution and occupation had failed. Rhode Island's shift from merchant to industrial capitalism was moving jobs and industries inland, and as new mills appeared along the Blackstone and Providence rivers, Newport's wharves rotted and crumbled from inactivity.

The process of emancipation in Rhode Island was painfully slow and protracted. Court records indicate that at least some African Americans were free from the 17th century on, but their activities and participation in Newport's economies are not yet understood. An act of the Rhode Island General Assembly in 1774 ended the importation of slaves into the colony, but as McLoughlin (1986[1978]: 106) points out, the law contained a clever proviso: slave traders caught in a poor market were permitted to retain slaves for up to a year, or until they were able to sell at a profit. Even the Assembly's half-hearted decision to ban slavery in 1784 only provided freedom for children born after 1 March of that year. The resulting confusion initially fragmented African Americans into divisions of free and enslaved persons with varying degrees of legal status; often these divisions occurred within families, as masters obstinately refused to release African Americans from bondage.

FIGURE 13. Grave marker for Portsmouth "Servt. of Mr. DAVID CHESEBROUGH for more than Forty Years" (1772). Stonecutter John Bull's epitaph echoes an identification of slave with master much more common in the first half of the 18th century.

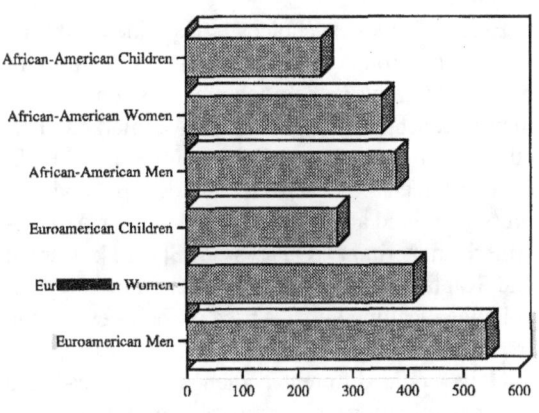

Average Surface Area (sq. in.)

FIGURE 14. During the Revolutionary War era, 1770–1800, the surface area of gravestones for white adult males began to form a distinct category, foreshadowing material expressions of patriarchy in 19th-century cemeteries (McGuire 1988).

African Americans were hardly powerless in the face of Euroamerican racism. Gutman (1976) has shown that Southern African Americans were able to maintain their family structure despite the pressures of overwhelmingly white society. Another response, available only to men, was to form benevolent societies, or fraternal groups that may have served as grassroots political organizations. Newport's African Union Society, one of the earliest benevolent societies in the United States, was founded in 1780. "The organization sought to record births, deaths, and marriages among Newport's blacks," write Gaines and Parkhurst (1992: 15), and "it was also concerned with the moral and religious condition of Newport's black community, and its members also went on record to oppose slavery." Death and burial also formed important aspects of the African Union Society, whose leadership issued decrees in 1790 and 1794 regulating the behavior and dress of its members at funerals (Robinson 1976).

The support networks of African-American benevolent societies did not survive long. By the late 1790s, the African Union Society crumbled under the external pressures of racism and the internal pressures of political infighting. McLoughlin describes the position of post-emancipation African Americans in Rhode Island succinctly:

> While most black Rhode Islanders were free after 1807, they remained the victims of prejudice and oppression in every sphere of life. They were segregated in the churches, kept out of the public schools, denied employment in the textile mills, and finally, in 1822, denied the right to vote (McLoughlin 1986[1978]:107–108).

Newport's political climate was not appreciably better for African Americans than that in other cities in Rhode Island, as competition for jobs in a depressed economy engendered a populist racism, the effects of which are seen in the Common Burying Ground.

The characteristics of the material culture of death and the readings they inspire point toward some of the underlying tensions during this time. Unlike monuments from the other periods, markers in the last sample are only identifiable as belonging to African Americans because of their location in the corner of the graveyard. Although the gravestones may have appeared similar to those of Euroamericans, the landscape of the burying ground still divided African Americans from whites. The color line did not disappear with emancipation; indeed, its effects were felt more keenly as contests between two groups of free people took shape in the material world.

This sharply-drawn and differently-constituted racism is evident in the 19th and perhaps even into the 20th century as African-American burials continued to be segregated at the north end of the burying ground. Despite varying degrees of integration in Newport's ecclesiastical cemeteries, markers for African Americans are not visible in other, white, sections of the secular Common Burying Ground.

Changes *are* apparent, however, in the African-American material culture of death in this time period. Although epitaphs are lengthier than they were previously, they rarely mention ethnicity. The two exceptions are the markers commemorating Dutchess (*sic*) Quamino (1804) and Dinah Neptune (ca. 1805), both of which include striking racially-grounded epitaphs memorializing the women. The marker for Dutchess Quamino is particularly effusive in its praise for the deceased, describing her as "a free black of distinguished excellence: intelligent, industrious, affectionate, honest, and of exemplary Piety." In an examination of African-American pauper records in Providence, Rhode Island, Coughtry and Coughtry (1985:111) noticed a similar phrase commonly used as a descriptive epithet. During the period 1804 through 1832, they found African Americans "invariably described as 'respectable' men and women 'of color'."

The tendency for a shrinking disparity in size between gravestones of African-American men and women and gravestones of Euroamerican women continued until little difference remained between the three types of markers (Figure 15). Erosion of size difference was related to the industrial production of markers, a trend that began in the 1820s and continues to the present day. The material culture of death became more restricted, with fewer choices available for all consumers as the idiosyncrasies of individual carvers disappeared. Moreover, the tendency of markers for Euroamerican men to form a separate and distinct

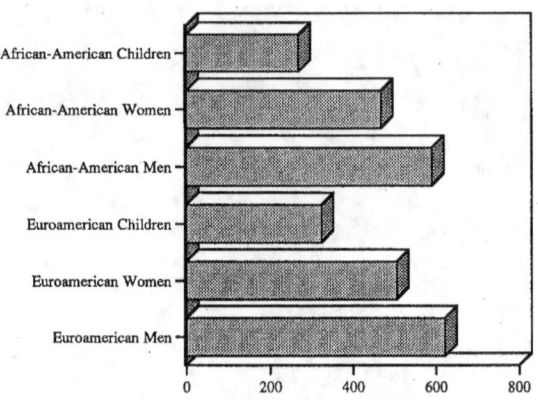

Average Surface Area (sq. in.)

FIGURE 15. By 1800–1830, industrial production rendered cross-cultural size differences invisible. Under the social conditions of industrial capitalism the difference in marker size became one of gender rather than of race.

category, first noticed in the Revolutionary period, continued to accelerate after the turn of the 19th century.

Even if market choices constrained African Americans from choosing a material culture of death containing iconographic expressions of ethnicity, consumers might still have marked their ethnicity in other ways. For example, they might have retained control over the epitaph and expressly ordered a text that referred to their African-American heritage (Quarles 1973[1961]; Kaplan and Kaplan 1988). Yet they chose not to select epitaphs recalling either Africa or their newly-won freedom.

How would different audiences have read this increasing homogeneity and uniformity in the material culture of death? By 1800–1830, both the actors and audiences for the performance of funerary ritual would have been exclusively African American. Euroamericans would have found little reason to enter the northern corner of the Common Burying Ground; indeed, the story of Mintus, Newport's "last colored undertaker" (Mason 1884:104–108) serves as a pertinent reminder of this separation. The patronizing description of the funeral ceremony is telling:

Perspectives from *Historical Archaeology*

It took Mintus some time to organize a funeral; but when everything was ready, he gave the signal to move, by walking ahead of the hearse . . . then he turned his head, and, jerking his thumb over his shoulder, exclaimed in a hoarse whisper, "Come along with that corpse!" (Mason 1884: 106–107).

Everything about Mintus—his clothing, his bearing, his actions in leading the funeral—is seen through white eyes as a heathenish ritual, one that is less directly threatening but worthy of contempt. If whites ridiculed African-American death rituals, how did African-American audiences view the masking of ethnicity in the landscape of the cemetery?

One interpretation uses assimilation to understand the erosion of difference. Those who were paying for grave markers may have wished to emphasize their families' participation in the culture of the new republic, forcing readers of epitaphs to admit that they, too, were part of this culture. Just as there are no ostensible differences in death, there should be no such differences in life—a hopeful message that later events would prove overly optimistic.

Alternatively, African Americans might have seen the presentation of "public selves" as an effort to legitimize their own identities in post-emancipation New England. These consumers of gravestones *did* see white Newporters as part of their audience, and they hoped to confront all readers with a realization of the equality of African Americans. African-American readers might have understood this message as an injunction to stand up for treatment as equals, and not to allow Euroamericans to create racial differences, even in the arena of the commemoration of death.

A third message may have been one of fear, a fear that riots in nearby Providence during the 1820s would certainly have justified. Possibly African Americans saw their counterparts' epitaphs as conscious efforts to avoid representation as African Americans, although the location of those texts in the corner of the burying ground would have rendered such efforts relatively powerless. African American readers of these texts would have experienced the sensibility that calling attention to one's self could bring down retribution,

especially for African Americans living in an overwhelmingly white society.

These three readings dramatically underscore the complexity of the color line dividing African Americans and whites while pointing to some of the tensions generated over the legal identity and status of African Americans in society. Many of the messages of interpretation emerge from these tensions, even into the present. One ought not to point specifically to changes in production or to attitudes of assimilation, confrontation, or fear to find the one reason why the masking of ethnicity occurred; all of these factors were operating simultaneously in Newport during the period 1800–1830. The major difference in grave markers between this period and the ones that preceded it were the audiences for the texts; this last period was one in which African Americans spoke directly to other African Americans. White Americans were neither the writers nor the readers of the material culture of death, although African Americans may have directed messages of confrontation or demands to be recognized directly at them.

African Americans found few responses to their protestations of equality. The frustration engendered by the lack of reaction, or the reaction of outright racism, was most poignantly expressed by Occramer Marycoo, who had been brought to Newport from Africa in 1760. At that time, according to Mason (1884:154), "he was still a savage and unable to speak other than the language of his tribe." Marycoo, whose captors gave him the name Newport Gardner, organized the Colored Union Church and Society. In 1825, at the age of 80, Marycoo finally gained sufficient means to return to Africa. At his departure, Marycoo said:

I go to set an example to the youth of my race; I go to encourage the young. They can never be elevated here; I have tried it for sixty years—it is in vain (Mason 1884:159).

The archaeological evidence from the Common Burying Ground suggests that at the time of Marycoo's embarkation, African Americans were engaged in a wide range of what might be termed resistive responses to whites. The masking of ethnic difference in the material culture of death was one way of attempting to legitimize identity, and to force fellow African Americans and Euroamericans alike to live up to the promises of the Revolution.

Discussion: Viewing the Color Line Through the Material Culture of Death

For any time period in the history of Newport, the material culture of death has multiple interpretations for readers of the gravestones and the burying ground landscape. Although the physical separation of burying places for Euroamericans and African Americans remained fixed in space, the messages carried by the texts generated a wide range of meanings for those who stopped to read them. Understanding these ranges of meanings provides historical archaeologists with an entry into the dynamics of the color line in coastal New England, and how African-American ethnicity shaped the context of daily life for both black and white residents of Newport, Rhode Island.

The interpretation of the material culture of death in Newport provided in this paper presents immediate questions for further research directed at developing the specific historical issues raised in this paper. Some questions are site-specific to the folklore and traditions of the Common Burying Ground. For example, to what extent were enslaved or free African Americans carving markers in the John Stevens Shop (Tashijan and Tashijan 1988)? Although Pompe (*sic*) Stevens, a slave working in the shop, signed a 1768 marker for Cuffe Gibbs, the extent to which African Americans were actually carving remains a tantalizing question worthy of investigation.

Other questions to pursue concern the ability of the diverse audiences of material culture to understand sentiments directed toward them. A study of comparative literacy in colonial Newport would reveal to what extent readers were able to read and experience fully the messages in the material culture of death. Still other questions, including the complicated changing legal status of African Americans in Rhode Island, require more extensive research into the documentary record. Finally, the demographic information contained in the markers offers extraordinary insight into mortality and kinship patterns of a Northern African-American community.

The results of these research efforts will ultimately lead historians and archaeologists alike to construct histories of Newport that are more inclusive of the city's African-American community than those that have been constructed to date. Tashijan and Tashijan close their analysis of the Common Burying Ground on a similarly hopeful note:

> In the final analysis, it is the existence of these gravestones in conjunction with external documentation that might eventually lead to a reconstruction of black community life in Newport . . . these gravestones call for a recognition of the textures and sensibilities of black communal life in eighteenth-century Newport (Tashijan and Tashijan 1988:190).

The use of hermeneutic theory to shed light on the color line raises a larger question of archaeological theory: How do efforts to understand the dialectic of the color line translate into the practice of historical archaeology? The implications of using Iser's (1978) focus on the readers of texts to construct archaeologies of the color line are significant, given the growing interest in a series of loosely-related topics lumped under the rubric "African-American archaeology," a phenomenon that eludes even the best efforts to define it (Singleton 1991).

With relatively few exceptions, the focus of African-American archaeology has centered on the experience of plantation slaves in the Caribbean and the American South. At the 1992 Society for Historical Archaeology Conference on Historical and Underwater Archaeology in Jamaica, for example, at least 100 papers could be classified as at least partially addressing African-American archaeology. Sixty-one of those papers dealt explicitly with plantation slavery, while only 17 considered free African Americans. (The remaining 22 papers fell into categories of overviews, artistic motifs, and theoretical discussions.) Of the 17 papers addressing the lives of free African Americans, only four were concerned with New England or the Northeast. The message is disturbing: for historical archaeologists, African Americans often exist principally as plantation slaves in the South or the Caribbean.

The intent here is emphatically *not* to dismiss studies of plantation slavery as irrelevant or meaningless. It must be acknowledged, however, that an archaeology that studies African-American experiences only through this particular mode of production is not addressing the range of variation, since, as Little (1992b) has shown, it effectively ignores the larger issue of the development of the world capitalist system in generating "the cultural, historical, social, and political processes that affected African Americans" (Singleton 1991:1).

The increase in attention toward defining African-American ethnicity through concepts like "plantation" has roused critics like Potter (1991), who argue that if historical archaeologists incorporated more reflexivity in their analyses, they would not be lulled into interpretations that gloss over the day-to-day realities of the color line. Similarly, Gaines and Parkhurst, in examining the historical records of Newport, conclude that the very act of trying to define an African-American community leads the researcher into troubling questions with ramifications in the present:

> Not only has the Newport African-American community's history received little attention, it is not even clear who that community is. . . . Furthermore, the color line has never been hard-and-fast: definitions of who is black vary considerably over time and by context. Our situation is in some ways comparable to that of a historian who sets out to study child labor and finds that some sources include 16-year-olds [*sic*] in statistics on children, others consider anyone 12 or older an adult, and many do not specify their definition (Gaines and Parkhurst 1992:2).

No reasonable person would deny that the increasing attention to African Americans in both the historical and archaeological records is a significant step toward interpretations of the past that are more inclusive than ones that have preceded them. Yet Potter's warnings about the dangers of objectifying African Americans have become increasingly appropriate. If the extensive publicity surrounding the discovery of Manhattan's "African Burial Ground" (Harrington 1993) has taught historical archaeologists a lesson, it is that the social and political realities of African-American archae-ologies entail not only dialogue, but proactive partnerships with the living descendants of the people they purport to study.

By shifting the focus of African-American archaeology toward an archaeology of contests over the color line, researchers might begin to see a more holistic picture of those contests, one that does not reduce African Americans to a collection of material traits with links to Africa. No one wrote more expressively about these contests than Du Bois, who believed that the challenge facing African-Americans was to merge the African and American aspects of their consciousness, to suppress the inherent feeling of "two-ness":

> In this merging, he [the African American] wishes neither of the older selves to be lost. He would not Africanize America, for America has too much to teach the world and Africa. He would not bleach his Negro soul in a flood of white Americanism, for he knows that Negro blood has a message for the world. He simply wishes . . . for a man to be both a Negro and an American, without being cursed and spit upon by his fellows (Du Bois 1990[1903]:9).

Paynter (1990) has argued that if archaeologists want to know what it was like to live in Massachusetts during the last 300 years, they need to understand the experiences of both African Americans and Euroamericans. Forms of reader-response theory might offer a promising entry point into discussions concerning the color line identified by Du Bois. By rediscovering the readers of material culture, historical archaeologists will gain insight not only into the construction of race in the United States, but also into the associated tensions that survive today.

ACKNOWLEDGMENTS

Many thanks to Robert Paynter, Jacqueline Urla, Kevin Sweeney, Mary Beaudry, and especially Martin Wobst for their responses to earlier versions of this paper. Part of the supplementary research for this project was accomplished under a Paul Cuffe Memorial Fellowship from the Munson Institute for American Maritime Studies at Mystic Seaport. I would also like to thank members of the former Reading Group in Post-Processual Archaeology at the University of Massachusetts for their comments, particularly Uzi Baram, J. Edward

Hood, Robert Paine, and Michael Volmar. John McCarthy, Lauren Cook, and Robert Fitts offered advice about the draft, as did Daniel G. Roberts, Edward L. Bell, and two anonymous reviewers for *Historical Archaeology.* The M.A. thesis on which this article was based was published in the Volumes in Historical Archaeology Series sponsored by the South Carolina Institute of Archaeology and Anthropology. Finally, Eve Sterne made many visits to the Common Burying Ground during the course of this study; this paper is for her, with love and appreciation.

REFERENCES

BAKER, VERNON G.
1978   Historical Archaeology at Black Lucy's Garden, Andover, Massachusetts. *Papers of the Robert S. Peabody Foundation for Archaeology* 8:110–121. Robert S. Peabody Foundation for Archaeology, Andover, Massachusetts.

BATTLE, C. A.
1932   Negroes on the Island of Rhode Island. Manuscript on file, Newport Historical Society, Newport, Rhode Island.

BARRET, JOHN
1987   Fields of Discourse: Reconstituting a Social Archaeology. *Critique of Anthropology* 7:5–16.

BEAUDRY, MARY C., LAUREN J. COOK, AND STEPHEN A. MROZOWSKI
1990   Artifacts and Active Voices: Material Culture as Social Discourse. In *The Archaeology of Inequality,* edited by Randall H. McGuire and Robert Paynter, pp. 150–191. Basil Blackwell, Oxford.

BELL, EDWARD L.
1990   The Historical Archaeology of Mortuary Behavior: Coffin Hardware from Uxbridge, Massachusetts. *Historical Archaeology* 24(3):54–78.
1991   Review of *Gravestone Chronicles: Some Eighteenth-Century New England Carvers and Their Work,* by Theodore Chase and Laurel K. Gabel. *New England Quarterly* 64(2):330–332.

BOWER, BETH
1991   Material Culture in Boston: The Black Experience. In *The Archaeology of Inequality,* edited by Randall H. McGuire and Robert Paynter, pp. 55–63. Basil Blackwell, Oxford.

BRIDENBAUGH, CARL
1976   *Fat Mutton and Liberty of Conscience.* Reprint of 1974 edition. Athenaeum, New York.

CHYET, STANLEY F.
1970   *Lopez of Newport: Colonial American Merchant Prince.* Wayne State University Press, Detroit, Michigan.

CONNELLY, EDWIN
1973   Plan of the Common Burying Ground, Newport, Rhode Island. Manuscript on file, Redwood Library, Newport, Rhode Island.

COUGHTRY, JAMIE, AND JAY COUGHTRY
1985   Black Pauper Records: Providence Rhode Island, 1777–1831. *Rhode Island History* 44(4):109–119.

CRANE, ELAINE FORMAN
1985   *A Dependent People: Newport, Rhode Island, in the Revolutionary Era.* Fordham University Press, New York.

CRAPANZANO, VINCENT
1992   *Hermes' Dilemma and Hamlet's Desire: On the Epistemology of Interpretation.* Harvard University Press, Cambridge, Massachusetts.

DEETZ, JAMES
1977   *In Small Things Forgotten: The Archaeology of Early American Life.* Anchor Press/Doubleday, Garden City, New York.

DEXTER, FRANKLIN BOWDITCH (EDITOR)
1901   *The Literary Journal of Ezra Stiles,* Vol. 1. Charles Scribner's Sons, New York.

DU BOIS, W. E. B.
1990   *The Souls of Black Folk.* Reprint of 1903 edition. Vintage Books, New York.

EAGLETON, TERRY
1983   *Literary Theory: An Introduction.* University of Minnesota Press, Minneapolis.

FRANKLIN, R. S.
1913   *Newport Cemeteries.* Special Bulletin of the Newport Historical Society, Newport, Rhode Island.

GADAMER, HANS-GEORG
1975   *Truth and Method.* Sheed and Ward, London.

GAINES, KEVIN, AND BETH PARKHURST
1992   African-Americans in Newport, 1660–1960. Manuscript on file, Rhode Island Historical Preservation Commission, Providence, Rhode Island.

GARMAN, JAMES C.
1992   "Faithful and Loyal Servants": The Masking and Marking of Ethnicity in the Material Culture of Death. South Carolina Institute of Archaeology and Anthropology, Charleston, South Carolina.
[1994] African Americans in the East Bay Region of Rhode Island: The Evidence from Probate Inventories. Report to be submitted to the Rhode Island Historical Preservation Commission, Providence, in preparation.

GREENE, LORENZO D.
1966 *The Negro in Colonial New England, 1620–1776.* Reprint of 1942 edition. Kennikat Press, Port Washington, New York.

GUTMAN, HERBERT G.
1976 *The Black Family in Slavery and Freedom, 1750–1925.* Pantheon Books, New York.

HARRINGTON, SPENCER P. M.
1993 Bones and Bureaucrats: New York's Great Cemetery Imbroglio. *Archaeology* 46(2):28–38.

HAUTENIEMI, SUSAN
1992 The W. E. B. Du Bois Site: Material Culture and the Creation of Race and Gender. Paper presented at the Annual Meeting of the Society for Historical Archaeology Conference on Historical and Underwater Archaeology, Kingston, Jamaica.

HOWE, GEORGE
1959 *Mount Hope.* Viking Press, New York.

ISER, WOLFGANG
1978 *The Act of Reading: A Theory of Aesthetic Response.* Johns Hopkins University Press, Baltimore, Maryland.

JOHNSEN, HARALD, AND BJORNAR OLSEN
1992 Hermeneutics and Archaeology: On the Philosophy of Contextual Archaeology. *American Antiquity* 57(3):419–436.

JORDAN, TERRY G.
1982 *Texas Graveyards.* University of Texas Press, Austin.

KAPLAN, SIDNEY, AND EMMA NOGRADY KAPLAN
1988 *The Black Presence in the Era of the American Revolution.* University of Massachusetts Press, Amherst.

KNIGHT, SARAH KEMBLE
1935 *The Journal of Madam Knight.* Facsimile reprint of the 1825 edition. Peter Smith, New York.

KRUGER-KAHLOULA, ANGELIKA
1989 Tributes in Stone and Lapidary Lapses: Commemorating Black People in Eighteenth- and Nineteenth-Century America. *Markers* 6:33–102.

LEONE, MARK P.
1984 Interpreting Ideology in Historical Archaeology: Using the Rules of Perspective in the William Paca Garden in Annapolis, Maryland. In *Ideology, Power and Prehistory,* edited by Daniel Miller and Christopher Tilley, pp. 25–35. Cambridge University Press, Cambridge and New York.

LITTLE, BARBARA J.
1992a Text, Images, Material Culture. In *Text-Aided Archaeology,* edited by Barbara J. Little, pp. 217–221. CRC Press, Boca Raton, Florida.

1992b Text-Aided Archaeology. In *Text-Aided Archaeology,* edited by Barbara J. Little, pp. 1–6. CRC Press, Boca Raton, Florida.

LITTLE, BARBARA J., KIM M. LANPHEAR, AND DOUGLAS OWSLEY
1992 Mortuary Display and Status in a Nineteenth-Century Anglo-American Cemetery in Manassas, Virginia. *American Antiquity* 57(3):397–418.

LOVECRAFT, HOWARD PHILLIPS
1983 *The Dream-Quest of Unknown Kadath.* Reprint of 1939 edition. Del Rey/Ballantine Books, New York.

MANN, THOMAS C., AND JANET GREENE
1962 *Over Their Dead Bodies: Yankee Epitaphs and History.* Stephen Greene Press, Brattleboro, Vermont.

MASON, GEORGE CHAPMAN
1884 *Reminiscences of Newport.* Charles E. Hammett, Jr., Newport, Rhode Island.

McCARTHY, JOHN P.
1990 African-American Acculturation as Reflected in the Cemeteries of the First African Baptist Church, Philadelphia: Population Dynamics and Social Stress in the Early Nineteenth Century. Paper presented at the Annual Meeting of the Council for Northeastern Historical Archaeology, Kingston, Ontario.

McGUIRE, RANDALL H.
1988 Dialogues with the Dead: Ideology and the Cemetery. In *The Recovery of Meaning: Historical Archaeology in the Eastern United States,* edited by Mark P. Leone and Parker B. Potter, Jr., pp. 435–480. Anthropological Society of Washington Series. Smithsonian Institution Press, Washington, D.C.

McLOUGHLIN, WILLIAM
1986 *Rhode Island: A History.* Reprint of 1978 edition. Norton, New York.

MROZOWSKI, STEPHEN A.
1981 Archaeological Investigations in Queen Anne Square, Newport, Rhode Island: A Study in Urban Archaeology. Unpublished M.A. thesis, Department of Anthropology, Brown University, Providence, Rhode Island.

MULLER, NANCY LADD
1992 "The House of the Black Burghardts": An Investigation of Race, Gender and Class at the W. E. B. Du Bois Boyhood Homesite. Ph.D. prospectus on file, Department of Anthropology, University of Massachusetts, Amherst.

PARKER PEARSON, MICHAEL
1982 Mortuary Practices, Society and Ideology: An Ethnoarchaeological Study. In *Symbolic and Structural Archaeology,* edited by Ian Hodder, pp. 99–113. Cambridge University Press, Cambridge and New York.

PARRINGTON, MICHAEL, AND JANET C. WIDEMAN
1986   The Archaeology of a Black Philadelphia Cemetery: Acculturation in an Urban Setting. *Expedition* 28(1): 55–62.

PAYNTER, ROBERT
1990   Afro-Americans in the Massachusetts Historical Landscape. In *The Politics of the Past,* edited by Peter Gathercole and David Lowenthal, pp. 49–62. Unwin Hyman, London.

PIERSEN, WILLIAM D.
1988   *Black Yankees: The Development of an Afro-American Subculture in Eighteenth-Century New England.* University of Massachusetts Press, Amherst.

POTTER, PARKER B., JR.
1991   What Is the Use of Plantation Archaeology? *Historical Archaeology* 25(3):94–107.

QUARLES, BENJAMIN
1973   *The Negro in the American Revolution.* Reprint of 1961 edition. Norton Library, New York.

RHODE ISLAND STATE ARCHIVES [RISA]
1774   An Account of the Number of Families and Inhabitants of the Town of Newport, 1774. Document on file, Rhode Island State Archives, Providence.

ROBINSON, WILLIAM H. (EDITOR)
1976   *The Proceedings of the Free African Union Society and the African Benevolent Society.* Urban League of Rhode Island, Providence.

ROVELAND, BLYTHE E.
1983   Houses of the Dead. Unpublished B.A. thesis, Department of Anthropology, State University of New York at Binghamton, Binghamton.

ST. GEORGE, ROBERT BLAIR
1985   Artifacts of Regional Consciousness in the Connecticut River Valley, 1700–1870. In *The Great River,* edited by William Hosley and E. Fox, pp. 28–39. Wadsworth Athenaeum, Hartford, Connecticut.

SCHMIDT, PETER R., AND STEPHEN A. MROZOWSKI
1989   Documentary Insights into the Archaeology of Smuggling. In *Documentary Archaeology in the New World,* edited by Mary C. Beaudry, pp. 32–42. Cambridge University Press, Cambridge and New York.

SCHUYLER, ROBERT L. (EDITOR)
1980   *Archaeological Perspectives on Ethnicity in America.* Baywood Monographs in Archaeology, Vol. 1. Baywood, Farmingdale, New York.

SHANKS, MICHAEL, AND CHRISTOPHER TILLEY
1987   *Social Theory and Archaeology.* University of New Mexico Press, Albuquerque.
1992   *Reconstructing Archaeology.* Second edition. Routledge, London and New York.

SHEFFIELD, WILLIAM P.
1876   *Historical Address of the City of Newport, Delivered July 4th, 1876.* John P. Sanborn and Co., Newport, Rhode Island.

SINGLETON, THERESA A.
1991   Editor's Notes. *African-American Archaeology* 1(3):1.

SWEENEY, KEVIN
1985   From Wilderness to Arcadian Vale: Material Life in the Connecticut River Valley, 1635–1760. In *The Great River,* edited by William Hosley and E. Fox, pp. 17–27. Wadsworth Athenaeum, Hartford, Connecticut.

TASHJIAN, ANN, AND DICKRAN TASHJIAN
1988   The Afro-American Section of Newport, Rhode Island's Common Burying Ground. In *Cemeteries and Gravemarkers: Voices of American Culture,* edited by Richard E. Meyer, pp. 163–195. UMI Research Press, Ann Arbor, Michigan.

TASHJIAN, DICKRAN, AND ANN TASHJIAN
1974   *Memorials for Children of Change.* Wesleyan University Press, Middletown, Connecticut.

TILLEY, CHRISTOPHER (EDITOR)
1990   *Reading Material Culture.* Basil Blackwell, Oxford.

VLACH, JOHN MICHAEL
1978   *The Afro-American Tradition in Decorative Arts.* Cleveland Museum of Art, Cleveland, Ohio.
1991   *By the Work of Their Hands: Studies in African-American Folklife.* University Press of Virginia, Charlottesville.

JAMES C. GARMAN
PUBLIC ARCHAEOLOGY LABORATORY, INC.
210 LONSDALE AVENUE
PAWTUCKET, RHODE ISLAND 02860

Harold Mytum

Mortality Symbols in Action: Protestant and Catholic Memorials in Early-Eighteenth-Century West Ulster

ABSTRACT

Material culture can carry many complementary and even conflicting messages simultaneously, to be read in varied ways by those observing it. Graveyard memorials link the living and the dead within a communal setting and are active in reinforcing conscious and unconscious values or in challenging them. The graveyard monuments of West Ulster offer an unusually rich sample of monuments with mortality symbols (skull, crossed bones, coffin, bell, and hourglass) as well as texts. Graveyards were the scenes of religious and social tension in 18th-century Ireland, and the memorials with their symbols and texts can be used to investigate the dynamics of identity played out in this arena. Although memorials were important in the dynamics of class and ethnic identities, emphasis is placed on religious identity here, an aspect of great importance in the past but one that has received less attention in historical archaeology than it deserves. Protestants and Catholics chose to use some of the same symbols on their memorials but assigned them meanings and associations appropriate to their theologies. Although they normally were buried in the same Anglican-controlled graveyard, symbol and text reflected and reinforced separate religious identities.

Introduction

One of the major themes in historical archaeology has focused analysis on divisions within society, and studies of mortuary monuments have reflected these interests. Particular attention has been paid to divisions based on class (McGuire 1988; Wurst 1991), ethnicity (Meyer 1993; Garman 1994), and the interrelationship of these two variables (Clark 1987). The study of mortuary monuments has tended to link religion with one of these other headings, particularly ethnicity (Nakagawa 1994), but it should be recognized that for many people in the past, religion was a major categorizing element in their world and an important feature of their self-definition. The ways in which religious belief and identity might be expressed

within the mortuary context can be complex. It may be subtle and not always explicitly stated on memorials (Nakagawa 1994; Mytum 2002a). This paper examines memorials from West Ulster, Ireland, where both Catholic and Protestant groups used graveyard monuments to make statements through text and symbol about their beliefs.

Burial monuments with inscriptions provide relatively well-dated examples of material culture (Mytum 2002b), often with close spatial definition. They are potent artifacts, consciously created to serve private commemorative purposes but also to act as a public and visible statement regarding both the deceased and their families. Whilst the emotional power of bereavement may be a factor in commemoration (Tarlow 1999), many cultural factors also affected the production, use, and meanings of the selected monuments. Archaeologists have studied gravestones in a generalizing manner, considering broad trends over time and space (Deetz and Dethlefsen 1965; Dethlefsen and Deetz 1966; Mytum 2003a, 2004e) and even with a cross-cultural comparative purpose (Cannon 1989). Monuments are also amenable to analysis where priority is given to the localized, temporally specific communication for which they were consciously constructed. This approach is taken here. James Garman (1994) has considered how African American memorials could have had a range of different meanings, depending on who was viewing the memorials; this can be seen to be equally relevant in the Irish context investigated here.

This study examines whether contemporary groups may have read differently the texts and symbols on 17th- and 18th-century memorials. An archaeological analysis takes account of the social and ideological context in which the monuments were created and the various constituencies that could observe the memorials. While Irish memorials of the early-18th century incorporated a range of symbols, concentration here will be placed on the most frequently used category—mortality symbols, already widely recorded and discussed within gravestone studies. These symbols are examined in the context of Protestant and Catholic commemorative practice to investigate whether the same symbols could have been used by both groups yet could have created different resonances, associations, and meanings due to each group's different theologies. Following standard archaeological methodology (Mytum 2000), the data from West Ulster presented here have been collected from seven burial grounds used by both Protestants and Catholics in the counties of Fermanagh and Monaghan (Figure 1).

Gravestones, Mortality Symbols, and Meanings

Many morta,lity symbols on gravestones are easily recognized, being either skeletal remains or related to the funeral process. The most ubiquitous is that of the skull, although many others occur (Table 1). The popularity of particular motifs, and their combination with others that may emphasize judgment and salvation, relates to religious persuasion. Use of particular motifs is also determined by regional styles that often incorporate other iconographic themes

FIGURE 1. Ireland, showing West Ulster and indicating counties Fermanagh (*F*) and Monaghan (*M*) where the survey has been largely concentrated. (Map by author.)

TABLE 1
MORTALITY SYMBOLS FOUND ON SCOTTISH MONUMENTS

Symbol	Comments
Angel of Death	May have wings and one or more of dart, hourglass, and scales
Axe	Indicating the cutting off of life
Bell	Handbell (deid bell) giving notice of death and used at the funeral
Bones	Crossed bones (two long bones) but also single long bone or jaw
Bow and arrow	As sometimes used by Angel of Death
Coffin	Shown in range of forms as in use at the time
Corpse	In winding sheet or lying in a coffin
Dart	Shown as an arrow or spear
Death	Active skeleton with dart or spear
Deathbed scene	Deceased, usually visited by Death
Death's head (skull)	In various profiles, with or without lower jaw
Father Time	Bearded figure, often with scythe and hourglass
Green man	Medieval symbol for physical corruption but possibly also with optimistic rebirth connotations
Hourglass	Vertical or horizontal, occasionally winged
Pick	Sexton's grave-digging tool
Scythe	As used by Father Time and Angel of Death
Skeleton	Lying or standing; see also Death with dart or spear
Snakes	Sin and Death as shown by the Fall of Man with Adam and Eve
Spade	Sexton's grave-digging tool; contemporary regional forms depicted
Spear or lance	A large version of the dart
Turf cutter	Sexton's grave-digging tool; contemporary regional forms depicted
Winged skull	On some 17th-century monuments; rare later

Perspectives from *Historical Archaeology*

such as kinship or occupation (Willsher and Hunter 1978). While these motifs were socially extremely important, here emphasis is placed on the choice and use of mortality symbols to state religious belief, with symbols evoking varied responses from those viewing them.

The symbolic power of mortality symbols was not constrained by denomination. The *danse macabre*, or dance of death, was continued after the Protestant Reformation in Catholic contexts (Ariès 1974), whilst Hans Holbein the Younger's illustrations of 1526 were particularly influential for Protestants (Llewellyn 1991). The medieval skeletal images in England and Scotland change from those representing the dead person to those indicating the active and sinister figure of death itself. After the reformation, the death figure and mortality symbols continue to be important on high-status internal memorials and in printed literature and are found with both Catholic and Protestant associations. Although these images reminded viewers of their own inevitable mortality, they did not symbolize the same religious messages. It is therefore necessary to explore the varied theological strands that could be woven using the same symbolic repertoire.

Protestant Tradition

Protestant treatment of death and commemoration was centered around the concept of judgment, based on the life and faith of the deceased, which could not be further ameliorated upon death. The role of the monument thus became one of celebration of the social persona of the deceased and of a didactic role, warning those still alive of the fate that awaited them (Llewellyn 2000). There were different perspectives, however, on the nature of judgment and the chances of salvation that changed over time but were also based on denominational interpretations. The most studied of these with regard to mortuary art and symbol is the Puritan element, although it must be remembered that the Anglican and some of the nonconformist traditions offered a less pessimistic view that therefore incorporated a lower level of mortality symbolism. This can be seen, for example, in the numerous tombs and ledgers in the Calder Valley, Yorkshire, England, of the 17th and early 18th centuries where mortality symbols are rare, cherubs frequent, and hearts (representing here

the soul of the deceased) ubiquitous (Brears 1981).

Puritan perspectives on death have been well studied and integrated with evidence from mortuary monuments (Stannard 1973, 1977; Watters 1981; Messer 1990). Edwin Dethlefsen and James Deetz (1966:508) saw the skull as linked to a strong Puritanical concern with judgment and mortality, unlike the later use of the cherub that epitomized a more optimistic anticipation of resurrection. Allan Ludwig (1966) also placed the use of the mortality symbols firmly within the Puritan tradition, with the decay of the flesh carrying with it the possibility of eternal damnation for those who were not within the elect, destined for a place amongst the saints. The division between the death's head and the cherub was straddled by the winged skull within New England, although other symbolic elements could also be used. Dickran Tashjian and Ann Tashjian (1974:62–63) note:

> The symbol of a winged skull conveys in didactic as well as figurative terms the concept of metamorphosis. The skull itself still remains a powerful icon of human mortality, a sign of irreversible change and decay … The *winged* skull symbolically looks forward to the Judgment Day, when, upon the Second Coming of Christ, the body bequeathed to the earth shall be reunited with its soul to ascend to heaven. Hence the exhortation engraved upon so many markers: "Arise ye dead." This eschatology, expressed primarily by the winged skull, is reinforced by other elements within the design whose animation is essentially metamorphic [emphasis in original].

The use of mortality symbols was extremely widespread in Scotland (Table 1), which can also be linked to the Presbyterian tenor of the church that developed out of a range of factions with varying Protestant inclinations (Dunbar 1996). This Scottish Calvinist emphasis provides a clear parallel to the New England situation, and so the popularity of mortality symbols can be explained in a similar manner. Indeed, Betty Willsher (1996:15) notes that the church emphasized that death of the sinful body was inevitable but balanced this with hope of salvation through grace on the day of judgment. In Scotland, the cherub therefore often can be found to counterbalance the mortality symbols, even from an early date. Rather than combine these themes in one symbol (the winged skull), two elements were often present on memorials, with the mortality symbols usually low down and the cherub towards the top (Figure 2). In this way, the mortal remains lie below, while the cherubic soul flies to heaven. Many earlier Scottish memorials only portrayed mortality symbols, where the great variety of such motifs and even the repeated use of some elements on the same monument created a clear statement (Table 1). Scottish stones often provided visually complex iconographical schemes, but they were similar in theology to those of New England.

American scholars have concentrated on English sources for parallels and origins for the Puritan mortality symbols. They have looked in those areas of Kent and East Anglia where such communities were significant and from which New England populations were drawn (Ludwig 1966; Benes 1977). This emphasizes population movements that were no doubt important, but other British evidence may provide potentially more relevant comparisons. The situation in Scotland and Scottish Ulster are such examples, where continued Presbyterian traditions more closely mirrored the theology of the Puritans. These situations provide alternative comparative regions where one of the dominant theological strands was similar to that of New England, and where movement of people provided a vehicle for the transfer of ideas and practices (Watters 1997; Mytum 2004b). In contrast, there were other contemporary theological viewpoints in Ireland and Europe that offered very different emphases on death and salvation and used the same symbols in significantly different ways.

Catholic Tradition

Archaeological and art-historical gravestone studies have concentrated on certain regions of predominantly Protestant settlement. It is appropriate that Protestant Reformation theology is applied to explain the meaning of such memorials, but this approach could be taken to imply that mortality symbols were a uniquely Protestant manifestation. This was certainly not the case, as the same symbols were widely applied within what was called the Catholic Counter-Reformation context. The domination of interpretation within a Protestant framework needs to be tempered with an analysis that provides a Catholic perspective.

The role of the Catholic Counter-Reformation, with its new theological emphases and its changed priorities in iconography, needs to be incorporated within a wider review of the use of mortality symbols. The impact of these theological shifts on the material culture of death has not been considered by archaeologists and has received merely passing note by other scholars (Janelle 1963:163–164; Knipping 1974). The Counter-Reformation reacted to the Protestant criticisms by removing excesses that had developed in the late medieval church, and by new vigor and commitment by both parochial clergy and dynamic orders such as the Jesuits. The latter concentrated on figural scenes, although symbols such as "IHS," the first three letters of Jesus in Greek, were much used (Smith 2002) and will be seen as one of the most significant, and no doubt widely understood, symbol of Catholic affiliation and devotion in Ireland. Although in some regions, the use of

FIGURE 2. Holy Rood churchyard, Stirling; Scottish memorial with mortality symbols and cherub. (Photo by author, 2002.)

Crucifixion images and symbols of the Passion of Jesus Christ (the time of the last days and death of Jesus) also were popular (Longfield 1944, 1954; Tait 2002).

Another strand of Counter-Reformation thought emphasized the mortality of the body and the need for prayer by those still alive. This intercession could reduce the time spent by the deceased's soul in purgatory. Indeed, the role of purgatory as a necessary phase of indeterminate length was a central part of Counter-Reformation theology (Ariès 1981:463). Images of human remains, or skeletal material itself, could be used to emphasize this point and to create environments where prayer was encouraged. These images could be in communal ossuaries (Ariès 1985:167–170), or in chapels decorated with human remains, often in imaginative and creative designs. The use of human charnel to create environments for commemoration and prayer continued into the 19th century and are still in use today (Ariès 1985:190–192). The use of actual skeletal elements could encourage prayer and supplication, and a similar response could be gained by the use of mortality symbols. The latter strategy was applied in Ireland, the former being more frequent in the Mediterranean region. Particularly the skull was often associated with prayer for the soul in Counter-Reformation contexts (Ariès 1985:236), which might explain its popularity on Catholic memorials of the early-18th century in West Ulster.

Mortality symbols such as the skull and hourglass also appeared in many vanities—paintings and engravings where still-life compositions included or were dominated by symbols of death. These could have a didactic theological role, although they developed to become secular romantic reminders of the hollowness of life and for a melancholy contemplation that could be emotional or philosophical (Ariès 1981:327–332, 1985:193,196–198). It is likely that mortality symbols on memorials with other Christian iconography were indeed designed to encourage a religious connotation. It may be that for some observers, Age of Enlightenment concepts might be evoked instead by such symbols.

The tradition in much of Catholic Europe for temporary inhumation, followed by disinterment of remains and their transfer to a familial or communal ossuary, meant that burial plots were used many times over. Memorials were not normally retained for any length of time, a custom that has limited the preservation of historic Catholic memorials (Mytum 2003b). Catholic symbolism used on 18th-century memorials is less well known and is even more reliant than elsewhere on the relatively small number of elite monuments that have survived within churches. Ireland, however, provides a window on popular Catholic iconographic culture, as it was an area of Catholic Europe where exhumation was not widely practiced. A few elite 17th-century tombs and a significant number of 18th-century memorials survive. The more affluent (and often Protestant) members of society tended to be those who erected large monuments, but sufficient numbers of the Catholic majority were able to commission stone memorials and erect them in the same graveyards used by Protestants. In this way, the various denominations can be compared within closed multidenominational environments.

Some symbols have clear Catholic associations and are important in identifying the religion of the deceased on Irish memorials. The most obvious and potent of these symbols is the cross. Protestants disliked what was seen at the time as a Papist symbol. Although it could occur occasionally even in Puritan New England contexts (Ludwig 1966:128–133), the cross is not found on Protestant memorials in Scotland (Willsher and Hunter 1978) and is very rare in England and Wales until the 19th century. In Ireland the cross was certainly recognized as a Catholic symbol, being displayed on the gabled roofs of Catholic churches but not on Protestant ones. Numerous stone wayside commemorative crosses were erected in 17th-century Ireland by Catholics desiring prayers for departed souls. For most Catholics the purpose of crosses was obvious but was further emphasized by the content of any inscriptions (King 1985). It is perhaps surprising that so many survive. Given their overt religious affiliation and purpose, crosses would have been easy targets for iconoclastic purging. This allowance of some Catholic symbols is also a feature notable in the graveyards themselves.

Another symbol, often linked with the cross, also indicated Catholic belief—the letters IHS, usually although not exclusively depicted with a cross rising from the horizontal crossbar of the *H*. Having a long tradition in Catholic iconography, the abbreviation was widely displayed in many stylistic forms across Counter-Reformation Europe (Ariès 1985:220,224; Blake et al. 2003). This symbol of Jesus and his sacrifice to gain eternal life for humanity had an obvious role on grave monuments, particularly as it encouraged prayer for the deceased to receive the gift of salvation. IHS often was used as lower-status external memorials began to appear in many regions of Europe, notably in Ireland (Longfield 1945; Grogan 1998; Mytum 2004c). IHS does not occur widely in Protestant memorial contexts until Anglo-Catholic High Church traditions developed in the 19th century. Its popularity coincided with a period when cross forms were also acceptable in Anglican contexts (Mytum 2000, 2002a). For the 18th century, IHS remains a reliable signal of Catholic religious affiliation; indeed in Scotland it was used on buildings as a sign of resistance by the Catholic minority (Bryce and Roberts 1993, 1996). For this study, the use of IHS is taken to be sufficient to indicate a Catholic memorial. All other Catholic indicators occur in addition to IHS and never without it.

In order to appreciate the role of religion and religious symbolism, the intimate relationship between denomination and power structures needs to be outlined. In Ireland the historical development of sectional interests has intimately linked the two most important variables of ethnicity and religion with class, dynastic succession, and occupation (Graham 1997).

Context of Irish Commemoration

Ireland in the early-18th century was a country divided into a number of groups defined by class and religion. The politically dominant group included the land-owning classes. These people were predominantly Protestant and of Anglican persuasion. The Anglican Church of Ireland was the established church, but it never captured the hearts of more than a minority of the population, although supporters belonged to all levels of society. Church of Ireland members were overwhelmingly Irish in that their families had been settled in the country for decades, if not centuries (Connolly 1997:48). Following the success of the Williamite campaign, culminating in the Battle of the Boyne in 1690, the threat

of Catholic Jacobite control was broken. In the following decades, the Protestant elite introduced various pieces of legislation through the Irish Parliament in Dublin that ensured its social and economic position by restricting the rights of opponents (Connolly 1992:263–313). Political security was also increased by the encouragement of settlement from England and Scotland. It was from the latter country that most came, and Ulster was the most frequent destination—the Plantation of Ulster that had already been proclaimed in the early-17th century (Bardon 1996:67–92). The Scots who came to Ulster as "planters" were overwhelmingly Presbyterian and created within Ulster a distinctive culture that has lasted to this day (Bardon 1996; Connolly 1997). Although many Ulster Scots later moved on to the New World (Leyburn 1962), the large numbers that remained across Ulster were demographically significant.

The various elements of discriminatory legislation passed through the Irish Parliament in Dublin have been termed the "Penal Laws," and they affected both religious and secular aspects of life. In 1695, the holding of arms by Catholics was forbidden, as was contact and exchange with foreign educators (Connolly 1992:267–268). These were security measures to both weaken the military strength of any uprising and to limit contact with overseas Catholic powers. Legislation was subsequently passed making interdenominational marriages always to the benefit of Protestants. The Banishment Act of 1697 provided a legal framework for the exclusion of those not only of religious orders but also bishops. As bishops were needed to ordain clergy and it was illegal from 1704 for clergy to enter the country, this should have led to a gradual decline in the numbers of parish priests through natural attrition (Connolly 1992:275). In practice, however, the Banishment Act was only briefly enforced with enthusiasm, and a diocesan structure was maintained with priests well distributed through the parishes, although often without buildings within which to worship. Several government returns identified clergy, and these numbers suggest a level of Catholic pastoral support not dissimilar to that within Ireland at the turn of the 20th century (Connolly 1992:150–151). The main purpose of all this legislation was to ensure the political dominance of the Protestant elite, rather than to destroy Catholicism; Catholic priests were still recognized in law, and marriages conducted by them were valid (Connolly 1992:156; McNally 1997:159). Levels of persecution varied, but gradually a Counter-Reformation post-Tridentine system of management and belief was established. It reduced the elements of magic and superstition within popular belief (Gillespie 1994), although this aspect continued as a substratum that surfaced most notably at times of illness and death.

In terms of landowning and therefore traditional political power, the Penal Laws affected Catholics most severely and led to some estates being confiscated; other Catholics changed their religious allegiance at least in name to maintain their families' inheritance. Most Catholic land had already been confiscated following the Williamite wars, however, and legislation was designed to maintain the Protestant ascendancy rather than create it (Connolly 1992; McNally 1997). Moreover, political activity was seriously restricted. The laws affected the elite group that had lost in the power struggle but did not greatly affect most of the population, except that their priests and bishops had to operate under constrained conditions.

The Penal Laws affected not only Catholics but also nonconformist sects such as Quakers and Presbyterians who were also discriminated against. Not until 1719 were they given legal rights to practice their religion. Nonconformists were still unable to own land or hold political office, and even their marriage ceremonies were not legally recognized until 1737, unlike those of Catholics (Connolly 1992:164). In Ulster, the fear that within the Protestant community the majority Presbyterians who would also gain political control over the Anglican elite ensured continued discrimination against them in law. The Presbyterians, more engaged in tenant farming or in the newly developing mercantile and industrial enterprises, were less affected by the constraints on property ownership. More serious for them was exclusion from traditional politics and payment of tithes to the established church, which they did not attend.

Both Catholics and nonconformists objected to control of burial grounds by Anglican clergy, payment of burial fees to the Church of Ireland, and frequent imposition of Anglican funeral services. These requirements led to clashes that could even turn to violence (Tait 2002:54–56). In many cases, however, the Anglican clergy could not or would not control burial of local Catholics or the involvement of Catholic priests. While the more dramatic clashes have tended to be recorded, an aura of laissez faire seems to have been the norm. To prevent clashes of Sunday service times, in many areas informal arrangements suggest a level of pragmatic cohabitation, which is supported by the widespread respect given to monuments of all denominations within the graveyards.

Ireland in the early-18th century was full of contradictions and conflicts at many different levels. Issues of ethnicity, religion, and class sometimes cross-cut each other but were often combined to create differences in perception and interest. The Penal Laws supported rather than created such distinctions, which also existed in similarly unequal sets of relations within Britain and Europe (Connolly 1992:312). The laws created particular problems with regard to the practice of religion, relevant here in the context of burial and commemoration, and they also reinforced attitudes of segregation and difference. These laws had an impact on individuals' desires for self-definition, a factor directly relevant to the design of funerary monuments. In the context of Ireland, the religious divisions largely mirror both class and ethnicity. The use of symbols across such mutually reinforcing divides can be seen to represent appropriation and reinterpretation of motifs familiar to all but evoking different responses, depending on the observer.

West Ulster

Ulster contained the largest number of Protestant plantation settlements within Ireland, and these were increased and strengthened during the 17th century with many Scottish families migrating across the narrow stretch of sea. While most families settled in eastern Ulster (Gillespie 1985), others made their way further west and were successful in carving out estates or in establishing businesses. Ulster was the most industrialized region of Ireland. In the early-18th century the economy was driven by the profitable linen industry, which involved Catholics as well as Protestants (Ó Mórda 1979; Cullen 1987). Flax was grown on numerous smallholdings and processed into linen that was woven by many small producers, creating relative affluence among a wide range of individuals. This affluence may provide one reason why a relatively large number of people were able to afford stone memorials in the early-18th century. Most of the local population would have been Catholic, with some Presbyterian Ulster Scots and a small minority Anglican Anglo-Irish elite.

Recent survey has begun to record and analyze data from a range of burial grounds in the counties of Monaghan and Fermanagh to explore early-18th-century commemorative strategies (Mytum 2004a). The graveyards were normally ancient Catholic church sites that had passed during the Reformation to Anglican control. Memorials are present in the 17th century but become common in the early decades of the 18th century, offering an unusually large sample of mortality symbols (Table 2). In addition, heraldic and trade symbols, cherubs, Adam and Eve scenes, and those with suns, moons, and stars occur sporadically (McCormick 1976, 1979; Mytum and Evans 2003), although these are not considered further here. Burial took place within church ruins and outside them (Mytum and Evans 2002), with two main categories of memorial in use—low table tombs or ledgers, and headstones. There were also some

wall monuments, a type already popular in Scotland (Figure 3). Some graves were marked with unshaped stones, either robbed from the rubble of the church ruin or brought into the graveyard from the field as a marker. These stones were rarely inscribed and, indeed, may have been moved and reused, but it is likely that most burials were not marked with any stone at all. Nevertheless, the inscribed memorials do provide an important source of information for the wealthier segments of West Ulster society. Some markers are preserved within family plots that have continued in use up to the present day (Mytum 2004d).

Low tombs and ledgers covered the grave with large slabs of carefully shaped stone. Slabs could be raised up as tombs, and several variations have been noted. Table tombs were ledger slabs set on small plinths or squat, square columns, although many of these supports have either sunk into the ground or have collapsed. Chest tombs also occur (Figure 4), although erosion of the lower elements has often led to the dismantling of the tomb and the laying of the inscribed and decorated top slab on the ground. It is hard to discern what proportion of these monuments were originally tombs. In the following discussion, all are called ledgers, as it is the top ledger slab that is always of relevance.

TABLE 2
MONMUMENT TYPES BY DATE, RELIGION, AND SYMBOL

| | Catholic | | | Protestant | | | Grand |
	Mortality	Other/None	Total	Mortality	Other/None	Total	Total
17th-century ledger	0	0	0	6	8	14	14
17th-century headstone	0	0	0	0	0	0	0
18th-century ledger	0	3	3	4	56	60	63
18th-century headstone	23	87	110	2	8	10	120
18th-century wheel-headed headstone	83	14	97	0	0	0	97
Grand Total	106	104	210	12	72	84	294

Note: Eighteenth-century stones are to 1769. After that date, mortality symbols were no longer used, and figures for comparative purposes would become skewed. No memorials after that date are included in the table. Ledgers also include chest and table tombs. Many have collapsed, sunk, or been dismantled, such that only the top inscribed slab survives, and the original form is uncertain.

FIGURE 3. Wall monument, with arms above the inscription and mortality symbols below; Aghalurcher, County Fermanagh. (Photo by author, 2003.)

Most ledgers are external memorials (Figure 5), but they can be used within roofed churches and occur in vaults, where they can be raised up on stone blocks, as with table tombs. One 17th-century example survives at Aghalurcher, County Fermanagh (Figure 6). The ledgers represent a class division, emphasized by the use of heraldry on a significant number of the stones. Ledgers are often placed together in discrete areas and in dynastic groups, emphasizing the multigenerational success of the family. Thus, at Killeevan, County Monaghan, armorial slabs are grouped to the east and north in the graveyard (Mytum and Evans 2002). At Aghalurcher the ledgers are densely packed in the southern and western sectors. Moreover, particular ledgers could commemorate several individuals, sometimes over a period of decades.

Burial within the church could be desirable for both Protestants and Catholics for different reasons. Some Protestants wished to be placed in prominent and central locations, and the church ruin provided this focus. For Catholics, being buried close to the altar was the motivation, among the medieval Catholic faithful and perhaps near the founding saint. Just as symbols may have been used by all groups but with different motivations and meanings, the same could apply to burial location. Most ledgers clearly or probably represent Protestants, but some represent important Catholics. One Catholic priest, possibly Tully Conolly, was commemorated on a ledger incorporating a chalice motif within the Killeevan church ruin where he had been pastor (Mytum and Evans 2002). The ledger was not a religious distinction but its link to class meant that using one was normally the preserve of Protestants (Table 2). Not all people desired the same type of burial place, however. Some Protestants, particularly Presbyterians who did not approve of burial within churches or in the pride associated with prominent locations, wished to be buried in marginal positions. Certainly some ledgers were placed away from the main burial areas, perhaps for this reason.

Most memorials in the early-18th century were not ledgers but were headstones. Two main forms can be identified in West Ulster (Figure 7). At this time the minority are of the slab type, with a range of profiles largely derived from the bedstead form and selected by all denominations (Table 2). These can be paralleled in Scotland, although such forms are also found in England and Wales. The other type is the wheeled cross (Figure 7), which is a distinctive West Ulster shape, not found elsewhere in Ireland, and selected only by Catholics (Table 2). The wheeled cross was produced during the first half of the 18th century, after which the slab form became universal; prior to that time, it was rare in West Ulster, although it was the form used widely elsewhere. Unshaped or irregularly formed stones were used at this time in some regions of Ireland (Mytum 2004c) but not in West Ulster.

The majority of wheeled crosses and a significant minority of the slab forms were carved on both sides (Figure 7), a phenomenon found widely in Scotland (Willsher and Hunter 1978) and elsewhere in Ulster as well as in some Scotch-Irish memorials in North America (Clark 1989). This characteristic suggests that Scottish influence affected the design principles

FIGURE 4. Chest tomb, St Augustine's Church, Londonderry, County Londonderry. (Photo by author, 2004.)

of the headstones, which were applied across denominations, although form in the case of wheeled-cross headstones indicated religious affiliation. The front face of the stone contained commemorative text. Some symbols also could be used there and were normally placed at the top of the stone, above the text. While a range of symbols has been recorded, the overwhelming majority portray the lettering IHS with cross, usually incised (Figure 7). The IHS monogram symbol with a cross extending from the horizontal crossbar of the *H* is a highly reliable indication of a Catholic memorial. IHS represents the first three letters of the name Jesus in Greek. It may also by this time have become associated with the phrase "*In hoc signo [vinces]*," "In this sign [victory]," which in association with the cross, makes a clear and positive Christian statement. The use of Latin indicates a Catholic liturgy. The selection

together of IHS and this phrase has been recorded in contemporary memorials in County Dublin (Mytum 2004c). The reverse of the West Ulster stones normally bears deeply carved symbols, of which those of mortality dominate, and these are discussed further below.

Within this limited range of monument types, and with selection based in part on class and on denomination, it is possible to analyze the use of mortality symbols and the meanings they were given by the various constituents of the West Ulster population.

Seventeenth-Century Protestant Memorials

Finbar McCormick (1983) has proposed that the inspiration for mortality symbols on Irish monuments came from Protestant Scottish designs, as the earliest use of such symbols is on memorials

FIGURE 5. Ledgers, some originally raised slightly above the surface by small stone blocks; Aghalurcher, County Fermanagh. (Photo by author, 2003.)

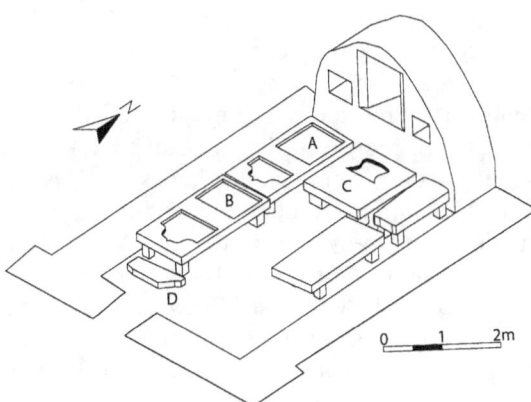

FIGURE 6. Burial vault with slabs, Aghalurcher, County Fermanagh: (*A*) Galbraith 1670, (*B*) Galbraith 1673, (*C*) 1688 Byron, (*D*) loose undated fragment. (Drawing by Kate Chapman, based on drawing by Claire Watson.)

for planters. A single example has been identified at Tydavnet, County Monaghan, to John Forster (d. 1677), and several have been noted at Aghalurcher, County Fermanagh (Bigger 1921).

The burial vault at Aghalurcher provides a valuable starting point for the analysis of mortality symbols in West Ulster, as it is the only intact surviving early example within the survey area (Figure 6). It therefore provides not only an in situ collection of 17th-century memorials but also those in very good condition. The Galbraith slab of 1670 has a marginal commemorative inscription that continues in the center of the slab with incised text, together with decorative panels in deeply carved false relief. The lower panel depicts a central skull and crossed bones, with a coffin below its head to the left, a bell to the left, and an hourglass to the right (Figure 6*A*; Figure 8). In Scottish and Ulster Scots mortuary ritual, the bell represents the "deid bell," rung to announce a death and at the time of the funeral (Table 1). The hourglass is a common motif indicating the shortness of life, a reminder to the living that the sands of time are running out (Willsher and Hunter 1978). Another Galbraith slab of 1672 (Figure 6*B*) is very similar, except that the mortality symbols are a mirror arrangement, with a coffin below with head to right, hourglass to left, and bell to right. A third slab in the vault has

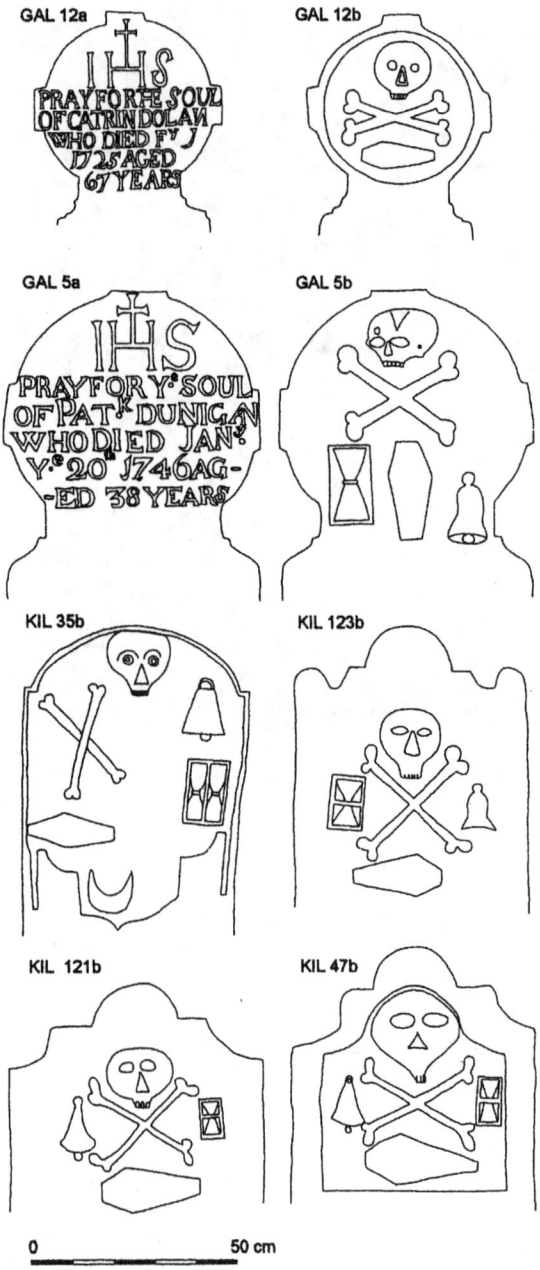

GAL 12a   GAL 12b

GAL 5a   GAL 5b

KIL 35b   KIL 123b

KIL 121b   KIL 47b

0   50 cm

FIGURE 7. Headstone types in West Ulster, showing (a) inscribed faces and (b) mortality symbols on the back; examples are from Galloon (GAL) and Killeevan (KIL). (Drawing by Kate Chapman, based on drawings by Carol Simmonds.)

mortality symbols. This simpler design is of an unusual shape, square rather than rectangular (Figure 6C). It has incised text at the top, with a deeply carved, false relief skull and crossed bones but no other mortality symbols.

The skull is a less common depiction, with a three-quarters view and no lower jaw. A loose, undated stone fragment within the vault has a skull and crossed bones flanked with two hourglasses (Figure 6D; Figure 9). This repeated use of the same motif on a monument is rare in Ireland but reflects Scottish custom. This fragment must have been part of a composite monument, the other elements of which have been lost, and it may have originally been in another location on the site.

External slabs at Aghalurcher also provide examples of early mortality symbols. Many of the incised inscriptions have been lost to erosion, even if the symbols remain because of their deeply cut forms. A wall monument displays the same arrangement of arms and mortality symbols but within a typically Scottish architectural wall slab frame and with only the skull and crossed-bone mortality symbols (Figure 3). A ledger, possibly from 1675, has an inscription at the top of the stone and a shield-shaped recess with the central skull and crossed bones, hourglass beneath, coffin upright to the left, and bell to the right. Another probable early stone has an inscription around the edge of the slab, with arms in high relief in the center of the stone and mortality symbols of skull, crossed bones, and coffin at the bottom of this design. Other slabs are discussed below as they are of the 18th-century. There can be no doubt that Protestants commissioned all these monuments. Moreover, the Galbraiths are known to have come from Scotland, descendants of Robert Galbraith, a Lord of Session in Edinburgh, and so provide a context for the transfer of this taste to West Ulster. The Galbraiths were also Anglicans, with Humphrey (d. 1676) an archdeacon of Clogher, even though he lived at Aghalurcher (McCormick 1983:283). It is likely that many of the other planter families were Presbyterian.

Stones in Scotland provide parallels for the Aghalurcher memorials in overall design and textual content as well as in the use of mortality symbols. A fine collection of slabs from 1618 onwards at Kilmadock, Perth, commemorating members of the Dog family, have marginal and other text augmented by coat-of-arms and mortality symbols (Christison 1902:288–293). This symbol is usually the skull and crossed bones and sometimes the skull alone on these

FIGURE 8. Mortality symbols on the Galbraith slab of 1670, Aghalurcher, County Fermanagh. (Photo by author, 2003.)

early stones, but coffins seem to be indicated on one memorial stone. At Logie-Pert, Angus, the hourglass is also recorded on a stone of 1664, and another of the same year also has a bell. These slabs depict a skull but no bones, and the other mortality symbols found but not used in West Ulster are the sexton's digging tools. Although David Christison (1902:372) suggests that the depiction of coffins was rare in Scotland, Betty Willsher and Doreen Hunter (1978:37) consider it more popular. They note that the coffin does not occur on its own as a mortality symbol, but pairs of coffins may be used in the 17th century, with the single coffin used as one of several mortality symbols in the 18th century. Indeed in Angus, the use of four symbols is common: usually the skull, crossed bones, and hourglass, and sometimes the coffin. A review of the evidence from the Laich of Moray (diFolco 1967) provides some further Scottish parallels. Death symbols cut in the same way as in West Ulster were placed in a panel at the foot of the slab. They included all the symbols seen in Ireland. The grave-digging tools may also be included, and some

of the symbols were duplicated, which is rarely a feature of West Ulster memorials.

What is notable in the Scottish data, however, is the far greater range of mortality symbols used and more variation in their combination (Table 1). The ways in which the symbols were placed within the overall design scheme of the memorials, which could include multiple use of the same motif (Willsher and Hunter 1978), displays a flexibility of design not seen in West Ulster memorials of any denomination. It would seem that a particular combination of mortality symbols was brought to West Ulster from Scotland and became common in the 17th century on elite memorials.

Seventeenth-Century Catholic Memorials

A small amount of evidence has survived indicating that, even in the 17th century, mortality symbols could be incorporated into Catholic memorials, but none have yet been recorded in West Ulster. They do not appear to be derived from any medieval Catholic heritage, however. Cadaver tombs depicting skeletons or partly

FIGURE 9. Mortality symbols on a tomb fragment with the hourglass represented twice, Aghalurcher, County Fermanagh. (Photo by author, 2003.)

decayed bodies (King 1990; Binski 1996) could have provided an inspiration, but they were relatively rare in Ireland (Roe 1969). Examples continue to be identified (Tait 2002:130). Instead, the use of mortality symbols was derived from the Scottish style, despite the differing religious affiliations. This evidence does not exist for West Ulster in the 17th century because of the effects of the plantations, but immediately south in County Meath on the edge of Scottish settlement some sculpture is available for study.

In northern County Meath a limited amount of Scottish settlement was identified through distinctive castle design features at Fennor and Robertstown Castle (King 1987:285). Several features of memorials in this region have Scottish parallels, as noted by Heather King (1987), but here attention will focus only on the mortality symbols. At St Bridget's graveyard in Robertstown, a grave slab of 1618 displays mortality symbols at the base. At Nobber, two slabs (ca. 1690 and ca.1700) display all five mortality symbols found in West Ulster: skull, crossed bones, coffin, bell, and hourglass. The 1686 O'Reilly tomb at Kilseer has the skull, crossed bones, and coffin on the end panel of the tomb. Unusually for Ireland, a cherub is also depicted on the same panel. Another end panel at Cruicetown, on a 1688 tomb, displays the now familiar five mortality symbols in high relief: skull, crossed long bones, hourglass, bell, and coffin. Features of Scottish Protestant monumental style were known in County Meath and, indeed, were adopted by leading families in the area on a number of tombs throughout the 17th century. Moreover, these families were all Catholic, being registered in the Civil Survey of 1654–1656 as Irish Papists. Although these tombs show no overt Catholic symbolism, the Catholic phrase "CRUX BONA CRUX DIGNA CRUX," "the cross [is] good, the cross [is] worthy," forms the beginning of the Cruicetown inscription. King (1987:290) notes that this inscription also indicates a strong Catholic Royalist stance, stating that the memorial was erected in the "reign of the most illustrious Prince, Our Gracious King James the Second." A longer version of the Latin inscription is known from a mid-18th-century stone at Balrothery, County Dublin (Mytum 2004c).

The County Meath stones contemporary with the West Ulster Protestant elite ledgers show how major Catholic families could appropriate the styles of the planters in the 17th century and use them for their own memorials. It is noteworthy in this context that the depictions of bells at Cruicetown and on two of the Nobber monuments show a long cord joined to the top of the bell. This is not found on the Scottish monuments and may indicate not the "deid bell," which was taken around the community and rung to signify a death (as implied in Protestant monuments) but, rather, was the Catholic priest's bell. This feature is not found on the Catholic memorials in West Ulster, where the Scottish form is retained on Catholic monuments. The same implication may have been drawn less obviously in that region dominated by Presbyterians.

Early-Eighteenth-Century Protestant Memorials

Ledgers continued to be used by the major plater families throughout West Ulster (Table 2). A minority continued to place mortality symbols carved in a group at the foot of the stone (Figure 10). These display the skull with crossed bones beneath and the hourglass bell and coffin.

FIGURE 10. Mortality symbols at the foot of a ledger of 1725, St. Columb's Cathedral burial ground, Londonderry, County Londonderry. (Photo by author, 2004.)

Some monuments display the heraldry and mortality symbols together, but generally there was a decline in the use of mortality symbols amongst this section of the population. The use of heraldry remains strong (Figure 11), but as the century progresses, undecorated stones become more frequent.

Positively identifying Protestant headstones can be problematic, but it is likely that many if not all those without the IHS symbol on the front (see below) may be of such a persuasion. It is likely that the Protestant section of the population with the means and status to erect headstones was small in many parts of West Ulster at this time. Not only were all the 97 wheeled headstones erected by Catholics, only two slab headstones out of 25 with mortality symbols so far recorded in the study area did not have had an IHS symbol (Table 2). Of those slab headstones with cherub or other motifs, or no symbols at all, only 8 have been noted

FIGURE 11. Ledger with coat of arms, Aghalurcher, County Fermanagh. (Photo by author, 2003.)

without the IHS above the commemorative inscription, compared to 87 with this Catholic symbol. This suggests that the use of headstones was an overwhelmingly Catholic preference and reflects on their majority population. Unfortunately, parish burial registers do not survive for the studied locations in West Ulster and are indeed rare for any part of Ireland in the 17th and 18th centuries.

Early-Eighteenth-Century Catholic Memorials

All the wheeled crosses and some of the slab headstones of this period can be identified as Catholic memorials (Table 2). The main defining characteristic is the use of IHS and the cross symbol. The content of the text can also demonstrate a clear Catholic theology. One indicative phrase is "Pray for the soul of," a direct reference to the place of the soul in purgatory, a concept alien to Protestant theology (Figure 7). The use of the Latin phrase "*Requiescat in pace*" is also a definitive sign at this period, the language aligning the monument with the Roman church. The abbreviation of that phrase, "R.I.P.," is used later on memorials of many denominations, also standing for "Rest in Peace." It forms part of a more sentimental 19th- and 20th-century attitude that includes likening death to sleep (Tarlow 1999). The use of "*Requiescat in pace*" does not have the sleep implication but, rather, is linked to ensuring a short and painless time in purgatory.

The mortality signs introduced by Protestant planters were taken over and applied in West Ulster, largely on the reverse sides of headstones. The ways in which they were applied were within a set of constraining rules that limit the mortality symbols used. The symbols were always chosen from the skull, crossed bones, coffin, bell, and hourglass. Other symbols such as sun, moon, and stars, or representations of churches or crosses also occurred with mortality symbols, but the wide range of mortality symbols used in Scotland are not found on the memorials (Table 2). Although only a relatively small number of memorials for planters survive, they also have the same limited range of symbols, which suggests that Catholic inspiration for mortality symbols did indeed come from what the planters used on their stones. Moreover, the planters' stones rarely used the same symbol more than once on the same monument (the one fragment in the Aghalurcher vault being an exception), even though in Scotland using multiple displays was frequent. The Irish Catholic memorials again share the planters' restraint, using each mortality symbol only once. This further emphasizes the source of inspiration and an attitude to symbolism that was accepted within the Catholic design aesthetic.

Once selected by Catholics, however, the meaning of the symbols was changed, and the theological inferences drawn from the symbols are distinct. No longer simply as a Protestant *momento mori* to encourage better behavior from those still alive, the symbols are active in creating a motivation to pray for the soul of the deceased in order to decrease the time the soul spent in purgatory. The living could affect the fate of the deceased in Catholic theology; in the Protestant theology, it was too late; the die had been cast. While the body decayed, a process that was inevitable and inexorable, and was represented on the symbols for both Protestant and Catholic memorials, the soul's destiny was disputed. In Protestant belief the soul's fate was ordained upon death, and actions and faith in life dictated the verdict. Within Catholic theology, the suffering of the soul in purgatory could be reduced by prayer. The symbolism still took a didactic role in warning of the frailty of the flesh, but there was some option for postmortem redemption that made Catholic memorials particularly socially active as a focus for intercession.

The limited range of mortality symbols used in West Ulster creats a distinctive local cultural form, particularly when used on the wheeled cross. Nevertheless, there is great creativity in the style of each symbol (Figures 12 and 13). The detail of the form of the skull, hourglass, and bell varies greatly, and even the long bones and coffin forms have many renderings. This variability may be linked to specific carver styles. This aspect of variability in monumental design and production is currently under investigation, using methodologies developed during the long period of research in this area of mortuary studies in New England (Slater 1976; Williams 2000; Luti 2002). It is clear, however, that a significant number of carvers were working during the early-18th century in

FIGURE 12. Wheeled-cross headstone with mortality symbols, Donagh, County Fermanagh. (Photo by author, 2002.)

FIGURE 13. Wheeled-cross headstone with mortality symbols, Edergole, County Monaghan. (Photo by author, 2002.)

West Ulster, using many local quarry sources and creating much minor variability within this very distinctive cultural form. Despite this fragmented production, there was a strong expectation regarding how some of the symbols should be used and significant structuring in the choices of symbol arrangement on the stones, irrespective of carver.

The majority of memorials display all five symbols, but their relative positions on the face of the stone show considerable variation (Figure 14). Some standardization is seen. It was normal to place the skull in the center top with crossed bones beneath, but the other symbols could be placed in various positions and orientations. The arrangements with the hourglass and bell on each side of the crossed bones (Figure 14A–D) and with the coffin beneath occur 51 times. Within this arrangement, the coffin head is equally likely to be to the left (26 cases) or to the right (25 cases). Likewise, placing the bell to the left and hourglass to the right is found in 29 stones, with the reverse in 22 cases. The coffin placed upright next to the crossed bones with the hourglass horizontal beneath (Figure 14E–F) is another popular arrangement with 26 examples. Probably significant is the fact that only a few examples (6) occur with the coffin and bell exchanging places, and it is notable that none has been found with the coffin on the right (Figure 14G–H). It would seem that a linear symbol, such as the coffin or hourglass on its side, was suitable as the bottom central symbol, although this placement has no obvious aesthetic explanation. The circular area provided on the wheeled cross could adequately accommodate a more vertical symbol, as can be seen on the few that did use the bell in such a position. Rather it would seem likely that placing the bell at the bottom was not seen as symbolically appropriate and, for some reason, was never chosen when the coffin was on the right of the long bones and the hourglass was to the left.

Considerable but not random variation occurs in the arrangement of symbols, but examination of correlates such as age and sex of the deceased does not suggest that the relative placing of symbols has any specific meaning. The presence of all the symbols, however arranged, provided the key prompt to remember the deceased and pray for their souls. Neverthe-

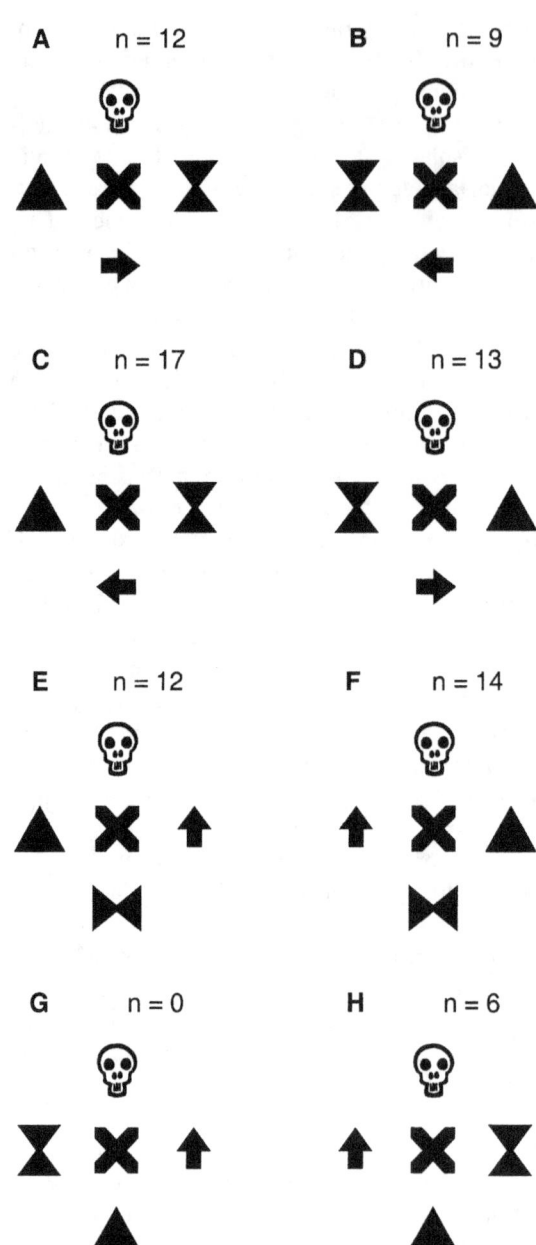

FIGURE 14. The most frequently occurring arrangements of five mortality symbols on wheeled crosses in West Ulster; for sites used in the sample, see Table 2. (Drawing by author.)

less, several patterns of arrangement were most common and suggest desired and acceptable compositions.

A minority of memorials contains only some of the mortality symbols (Figure 14). Some of the headstones are very small, so rather than carve tiny representations of all the symbols, a few were selected and portrayed at a large enough size to be visible from a distance; such cases could exclude the skull symbol. Symbol choice may indicate which symbol could be taken most readily to represent the whole. Yet, many of the stones were large enough to display all the motifs, and still one or more was excluded. When four symbols are present, the hourglass is the most frequently omitted in 15 examples (Figure 14*J, L, M*), with the hour-glass occurring instead of the bell in only one arrangement that has been recorded seven times (Figure 14*I*). While two of these arrangements (Figure 15*I, J*) merely omit a symbol from the lowest register of the design (11 cases), others (Figure 15*L, M*) have a vertical emphasis made asymmetrical by placing the bell on the right of the crossed bones (11 cases). A few arrangements with three and two symbols have also been noted at least three times (Figure 15*K, N*); other rarer combinations have also been recorded but are not discussed here. Some of the arrangements may have been popular for specific carvers, but it is clear that all the frequently occurring combinations were produced by many different carvers and that the cultural preferences should not be linked to production. The standard position of the skull and crossed bones found on the five-symbol stones was maintained on these less richly decorated large stones. That might suggest their primacy in selection, the motifs used around these varying in number as well as arrangement. Only with two symbols does the skull no longer always make an appearance. The only ubiquitous symbol is the long bones, convenient shorthand for death and decay.

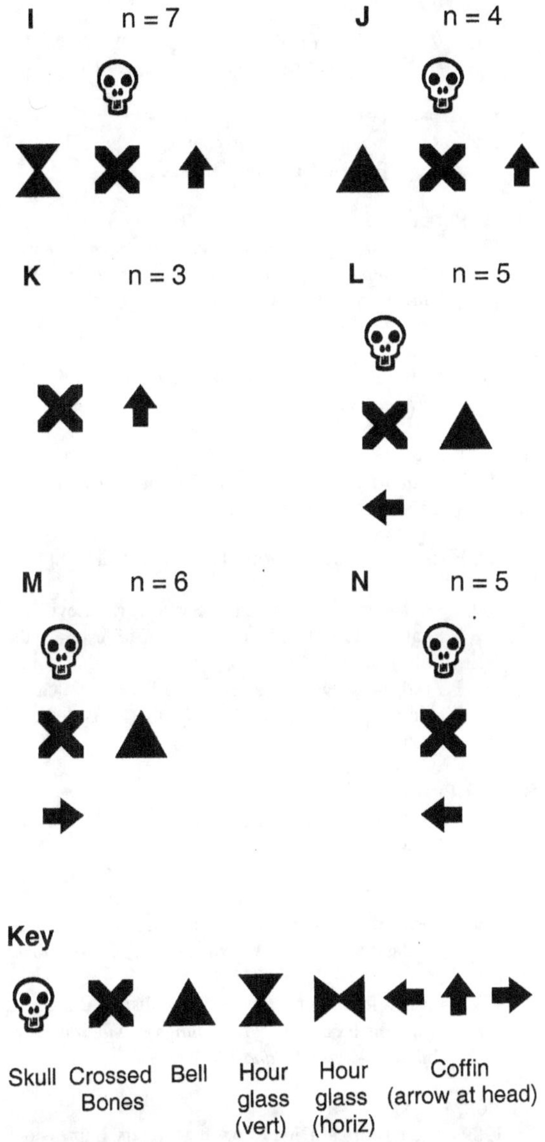

Conclusions

Many Irish graveyards were used by both Protestants and Catholics in the 18th century and were arenas for religious tension regarding control of burial rites. In some regions of Ireland, stone burial markers became common in the early-18th century, and in West Ulster the numerous memorials of this period allow analysis of assimilation, competition, and contrasting religious identities. The Protestant memorial culture owed a great deal to antecedents in Scotland, where a rich repertoire of symbols can be identified. A subset of the mortality symbols was reproduced in Ireland and was applied to monuments of the Protestant planter elite. These same symbols were appropriated by the Catholic population and used on monuments in Meath, where the Catholic elite still survived, and in West Ulster on headstones purchased by moderately successful individuals of lesser status. The forms of the headstones could also reproduce Protestant forms, and the Scottish tradition of carving on both faces of the stone was widely

FIGURE 15. The most frequently occurring arrangements of four or fewer mortality symbols on wheeled crosses in West Ulster; for sites used in the sample, see Table 2. (Drawing by author.)

adopted. A new shape, the wheeled cross, was developed as a Catholic form and would have been recognized as such by all. Moreover, the use of IHS and phrases such as "Pray for the soul of" demonstrates that the Catholic nature of the individuals and families commemorated and the active role memorials played in perpetuating that faith was not prevented. No memorials show signs of damage in removing offending texts. In this arena of competition over control of burial (and the income so derived), no attempt by the Protestant elite was made to deny the chosen forms of Catholic commemoration. The Catholic use of symbols that were familiar to and used by the Protestants may have partly assuaged any perception of difference, although texts indicate clear theological separation.

Archaeologists must continue to analyze symbolic patterning with regard not only to their commissioners and creators but also to the variety of audiences that might read them. In this Irish context, similar symbols carried different meanings to the various components of the population. The Irish graveyard was redolent with identities of class, ethnicity, and religion, even though these largely overlapped. Then as now, religion was often held up in Ireland as the most crucial identifier. Other structuring principles such as gender and class were also important, but at the time religion was the most significant and primary division. In West Ulster it is possible to explore this relationship through text, symbol, and mortuary monuments and see that for all the documented conflicts, there were aspects of commemorative practice that allowed diversity of material expression in text and symbol within any one burial ground and across the region.

Acknowledgments

The data used in this paper have been collected as part of the University of York Castell Henllys Field School, directed by the author. Many students produced the necessary written and drawn records under the supervision of Robert Evans, who has provided much stimulating discussion of the issues covered in this paper. Carol Simmonds assisted in the field and produced the illustrations used in Figure 7. Claire Watson surveyed and drew up the Aghalurcher vault, and Kate Chapman produced the final drawing for Figure 6 as well carried out a comprehensive check of all the field records prior to the analyses presented here. I also thank Finbar McCormick for generously sharing his knowledge of West Ulster graveyards.

References

Ariès, Philippe
1974 *Western Attitudes toward Death from the Middle Ages to the Present*, Patricia M. Ranum, translator. Johns Hopkins University Press, Baltimore, MD.
1981 *The Hour of Our Death*, H. Weaver, translator. Knopf, New York, NY.
1985 *Images of Man and Death*, Janet Lloyd, translator. Harvard University Press, Cambridge, MA.

Bardon, Jonathan
1996 *A Shorter Illustrated History of Ulster*. Blackstaff Press, Belfast, Northern Ireland.

Benes, Peter
1977 *The Masks of Orthodoxy: Folk Gravestone Carving in Plymouth County, Massachusetts, 1689–1805*. University of Massachusetts Press, Amherst.

Bigger, Francis J.
1921 Aghalurcher Churchyard. *Ulster Journal of Archaeology*:49–58.

Binski, Paul
1996 *Medieval Death: Ritual and Representation*. Cornell University Press, New York, NY.

Blake, Hugo, Geoff Egan, John Hurst, and Elizabeth New
2003 From Popular Devotion to Resistance and Revival in England: The Cult of the Holy Name of Jesus and the Reformation. In *The Archaeology of the Reformation 1480–1580*, David Gaimster and Roberta Gilchrist, editors, pp. 175–203. Society for Post-Medieval Archaeology and Maneys, Leeds, England, UK.

Brears, Peter C. D.
1981 Heart Gravestones in the Calder Valley. *Folk Life* 19:84–93.

Bryce, Ian B. D., and Alasdair Roberts
1993 Post-Reformation Catholic Houses of North-East Scotland. *Proceedings of the Society of Antiquaries of Scotland* 123:363–372.
1996 Post-Reformation Catholic Symbolism: Further and Different Examples. *Proceedings of the Society of Antiquaries of Scotland* 126:899–909.

Cannon, Aubrey
1989 The Historical Dimension in Mortuary Expressions of Status and Sentiment. *Current Anthropology* 30(4):437–458.

CHRISTISON, DAVID
1902 The Carvings and Inscriptions of the Kirkyard Monuments of the Scottish Lowlands. *Proceedings of the Society of Antiquaries of Scotland* 36:280–457.

CLARK, EDWARD W.
1989 The Bigham Carvers of the Carolina Piedmont: Stone Images of an Emerging Sense of American Identity. In *Cemeteries and Gravemarkers: Voices of American Culture*, Richard E. Meyer, editor, pp. 31–59. UMI Research, Ann Arbor, MI.

CLARK, LYNNE
1987 Gravestones: Reflectors of Ethnicity or Class? In *Consumer Choice in Historical Archaeology*, Suzanne M. Spencer-Wood, editor, pp. 383–395. Plenum Press, New York, NY.

CONNOLLY, SEAN J.
1992 *Religion, Law, and Power: The Making of Protestant Ireland 1660–1760.* Clarendon Press, Oxford, England, UK.
1997 Culture, Identity, and Tradition: Changing Definitions of Irishness. In *In Search of Ireland: A Cultural Geography*, Brian Graham, editor, pp. 43–63. Routledge, London, England, UK.

CULLEN, L. M.
1987 *An Economic History of Ireland since 1660,* 2nd edition. Batsford, London, England, UK.

DEETZ, JAMES F., AND EDWIN DETHLEFSEN
1965 The Doppler Effect and Archaeology: A Consideration of the Spatial Aspects of Seriation. *Southwest Journal of Anthropology* 21(3):196–206.

DETHLEFSEN, EDWIN, AND JAMES F. DEETZ
1966 Death's Heads, Cherubs, and Willow Trees: Experimental Archaeology in Colonial Cemeteries. *American Antiquity* 31(4):502–510.

DIFOLCO, JOHN
1967 Kirkyards in the Laich of Moray: An Illustrated Survey. *Proceedings of the Society of Antiquaries of Scotland* 99:211–254.

DUNBAR, JOHN G.
1996 The Emergence of the Reformed Church in Scotland, ca. 1560–ca. 1700. In *Church Archaeology: Research Directions for the Future*, John Blair and Carol Pyrah, editors, pp. 127–134. Research Report, No. 104. Council for British Archaeology, York, England, UK.

GARMAN, JAMES C.
1994 Viewing the Color Line through the Material Culture of Death. *Historical Archaeology* 28(3):74–93.

GILLESPIE, RAYMOND
1985 *Colonial Ulster: The Settlement of East Ulster 1600–1641.* Cork University Press for the Irish Committee of Historical Sciences, Cork, Republic of Ireland.

1994 Irish Funeral Monuments and Social Change 1500–1700: Perceptions of Death. In *Ireland: Art into History*, Raymond Gillespie and Brian P. Kennedy, editors, pp. 155–168. Town House, Dublin, Republic of Ireland.

GRAHAM, BRIAN (EDITOR)
1997 *In Search of Ireland. A Cultural Geography.* Routledge, London, England, UK.

GROGAN, EOIN
1998 Eighteenth-Century Headstones and the Stone Mason Tradition in County Wicklow: The Work of Dennis Cullen of Monaseed. *Wicklow Archaeology and History* 1:41–63.

JANELLE, PIERRE
1963 *The Catholic Reformation.* Bruce Publishing, Milwaukee, WI.

KING, HEATHER A.
1985 Irish Wayside and Churchyard Crosses, 1600–1700. *Post-Medieval Archaeology* 19:13–34.
1987 Seventeenth-Century Effigial Sculpture in the North Meath Area. In *Figures from the Past: Studies on Figurative Art in Christian Ireland*, E. Rynne, editor, pp. 283–307. In honour of Helen M. Roe. Glendale Press for the Society of Antiquaries of Ireland, Dun Laoghaire, Republic of Ireland.

KING, PAMELA M.
1990 The Cadaver Tomb in England: Novel Manifestations of an Old Idea. *Church Monuments* 5:26–38.

KNIPPING, JOHN
1974 *Iconography of the Counter Reformation in the Netherlands.* B de Graaf, Nieukoop, Netherlands.

LEYBURN, JAMES G.
1962 *The Scotch Irish: A Social History.* University of North Carolina Press, Chapel Hill.

LLEWELLYN, NIGEL
1991 *The Art of Death: Visual Culture in the English Death Ritual ca. 1500–ca. 1800.* Reaktion Books, London, England, UK.
2000 *Funeral Monuments in Post-Reformation England.* Cambridge University Press, Cambridge, England, UK.

LONGFIELD, ADA K.
1944 Some Eighteenth-Century Irish Tombstones, II, Miles Brien. *Journal of the Royal Society of Antiquaries of Ireland* 74:63–72.
1945 Some Eighteenth-Century Irish Tombstones, III, James Byrne and His School. *Journal of the Royal Society of Antiquaries of Ireland* 75:76–88.
1954 Some Eighteenth-Century Irish Tombstones, VII, Clonmel, Kiltoom, Seir Keiran, etc. *Journal of the Royal Society of Antiquaries of Ireland* 84:173–178.

LUDWIG, ALLAN I.
1966 *Graven Images: New England Stonecarving and Its Symbols, 1650–1815.* Wesleyan University Press, Middletown, CT.

LUTI, VINCENT F.
2002 *Mallet and Chisel: Gravestone Carvers of Newport, Rhode Island, in the Eighteenth Century.* New England Historic Genealogical Society, Boston, MA.

MCCORMICK, FINBAR
1976 A Group of Eighteenth-Century Clogher Headstones. *Clogher Record* 9(1):5–16.
1979 A Group of Tradesmen's Headstones. *Clogher Record* 10(1):12–22.
1983 The Symbols of Death and the Tomb of John Forster in Tydavnet, Co. Monaghan, *Clogher Record* 11(2):273–286.

MCGUIRE, RANDAL H.
1988 Dialogues with the Dead: Ideology and the Cemetery. In *The Recovery of Meaning*, Mark P. Leone and Parker B. Potter, editors, pp. 435–480. Smithsonian Institution Press, Washington, DC.

MCNALLY, PATRICK
1997 *Parties, Patriots, and Undertakers: Parliamentary Politics in Early Hanoverian Ireland.* Four Courts Press, Dublin, Republic of Ireland.

MESSER, STEPHEN C.
1990 Individual Responses to Death in Puritan Massachusetts. *Omega: Journal of Death and Dying* 21(2):155–163.

MEYER, RICHARD E. (EDITOR)
1993 *Ethnicity and the American Cemetery.* Bowling Green State University Popular Press, Bowling Green, OH.

MYTUM, HAROLD
2000 *Recording and Analysing Graveyards.* Practical Handbook, No. 15. Council for British Archaeology, York, England, UK.
2002a A Comparison of Nineteenth and Twentieth Century Anglican and Nonconformist Memorials in North Pembrokeshire. *The Archaeological Journal* 159:194–241.
2002b The Dating of Graveyard Memorials: Evidence from the Stones. *Post-Medieval Archaeology* 36:1–38.
2003a Death and Remembrance in the Colonial Context. In *The Archaeology of the British*, Susan Lawrence, editor, pp. 156–173. Routledge, London, England, UK.
2003b The Social History of the European Cemetery. In *Death and Dying*, Clifford D. Bryant, editor, pp. 801–809. Sage, Thousand Oaks, CA.
2004a Graveyard Survey in West Ulster. *Church Archaeology* 5/6:112–114.
2004b Ireland, Scotland, and America: The Construction of Identities in Mortuary Monuments by the Ulster Scots in the Seventeenth and Eighteenth Centuries. Paper given at Ireland and Britain in the Atlantic World, a joint conference of the Irish Post-Medieval Archaeology Group and the Society for Post-Medieval Archaeology, Derry, Northern Ireland, February 2004. Proceedings to be published in Irish Post-Medieval Archaeology Group monograph by Wordwell, Dublin, Ireland.
2004c Local Traditions in Early Eighteenth-Century Commemoration: The Headstone Memorials from Balrothery, County Dublin, and Their Place in the Evolution of Irish and British Commemorative Practice. *Proceedings of the Royal Irish Academy* 104C:1–35.
2004d A Long and Complex Plot: Patterns of Family Burial in Irish Graveyards from the Eighteenth Century. *Church Archaeology* 5/6:31–41.
2004e *Mortuary Monuments and Burial Grounds of the Historic Period.* Kluwer Academic/Plenum, New York, NY.

MYTUM, HAROLD, AND ROBERT EVANS
2002 The Evolution of an Irish Graveyard during the Eighteenth Century: The Example of Killeevan, Co. Monaghan. *Journal of Irish Archaeology* 11:131–146.
2003 Killeevan, County Monaghan and Galloon, County Fermanagh. *Clogher Record* 18(1):1–31.

NAKAGAWA, TADASHI
1994 Louisiana Cemeteries: Manifestations of Regional and Denominational Identity. *Markers 11*:28–51. Association for Gravestone Studies, Worcester, MA.

Ó MÓRDA, PILIP
1979 The Linen Industry in the Clones Area (1660–1840). *Clogher Record* 10(1):144–153.

ROE, HELEN M.
1969 Cadaver Effigial Monuments in Ireland. *Journal of the Royal Society of Antiquaries of Ireland* 99:1–19.

SLATER, JAMES A.
1976 Principles and Methods for the Study of the Work of Individual Carvers. In *Puritan Gravestone Art: The Dublin Seminar for New England Folklife, Annual Proceedings, 1976*, Peter Benes, editor, pp. 9–13. Boston University Press, Boston, MA.

SMITH, JEFFREY C.
2002 *Sensuous Worship. Jesuits and the Art of the Early Catholic Reformation in Germany.* Princeton University Press, Princeton, NJ.

STANNARD, DAVID E.,
1973 Death and Dying in Puritan New England. *American Historical Review* 78:1305–1330.
1977 *The Puritan Way of Death: A Study in Religion, Culture, and Social Change.* Oxford University Press, Oxford, England, UK.

TARLOW, SARAH
1999 *Bereavement and Commemoration: An Archaeology of Mortality.* Blackwell, Oxford, England, UK.

TASHJIAN, DICKRAN, AND ANN TASHJIAN
  1974 *Memorials for Children of Change: The Art of Early New England Stonecarving.* Wesleyan University Press, Middletown, CT.

TAIT, CLODAGH
  2002 *Death, Burial and Commemoration in Ireland, 1550–1650.* Palgrave Macmillan, Basingstoke, England, UK.

WATTERS, DAVID H.
  1981 *"With Bodilie Eyes": Eschatological Themes in Puritan Literature and Gravestone Art.* UMI Research Press, Ann Arbor, MI.
  1997 Fencing ye Tables: Scotch-Irish Ethnicity and the Gravestones of John Wright. *Historical New Hampshire* 52(1–2):2–17.

WILLIAMS, GRAY
  2000 By Their Characters Shall You Know Them: Using Styles of Lettering to Identify Gravestone Carvers. *Markers 17*:162–205. Association for Gravestone Studies, Worcester, MA.

WILLSHER, BETTY, AND DOREEN HUNTER
  1978 *Stones: Eighteenth-Century Scottish Gravestones.* Cannongate Books, Edinburgh, Scotland, UK.

WURST, LOU ANN
  1991 "Employees Must Be of Moral and Temperate Habits": Rural and Urban Elite Ideologies. In *The Archaeology of Inequality*, Randall H. McGuire and Robert Paynter, editors, pp. 125–149. Blackwell, Oxford, England, UK.

HAROLD MYTUM
UNIVERSITY OF LIVERPOOL
SCHOOL OF ARCHAEOLOGY, CLASSICS, AND EGYPTOLOGY
HARTLEY BUILDING
UNIVERSITY OF LIVERPOOL
LIVERPOOL L693GS, ENGLAND, UK

Paul Prince

Cultural Coherency and Resistance in Historic-Period Northwest-Coast Mortuary Practices at Kimsquit

ABSTRACT

This paper analyzes the mortuary practices of the Kimsquit people of the central coast of British Columbia as seen at a cemetery dating approximately A.D. 1850–1927. The cemetery gives the outward appearance of rapid change in burial mode, grave goods, and grave monuments, coincident with increasing acculturative pressures. When considered within the context of written records of the Kimsquit people's attitude to Euro-Canadian culture, the use of manufactured goods evident at associated domestic sites, and the ideology behind mortuary practices, it can be argued that there was a continuance of attitudes towards death, wealth, and descent in the mortuary complex. The patterns observed here support the position that creative changes may occur under conditions of intense colonial pressure, and they are directed by underlying structures of long-term history, such that change can be a more effective strategy towards cultural survival than extreme conservatism.

Introduction

This paper discusses mortuary practices at a native cemetery in the locality of Kimsquit on the central coast of British Columbia. The cemetery was used from approximately A.D. 1850–1927 by the Kimsquit people who were one of three Bella Coola nations, the others being Nuxalk and Talio. The archaeological and ethnohistoric records of this area indicate that the Kimsquits resisted increasingly intense acculturative pressures during the late-19th and early-20th-centuries in innovative ways that were consistent with long-term patterns in their culture. Proceeding from a discussion of culture contact to variation in burial mode, grave goods, and mortuary monuments, it is argued that resistance to acculturation was also expressed in mortuary practices in a manner that maintained cultural coherency, particularly in ideology and attitudes to material culture, death, social status, and descent, despite the surficial appearance of rapid change.

Culture Contact at Kimsquit

Kimsquit is located near the head of Dean Channel at the mouth of the Dean River. Philip Hobler of Simon Fraser University excavated four habitation sites there in 1971 and 1972 (Figure 1) (Hobler 1972, 1982, 1986). Three of these are village sites that were occupied in a sequence. Based on the dates of manufacture and availability of European goods at these sites, native oral tradition, and European descriptions of the area (Hobler 1986; Prince 1992, 2002), a rough chronology is as follows. Site FeSr-4, Nutsqwalt, was occupied sometime between 1770 to 1830; FeSr-7, Nutal, 1780–1850; and FeSr-1, the village of Anutlitx, 1850–1927. The fourth site, FeSr-5, Axeti, is a refuge site used intermittently between 7000 B.C. and A.D. 1790 (Hobler 1982:8; Prince 1992:111). The cemetery,

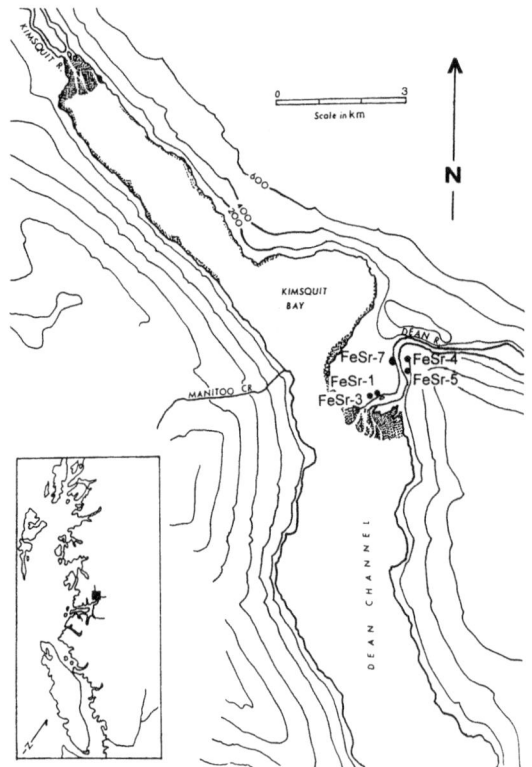

FIGURE 1. Location map of the Kimsquit cemetery (FeSr-3) and habitation sites on the lower Dean River.

site FeSr-3, was clearly contemporary with the most recent village, Anutlitx. It lies immediately southwest (250 m) of Anutlitx and is too distant from the other Dean River settlements to have been used by their occupants.

Together, the archaeological assemblage of the four habitation sites provides a material record of contact with Europeans and the means by which new materials were accommodated (Prince 1992, 2002). George Vancouver made the first documented visit by a European to Kimsquit by longboat in 1793 (Vancouver 1798 [2]:267). Kimsquit was distant from the main routes of navigation for other early-European mariners and difficult to reach by sail ship, due to its fjord location. Therefore, Kimsquit's participation in the bustling maritime fur trade of the late-18th and early-19th centuries was probably mainly through native middlemen further down Dean Channel or at Millbanke and Fitz Hugh Sounds (Figure 2), which were regular ports of call (Howay 1973). Emphasis shifted to the land-based fur trade on the central coast in 1833 with the establishment of Fort McLoughlin at Bella Bella, followed by smaller posts that operated intermittently at Bella Bella and Bella Coola in the 1850s to 1910s (Hobler and Bedard 1989; Prince 1992:46). People from Kimsquit periodically visited these posts, where interaction with Europeans was brief and businesslike and often mediated by local middlemen (Tolmie 1963:292, 303, 307). These fur-trade posts operated for a time in conjunction with trading steamships, which visited remote villages directly. Contact between Kimsquit and steamships can be expected to have been more frequent, but records are very sparse (Dunn 1844; Compton 1869). As a result of the fur trade, the Kimsquit people received goods that were useful, like metals and firearms, or that had meaning within indigenous prestige and value systems, but they were not influenced to accept European values or customs (Prince 1992; 2002). European descriptions of Kimsquit from this time indicate the people were particularly conservative. The archaeological assemblages of the early sites, Axeti (FeSr-5), Nutsqwalt (FeSr-4) and Nutal (FeSr-7), indicate material life and activities were little changed. European trade metals were heavily recycled and fashioned into ornaments and tools with indigenous analogues, employing preexisting methods of manufacture, while items of indig-

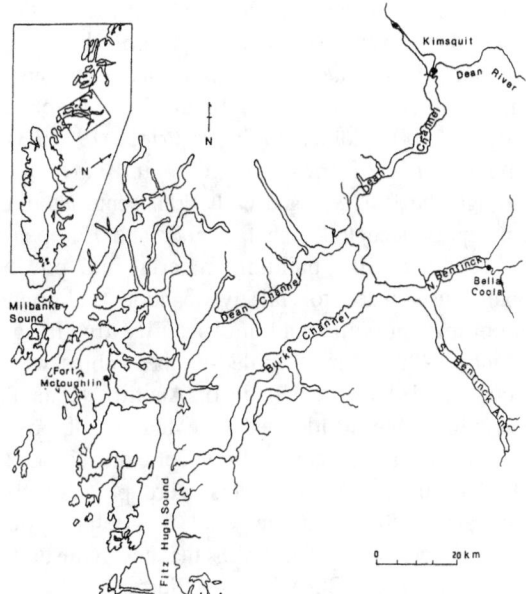

FIGURE 2. Map of the central coast of British Columbia.

enous technology were slow to be replaced (Prince 1992; 2002). The most significant technological change would seem to be the replacement of stone adzes with reworked copper implements late in the first half of the 19th century.

The Kimsquit people eventually gained a reputation for being backwards and uncooperative with the colonial government of British Columbia, and intense, but unsustained, efforts were made at pacification and assimilation in the late-19th century. The Royal Navy became an instrument for paving the way for Euro-Canadian colonization and development projects in the 1870s (Gough 1984). Canadian Pacific Railway surveyors requested a Royal Navy presence at Kimsquit in 1874 to mitigate potential hostilities prior to their surveys of the Dean and Kimsquit Valleys (Smith 1874:42, 66). On a separate occasion, in 1877, the Royal Navy shelled the village of Anutlitx, ostensibly on allegations of piracy and murder against some of the residents but, in effect, to demonstrate colonial power (Harris 1877a, 1877b; Powell 1882; Gough 1984:198). Less brutal efforts at instilling change in native values, social structure, ideology, and economy were made by missionaries and Indian agents, beginning in the 1880s (Canada 1882; Glad Tidings Logbook 1887; Kennedy and Bouchard 1990:337) and through the establishment of two local fish canneries around 1900 (Hobler 1972:89; Prince 1992:63). The records of these agencies indicate that through the late-19th and early-20th centuries, the Kimsquits accepted cash for labor and European conveniences like building material and power boats but refused to entirely abandon traditional economic pursuits and multifamily dwellings (Prince 1992). Small, milled-lumber cabins were slowly added to the village of Anutlitx (Canada 1912:203), but residences were mainly of post-and-beam planked construction until the village's abandonment. Missionaries were particularly frustrated. Reverend Pierce of the Bella Coola mission recalled in the 1930s that the Kimsquits never accepted Christianity (Pierce 1933:48). However, Indian Affairs records and the memoirs of Reverend Crosby, the Methodist mission chairman, suggest that some Kimsquit people may have experimented with Christianity in the 1910s (Crosby 1914:194; Canada 1916 [1]:228; Prince 2002). Factionalism and syncretism surely occurred in Kimsquit beliefs.

The archaeological assemblage of the late-19th and early-20th centuries at Anutlitx (FeSr-1) shows a near total replacement of indigenous material culture, but the bulk of it is associated with woodworking and construction, activities of long importance, and much of the remainder is of ambiguous significance (Table 1). Many domestic items, ceramic tableware for instance, were valued historically within the prestige system on the Northwest Coast (Blackman 1976:407; Marshall and Maas 1997) and functioned in Nuxalk food presentation as communal dishes, analogous to indigenous wooden vessels (McIlwraith 1948 [2]:528). The practice of refashioning metal goods into useful implements and ornaments also continued at Anutlitx. These points are consistent with written impressions of the Kimsquit's selective attitude towards Euro-Canadian culture (Prince 1992:65–67).

Kimsquit was eventually abandoned around 1927, probably more as a result of population decline than cultural erosion. A smallpox epidemic that swept the Northwest Coast in 1862–1863 took a drastic toll, and census records indicate subsequent outbreaks of flu, measles, and tuberculosis severely affected the viability of the community in the 1910s, when the population dipped below 50 (Prince 1992:68–72). Unsuccessful attempts were made to recruit new members, especially children (Canada 1901:271), before the survivors finally took refuge at Bella Coola, where they lent their traditions to the identity of the Nuxalk Nation.

Cultural Coherency and Resistance

The material and ethnohistoric record at Kimsquit provides an important counterpoint to arguments that Northwest Coast people lost their ability under intense direct contact to maneuver (Fisher 1977). Robin Fisher's argument, like many other culture contact studies that were guided by acculturation theory, was that during the fur trade natives freely adopted new materials, technology, and wealth, which contributed to a cultural fluorescence without significant "disruptive" effects. But when the intention of Europeans shifted to colonization, resource extraction, and the administration of law and government, native societies were overwhelmed, marginalized, and ultimately fell into demise.

More recent thinking on culture contact in other parts of North America argues that intense efforts to direct change by white colonial administrations were often met with innovative responses that contributed to the creation and reaffirmation of native cultural systems, rather than to assimilation (Sider 1987:11; Roseberry 1989). Of particular relevance to this study, archaeologists have demonstrated that foreign material items continued to be integrated within native contexts in a manner that fit or redefined underlying ideological and social structures, with or without physical modification (Wilson and Rogers 1993; Lightfoot 1995). Kenneth Lightfoot (1995:207) concludes that artifact frequencies alone are not conclusive of the degree and direction of cultural change, and a broader contextual approach is required. Ideas and practices, even Christianity, could also be adopted and experimented with if compatible with underlying indigenous ideological and social structures and goals (Sahlins 1981; Bolt 1992). In its broadest sense, these observations reflect the resiliency of culture and the ability of cultural traditions and identities to be redefined

TABLE 1
ARTIFACTS BY FUNCTIONAL GROUP AND ORIGIN AT FESR-1, ANUTLIX

Artifact Group and Type	Euro-Canadian	Modified Euro-Canadian	Local Material
Domestic Group			
Glass Bottles	57		
Ceramics	33		
Utensils	3		
Clock Parts	2		
Wood Stove	1		
Lantern	2		
	98		
Construction-Hardware Group			
Nails and Fasteners	219	6	
Architectural Hardware	7		
Tools	2	–	
	228	6	
Hunting Group			
Cartridge Cases	3		
	3		
Clothing Adornment Group			
Buttons & Fasteners	23		
Beads	16		
Ornaments	1	6	
	40	6	
Miscellaneous	23		4
TOTAL	392	12	4

to incorporate changing conditions in the world (Hobsbawm 1983; Upton 1996; Lightfoot et al. 1998).

The archaeological and ethnohistoric records of the domestic sites at Kimsquit have been interpreted from the above perspective. Foreign material culture and ideas were adopted according to underlying social and ideological structures (principles of rank, extended family, and group identity being particularly important) and used within traditional social and economic contexts, which themselves were subject to redefinition but remained distinct from those of Euro-Canadians (Prince 1992, 2002). Given what Euro-Canadians described as a stubborn adherence by the Kimsquit people to paganism, it might be expected that the mortuary complex at Kimsquit would be nearly static. Instead, material evidence at the cemetery shows there was a rapid change in burial mode, the form of monuments, and the addition of European grave goods. On the surface, these data may seem to represent a transition in native belief and practice, stemming from the influence of missionaries and Indian agents and the increasing reliance on European goods. Historic native burial practices, however, should also be interpreted within broad social, spatial, and temporal contexts (Lightfoot 1995:207). When such an approach is taken, a different pattern emerges at the Kimsquit cemetery.

Investigations at the Kimsquit Cemetary

The Kimsquit cemetery (FeSr-3) covers an area of approximately 1,150 m², ranging along a low terrace and broad forested plain on the Dean River delta. The terrace runs along the north edge of the cemetery and is probably a remnant of an old slough channel, exiting to the river south of Anutlitx. Burial features are densest southwest of the terrace in an area referred to here as the core, as shown in Figure 3, and described further below.

The cemetery was photographed repeatedly towards the end of its use, from 1920 to 1924, by Harlan Smith, then of the Geological Survey of Canada, Archaeology Section. Smith concentrated on illustrating native mortuary art and monuments, but his photographs are useful for assessing the range of mortuary styles and media, and the contexts in which they occur. The site was re-recorded in 1971 by Hobler who mapped the cemetery, recorded gravestone inscriptions, and conducted an inventory of visible grave goods without disturbing the graves. This combination of fieldwork has produced a record of circular and elongated grave depressions and small cabin-like grave houses (Table 2). There are also several variations on grave monuments, including carved wooden crests, poles and canoes, and Christian-like crosses and gravestones, as well as a large quantity of European-manufactured grave goods.

Burial Modes

A total of 261 graves have been documented at the cemetery. Of these, 210 (80%) are indicated by circular depressions. These are found throughout the cemetery but are particularly dense along the edge of the terrace and are the only grave style present above the terrace.

Thomas McIlwraith's ethnography of the Nuxalk describes circular graves as representing the placement of a body in a squatting position

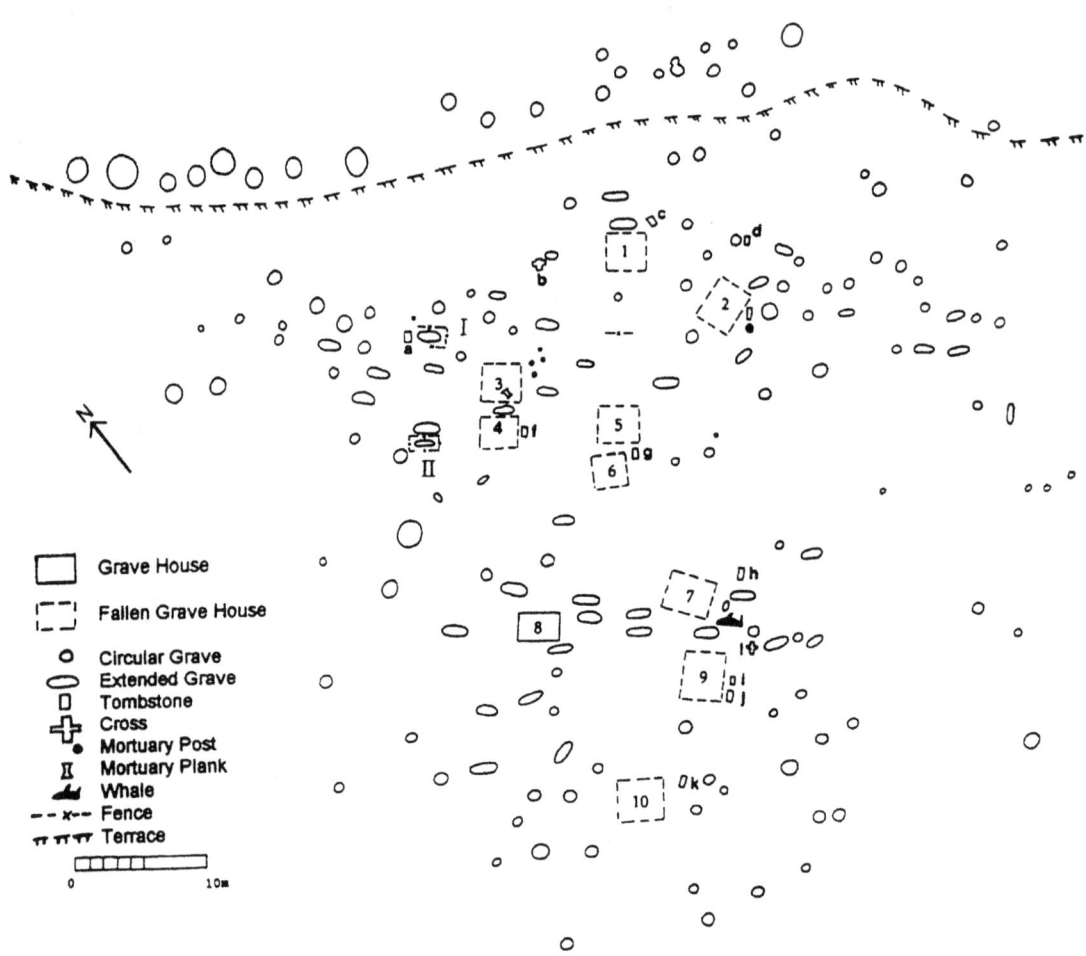

Grave House
Fallen Grave House
o Circular Grave
⬯ Extended Grave
◻ Tombstone
✚ Cross
• Mortuary Post
II Mortuary Plank
🐋 Whale
-- x -- Fence
⊤⊤⊤⊤ Terrace

0   10m

FIGURE 3. Plan of the core of the Kimsquit cemetery. Lettered grave monuments are keyed to the epitaphs in Table 3.

TABLE 2
DATES OF BURIAL MODES, ASSOCIATED MONUMENTS, AND EUROPEAN CONTACTS

Approximate Date	Burial Mode	Associated Monuments	Mode of Contact
1850–1880	Circular/Squatting	Planks	Fur Traders, Surveyors, Navy
1880–1927	Extended	Poles, Fences, Crosses, Gravestones	Missionaries, Indian Agents, Fish Canneries
1900–1927	Grave Houses	Planks, Poles, Crests, Potlatch Symbols, Crosses, Gravestones	Missionaries, Indian Agents, Fish Canneries

into a snug bentwood box. Burial was then made in a hole large enough to accommodate the box but not overly large (McIlwraith 1948 [1]:437, 445–446). The body was placed facing east. Excess back-dirt from the grave was spread level with the surrounding ground surface rather than being mounded over the grave (McIlwraith 1948 [1]:449). The eventual decay and collapse of the box would result in a circular depression. McIlwraith's informants indicated the primary earlier mortuary practice was to elevate mortuary boxes in trees, scaffolds, or poles (McIlwraith 1948 [1]:450). Other early modes of disposal included the occasional placement of bodies into caves or rock clefts (McIlwraith 1948 [1]:751) and, perhaps, the placement of mortuary "boxes on the ground covered by a sort of small tent" (Compton 1869:28), although the veracity of this last statement is uncertain. McIlwraith's informants further indicated that when European digging tools became widely available, burial replaced other modes of disposal for practical reasons, such as deterring scavengers, (McIlwraith 1948 [1]:451). Circular depressions are thus felt to be the oldest burial mode represented at FeSr-3, and the terrace is probably the oldest part of the cemetery, beginning in the mid-19th century.

Forty-one (15.7%) of the graves are elongated depressions. These represent the practice of placing bodies into rectangular coffins in an extended position and then into a grave of an appropriate size and shape. This grave style is limited to the central core of the cemetery. McIlwraith (1948 [1]:452) indicates coffins became common once milled lumber and metal fasteners and nails were widely available. This places coffin use in the late-19th and early-20th centuries. Compared with the time-consuming process of making a hand-hewn plank and kerfing it into a box, the use of these new materials and the rectangular coffin form may have been adopted for convenience. The rectangular coffin also obviated the difficulty of forcing a body into a squatting position, which involved binding and sometimes breaking limbs (McIlwraith 1948 [1]:437, 452).

Grave houses were occasionally erected over burials. Hobler recorded the remains of 10 such houses (3.8% of all graves), all from the central core. Smith's photographs indicate one other house, which probably decayed beyond surface recognition. These structures are small (2.5–3 m by 3–4 m) cabins, constructed of milled lumber, with gabled roofs, glass windows, and a hinged door (Figure 4). The grave houses of the Bella Coola nations were typically erected above an extended coffin burial (McIlwraith 1948 [1]:453). Although many of the grave houses at Kimsquit had collapsed, Hobler noted no coffins or human remains. Given that some of the headstones associated with grave houses memorialize more than one family member, some houses may have covered more than one burial. This was reportedly the custom of the nearby Heiltsuk nation (Large 1905:100). The origin of grave houses lies to the north, where the Haida constructed mortuary house crypts along the lines of post-and-beam planked houses prior to European contact (Vastokas 1966:120). In post-contact times, variations on mortuary houses were adopted by people to the south, including the central coast of British Columbia (Vastokas 1966:123). Grave houses were introduced to Kimsquit by the Heiltsuk people, with whom they had close ties, around 1900 (Large 1905:100) and were used into the 1920s. They, thus, are not a Euro-Canadian introduction and may be an elaboration of the tented graves mentioned by Compton, facilitated by the availability of modern building materials and tools.

The transitions between the three types of burial roughly correspond to increasing pressures in the mode of European contact, such as direct

FIGURE 4. Grave house 10 and associated monuments, including tombstone *k* (Jesse Robson). (Photo by Harlan Smith, 5 August 1920; courtesy of the Canadian Museum of Civilization, Ethnology Division, #49010.)

placement of the dead and direction (eastward) for departure of the soul.

Given the pressure exerted upon the Kimsquits by Indian agents to abandon extended-family longhouses and adopt smaller nuclear-family dwellings, it is interesting that much of the building material provided for this purpose went into construction of conspicuous dwellings for the dead instead. This is consistent with long-held attitudes regarding European materials as media to be used to meaningful ends and not necessarily for their supplier's intent. The resemblance of the grave houses to Euro-Canadian domestic architecture may be a reflection of the forms permitted by the building materials and, perhaps, a measure of status afforded by the display of foreign styles. This need not contradict the Kimsquit's resistance to new dwelling styles as there is no necessary concomitant change in social structure (nuclear family residence). The use of grave houses can actually be viewed as reaffirming traditional values in two senses: (1) by demonstrating the wealth and status of the deceased's relatives who erected the grave house; and (2) by providing a comfortable dwelling for the ghost of the dead, which, according to McIlwraith (1948 [1]:497), was believed to descend to an underworld village as described further below.

Grave Goods

The disposal of an individual's personal possessions at the grave site was an important part of the funeral ritual of the Bella Coola nations. The deceased's personal possessions, especially things used exclusively by them, like clothes, cooking utensils, tools, rifles, furniture, and any food they had prepared, including stores of salmon and berries, were burned at the grave side in two stages: on the day of the funeral and four days later (McIlwraith 1948 [1]:449–452). Any nonburnable, European-manufactured items were left on the fire or placed in a grave house, if one was erected. The idea behind this ritual disposal was, first, that reuse of these items would cause sickness among the living and, second, that these items would fall through the cemetery to the underworld where ghosts expected to use them. Those burned on the day of the funeral were distributed among the ghosts of the underworld,

visits by traders, the acculturative efforts by Indian agents and missionaries, and the beginnings of wage labor (Table 2). The changes have less to do with white influences on belief, however, than they do with opportunities made available by new technology in terms of discouraging scavengers, conserving labor, or displaying status. The burial ritual and values behind internment remained essentially unchanged. The change from a squatting position to an extended position for the body would seem to signal a radical cultural change, as position of the body is often governed by ideology. Extended burials and grave houses, however, tend to share a common orientation, roughly southeast-northwest, representing a continuation of belief in the proper

Perspectives from *Historical Archaeology*

while the deceased was in a limbo-like state (McIlwraith 1948 [1]:497). Goods burned on the fourth day were exclusively for the ghost of the deceased (McIlwraith 1948 [1]:452, 499). If the ghosts did not receive these goods, they could inflict illness on the community. The taboo against reuse of materials extended to anything the corpse was in close contact with, including canoes, if the body had been shipped to the village for burial (McIlwraith 1948 [1]:454).

Harlan Smith's photographs show many of the goods associated with grave houses, including utensils, furniture, tools, and sewing machines as well as canoes deposited in the cemetery (Tepper 1991:22–26). The assemblages of grave goods Hobler recorded are undoubtedly affected by 50 years of post-abandonment decay and disturbance, but rough patterning in their distribution and composition is still observable. The greatest number and variety of goods are directly associated with the grave houses (Table 3). Details of artifact manufacture and type useful for fine-grained temporal comparisons were most often not noted, but it is apparent that most of the material is broadly of late-19th and early-20th century manufacture, blue and white or gray graniteware being common, which corresponds to the period of grave-house construction. The grave-house goods are also nearly exclusively domestic household items, reflecting the rule against their reuse and their perceived utility to the deceased in the underworld. This pattern stands in contrast to the goods disposed of in the village midden (Table 1) where domestic items are underrepresented and may indicate a tendency to curate such items for disposal with the dead.

Several small assemblages of goods are loosely provenienced to the depressions between and around the periphery of the grave houses in the core of the cemetery (Table 3). The majority of the depressions in these areas are elongated, and it is likely that most of the artifacts are associated with them, rather than the few circular depressions. These goods also are primarily domestic items of the late-19th and early-20th centuries, representing the overlap in use of grave houses and extended burials.

Artifacts are not generally associated with the depressions along the terrace, probably because there were very few nonburnable items to dis-

pose of during the time circular graves were dug, that is before the glut of Euro-Canadian goods in the late-19th century (Hobler 1972:91). The few items that are present are domestic, except for a canoe, but are not temporally sensitive.

Overall, the assemblages of grave goods show a broad trend towards increased access to non-burnable Euro-Canadian goods, but the pattern of their disposal remained constant. A further consistency can be noted in the grave goods by grouping the items into broad functional categories (Figure 5). The majority of the goods represented (56.4% of 117) are receptacles of some kind: buckets, basins, tubs, kettles, pots, or pitchers. The next most common category is tableware at 20%. This marked predominance of receptacles relates not only to the rule against reuse of the deceased's belongings making people ill but also to long-standing taboos, noted by Alexander Mackenzie (1967:283–284) in the Bella Coola Valley in 1793, against the contamination of salmon rivers with unclean items. All of these receptacles would have been used to retrieve and dispose of water from the Dean River, and nothing in the Kimsquits' beliefs could be more harmful to the river than contamination by a ghost. While the abundance of receptacles represents the adoption of new elements of European technology, their use and disposal is consistent with long-held indigenous beliefs. The same can be said of all of the grave goods, if they are considered within the context of attitudes towards the accumulation and disposal of wealth: material possessions were more valued for the generosity and status they symbolized when disposed of ritually than for the physical comfort they brought (Kennedy and Bouchard 1990:329). The disposal of relatively expensive goods in the cemetery, like sewing machines and beds, was both a form of redistribution to the underworld and a conspicuous display of the wealth of the deceased and their kinsmen who could afford to replace or do without them.

Memorials

Two broad categories of grave memorials were erected: various traditional mortuary carvings and poles, and the European introductions—tombstones, wooden crosses, and picket fences (Table 2). Traditional mortuary markers

TABLE 3
INVENTORY OF GRAVE GOODS

Grave	Material	Artifact Type
House 1	iron: ceramic:	1 kettle, 1 stove, 1 box 3 cups, 1 saucer, 1 vase
House 2	composite:	1 sewing machine
House 3	wood: iron:	2 table legs 1 bucket
House 4	ceramic: graniteware:	1 cup 1 bucket
House 5	iron: graniteware: glass: ceramic:	1 lantern base, 1 stove, 2 kettles 1 soup ladle, 1 cup, 2 washbasins 1 basin, 1 lantern chimney 1 jar
House 6	iron: graniteware: ceramic: composite: other:	1 kettle, 1 saucer, 1 shovel 1 pot, 2 buckets, 1 washbasin 3 dishes, 1 doorknob 1 mirror, 1 sewing machine 1 comb
House 7	iron: graniteware: glass: 1 pitcher ceramic: 1 jar composite:	1 washtub, 1 pot, 1 kettle, 1 bowl, 1 unid 3 basins, 2 pitchers, 1 teapot, 1 ladle 1 sewing machine
House 8	iron: graniteware: glass: composite:	1 box, 1 pan 1 bucket 1 plate 1 sewing machine
House 9	iron: graniteware: glass: composite: other:	2 buckets, 2 washtubs, 1 bed frame 1 coffeepot, 1 teakettle, 1 bucket, 2 basins, 1 pot, 1 bowl 1 jar 1 sewing machine 1 clock part
House 10	iron: composite:	1 teakettle, 1 shovel, 1 bed frame 1 sewing machine
Fenced Plot I	iron: graniteware:	1 box 1 bucket
Fenced Plot II	graniteware: ceramic:	1 bucket 1 doorknob
Elongated depressions between Houses 7–9	iron:	1 pot, 1 bucket
Elongated depressions between Houses 7–8	graniteware: glass: 1 vase wood:	4 teakettles, 2 pitchers, 1 washbasin 1 washtub
Depressions between Houses 6–8	iron: graniteware:	1 pot 1 washbasin
Depressions between Houses 2–5	iron:	1 teakettle, 1 box
Depressions south of House 7	iron: graniteware: ceramic:	1 box, 1 bucket 1 bowl 1 cup
Depressions near headstone *d*	iron: 1 box, 1 cauldron graniteware:	 1 bucket
Area between monument *b* and Houses 1–2	iron: graniteware: brass:	1 bucket, 1 pot, 1 cauldron 1 coffeepot, 1 kettle, 1 washbasin, 1 casserole pan 1 clock
Circular depressions on terrace	iron: wood:	4 kettles, 4 teapots 1 canoe

Note. Grave house and monument proveniences are keyed to Figure 3.

Perspectives from *Historical Archaeology*

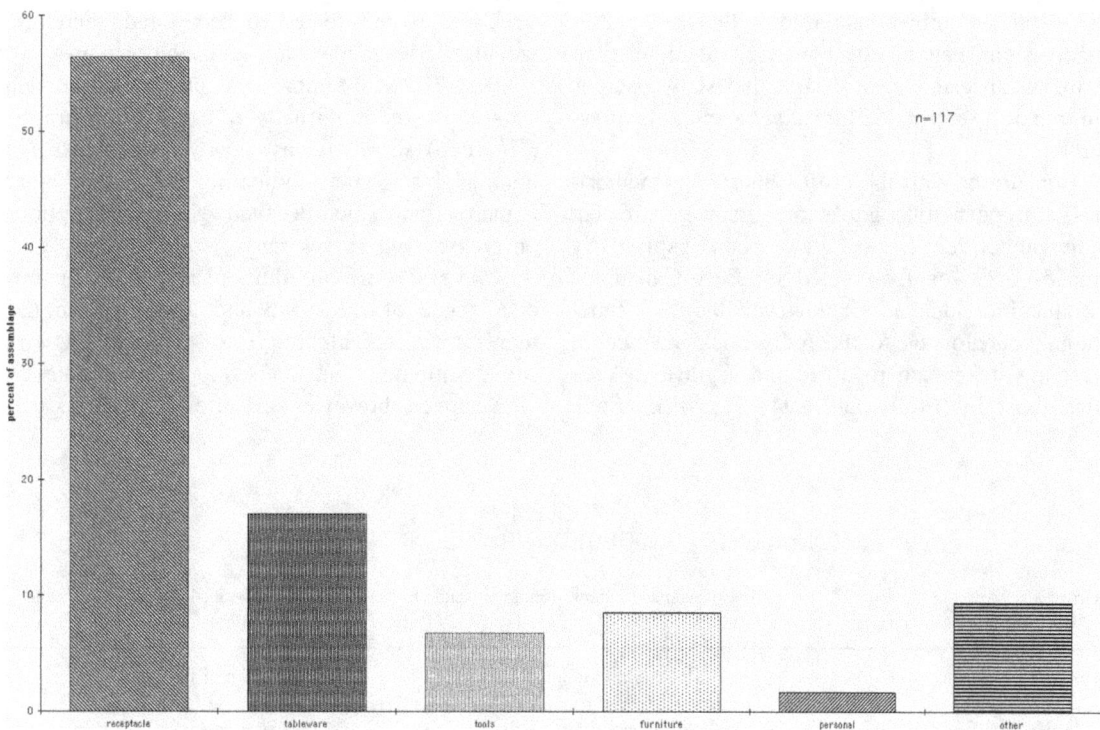

FIGURE 5. Proportions of grave goods by function in archaeological inventory of the Kimsquit cemetery.

were of two functional types. The first type includes posts or planks carved and painted with one or more of the deceased's crests to commemorate their ancestry. Often an individual's male and female lines of descent were both represented (McIlwraith 1948 [1]:461). A subtype, fulfilling the same function, includes carvings of crests attached to the grave-house front, such as the eagle attached to House 10 (Figure 4) or placed on the ground, such as the whale in front of House 7 (Figure 3). A second type of monument was left to commemorate the ceremonies the deceased had hosted. These include plain poles erected around the grave for each ceremony and representations of goods distributed by the deceased, such as canoes, paddles, coppers, or slaves, which were either attached to poles or grave houses (Figure 6) (McIlwraith 1948 [1]:462–463).

The distribution of monuments discussed here is based on those mapped by Hobler in 1971 and additional monuments evident in Smith's photographs but not archaeologically observed (Table 4). The majority of the aboriginal monuments are in the core of the cemetery and are

associated with grave houses. Crests and potlatch memorabilia are often directly affixed to the house. These clearly represent a continuation of the importance of the potlatch and the commemoration of ancestral descent and rights, long after attempts at conversion and the potlatch ban passed in 1884, which was intended to curtail its practice throughout the coast of British Columbia (Fisher 1977:207). Poles, whether plain or decorated with crests and coppers, are more difficult to associate with individual graves but also tend to be clustered in front of grave houses (Figure 6), as both kinds are reflections of the status of the individual families. Some were erected at non-grave-house burials, that is, near extended depressions, a clear example of which is a plain pole at fenced plot I. This grave also has a headstone dated 1895, which indicates the practice of erecting poles in the cemetery is at least that old. The practice is likely much older, to judge from historical and ethnographic references to crest art, poles, and the potlatch (Drucker 1955:193; Mackenzie 1967:287). Earlier 19th-century wooden monuments may have simply decayed.

The only memorial isolated with the circular depressions beyond the core is a plank painted with an ancestral crest design that showed signs of repair (Tepper 1991:25), enhancing its preservation.

Concurrent with the use of aboriginal memorials, European-style grave markers were erected. The picket fences may have been inspired by fences occasionally erected by Euro-Canadians around individual plots; however, they are functionally analogous to the indigenous practice of erecting stakes and ropes around a grave to keep the ghost in (McIlwraith 1948 [1]:449). Such structures were allowed to decay and, therefore, would not be represented archaeologically.

In 1971, 10 tombstones and two wooden crosses were standing. Smith's photographs (Figure 6) show at least one wooden cross not mapped by Hobler, indicating they were more numerous and since decayed. Dated inscriptions on crosses and stones range from 1895 to 1917, but several bore no date (Table 5). The co-occurrence of European and aboriginal monuments may indicate religious factionalism with some community members adopting Christianity. Gravestones, however, are often directly associ-

TABLE 4
MONUMENTS ASSOCIATED WITH INDIVIDUAL GRAVES

Grave	Archaeological Monuments and Date	Additional Monuments Visible in Smith Photos
House 1	Headstone c, n.d.	Several poles[a]
House 2	Headstone e, n.d.	Several poles[a]
House 3	1 painted plank; 4 posts[b]	
House 4	Headstone f, 1913	
House 5	Headstone g, n.d.[c]	1 canoe on house
House 6		1 plain pole, 1 frog crest pole, 1 pole with copper and 2 canoes, 2 coppers on house, 4 canoes on house
House 7	Headstone h, 1907; 1 whale	pole with 3 coppers, 3 coppers on house, 1 painted paddle
House 9	2 headstones, i, 1913; j, 1913; cross l, 1912[d]	1 cross, SQUIN[A]S
House 10	headstone k, 1917	eagle crest on house
Fenced Plot I	headstone a, 1895; picket fence; 1 pole	
Fenced Plot II	picket fence	
Depressions near Headstone d	Headstone d	
Area between Houses 1–2 and Monument b	wooden cross b	
Circular depressions along terrace	1 painted plank	

Note. Grave and monument proveniences are keyed to Figure 3.
[a] Precise association uncertain.
[b] Posts could be associated with nearby elongated depressions.
[c] Headstone is clearly associated with House 5 in photos; archaeological relationship is obscured by collapse of houses.
[d] Perhaps associated with nearby elongate depression.

FIGURE 6. Wide-angle view of grave houses, showing associated mortuary poles, crests, representations of potlatch goods, wooden crosses, and tombstones. Shown (*left to right*) are wooden cross I, House 7, tombstone *h*, Houses 6 and 5, an unmapped house, and House 1. (Photo by Harlan Smith, 5 August 1920; courtesy of the Canadian Museum of Civilization, Ethnology Division, #49013.)

ated with grave houses, which display aboriginal crests and potlatch memorabilia (Table 4), suggesting that Christian and traditional elements were also syncretized in mortuary practice and belief. In fact, it is not clear how much of Christianity is represented by these grave monuments. Only one headstone has an epitaph that makes reference to Christianity, but the Kimsquit name of the person buried there is given precedence (Table 5). Both known crosses also bore native names (Tables 4 and 5). McIlwraith (1948 [1]:463) indicates further that the Nuxalk frequently depicted crests on gravestones, making them consistent with previous forms of mortuary monuments, although the frequency with which this was done at Kimsquit is unknown. It is suggested here that gravestones and crosses were adopted within the Kimsquits' belief system merely as another style of monument to the deceased and their living relatives. Richard Garvin (2000) has offered a similar interpretation of gravestones at the more heavily missionized Gingolx Nisga'a community cemetery, based on consistency in the representation of ancestral crests and, thus, rules of descent.

One-half of the inscriptions at the cemetery give prominent credit to the sponsor, parents, or kinsmen of the deceased who erected the monument. While this practice is not unique to Kimsquit and the sample of gravestones is small, the frequency of its occurrence is interesting and may be informative of the motives behind the adoption of these memorials. Tombstones would have been expensive to have inscribed and imported to Kimsquit. Garvin (2000) indicates tombstones at Gingolx were commissioned at Victoria at a cost of up to $300. Costs for the Kimsquit people can be expected to have been comparable. The erection of gravestones was, thus, a visible indication of the wealth and standing of the sponsor, analogous to the longstanding practice of staging a memorial potlatch and commissioning totem poles. As anecdotal support for this interpretation, the Pollards, who are given credit for one of the headstones (Table 5), were particularly prominent at Kimsquit and adept at seizing opportunities to display their generosity and status (McIlwraith 1948 [2]:525; Prince 1992:66–67; Black 1997:85). Three of the uncredited gravestones were erected in 1913 in memory of the four victims of a shootout between factions of the community that supported either Jim Pollard or his rival Joe Saunders for a chiefly title (*Van-*

couver Daily World 1913:6; Prince 1992:73–74). The sponsors of these memorials may have been too numerous or felt it inappropriate to claim credit for these monuments, so that variation from the practice of acknowledging sponsors of funerary monuments may be an exceptional circumstance.

Discussion

The Kimsquit cemetery saw the rapid addition of Euro-Canadian materials into the mortuary complex, including coffins and hardware, building material, headstones, crosses, and a wide range of grave goods. This parallels the situation at the associated village of Anutlitx (FeSr-1) where Euro-Canadian materials dominate the artifact assemblage. Much of the material at Anutlitx, however, was likely adopted for convenience, expediency, and, in some cases, prestige. This was most certainly the case at earlier Kimsquit villages where Euro-Canadian materials were gradually added to the material culture and were most often refashioned (Prince 1992). At the immediately previously occupied village of Nutal (FeSr-7), 82% (N=77) of the Euro-Canadian material was recycled. At Anutlitx,

too, indigenous technological practices were transfered to new materials, such as grinding and polishing metal implements rather than stone, bone, or wood. Despite the large number of unmodified trade goods, domestic and economic life remained little changed, to judge from historical accounts and the context from which the assemblage was recovered—a shell midden in front of post-and-beam planked houses.

The same kind of transference and adaptation can be argued for the mortuary practices and grave goods assemblage at the cemetery. The only real changes in burial practices evident seem to have been the switch to extended burials and their eventual combination with grave houses. These changes are argued to represent the adaptation of new technologies and ideas to the conservation of labor that formerly went into preparing a bound corpse and an elaborately constructed bentwood box, and the eventual transference of this effort to a more conspicuous display of status—a grave house. It was further argued that consistencies over time in the erection of mortuary markers and in orientation of graves indicate that attitudes to death and the afterlife continued to be defined by the ideology of the Kimsquits.

TABLE 5
GRAVE MONUMENT INSCRIPTIONS

Map Reference	Date	Epitaph	Monument Type
a	1895	GEORGE\AN NU SE A LAIK\DIED\DEC 25, 1895\AGED 35 YEARS\WITH CHRIST IN HEAVEN	Headstone
b	none	DIED\CHARLES KILTAKOWER	Wooden Cross
c	none	SILAS JAMES\LUCY SUSKIS\CHILDREN OF\JAMES BALLART\KIMSQUIT	Headstone
d	none	IN\MEMORY OF\JIMMIE JOSEPH\SON OF SALLY	Headstone
e	none	IN\MEMORY OF\JOE\THOMPSON\MARTHA\GEORGE\CHILDREN OF\MARY AND ANEKA	Headstone
f	1913	WATSEE\GUS\DIED SEPT 10, 1913\AGED 37	Headstone
g	none	IN MEMORY OF\SALLY\DAUGHTER OF\CAPTAIN JACK\ERECTED BY\MRS. JAMES POLLARD	Headstone
h	1907	IN\MEMORY\OF\MARTHA\DIED\DEC 25 1907\JOHNEY\AGED 20 YEARS\SAM AGED 14 YEARS\ERECTED BY\THEIR PARENTS\MR AND MRS BILLEY	Headstone
i	1913	IN MEMORY OF\GEORGE PAUL\KILLED SEPT 10, 1913	Headstone
j	1913	IN MEMORY OF\CHAS WILSON\AND\EMMA WILSON\HIS WIFE\KILLED SEPT 10, 1913	Headstone
k	1917	IN\LOVING MEMORY\OF\JESSE ROBSON\BORN FEB 1892\KILLED\MAY 11, 1917\SHE WAS KIND AND GENTLE\AND LOVED BY ALL\ERECTED BY B. G. ROBSON	Headstone
l	1912	FANNY DANIEL\AGED 6\DIED\AUG 27, 1912	Wooden Cross

Perspectives from *Historical Archaeology*

The Euro-Canadian goods, grave monuments, and building materials represented at Kimsquit were all adapted to uniquely native contexts in accordance with deeply entrenched values. They did not disrupt the preexisting mortuary system. If anything, their use indicates a reaffirmation of aboriginal traditions, despite an outward resemblance to Euro-Canadian culture. The disposal of pots and pans at a grave, the use of Western architecture for a grave house, and the erection of ancestral crests and potlatch memorabilia alongside headstones all reflect the assertion and redefinition of native identity in the face of acculturative pressures. These changes indicate that mortuary traditions can be dynamic yet consistent with preexisting value systems. Mortuary media are universally a powerful tool for signaling the status, aspirations, social bonds, and values of the living and exhibiting trends that are best understood within the history of the socioeconomic milieu in which they are situated (Cannon 1989). At Kimsquit, mortuary media signified all of these. Changes are best understood in the context of redefining traditions in order to maintain cultural coherency and resist assimilation.

Their mortuary complex was so integral to the function and identity of Northwest Coast cultures that colonial powers recognized the need to abolish the memorial potlatch in order to achieve their agenda of assimilation. To the Bella Coola nations, the memorial potlatch served to relieve grief, enhance the social importance of the sponsors (McIlwraith 1948 [1]:473–474), and bring order out of death and loss. It is, therefore, not surprising that the Kimsquit people not only risked jail to continue this practice (McIlwraith 1948 [1]:473) but added new elements to preserve it.

Conclusions

Changes in mortuary practice at Kimsquit appear to have been rapid, but they were consistent with preexisting values and beliefs. In particular, beliefs in ghosts, the afterlife, the proper disposal of wealth, and commemoration of the deeds, ancestry, and status of the deceased and their kin were strictly adhered to. The changes in burial mode, kinds of grave goods, and forms of monuments are largely superficial and opportunistic, representing the seizing of elements of Euro-Canadian culture that were usefully adapted to long-held native values. Mortuary media and practices were manipulated by the survivors in order to maintain cultural coherency and resist assimilation by Euro-Canadian culture. Further, if people died believing they would descend to an underworld where their ghosts would lead an existence mirroring their lives, as McIlwraith (1948 [1]:497–499) describes, then perhaps there was also resistance in death.

ACKNOWLEDGMENTS

I wish to thank Philip Hobler of Simon Fraser University for providing continued access to his Kimsquit material and for his enthusiasm and advice on my research. I also thank Jerome Cybulski of the Canadian Museum of Civilisation and Joan Vastokas of Trent University for sharing some of their thoughts and information on historic-period Northwest Coast burial practices. Thanks to Aubrey Cannon of McMaster University for reading an earlier draft of this paper and making several useful suggestions. The editors and reviewers of this journal also made comments that improved my paper. I gratefully acknowledge the Canadian Museum of Civilisation Library Division for permission to reproduce the photographs used in this paper.

REFERENCES

BLACK, MARTHA
    1997 *Bella Bella: A Season of Heiltsuk Art*. Royal Ontario Museum, Toronto, Ontario.

BLACKMAN, MARGARET
    1976 Creativity in Acculturation: Art, Architecture, and Ceremony from the Northwest Coast. *Ethnohistory*, 23(1):387–413.

BOLT, CLARENCE
    1992 *Thomas Crosby and the Tsimshian: Small Shoes for Feet Too Large*. UBC Press, Vancouver, British Colombia.

CANADA, DOMINION OF
    1882 *Annual Report of the Department of Indian Affairs for the Year 1881*. Maclean, Roger and Company, Ottawa, Ontario.
    1901 *Annual Report of the Department of Indian Affairs for the Year 1900*. Maclean, Roger and Company, Ottawa, Ontario.
    1912 *Annual Report of the Department of Indian Affairs for the Year 1911*. Maclean, Roger and Company, Ottawa, Ontario.
    1916 *Report of the Royal Commission on Indian Affairs for the Province of British Columbia, Volume I*. Acme, Victoria, British Columbia.

CANNON, AUBREY
1989 The Historical Dimension in Mortuary Expressions of Status and Sentiment. *Current Anthropology,* 30(4):437–459.

COMPTON, PYMS NEVINS
1869 An Account of an Early Trip to Fort Victoria and of Life in the Colony. British Columbia Archives, Add. Mss. 2778. Victoria, British Columbia.

CROSBY, THOMAS
1914 *Up and Down the North Pacific Coast by Canoe and Missionship.* Frederic Clarke Stephenson, Toronto, Ontario.

DRUCKER, PHILIP
1955 *Indians of the Northwest Coast.* American Museum of Natural History, Garden City, NY.

DUNN, JOHN
1844 *History of the Oregon Territory and the British North American Fur Trade.* Edwards and Hughes, London, England.

FISHER, ROBIN
1977 *Contact and Conflict: Indian-European Relations in British Columbia, 1774–1890.* University of British Columbia Press, Vancouver.

GARVIN, RICHARD
2000 Anthropological Archaeology at the Gingolx Cemetery. Paper presented at the 33rd Annual Meeting of the Canadian Archaeological Association, Ottawa, Ontario.

GLAD TIDINGS LOGBOOK
1887 Logbook of the "Glad Tidings." British Columbia Archives, Microfilm, Reel 31a. Victoria, British Columbia.

GOUGH, BARRY
1984 *Gunboat Frontier: British Maritime Authority and Northwest Coast Indians, 1846–1890.* University of British Columbia Press, Vancouver.

HARRIS, LT. G. R.
1877a Proceedings of the H.M.S. "Rocket." British Columbia Archives, Record Group 10, V3604 F2314. Victoria.
1877b Letter to Lt. Governor Richards Reporting Proceedings and Return of H.M.S. "Rocket," 6 April 1877. British Columbia Archives, Record Group 10, V3604 F2314. Victoria.

HOBLER, PHILIP
1972 Archaeological Work at Kimsquit. In *Salvage '71,* Roy Carlson, editor, pp. 85–106. Department of Archaeology, Simon Fraser University, Burnaby, British Columbia.
1982 Introduction. In *Papers on Central Coast Archaeology,* Philip Hobler, editor, pp. 1–12. Department of Archaeology, Simon Fraser University, Burnaby, British Columbia.

1986 Measures of the Acculturative Response to Trade on the Central Coast of British Columbia. *Historical Archaeology,* 20(2):16–26.

HOBLER, PHILIP, AND BETH BEDARD
1989 Bella Coola Villages in History and Prehistory: A Preliminary Report on the 1988 Season. Report to the Social Sciences and Humanities Research Council of Canada, Ottawa, Ontario.

HOBSBAWM, ERIC
1983 Introduction: Inventing Tradition. In *The Invention of Tradition,* Eric Hobsbawm and T. Ranger, editors, pp. 1–14. Cambridge University Press, Cambridge, England.

HOWAY, F. W.
1973 *A List of Trading Vessels in the Maritime Fur Trade 1785–1825.* Limestone Press, Kingston, Ontario.

KENNEDY, DOROTHY, AND RANDALL BOUCHARD
1990 Bella Coola. In *Handbook of North American Indians, Volume 7 Northwest Coast,* Wayne Suttles, editor, pp. 323–339. Smithsonian Institution, Washington, DC.

LARGE, R. W.
1905 Mortuary Customs in British Columbia. In *Annual Archaeological Report of Ontario, 1904, Being an Appendix to the Report of the Minister of Education Ontario,* pp. 100–101. L.K. Cameron Publishing, Toronto, Ontario.

LIGHTFOOT, KENNETH
1995 Culture Contact Studies: Redefining the Relationship Between Prehistoric and Historical Archaeology. *American Antiquity,* 60(2):199–217.

LIGHTFOOT, KENNETH, ANTOINETTE MARTINEZ, AND ANN SCHIFF
1998 Daily Practice and Material Culture in Pluralistic Social Settings: An Archaeological Study of Culture Change and Persistence from Fort Ross, California. *American Antiquity,* 63(2):199–222.

MACKENZIE, ALEXANDER
1967 *Alexander Mackenzie's Voyage to the Pacific Ocean in 1793.* Citadel Press, New York, NY.

MARSHALL, YVONNE, AND ALEXANDRA MAAS
1997 Dashing Dishes. *World Archaeology,* 28(3):275–290.

McILWRAITH, THOMAS
1948 *The Bella Coola Indians,* Two Volumes. University of Toronto Press, Toronto, Ontario.

PIERCE, WILLIAM HENRY
1933 *From Potlatch to Pulpit, Being the Autobiography of William Henry Pierce.* Vancouver Bindery, Vancouver, British Columbia.

POWELL, I. W.
1882 Correspondence Outward, 28 Sept 1882. British Columbia Archives, Record Group 10, V3604 F2314. Victoria.

PRINCE, PAUL
1992 A People with History: Acculturation and Resistance at Kimsquit. Masters Thesis, Department of Archaeology, Simon Fraser University, Burnaby, British Columbia.
2002 Contact, Resistance, and Cultural Survival at Kimsquit. In *Papers in Central Coast Archaeology, Volume 2*, Philip Hobler, editor. Simon Fraser University Archaeology Press, Burnaby, British Columbia, in press.

ROSEBERRY, WILLIAM
1989 *Anthropologies and Histories: Essays in Culture, History, and Political Economy*. Rutgers University Press, New Brunswick, NJ.

SAHLINS, MARSHALL
1981 *Historical Metaphors and Mythical Realities*. ASAO Publication 1, University of Michigan Press, Ann Arbor.

SIDER, GERALD
1987 When Parrots Learn to Talk and Why They Can't: Domination, Deception, and Self Deception in Indian-White Relations. *Comparative Studies in Sociology and History*, 29:3–23.

SMITH, MARCUS
1874 Diary 1873–74. British Columbia Archives, Add. Mss. 748. Victoria.

TEPPER, LESLIE (EDITOR)
1991 *The Bella Coola Valley: Harlan I. Smith's Fieldwork Photographs, 1920–1924*. Canadian Museum of Civilization, Mercury Series Paper 123, Hull, Quebec.

TOLMIE, WILLIAM FRASER
1963 *The Journals of William Fraser Tolmie, Physician and Fur Trader*. Mitchell Press, Vancouver, British Columbia.

UPTON, DELL
1996 Ethnicity, Authenticity, and Invented Traditions. *Historical Archaeology*, 30(2):1–7.

VANCOUVER DAILY WORLD
1913 Four Killed in Battle on Kimsquit Inlet. *Vancouver Daily World*, 13 September 1913, (2)11:6.

VANCOUVER, GEORGE
1798 *A Voyage of Discovery to the North Pacific Ocean and Round the World: In Which the Coast of North-West America Has Been Carefully Examined and Accurately Surveyed, Vol 2*. G. G. and J. Robinson, London, England.

VASTOKAS, JOAN
1966 *Architecture of the Northwest Coast Indians of America*. Doctoral Dissertation, Department of Art, Columbia University, New York. University Microfilms International, Ann Arbor, MI.

WILSON, SAMUEL, AND J. DANIEL ROGERS
1993 Historical Dynamics in the Contact Era. In *Ethnohistory and Archaeology: Approaches to Post-Contact Change in the Americas*, Samuel Wilson and J. Daniel Rogers, editors, pp. 3–15. Plenum press, New York, NY.

PAUL PRINCE
DEPARTMENT OF ANTHROPOLOGY
TRENT UNIVERSITY
PETERBOROUGH, ON, CANADA K9J 7B8

DAVID V. BURLEY

Contexts of Meaning: Beer Bottles and Cans in Contemporary Burial Practices in the Polynesian Kingdom of Tonga

ABSTRACT

Interpretations of symbolic meaning and nonverbal communication have gained a strong foothold in the field of historical archaeology as post-processual theory becomes more
widely accepted. Through an examination of beer bottles
and beer cans used as components of grave decoration in the
Polynesian kingdom of Tonga, the potential pitfalls of this
approach can be illustrated. In "recovering mind," care
must be taken to ensure cause, motivations, and rationalizations are not solely a product of one's own cultural milieu.

Introduction

The past, just like foreign cultures, for ethnographers, is
entered through the imagination—the agreed on source of
all hypotheses. This process includes, inevitably, the repli-
cation of the scientist's social structure . . . (Leone 1981:13).

Archaeologists are a product of culture and their
interpretations of the past, as suggested in the
above quote by Mark Leone, are influenced by
their cultural milieu. As the discipline moves further into a post-processualist theory, one in which
"recovering mind" becomes as important as historical chronology, greater and greater emphasis is
placed on intellectual ingenuity or, as Leone might
argue, imagination (Leone 1982; Little and
Shackel 1992). Hodder (1986) and others (Shackel
and Little 1992) illustrate that the greatest advances in this type of work in North America are
by historical archaeologists. The reasons for this
are several, but the availability of the written word
is a key factor for interpretations of symbolic and
ideological structures. Perhaps equally important,
historical archaeology deals with a recognizable

material culture that, one presumes, can be interpreted within accepted contexts of meaning.

In the following paper, the question of symbolic
meaning of material culture is brought into focus
through an examination of beer bottles and cans
used in contemporary grave architecture in the
Polynesian kingdom of Tonga. Beer bottles and
cans are one component of material culture with
which many archaeologists confess a degree of familiarity, and one is naturally intrigued by their
potential metaphorical association with funerary
rites. In the case presented here, however, meaning
has little relationship to such a Western frame of
reference. In presenting these data, this paper is not
intended as a theoretical opposition to "recovering
mind." Rather it may be viewed as a cautionary
tale for those interested in refining archaeological
interpretations of the past as they may be config-
ured by one's own cultural perceptions. Second, by
virtue of Rathje's (1979) rationalizations for modern material culture studies, this paper documents a
material record of the present for future archaeological use. There is every expectation that some
other archaeologist will find these materials in context, perhaps after the practice has ceased to exist,
and be as puzzled as the author in his first experiences with Tongan cemeteries.

The Kingdom of Tonga

Tonga is situated on the western periphery of the
Polynesian triangle, east of Fiji and southwest of
Samoa (Figure 1). The kingdom incorporates over
160 islands of which about 40 currently have inhabitants. With the exception of scattered outliers,
the islands are clustered into three principal
groups—Tongatapu, Ha'apai, and Vava'u. Tongatapu, the largest of the islands, has the vast majority of population and, from at least the 11th
century A.D., has been the center of political control for the kingdom's paramount chiefs (Gifford
1929:48–102). The practices to which this paper
refers have been observed in all three of these island groups and, thus, must be considered a widespread and culturally acceptable form of behavior.

Even a basic introduction to Tongan history, an-

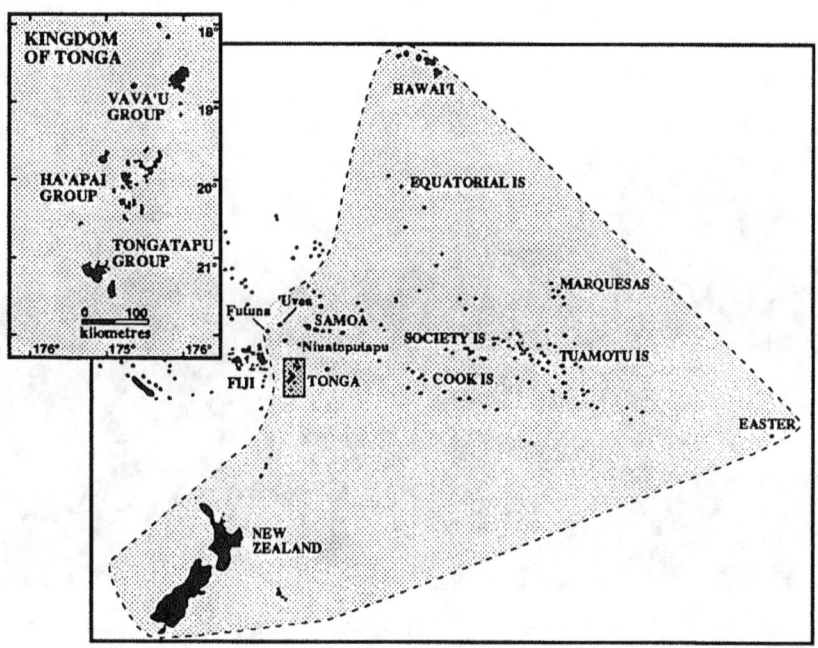

FIGURE 1. Polynesian Triangle and the kingdom of Tonga.

thropology, or archaeology is far beyond the limits or needs of the present paper. Suffice it to say that Tonga, as one of the few surviving Polynesian kingdoms, is relatively well documented by Western scholars beginning in the early 1920s and continuing through to the present (e.g., Kirch 1984; Ferdon 1987; Gailey 1987; Campbell 1992). Tonga has a long history of European contact beginning in the 17th century, and by the 1830s the onslaught of missionaries, merchants, and European colonial interests throughout the South Pacific ensured regular interaction. In 1875 the chiefly political structure was transformed into a constitutional monarchy complete with a king and nobles (Marcus 1980). Since then, Tonga has gone through a succession of four monarchs, protectorate status under Great Britain, acceptance into the British Commonwealth, a process of cash monetization and, one might conclude, full entry into a Westernized economy and lifestyle. Despite over 350 years of contact, and the zealous and competitive efforts of numerous religious denominations, traditional

practices and values do continue to persist in many aspects of Tongan culture. One such aspect is burial patterns, albeit with several transformations.

Traditional Tongan social structure was highly stratified, and this was symbolically reproduced in Tongan funerary rites, among other things (Burley 1993). At the upper end of the sociopolitical scale were the paramount chiefs and their immediate lineage. From the 10th to 19th centuries A.D., the sacred kings of the chiefdom were the *Tu'i Tonga,* a lineage originating with the union of a Tongan woman and a sky god (Gifford 1929:52). The *Tu'i Tonga* were buried in elaborate tombs known as *langi,* a word also referring to sky or heaven (Churchward 1959:282). These tombs were large, rectangular earthen mounds faced with heavy dressed blocks of beach-stone, often in tiers (Kirch 1990). In later years two other chiefly lineages emerged as secular rulers over the kingdom, and they, too, were buried in a like manner. Lesser chiefs and chiefly attendants were deposited in smaller mounds lacking the labor input of the

FIGURE 2. Beer bottle graves—Mu'a, Tongatapu, kingdom of Tonga (a stone faced *langi* is in the background).

langi, particularly in the characteristics of stone facings, yet they continued to be reasonably impressive structures. Finally, members of the commoner or *tu'a* class are said historically to have been buried "anywhere," without much concern for location or long-term maintenance of the grave (Gifford 1929:201). By at least the mid-1800s, many of the *tu'a* burials were being placed in large cemeteries that today are generally referred to as *mala'e.* The *mala'e,* and the practices of *tu'a* interment, are of interest here.

Beer Bottles and Cans: Symbolic Connotations in Tongan Grave Architecture

One's first observation of Tongan burial practices occurs almost immediately upon leaving the airport on the main island of Tongatapu. Each village, and frequently each extended family within a village, has its own *mala'e,* resulting in literally hundreds of plots on Tongatapu alone. Tongan *mala'e* incorporate a range of burial markers from those with brightly colored banners, to grave houses, to tombstones that would be comfortably at home on a European landscape. All graves are covered by simply constructed mounds of white coralline sand that become superimposed over time and form larger tumuli. Notwithstanding the different types of burial markers, each of these sand mounds may be decorated with a variety of materials including beer bottles and, to a lesser extent, cans (Figures 2, 3).

Graves with beer bottle decorations almost always employ them as a border to the mound, with variations on this theme. Positioned upside down in the sand and buried to the shoulder, they often provide a retaining wall to hold the mound in place. Variations include single or double tiered walls having either a rectangular or oblong shape (Figure 2). To a lesser extent, bottles are used as corner posts, or in a few cases they totally cover the grave in a blanket-like fashion. Scattered bottle piles are also found in many *mala'e,* a result of occasional clean-up activities in which earlier grave mounds that have collapsed are cleared off. Graves with beer cans are not so numerous, but in their usage are similar (Figure 3). A variation re-

FIGURE 3. Beer can grave, Nieafu, Vava'u, kingdom of Tonga.

corded on the grave of one individual that appeared particularly intriguing, as to be noted later, was a scatter of intentionally crumpled cans.

The introduction of alcohol into Tonga has long historical time depth, beginning with the voyages of Captain James Cook in 1773 (e.g., Beaglehole 1969:253). Indeed by 1904, beer, wine, and spirits accounted for over 24 percent of the value of all imports (British Foreign Office 1906), and on this basis one might suspect its usage to have caught on rather quickly. However, in these early years of the 20th century few Tongans had the financial ability to purchase alcohol, and the greatest quantity was no doubt consumed by the European community of merchants, whalers, diplomats, and visitors. Since 1975 ever-increasing numbers of Tongans have temporarily emigrated to Australia, New Zealand, or the United States for employment (Cowling 1990a), and as a consequence alcohol is gaining wider social acceptance. Recently under license to the Pripps Brewing Company of Sweden, Crown Prince Tupouto'a has developed a domestic brewery giving its product the name Royal Beer.

With a few minor exceptions, all of the bottles used in grave construction have originated from a single source, the Steinlager Brewing Company of Auckland, New Zealand. These are 26-oz. containers that in Tonga have been sold as disposables without deposit. Similarly, aluminium beer cans stemming from either the Foster or Victoria Bitters Brewing company of Australia litter the landscape. Only in the past three years has a refund been paid for the return of aluminium tins, and this is sufficiently small (1¢) to ensure that recycling is a minor activity, and occurs only on the island of Tongatapu. When exactly the Steinlager and Foster's invasion began has not been determined, but it probably post-dates 1960 and, in part, has been stimulated by Tongans returning from overseas employment. Here it is important to note that, despite the presence of alternatives, including Pepsi, Coke, and similar soft drink containers, only those associated with beer have been consistently found in grave decoration.

Even with the growing number of Tongans exposed to Western influences, contemporary society remains rigidly devote, with most church denominations opposed to the use of alcohol in any fashion. *Kava,* made from the crushed root of the pepper shrub (*Piper methysticum*), continues to be the favored national drink and one integrated into the kingdom's social and political fabric. The position of chiefs within the *kava* circle symbolically defined rank and status, and the *kava* ceremony was the means by which title was conferred. Even today the king's *kava* circle serves as a form of Tongan court in which the relative status of nobles and chiefly attendants is disclosed (Gifford 1929:166–168). Consequently alcoholic beverage containers as a component of grave architecture seem not only anomalous but a structural opposition to ritual and traditional custom. Since they serve as a social metaphor in funerary practices, an explanation was sought within a framework of symbolic meaning. Several potential interpretations are worthy of note.

Tongan society today, as in the past, is highly stratified with many aspects of behavior predicated upon considerations of status, either for its acquisition or through proscription. Beer drinking in one sense represents a component of Western culture, a culture generally viewed by Tongans as prosperous and to be emulated. With many young adults now familiar with Western lifeways as a result of overseas experiences or through television, the kingdom is in a state of rapid transition, particularly as it is reflected in consumer demands for Western-style houses, vehicles, VCRs, and the like. In its association with the European, then, beer potentially forms a symbol of modernism and progress, church prohibitions notwithstanding. Within this context, it might further be suggested that beer containers in grave architecture symbolically encode statements on the lifestyle of the deceased, and aspirations of the extended family.

The purchase of beer continues to constitute a cash expense beyond the economic means of most Tongan households. Beer drinking exhibits a level of economic status and, as such, is a form of conspicuous consumption in a highly status-conscious society. One's economic position can be publicly displayed in a bar, and it is worthy of note that many Tongans who drink beer consume expensive imports as opposed to the cheaper locally-produced variety for just this reason. Several private clubs also exist, which are generally ranked relative to the status of their members and at which beer and other alcohols are consumed. These too are highly elitist in their membership, with the Nuku'alofa Club, among whose members are the crown prince and the business elite of the kingdom, at the upper end. Beer, in these contexts, has a symbolic association with the economically privileged class.

The structural patterning of beer containers on graves further emphasizes the symbolic presentation of status. Bottles and cans form single and tiered boundaries around the burial mound, and in this alignment they create a miniaturized form of the chiefly burial tomb (Figure 2). They are a substitute for the stone facings of the *langi,* and they have become an integral component of architectural form. Beach-stone facing slabs required intensive labor investment, were a sole prerogative of chiefly position, and their presence at a grave site created a powerful statement of rank and status (Burley 1993). Though one can hardly argue such a message is being conveyed through bottles, the structural parallel is of note, especially in light of other overlapping meanings.

Finally, on a majority of Tongan graves where bottles are employed they are brown, despite the current use of green bottles by the Steinlager Company. This consistent use of brown bottles is so noticeable that it is difficult to ignore the potential for color symbolism. Cross-cultural meaning of color is a topic well studied in anthropology and other fields (Rapoport 1982:111–116). In this particular context, a structuralist interpretation of color may be framed as follows: brown is to death as green is to life. This interpretation seems further supported by the presence of black basalt pebbles that are strewn over the top of many graves, whether surrounded by beer containers or not. Extending this type of interpretation even further, crumpled beer cans as described earlier might also be taken as a symbolic representation of death.

In light of the above, beer containers on graves could be interpreted as an active component of nonverbal communication integrated within a clearly defined social metaphor. Other anthropologists who have viewed Tongan grave decorations have also felt them to be laden with symbolic overtones. Cowling (1990b:79), for example, has gone so far as to state that these decorations are "not only intended to impress others with the status or generosity of a family, they are clearly intended as a message to the dead." Unfortunately, Tongans disagree, despite the assurances with which Western academics may present their conclusions. Repeated discussions with a variety of informants revealed only that beer bottles and cans are a form of decoration like all other decorations.

Tongan Graves and Tongan Culture: Meaning as Constituted

Early historical descriptions of Tongan burial practices are related largely to the chiefly class, and specific inferences about *tu'a* mortuary rites as they might have existed prior to conversion to Christianity are difficult to make. Gifford (1929: 201) has stated that commoners tended to be buried in convenient areas, usually the tract of land on which they lived. He also notes that, occasionally, children or loved ones were buried beneath the floor of a dwelling house, so that "the deceased might sit with them in the home circle" (Gifford 1929:201). Both practices are evident in the archaeological record of Tonga, with numerous small burial plots scattered over the landscape and the occasional presence of burials within house floor or midden deposits (Spenneman 1986; Burley 1992). Archaeological sites of the late prehistoric period in Tonga also suggest the underlying structure of grave architecture has remained the same over the past three or four centuries. This includes the use of coral sand for filling of the excavation and mound construction, as well as mound decoration with shell, coral gravel, and black basalt pebbles.

In 1920, W. C. McKern ([ca. 1925]:795–809) gathered data on 20th-century Tongan funerals relative to formal rules of behavior, treatment of the deceased, and grave construction (cf. Gifford 1929:196–203). Of the latter, three essential components are present, each with an associated set of rituals and proscriptions. These include: (1) the excavation for and interment of the body; (2) the infilling of the burial pit and construction of a white sand/gravel mound; and (3) the shaping of the mound and its decoration. This tripartite series of events continues to characterize Tongan burial practices today.

Of the three, that with the greatest import appears to be the building of the mound. Without it, as Tongans will readily state, an individual can neither be properly interred nor given due respect in the Tongan manner. Upon the death of an individual, the grave is dug and interment takes place almost immediately, along with the acquisition and placement of sand for the mound (Gifford 1929:200). The long-term use of coral sand for grave fill and burial mound construction has led to problems on islands with larger populations, one recognized today on Tongatapu with prohibitions on sand removal from beaches. In one case recorded in the Ha'apai islands, a late prehistoric burial mound without known ancestral affiliation was mined for this material until skeletal remains began to be encountered. Sand mounds in *tu'a* burial are traditional, required, and as far as could be ascertained, have no symbolic meaning beyond being a defined stage in the funerary ritual. McKern ([ca. 1925]:802) has suggested these mounds served a parallel function to the covering of the body with a mat or *tapa*, traditional bark cloth. In this capacity they were a means to protect the living from the dead.

Mound decoration does not take place at the time of its construction but represents a final activity that must be preceded by appropriate feasting and gift distribution. Dependent upon the status of the person, the intervening period between burial and grave decoration may be as little as a few days or as much as two years (McKern [ca. 1925]:804). The decoration of the grave involves two aspects, the shaping of the sand mound, often into tiers, and its embellishment through the use of shell, coral, volcanic pebbles, or any other materials deemed appropriate, from seeds to plastic flowers. McKern ([ca. 1925]:806) states that in former times the number of terraces on a grave "corresponded after a fashion to the rank of the one buried there." Similarly, chiefly as opposed to commoner graves in earlier days were distinguished by the presence of coral gravel and black volcanic pebbles (Gifford 1929:201). By the 20th century, such distinctions no longer held true with "anyone" able to lavishly decorate the grave of a relative "providing he can afford to supply the necessary materials, entertainment and feasting" (McKern [ca. 1925]:808).

The process of decorating the grave is undertaken by women. Presently there are no requisite materials nor do there seem to be traditional templates for exclusive use based on rank or other social dimensions. Modern burials differ from earlier ones predominantly through the extent to which graves are decorated, in the proliferation of materials now being employed, and in the elaboration of designs. Gifford (1924:283) interestingly attributes the introduction of new geometric design elements in 1920 to "the coloured linoleum and tile advertisements of magazines."

Beer bottles and cans, as integrated into the process of decoration, are but two of many potential materials. As earlier described, they most frequently are used to define the perimeters of a mound and, if imaginatively used, they can produce an appealing aesthetic. In this context Tongans place emphasis not on the symbolism of individual components of grave decoration, but on the act of decoration itself, and on the feast that is to follow. In seeking social metaphor in alcohol consumption, the author had transferred meaning from content (beer) to container (bottle/can). This basic association does not exist in the Tongan mind any more so than clam shells on a grave bespeak of an individual's food preferences. When informants stated that beer bottles and cans were used solely for decoration, they were, in fact, stating a truism.

Symbolic considerations of status and an individual's lifestyle aside, the color symbolism alluded to earlier would seem a more solid interpretation. Brown bottles dominate grave decoration throughout Tonga, despite the presence of green alternatives. With the association of brown is to death as green is to life, a near universal association appears apparent. Again this configuration was denied by Tongan informants, though a few thought it had far greater merit than other interpretations of beer bottles and cans with which they were being confronted. Through consideration of other contexts of meaning an alternative explanation may be offered, though in this case the context is historical rather than perceptual. In the late 1970s, Slake, an indigenous soft drink manufacturing company, was established on Tongatapu. Lacking a dedicated bottle supply, the company began, and continues, to recycle green Steinlager bottles—with the exception of the non-refillable, 750-ml bottle currently in use—and offer a refund for their return. While this circumstance has not been empirically verified as a dominant factor affecting color skew in the archaeological record of bottles in Tongan *mala'e,* its implications are nonetheless significant.

Conclusions

The use of beer cans and bottles as decorative materials for Tongan graves seems a curiously strange custom to a Western mind that associates container with content. Believing this practice to have originated in social metaphor in which an individual's status or lifestyle was actively portrayed, a number of interpretations were presented, each grounded in cultural or historical rationalization. Yet to the Tongans none of these has merit. Rather, bottles and cans are an aesthetic and structural medium that are easily available on the Tongan landscape and can be integrated into the process of grave decoration. Interpretations to the contrary say more about the symbolic associations of the archaeologist than they do about cultural meaning in Tongan mortuary practice.

This paper has been offered in part as a cautionary tale about the complexities of "recovering mind" and the potential for an interpretation of symbolic text in material culture where none may exist. Many North American historical archaeologists could, no doubt, question the relevancy of a study carried out in the western Polynesian kingdom of Tonga as it relates to their own research endeavors. Insofar as those within the discipline are constantly interpreting ethnic configurations of landscape, status, and other material correlates, parallels do hold forth. Indeed, as hinted at by Leone in the introductory quote (cf. Deetz 1977:23), historic behaviors and events, even when they originate with one's own ancestry, may be as far removed from contemporary frameworks for understanding as Tongan mortuary rites. Care must be taken to ensure cause, motivations, and rationalizations are not solely a product of one's own cultural milieu.

ACKNOWLEDGMENTS

I wish to acknowledge the Social Sciences and Humanities Research Council of Canada through which I have received funding to conduct archaeological fieldwork in Tonga. I am grateful to Andrew Barton and two anonymous reviewers for comments on the manuscript draft. Finally I wish to thank Ronn Michael and Jim Ayres for encouraging me to revise this paper for publication after it was presented at the Society for Historical Archaeology Conference on Historical and Underwater Archaeology meetings in Richmond, Virginia.

REFERENCES

BEAGLEHOLE, JOHN C. (EDITOR)
1969   *The Journals of Captain James Cook on His Voyages of Discovery; The Voyage of the* Resolution *and* Adventure, *1772–1775.* Published for the Hakluyt Society. Cambridge University Press, Cambridge.

BRITISH FOREIGN OFFICE
1906   Annual Report for Tonga, 1904 and 1905. Report prepared by Mr. Consul Hamilton Hunter. On file, Catholic Church Library, Nuku'alofa.

BURLEY, DAVID V.
1992   Archaeological Research in the Ha'apai Islands Kingdom of Tonga: Activities of the 1991 Field Season. Report on file, Department of Archaeology, Simon Fraser University, Burnaby.
1993   Chiefly Prerogatives Over Critical Resources: Archaeology, Oral Traditions and Symbolic Landscapes in the Ha'apai Islands, Kingdom of Tonga. In *Culture and Environment: A Fragile Co-existence,* edited by R. Jamieson, S. Abonyi, and N. Mirau, pp. 437–443. University of Calgary, Calgary.

CAMPBELL, I. C.
1992   *Island Kingdom, Tonga Ancient and Modern.* Canterbury University Press, Christchurch.

CHURCHWARD, CLERK M.
1959   *Tongan Dictionary.* Government Printing Press, Nuku'alofa, Tonga.

COWLING, W. E.
1990a   Motivations for Contemporary Tongan Migration. In *Tongan Culture and History,* edited by P. Herda, J. Terrell, and N. Gunson, pp. 187–205. Australian National University, Canberra.
1990b   Eclectic Elements in Tongan Folk Belief and Healing Practice. In *Tongan Culture and History,* edited by P. Herda, J. Terrell, and N. Gunson, pp. 72–92. Australian National University, Canberra.

DEETZ, JAMES
1977   *In Small Things Forgotten: The Archaeology of Early American Life.* Anchor Press/Doubleday, New York.

FERDON, E. N.
1987   *Early Tonga as the Explorers Saw It, 1616–1810.* University of Arizona Press, Tucson.

GAILEY, CHRISTINE W.
1987   *Kinship to Kingship: Gender Hierarchy and State Formation in the Tongan Islands.* University of Texas Press, Austin.

GIFFORD, EDWARD W.
1924   Euroamerican Acculturation in Tonga. *Journal of the Polynesian Society* 33:281–292.
1929   Tongan Society. *Bulletin* 61. Bernice P. Bishop Museum, Honolulu.

HODDER, IAN
1986   *Reading the Past: Current Approaches to Interpretation in Archaeology.* Cambridge University Press, Cambridge.

KIRCH, PATRICK V.
1984   *The Evolution of the Polynesian Chiefdoms.* Cambridge University Press, Cambridge.
1990   Monumental Architecture and Power in Polynesian Chiefdoms: A Comparison of Tonga and Hawaii. *World Archaeology* 22(2):206–222.

LEONE, MARK P.
1981   Archaeology's Relationship to the Present and the Past. In *Modern Material Culture: The Archaeology of Us,* edited by Richard A. Gould and Michael B. Schiffer, pp. 5–14. Academic Press, New York.
1982   Some Opinions About Recovering Mind. *American Antiquity* 47:742–760.

LITTLE, BARBARA J., AND PAUL A. SHACKEL (EDITORS)
1992   Meanings and Uses of Material Culture (Special Issue). *Historical Archaeology* 26(3).

MARCUS, G.
1980   *The Nobility and the Chiefly Tradition in Modern Tonga.* The Polynesian Society, University of Hawaii Press, Honolulu.

McKERN, W. C.
[ca.   Tongan Material Culture. Report of the Bayard Do-
1925]   minick Expedition to the Kingdom of Tonga, 1920–

1921. Report on file, Bernice P. Bishop Museum, Honolulu.

RAPOPORT, AMOS
1982   *The Meaning of the Built Environment: A Nonverbal Communication Approach.* Sage Publications, Beverly Hills.

RATHJE, WILLIAM L.
1979   Modern Material Culture Studies. *Advances in Archaeological Method and Theory* 2:1–37. Michael B. Schiffer, editor. Serial Publication Series. Academic Press, New York.

SHACKEL, PAUL A., AND BARBARA J. LITTLE
1992   Post-Processual Approaches to Meanings and Uses of Material Culture in Historical Archaeology. In Meanings and Uses of Material Culture (Special Issue), edited by Barbara J. Little and Paul A. Shackel. *Historical Archaeology* 26(3):5–11.

SPENNEMAN, D. H.
1986   Archaeological Fieldwork in Tonga, 1985–86. *Tongan Dark Ages Research Programme, Report* No. 7. Department of Prehistory, Australian National University, Canberra.

DAVID V. BURLEY
DEPARTMENT OF ARCHAEOLOGY
SIMON FRASER UNIVERSITY
BURNABY, BRITISH COLUMBIA V5A 1S6
CANADA

Timothy B. Riordan

"Carry Me to Yon Kirk Yard": An Investigation of Changing Burial Practices in the Seventeenth-Century Cemetery at St. Mary's City, Maryland

ABSTRACT

Fifty-seven burials were excavated in the 17th-century cemetery at St. Mary's City, Maryland. Through a unique combination of the structural history of the site and a detailed recording process, the burials are assigned to three 30-year periods, spanning ca. 1638–1730. This data is used to investigate changes in the use and construction of coffins, the function of copper pins, and the evolution of hand placement in the burials. These trends are related to larger changes in English burial practices.

Introduction

In England, the 17th century was an important period of change in traditional burial practices (Gittings 1984:13–14; Litten 1992:12–13). This change has been seen as part of a larger trend emphasizing the individual (Ariés 1981:602–603). Burial in a wooden coffin, a 16th-century innovation, became a universally accepted part of the ritual. Along with coffin burial, a shift occurred from an untailored shroud towards readymade burial clothing. Regional traditions gave way to accepted standards of what constituted a decent burial. Many of these changes have physical aspects that are reflected but generally ignored in the archaeological record.

Excavations in the 17th-century Catholic cemetery at St. Mary's City, Maryland, offered a unique opportunity to observe these changes in a colonial setting. The cemetery was the community's main burial ground for approximately 100 years, ca. 1638–1730. During that time, a series of chapels were built on the property. The brick chapel (ca. 1667) was constructed in the middle of the cemetery. It was closed in 1704 by order

of the government, and the Jesuits tore it down several years later. Beginning in 1983, Historic St. Mary's City conducted investigations in the Chapel Field, identifying the location of the brick chapel and exposing its foundation (Riordan et al. 1994). As preparation for the reconstruction of the brick chapel, museum archaeologists cleared a 10 ft. wide corridor around the foundation of any archaeological resources. This work included excavation of 57 burials.

While no burials were marked by tombstones, it was possible to place each grave into a shorter time period by recording its specific characteristics. The sequence was divided into three periods, based on the history of the brick chapel: early (ca. 1638–1667), middle (ca. 1667–1704), and late (ca. 1704–1730). Burials in the early period had little or no rubble in their fill and were oriented to either the early wooden chapel or close to due east. All of the burials cut through by the foundation of the brick chapel share these characteristics. Middle-period burials are oriented within a degree or two of the orientation of the brick chapel (111° from true north). They have a large amount of brick rubble from the chapel's construction but do not have any mortar or plaster. Finally, late period burials have large amounts of rubble of all types. Each of the periods is roughly 30 years long, and the sequence spans the period of greatest change in English burial customs.

The opportunity to study these changes over time would be lost without a detailed methodology designed to maximize the amount of information from each burial. As part of the normal excavation technique, each coffin stain was carefully mapped. The nails were described in detail, noting the location of the head, its elevation, the orientation of the shaft, and any adhering wood. The same treatment was given to the numerous copper pins found on the skeletons. This attention to detail, combined with the burial sequence, has produced a remarkable body of data for observing developments in mortuary customs in a colonial setting.

The present study focuses on three aspects of the burial program that underwent major changes in the period under consideration. Use of wooden coffins for burial was becoming the accepted norm, bringing along different ways of making coffins. This paper looks at the use and construction of coffins to investigate chronological trends and technological innovations. Secondly, the use of copper straight pins, so-called shroud pins, in the burial ritual is investigated. These artifacts are frequently found in colonial burials, but their function is assumed rather than proved. A new interpretation, tied to larger changes in burial ritual, is presented here. Finally, an investigation of changes in hand placement of English burials is reported

Coffin Use in England and Colonial America

During the middle ages, the most common form of burial called for placing the tightly shrouded corpse directly into the ground without a coffin. Numerous contemporary illustrations depict this manner of burial (Hazlitt 1905[1]:250; Ariés 1985:117–119,131; Litten 1992:58,59,64). Although there is little information available about the use of wooden coffins during this time, this does not imply that coffins were not made and used. Julian Litten (1992:89) shows a rectangular wooden coffin dating to the 14th century. It may be a reusable communal coffin, used only for transporting the shrouded corpse to the church and grave but not for burial. The use and reuse of such coffins continued well into the 17th century in England (Geddes 1976:118; Litten 1992:98).

The documented use of communal coffins confuses the issue of when the practice of burial in wooden coffins began. A number of illustrations from 15th-century France show trapezoidal, gable-lidded coffins that were covered with a pall during a requiem Mass (Ariés 1985:124; Litten 1992:149). These visuals have been interpreted to mean that wooden coffins were being used in burial rituals, but no illustrations actually show coffins being buried even though pictures of the burial of shrouded bodies are common. In fact, Litten (1992:58) presents an illustrated page (ca. 1423) showing a complete sequence from death, through the Mass, to the burial. At the requiem Mass, a pall covers the typical coffin; yet at the burial, the shrouded body is placed into the grave without a coffin.

Until archaeological evidence of these coffins is reported, the issue will remain uncertain.

The use of wooden coffins shows a marked increase during the reign of Queen Elizabeth (Litten 1992:12). By the early-17th century, coffins become standard burial equipment for all but the poorest people. Clare Gittings (1984:235–241) surveys probate accounts for three English counties from ca. 1580–1650 and finds evidence for the increasing use of coffins. Her analysis shows 22% coffin use in the 1580s but almost 90% in the 1640s. While the use of such probate accounts clearly introduces a bias towards the wealthier members of society, there is an obvious increase in coffin use in early-17th-century England. Lois Green Carr (n.d.) reviewed probate accounts during the period 1638–1705 for 10 counties in Maryland. The sample included 457 accounts that showed expenses for funerals, and 91% of these mention a coffin. When viewed chronologically, a trend towards increasing use of coffins is evident. In those accounts dated before 1670, only 79% mention coffins, while 97% of the accounts dated after 1700 have such an expense.

Similar results were found in the cemetery at St. Mary's City. Of the 47 grave shafts where preservation was sufficient to note the characteristic, 32 (68%) had evidence of coffins. The trend in coffin use is clear when these burials are considered within the framework of the cemetery chronology (Table 1). Presence of a coffin varies according to several factors, including time period, sex, and age. The general rule is for all adult burials to have coffins. In the early period, however, 61% (11 of 18) of the adults were uncoffined shroud burials. Not surprisingly, given the demographics of the Chesapeake, the

TABLE 1
COFFIN USE: ST. MARY'S CITY CEMETERY
(CA. 1638–1730)

Period	No. of Graves	Percentage of Total	No. of Coffins	Percentage of Period
Early period	23	48.9	10	43.5
Middle period	20	42.6	18	90.0
Late period	4	8.5	4	100.0
Total	47	100.0	32	

majority of the uncoffined adults were male. Of the five infant burials dating to the early period, three were in coffins. By the time the brick chapel was built (ca. 1667), a coffin was required for all adults. The only middle-period burials that show no evidence of a coffin are two infants, yet five other infants dating to the middle period are buried in coffins. All of the late period burials are adults who are buried in coffins. Over the course of 100 years, coffin use went from less than half to universal use.

Coffin use in the cemetery at St. Mary's City shows some interesting contrasts to other reported cemeteries in the Chesapeake. The early period graves, with less than 50% coffin use, are comparable to the site of Martin's Hundred (1619–1622), which had 33% coffin use (Noël Hume 1982:74–83). It may be that until the last quarter of the 17th century, the use of coffins, while common, was restricted to the more wealthy or prominent members of a community. By the later 17th century, coffin use, as represented by the middle-period burials, becomes universal for adults. Similar results have been found at Middle Plantation (ca. 1664–1700) in Maryland with 100% coffin use (Doepkins 1991:134–135) and Clifts Plantation (ca. 1670–1730) in Virginia with 94% coffin use (Neiman 1980:128–140). In contrast, coffin use at the contemporary Patuxent Point cemetery (ca. 1660–1670) in Maryland is very low with only 44% use (King and Ubelaker 1996:39–40). Such small, rural cemeteries, particularly those where the landowner was probably not resident, are more likely to retain older, perhaps cheaper, mortuary patterns. The location of the St. Mary's cemetery in the provincial capital must be considered in assessing its relationship to other cemeteries in the Chesapeake.

Another characteristic, notable from the nails and wood stains, was the shape of the coffin. Until recently, all colonial coffins were thought to be of the standard hexagonal or "single break shape," with a flat lid (Habenstein and Lamars 1962:254–256). Discoveries at Martin's Hundred showed that coffins not only could be made in other shapes, like trapezoidal, but they could have gabled lids as well (Noël Hume 1982:38–41,76–80). Even knowing about the possibility of different coffin shapes occurring, the excavators were not ready for the variety found in the chapel cemetery.

Seven distinct types of coffins were evident in the St. Mary's sample, based on shape of the box and lid style (Figure 1). There are three types of hexagonal coffin: one with a flat lid (HF) and two varieties of gable lid (HG). The rectangular shape was only found with a flat lid (RF). Tapered coffins occurred with both flat and gabled lids (TF, TG). Finally, there was the anthropomorphic shaped coffin with a flat lid (AF). This coffin is narrow at the foot, like the tapered and hexagonal types and expands up to the shoulders. At the shoulder, there is a sharp inward angle, and the head is contained within a small box. Careful attention to the wood stain and nail patterns can add much to understanding the evolution of coffin types.

The seven types found in St. Mary's show significant variation in frequency through time (Table 2). Hexagonal types are almost absent from the early period but become the dominant type by the mid-17th century. They are the only type found in the 18th-century sample. This shape was a recent innovation in the early-17th

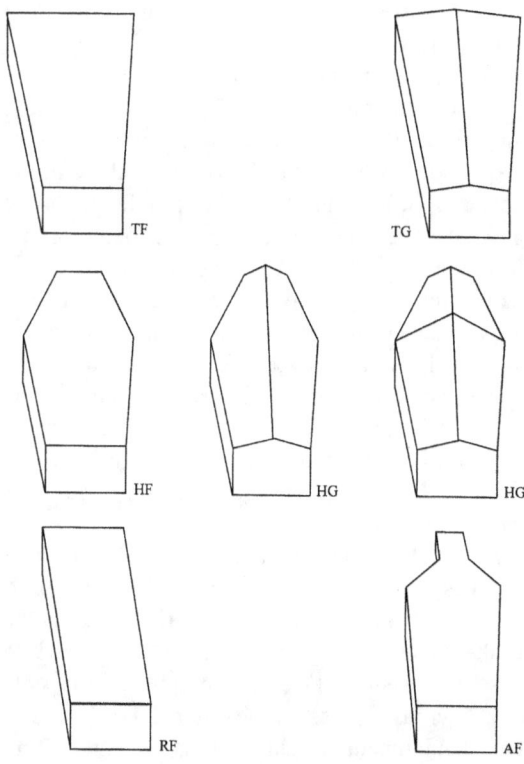

Figure 1. Coffin shapes. (Drawing by author, 1999.)

TABLE 2
COFFIN TYPES: ST. MARY'S CITY CEMETERY (CA. 1638–1730)

Period	HF	HG	H?	RF	TF	TG	AF	U	Total
Early period	1	-	-	2	1	-	3	3	10
Middle period	7	4	-	3	-	1	-	3	18
Late period	1	2	1	-	-	-	-	-	4
Total	9	6	1	5	1	1	3	6	32

century, and the trend to increasing use of hexagonal coffins mirrors contemporary English practice (Litten 1992:96–97). Rectangular coffins are significant in the early period, less so in the middle period, and are not found in the late period. The most unusual coffin type is the anthropomorphic coffin. Not only is this type present in the early period, but also it is the most common type. Several lead coffins of this shape are known from English vaults, but this may be the first wooden coffin of the type found archaeologically (Litten 1992:101).

The choice of a particular coffin type shows a strong correlation to age at death. In the early period, adults are buried in anthropomorphic and tapered coffins. Of the three infants, two are buried in rectangular coffins. At least one of these (and possibly both) is a recycled box, not originally intended for a coffin. The only hexagonal coffin in the early period contains the other infant burial. In the middle period, 9 of the 11 adults are buried in hexagonal coffins. The others are buried in a tapered coffin and a rectangular box, but the latter is a reburial and not a true coffin. Infant burials in this period are evenly split between rectangular and hexagonal coffins. Both of the rectangular coffins used for infant burials in this period appear to be intentionally made as coffins and are not recycled boxes. All of the coffins in the later period are hexagonal.

Within the cemetery, there is a distinct trend towards a hexagonal coffin as the accepted burial container. In the early period, only 14% of the identifiable coffins are hexagonal, while these represent 73% of the middle period coffins. Increasing use of hexagonal coffins, and the abandonment of other forms, is part of the standardization of the English funeral that was progressing through the 17th century. Whether standardization represents the breakdown of regional burial patterns or a growing sophistication on the part of carpenters hired to make coffins cannot be demonstrated at present. It is clear, however, that in the early-17th century, several different styles of coffins were deemed acceptable as burial containers, and by the end of the century, there was only one acceptable style.

Other cemeteries in the Chesapeake, while used for much shorter periods, have produced similar results. Cemeteries dating before 1650, such as Martin's Hundred, Flowerdew Hundred, and Jordan's Journey, show evidence of tapered and possibly rectangular coffins but no hexagonal ones (Noël Hume 1982:74–83; McLearnen and Mouer 1993). The exclusive use of hexagonal coffins in the late-17th century and the 18th century has been seen at Middle Plantation and at Patuxent Point (Doepkins 1991:134–135; King and Ubelaker 1996:39). A single rectangular coffin is reported from Clifts Plantation, Virginia, along with 15 hexagonal coffins (Neiman 1980:130). By the late-17th century in the Chesapeake, as in England, use of a hexagonal coffin was part of a standardized funeral.

Coffin Construction Techniques

Typically, archaeological reports describe the presence or absence of coffins and usually go far enough to describe the shape of the coffins. This level of analysis misses some of the most important information concerning the burial container. Unless the burial has been heavily disturbed, the location and orientation of the nails can provide vital data on coffine construction. One of the earliest demonstrations of the importance of this type of analysis was Ivor Noël Hume's (1982:76) discovery of gable-lidded coffins at Martin's Hundred, based on the finding of a row of nails down the center of the burial.

A basic understanding of coffin carpentry can aid in analyzing archaeological remains. Leaving aside the lid, for the moment, a simple coffin consists of five pieces of wood—a base, two sides, and two ends. The base is prepared first because it gives shape and form to the rest of the box. The sides are then nailed to the edge of the base. This procedure results in the side nails lying flat and perpendicular to the main axis of the coffin. While it would be possible to nail the sides on top of the base, this was never done because of the risk that in lifting the coffin, the base could fall off (Litten 1992:92).

Significant variation occurs with the closure of the ends. The earliest closure, termed the inserted end board, has the sides cut to the same length as the base. After the sides are attached, the end is inserted into the U-shaped opening. This board is attached by nails driven through the sides and the base. The nail pattern for this closure shows nails on the sides, perpendicular to the main axis, and nails standing upside down at the base (Figure 2). The earliest surviving coffin, a 14th-century communal coffin in England, shows this closure (Litten 1992:89).

A second method of closing the box is to butt the end up against the base and side boards. The end board is attached with nails driven through the end and into the other pieces. This is referred to as a butted end board. The nail pattern for a butted end board shows nails oriented parallel to the main axis of the coffin (Figure 2). These nails are at the base and run up the sides. This pattern, while simple to construct, is not as strong as the others.

Carpentry that is more complex is required for the third type of closure, known as a combined end board. This method uses aspects of the other two. The sides are made slightly longer than the base, and the end is fitted into this space. The end is butted against the base but is inserted between the sides. The nail pattern for this type has nails along the base that are parallel to the main axis of the coffin and nails up the sides that are perpendicular to the main axis (Figure 2). The earliest reported coffin using the combined end pattern may be that of Sir William Allestree, dated 1655 (Litten 1992:98). This type is the most common pattern reported in the archaeological literature (Neiman 1980:140;

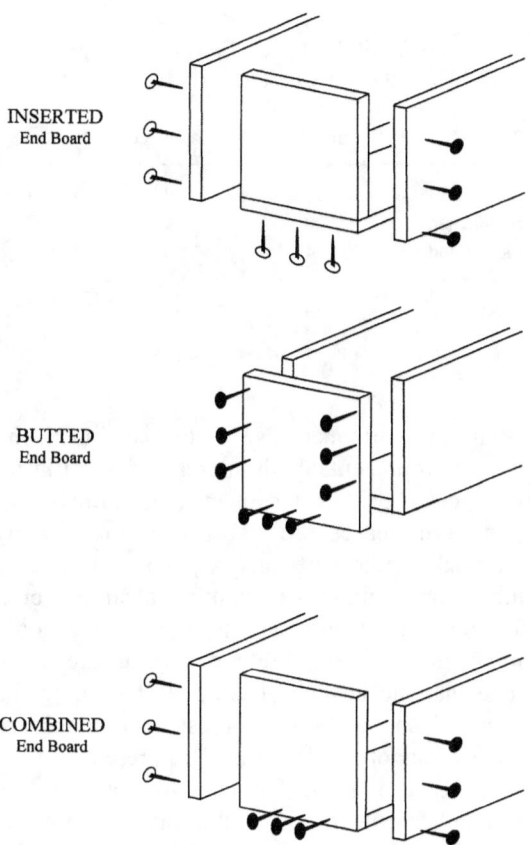

Figure 2. Coffin construction techniques and nail patterns. (Drawing by author, 1999.)

Parrington et al. 1989:145; Reeve and Adams 1993:78; LeeDecker et al. 1995:53).

All three of these treatments leave unique nail patterns that are discernible in the archaeological record. It is vital that the excavation methods be sensitive enough to record these important differences. In the cemetery at St. Mary's, the excavated data provide significant insights on coffin construction over time. It was possible to make 50 observations on end closure (Table 3). By far, the most common closing technique is the inserted end board, which accounts for almost 70% of the observed end patterns. In the early period, the inserted end board makes up 83% of the observations, but this falls to 50% by the late period. The combined end pattern, which makes up only 8% of the sample in the early period, represents 50% of the late period sample. The butted end board is uncommon in all periods.

Period	Inserted	Combined	Butted
Early period	10	1	1
Middle period	20	7	3
Late period	4	4	0
Total	34	12	4

The more frequent use of the combined end pattern represents both increasing familiarity with and sophistication in making coffins. This pattern increases the stability of the box by interlocking the parts and requires considerably more forethought than making a simple box. The combined end pattern begins to become important in the middle period at the same time that the hexagonal coffin is becoming the standard shape. Whether these two things are related cannot be determined at present.

The type of lid that is used to close the box is another characteristic that can be observed archaeologically. Until Noël Hume's (1982:76) work at Martin's Hundred, most archaeologists were unaware that coffins could have anything but a flat lid. Even today, there is considerable skepticism that colonial carpenters were capable of making a gable lid (LeeDecker et al. 1995:50). In fact, the gable lid was common well into the 19th century (Pike and Armstrong 1980:132,153; Parrington et al. 1989:139–149).

Whether flat or gable, the lid must reflect the shape of the base and must be made larger to cover both the base and the sides. The lid is nailed to the top edge of the sides. Archaeologically, this technique leaves a number of nails standing vertically with their heads at the top. While the coffin often collapses in on itself, the lid nails are often found in place because the sides support them. The elevation of their heads can provide a minimum height for the sides of the coffin.

Gable lids require more detailed carpentry than do flat lids. In a straight-sided coffin, the gable lid is composed of two pieces of wood that are laid on the gable-shaped end board. The top edges of these boards can either be butt jointed or mitered to provide a clean joint at the peak of the lid. The boards are joined to the coffin with vertical nails on the sides and ends, along with a line of angled nails running down the coffin centerline. When the coffin sides are angled rather than straight, the geometry becomes more complex. Researchers have observed two distinct types of gable-lidded, hexagonal coffins. Litten (1992:plate 11) illustrates a hexagonal coffin with a gable that runs in one plane from head to foot. This type would have a nail pattern similar to the rectangular, gable-lidded type. Martha Pike and Janice Armstrong (1980:132,153) show two hexagonal coffins that have gables running straight up to the chest and then sloping down to the head at a noticeable angle. It is not certain how this type of lid was constructed. The angle could have been created by kerfing the boards and then bending them. Alternately, the lid could be made from four boards that were mitered at the angle. There is good evidence of this form in the 19th century. The lid is made of pairs of boards, joined along the centerline by pairs of nails going in opposite directions. Two of the boards make the ridge from the foot to the chest, and the others make the ridge from the chest to the head. The two sections are butted against each other but not joined (Parrington et al. 1989:145). It is not known if this nail pattern was followed earlier than the 19th century.

Within the cemetery at St. Mary's, construction of the gable lids proved to be more complex than anticipated. Four different methods were observed in just seven examples (Figure 3). The most common construction reveals a number of nails along the centerline of the coffin from the foot end to the shoulder area. These nails often appear to be paired with heads on opposite sides. No centerline nails are found between the shoulder and head end. In addition, a number of nails, usually three on each side, are found angling back from the shoulder area. These nails joined separate boards to the main lid and created a diamond-shaped lid rather than a straight gable. There were three examples of this technique, all made on hexagonal coffins.

The other three construction techniques are each represented by one example. There was one coffin whose gable lid was too disturbed to determine its construction. The first of these was a hexagonal coffin with a line of nails all along the centerline, similar to those from Mar-

344

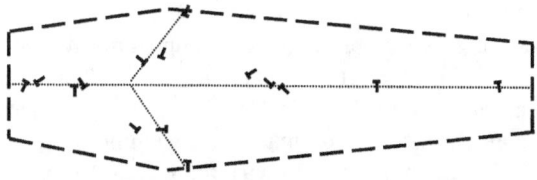

HEX W/DIAMONDBACK GABLE LID
Nail Pattern

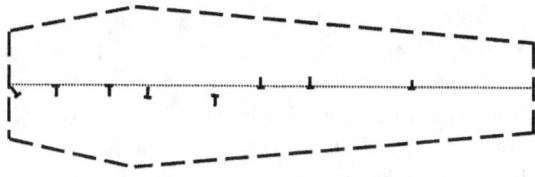

HEX W/STRAIGHT GABLE LID
Nail Pattern

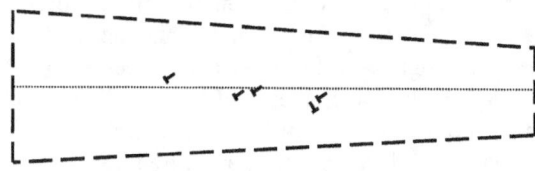

TAPERED W/GABLE LID
Nail Pattern

Figure 3. Gable-lid nail patterns. (Drawing by author, 1999.)

tin's Hundred. A tapered coffin was found with centerline nails only near the mid length of the lid, evenly spaced from either end. Finally, a hexagonal coffin showed evidence of a gable in its profile but had no centerline nails. This was the coffin of an 8 to 9 year old juvenile and is much shorter than the other coffins. It may be that the lid was only joined on the ends.

Gable lids comprise a little over one-quarter of all the coffins whose lid construction can be determined. All seven of these are found in the middle and late periods. More importantly, they seem to become more popular over time, being 33% of the middle period lids and 66% of the late period lids. Overall, the sample size is too small to make any firm conclusions.

Within the sample, there seems to be an association of the combined end pattern with gable-lidded coffins. Of the 12 observed examples

of this closure, 9 (75%) are on gable-lidded coffins. The inserted end board is even more closely associated with flat-lidded coffins. Of the 34 examples of inserted end boards, 32 (94%) are on flat-lidded coffins. While these relationships seem very strong, they must be accepted with caution for the time being. It has already been noted that gable lids are more common during the later part of the 17th and into the 18th century—the same time that the combined end pattern is more common. It may be that they are independent developments in two separate aspects of coffin construction.

Over the period that the cemetery at St. Mary's City was being used, significant changes in the use and construction of wooden coffins have been noted. The trend is clearly towards a standardized burial container. While there is great variation in shape and construction during the first half of the 17th century, the end of the century is characterized by a much narrower selection. Along with standardization, a greater sophistication in carpentry appears to be applied to construction. The hexagonal shape, combined end board, and gable lid appear to be integral parts of this overall trend.

Function of "Shroud" Pins

A common artifact found in colonial burials is the simple copper or brass straight pin. These are often identified as shroud pins and, if they are interpreted at all, are assumed to be for closing and holding the edge of the wrapped shroud (King and Ubelaker 1996:38–39). A notable exception to this line of reasoning is Fraser Neiman's (1980:140) observation that 22 of the 32 pins he found were on the skull or upper body. As with the coffins, an understanding of accepted burial clothing and careful recording of pin placement provide unexpected and useful data.

Tradition dictated that the deceased would not be buried in their normal clothing. Late medieval burial clothing can be seen on monuments and in paintings. Burial clothing consisted of a long sheet, often of linen, wrapped around the body. Litten (1992:57–72) discusses the development of this garment from a regular sheet to a fully tailored garment in the 18th century. The winding sheet was most often tightly wrapped, and strips of cloth were used to secure the sheet at the head and feet. Often additional strips were tied around the legs to make the body stiffer (Ariés 1985:118; Litten 1992:61,65). Sometimes the winding sheet was sewn along its edge (Ariés 1985:117). There is little evidence in the literature to support the idea that pins were used to fasten an adult shroud.

Beneath the winding sheet, the deceased in the middle ages did not wear any other clothing (Ariés 1985:116; Litten 1992:59). During the wake, the winding sheet was often parted to show the face of the deceased. Sometimes a face cloth was placed over the exposed head and pinned to the shroud. By the 1630s, it was common for the body to be dressed in a shirt and cap under the winding sheet (Litten 1992:76). The standard 17th-century English burial included "a sheet, shirt and cap" (Gittings 1984:112). Chin cloths, designed to keep the mouth closed, were pinned to the cap. The remarkable preservation of some of the bodies in the vault at Christ Church, Spitalfields, London, demonstrates the use of both face and chin cloths (Reeve and Adams 1993:110–119). These differences in burial clothing are reflected in the use and placement of pins within the burial.

Copper or brass straight pins are common in the St. Mary's cemetery burials. Of the 36 burials sufficiently preserved to assess this characteristic, 27 graves (71%) have pins in direct association with the skeleton. The number of pins included in a burial varies widely, with 9 burials having no pins at all and several burials having 10 or more. One infant burial from the middle period with 18 pins had the highest total. Pins seem to be more common in infant burials than in adult burials. The adult burials averaged 3.5 pins per grave, while the infant

burials average 8.8 pins per grave. Pins also seem to be more common through time for both types of graves (Table 4). The apparent decline in the number of pins during the late period may be a factor of inadequate sample size.

Although no fabric was recovered from any burials, it was possible to determine if a tightly wrapped shroud was used. If the toes were preserved in anatomical position, showed signs of confinement, and the knees were close together, this was taken as indicative of a tightly wrapped shroud. If the toes had collapsed, the knees were apart, and the tibiae had rolled sideways, this was taken as indicative of no tightly wrapped shroud. Obviously, this method cannot distinguish the presence of a loosely wrapped shroud, but no contemporary illustrations show such a garment. Using these observations, a dramatic trend is noticeable in the cemetery (Table 5). Shroud use, which is at 69% in the early period, falls to 30% in the middle period and to 25% in the late period. This change from use of a tightly wrapped shroud agrees with the change to burial clothes in England. This trend has implications for the use of straight pins in burials. While these pins are often referred to as "shroud" pins, they seem to become more common just at the time that evidence of shroud use is declining.

The actual distribution of pins reveals a more complex pattern of use. Of the 163 pins directly associated with the skeletons, 125 (77%) are found on or around the skull. The proportion of pins in the head area is about the same for both adults (78.5%) and infants (74%). This concentration probably reflects the use of caps, chin cloths, and face cloths. Similar concentrations of pins in the head area have been noted at other

TABLE 4
AVERAGE NUMBER OF PINS BY TYPE OF BURIAL:
ST. MARY'S CITY CEMETERY (CA. 1638–1730)

Period	Adult Graves		Infant Graves	
	No. of Pins	Av.	No. of Pins	Av.
Early period	32	2.5	25	8.3
Middle period	47	4.7	45	9.0
Late period	14	3.5	0	0.0
Total	93	3.5	70	8.8

Period	Shrouded	No Shroud
Early period	9	4
Middle period	37	
Late period	1	3
Total	13	14

17th-century cemeteries in the Chesapeake. At the Clifts Plantation cemetery, 66% of the pins or stains were found in the head area, while at Patuxent Point, around 80% appear to have been in this area (Neiman 1980:140; King and Ubelaker 1996:133–182).

In the St. Mary's graves, the pins do not occur randomly in the head area but are found in two distinct patterns (Figure 4). The most common pattern, observed in five burials, has lines of two to five pins, all oriented in the same direction, on opposite sides of the skull. The pins are commonly spaced within a 2 in. area. Their location and symmetry suggests these were used to attach a chin cloth to a

cap. The second pattern has pins all around the skull, and it was observed in three burials. These may represent the use of a face cloth that was pinned to the shroud. There appears to be a temporal distinction between the two patterns. Evidence of the face cloth was only being found in early period burials, and evidence of the chin cloth was being observed in middle and late period burials. The use of a cap and chin cloth for burial were gaining popularity in England during the middle of the 17th century, and the St. Mary's burials may reflect this trend.

Outside of the head area, the use of pins is sporadic but may reveal some pattern. Five burials each contain a single pin on the chest, and one burial has a pin over each clavicle. The significance of this pattern is unknown, but it seems to have been common. Another unexplained pin location is at the wrists. There are four burials where a single pin was found in the wrist area, three on the left wrist and one on the right wrist. In addition to these, there are single pins found on the pelvis in two cases, on the knee in two cases, and at the feet in a single case. It is clear that while pin use was common in the head area, significant use also occurred in other parts of the burial. Further research may identify reasons for these patterns in use of pins.

Changes in Hand Placement

An important aspect of preparing a body for burial was positioning the hands of the deceased. Information on this aspect comes from excavated graves and from tomb memorials, since there seems to be little written tradition regarding the positioning of the arms or the placement of the hands. In the middle ages, hand placement was variable with at least four different positions recorded (Daniell 1997:118). Use of a particular placement might represent regional or status-related trends, but not enough research has been done to make any definite statements. By the 17th century, the most common placement in British burials is with the hands crossed on the pelvis, usually with the right hand on top of the left hand. This positioning is found from Anglo-Saxon times onward (Ariés 1985:117; Rodwell 1989:164,171; Litten 1992:36,60,63,67). A second common placement is to lay the arms out by the side

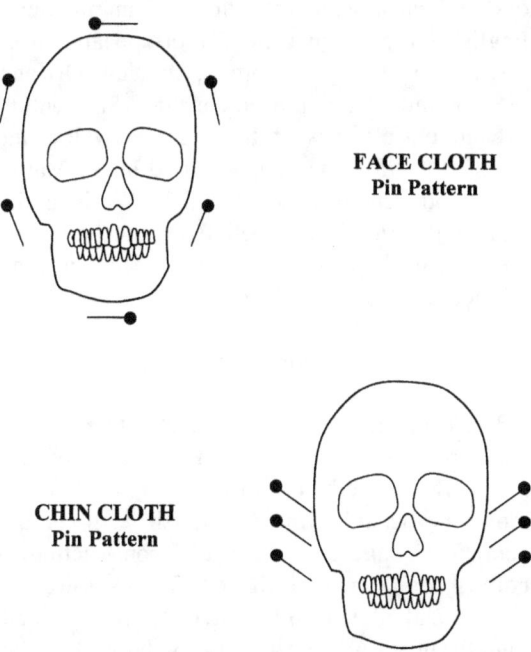

FACE CLOTH
Pin Pattern

CHIN CLOTH
Pin Pattern

Figure 4. Copper pin pattern. (Drawing by author 1999.)

of the body (Koch 1983:203; Litten 1992:203). Placing the arms across the chest with the hands on the shoulders seems to have been common in the middle ages but went out of fashion before the 17th century (Litten 1992:60). Finally, the hands were often placed on the chest as if clasped in prayer. Again, this was common in medieval burials but was abandoned in the 15th century in Britain (Rahtz 1981:119; Ariés 1985:49). Placement of the hands on the chest was still common in 17th-century Spanish burials in Florida (Koch 1983:203).

Hand placement is one of the characteristics carefully noted during excavation. This feature could be observed in 28 adult burials. Three distinct hand placements were noted: on the pelvis, on the thighs below the pelvis, and by the sides of the thighs (Table 6). In the early period, hand placement varied widely. This variation did not correlate to sex or use of a coffin but was evenly distributed across all other variables. In the middle and late periods, the pelvis became the primary placement site. This placement was also seen in the contemporary cemetery at Patuxent Point, Maryland, where 73% of the burials were found with their hands crossed on the pelvis (King and Ubelaker 1996). In the St. Mary's cemetery, when the hands were crossed on the pelvis, the right hand was always on top of the left, following an established English tradition. There are only two examples where the hands were on the pelvis and not crossed, both from the middle period. Whether this was intentional or due to movement after the coffin was closed is unknown.

Once again, there appears to be a trend in the St. Mary's data towards a standardization of the burial program. Placement of the hands on the thighs or at the sides may be part of

the variation existing in regional burial patterns, and they represent the majority of observed placements in the early period. In contrast, positioning the hands on the pelvis makes up only 43% of the early period observations. By the middle period, this ratio rises to 80%. As with other characteristics, burials in the cemetery at St. Mary's City carefully follow changes occurring in England at the same time, leading to an accepted manner of burial.

It is here that an important point, mostly overlooked in this paper, is reintroduced. Burials at St. Mary's City are Catholic internments. In the 17th century, English Catholics were a despised and distrusted minority in England. While the reasons for the settlement of Maryland are varied, for Catholics an important one was freedom from the restraints their minority status imposed upon them. The very existence of a Catholic church in an English colony is an anomaly. Being free of other restraints, English Catholics might be expected to follow a Catholic burial program.

Some significant evidence about burials in other Catholic colonies clarifies this point. Numerous burials have been excavated from 17th-century sites in Spanish Florida. Hand placement here follows an old Catholic tradition with the hands most often crossed over the chest (Larsen 1993; Koch 1983). This placement of the hands, which is known from medieval English burials, had generally disappeared from England by the 17th century. In New Orleans, the common hand placement for 18th-century French burials was at the sides (Owsley and Orser 1984:95). The people buried at St. Mary's were both Catholic and English. While maintaining the rituals and beliefs of their religion, they retained the material culture and customs of their English homeland.

Summary

The combination of a unique structural history and an intense recording method has produced a remarkable body of information on evolving mortuary behavior in an English 17th-century context. Change in the use and construction of coffins has been investigated. Trends toward a more standardized coffin have been postulated. Significant insights on the use of burial clothing during the period have been formulated. Analysis

TABLE 6
HAND PLACEMENT:
ST. MARY'S CITY CEMETERY (CA. 1638–1730)

Period	Pelvis	Thighs	Sides
Early period	6	3	5
Middle period	8	1	1
Late period	4	0	0
Total	18	4	6

of body placement has demonstrated that the colonists' emphasized their English origins over their Catholic religion, even though the unrestricted practice of their religion was the reason many of them emigrated to Maryland.

While many cemeteries were not used for such a long period or do not provide the temporal control seen in the St. Mary's City cemetery, all burials can produce useful and detailed insights on burial practices. There is no doubt that the skeleton tells researchers much about the person buried in the grave and potentially the society of which that person was a part. The rest of the material from the grave, such as nails, pins, wood, and soil stains, however, also have as much to tell about burial practices. It is vital that any burial excavation recover this data through detailed provenience information. Thus far, not enough emphasis has been placed on these aspects of the burial ritual.

References

Ariés, Philippe
  1981 *The Hour of Our Death*. Allen Lane, London, England, UK.
  1985 *Images of Man and Death*. Harvard University Press, Cambridge, MA.

Carr, Lois Green
  n.d. Probate Mortuary Data File. Manuscript, Department of Research, Historic St. Mary's City, MD.

Daniell, Christopher
  1997 *Death and Burial in Medieval England*. Routledge, London, England, UK.

Doepkins, William P.
  1991 *Excavations at Maureen Duvall's Middle Plantation of South River Hundred*. Gateway Press, Baltimore, MD.

Geddes, Gordon E.
  1976 *Welcome Joy: Death in Puritan New England*. UMI Research Press, Ann Arbor, MI.

Gittings, Clare
  1984 *Death, Burial, and the Individual in Early Modern England*. Croom Helm, London, England, UK.

Habenstein, Robert W., and William M. Lamars
  1962 *The History of American Funeral Directing*, revised edition. Bulfin Printers, Milwaukee, WI.

Hazlitt, W. Carew
  1905 *Faiths and Folklore of the British Isles*. 2 Vols. Reprinted in 1965 by Benjamin Bloom, New York, NY.

King, Julia A., and Douglas H. Ubelaker
  1996 *Living and Dying on the Seventeenth-Century Patuxent Frontier*. Maryland Historical Trust Press, Crownsville, MD.

Koch, Joan K.
  1983 Mortuary Behavior Patterning and Physical Anthropology in Colonial St. Augustine. In *Spanish St. Augustine: The Archaeology of a Colonial Creole Community*, Kathleen Deagan, editor, pp. 187–227. Academic Press, New York, NY.

Larsen, Clark Spencer
  1993 On the Frontier of Contact: Mission Bioarchaeology in La Florida. In *The Spanish Missions of La Florida*, Bonnie G. McEwan, editor, pp. 357–375. University Press of Florida, Gainesville.

LeeDecker, Charles H., Jonathan Bloom, Ingrid Wuebber, and Marie-Lorraine Pipes
  1995 Final Archaeological Excavations at a Late Eighteenth-Century Family Cemetery for the U.S. Route 113 Dualization, Milford to Georgetown, Sussex County, Delaware. Delaware Department of Transportation Archaeology Series, No. 134. Report to the Delaware Department of Transportation, Dover, from the Cultural Resource Group, Louis Berger & Associates, East Orange, NJ.

Litten, Julian
  1992 *The English Way of Death: The Common English Funeral Since 1450*. Robert Hale, London, England, UK.

McLearnen, D. C., and L. D. Mouer
  1993 Jordan's Journey II: A Preliminary Report on the 1992 Excavations at Archaeological Sites 44PG302, 44PG303, and 44PG315. Report to the Virginia Department of Historic Resources, Richmond, from the Archaeological Research Center, Virginia Commonwealth University, Richmond.

Neiman, Fraser D.
  1980 Field Archaeology of the Clifts Plantation Site, Westmoreland County, Virginia. Manuscript, Virginia Department of Historic Resources, Richmond.

Noël Hume, Ivor
  1982 *Martin's Hundred*. Alfred A. Knopf, New York, NY.

Owsley, Douglas W., and Charles E. Orser, Jr.
  1984 An Archaeological and Physical Anthropological Study of the First Cemetery in New Orleans, Louisiana. Manuscript, Department of Geography and Anthropology, Louisiana State University, Baton Rouge.

Parrington, Michael, Daniel G. Roberts, Stephanie A. Pinter, and Janet C. Wideman
  1989 The First African Baptist Church Cemetery: Bioarchaeology, Demography, and Acculturation of Early-Nineteenth-Century Blacks. 3 Vols. Report

prepared for the Redevelopment Authority of the City of Philadelphia, from John Milner Associates, Philadelphia, PA.

PIKE, MARTHA V., AND JANICE GRAY ARMSTRONG
1980 *A Time to Mourn: Expressions of Grief in Nineteenth-Century America*. The Museums at Stony Brook, Stony Brook, NY.

RAHTZ, PHILIP
1981 Artefacts of Christian Death. In *Mortality and Immortality: The Anthropology and Archaeology of Death*, S. C. Humphreys and Helen King, editors, pp. 117–136. Academic Press, New York, NY.

REEVE, JEZ, AND MAX ADAMS
1993 *The Spitalfields Project*, vol. 1, *The Archaeology: Across the Styx*. CBA Research Reports, no. 85. Council for British Archaeology, London, England, UK.

RIORDAN, TIMOTHY B., SILAS D. HURRY, AND HENRY M. MILLER
1994 Birth of an American Freedom: Religion in Early Maryland. Completion report for NEH Grant RO-22102-90. Report to National Endowment for the Humanities, Washington, DC, from Department of Research, Historic St. Mary's City, MD.

RODWELL, WARWICK
1989 *The Archaeology of Religious Places*. University of Pennsylvania Press, Philadelphia.

TIMOTHY B. RIORDAN
RESEARCH DEPARTMENT
HISTORIC ST. MARY'S CITY
PO BOX 39
ST. MARY'S CITY, MD 20686

Francine W. Bromberg
Steven J. Shephard

The Quaker Burying Ground in Alexandria, Virginia: A Study of Burial Practices of the Religious Society of Friends

ABSTRACT

The values of humility and simplicity are two central tenets of the members of the Religious Society of Friends that set them apart from the rest of society. Adherence to these tenets by Alexandria Quakers living in the 18th and 19th centuries is evidenced in the archaeological investigation of the old Quaker Burying Ground in Old Town Alexandria, Virginia. In preparation for the construction of a library addition on the cemetery property, City of Alexandria archaeologists conducted excavations in 1993 to 1995 and identified 159 burial features, 66 of which were excavated. Although preservation of the remains was poor, information on interment practices, coffin types, burial goods, and health was recovered. Analysis of the Quaker Burying Ground data and comparisons with other historical cemetery excavations suggest that Alexandria's Quaker community largely rejected the ostentatious burial rituals, known as the "beautification of death" movement, of the dominant culture.

Introduction

Alexandria, Virginia, has a long commitment to increasing the public's awareness and understanding of its rich historical and archaeological past. Situated across the Potomac River from Washington, DC, the city was founded in 1749, and echoes of the past reverberate in the many structures of the Old Town area along the waterfront, nominated as a National Historic Landmark District in 1946. Since 1975, the city has continuously supported an active archaeology program. In 1989, Alexandria's city council passed the Archaeological Protection Code, which ensures that appropriate preservation actions will be taken prior to construction activities affecting significant archaeological sites. The task of enforcing the code became one of the functions of Alexandria Archaeology, a division of the city government's Office of Historic Alexandria. The staff reviews all of the building projects in the city to evaluate whether they have the potential to destroy significant archaeological resources; if there is a possibility for resources to be present, the developer is required to hire an archaeological consultant to conduct an investigation. In the case of small projects (such as the addition to a house) or city construction projects, Alexandria Archaeology is responsible for doing the work.

In 1992, the city initiated plans to replace a 1954 addition to the Kate Waller Barrett Library located at the corner of Queen and Columbus streets in its old and historic district (Figure 1). Given Alexandria Archaeology's role as the enforcer of the Archaeological Protection Code, the staff notified the city's planning department that archaeological work would be required prior to the library construction. This was the location of an historical period Quaker cemetery that was registered as archaeological site 44AX132 with the Virginia Department of Historic Resources (Figure 2). The existing library had only a small basement area, and it was predicted that graves would remain preserved under the building's floor and foundation.

The library addition project presented a unique opportunity for Alexandria Archaeology to focus on gaining an increased understanding

FIGURE 1. Front of Kate Waller Barrett Library in 1994. (Photo by Alexandria Archaeology.)

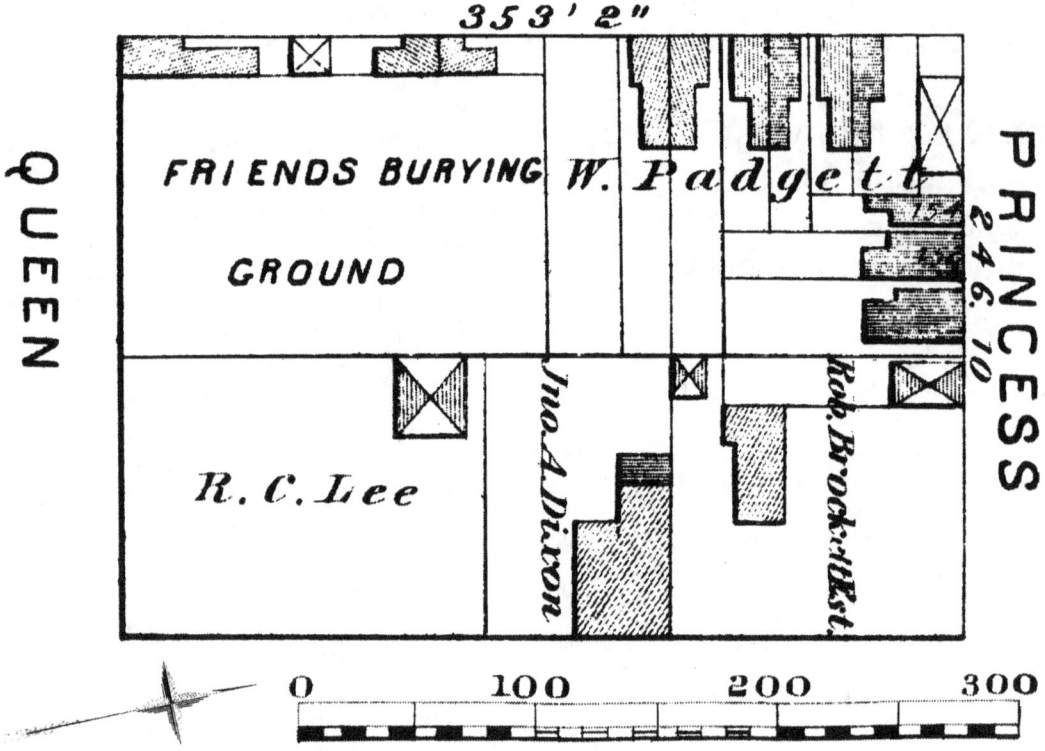

FIGURE 2. Friends Burying Ground on the 1877 Hopkins Map.

of the 18th- to 19th-century Quaker community in the city. The beliefs and practices of the Quakers set them apart from the mainstream culture of the time. Quakerism arose in the mid-17th century as a spiritual concept that afforded every individual his or her own access and connection to God. This spiritual egalitarianism contrasted sharply with the traditional reliance on authority, which was characteristic of the Puritans and other Calvinist sects. The emphasis on individual spirituality created an ideology based on a utopian belief in equality, and it fostered characteristic modes of behavior that prohibited expressions of social distinction. The Quakers demonstrated their egalitarianism through exterior symbols, such as simplicity in speech and dress, and through their principles, such as pacifism and the refusal to take oaths. This behavior both defined the Quakers as a distinct social group and preserved a sense of the Quaker identity.

Despite their utopian ideals and the behaviors that set them apart, the Quaker community was thoroughly integrated into Alexandria society. It was not a utopian community in the sense of a society that lives apart from the mainstream. Instead, the Quakers were among the most well-to-do members of the town, many serving as merchants who boosted trade during the early years of the city's development. Throughout the 19th century, the Quakers went on to promote many causes that led to community and societal improvements, including the creation of schools and libraries; the development of the Alexandria Canal, Little River Turnpike, and the Alexandria Water Company; and the relief of oppressed minorities. Many of the town's prominent Quakers engaged in real estate transactions that enabled free African Americans in the community to purchase their own property. Members of the Alexandria community were among the major forces involved in activities that focused on the betterment of the town and the individuals who lived in it.

One of the major research goals of the Quaker Burying Ground project was to examine how successful the community was in strictly adhering to the ideological tenets of the faith, given the integration of the Quakers into Alexandria society. The cemetery was used throughout a period when elaborate, ostentatious mourning rituals became commonplace as the country industrialized throughout the course of the 19th century. The question arose regarding the Quaker's continued adherence to the principles of simplicity with the changing tenor of the times. Since the characteristics of simplicity can be judged from an examination of material culture, the project was uniquely suited to address this issue. It afforded the opportunity to compare the espoused values of the Quakers with their behavior, as evidenced by the analysis of the material goods and features discovered during the archaeological investigation.

Beliefs and Practices of the Religious Society of Friends

The Quaker faith originated as a revolutionary spiritual concept first outlined by George Fox in London in 1647. Followers referred to themselves as Children of the Light or Friends of God and spoke with great passion on London street corners. They enjoined others to

> be not satisfied with outward ceremonies and old forms . . . no longer look outward for sermons and hymns, organs, whistles and pipes, bells, cushions, altars and fonts to change your lives . . . there is some thing of God in *you* . . . turn your mind *within* . . . examine your heart . . . try your ways, with the Light Christ Jesus has enlightened *you* [emphasis in original] (Worrall 1994:1).

Believers in this new way of relating to God were first given the name of Quakers in 1650 by Justice Bennet of Derby, when Fox ordered the judge and others in the courtroom "to tremble at the word of the Lord" (Clarkson 1806[1]:vi).

The central conviction of the faith is that God is in every human being. This "divine seed" is manifested through an inward light, the "Christ within," which comes through "a still small voice inside" as one listens in silence. A Friend's life then is carried out in harmony with what is perceived while listening, which is referred to as "minding the light" or "walking in the light" (Worrall 1994:23,301).

The Friends' ideology espoused the principle that every individual has equal access to a communion with God. This spiritual egalitarianism was a radical departure from the religious beliefs and practices of the 17th century, which emphasized the holy trinity and the Bible as the authority for behavior. It called for a fundamental change in thinking that challenged contemporary assumptions and threatened to change the structure and organization of contemporary institutions (Kunze 1994:1). With spiritual equality came the rejection of the Calvinistic principle that only a few people would be saved, and Quakers cast aside many other elements sacred to English Christianity, including baptism, communion, singing psalms, holy places, churches as places of worship, and a strict Sabbath day.

The sense of equality, called "the bedrock of the Quaker value system" (Baltzell 1979:102), extended into many of the more secular realms of Quaker life. The Friends proclaimed their equality through their language and simplicity in dress. They were "levelers of authority" (Baltzell 1979:103) and refused to perform deferential actions toward the rich and powerful (Baltzell 1979:103–104). There was equality between males and females, and women were seen as equal partners not only in aspects of religious life but also in marriage (Kunze 1994:225). Loyalty to the Christ within superseded loyalty to the state, and the religious conscience of the faithful forbade them from taking oaths (Kunze 1994:225). The Friends did not serve in the military, for the statement of the peaceful principle of Quakerism, first published in 1660, denounced all war and violence (Kunze 1994:5). The behavior of the Quakers set them apart and defined them as a distinct social group (Tully 1977:143). Some historians have contended that Quakerism was "fundamentally a way of life," rather than "a system of thought or doctrine" (Kunze 1994:81).

In the context of its origins, the rise of Quakerism can be seen as an attempt to create a utopian community, where equality, simplicity, and harmony prevailed. Certainly, the idea of what constitutes utopia has changed over time, with the politico-religious ideals of the 16th and 17th centuries giving way to the utopian socialism of the 18th-century Enlightenment and, later, to the economic idealism of the late-19th century (*Columbia Encyclopedia* 2001). Quakerism arose in the context of the political and religious idealism of England's 17th-century philosophers. By establishing a new order based on the purity of the primitive church, early Quakers sought to separate from what they considered the sinful, decadent world of Restoration England and to set up an anti-establishment, antihierarchical community, where each individual, living in consonance with the doctrine of the inner light, could achieve a state of perfection (Kunze 1994:125–126).

The embodiment of these principles in later times, relevant for the purposes of this article, can be seen in a short volume of instruction for Quaker youth entitled *The Young Friend's Manual*, written by Quaker Benjamin Hallowell who lived in Alexandria in the early-19th century. Hallowell (1867:107–108) set down the "cardinal principles and testimonies" of Quakerism in accordance with the characteristics of the true Christian Church in the apostolic age as the following:

1. A pure, spiritual worship.
2. A free Gospel ministry.
3. Religious liberty.
4. A testimony against war and oppression.
5. A testimony against oaths.
6. A testimony against vain fashions, corrupting amusements and flattering titles.

Hallowell (1867:62) described the results of living by these precepts:

> Under the influence of this Divine spirit, there can be no war, no slavery, no oppression of any kind, no intemperance, no deception, no injustice, no impurity, no tale-bearing or detraction, no vanity, pride, ostentation, extravagance, nor anything that could hurt or destroy.

The nature of the Quaker community, permeated by the value of equality, is evident in the structure of the meeting with regard to both worship and business. Since the relationships among the Friends were derived from the consensual association of equals, the meeting made decisions through reaching a consensus. As Alan Tully (1977:144) stated, "the achievement of unanimity among Friends was as much an end as the attainment of more specific goals."

Powerful bonds existed among the members of the community. Benevolence was extended to all, and the meeting structure allowed for the distribution of relief to the poor, for loans to those in need, for advice on employment, and even for arbitration in economic matters (Tully 1977:144). Hallowell (1867:181–182) elaborates:

> Joined into a religious association by the bond of these precious religious principles and testimonies, with a consequent concern to extend a mutual care over each other, and to bear one another's burdens, certain rights and privileges became attached to individual members, *such as* [emphasis in original], that the poor should have all needed attention and assistance; their children be freely educated, and properly cared for; and a member who removed from one branch of the organization to another, should be furnished with a certificate, which entitled him to the care and kindness, as well as to all the rights and privileges of those among whom his lot might be cast.

The rights and privileges of membership in the community were extended to the offspring of the faithful by a principle known as "birthright," which ensured that children of Friends were cared for in the event of death or disability of their parents (Hallowell 1867:132–133).

The community organization derived from a code of conduct spelled out in the Book of Discipline, which aided in ordering the activities of daily life in accordance with the precepts of the religion (Hallowell 1867:130; Tully 1977:146). The rules and regulations of the discipline frequently changed as circumstances and conditions changed in the society (Hallowell 1867:130). Members of the meeting were charged with making decisions about compliance and noncompliance with the rules of discipline (Hallowell 1867:136; Tully 1977:146). Attempts were made to reform and restore those who had deviated from the acceptable behavior, but "when they *would not be reclaimed*, they ... were said to be 'disowned' [emphasis in original]" (Hallowell 1867:136).

Several documents provide specific insights into what life might have been like for 19th-century Quakers. In particular, the work of abolitionist Thomas Clarkson, *A Portraiture of Quakerism. Taken From a View of the Education and Discipline, Social Manners, Civil and Political Economy, Religious Principles, and Character of the Society of Friends*, published in 1806, gives details about the practices, beliefs, and daily activities of the Quakers. Clarkson (1806[1]:242), who was not a Quaker,

Perspectives from *Historical Archaeology*

described the Quaker simplicity in wearing apparel (Figure 3):

> The men wear neither lace, frills, ruffles, swords, nor any of the ornaments used by the fashionable world. The women wear neither lace, flounces, lappets, rings, bracelets, necklaces, ear-rings, nor any thing belonging to this class. Both sexes are also particular in the choice of the colour of their clothes. All gay colours, such as red, blue, green and yellow, are exploded.

Clarkson (1806[1]:255,263) goes on to state that although there is some variety in dress among the Quakers, even the wealthiest among them adhere to the tenets of their faith as far as clothing is concerned:

> [E]ven among the richest of Quakers, there is frequently as much plainness and simplicity in their outward dress, as among the poor; and where exceptions exist, they are seldom carried to an extravagant, and never to a preposterous extent. . . . They have discarded all superfluities and ornaments, because they may be hurtful to the mind.

Clarkson's work has particular relevance for the Quaker Burying Ground project, since it provides a brief description of 19th-century Quaker beliefs and customs relating to death and cemeteries:

> When they die, they are buried in a manner singularly plain. The corpse is deposed in a plain coffin. . . . The Quakers are of the opinion that funeral processions should be made, if any thing is to be made of them, to excite serious reflections, and to produce lessons of morality in those who see them. This they conceive to be best done by depriving the dead body of ornaments and outward honours. For, stripped in this manner, they conceive it to approach the nearest to its native worthlessness of dust . . . (Clarkson 1806[2]:23,25).

Clarkson went on to describe how the coffin is taken to the meetinghouse and graveyard attended by friends and relations. Mourners wear "nothing different at this time in their external garments from their ordinary dress," and there is no "pomp or parade" in the funeral procession (Clarkson 1806[2]:25). At the meetinghouse, the coffin is placed in full view of the congregants who remain silent or may speak as is their desire. The coffin is then taken to the cemetery and placed beside the open grave. Another period of silence is observed; then the coffin is lowered into the grave, and this action is followed by another

FIGURE 3. Portrait of Quaker Robert Miller illustrating simplicity of dress. (Alexandria Library, Our Town Collection.)

silent pause. Clarkson (1806[2]:26) relates that the pauses are customary so that "spectators may be more deeply touched with a sense of their approaching exit, and their future state." He concludes by stating that "the act of seeing the body deposited in the grave is the last public act of respect which the Quakers show to their deceased relations. This is the whole process of the Quaker funeral" (Clarkson 1806[2]:26).

A similar description of the simplicity expected in a proper Quaker burial comes from a 1794 document approved by the Yearly Meeting of Friends held in Baltimore:

> Whereas at some burials, where people come far, there may be occasion for some refreshments, yet let that be done with such moderation, gravity, and solidity, as becomes the occasion; and if any appear otherwise, let such be reproved and dealt with as is advised in cases of misbehavior, or indecencies at marriages: And it may be further noted, that any excess in this case, and making so solemn a time as this ought to be,

and in its nature really is, appear as a festival, must be burdensome and grievous to the sober Christian mind, which will of course, at such times, be under a far different exercise. (Society of Friends 1794:8; Miller 1994:8)

The traditional Quaker views did not condone the use of gravestones or monuments. Clarkson reported (1806[2]:29) that this was not considered the appropriate way for Quakers to honor a dead relative or friend; instead, Friends were encouraged to "let all his good actions live in your memory; let them live in your grateful love and esteem; so cherish them in your heart, that they may constantly awaken you to imitation. Thus you will show, by your adoption of this amiable example, that you really respect his memory."

It was thought that erecting impressive monuments to the departed could solicit a "superstitious veneration" and exaggerated regard for the dead, which would lead to a "deviation from the truth" (Clarkson 1806[2]:30). The subject of the appropriateness of grave markers actually became a major issue in the Pennsylvania Quaker community in the early-18th century. In 1706–1708, the Pennsylvania Yearly Meeting declared that existing gravestones and monuments should be torn down, no more should be erected, and that any Quaker who opposed the policy should be dealt with as a "disorderly person" (Tully 1977:153). The results of this policy were quite variable in that some meetings complied, while many did not. Still, the sentiment was echoed in *The Revised Discipline* document approved by the Baltimore Yearly Meeting in 1794. It characterized "hewn or carved gravestones or any other sort of superfluous or ornamental monuments" as "wrong and of evil tendency" (Society of Friends 1794:18; Miller 1994:9). Writing of the early-19th-century burial customs at Goose Creek Meeting in Prince William County, Virginia, not far from Alexandria, John Janney indicated that "a plain slab, got from the nearest quarry, with the initials and date of death, and sometimes birth, rudely picked in with some domestic tool, were all that was allowed" (Janney and Janney 1978:95). By 1913, however, the Baltimore Yearly Meeting did allow "modest memorial stones or tablets to mark the resting place of the departed," although "monuments for the purposes of distinction" were still not condoned (Society of Friends 1913; Miller 1994:9).

Simplicity was also the rule when it came to coffins. Clarkson (1806[2]:28) relates that "the Quakers have no sepulchers or arched vaults under ground [sic] for the reception of their dead. There has been here and there a vault, and there is here and there a grave with sides of brick; but the coffins, containing their bodies, are usually committed to the dust." William Frost (1973:43–44), another scholar who studied Quaker customs, wrote, "most Friends preferred to have the wood coffin placed next to the earth. Since the person was dust in the beginning and would return to dust shortly, elaborate care of the physical remains was sacrilegious." Janney described a simple shouldered wooden coffin with a peaked or gabled top as the preferred burial receptacle for his fellow congregants at Goose Creek during the early-19th century. Even as late as 1913, the Baltimore Yearly Meeting was reiterating that Quakers should use moderation in choosing a burial case and should "avoid costly caskets or coffins and other unnecessary expenditures," thereby setting an example that "would be most salutary on those less able to bear these unnecessary expenses" (Society of Friends 1913; Miller 1994:9).

It has been suggested that this attitude toward preservation after death may also be reflected in the Friends' allowing cemeteries to be used for purposes other than burial. For example, it has been reported that when a meetinghouse in Philadelphia was constructed on the site of an old Quaker burial ground in 1803–1804, "the members of the meeting were neither disturbed by the prospect of invading the graveyard nor dismayed by the skeletal remains that the excavations produced" (Cotter et al. 1992:200).

Quakers in Virginia and Alexandria

The first Quaker to bring the Friends' message to Virginia is thought to have been Elizabeth Harris, who came to the colony in September 1655 (Worrall 1994:4). The practices of the 17th-century Virginia Quakers set them apart and marked them for persecution by the colonial governors. In the 1660s, Virginians were forbidden to have Quakers in their homes or distribute Friends' literature. Rules forbade marriages without Church of England officiants and extracted heavy penalties for nonorthodox baptisms, missing church or military exercises, and assembling for Quaker worship. Greater acceptance began to occur with the passage of the Toleration Act in Virginia in 1699, which ended actual persecution but did not really provide true religious freedom (Worrall 1994: 86). Quakers continued to be fined and jailed and to have their property seized if they did not perform military duties or pay church taxes into the early 18th century.

It is difficult to determine the exact years when the first Friends began living in Alexandria. They had ties with the Quakers who had begun to move into northern Virginia from Maryland and Pennsylvania. The Fairfax Meeting was established in 1745, and the minutes from the 1750s, 1760s, and 1770s include the names of individuals who eventually became associated with Alexandria. The Alexandria Preparatory Meeting, which first met at the home of Jonathan Butcher in 1783, was established under the Fairfax Meeting. At this time, there may have been eight Quaker families living in the town. In 1785, one of the founding members, Benjamin Shreve, donated a lot (currently 311 S. St. Asaph Street) for use as a meetinghouse (Cox 1976:163). The land for a second meeting house was purchased in 1798 at the southwest corner of Wolfe and S. St. Asaph streets, just a half block to the south of the original structure. The new building was completed for use in 1810, eight years after the Alexandria Monthly Meeting was formally established with the participation of 21 families as charter members (Bromberg et al. 2000:54–55).

While Alexandria's Quakers formed a distinct social group, they were fully integrated into the community. In fact, the majority of the heads of Quaker households in Alexandria were merchants who had great influence in the community and helped to boost its economy as the port and town expanded during the early 19th century (Anderberg 1996). They traded internationally and stocked their warehouses with a wide array of goods. They engaged in buying and selling property, farming, milling, and serving as officers in cultural institutions, city government, and businesses designed to improve the town's economy. More specifically, throughout the late-18th and 19th centuries, Quakers played a major role in the formation of the Alexandria Library Company and the Lyceum Company, the creation of numerous schools, the promotion of Little River Turnpike, the construction of the Alexandria Canal, the development of the first railroad line—the Orange and Alexandria—to enter the town, the founding of the Female Orphan Asylum to assist the homeless, the establishment of the Alexandria Water Company, and the opening of the steam-powered Mount Vernon Cotton Factory—the largest business in town at the time (Bromberg et al. 2000:44–94).

The enslavement of African Americans was a major concern for Alexandria's Friends prior to the Civil War. Members of the community bought and then freed slaves, and sold property to free blacks, helping to create stable African American neighborhoods that survived into the mid-20th century (Bromberg et al. 2000:73). Just south of Alexandria, Quakers from New Jersey, Pennsylvania, and New York purchased the Woodlawn estate and neighboring lands to set up a lumbering and farming community, where they hoped to demonstrate that slavery was not necessary for a prosperous economy (Worrall 1994:354–355). Woodlawn became a preparatory meeting under the Alexandria Monthly Meeting (Anderberg 1988:8).

The property that became the Quaker Burying Ground is located within the original boundaries of Alexandria as established by the Virginia Assembly in 1749. Just one year after the first meeting of the Alexandria Preparatory Meeting in the city, a lot near the corner of Queen and Columbus streets was sold by Thomas West to the Alexandria Meeting of the Religious Society of Friends on 8 May 1784, for use as a place of burial (Miller 1993:1). Documentary records indicate that plots in the cemetery were acquired by meeting members at this time (*Alexandria Gazette* 1933). Although the date of the first burial is not known, the earliest definite reference to a burial on the property comes from an obituary for Benjamin Shreve who died 17 November 1801 (*Alexandria Times* 1801). Burials continued in the cemetery through the 19th century. A list of tombstone inscriptions, compiled by Carrie White Avery in 1923, indicates that 43 headstones with dates ranging from 1831 to 1896 were present on the site at the time of her recordation (Avery 1923:208; Pippenger 1992:64; Powell 1995:165–167).

During the Civil War, the Union Army used the Alexandria Meeting House as a hospital. After the war, monthly meetings were divided among Woodlawn, Washington, and Alexandria. By 1887, however, the Alexandria Meeting House property had been sold, and at the present time, the Alexandria Monthly Meeting continues at Woodlawn (Bromberg et al. 2000: 90–91). By 1913, it is clear that the Quaker Burying Ground was no longer being used, for meeting members were attempting to find a socially beneficial use for the property. It was considered for use as a hospital at that time and as a bird sanctuary in 1918. By 1921, the meeting approved its use as a children's playground. Then, in 1937, the property was leased to the City of Alexandria for $1.00 for use as a library for 99 years. It is possible that the 1930s decision by the Alexandria Monthly Meeting to allow construction of the library on the graveyard may be an example of the Quaker's lack of concern for the physical remains and preservation of the body and their greater emphasis on the spiritual.

Mainstream Attitudes toward Death

A guiding principle of the Quaker Burying Ground investigation was that the burials had to be interpreted in the context of late-18th-through 19th-century life and attitudes toward death as well as in the context of the Quaker's lifestyle and philosophy. The Quaker cemetery was used throughout the period when the concepts, collectively known as the beautification of death movement, became integral to the 19th-century view of death in America. The movement began in the late-18th century with an increasing trend toward the idealization of death and heaven. Death was romanticized in ritual and in verse. The changing attitudes were reflected in the material objects for memorializing the dead. Instead of the grim skeletons and personifications of death and time characteristic of the colonial period, mortuary artifacts began to incorporate the symbols of melancholy beauty of the romantic era: angels, urns, foliage, etc. (Stannard 1975; Farrell 1980; Bell 1990:55–58). The "beautification of death" movement reached the pinnacle of its expression in the elaborate, ostentatious mourning rituals practiced by middle-class Victorians in the second half of the 19th century (Farrell 1980: 34). Hallmarks of the period include elaborate mourning clothes, ornate grave markers with

sentimental inscriptions, and highly decorated burial containers (Bell 1990:57, 1994:23). Rectangular caskets replaced the coffin, or hexagonal form of burial container, and there was an increased emphasis on preservation of the body (Habenstein and Lamers 1981:165–168). Adoption of the term *casket*, connoting a jewelry box, epitomized the sentimental approach to heaven and death associated with the movement (Farrell 1980:10). The new shape emphasized presentation over mere encasement and avoided the unpleasant feeling associated with the hexagonal coffins, which, by their very form, reminded mourners of the dead body inside (Lang 1984:31).

As the industrial revolution progressed, home and heaven were increasingly idealized to provide comfort in the face of the upheaval and uncertainties of the changing times (Pike and Armstrong 1980:17). The increased sentimentality with regard to the concepts of death and dying created a market for the trappings of the beautification of death. At the same time, improvements in technology and transportation enabled the trappings to become affordable to all segments of the population (Bell 1990:57). Catalogs advertising mass-produced hardware and burial receptacles became more common as the 19th century progressed (Crane, Breed & Co. 1858; Russell & Erwin Manufacturing Company 1865; Sargent & Co. 1869, 1871; Columbus Coffin Company 1882; National Casket Company 1891). The accessibility and affordability of these trappings in turn fueled the pervasive acceptance of the concepts of the beautification of death in so many levels of American society (Bell 1990:57).

The Quakers were a well-educated, well-to-do community in Alexandria, able to afford the material goods available at the time. The results of the Quaker cemetery investigation will be examined to gain an understanding of the extent to which the Quakers in Alexandria adopted the trappings of the beautification of death movement, some of which contrasted with the tenets of simplicity and humility so central to their faith. The archaeological work yielded information on issues related to preservation, gravestone type and inscriptions, type of burial container, levels of coffin decoration, and, to a lesser extent, clothing styles, which provide insight into this question.

Project Background

The original library building opened in August 1937, and an addition on the side of the building was constructed in 1954. East and west wings were added in 1964 (Figure 4). Documentary sources indicated the possibility that some graves had been removed for reburial both in the 1920s and just prior to the 1937 construction. The 1992 construction plans called for the demolition of the 1954 portion of the structure and its replacement by a new northern addition.

In 1992, nine gravestones and one monument remained on the property. It was possible that one of these, that of James H. Miller, a 14-month-old infant who died in 1854, actually marked a grave location. The remaining eight stones were lined up parallel to the east wall of the 1954 library addition. They had been moved to this location after the demolition of

a row of townhouses built in the 1860s on an 18-ft. strip of land along the western boundary of what is now the library lot. Photographs and maps showing the alley behind these townhouses in the late 1950s or early 1960s show these stones, and six others, incorporated into a brick wall that appears to have surrounded the cemetery and also served as the rear wall of the townhouses. Archaeological investigation in this area of the site resulted in the discovery that some burials actually extended under the 1860s houses, even though this 18-ft. strip of land was not within the official cemetery boundaries. In 1996, this land was deeded by the city to the Alexandria Monthly Meeting in exchange for a 30-year extension of the original 99-year lease.

As stewards of the cemetery, the current members of the Alexandria Monthly Meeting were concerned about the impact of the proposed construction on the potential burials

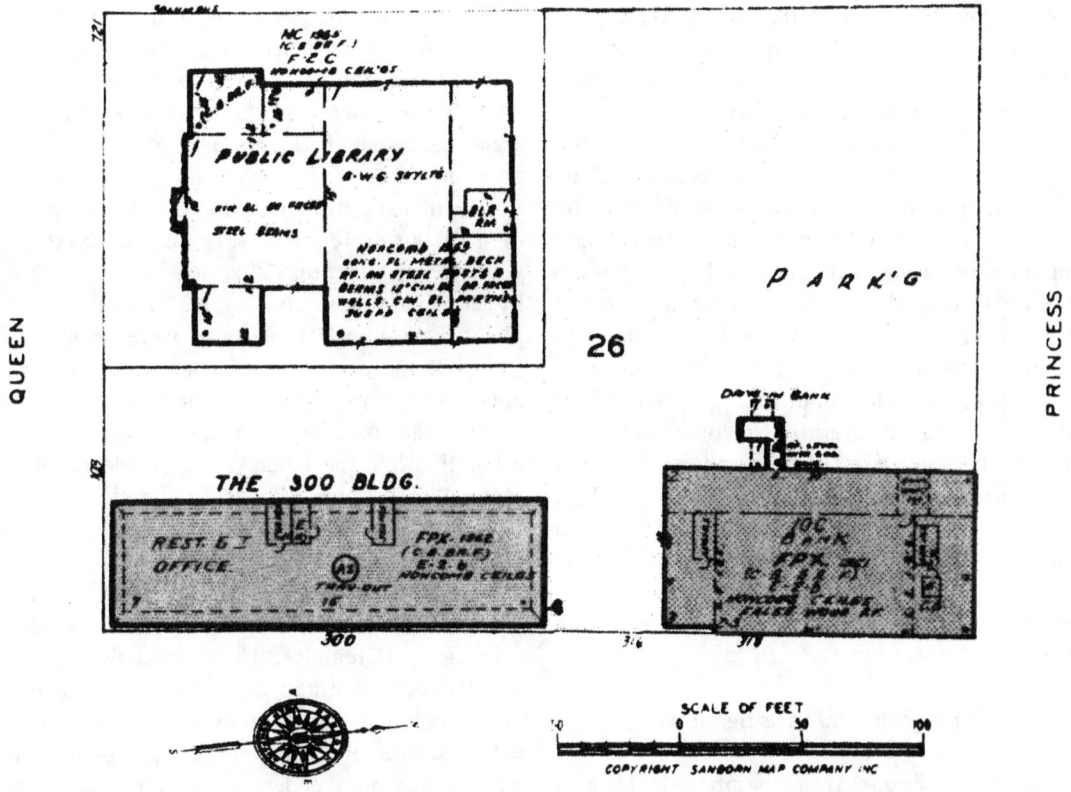

FIGURE 4. 1977 Sanborn Map with original 1937 library plus 1954 addition and 1964 wing additions. (Copyright 1977, The Sanborn Map Company, The Sanborn Library, LLC. All Rights Reserved. Further reproductions prohibited without prior written permission from The Sanborn Library, LLC.)

still remaining on the property. They knew, however, that the Quakers in 1937, who were no longer using the site as a cemetery at that time, were intent on ensuring that the property be used for some socially beneficial purpose; for a while it had served as a playground, and it was also considered as the site for a hospital. Wishing to honor the 1937 agreement between the city and the Quakers, the current meeting members decided to allow construction of the library addition, provided that appropriate preservation measures were instituted. A commitment was made to maintain respect and privacy for the remains. Measures were set out in a formal Memorandum of Agreement signed by both meeting trustees and city officials, and in the permit application required by the State of Virginia for the archaeological removal of burials. The documents stipulated that the goal was to preserve as many of the burials in situ as possible, and the building was designed to maximize this number. Only those graves that would be disturbed by construction activities were to be removed.

With the library construction project, the Quakers of today have continued to support the community by establishing a working partnership with the city in order to balance stewardship of the burying ground with the continuation of the public library, presumably the desire of their 1937 predecessors. As work progressed, the meeting's concern for minimizing intrusion and maximizing privacy on the site began to take specific form. The Quaker community decided to limit examination of the human remains to recording the information as it was uncovered under normal field conditions; no additional laboratory analysis was to be conducted. All the remains, both skeletal and artifactual, would be reburied on site as soon as possible. With regard to the issue of privacy, the meeting also requested that the investigation be kept "low profile," that the public not be allowed on site, and that no photographs of human remains be shown publicly.

Archaeological Investigations

Fieldwork began in December 1993 and continued through one of the worst winters on record, with the majority of the field investigation completed by the following June.

Site monitoring of the actual construction activities continued until March 1995. Methods used to conduct the fieldwork were linked to the construction plans for the new addition (Figure 5). The addition had been designed to minimize ground disturbance: the size of the basement and elevator areas was minimized, and the foundation consisted of deep concrete pilings enclosed in pile caps with shallow-grade beams running between the pile caps. The design allowed for the preservation of more graves in situ than would have been possible with a more standard continuous-footing foundation plan. The archaeological investigation was confined to the areas that would be disturbed by construction activities. A backhoe, monitored by the authors, excavated along the utility and foundation lines and removed the dirt from the basement area to expose the natural clay subsoil, which was capped by up to 4 ft. of fill. The subsoil within the foundation and utility lines and in the basement area was troweled so that the surface could be examined for evidence of grave shafts. In the grade beam areas, the impact of the construction was shallow enough that disturbance of the burials could be avoided and left in place. The depth of the construction impact in the basement and piling areas necessitated the removal of all graves in those locations.

The investigation resulted in the discovery of 159 burial features (Figure 6). Sixty-six were located in areas that would be disturbed by construction activities and required complete excavation; 64 of these were intact burials. (Of the remaining two features, one probably resulted from a grave shaft being dug too close to an existing burial and never contained a burial, while the other yielded evidence of the removal of a burial prior to the library construction.) Ninety-three burials (58% of those discovered) were left in place.

Of the 64 intact burials unearthed during the investigation, 32 were identified as adults (9 males, 10 females, 13 of unknown gender) and 9 were identified as children on the basis of osteological examination, coffin size, and/or the inclusion of gender-related personal items. Neither age nor gender was determined for the remainder. While a complete presentation of the osteological study is beyond the scope of this article, it is perhaps noteworthy that the limited

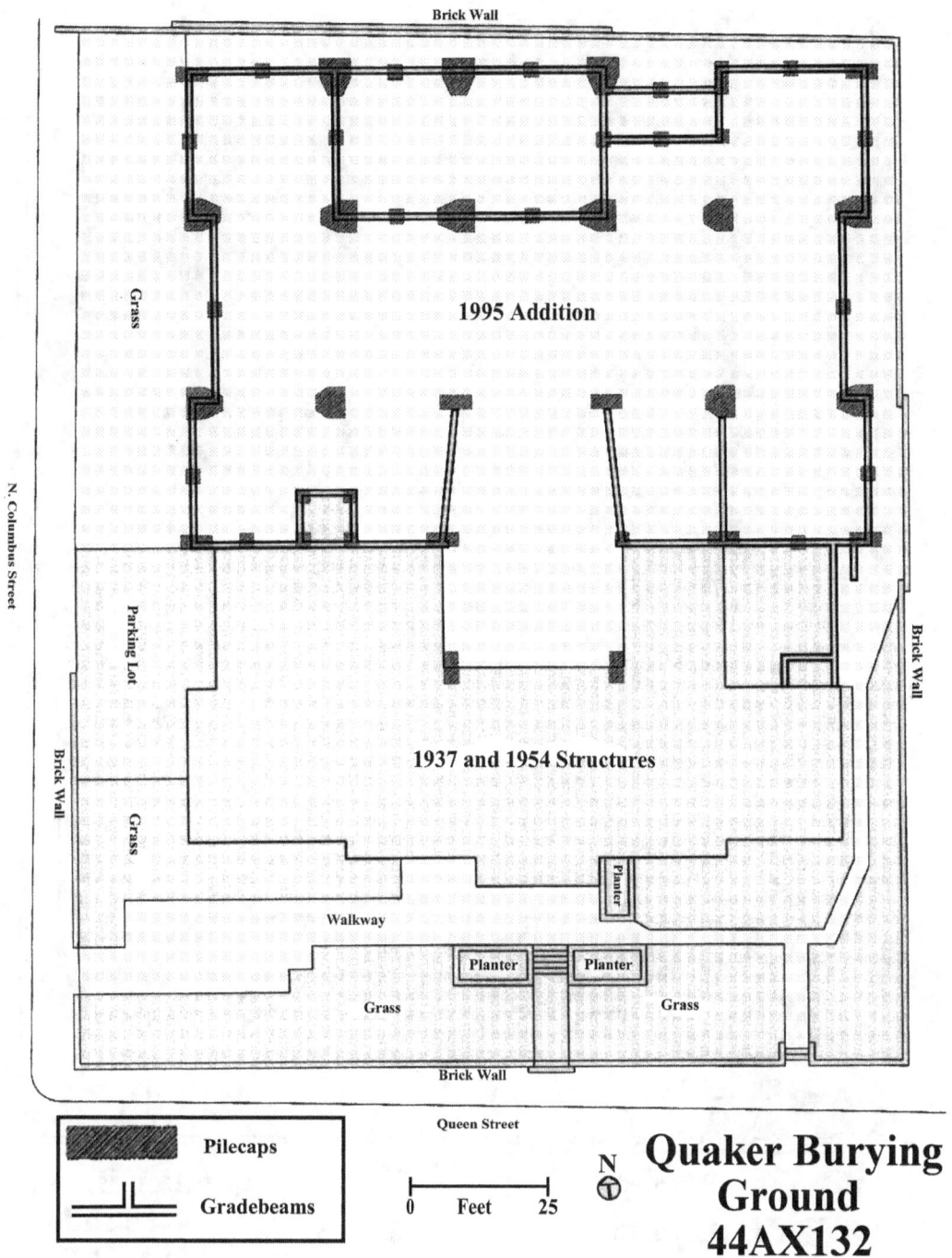

Brick Wall

1995 Addition

N. Columbus Street

Grass

Parking Lot

Brick Wall

Grass

1937 and 1954 Structures

Planter

Walkway

Brick Wall

Planter

Planter

Grass

Grass

Brick Wall

Queen Street

Pilecaps

Gradebeams

0   Feet   25

N

Quaker Burying Ground 44AX132

FIGURE 5. Barrett Library 1995 addition foundation plan showing pile cap and grade-beam construction. (Drawing by Alexandria Archaeology.)

dental analysis suggested a confirmation of the high socioeconomic status of Alexandria's 19th-century Quakers. As might be expected among groups of higher socioeconomic status, the Friends sought out dental care as shown by the presence of fillings in several teeth and the fact that two well-made dental plates were found. Examination of the human remains, however, suggests that seri-

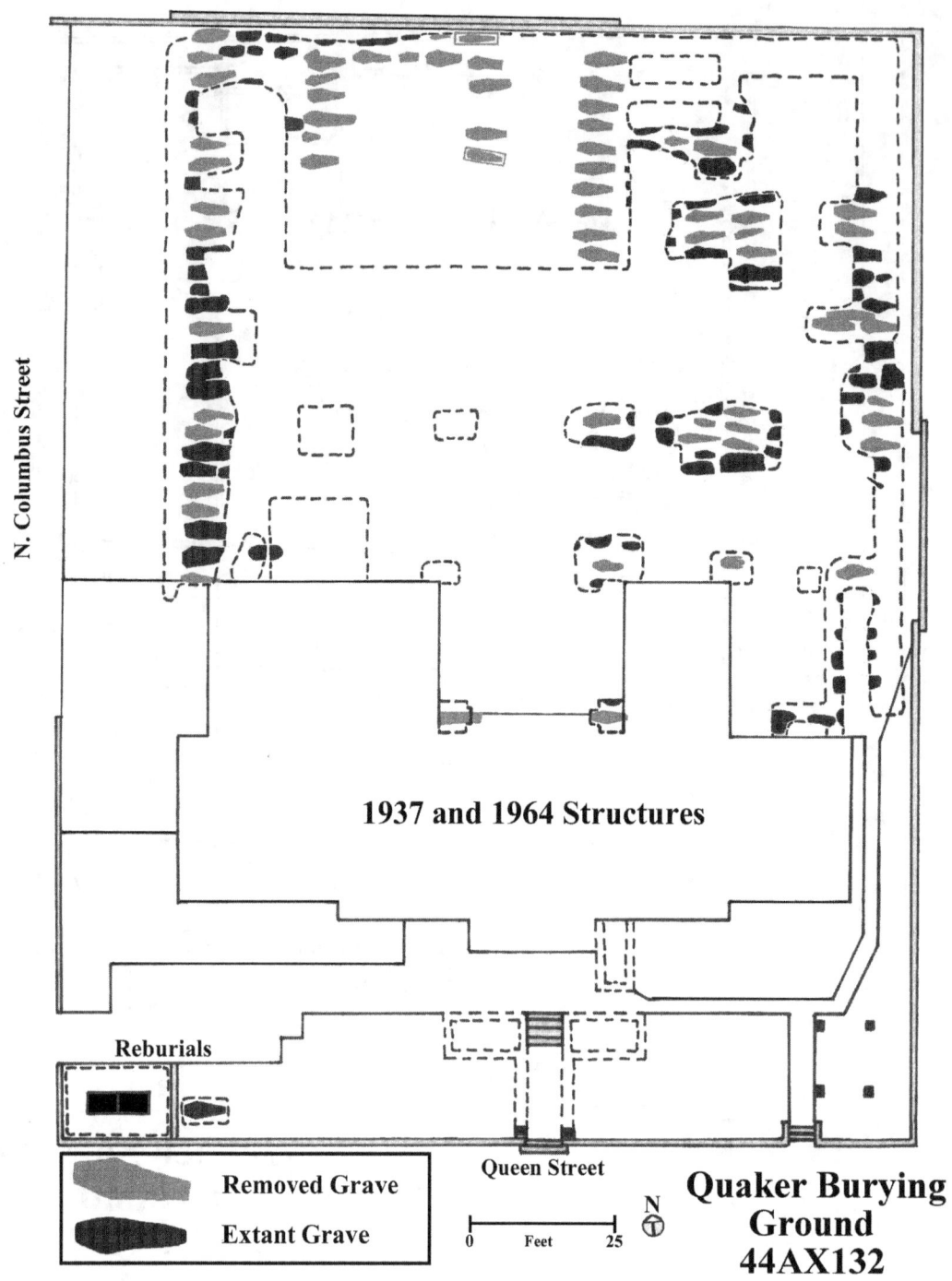

N. Columbus Street

1937 and 1964 Structures

Reburials

Removed Grave

Extant Grave

Queen Street

0   Feet   25   N

Quaker Burying
Ground
44AX132

FIGURE 6. Quaker Burying Ground base map showing locations of 158 graves and the reburial sites. (Drawing by Alexandria Archaeology.)

ous childhood diseases affected even this educated and economically successful population. Hypoplastic lines indicative of episodes of malnutrition or illness at early ages were present.

Analysis: Preservation Issues

The vast majority of the burials at the site (62 of 64 excavated) were in simple wooden coffins in which the advanced stages of decomposition provided a testament to the Quaker philosophy of "dust to dust." The excavation provided evidence for a number of unusual burials and burial methods, most of which functioned, at least in part, to prolong preservation of the burial in the ground. One was a burial in a cast-iron coffin placed within a wooden coffin box (Figures 7 and 8), and another was a burial in a wooden hexagonal coffin placed in a brick vault (Figure 9). Both of these burials occurred in the second half of the 19th century at a time when there was an increased emphasis on preservation of the body, as evidenced by the invention of the iron coffin (patented in 1848 by Almond Fisk) and

FIGURE 7. Burial 6, iron coffin with damaged head end (prior to removal of fill dirt), inside wooden coffin box. (Photo by Alexandria Archaeology.)

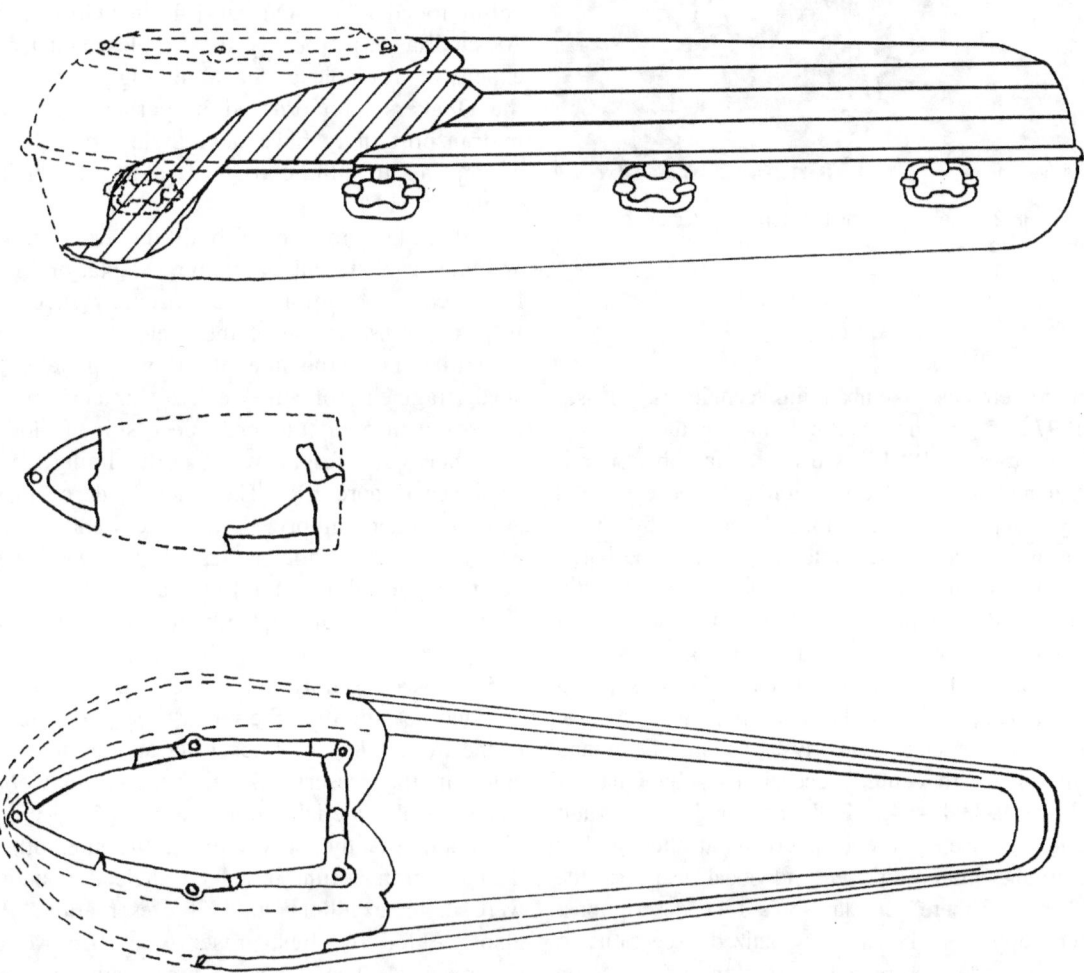

FIGURE 8. Burial 6, sketch of iron coffin. (Drawing by Judy Lebio.)

FIGURE 9. Brick coffin vault of Burial 19. (Photo by Alexandria Archaeology.)

improvements in embalming techniques (Slusser 1997:2). The iron coffin found on the site was dated to after 1854, based on the fact that simplified metallic burial cases similar to the excavated style apparently began to be produced by Fisk's licensed manufacturers after that time. The burial vault dated to after 1850, for the associated coffin contained mass-produced white metal hardware of a type that was manufactured during the second half of the 19th century. Creating a brick lining or vault around a coffin at the bottom of a grave shaft was practiced as early as colonial times and into the 19th century, occasionally by Quakers (Frost 1973:43–44). Both the burial in the vault and the use of the iron coffin at the Quaker Burying Ground represent individual decisions, the "here and there" of Clarkson's 1806 descriptions; they appear to be the personalized exceptions to the attitudes expressed by the majority of the Quaker population.

It is also possible that the use of the iron coffin relates more to a need to transport a body back to Alexandria from the place of death, suggesting a desire for preservation prior to burial rather than a real concern for increased preservation of the burial in the ground. Clearly, the efficacy of metallic burial cases for use in transporting a body related to their increasing popularity throughout the latter half of the 19th century, particularly as Civil War fatalities created a special need for this service. Although only a small number of metallic coffin burials have been studied in detail, the fact that forensic anthropologists at the Smithsonian Institution have recently compiled a list of about 50 that have been discovered attests to the fact that their use became widespread in the mid- to late-1800s, especially after mass production reduced costs (Owsley and Mann 1992:5). It is perhaps noteworthy in this light that the style of iron coffin found at the Quaker Burying Ground in Alexandria was probably the simplest and least expensive available at the time, suggesting that the Quakers who ordered it, perhaps for use in transport, may have nevertheless still been attempting to adhere to the traditional tenets of the Friends.

With regard to use of both the iron coffin and the brick burial vault, the adaptations for increased preservation were extremely successful. The preservation of the skeleton of a man who died after the age of 50 was excellent; small fragments of adipocere, a fair amount of hair, as well as a full three-piece suit of clothing, shoes, and fragments of coffin lining were preserved (Figure 10). The claim made by Fisk and the other authorized manufacturers of the iron coffin—"that the bodies of the dead have been preserved in Metallic Burial Cases for months, and not unfrequently for years, without any perceptible change" (Crane, Breed & Co. 1858)—was certainly not without merit.

While not affording the remarkable preservation of the iron coffin, the brick vault appears to have aided in the preservation of both coffin wood and skeletal material. Burial 19, a 55–65-year-old man, was the only one on the site, other than the iron coffin, in which skeletal remains were in an excellent state of preservation. It also yielded the best-preserved coffin wood (Figure 11). The increased preservation in the vault, which was filled with water at the time

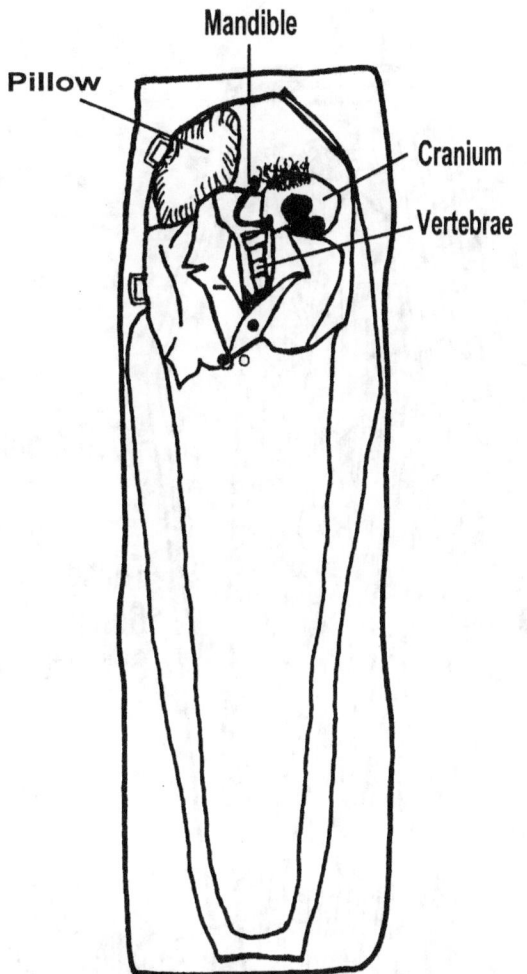

Pillow

Mandible

Cranium

Vertebrae

FIGURE 10. Burial 6, sketch of remains visible within the iron coffin. (Drawing by Alexandria Archaeology.)

layer of protection over the coffin served to help delay the slumping of the ground surface. Like the iron coffin and vault, the use of planks is documented in only one instance at the Quaker cemetery, Burial 11, and thus appears to be a case of individual preference.

The use of an outside box surrounding the coffin, discerned in 19 burials at the site, represents a more common practice, presumably also related to the urge to prolong preservation (Figure 12). At the Quaker Burying Ground, outside boxes were discovered in all of the excavated areas of the cemetery with all types of coffins. The iron coffin was enclosed in a wooden box as were numerous gabled and apparently flat-topped wooden coffins. Decorated and undecorated as well as hinged and unhinged coffins were also buried in boxes, and they were found in association with both child and adult burials. While use of boxes is occasionally mentioned in reports on other cemetery excavations, information is scant. The lack of extensive reporting on the subject may relate to the difficulty in distinguishing the box from the coffin in the field when the wood is decomposed and the fit is tight.

The origin of the use of the outside coffin box, precursor to the modern concrete vault, remains unknown (Coffin 1976:101; Habenstein and Lamers 1981:193). They were definitely used as early as the colonial period, but the prevalence of their use during the late-18th and early-19th centuries is uncertain. It is possible that the box represents an added expense and is therefore associated with burials of members of wealthier socioeconomic groups. Several possible explanations have been suggested for their use: as an extra layer of protection from the elements, as an aid to slowing down the slumping in the ground surface of a cemetery that occurs as a result of decomposition, and as an aid in the preparation of the grave shaft prior to burial. During the second half of the 19th century, when coffins and caskets were being mass-produced and transported from factories for use in cemeteries across the country, they would have served as protective shipping boxes for the coffins (Habenstein and Lamers 1981:187).

Perhaps one of the most perplexing practices discerned during excavation of the Quaker Burying Ground relates to the use of gray marine clay to encase the coffin in the shaft. Fifteen

of excavation, probably relates to the alkaline conditions created by the brick and mortar, which prevented the growth of sulfate-reducing bacteria, the cause of decay in water-logged conditions (Magid and Young 1995:4).

Although not a dramatic example, the practice of covering the coffin with planks in the grave shaft represents another attempt to prolong preservation. While not commonly found, this burial method has been recorded in various other historical cemetery excavations (Swauger 1959:39). Sometimes called "grave arches," the planks aided in keeping the coffin intact in the ground by providing additional support so that the lid was not as likely to collapse inward from the pressure of the dirt above. This extra

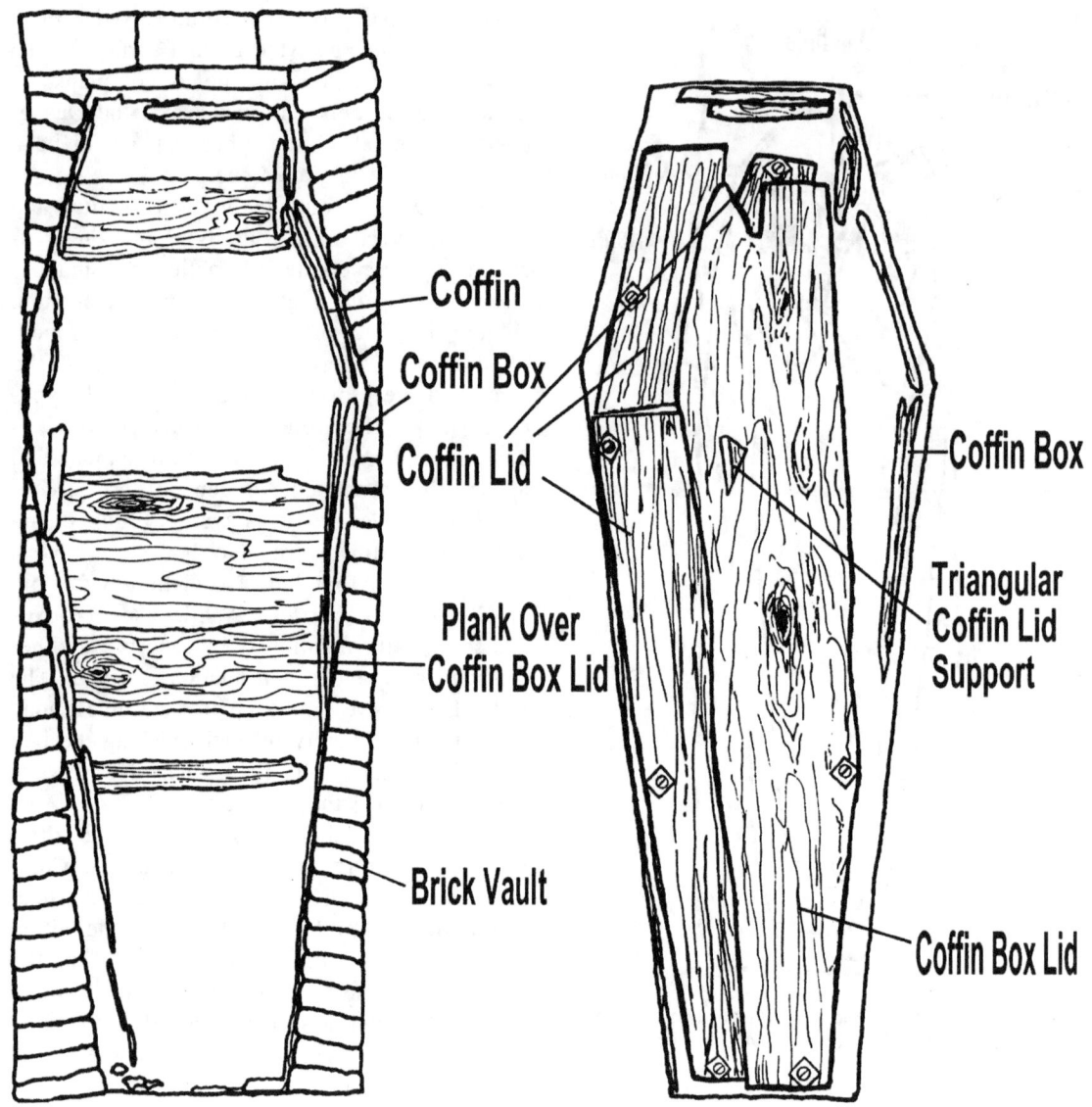

FIGURE 11. *(Left)* Burial 19, interior of vault with planks, coffin, and coffin box wood; *(right)* coffin and coffin box wood decorated with plates and screw/tacks. (Drawing by Alexandria Archaeology.)

of the excavated burials and 9 unexcavated grave shafts showed the use of this technique. Given the impervious quality of clay, it is thought that use of this material may also represent an attempt to aid in the preservation of the burial. The gray clay was placed in the burial shaft to act as a shield around the coffin, presumably to prevent the penetration of water. Given the philosophy of "dust to dust," it would seem unlikely that Quakers would engage in this practice, which would require a considerable

expenditure of time and effort. It is noteworthy that to the writers' knowledge, this practice has not been recorded in historical documents or during any other cemetery excavations.

Gray marine clay is found buried in pockets throughout the City of Alexandria. Given the fact that the use of gray clay was confined to an area in the east central and northeast sections of the excavated portion of the cemetery, it is tempting to speculate that it was not intentionally used but was merely present on the site in

Perspectives from *Historical Archaeology*

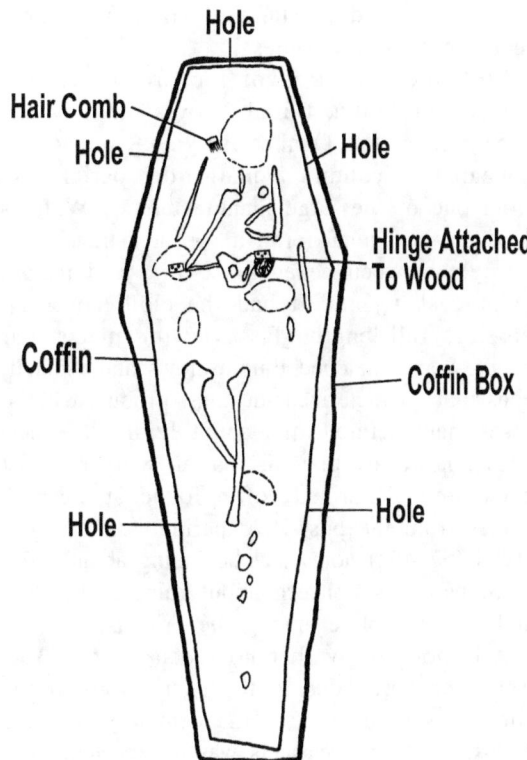

Hole

Hair Comb

Hole

Hole

Hinge Attached
To Wood

Coffin

Coffin Box

Hole

Hole

FIGURE 12. Burial 42, showing coffin sides (with drilled circular holes) and coffin box outline. (Drawing by Alexandria Archaeology.)

layers penetrated by the excavation of the burial shafts. If this scenario were correct, gray clay could have been included in the back dirt as the grave shafts were backfilled after burials. It was clear from the excavation that the gray marine clay did not occur naturally on the site and that its use was intentional. It was invariably discovered surrounding the coffins, at the bottom of the burial shafts, which were cut into the typical light yellowish brown clay subsoil found throughout the site. Use of the gray marine clay would have required it to be excavated from a borrow pit somewhere else in the city and brought to the cemetery for use.

Unlike the vault and iron coffin, however, the use of gray clay does not appear to have actually contributed to the preservation of the burials. If the purpose was to preserve, the technique was unsuccessful. Of the 15 excavated burials associated with gray clay, 7 exhibited coffins in poor states of preservation, and the skeletal remains were also poorly preserved in all but 3 cases.

Analysis: Coffin Types

The analysis of the coffin types from the Quaker Burying Ground excavations suggests Friends preferred a traditional style and eschewed the ready-made coffins and caskets that became more common as industrialization increased and the beautification of death movement reached its pinnacle. All but one of the wooden coffins excavated from the Quaker Burying Ground exhibited a tapered hexagonal shape. There were two basic types, those with flat lids (75%) and those with gabled lids (25%). Examination both in the field and in the lab indicated that despite the common shape, a number of variations existed: lids were either flat or gabled; lid supports were sometimes present; hinges that allowed the coffin to be open for viewing were often noted; end boards could be angled or "dropped"; gabled coffins sometimes had drilled holes in the end and/or sideboards; and end boards occasionally exhibited rabbeted edges for attachment to the bottom. Distinguishing some of these styles in the field was difficult because the preservation of coffin wood at the site was generally poor.

The gabled type of coffin, found in 16 of the burials at the site, may have been more common in the first half of the 19th century, but it continued to be used after mid-century, since three of the gabled coffins at the site contain hardware dating to 1850 or later. The historical account of John Jay Janney makes reference to the use of this style in rural Virginia Quaker communities in the early-19th century (Janney and Janney 1978). Refinement regarding the dates of use of the gabled coffin style may be one benefit of paying more attention to looking for evidence of this coffin type in the field. Temporal implications of other variations in coffin style are unknown and may also be revealed by increased consistency in recording field information.

It is possible that gabled coffins were more often reserved for adult burials. Of the 9 burials identified as children, only 1 (11%) was interred in what appeared to be a gabled style of coffin, while 10 burials identified as adults (32%) fell into this category. There did not appear to be any significant gender difference with regard to the gabled coffin burials. Of the 8 individuals in wooden coffins identified as adult males, 2 (25%) were in gabled coffins, as were 3 of the 10 (30%) identified as females.

One of the most conspicuous variations in coffin style involved the use of coffin hinges. Observed on both gabled and flat coffin lids at the site, the hinges were placed across the shoulder area of the coffins and allowed the upper portion of the lid to be opened so that the face of the deceased could be viewed. Thirty-nine of the coffins from the Quaker Burying Ground exhibited evidence for hinges. Thus, viewing of the deceased, an integral part of the beautification of death movement, appears to have been an important part of the burial ritual for Alexandria's 19th-century Quakers. When the two coffins with glass plates (Burials 6 and 37) are added to the number of hinged coffins, it becomes evident that more than 65% of the burials at the site allowed for viewing without the complete detachment of the lid.

Some of the variations in coffin style may relate to the fact that many of the coffins were individually made to order at the time of death. This possibility is further demonstrated by an analysis of the sizes of the various coffins found at the site. Coffin lengths ranged from 2.7 to 7.05 ft. but clustered into three general sizes: 10% were 2-1/2 to 3-1/2 ft., 10% were 4-1/2 to 5-1/2 ft., and 80% were 5-3/4 to 7 ft. long. The width of the coffins varied as well. When the length and width measurements for each coffin were graphed, the result was a scatter of points with only limited clustering (Figure 13). This suggests that there was little standardization in the size of the coffins and that the majority of the coffins were being individually handcrafted.

Made-to-order coffins would certainly have been the rule during the early-19th century. In Alexandria, they would have been obtained from the numerous cabinetmakers (22 listed in the 1834 Directory of Alexandria) working in the city, who, like their counterparts in other jurisdictions, would have gone on to perform the necessary funerary services. After about 1850, some of the local cabinetmakers might have begun to have ready-made coffins in standard sizes in stock for immediate sale, and standard-sized metallic burial cases could have been ordered from the manufacturers of Fisk's coffins. By the 1870s, wooden coffins could

also be ordered in standard sizes from large manufacturing companies.

With the exception of the previously discussed iron coffin, Burial 37 was the only one excavated at the Quaker Burying Ground that appeared to contain a mail-order burial case from one of the large manufacturers. With its modified hexagonal form, it appeared transitional in style between hexagonal coffins and rectangular caskets, and it had the cloth covering, possible full-length glass viewing plates, bar handles, and matched thumbscrews and escutcheons that characterized the mass-produced burial cases manufactured after about 1870. It is perhaps noteworthy that this burial, with the most elaborately decorated coffin found at the site, comes from the post-1870 period. Jay Worrall (1994:457–458) notes that beginning about 1870, there was less concern about rules of conduct and less discipline among the Friends.

It is noteworthy that no rectangular caskets were uncovered during the excavations at the site. Given the use of the cemetery into the 1890s, the lack of caskets was unexpected. The rectangular form was probably first used around 1850 and began to replace the hexagonal "shouldered" style about 1860 with more frequent use beginning in the 1870s. The increasing popularity of the form is tied to the beautification of death phenomenon, in that the term *casket* suggested a container for something valuable, a treasure or a jewel.

Other excavations of cemeteries with burials dating to the late-19th century generally report the presence of caskets as well as hexagonal coffins (Blakely and Beck 1982; Crowell et al.

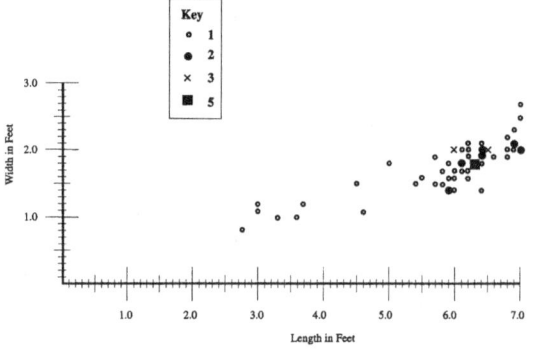

FIGURE 13. Graph of hexagonal wood coffin sizes. (Drawing by Alexandria Archaeology.)

1991; Elia and Wesolowsky 1991). One family cemetery in Manassas, Virginia, serves as a particularly good basis for comparison with the Quaker Burying Ground because it includes burials of a wealthy family, which, although rural, was probably similar in status to the Friends living in Alexandria. The excellent comparative nature of the data is enhanced by the fact that most of the burials from the site are datable, based on their association with in-situ gravestones with inscriptions. At this Weir family cemetery, investigators noted the presence of six rectangular coffins, including one for an 1852 burial, out of a total of 15 burials dated to the second half of the 19th century (Little et al. 1992:403). Similarly, the Anglican cemetery of Old St. Paul's in Philadelphia offers a good comparative source, given the comparable socioeconomic status of the Quaker and Anglican groups. In Old St. Paul's, where burials occurred from 1788 to 1871, the plain wooden hexagonal coffins of the late-18th century gave way to elaborate rectangular caskets with ornate handles and glass plates by the end of the period of the cemetery's use (Cotter et al. 1992:200).

Several explanations, taken separately or in combination, could help to account for the lack of rectangular caskets found during excavations at the Quaker Burying Ground. First, with the decreasing number of members in the Quaker community after 1870, it is probable that there were fewer burials in the cemetery at a time when the rectangular form was increasing in popularity. The fact that only two burials definitely dating to after 1870 were discovered during the investigation is in keeping with this theory. It is also conceivable, given the possibility of some temporal organization of the cemetery, that a section of more recent burials containing a larger proportion of rectangular caskets could exist in the unexcavated parts of the burial ground. Indeed, large sections of the cemetery, including the area under the 1937 building and most of the front yard, were not investigated as part of this project.

Certainly there were a number of local cabinetmakers in Alexandria and Washington, DC, who could have supplied burial cases to the local Quaker population. The traditional hexagonal style would have been available into the late-19th century. Despite the trend toward use of the rectangular casket, even some of the large manufacturers at the time were offering a steam-bent burial case, which tended to have a hexagonal shape. As late as the 1890s, local cabinetmakers were most probably still providing hexagonal coffins for their communities throughout much of the country. This may have been especially true of Alexandria, which did not grow into a major urban center. Whether these local cabinetmakers were also manufacturing rectangular styles, which were becoming increasingly popular after 1870, remains in question. A list of funeral-related items of cabinetmakers from Washington, DC, from the Census of Manufacturers for 1850, 1860, 1870, and 1880 does not include any reference to caskets. Instead, all products are listed as "coffins," perhaps indicating that the newer form was not yet popular in the local area. Since no other definite 19th-century burials have been excavated in Alexandria, it is unknown if burial grounds for other religious groups in the city would also exhibit this lack of the casket form. If this were the case, the lack of the rectangular casket might reflect a conservatism on the part of Alexandria's citizenry, in general, rather than an indication of the maintenance of the traditional form only within the Society of Friends.

The lack of rectangular caskets may also be a manifestation of the Alexandria Friends' preference for a more traditional style of coffin and is perhaps related to Quaker philosophy, which espouses simplicity in order to seek "inner light" by avoiding the distractions from the world. As described by Clarkson in 1806 ([2]: 25), this philosophy entailed burial "in a manner singularly plain. The corpse is deposited in a plain coffin." Burial rituals of the Quakers, "by depriving the body of ornaments and outward honours," were designed to "excite serious reflections, and to produce lessons of morality in those who see them" (Clarkson 1806[2]:23).

Analysis: Coffin Ornamentation

As late as 1913, the Baltimore Yearly Meeting expressed the need for simplicity with regard to coffin ornamentation (Society of Friends 1913; Miller 1994:10):

> Friends are affectionately admonished to be careful to avoid costly caskets or coffins and other unnecessary expenditures. We believe if those in affluent

circumstances would observe moderation in these respects, the example would be most salutary on those less able to bear these unnecessary expenses.

Excavations at Alexandria's Quaker cemetery suggest that the Alexandria Monthly Meeting took this admonishment to heart. The lack of coffin ornamentation is particularly true for the Quaker burials dated to the late-18th and early-19th centuries. There is no evidence for the use of any decorative coffin hardware on the site prior to 1850. Throughout the first half of the 19th century, there was a strict faithfulness to the Quaker principle of plainness with regard to coffin ornamentation. Non-Quaker groups, even those of lower socioeconomic status, occasionally found a way to decorate their coffins during this period, as evidenced by the metal ornamentation present on 8 (18%) of 45 coffins excavated from Philadelphia's First African Baptist Church cemetery in use from 1823 to 1842 (Parrington et al. 1989).

These trappings of the beautification of death movement were thus available and inexpensive enough that all segments of the society could afford them. As the wealthy merchants of the town during this period, certainly the Quakers would have had access to and would have been able to afford these coffin decorations, but they chose not to use them. Frost (1973:43) has reported the use of elaborate coffin hardware, including handles and name plates, by some of Philadelphia's wealthy Quaker families, even in the colonial period. The Friends of Alexandria seem to be more traditional on this issue than their Philadelphia counterparts through the early part of the 19th century.

All of the decorative coffin hardware excavated from the Quaker Burying Ground dates to post-1850. The coffins with decorative elements included 5 with handles, 17 with decorative hinges, 8 with screw/tacks matched with coffin plates, and 13 with screw/tacks alone (Table 1). In all, 21 (33%) of the 63 wooden coffins

TABLE 1
LEVELS OF COFFIN DECORATION

Burial Number	Handles	Hinges	Screw/Tacks	Coffin Plate	No. of Types of Decorative Elements	Total No. of Decorative Elements	Level of Decoration
1	4	4	8	6	4	22	moderate
2			1	1	2	2	minimal
4			46		1	46	moderate
5		½	39		2	40	moderate
7 (upper)		4	33		2	37	moderate
7 (lower)		4	32		2	36	moderate
8	6	3½	46		3	56	moderate
19	6	5	7	7	4	25	moderate
20		4	4		2	8	minimal
26		4	9		2	13	minimal
27		stains	51+		2	53	moderate
37	6		7	5	3	18	minimal
50		4	5		2	9	minimal
51		4	10	8	3	22	moderate
80		2	4		2	6	minimal
92			6		1	6	minimal
103		4	11		2	15	minimal
104		4	10		2	14	minimal
108		4	3	7	3	14	minimal
109	6	3	6	6	4	21	moderate
128		3	6	4	3	17	minimal

Perspectives from *Historical Archaeology*

excavated had decorative elements. While at first this percentage may seem relatively high for a group espousing simplicity, its significance can be understood only through comparison with the percentages of decorative coffins found at other 19th-century burial grounds (Table 2). At the Weir cemetery in Manassas, Virginia, used from the 1830s until the early-20th century by a wealthy plantation family, for example, 18 of 24 burials (75%) showed some form of ornamentation on the burial containers (Little et al. 1992:414). Even at a potter's field in use between 1831 and 1872 in Uxbridge, Massachusetts, 14 of 45 coffins (45%) had some form of decorative hardware (Bell 1990; Elia and Wesolowsky 1991; Little et al. 1992: 414). The percentage of decorated coffins at the Quaker Burying Ground is significantly lower than that at the Weir family cemetery and is even lower than the percentage at the Uxbridge potter's field. It appears that mass production of coffin hardware made it available to all segments of the population. It would

have been affordable even to those of low socioeconomic status, but the Quakers apparently often chose not to make use of it. It is true that the Quaker Burying Ground was in use about 40 years earlier than Uxbridge and Weir, and the effect of this fact on the percentages cannot be determined. Nevertheless, given the high status of the Quaker community in Alexandria, as evidenced by Lorna Anderberg's (1996) work, this relative lack of ornamentation seems to attest to the continued devotion to simplicity as a Quaker ideal.

The relative simplicity of the coffins from the Quaker Burying Ground can be further illustrated by comparing the degree of ornamentation of coffins on the site with the levels of coffin decoration noted at other historical cemeteries. Little and colleagues (1992) devised a measure for effecting this comparison in the analysis of the Weir family cemetery. The method involves charting the overall number of decorative elements for each coffin excavated as well as the number of types of decorative elements on

TABLE 2
COFFIN ORNAMENTATION: CEMETERY COMPARISONS

Decorated Coffin Percentages:

Cemetery	Percent
Quaker Burying Ground	33
Weir Family Cemetery	75
Uxbridge Potter's Field	45

Levels of Decoration for Post-1850 Coffins:

Cemetery	% Minimally Decorated	% Moderately Decorated	% Elaborately Decorated
Quaker Burying Ground	52	48	0
Weir Family Cemetery	40	40	20
Uxbridge Potter's Field	64	36	0

Maximum Decoration:

Cemetery	Types of Decorative Elements	No. of Decorative Elements
Quaker Burying Ground	4	56
Weir Family Cemetery	9	97
Uxbridge Potter's Field	3	49

each (with handles, screws, tacks, plates, and name plates, each representing a type). For the purposes of this analysis, coffins with fewer than 20 decorative elements and fewer than 4 types of decoration were considered minimally decorated, those with 20–60 decorative elements and up to 4 types of decoration were considered moderately decorated, and those with more than 60 decorative elements were considered elaborately decorated. When the 15 late-19th-century coffins unearthed at the Weir cemetery were considered in this manner, the number of types of decorative elements on a single coffin ranged from 1 to 9, and the overall number of decorative elements per coffin varied from 1 to 97. Nine (60%) of the coffins had more than 20 decorative elements (3 elaborately ornamented with from 60 to 97 elements and 6 moderately ornamented with from 20 to 49 decorations). Six (40%) were minimally decorated, with fewer than 20 elements. In terms of the number of types of decorative hardware on the coffins, eight had between one and three types, whereas seven had between four and nine types. The most elaborately ornamented coffin had 97 elements, with 7 types of decoration (Little et al. 1992:402–403).

Table 1 shows these data for the 21 decorated post-1850 coffins excavated at the Quaker Burying Ground, and Table 2 presents comparisons with the Weir and Uxbridge cemeteries. The total number of decorative elements on a coffin at the Quaker cemetery ranged from 2 to 56; the coffin with the greatest amount of ornamentation thus had only slightly more than half as many decorative elements as the most highly decorated of the Weir coffins. Ten of 21 (48%) of the Quaker coffins exhibited more than 20 decorative elements, whereas 60% of the Weir coffins fell into this category. In addition, the Quaker cemetery had a maximum of four types of decoration per coffin, in contrast to the nine types found at the Weir family burial ground.

Comparisons with data from the Uxbridge cemetery indicate that the Quaker Burying Ground coffins (with 52% minimally decorated and 48% moderately decorated) were slightly more ornamented than those in the potter's field, where 64% had minimal decoration and 36% fell into the moderately decorated category. In addition, the most highly decorated coffins at the Quaker Burying Ground appear to exhibit only slightly more ornamentation than the most elaborate coffins found in the pauper's cemetery at Uxbridge. At the potter's field, the two most elaborately decorated burials had 48 elements of 3 different types and 49 elements of 2 types of decoration, respectively. The coffin with the most ornamentation at the Quaker Burying Ground had a total of 56 decorative elements of 3 types.

With regard to adhering to the value placed upon humility, it is noteworthy that no intact engraved breastplates or name plates were found at the Quaker Burying Ground, although a few of the coffins did have screws in locations suggestive of this type of decoration. Assuming that some coffins may have been ready-made by this time, it is possible that these coffins actually had only the screws, i.e., that by choice, name plates were not used, but the screws remained in place at the time of burial merely to cover the attachment holes. Investigators at other cemetery sites dating to this period often report the presence of name and breastplates (McKillop 1995).

One additional consideration regarding the decorative coffin hardware should also be mentioned. Hinges, screw/tacks, and even handles all had functional as well as decorative purposes. Hinges allowed for the lid of the coffin to be opened for viewing of the deceased, and screw/tacks served to attach the lid (Figure 14). In this light, it is noteworthy that only 6 of the coffins at the site exhibited more than 10 screw tacks, and it is probable that from 6 to 10 screws would be needed to fasten the coffin lid securely. The screw/tacks and hinges may have been used as much for their functional as for their decorative value. Handles occurred on only five coffins (24% of those decorated, as compared with 50% at Weir), and it is of note that five undecorated coffins and one with decorated hinges had holes in the end and side boards that could have served the same function as handles. The holes could provide a method to lift the coffin, without the added ornamentation of handles. Indeed, the styles of hardware found at the site were, for the most part, among the simplest available at the time. Given the fact that some coffins may have been purchased ready-made beginning in the 1850s, it is possible that the use of the coffin hardware may also result in part from the availability

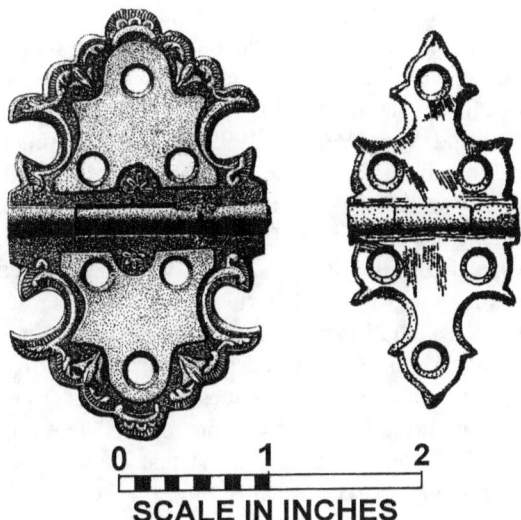

0   1   2
SCALE IN INCHES

FIGURE 14. Decorative coffin hinges. (Drawings by Andy Flora and Carrie Feldman.)

of coffins with these items already attached to serve their functional roles.

The widespread use of decorative coffin hardware in the 19th century has been considered a manifestation of the phenomenon known as the beautification of death, characterized by sentimental and melancholy views of death and heaven. The archaeological recovery of

0   1   2
SCALE IN INCHES

FIGURE 15. Coffin handle (one of four), copper alloy and silver-plated, Burial 1, James Miller who died in 1854, age 14 months. (Drawing by Andy Flora.)

decorative hardware from the Quaker Burying Ground, especially such types as the cupid and angel coffin handles, suggests that Alexandria's 19th-century Quaker population was influenced by the values of the beautification of death movement. Their adoption of the material trappings of the movement reflects moderation, indicating a continuation of the values of simplicity inherent in the Quaker philosophy (Figure 15). None of the coffins from the first half of the 19th century exhibited ornamentation, and the percentage of definite post-1850 coffins with decorative hardware was significantly lower than that found both in a family cemetery where individuals of comparable status were interred and in a potter's field. Moreover, the Quaker coffins that were decorated had considerably less ornamentation than those in a comparative sample from the Weir family cemetery and only slightly more ornamentation than those found at a potter's field. The overall picture of the burials at the Quaker Burying Ground is one that shows a continuing attempt to uphold the traditional values of the Religious Society of Friends.

Analysis: Gravestones

A strict adherence to Quaker philosophy would necessitate an avoidance of the use of gravestones. The issue actually resulted in a great deal of controversy among early-18th-century Pennsylvania Quakers and was eventually resolved by allowing the separate meetings to make their own decisions on the desirability of allowing gravestone use. In 1794, it was explicitly stated that use of gravestones was not condoned by the Baltimore Yearly Meeting: "It appears to this meeting, to be wrong and of evil tendency to have hewn or carved grave-stones, or any other sort of superfluous or ornamental monuments over, or about the graves on any of Friends burying grounds" (Society of Friends 1794:18; Miller 1994:9).

By 1913 the policy with regard to gravestones had clearly changed. As indicated in the *Principles, Advice and Rules of Discipline of the Baltimore Yearly Meeting of Friends*, by that time gravestones were permitted, provided they adhered to Quaker tenets of humility, simplicity, and plainness (Society of Friends 1913; Miller 1994:9):

Friends are also enjoined, to maintain our testimony against affixing monuments for the purpose of distinction, to graves, in any of our burying grounds that would involve our testimony for the maintenance of simplicity and plainness in this direction. This is not intended, however, to prevent the erection of modest memorial stones or tablets to mark the resting place of the departed; which are to be of such dimensions only, as to admit of placing thereon, the name and date of the birth, and death of the deceased.

Nine stones, plus a monument to Elisha Cullen Dick, were visible on the site when the archaeological work began in 1994 (Figures 16 and 17). Only one headstone was in situ, marking the grave of the infant, James Miller, who died in 1854. The eight other stones had been moved, but based on their recorded positions in the 1960s, a number of them may be associated with burials discovered during the excavation. During the course of the investigation, an additional 25 gravestones and gravestone fragments were recovered.

It is noteworthy that the earliest stone recorded from the site dates to the 1830s. It is possible that earlier grave markers, perhaps some made of wood, were present on the site prior to the 1830s but did not survive intact or were no longer visible in the 1920s when Avery (1923: 208) and Mary Powell (1995:165–167) recorded the inscriptions. If the markers inscribed with "J B" and "J J" refer to the burials of John Butcher and Jonathan Janney in 1811 and 1796, respectively, then clearly stones were being used in the late-18th and early-19th centuries, but these associations are far from definite since no dates were included. Historical records indicate that Dr. Dick requested that his grave remain unmarked at the time of his death in 1825; this request does suggest that some graves were being marked by this time. Like the use of totally undecorated coffins prior to the 1850s, the probable limited use of gravestones in the 18th and first quarter of the 19th centuries may be another example of the Alexandria Friends upholding traditional Quaker values.

The styles and iconography of gravestones often reflect the beliefs and values of a society (Deetz 1977; Crowell 1979). As with coffin decora-

FIGURE 16. Eight original headstones along the wall of the library in 1994. (Photo by Alexandria Archaeology.)

Perspectives from *Historical Archaeology*

tion, when the use of gravestones became more common at Alexandria's Quaker Burying Ground, both styles and inscriptions expressed the simplicity so central to Quaker philosophy. All of the gravestones that remained intact on the site into the middle of the 20th century were relatively simple in shape. Most were simple rounded or pointed headstones, and two were small, flat rectangular breast stones. The only stone found with a decorative element was a fragment, which apparently marked the grave of Mary Deakins; it contained a simple leaf design. All others were plain, with simple chiseled written inscriptions.

The gravestone types found at the Quaker Burying Ground represent some of the simplest styles available at the time. In addition to the rounded headstone and breast stone, common styles from the 1830s to the 1860s include the squared headstone, the pointed arch, and the pedestal stone, often topped with an obelisk, urn, or other carved feature. During this period, symbolic decorative elements were common on stones, including the urn, willows, and other flowers and plants, angels, lambs, and the human hand. By the 1840s, raised lettering for inscriptions also became common. In the 1870s, great differentiation and incredibly elaborate gravestones appear (Crowell 1980:29–33). Only simple, rounded headstones and small breast stones, with chiseled inscriptions and largely without any decorative symbolic elements, were found at the Quaker cemetery.

Like the gravestone styles, the inscriptions themselves reflect Quaker tenets of simplicity and humility. Nineteen of the recorded inscriptions indicate only name or initials with date of death. Another 16 also include date of birth or age at the time of death, and 2 add information about relationships. One inscription records merely name and age. Only four of the inscriptions have any phrasing indicating memorialization. Thus, the lengthy inscriptions and memorial sentiments common on gravestones of the period are lacking at the Quaker Burying Ground.

Analysis: Clothing and Personal Items

The style of dress of the Quakers would have set them apart from their contemporaries. The poor preservation of clothing remains, which was limited to buttons and fasteners in all but one grave, provides little insight into the practices of the Quaker community in Alexandria.

FIGURE 17. James Miller headstone (1854) near the north boundary wall of the library in 1994. (Photo by Alexandria Archaeology.)

In the 19th century, a corpse might be wrapped in a shroud or winding sheet, buried in regular clothing, or dressed in a burial robe. The use of shrouds is an ancient and traditional practice. Frost (1973:43) mentions the use of linen or wool shrouds among Quaker families. The practice of burying the dead in regular clothing occurs as early as the 18th century in America. Ann Ritson (1809:110) describes a Quaker burial in Norfolk in which the body is "dress'd in the clothes they us'd to wear." Burial robes appear in the later 19th century with formation of the modern funeral industry. Burial robes are specialized garments sold by undertakers, which look like street clothing when seen in an open coffin. They are of one piece and split in the back for ease in dressing the corpse (Columbus Coffin Company 1882:63).

In the archaeological record, burial robes would be indistinguishable from street clothing, unless the fabric was well preserved.

At Alexandria's Quaker Burying Ground, clothing remains were found in the graves of 14 adult individuals, including 9 males, 2 females, and 5 of unknown sex. Buttons were also found in the graves of one infant and one child. The absence of personal artifacts in 39 of 64 excavated coffins (59%) may in itself speak to the simplicity of dress. This phenomenon may also be a factor of preservation (cloth-covered bone and shell buttons may completely deteriorate in some graves) or of the time period (for instance, buttons were uncommon on women's clothing prior to the 1830s).

The male burials included buttons, fabric, and a small buckle, indicative of coats, vests, shirts, trousers, and underwear. Clarkson (1806[1]: 241) wrote that men's buttons were generally of "alchymy" (plated) or the same color as their clothes, and in the Quaker Burying Ground, they were indeed of plain brass, black vulcanized rubber, or black fabric.

The female burials included buttons from a dress or gown and a bodice or blouse. Contrary to what might be expected—because the use of jewelry was not condoned by the Quaker community—one female wore a simple gold ring. Plain tortoiseshell hair combs were found with seven of the Alexandria Quaker burials (Figure 18). Quaker women in the 19th century generally wore their hair up, swept away from the face and nape of the neck, and tucked under a bonnet. The hair could be held in place with a plain comb or combs (Gunmere 1968:144). As was common with Quaker clothing, these combs were plain but of the finest material (Gunmere 1968:163). Tortoiseshell combs such as these were more costly than combs of horn, which were processed to resemble tortoiseshell after 1805 (Haertig 1983:31) or celluloid, a material invented in 1869 (Friedel 1988:34). While some Quaker women used fashionable high-backed combs, made to show above the knots of hair (McLennan 1937:531), none of these ornate combs was found at the cemetery site. The comb styles were all plain, but they were all made of tortoiseshell, the more expensive material for hair combs available at the time.

While no clothing remains were found in the other burials (except for the iron coffin discussed earlier), this does not present conclusive evidence of the use of shrouds rather than street clothing. The use of shrouds may be indicated in the burial record by the placement of pins in certain positions and the absence of buttons and other clothing remains. However, a single pin such as that found in Burial 7 may have been used to fasten other items of clothing, and clothing may be fastened with cloth ties, drawstrings, or hooks and eyes rather than buttons.

The analysis of clothing remains from the Quaker Burying Ground does not provide conclusive evidence concerning the adherence of the community to the tenets of simplicity. For the most part, however, the remnants of clothing found at the site do not provide indications to the contrary. The single exception is the simple ring, probably a wedding band.

Other grave goods were found in the burials of the cemetery, but any connections to the Quaker belief system are unclear. One burial contained seven cobbles placed around the edges of the top of the coffin in the grave shaft. An eighth cobble was found in the center of the east end of the coffin; it had apparently been placed over the head area of the coffin lid and had fallen in when the lid collapsed. The meaning of the ritual placement of these stones on the coffin is unknown, although it

FIGURE 18. Tortoiseshell hair comb. (Photo by Alexandria Archaeology.)

is a custom for stones to be placed on top of Jewish gravestones. In another burial, an iron skeleton key, adhering with corrosion to a piece of wood, was found near the left shoulder of an adult male (Figures 19 and 20). The meaning of the key is unclear. It may be the key to a house, place of business, or a chest, or it may be symbolic of the "key to heaven" mentioned in the Bible (Matthew 16:19). Another burial contained five small fragments of clear (slightly tinted), very thin curved glass found in the chest area of a female. The curve and thinness of the glass suggests a small medicine vial, which may have been used to hold scent or tears.

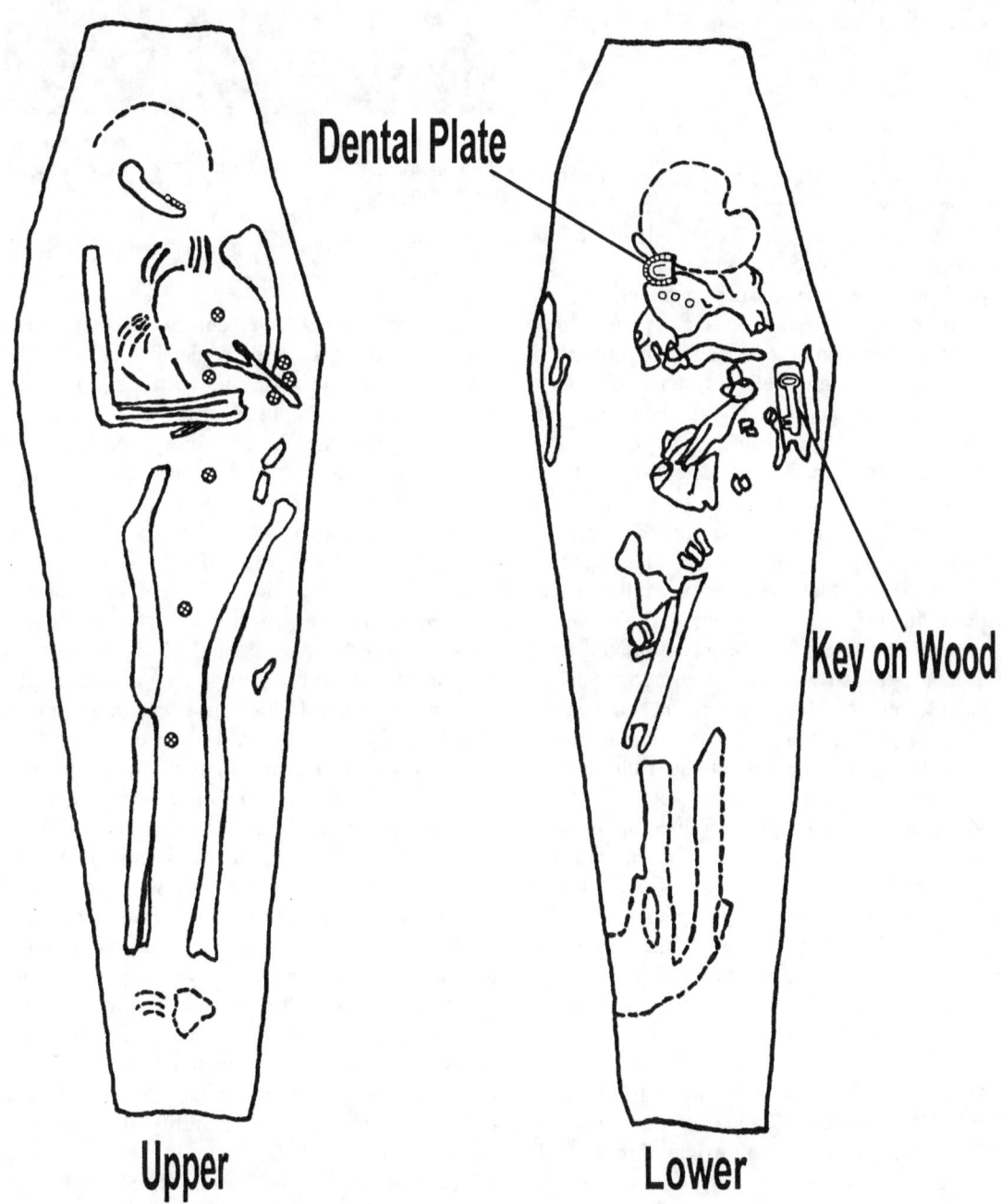

Dental Plate

Key on Wood

Upper

Lower

FIGURE 19. Burial 7, showing the key in a stacked burial. (Drawing by Alexandria Archaeology.)

FIGURE 20. Iron skeleton key on wood fragment found near the right hand of the lower burial, Burial 7. (Photo by Alexandria Archaeology.)

FIGURE 21. Ironstone plate, with gilt script "E," found in the abdominal area of Burial 103. (Photo by Alexandria Archaeology.)

Its inclusion in the grave probably relates to a sentimental mourning custom and may be one instance of evidence of a ritual relating to the beautification of death movement.

While not related to issues of simplicity, one other grave item found at the cemetery may provide evidence of the strong commitment of the Quakers to their belief system. An ironstone plate was placed over the abdominal area of an adult female in Burial 103 (Figure 21). The plate, with a plain rim, dates to the 1860s or later. A gilt initial *E*, in script, was added at the center after the plate was glazed and fired. A portion of the plate rim is missing, suggesting that the plate was purposefully broken prior to inclusion in the grave. The presence of plates in burials has been associated with traditional African and African American burial practices into the 20th century in some areas, as well as with customs in parts of the British Isles at least until the end of the 18th century. While there was not sufficient skeletal material to allow for osteological determination of race, given the Quaker's championship of abolition and African American rights, it would not be out of keeping with Quaker sympathies for African Americans, perhaps even if they were not members, to be buried in the cemetery.

Summary and Conclusions

Archaeological investigation of the Quaker Burying Ground at 717 Queen Street in Alexandria, Virginia, provided insight into the life and death of an important segment of the population of the city during the late-18th and 19th centuries. As merchants who moved into Alexandria in the 18th century, Quakers were active participants in the trade that boosted the town's economy. As the 19th century progressed, they championed causes that brought about improvements to society, such as the creation of schools and libraries, the enhancement of municipal health systems, and the relief of oppressed minorities. The first meeting of the Religious Society of Friends in Alexandria was held in 1783, and the following year the Alexandria Monthly Meeting purchased the site on the corner of Queen and Columbus streets for use as a cemetery. Burials continued on the property into the 1890s. In 1937, the Alexandria Monthly Meeting leased the cemetery land to the City of Alexandria for use as the site of a library. The archaeological investigation, necessitated by construction of a new addition to the library, resulted in the discovery of 159 burial features on the site. It was determined that 66 of these features required excavation because they would be disturbed by construction activities. The excavation yielded significant information about the Friends living in Alexandria during the 18th and 19th centuries and provided a basis for understanding the extent to which the Quaker community adhered to the tenets of simplicity and humility that were so central to their belief system.

The majority of the burials discovered were wooden coffins placed in grave shafts and attest to the Quaker's belief in "commit[ing the body] to the dust" (Clarkson 1806[2]:28). However, there was evidence for a number of burial practices that tended to indicate a concern for prolonging preservation in the ground. One iron coffin burial was found in the cemetery containing the well-preserved remains of an older adult male interred after 1854. Metal coffins were reasonably expensive, and this one may have been used to transport this individual back to Alexandria for interment. A buried, vaulted brick structure surrounded the hexagonal wooden coffin of another of the adult male burials. Planks had been placed across the top of another coffin, probably to prevent the ground from slumping as the coffin decayed. These instances seem to represent exceptions and do not appear to have been normal occurrences at the cemetery. Outside coffin boxes had been used in 19 instances. The use of marine clay to encase numerous coffins, possibly as an attempt at prolonging preservation, is a technique that, to the writers' knowledge, has not been reported for other historical cemeteries.

The artifact analysis suggests that Alexandria's Friends attempted to uphold the value of simplicity central to their philosophy during the 18th and 19th centuries. While Quakers may have been influenced by the beautification of death phenomenon of the 19th century, their adoption of the material trappings of the movement was tempered with moderation. Coffins were primarily of the traditional hexagonal style and did not exhibit excessive ornamentation. In fact, there were no decorative coffins found that dated to the first half of the 19th century. When present, gravestones also tended to be simple with inscriptions generally limited to name, date of death, and sometimes date of birth or age. In accordance with Quaker traditions of humility, no name plates were recovered and only one piece of jewelry, a simple wedding band, was found. For the most part, clothing items, including buttons and hair combs, were also relatively plain. The only other grave goods were a tiny glass bottle (a vial for scent or tears?), an iron key (to a house, chest, or business, or, even more speculatively, to the "kingdom of heaven"?), and an ironstone plate (found in the abdominal area of an adult female). Plates included in graves have been associated with African American traditions, and this may be such a burial. Inclusion of an African American in the cemetery would be very much in keeping with the supportive relationship Quakers had with this ethnic minority in the 18th and 19th centuries.

Acknowledgments

Many people assisted in the completion of the Quaker Burying Ground project. We would particularly like to thank the Alexandria Monthly Meeting for their support in the preservation of the Quaker cemetery. The meeting continues today as a vibrant community, faithful to the ideals of peace and equality. This project was a collaborative effort and involved the entire staff of Alexandria Archaeology. In particular, we would like to credit Alexandria city archaeologist Pamela Cressey for her work in pulling together so much information about the history of the Quaker community in Alexandria and Barbara Magid for the analysis of the clothing and personal items. The staff from various Alexandria city departments, including the Department of General Services, the Department of Transportation and Environmental Services, and the Office of Historic Alexandria helped to make the project a success. More than 25 crew members were hired to help with the excavation, and more than 50 volunteers, interns, and George Washington University field school students contributed hundreds of hours working to excavate the site under adverse weather conditions, to process and catalog the materials in the laboratory, and to help with the graphics and illustrations.

References

ALEXANDRIA GAZETTE
  1933   Leadbeater Relics on "Block" Today. *Alexandria Gazette*, 19 July. Alexandria, VA.

ALEXANDRIA TIMES
  1801   Obituary of Benjamin Shreve. *Alexandria Times*, 20 November. Alexandria, VA.

ANDERBERG, LORNA
  1988   Chronology of Events of the Alexandria Quaker Meeting. Manuscript, Alexandria Archaeology, Alexandria, VA.
  1996   A Comparison of Alexandria Quakers to the Population of White Alexandria. *Alexandria Archaeology Publications*, No. 28. Alexandria Archaeology, Alexandria, VA.

AVERY, CARRIE F. WHITE
  1923 Genealogical Records. Manuscript, Barrett Library, Alexandria, VA.

BALTZELL, EDWARD DIGBY
  1979 *Puritan Boston and Quaker Philadelphia: Two Protestant Ethics and the Spirit of Class Authority and Leadership*. The Free Press, New York, NY.

BELL, EDWARD L.
  1990 The Historical Archaeology of Mortuary Behavior: Coffin Hardware from Uxbridge, Massachusetts. *Historical Archaeology* 24(3):54–78.

BLAKELY, ROBERT L., AND LANE A. BECK
  1982 Bioarchaeology in the Urban Context. In *Archaeology of Urban America, the Search for Pattern and Process*, R. S. Dickens, editor, pp. 175–207. Academic Press, New York, NY.

BROMBERG, FRANCINE W., STEVEN J. SHEPHARD, BARBARA H. MAGID, PAMELA J. CRESSEY, TIMOTHY DENNEE, AND BERNARD K. MEANS
  2000 "To Find Rest from All Trouble": The Archaeology of the Quaker Burying Ground, Alexandria, Virginia. *Alexandria Archaeology Publications*, No. 120. Alexandria Archaeology, Alexandria, VA.

CLARKSON, THOMAS
  1806 *A Portraiture of Quakerism. Taken from a View of the Education and Discipline, Social Manners, Civil and Political Economy, Religious Principles, and Character of the Society of Friends*, Vols. 1–3. Samuel Stansbury, New York, NY.

COFFIN, MARGARET M.
  1976 *Death in Early America: The History and Folklore of Customs and Superstitions of Early Medicine, Burial, and Mourning*. Thomas Nelson, New York, NY.

COLUMBIA ENCYCLOPEDIA
  2001 Utopia. *Columbia Encyclopedia*, 6th edition. Bartleby.com, Great Books Online. <http://www.bartleby.com/65/ut/Utopia.html>.

COLUMBUS COFFIN COMPANY
  1882 *Columbus Coffin Company's Illustrated Catalogue. Wood and Cloth Covered Coffins and Caskets. Undertaker's Hardware and Supplies, Linings, and General Supplies*. Columbus Coffin Company, Columbus, OH.

COTTER, JOHN L., DANIEL G. ROBERTS, AND MICHAEL PARRINGTON
  1992 *The Buried Past, An Archaeological History of Philadelphia*. University of Pennsylvania Press, Philadelphia.

COX, ETHELYN
  1976 *Historic Alexandria, Virginia, Street by Street*. Historic Alexandria Foundation, Alexandria, VA.

CRANE, BREED & CO.
  1858 Catalog. Crane, Breed & Co., Cincinnati, OH.

CROWELL, ELIZABETH A.
  1979 Tombstones in Colonial America. Manuscript, Alexandria Archaeology, Alexandria, VA.
  1980 South Carolina Gravestones, 1830–1860. Manuscript, Alexandria Archaeology, Alexandria, VA.

CROWELL, ELIZABETH A., HOLLY HESTON, MARK WALKER, MADELAINE PAPPAS, AND CHRISTOPHER MARTIN, WITH DOUGLAS OWSLEY AND ROBERT MANN
  1991 *Archaeological Excavation of Burials at the Marshall/Jones Family Cemetery Compressor Station #167, South Hill, Virginia*. Engineering-Science, Chartered, Washington, DC.

DEETZ, JAMES
  1977 *In Small Things Forgotten*. Anchor Press/Doubleday, Garden City, New York, NY

DIRECTORY OF ALEXANDRIA, D.C.
  1834 Directory of Alexandria, D.C. In *A Full Directory for Washington City, Georgetown, and Alexandria*. E. A. Cohen & Company, Washington, DC.

ELIA, R. J., AND A. B. WESOLOWSKY (EDITORS)
  1991 Archaeological Excavations at the Uxbridge Almshouse Burial Ground in Uxbridge, Massachusetts. *BAR International Series*, 564. British Archaeological Reports, Oxford, England.

FARRELL, JAMES J.
  1980 *Inventing the American Way of Death, 1830–1920*. Temple University Press, Philadelphia, PA.

FRIEDEL, ROBERT
  1988 *A Material World*. Catalogue of an Exhibition at the National Museum of American History, Smithsonian Institution, Washington, DC.

FROST, J. WILLIAM
  1973 *The Quaker Family in Colonial America, a Portrait of the Society of Friends*. St. Martin's Press, New York, NY.

GUNMERE, AMELIA MOTT
  1968 *The Quaker: A Study in Costume*. Benjamin Blom, New York, NY.

HABENSTEIN, ROBERT W., AND WILLIAM M. LAMERS
  1981 *The History of American Funeral Directing*, 2nd revised edition. National Funeral Directors Association, Milwaukee, WI.

HAERTIG, EVELYN
  1983 *Antique Combs and Purses*. The Newport Press, Santa Ana, CA.

HALLOWELL, BENJAMIN
  1867 *The Young Friend's Manual: Containing a Statement of Some of the Doctrines and Testimonies of Friends, and of The Principles of Truth Professed by That Society*. T. Ellwood Zell, Philadelphia, PA

JANNEY, ASA MOORE, AND WERNER J. JANNEY (EDITORS)
1978 *John Jay Janney's Virginia, An American Farm Lad's Life in the Early-Nineteenth Century*. EPM Publications, McLean, VA.

KUNZE, BONNELYN YOUNG
1994 *Margaret Fell and the Rise of Quakerism*. Stanford University Press, Stanford, CA.

LANG, KATHRYN ANN
1984 Coffins and Caskets: Their Contribution to the Archaeological Record. Master's thesis, Department of Anthropology, University of Idaho, Moscow, ID.

LITTLE, BARBARA J., KIM M. LANPHEAR, AND DOUGLAS W. OWSLEY
1992 Mortuary Display and Status in a Nineteenth-Century Anglo-American Cemetery in Manassas, Virginia. *American Antiquity* 57(3):397–418.

MAGID, BARBARA H., AND LISA A. YOUNG
1995 Conservation and Differential Preservation in a Nineteenth-Century Cemetery in Alexandria, Virginia. Paper presented at the 28th Conference on Historical and Underwater Archaeology, Washington, DC.

McKILLOP, HEATHER
1995 Recognizing Children's Graves in Nineteenth-Century Cemeteries: Excavations in St. Thomas Anglican Churchyard, Belleville, Ontario, Canada. *Historical Archaeology* 29(2):77–99.

McLENNAN, ELISABETH
1937 *A History of American Costume, Book I, 1607–1800*. Tudor Publishing Co., New York, NY.

MILLER, T. MICHAEL
1993 Boning Up on the Quaker Cemetery. Manuscript, Alexandria Archaeology, Alexandria, VA.
1994 Further Reflections on the Friends Cemetery at 717 Queen Street, Alexandria, Va. Manuscript, Alexandria Archaeology, Alexandria, VA.

NATIONAL CASKET COMPANY
1891 Catalog. National Casket Co., Buffalo, New York. Reprinted in 1984 in *Trade Catalogues at Winterthur*, E. R. McKinstry, compiler, Item 638, Clearwater, NY.

OWSLEY, DOUGLAS W., AND ROBERT W. MANN
1992 Multidisciplinary Investigations of Two Iron Coffin Burials. Paper presented at the International Conference on Mummy Studies, Santa Cruz de Tenerife, Canary Islands.

PARRINGTON, MICHAEL, DANIEL G. ROBERTS, STEPHANIE PINTER, AND JANET C. WIDEMAN
1989 *The First African Baptist Church Cemetery: Bioarchaeology, Demography, and Acculturation of Early-Nineteenth-Century Philadelphia Blacks*, Vols. 1 and 2. John Milner Associates, Philadelphia, PA.

PIKE, MARTHA V., AND JANICE GRAY ARMSTRONG (EDITORS)
1980 *A Time to Mourn: Expressions of Grief in Nineteenth-Century America*. Museums at Stony Brook, Stony Brook, NY.

PIPPENGER, WESLEY E.
1992 *Tombstone Inscriptions of Alexandria, Virginia (Volume 3)*. Family Line Publications, Westminster, MD.

POWELL, MARY
1995 History of Old Alexandria, Virginia, from July 1, 1749, to May 24, 1861. Family Line Publications, Westminster, MD. [Originally published in 1928.]

RITSON, ANN
1809 *A Poetical Picture of America, Being Observations Made During a Residence of Several Years at Alexandria and Norfolk, in Virginia*. Vernon, Hood and Sharpe, London, England.

RUSSELL & ERWIN MANUFACTURING COMPANY
1865 *Illustrated Catalog of American Hardware of the Russell and Erwin Manufacturing Company*. Reprinted in 1980 by the Association for Preservation Technology, New Britain, CT.

SARGENT & CO.
1869 *Price List and Illustrated Catalogue of Hardware*. Sargent & Co., New York, NY.
1871 *Price List and Illustrated Catalogue of Hardware*. Sargent & Co., New York, NY.

SLUSSER, H. ROBERT
1997 The Quaker Cemetery Cast Iron Coffin in Relation to the Development of Coffins and Caskets in North America. *Alexandria Archaeology Publication*, No. 121. Alexandria Archaeology, Alexandria, VA.

SOCIETY OF FRIENDS
1794 *The Revised Discipline approved by the Yearly Meeting of Friends held in Baltimore for the Western shore of Maryland and the Adjacent Parts of Pennsylvania and Virginia*. John Hayes, printer, Baltimore, MD.
1913 *Principles, Advice, and Rules of Discipline of Baltimore Yearly Meeting of Friends*. The Lord Baltimore Press, Baltimore, MD.

STANNARD, DAVID E.
1975 *Death in America*. University of Pennsylvania Press, Philadelphia, PA.

SWAUGER, JAMES L.
1959 An American Burial Technique of the Early-Nineteenth Century. *Pennsylvania Archaeologist* 29(1):38–39.

TULLY, ALAN
1977 *William Penn's Legacy, Politics and Social Structure in Provincial Pennsylvania, 1726–1755*. Johns Hopkins University Press, Baltimore, MD.

WORRALL, JAY, JR.
    1994 *The Friendly Virginians, America's First Quakers.*
          Iberian Publishing Company, Athens, GA.

FRANCINE W. BROMBERG
ALEXANDRIA ARCHAEOLOGY
105 N. UNION STREET
ALEXANDRIA, VA 22314

STEVEN J. SHEPHARD
ALEXANDRIA ARCHAEOLOGY
105 N. UNION STREET
ALEXANDRIA, VA 22314

Christina J. Hodge

Faith and Practice at an Early-Eighteenth-Century Wampanoag Burial Ground: The Waldo Farm Site in Dartmouth, Massachusetts

ABSTRACT

Recent archaeological interpretations of colonial Native American cemeteries in southeastern New England typically focus on the interplay of resistance and accommodation and creative reimagining of Native practices in the face of Anglo-American oppression. Resistance is tracked primarily via "traditional" mortuary ceremonialism. The Waldo Farm cemetery in Dartmouth, Massachusetts, is unlike any other archaeologically known colonial Native burial ground in the region. Native burial practices there seem indistinguishable from local Anglo-American practices. How may one approach the interpretation of such a site? Postcolonial concepts such as hybridization, mimicry, and appropriation, which emphasize the interdependence of domination and resistance, are used. The local cultural context, especially the religious context, of the Waldo site may explain mortuary choices there.

Introduction

Archaeology is inescapably materialistic, but a purely materialistic view of colonial Native New England has long been abandoned by researchers who recognize that archaeologists ultimately study people, not things (Leone and Potter 1988). Recent studies of Native sites in the region emphasize the social significance of material culture and landscape as it communicates, reflects, and changes cultural systems (Johnson 2000; Murray 2000; Nassaney 2000, 2003; Robinson 2000; Rubertone 2001; Clements 2003). The majority of known Native sites from colonial (post-Contact and pre-Revolution) eastern Massachusetts, as in southeastern New England as a whole, are cemeteries (Grumet 1995:113,117). Archaeological study of these burial grounds refutes the idea that Natives were passive victims of the religious and social domination associated with British colonialism.

Interpretations of post-Contact Native burial practices in southeastern New England strongly rely on differences between Anglo-American and Native American ceremonialism (Brenner 1988; Nassaney 1989, 2000; Turnbaugh 1993; Bragdon 1996; Robinson 2000; Rubertone 2001). Diagnostic differences occur in the spatial organization of the burial ground, positioning of the body, grave-shaft shape and orientation, choice of burial markers, and the presence of grave goods, coffins, and shrouds. Items of Native and European manufacture are consistently found in colonial cemeteries of non-Christian *and Christian* Natives (Salwen 1978; Gibson 1980b; Brenner 1984; Grumet 1995; Bragdon 1996). Archaeologists investigate patterns of change and continuity in mortuary practices. These behaviors speak to creative, culturally situated responses to colonial oppression and marginalization.

Native practices that developed during the Late Woodland and early-Contact periods (ca. A.D. 1000–1600) are described as "traditional," which should be glossed as "non-Anglo and non-Christian." The term is used in favor of "pre-Contact" or "prehistoric" because certain of the practices it refers to developed during proto- and early-Contact times. For example, the use of grave goods predates the arrival of Europeans in southeastern New England but continued, and even intensified, after Contact (Bragdon 1996:232). In addition, the creation of designated burial grounds in the region is closely associated with proto-Contact times (Bragdon 1996:232; Nassaney 2000:414). The term does not imply that behaviors introduced by Anglo-Americans were not themselves "traditions" or that they were somehow less authentic than non-Christian Native practices.

The need for an expanded interpretive approach to colonial Native burials is demonstrated by the Waldo Farm cemetery. This little-known burial ground is located on the Slocums River in Dartmouth, a southeastern Massachusetts coastal town (Figure 1) (Peabody

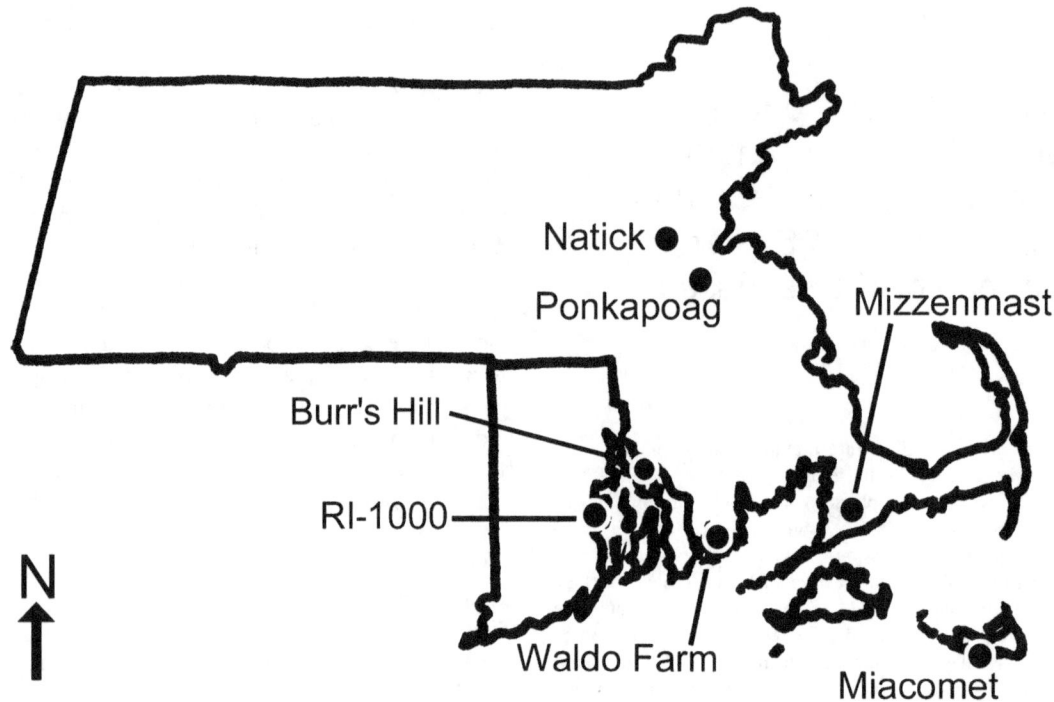

FIGURE 1. Massachusetts and Rhode Island, showing the approximate locations of archaeological sites mentioned in the text. (Drawing by author, 2004.)

Museum of Archaeology and Ethnology [PMAE] 1924; Hodge 1998). The cemetery served Christianized Wampanoags during the early-18th century. Aside from the human remains themselves and the location of the cemetery within a Native enclave, there is nothing to distinguish the Waldo burials from those of their non-Native neighbors. The site is therefore unique among archaeologically known Native cemeteries of the period and area. The specific goal of understanding mortuary behavior at Waldo Farm necessitates a broad conception of post-Contact Native mortuary ceremonialism in southeastern New England, one in which grave goods and other traditional material practices do not obviously play a part.

Colonial Native cemeteries in southeastern New England are characterized by an unequal distribution of grave goods of both Native and European manufacture and typically show at least a partial retention of other traditional burial practices (Bragdon 1996:233; Nassaney 2000:414–416). Modern studies assert that the maintenance of in-group social structures, such as hierarchies and gender roles, is related

(although not necessarily in a direct or obvious way) to the choice and unequal distribution of funerary objects (Brenner 1984:229, 1988: 148,176; Turnbaugh 1984:6–7,19; Crosby 1988: 192; Nassaney 2000:425–426; Rubertone 2001: 139–164). These conclusions are well argued and sound. Archaeologists focus so pointedly on grave goods, however, that the study of colonial Native cemeteries seems reliant on them. While this approach is supportable at most burial grounds, an interpretation dependant on grave goods, or other non-Anglo burial practices, is not possible at the Waldo Farm cemetery.

Physical evidence indicates Waldo Farm Natives adopted the burial customs of the surrounding Anglo-American community. Does this mean they embraced conformity to cultural domination and not resistance? By relinquishing their traditional practices did they, by implication, relinquish their values? Relying on archaeological evidence alone, it is difficult to identify resistance or material correlates of a distinct Native identity among the Slocums River Wampanoag community. These elements *are* found by a close interrogation of other sources, including Anglo-American folk history, historical documentation, and tribal oral history, as well as by an interpretive concern for cultural landscapes. The challenge, then, is to reconcile archaeological and nonarchaeological sources by fashioning a coherent interpretation of the Waldo Farm cemetery, one that explains the absence of grave goods in light of accommodation, ambivalence, and a persistent Wampanoag identity.

The Waldo Farm Cemetery, Dartmouth

Historical Context:
An Introduction to Seventeenth- and Eighteenth-Century Dartmouth

Dartmouth lies within traditional Wampanoag territory (Grumet 1995:117). Few specifics are known about the Natives who occupied Dartmouth during the Late Woodland (ca. 1000 B.C.–A.D. 1500) and early-Contact (ca. A.D. 1500–1600) periods (Herbster and Cox 2002). It is probable they practiced the same lifeways as other Natives in coastal areas of southern New England. These populations were likely loosely organized along kinship lines into small, mobile groups of shifting composition (Bragdon 1996:41–43,157). Whether these groups were more egalitarian or hierarchical and whether the arrival of Europeans in southern New England initiated or merely accelerated their development into chiefly societies are currently contested issues (Bragdon 1999). The first recorded European contact in Dartmouth took place in 1602 when English explorer Bartholomew Gosnold and his party are said to have landed on Round Hill (Ricketson 1858:18). These Englishmen were surprised to find the local Wampanoags already knew "diverse Christian words" and wore articles of European clothing (Archer [1602] in Salisbury 1982:87).

The leaders of Plymouth Colony purchased what is now known as Old Dartmouth, which included the modern towns and cities of Westport, Dartmouth, New Bedford, Acushnet, and Fairhaven in Massachusetts, and eastern strips of Tiverton and Little Compton in Rhode Island, from the Wampanoag sachem Massasoit in 1652 (Figure 2). Many parcels of this frontier property were sold to religious dissidents whom Puritan leaders in both the Plymouth and Massachusetts Bay colonies considered

undesirable, including members of the Religious Society of Friends (a.k.a. Friends or Quakers) and Baptists. The area of modern Dartmouth and New Bedford was a Quaker enclave within Old Dartmouth. To avoid persecution, Friends first settled there in 1657, just one year before Quakerism was made a capital offense in Boston (Hallowell 1883:46). Massasoit's son Metacom, also known as King Philip, and colonists officially defined the township's boundaries in 1664. In that year "Dartmouth" (Old Dartmouth) was incorporated (New Plymouth Colony 1968a:72).

Although geographically close to several Puritan communities, the settlers in Dartmouth were marginalized Anglo-Americans with different beliefs and values from the dominant, Puritan colonial authorities. Friends in 17th-century New England were, in part, defined by their (more or less disruptive) methods of public religious testimony (Chu 1985:61,94; Pestana 1991:150–151,155–156; Kamensky 1997:117–126). Tensions between Old Dartmouth Friends and Plymouth authorities persisted during the colonial period, causing great consternation among Plymouth leaders. Dartmouth Friends repeatedly refused to pay tax for a Puritan minister they did not want, improperly observed the Sabbath, refused to serve in the military, and stubbornly preserved the scattered settlement pattern they felt suited their agrarian interests (New Plymouth Colony 1968a, 1968b). By the late-17th and 18th

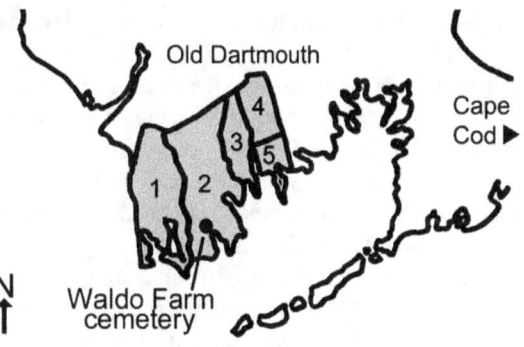

FIGURE 2. Boundaries of the Old Dartmouth township (shaded) and its modern constituent towns and cities within Massachusetts: (1) Westport, (2) Dartmouth, (3) New Bedford, (4) Acushnet, (5) Fairhaven. The approximate location of the Waldo Farm site is marked. (Drawing by author, 2004.)

centuries, however, authorities at the county and town level were increasingly tolerant of Friends, who were respected, productive citizens and provided no identifiable threat to the social order (Chu 1985:7,13,94).

To protect their land and lifeways from intensifying English encroachment, Wampanoags loyal to the sachem Metacom wreaked much destruction throughout New England, beginning in summer 1675. Reports state that approximately 30 houses in Old Dartmouth were burned, and records number four settlers murdered in the township (Ricketson 1858: 343–344; Ellis 1892:24–25; Lepore 1998:78). Natives' violence was matched by the colonists' retaliation (Lepore 1998:78,119–121). The conflict, known as King Philip's War, lasted into 1676 and manifestly altered cultural relations in New England. Neither its Native instigators nor those Natives (Christian and non-Christian) who fought for the colonists emerged unscathed. Captured Wampanoags from the Dartmouth area were among those sent as slaves to the West Indies after the war (Ricketson 1858:343). This group of exiles likely included members of the Slocums River population or their kin.

Little documentation describes relations between Wampanoags and settlers in Dartmouth during colonial times. Existing original sources are practically mute on the subject, probably because a 1725 fire destroyed many records of the old township (Ricketson 1858: 179–180). There is a 1703 reference, when Ebenezer Allen was disowned from the Dartmouth Friends meeting for "beating and abusing an Indian" (Dartmouth Monthly Meeting of Friends 1703:12). The incident suggests Dartmouth Natives suffered some of the same demoralizing fates as other Wampanoags: those implicated in King Philip's War were sent into slavery, and those who remained were pushed to the fringes of land and society, marginalized by Anglo-American law and custom.

During the 18th century, most Native American groups in New England lived in permanent settlements on reservation or mission land within English towns and continued to hunt and gather in the less settled areas (Cronon 1983:103; Grumet 1995:123,128). Archaeology shows that residents of the approximately 20 18th-century Wampanoag "Indian towns" "maintained dispersed settlement patterns rather than move into nucleated towns of the type occupied by neighboring colonists" (Grumet 1995:128). A settlement similar to this model reportedly existed along the Slocums River in Dartmouth as late as 1770 or 1780, although it was within Anglo township boundaries (Ricketson 1858:95; King and Russell 1864:3).

Archaeological Evidence from the Waldo Farm Site

The Waldo Farm cemetery (state site no. DAR-HA-05) is located on the west bank of the Slocums River in South Dartmouth (Figure 3) (Massachusetts Historical Commission [MHC] 1995b). It is significantly disturbed, and all physical remnants likely have been destroyed by excavation and farming. The site was discovered by landowner John Lincoln Waldo in 1922 when he began to clear a new field adjacent to the Slocums River marshes (PMAE 1922). At that time, Waldo donated the remains of three individuals to the Peabody Museum at Harvard University.

In 1924, Harvard graduate student Harry L. Shapiro (best known for his later anthropological work at the American Museum of Natural History in New York) excavated the cemetery site at Waldo's request. An extant, isolated clearing on the former Waldo property may be the site of the former burial ground. Its location corresponds with the site location described in Shapiro's field notes and map. Shapiro removed at least 34 individuals from the Waldo Farm cemetery and transferred them to the Peabody Museum in 1924. These individuals have been osteologically identified as Native American (PMAE 1924). The Peabody Museum repatriated remains from Waldo Farm to Wampanoag representatives in late 2003 under the Native American Graves Protection and Repatriation Act.

Peleg Slocum moved to Dartmouth no earlier than 1683 and donated lands and funds for Old Dartmouth's first Anglo-Quaker meetinghouse in 1698 (Ricketson 1858:37; Clark 1955:8). He was prominent in town affairs, a supportive member of the Religious Society of Friends, and a Public Friend (roughly equivalent to a minister) (Clark 1955). According to Shapiro's informants, land for the Waldo Farm cemetery and a nearby Native meetinghouse was given

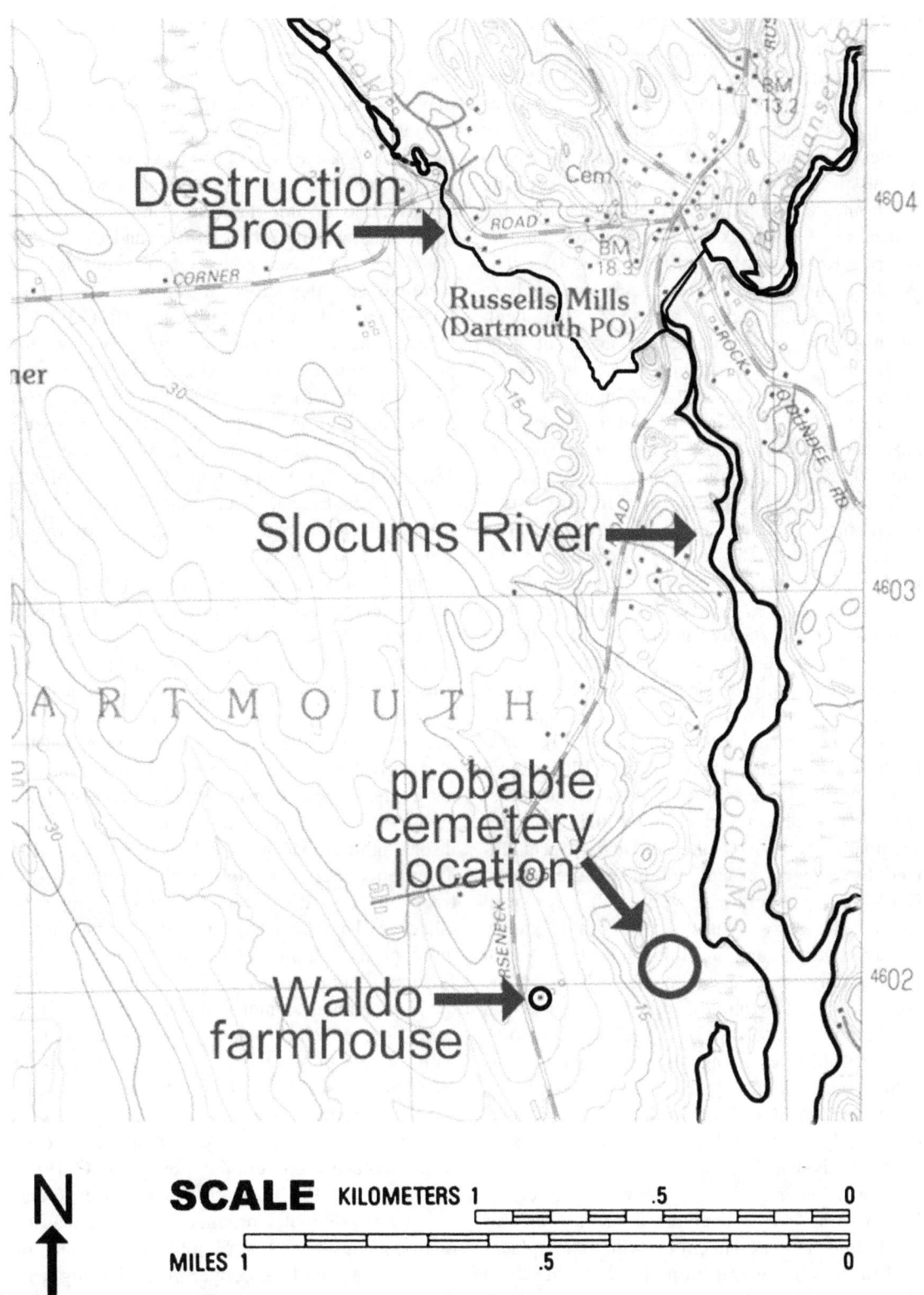

FIGURE 3. The Waldo Farm area of Dartmouth, showing the locations of the Destruction Brook, Slocums River, Waldo farmhouse, and Waldo Farm cemetery (after United States Geological Survey 1985).

by Slocum to those Dartmouth Wampanoags whom Slocum and his wife Mary Holder had converted sometime around 1700 (PMAE 1924). The Waldo site *is* on land that once belonged to Slocum. Although records do not suggest Slocum ever gave up legal possession of the property, a 1751 indenture describing his homestead mentions "the Indian meeting house" as a landmark (Bristol County Southern District Registry of Deeds 1751:5.440). The Waldo Farm site is on Horseneck Road, whose name supposedly derives from the Native appellation *hassanegk* (meaning cave, cavern, or stone enclosure; in this case, an old cellar) (Worth 1908:7). This road was a Wampanoag track dating to at least the 17th century and probably earlier (Worth 1908; Crane 1910; Herbster and Cox 2002:108).

Others have identified the Slocums River Indian meeting house as the Dartmouth Native church at "Nukkehkummees" (Worth 1908:8; Goddard and Bragdon 1988:13; Glennon 2001: 49; Herbster and Cox 2002:39). This identification is almost certainly incorrect. The Nukkehkummees community was visited by the Reverend Samuel Danforth, on behalf of the Puritan Society for the Propagation of the Gospel, in 1698 (Rawson and Danforth 1698:130). Danforth (Rawson and Danforth 1698:130) stated, "the word is preached here [at Nukkehkummees] twice every sabbath" by pastor William Simons. Wampanoags in a Quaker enclave, Christianized by Friends, would not have fallen under Danforth's purview and would not have been "preached" to by a Puritan. Simons is known to have lived among and ministered to a Native Puritan praying town on Sconticut Neck in the area of Old Dartmouth that is now modern Fairhaven (Smith 1992a, 1992b). Danforth was probably describing *that* community in his 1698 report. Confusion between the boundaries of modern and Old Dartmouth in early histories (principally Winthrop 1826) is to blame for subsequent misidentifications.

As with other Native cemeteries in the region, Waldo Farm "was not remote from the world of the living but was integrated with other places within this ancestral homeland. The dead shared the cultural landscape with the living" (Rubertone 2001:127). An 1864 state senate report indicates that, until at least 1770, the land along both banks of the Slocums River was occupied exclusively by Wampanoags and that there were two burial grounds there (King and Russell 1864:3); the Waldo site was likely one of them. The second burial ground may be represented by state site no. DAR-HA-04 (MHC 1995a), and/or PMAE accession 32-98 (PMAE 1932), and/or a woodland knoll to the southwest of Waldo Farm that reportedly contains fieldstone markers (Herbster and Cox 2002: 108). Use of these cemeteries probably did not continue into the late-18th century. An active burial ground or meetinghouse should have legally encumbered the Slocum property, but no restriction was noted on the 1751 indenture. Evidence, therefore, suggests use of the Waldo Farm burial ground began ca. 1700 and ended by the early 1750s, more certainly by the late-18th century, as Wampanoag occupation of the Slocums' banks ended and Natives in the town dispersed (King and Russell 1864:3; Herbster and Cox 2002:53–54).

The burials themselves are not useful for further determining antiquity. Shapiro hoped to recover associated funerary objects from the Waldo cemetery but found none (PMAE 1924). Preservation was generally poor, but the absence of *any* durable grave goods (ceramic, glass, or stone) makes Waldo Farm unique among archaeologically known, contemporary Native cemeteries in the region (Gibson 1980b; Brenner 1984, 1986, 1988; Grumet 1995; Nassaney 2000; Robinson 2000; Rubertone 2001). There is a clear divergence between Native and Anglo burial traditions regarding the inclusion of funerary objects. Their absence at Waldo Farm places those burials within a Christian tradition.

Copper staining was uniformly located on 11 of 27 individual cranial remains from the Waldo cemetery (40.7%). This pattern is consistent with the use of shrouds and shroud pins (Hodge 1998:66, 124–129), although no pins were found. Shroud pins are typically straight, made of copper or copper alloy, and are recovered from the neck and cranial areas (MHC 1988; Carlson et al. 1992:44). They have been found at several colonial Christian Native cemeteries in Massachusetts. For example, a fragment of shroud cloth with a copper pin adhering was recovered at the Ponkapoag praying town cemetery in Canton, Massachusetts (PMAE 1969). The shape (round to oval, some with irregular borders) and size (generally around 2 x 3 cm) of the cuprous stains from Waldo Farm support this identification. The use of copper shroud pins is a Christian practice, but these objects do have potential for non-Christian import. Copper was traditionally a favored material for Wampanoag grave goods, associated with trade, prestige, and color symbolism (Groce 1980; Bragdon 1996:236–237).

For southeastern New England Natives, a combination of European and Native clothing items had become "the dominant style" by the 18th century (Dillon 1980:106). Clothing artifacts are regularly found among grave goods in Native burials of the period (Gibson 1980b; Brenner 1988). Quakers, however, did not typically clothe the corpse for burial in the 18th century (Bromberg et al. 2000:540). There is no clear evidence of clothing at Waldo Farm. No leather or fasteners of any kind were recovered from the site, and the one fragment of seamed homespun is interpreted as a remnant of shroud cloth. Not all clothing required durable fasteners, but one would expect some staining on osteological remains if metal clothing fasteners were buried with the deceased. We know that copper shroud pins regularly produced such stains on remains from the site. One would expect similar cupric or ferrous stains from buttons, hooks, or buckles in the cuff, chest, waist, or foot areas.

Well-defined copper stains, each approximately 1 cm square in area, *were* found on the axial and appendicular elements of one adult male from the site. Two stains were found on the right femur, one on the left femur, one on a lumbar vertebra, and one on a metatarsal (Hodge 1998:66–68,118). It is conceivable these stains were caused by small clothing fasteners or decorative elements. The use of "extra" shroud pins cannot be ruled out, however, although shroud pin stains were typically larger than those on this individual and confined to cranial areas. Alternately, aside from the overall lack of grave goods and of other similar stains, there is also nothing to prove these stains were not caused by a few, small, copper grave goods. Even if these stains are the result of interred objects, all other burials recovered from the site yielded no such evidence. The overall lack of grave goods still sets Waldo Farm apart from contemporary Native burial sites.

Shapiro noted that "although no artifacts were found interred with the bodies, several pieces of homespun or at least early cloth of the seventeenth century were brought back" from the Waldo burial ground (PMAE 1924). One such piece, of finely woven linen, survived in the Waldo Farm accession. This fabric was recovered with human hair and is likely a remnant of the reported shroud cloth (Hodge 1998:70–73). Shrouds were a typical element of 17th- and 18th-century Quaker (and other Christian) burials (Bromberg et al. 2000:177). Textiles were also traditionally used in Wampanoag interments. Early ethnographic accounts indicate "the corpse was either sewn into a mat, wrapped in the mat upon which the person had died, or simply placed in the grave and covered with mats" (Bower 1980:90). Although these mats were originally woven of plant materials, the practices/ideological motivations would be easily transferable to cloth.

Interments at Waldo Farm were all supine, also consistent with Christian practices and the use of shrouds and shroud pins. There was no clear evidence to indicate that the individuals at Waldo Farm were buried in coffins, however. No nails or soil staining from wood or iron were identified during excavation. Neither were fragments of coffin wood recorded, although one small nonplanar wood fragment is part of the site accession (PMAE 1924). Shrouds and coffins were used (not always together) by Friends of the period as well as by other Christians (Fischer 1989:520; Bromberg et al. 2000:177). Wooden, rectangular burial containers were not traditionally used by Natives of the region, although wood planks were sometimes used on or in burials (Bower 1980:90).

Shapiro described grave markers at the cemetery as plain fieldstone, and he noted a head- and footstone for every grave on his sketch plan (Figure 4) (PMAE 1924). Similar markers are still present in Peleg Slocum's family cemetery, which was used from ca. 1700 to 1864 (Lund 1997:337). Anglo-American Friends in 17th- and 18th-century Dartmouth (and elsewhere) frequently used rough fieldstone or other simple grave markers, or none at all, because of their ideals of simplicity and austerity (Ricketson 1858:266–267; Lowry 1940; Lund 1997: 175,297–298). The 1785 *Rules and Discipline of the* [New England] *Yearly Meeting* (Society of Friends 1785:51) addressed some of its wayward members on this subject, advocating a return to

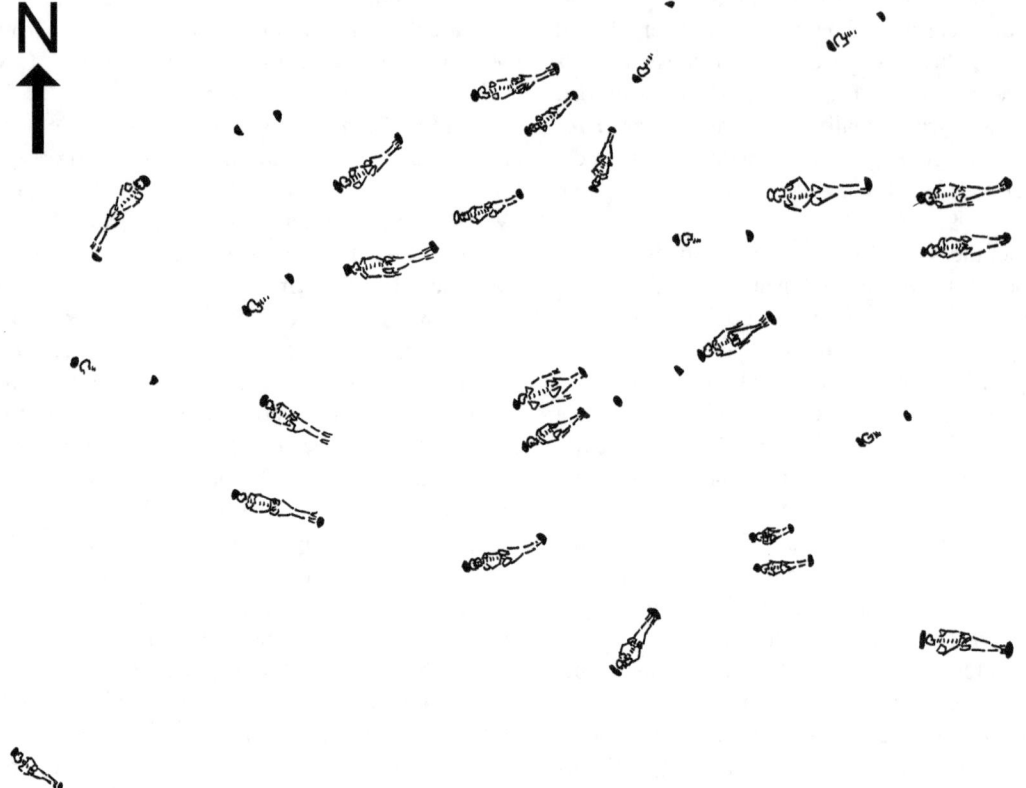

FIGURE 4. Sketch plan of burials and gravestones at the Waldo Farm cemetery, no scale (after Harry L. Shapiro's site sketch in PMAE 1924).

previous simplicities and censuring "the vain and empty custom of inscriptions, tomb-stones, &c." Pre-Contact Native traditions of grave marking did not typically include single field-stones (Bower 1980:90; Bragdon 1996:233–234). The use of such markers is most closely associated with colonial Anglo-Americans, by the 18th century specifically with Friends (Stannard 1977: 111–122).

The Waldo cemetery was located not just near the river and within the Wampanoag settlement but also supposedly near the Meetinghouse funded by Slocum. Quaker and other Christian burial grounds were typically located near their places of worship or, in the case of family plots, their homes (Lund 1997). According to Shapiro's site sketch, the cemetery was not regularly shaped or bounded, although the riverbank did immediately border the cemetery to the northeast. The cemetery's location by, and orientation to, the river likely held symbolic meaning for Dartmouth Wampanoags. The

intersection of land and water may be described as "a metaphorical threshold between this world and the other in terms of Northeastern Woodland Indian cosmology" (Rubertone 2001:128).

Not all of the 32 interments (34 individuals) Shapiro excavated are represented on his map, and he did not excavate, or draw, all the graves at the site (in particular he avoided children's graves with poor preservation) (PMAE 1924). Over 17% of drawn Waldo burials seem to have the head to the west and therefore closely conformed to Christian practices (Table 1) (Bromberg et al. 2000:9–14). This orientation was adopted so an individual may face the rising sun on Judgment Day, and it is not surprising to find this pattern represented at a Christian Native cemetery. However, this scheme was not universally followed, even by Anglo-Americans in the colonies; natural and cultural landscape features also affected burial orientation (for example Noël Hume 1982:77; Gibb 1996:207; Riordan 1997:31).

TABLE 1
BURIAL ORIENTATION

Orientation of Head	Number of Burials	Percent of Total
Southwest	17	58.6%
West	5	17.2%
Northwest	4	13.8%
Northeast	1	3.4%
Unknown	2	6.9%
TOTAL	29	100.0%

Source: As drawn by Harry L. Shapiro (Figure 4).

Waldo Farm burials admittedly exhibit a range of west/southwest orientations (Figure 4), so that distinguishing between these two directions is sometimes difficult. Almost 60% of drawn burials seem to be oriented with the head to the southwest. This orientation may have derived from dominant landscape features, i.e., the river and its banks. It also possessed cosmological significance for Natives in southeastern New England through its association with the sacred being Keihtan (a.k.a. Cautantowwit) and his dwelling place. It was said that corn comes from Cautantowwit, and that good souls journey to the being's home upon death (Bragdon 1996:188,235). At some colonial non-Christian Native burial sites, orientations were loosely southern rather than strictly southwestern (Gibson 1980a:13).

Although reliably associated with burial and renewal, the southwest was not the only significant direction according to traditional Wampanoag beliefs. Each of the four cardinal directions had its own particular vital force (not associated with burial orientation in existing studies) (Bragdon 1996:185,235). The northeast was associated with Hobbomok (a.k.a. Abbomocho), Keihtan's counterpart. As the latter's dwelling was a positive place of afterlife, the former's was largely a negative (Crosby 1988:190; Bragdon 1996:188–190). Just over 17% of burials at Waldo Farm are oriented to the northwest or northeast. If typical grave orientation has positive associations within both non-Christian and Christian traditions, then aberrant grave orientation among colonial Native and Anglo-American populations may have been associated with spiritual contamination or imbalance. At Waldo Farm, however, the prevalence of north-facing graves makes this scenario less likely.

Interpreting burial orientation is problematic, particularly when a range of orientations is present. Certainly, one should avoid postulating a one-to-one correlation between grave orientation and ideological system, especially where multiple ideologies may have coexisted. The Waldo Farm cemetery's liminal location as well as grave orientations (to the southwest or otherwise) likely *were* meaningful outside of the larger Christian tradition. Irregular orientation and boundaries, however, also put the burial ground *within* the Quaker tradition, not outside of it. While Quakers and other Christians ideally buried their dead in rows (Bromberg et al. 2000:9–14,179), this practice was apparently not closely followed by New England Quakers. The Society of Friends (1785:51) urged its members to bury in rows, suggesting problems were created by a widespread failure to do so. Early Friends are generally known for *not* following burial strictures very carefully (Bromberg et al. 2000:179).

The reuse of grave shafts, and disturbance of earlier interments, was not scrupulously avoided in Anglo-Christian contexts until the 19th century (Deetz 1996:123–124). Burials at Peleg and Mary Slocum's own meeting cemetery (at Apponegansett, first used in 1706) are described as "haphazard"; "quite often when digging a new grave, people would be put in the same opening, covered up again and forgotten" (Berish 1991:11). How, then, should one interpret the two instances of possible multiple interment at Waldo Farm? According to PMAE records (1924), an adult female and a child were interred in Grave 11 and an adult male and female in Grave 21. Like so much evidence from the site, these burials provide no interpretive closure. No multiple burials are noted and burials are not numbered on Shapiro's site map (Figure 4) or in his site report (PMAE 1924). Neither does he discuss positive or negative evidence of grave disturbance or secondary interment, although from the apparent articulation and completeness of the remains they are inferred to have all been recovered *in situ*. Would he have distinguished between individuals "put in the same opening" simultaneously and at different times? Multiple interments were not the norm for traditional Native burials after Contact, but they were known (Gibson 1980a:13). As mentioned, they are also consistent with burial practices of colonial Anglo-American Friends.

On all fronts, then, it is problematic to infer strict Christian or non-Christian belief systems at Waldo Farm. At the site, extended burial postures and an absence of grave goods fall within a broad Christian tradition, while the presence of fieldstone grave markers is associated with 18th-century Quaker death ways. The location of the cemetery and its irregular layout, possible multiple interments, and use of shrouds potentially fall within both Quaker *and* traditional Native belief systems. Material practices at Waldo Farm should be viewed with an open mind, as ambivalent evidence, possibly incorporating (or at least leaving room for) multiple religious traditions.

Comparative Native Burial Sites

The Waldo Farm burials do not resemble those of their Christianized contemporaries in southeastern New England. Tribal identity may be implicated in some aspects of cultural expression, but it is unlikely that differences in tribal belief systems explain the unique suite of mortuary customs seen at Waldo Farm. Massachusetts and Wampanoags had similar cultural systems, spiritual practices, lifeways, political organizations, and material culture; they also spoke the same language (Goddard and Bragdon 1988). A survey of archaeologically known, non-Christian Wampanoag burial grounds (Gibson 1980b; Brenner 1984), non-Christian Massachusett burial grounds (Willoughby 1924; Brenner 1984), and Christian burial grounds used by Puritan-influenced communities of both Wampanoags and Massachusetts (PMAE 1969; Brenner 1984, 1986, 1988; Baker 1992) shows these diverse communities all used grave goods during the 17th and early-18th centuries.

If, as Jill Lepore (1998:81) argues, "the principal cultural anxiety behind King Philip's War was confusion of identity," if it was this war that fixed previously moveable sociocultural boundaries, then perhaps the mixing of material symbols (such as placing "European" objects in "Native" graves, or placing any objects in "Christian" graves) was not an acceptable or effective social strategy for some Natives after the war. This scenario does not fully explain the lack of grave goods at Waldo Farm, however, because the site's use overlapped that of Puritan Native cemeteries where traditional mortuary ceremonialism seemingly persisted well into the 18th century.

Excavated Christian Native burial grounds from 18th-century southern New England are admittedly rare, but there are no conclusive similarities between them and the Waldo site. Probable *terminus post-* and *ante-quem* dates at Waldo Farm (ca. 1700–1750) overlap with dates at praying town cemeteries in Natick (1651–ca. 1750) and Ponkapoag in Canton (1652–1720), but numerous grave goods were recovered from both of these burial grounds (PMAE 1969; Brenner 1984; Baker 1992). The Mizzenmast Road Indian Cemetery (MAS-HA-20) in Mashpee, Massachusetts, dates from the 17th through 19th centuries (MHC 1999). It is assumed to be a Christian cemetery due to the presence of coffins and the spatial arrangement of graves. Here, again, material evidence of indigenous belief systems was noted by archaeologists (although not elaborated in their public site report) (MHC 1999). It is, unfortunately, impossible to phase burials at any of these Christian sites, making changes in mortuary offerings over time difficult to detect.

Finds from the Miacomet Indian Burial Ground on Nantucket Island, Massachusetts, (state site no. NAN-HA-02) most resemble those at Waldo Farm. During archaeological mitigation, two burials at this Puritan praying town were excavated to exposure but not removed. The only artifacts recovered from the first burial were coffin nails and from the second burial, a few buttons, a probable leather cuff fragment, and probable shroud pins (MHC 1980; Carlson et al. 1992:37–44). There is no way firmly to date the first interment. The second, dated ca. 1725–1775, is roughly contemporary with Waldo Farm (Carlson et al. 1992:44). Miacomet may have been used from 1693 to 1822, but historic documents, grave marking patterns, and demographics of the cemetery population strongly suggest the majority of burials resulted from a 1763–1764 epidemic (Carlson et al. 1992:40). Mortuary ceremonialism was probably altered or abbreviated due to the resultant stress. In addition, the cemetery is not really "known" archaeologically, as only 2 of 200 to 600 graves were exposed (Carlson et al. 1992:48). The possibility of differential burial treatment is unexplored. As a comparative dataset, therefore, Miacomet has several shortcomings.

King Philip's War manifestly altered cultural relations and, thereby, the lives of colonial New Englanders (Lepore 1998). Due to a lack of comparative data and ambiguous dating, however, a comparative interpretation of Native Christian cemeteries was not pursued based on pre- or postwar date. Instead, the clearest association was explored—that of grave good deposition and Anglo-American religious influence. Waldo Farm is the only archaeologically known Native cemetery from eastern Massachusetts, at least partially predating 1750, where no grave goods or clothing items have been recovered. It is also the only excavated cemetery where the local European religion was Quakerism and where Native and Anglo oral traditions indicate the Natives themselves subscribed to Quaker beliefs. The Waldo Farm site is intelligible only within localized contexts of settlement patterns, land use, and religious practices.

Documentary, Folk, and Oral Evidence of the Waldo Farm Community

Grave goods cannot be used to discuss acquisition strategies, differential object deposition, or the reinforcement of Native hierarchies, gender roles, and other social structures contra the Anglo-American hegemony. The Waldo site, however, can be addressed through concepts of identity and place. A local Anglo-American folktale illustrates this meaningful conflation of place and people. It closely associates the Slocums River landscape with Wampanoags, although the Native presence is presented as incomprehensible, unpredictable, and threatening. According to the legend, a brook one mile north of the Waldo Farm cemetery takes its name from an iconic Native/settler conflict:

> A small stream called Destruction Brook flows into the larger Paskamansett River [which south of this intersection is the even larger Slocums River; Figure 3] . . . . On either bank of the stream, at frequent intervals, are quaking bogs of the type locally reputed to be 'bottomless,' while occasional small stretches of quicksands await the unwary . . . . According to the legend it was

> a common, if reprehensible, practice of the Indians to harass early settlers of the district by forays and night raids, running off the livestock of the scattered farms . . . and drive them into the bogs to their destruction. From this vengeful practice arose the name—Destruction Brook (Wilson 1988).

The reference to "scattered farms" suggests these alleged assaults took place before or during King Philip's War (1675–1676). (David Silverman [2003] provides a more balanced account of Wampanoag/livestock relationships, both hostile and productive.)

In 1864, the Massachusetts state senate published its findings regarding a land claim posed by Wampanoags in modern Dartmouth. These Natives argued "that the Indian title to the land in question [between Narragansett and Massachusetts Bays] has never been extinguished, and that it now belongs to them as descendants and heirs of the original Wampanoags" (King and Russell 1864:3). The Natives' case was supported by living witness testimonials and affidavits from deceased witnesses. Affidavits from two Dartmouth Wampanoags, who were 88 and 91 years old in 1859, describe the Waldo Farm area in detail. Their statements are summarized in the report:

> A portion of the lands in Dartmouth and Westport were at their earliest recollection occupied exclusively by the Indians. These affidavits relate more particularly to the lands in Dartmouth lying along the shores of Slocum's River. Upon both sides of this river great numbers of Indians lived in their wigwams, and improved their lands as cornfields and hunting and fishing grounds. There were also two Indian burial grounds upon the lands which they occupied. The living witnesses testified to this Indian occupancy, but at the time to which their testimony related the wigwams were few, and the number of Indians had become greatly diminished. The last Indian who dwelt in this locality died about sixty years ago . . . . Since the periods above named the Indians have been scattered through the towns of Dartmouth and Westport (King and Russell 1864:3).

The report's authors agree that the Wampanoags never relinquished their possession of the Slocums River banks until perhaps 60 years previously, ca. 1800, since "the character of the occupancy which according to the affidavits of the two aged persons, existed nearly a hundred years ago, was such as to indicate an Indian possession for a long time anterior to that period . . . [at least] continuously from the time of the early settlers" (King and Russell 1864:9). Nevertheless, the senate committee found that Plymouth Colony acts, deeds, and conveyances supported the commonwealth's title to these lands.

In the 18th century, almost all Natives in southeastern New England lived in their own towns or in designated areas of settler towns, even using wooden-frame houses built in planned towns according to the British model (Grumet 1995:114). In contrast, the Slocums River banks were not officially reserved for or owned by the Wampanoags. Peleg and Mary Slocums' spiritual patronage, marked on the landscape by the Native meetinghouse and Waldo cemetery, may have legitimized the tribe's continuing presence in the eyes of town officials, however. Faith and community likely supported the "great numbers" of Dartmouth Wampanoag who lived "in their wigwams" while farming, hunting, and fishing along both the Slocums' banks prior to the 19th century (King and Russell 1864:3).

There is no indication that this unplanned, unofficial settlement had a government-appointed minister or overseer, another characteristic of most 18th-century Native communities in Massachusetts (Grumet 1995:123; Mandell 1996: 114; O'Brien 1997:91). Friends and other Anglo-Americans in Dartmouth were, in fact, historically opposed to colonial government's interference in local affairs. Seventeenth-century Friends in Dartmouth had themselves resisted nucleated settlement before King Philip's War. Perhaps it is not surprising Wampanoags seem to have retained a more dispersed settlement pattern longer there than elsewhere.

Throughout the colonial period, "tradition . . . became localized and embedded in a particular landscape," and "the land itself becomes the most potent and enduring symbol of and metaphor for both group and personal identities" (Crosby 1988:199). As discussed above, the Waldo site's riverbank location likely situated the place within a Native spiritual landscape (Tuma 1985:101–102; Bragdon 1996:235–236). Historical sources describe a strong Native presence in the area, predating and coeval with the cemetery. The Destruction Brook legend and Land Claim Report are biased and skewed representations, first- and secondhand accounts recorded within an Anglo-American tradition. Even so, they speak to a specific identity of

place that links Waldo Farm to a Wampanoag identity. Wampanoags felt (and continue to feel) that the Slocums River banks in modern Dartmouth, and the Waldo Farm cemetery itself, connect them to their ancestors (Edith Andrews 2002, pers. comm.; Ramona Peters 2002, pers. comm.).

The Postcolonial Project at Waldo Farm: Discourse, Mimicry, and Appropriation

The expression of individual identities is closely related to the cultural interaction and re-evaluation that is inherent in any colonial encounter. The process of "becoming colonial" recursively affects all groups involved as an inescapable hybridity blurs cultural boundaries (St. George 2000). This process is a central concern of colonial studies, postcolonial theory in particular (Ashcroft et al. 1995; St. George 2000). Postcolonial epistemology emphasizes the dynamic creation of identities through cross-cultural discourse. Identity is recognized as multiply constituted and experienced; colonialism existed not as an "abstract force" but through daily, lived practice in the material world (Stoler 1989:135).

In general, archaeologists have avoided the epistemology (Rowlands 1998:327). This may be due to an inherent prioritization of the ideational over the physical (material) in postcolonial theory's more developed writings, which are deeply grounded in literary criticism and textual analysis (Ashcroft et al. 1995; Gosden 2001). Historical archaeology's tendency to engage the *longue durée* on a theoretical rather than practical level may also be a factor (Lightfoot 1995; Gosden 2001). Postcolonial theorists agree on few points, but none argue that their methods are anything but heterogeneous, contentious, and fractioned, another problem with the approach's cross-disciplinary adoption (Ashcroft et al. 1995; Rowlands 1998; Gosden 2001).

The benefits of an articulated postcolonial viewpoint outweigh these risks. Postcolonial theory mandates the critical investigation of colonizer and colonized interaction in its multiple, dynamic, and situationally dependant forms. These relationships constitute a colonial "discourse," which may be understood as a "complex of signs and practices that organize social existence and social reproduction within colonial relationships"; "it is through the discourse itself that the [colonial and postcolonial] world is brought into being" (Ashcroft et al. 2000:42,71). This discourse is not straightforward but is inherently conflicted as colonizer and colonized groups use and redefine aspects of each others' cultures and identities. Hybridization, or creolization, of indigenous and foreign cultures is an inescapable outcome of the colonial process (Bhabha 2000b:112). Further, that hybridization may be "the most common and effective form of subversion" of the colonizers' power (Ashcroft et al. 1995:9).

Much work in historical archaeology, although not avowedly postcolonial, is allied with the postcolonial project in spirit. The idea of multiplicity and hybridization within colonial discourse, described as ambivalence, accommodation, or a middle ground of negotiation between dominant and subaltern cultures, has been explored in disparate colonial contexts (for example Nassaney 1989, 2000; Deagan 1990; White 1991; Garman 1998; Lightfoot et al. 1998; Murray 2000; Loren 2001, 2003; Silliman 2001; Trigg 2003). This study of Waldo Farm has a postcolonial orientation in that it seeks to understand localized, convoluted, and contradictory colonial discourse at the site. The Waldo Farm cemetery is approached through postcolonial concepts and, therefore, postcolonial terminology is used to describe behaviors at the site. In particular, the notions of "mimicry" and "appropriation" developed by postcolonial writer Homi K. Bhabha (2000a, 2000b) are adopted.

Appropriation is a subaltern group's *transformation* and redefinition of ideational or material symbols of a dominating discourse (Ashcroft et al. 2000:19–20; Bhabha 2000a, 2000b). Bill Ashcroft and colleagues (2000:19) emphasize appropriation's strategic potential for subaltern groups, clarifying that "the dominated or colonized culture can use tools of the dominant discourse to resist its political or cultural control." There is thus an interdependence between symbols of domination and resistance. For example, New England Natives sometimes deposited a brass kettle in place of a ceramic pot over the deceased's head, and shaped sheet-metal pendants were included as items of personal adornment along with trade rings and beads (Gibson 1980b; Brenner 1984, 1986, 1988; Murray 2000). European materials were endowed with

new meanings by indigenous peoples, and an individual's influence within Native society could be augmented, his or her identity could even be reshaped, by the capacity to obtain and manipulate such objects (Loren 2003). The dependence on European objects for social statements about power and status, however, also reinforced colonial authorities' socioeconomic control.

The situation is equally complex when elements of a colonizer's discourse are not "misused," i.e., when Natives do not appropriate items of European material culture but, as at the Waldo site, seem to behave in ways contemporary Europeans would themselves have sanctioned. Throughout the colonial period, some Natives in eastern Massachusetts participated in the Puritan religion, owned Bibles, wore English clothes, built English-style houses, organized their land and towns according to English models, and used pine coffins to bury their dead in rectangular graves (Conkey et al. 1978; Bragdon 1993; Morrison 1995). Superficially, these behaviors constitute mimicry, the *adoption* by colonized groups of ideational or material elements of a colonizer's discourse of domination (Ashcroft et al. 2000:139–142; Bhabha 2000a, 2000b).

Like appropriation, however, mimicry is a "doubled discourse . . . that both nominally obeys and paradoxically undercuts the assumed authority of imperial presence" (St. George 2000: 11). Social domination of colonized by colonizer depends on (often stereotypical) distinctions between these groups, distinctions that break down when the former imitates the latter (White 1991; Spivak 1995; Bhabha 2000a, 2000b; Loren 2001; Silliman 2001). Mimicry and appropriation are not *alternate* interpretive choices but are conceived as *interdependent* and inseparable.

Faith and Practice: Interpretation
of the Waldo Farm Cemetery

As David Hall (2000:159) observes, "no one has or believes a 'religion.' Instead, the religious lies in what we do—in practices and in the meanings that energize such practices." The implications of this assumption for archaeologists, particularly those studying religious communities or avowedly religious colonialisms, are clear. Religious faith is constituted through the practices of daily life and is situated in the physical, i.e., the material, world. Religious differences among colonizing factions will therefore manifest in the discourses they employ. The same is true for colonized groups with varying religious practices. Localized religious identities are therefore directly implicated in the creation and material expression of hybrid colonial cultures.

There has been a recent shift in historical and anthropological studies of colonialism away from a focus on its political and economic effects toward the examination of identity construction within and between colonizer and colonized groups (Rowlands 1998:327). Ann Stoler (1989:136) cautions that "anthropologists have taken the politically constructed dichotomy of colonizer and colonized as given, rather than as an historically shifting pair of social categories that needs to be explained . . . colonizers and their communities are frequently treated as diverse but unproblematic, viewed as unified in a fashion that would disturb our ethnographic sensibilities if applied to ruling elites of the colonized." Colonizing societies were divided along lines of economics, class, gender, politics, religion, location, and race. These divisions were not static, exclusive, or consistent.

The first Plymouth settlers, for example, were not representative transplants of contemporary English society. They did not have the same wants as their contemporaries in England but were deliberately seeking to create, for themselves, new identities in a new social order. These settlers were beset by factionalism, strife, maneuvering, and conflict *within* their community as well as *between* it and other interest groups in England, New England, and the other American colonies, including investors, trade companies, churches, and the crown (Trigger 1985; Innes 1995; Norton 1996; Demos 2000; Hall 2000). This is not to say that the Pilgrims had no common cultural ground with their contemporaries in England but that one cannot consider their beliefs to be those of the English ruling class or representative of a homogenous "English society." Uncritically grouping both Friends and Puritans as hegemonic "Europeans" does not reflect categories of the time, which consisted of numerous special interest groups of Europeans and Natives.

If one recognizes the existence of different Anglo-American factions (such as the Puritan church and the Religious Society of Friends, merchants and farmers, urban and rural dwellers) and of different Native American factions (such as Christians and non-Christians, tribal groups, kin groups, ruling lineages), one must also recognize that these groups negotiated their interactions in different ways. They would therefore generate different types of localized colonial cultures with correspondingly different beliefs, behaviors, and patterns of material culture. An understanding of practices at the Waldo Farm cemetery depends on an understanding of the cross-cultural implications of Anglo-American pluralism, specifically *religious* pluralism, in early Massachusetts. It is therefore reasonable to propose that the lack of durable grave goods at the Waldo site may be explained by the specific religious beliefs of the Wampanoag community that used the cemetery and the Anglo-American community with whom they coexisted.

The Society of Friends was founded upon a conviction that the light of God dwells equally within every man, regardless of "race" or religious persuasion (although, for centuries, this did not result in recognition of complete social, economic, or political equality). For Puritans, only an unknown, predestined few were among God's chosen. The rest of humanity, whatever their actions, would be damned in the next world. Quaker testimony also differed from Puritan in that it affirmed an individual's ability and right to communicate directly with God. As a consequence, Friends tended to be egalitarian and individualistic where Puritans tended to be hierarchical and communal, and the former typically embraced an anti-institutional and anti-authoritarian stance (Baltzell 1979), certainly evident in Dartmouth's history. This orientation may have made the Quaker faith attractive to those Wampanoags exposed to it if, as Michael Nassaney (2003:30) argues, after Contact many Native "men and women sought direct communication with spirit beings in an attempt to regain control over their destinies."

The Puritans' faith in hierarchy and institutional control guided their approach to converting New England's Natives. The Puritan "praying towns" were established by colonial authorities to control local Native populations, particularly their land use patterns, mobility, religion (including burial practices), social behavior (marriages, relationships, gatherings), social organization, and appearance (dress, hair, and other physical manifestations of "traditional" Native identity). Throughout the 18th century, even for Natives living outside of praying towns, "Massachusetts provincial authorities continued to insist on appointing or approving all Indian leaders and on approving all laws and ordinances enacted by Indian people. In effect, they regulated all relations between Native people and non-Indians" (Grumet 1995: 125). Even so, Puritan attempts at cultural domination, although destructive, were not entirely successful; the continuing use of grave goods at praying towns like Natick and Ponkapoag attests to this.

The Quaker approach to Native spirituality contrasted sharply with the Puritan due to the groups' differing beliefs. The Friends had no central, authoritative body, such as the Puritan's Society for the Propagation of the Gospel, to oversee endeavors like the praying towns. Quakers did not even establish missions among Natives until the 1790s. Earlier, "individual Friends, under a 'concern,' preached the Gospel" to both Natives and other Anglo-Americans (Kelsey 1917:19). In a key difference from Puritanism, Quaker founders encouraged men and women with no formal theological training, like Peleg and Mary Slocum, to preach the faith publicly. Meetings for worship were led by elders, but no pastor held privileged communion with God. Regular burial orientation at other colonial cemeteries has been associated with the presence of a minister (Brick Chapel, St. Mary's City, Maryland) or tribal mortician (RI-1000, North Kingstown, Rhode Island) (Riordan 1997: 34; Nassaney 2000:416). Perhaps the irregular grave orientation at Waldo Farm relates to the absence of a similar authority figure within the community, as expected per Quaker practices. In general, the traditional authority of Native tribal leaders waned, was suppressed, and was refigured throughout the 17th and 18th centuries (Crosby 1988:192).

The paucity of objects in Native graves dating before the mid-16th century is sometimes interpreted as evidence of a more egalitarian social structure than was present at Contact (Brenner 1988:154; Bragdon 1996:232). In turn, grave goods from later interments are believed to reflect differing status in hierarchically

organized communities (for example Gibson 1980b; Brenner 1984; Rubertone 2001). Friends' tenets emphasized nonhierarchical social and spiritual relations and, ideally, would have engendered a more egalitarian social system. The dearth of grave goods at Waldo Farm may, therefore, reflect a lack of tension surrounding social hierarchy. In this respect, at least, burials at Waldo Farm are more similar to *pre*-Contact graves in southeastern New England than to contemporary interments. An alternate hypothesis is that Natives of the period chose other ways to express social structures like hierarchies and gender roles (Bragdon 1996:232). Other possibilities must also be considered.

Waldo Natives may have appropriated the Friends' egalitarian burial practices to mask what inequalities did exist among them. They may have mimicked Friends' burial styles as a way of legitimizing their lifeways to religiously minded townspeople while using both Anglo-style cemeteries and Native-style wigwams to signify their autonomy along the Slocums River. Alternately, the population may have felt their sociocultural stability was little jeopardized in Dartmouth at the time the Waldo cemetery was in use. This perception would have rendered the marking of social status, through non-Christian mortuary ceremonialism or other means, less imperative for maintaining or changing their social system. At least some Dartmouth settlers distanced themselves from their Wampanoag neighbors and felt threatened by them (seen in the Destruction Brook legend). Dartmouth's Anglo-American population did not threaten the local Natives with the same *institutionalized* domination as did Puritans in nearby settlements, however.

It has been argued that the adoption of European burial practices by a Native group can most productively be studied not as the rejection of pre-Contact beliefs but as the integration of new beliefs (Gibson 1980a:13). Quaker burial practices were different from those of their Christian contemporaries (Bromberg et al. 2000:178), potentially allowing more ideological overlap with traditional Native practices. Indigenous belief systems were challenged and undermined by the intense cultural stresses of the 17th century (Contact, economic shifts, epidemic disease, war, displacement) (Brenner 1988; Crosby 1988; Mandell 1996; O'Brien

1997), perhaps making Quakerism attractive to its early Native practitioners.

Introduced ideologies, however, could foster loss/absence as well as gain/presence. Among southeastern New England Natives, traditional "rituals surrounding the dead were highly elaborated" (Bragdon 1996:233). Friends' burials were "in a manner singularly plain" (Clarkson 1806:25). Unlike Natives in southeastern New England (Crosby 1988:191; Bragdon 1996: 171,173,197–198,233–234), Anglo-American Friends traditionally memorialized their dead via personal reflection, not via altered dress or behavior. They did not construct wooden structures or otherwise distinguish the graves of their elders, did not avoid the homes of their dead, and did not link the bodies of their ancestors to cycles of renewal and the fecund earth.

At the Waldo Farm cemetery, the most obvious distinction in material relations, and in the spiritual and social relations with which they were linked, is reflected by the absence of grave goods. Friends believed ownership of few, simple, plain goods "suppressed" worldly distractions from the will of God, allowing one better to heed the guidance of one's Inner Light (Bromberg et al. 2000:177–178). Using objects in burials to reflect social position, gender, and status or including objects for use in the afterlife (Bragdon 1996:236–241) would have been anathema to them. Relatedly, Friends devalued funerary trappings and an individual's physical body in favor of his or her spiritual legacy (Bromberg et al. 2000:177–180,533). While some aspects of Friends' mortuary customs were intelligible within non-Christian Wampanoag traditions, others were a stark departure from those traditions. That the Waldo Farm population found a viable balance between old and new ways (Nassaney 2003:30), at least for a time, is attested to by its perseverance along the Slocums' banks.

The local context of Quakerism could best explain why the mortuary practices of the Waldo Farm population differ from those of their Puritan-influenced contemporaries currently known through archaeology. Quaker beliefs informed Dartmouth settlers' daily choices and actions, including their relationships with Native Americans. It is probable that Natives exposed to Quaker beliefs would ideologically and materially appropriate and mimic elements of those local lifeways. The mortuary remains at Waldo Farm are one aspect of this ambivalent colonial discourse. For Dartmouth Wampanoags, many Quaker practices already had, or could be glossed or layered with, traditional meanings. There is no way to separate Christian from non-Christian in such a context, nor would this be a productive exercise (as it is unclear such a separation was maintained by the individuals themselves).

Specific motivations are not accessible through archaeology alone, and no sources recount the reasoning behind mortuary ceremonialism at Waldo Farm; all, none, or any combination of the above hypotheses could be true for different individuals who experienced the site. The point is that this realm of interpretive possibilities opens only when one moves beyond grave goods and "traditional" material behaviors and recognizes the ambivalence inherent in indigenous mimicry and appropriation of foreign behaviors. Localized religious contexts were integral to multicultural colonial societies and should not be ignored.

Discussion

Kathleen Bragdon (1991:120) has argued that "Christianity played a positive role in the maintenance of distinct native communities in the eighteenth century." The Waldo Farm site supports this contention and elaborates on it. Natives' choices at Waldo Farm must have been affected by their exposure to Christian, specifically Quaker, ideology. Quaker spirituality and personal concerns perhaps elicited a different response among these men and women than a more institutionalized Puritan conversion would have. This possibility, coupled with expressions of egalitarianism, likely influenced the unusual burial patterns at the Waldo Farm cemetery. It is clear that mortuary practices, spirituality, and an abiding sense of place were integral to identity construction and maintenance among the community there.

An investigation of religious identity can resituate Europeans (and European ideologies) among "Christianized" Native groups. A richer conceptualization of mortuary strategies results, providing new interpretative venues. To this end, one must understand how people supported and undermined their social systems through religious beliefs and identities of place. Central to this approach are the questions: What religious interest groups made up local colonial cultures? How did they each view and define themselves in relation to other groups? Did these definitions and religious alliances change over time and why? How might conceptions of religious propriety on a community level affect the identification and interpretation of Native resistance through mortuary behaviors? The spiritual context of burial practices has great interpretive significance for Waldo Farm, but localized religious contexts also affected cultural identity and daily practice. A religion-based approach may deepen our understanding of other 18th- and even 17th-century Native burial sites, as well as domestic sites.

This study also illustrates the potential contributions of an adapted postcolonial theory to archaeological studies of historical America. The Waldo site highlights a necessary component of archaeological approaches to colonial cemeteries: recognition of the interdependence of resistance, domination, mimicry, and appropriation in daily practice. Archaeological conceptions of Native resistance should share in postcolonial theory's concern with localized colonial discourses and the accommodations that exist within acts of both appropriation and mimicry.

ACKNOWLEDGMENTS

It was the Waldo Farm site that guided me to pursue a career in historical archaeology in 1997, and I wish to thank all those who have helped me better articulate thoughts about it over the years. Most recently, Associate Editor William Turnbaugh, Michael Nassaney, Mark Warner, and an anonymous reviewer provided invaluable suggestions on the draft of this article. My graduate advisor Mary Beaudry, as well as Diana Loren, Christa Beranek, Janice Hodge, and Barry Hodge, read and usefully commented on earlier versions of the paper (including one given at the 2002 Society for Historical Archaeology Annual Conference in Mobile, Alabama). Elizabeth Chilton advised my first work on the site, my bachelor's thesis. For that project, Dartmouth historians/residents Judith Lund and Virginia Morrison shared their local knowledge with me. I also gratefully acknowledge those representatives of the Wampanoag people who have spoken with me about the site and their ancestors: Ken Perry Alves, Edith Andrews, and Ramona Peters.

REFERENCES

ASHCROFT, BILL, GARETH GRIFFITHS, AND HELEN TIFFIN
  1995   Introduction. In *The Post-Colonial Studies Reader*, Bill Ashcroft, Gareth Griffiths, and Helen Tiffin, editors, pp. 7–11. Routledge, New York, NY.
  2000   *Key Concepts in Post-Colonial Studies*. Routledge, New York, NY.

BAKER, BRENDA J.
  1992   Pilgrim's Progress and Praying Indians: The Biocultural Consequences of Contact in New England. Manuscript, Department of Anthropology, University of Massachusetts at Amherst.

BALTZELL, EDWARD D.
  1979   *Puritan Boston and Quaker Philadelphia: Two Protestant Ethics and the Spirit of Class Authority and Leadership*. Free Press, New York, NY.

BERISH, GEORGE T.
  1991   *The Quaker Meetinghouse at Apponegansett*. Dartmouth Monthly Meeting of Friends, South Dartmouth, MA.

BHABHA, HOMI K.
  2000a Of Mimicry and Man: The Ambivalence of Colonial Discourse. In *The Location of Culture*, pp. 85–92. Routledge, New York, NY.
  2000b Signs Taken for Wonders. In *The Location of Culture*, pp. 102–122. Routledge, New York, NY.

BOWER, BETH
  1980   Aboriginal Textiles. In Burr's Hill: A Seventeenth-Century Wampanoag Burial Ground in Warren, Rhode Island, Susan G. Gibson, editor, pp. 88–91. *Studies in Anthropology and Material Culture*, Vol. 2, Haffenreffer Museum of Anthropology, Brown University, Providence, RI.

BRAGDON, KATHLEEN J.
  1991   Native Christianity in Eighteenth-Century Massachusetts: Ritual as Cultural Reaffirmation. In New Dimensions in Ethnohistory: Papers of the Second Laurier Conference on Ethnohistory and Ethnology, Barry Gough and Laird Christie, editors, pp. 118–126. *Canadian Ethnology Service Mercury Series Paper 120*. Canadian Museum of Civilization, Quebec.
  1993   The Material Culture of the Christian Indians of New England, 1650–1775. In *Documentary Archaeology in the New World*, Mary C. Beaudry, editor, pp. 126–131. Cambridge University Press, New York, NY.
  1996   *Native People of Southern New England, 1500–1650*. University of Oklahoma Press, Norman.
  1999   Ethnohistory, Historical Archaeology, and the Rise of Social Complexity: Case Studies in Native New England. In *Old and New Worlds*, Geoff Egan and Ronald L. Michael, editors, pp. 84–96. Oxbow Books, Oxford, UK.

BRENNER, ELISE M.

1984 *Strategies for Autonomy: An Analysis of Ethnic Mobilization in Seventeenth-Century Southern New England.* Doctoral dissertation, University of Massachusetts at Amherst. University Microfilms International, Ann Arbor, MI.

1986 Archaeological Investigations at a Massachusetts Praying Town. *Bulletin of the Massachusetts Archaeological Society*, 47(2):69–78.

1988 Sociopolitical Implications of Mortuary Ritual Remains in Seventeenth-Century Native Southern New England. In *The Recovery of Meaning*, Mark P. Leone and Parker B. Potter, Jr., editors, pp. 147–181. Smithsonian Institution, Washington, DC.

BRISTOL COUNTY SOUTHERN DISTRICT REGISTRY OF DEEDS

1751 Indenture to Slocum Property. Book 5, pp. 440–454. Bristol County Southern District Registry of Deeds, New Bedford, MA.

BROMBERG, FRANCINE W., STEVEN J. SHEPHARD, BARBARA H. MAGID, PAMELA J. CRESSEY, TIMOTHY DENNÉE, AND BERNARD K. MEANS

2000 "To Find Rest from All Trouble": The Archaeology of the Quaker Burying Ground Alexandria, Virginia. *Alexandria Archaeology Publication Number 120.* Alexandria, VA.

CARLSON, CATHERINE CARROLL, ELIZABETH A. LITTLE, D. RICHARD GUMAER, LEONARD W. LOPARTO, AND BRENDA J. BAKER

1992 Archaeological Survey and Historical Background Research for the Miacomet Indian Village and Burial Ground, Nantucket, MA. Report to Massachusetts State Historic Preservation Office, Boston, from Anthropology Department, University of Massachusetts at Amherst.

CHU, JONATHAN M.

1985 *Neighbors, Friends, or Madmen: The Puritan Adjustment to Quakerism in Seventeenth-Century Massachusetts Bay.* Greenwood Press, Westport, CT.

CLARK, BERTHA W.

1955 Slocum Family History. Manuscript, Rhode Island Historical Society, Providence.

CLARKSON, THOMAS

1806 *A Portraiture of Quakerism, Taken from a View of the Education and Discipline, Social Manners, Political and Civil Economy, Religious Principles and Character of the Society of Friends*, Vol. 2. Samuel Stansbury, New York, NY.

CLEMENTS, JOYCE M.

2003 Thrust Forward into New Relations: The Transformation of Women's Lives in an Eighteenth-Century Praying Town. Paper presented at the Council for Northeast Historical Archaeology Annual Conference and Meeting, Lowell, MA.

CONKEY, LAURA E., ETHEL BOISSEVAIN, AND IVES GODDARD

1978 Indians of Southern New England and Long Island: Late Period. In *Handbook of North American Indians*, Vol.

15, *Northeast*, Bruce G. Trigger, editor, pp. 177–189. Smithsonian Institution, Washington, DC.

CRANE, BENJAMIN, BENJAMIN HAMMOND, AND SAMUEL SMITH

1910 *The Field Notes of Benjamin Crane, Benjamin Hammond, and Samuel Smith.* New Bedford Free Public Library, New Bedford, MA.

CRONON, WILLIAM

1983 *Changes in the Land: Indians, Colonists, and the Ecology of New England.* Reprinted in 1996 by Hill and Wang, New York, NY.

CROSBY, CONSTANCE A.

1988 From Myth to History, or Why King Philip's Ghost Walks Abroad. In *The Recovery of Meaning*, Mark P. Leone and Parker B. Potter, Jr., editors, pp. 183–209. Smithsonian Institution, Washington, DC.

DARTMOUTH MONTHLY MEETING OF FRIENDS

1703 Dartmouth Monthly Meeting of Friends Minutes, 1684–1792. Microfiche, Rhode Island Historical Society, Providence.

DEAGAN, KATHLEEN A.

1990 Accommodation and Resistance: The Process and Impact of Spanish Colonization in the Southeast. In *Columbian Consequences Volume 2: Archaeological and Historical Perspectives on the Spanish Borderlands East*, David Hurst Thomas, editor, pp. 297–314. Smithsonian Institution Press, Washington, DC.

DEETZ, JAMES

1996 *In Small Things Forgotten: An Archaeology of Early American Life*. Expanded and revised from 1977 edition by Doubleday, New York, NY.

DEMOS, JOHN

2000 *A Little Commonwealth: Family Life in Plymouth Colony*, 2nd edition. Oxford University Press, New York, NY.

DILLON, PHYLLIS

1980 Trade Fabrics. In Burr's Hill: A Seventeenth-Century Burial Ground in Warren, Rhode Island, Susan G. Gibson, editor, pp. 100–107. *Studies in Anthropology and Material Culture*, Vol. 2. Haffenreffer Museum of Anthropology, Brown University, Providence, RI.

ELLIS, LEONARD BOLLES

1892 *History of New Bedford and Its Vicinity, 1602–1892.* D. Mason Co., Syracuse, NY.

FISCHER, DAVIE HACKETT

1989 *Albion's Seed: Four British Folkways in America.* Oxford University Press, New York, NY.

GARMAN, JAMES C.

1998 Rethinking "Resistant Accommodation": Toward an Archaeology of African American Lives in Southern New England, 1638–1800. *International Journal of Historical Archaeology*, 2(2):133–160.

GIBB, JAMES G.
1996 The Archaeology of Wealth: Consumer Behavior in English America. In *Interdisciplinary Contributions to Archaeology*. Plenum Press, London, UK.

GIBSON, SUSAN G.
1980a Introduction. In Burr's Hill: A Seventeenth-Century Burial Ground in Warren, Rhode Island, Susan G. Gibson, editor, pp. 9–24. *Studies in Anthropology and Material Culture*, Vol. 2. Haffenreffer Museum of Anthropology, Brown University, Providence, RI.

GIBSON, SUSAN G. (EDITOR)
1980b Burr's Hill: A Seventeenth-Century Burial Ground in Warren, Rhode Island. *Studies in Anthropology and Material Culture*, Vol. 2. Haffenreffer Museum of Anthropology, Brown University, Providence, RI.

GLENNON, BEVERLY M.
2001 *Dartmouth: The Early History of a Massachusetts Coastal Town*. Garrison Wall, Dartmouth, MA.

GODDARD, IVES, AND KATHLEEN J. BRAGDON
1988 Native Writings in Massachusett. *Memoirs of the American Philosophical Society*, Vol. 185. Philadelphia, PA.

GOSDEN, CHRIS
2001 Postcolonial Archaeology: Issues of Culture, Identity, and Knowledge. In *Archaeological Theory Today*, Ian Hodder, editor, pp. 241–261. Polity Press, Cambridge, UK.

GROCE, NORA
1980 Ornaments of Metal: Rings, Medallions, Combs, Beads, and Pendants. In Burr's Hill: A Seventeenth-Century Wampanoag Burial Ground in Warren, Rhode Island, Susan G. Gibson, editor, pp. 108–117. *Studies in Anthropology and Material Culture*, Vol. 2. Haffenreffer Museum of Anthropology, Brown University, Providence, RI.

GRUMET, ROBERT S.
1995 *Historic Contact: Indian People and Colonists in Today's Northeastern United States in the Sixteenth through Eighteenth Centuries*. University of Oklahoma Press, Norman.

HALL, DAVID D.
2000 From "Religion and Society" to Practices: The New Religious History. In *Possible Pasts: Becoming Colonial in Early America*, Robert Blair St. George, editor, pp. 148–159. Cornell University Press, Ithaca, NY.

HALLOWELL, RICHARD P.
1883 *The Quaker Invasion of Massachusetts*. Houghton, Mifflin, and Company, Boston, MA.

HERBSTER, HOLLY, AND DEBORAH C. COX
2002 Archaeological Reconnaissance Survey Town of Dartmouth, Massachusetts. Report to Dartmouth Historical Commission, Dartmouth, and Massachusetts Historical Commission, Boston, from Public Archaeology Laboratory, Inc., Pawtucket, RI.

HODGE, CHRISTINA J.
1998 Out of the Silence: An Investigation of Mortuary Practices and Cultural Relations at the Waldo Farm Cemetery Site in Dartmouth, Massachusetts. Bachelor's thesis, Department of Anthropology, Harvard University, Cambridge, MA.

INNES, STEPHEN
1995 *Creating the Commonwealth: The Economic Culture of Puritan New England*. W. W. Norton and Company, New York, NY.

JOHNSON, ERIC S.
2000 The Politics of Pottery: Material Culture and Political Process among Algonquians of Seventeenth-Century Southern New England. In *Interpretations of Native North American Life: Material Contributions to Ethnohistory*, Eric S. Johnson and Michael S. Nassaney, editors, pp. 118–145. University Press of Florida, Gainesville.

KAMENSKY, JANE
1997 *Governing the Tongue: The Politics of Speech in Early New England*. Oxford University Press, New York, NY.

KELSEY, RAYNER WICKERSHAM
1917 *Friends and the Indians 1655–1917*. The Associated Executive Committee of Friends on Indians Affairs, Philadelphia, PA.

KING, GEORGE A., AND A. L. RUSSELL
1864 Report of Geo. A. King and A. L. Russell on the Dartmouth Indian Land Claim. Commonwealth of Massachusetts Senate Report. In *Senate-No. 2*, pp. 1–12. Massachusetts General Court, Boston.

LEONE, MARK P., AND PARKER B. POTTER, JR.
1988 Native Americans and Europeans in Seventeenth-Century Southern New England. In *The Recovery of Meaning*, Mark P. Leone and Parker B. Potter, Jr., editors, pp. 141–146. Smithsonian Institution, Washington, DC.

LEPORE, JILL
1998 *The Name of War: King Philip's War and the Origins of American Identity*. Random House, New York, NY.

LIGHTFOOT, KENT G.
1995 Culture Contact Studies: Redefining the Relationship between Prehistoric and Historical Archaeology. *American Antiquity*, 60(2):199–217.

LIGHTFOOT, KENT G., ANTOINETTE MARTINEZ, AND
ANN M. SCHIFF

 1998 Daily Practice and Material Culture in Pluralistic Social
 Settings: An Archaeological Study of Culture Change
 and Persistence from Fort Ross, California. *American
 Antiquity*, 63(2):199–222.

LOREN, DIANA DIPAOLO

 2001 Social Skins: Orthodoxies and Practices of Dressing in
 the Early Colonial Lower Mississippi Valley. *Journal
 of Social Archaeology*, 1(2):172–189.
 2003 Refashioning a Body Politic in Colonial Louisiana.
 Cambridge Archaeological Journal, 13(2):231–237.

LOWRY, ANN GIDLEY

 1940 *Quakers and Their Meeting House at Apponegansett.*
 Old Dartmouth Historical Sketch, No. 70. Old
 Dartmouth Historical Society, New Bedford, MA.

LUND, JUDITH NAVAS

 1997 *Burials and Burial Places in the Town of Dartmouth,
 Massachusetts.* Dartmouth Cemetery Commission,
 Dartmouth Historical Commission, New Bedford,
 MA.

MANDELL, DANIEL R.

 1996 *Behind the Frontier: Indians in Eighteenth-Century
 Eastern Massachusetts.* University of Nebraska Press,
 Lincoln.

MASSACHUSETTS HISTORICAL COMMISSION (MHC)

 1980 Miacomet Indian Village and Burial Ground, Nantucket.
 Manuscript, NAN-HA-2, Massachusetts Historical
 Commission, Boston.
 1988 Santuit Pond Road Cemetery, Mashpee. Manuscript,
 MAS-HA-4, Massachusetts Historical Commission,
 Boston.
 1995a Paskamanset River Burial, Dartmouth. Manuscript,
 MAS-DA-04, Massachusetts Historical Commission,
 Boston.
 1995b Waldo Farm Cemetery, Dartmouth. Manuscript,
 MAS-DA-05, Massachusetts Historical Commission,
 Boston.
 1999 Mizzenmast Road Mashpee Indian Cemetery.
 Manuscript, MAS-HA-20, Massachusetts Historical
 Commission, Boston.

MORRISON, DANE

 1995 *A Praying People: Massachusett Acculturation and
 the Failure of the Puritan Mission, 1600–1690.* Peter
 Lang, New York, NY.

MURRAY, DAVID

 2000 *Indian Giving: Economics of Power in Indian-White
 Exchanges.* University of Massachusetts Press,
 Amherst.

NASSANEY, MICHAEL S.

 1989 An Epistemological Enquiry into Some Archaeological
 and Historical Interpretations of Seventeenth-
 Century Native American-European Relations. In
 Archaeological Approaches to Cultural Identity,
 Stephen J. Shennan, editor, pp. 76–93. Unwin Hyman,
 Boston, MA.

 2000 Archaeology and Oral Tradition in Tandem:
 Interpreting Native American Ritual, Ideology, and
 Gender Relations in Contact-Period Southeastern New
 England. In *Interpretations of Native North American
 Life: Material Contributions to Ethnohistory*, Eric S.
 Johnson and Michael S. Nassaney, editors, pp. 412–431.
 University Press of Florida, Gainesville.
 2003 The Material Lives of Native Men and Women in
 Seventeenth-Century Southeastern New England. Paper
 presented at the 36th Annual Conference on Historical
 and Underwater Archaeology, Providence, RI.

NEW PLYMOUTH COLONY

 1968a *Records of the Colony of New Plymouth in New
 England, 1620–1691*, Vol. 4, *Book 4th.* AMS Press,
 New York, NY.
 1968b *Records of the Colony of New Plymouth in New
 England, 1620–1691*, Vol. 4, *Book 5th.* AMS Press,
 New York, NY.

NOËL HUME, IVOR

 1982 *Martin's Hundred.* Alfred A. Knopf, New York, NY.

NORTON, MARY BETH

 1996 *Founding Mothers and Fathers: Gendered Power and
 the Forming of American Society.* Alfred A. Knopf,
 New York, NY.

O'BRIEN, JEAN M.

 1997 Dispossession by Degrees: Indian Land and Identity in
 Natick, Massachusetts, 1650–1750. *Cambridge Studies
 in North American Indian History*, Frederick E. Hoxie
 and Neal Salisbury, editors. Cambridge University
 Press, Cambridge, England.

PEABODY MUSEUM OF ARCHAEOLOGY AND ETHNOLOGY
(PMAE)

 1922 Accession records 22-44. Manuscript, PMAE, Harvard
 University, Cambridge, MA.
 1924 Accession records 24-2. Manuscript, PMAE, Harvard
 University, Cambridge, MA.
 1932 Accession records 32-98. Manuscript, PMAE, Harvard
 University, Cambridge, MA.
 1969 Accession records 969-37. Manuscript, PMAE,
 Harvard University, Cambridge, MA.

PESTANA, CARLA GARDINA

 1991 *Quakers and Baptists in Colonial Massachusetts.*
 Cambridge University Press, New York, NY.

RAWSON, GRINDAL, AND SAMUEL DANFORTH

 1698 Account of an Indian Visitation A.D. 1698. Reprinted
 in 1809 in *Collections of the Massachusetts Historical
 Society 1st Series*, Vol. 10, pp. 129–134. Massachusetts
 Historical Society, Boston.

RICKETSON, DANIEL

 1858 *The History of New Bedford, Bristol County,
 Massachusetts, Including a History of the Old
 Township of Dartmouth and the Present Townships
 of Westport, Dartmouth, and Fairhaven, from Their
 Settlement to the Present Time.* Daniel Ricketson,
 New Bedford, MA.

RIORDAN, TIMOTHY B.
1997 The Seventeenth-Century Cemetery at St. Mary's City: Mortuary Practices in the Early Chesapeake. *Historical Archaeology*, 31(4):28–40.

ROBINSON, PAUL A.
2000 One Island, Two Places: Archaeology, Memory, and Meaning in a Rhode Island Town. In *Interpretations of Native North American Life: Material Contributions to Ethnohistory*, Eric S. Johnson and Michael S. Nassaney, editors, pp. 98–411. University Press of Florida, Gainesville.

ROWLANDS, MICHAEL
1998 The Archaeology of Colonialism. In *Social Transformation in Archaeology: Global and Local Perspectives*, Kristian Kristiansen and Michael Rowlands, editors, pp. 327–334. Routledge, New York, NY.

RUBERTONE, PATRICIA E.
2001 *Grave Undertakings: An Archaeology of Roger Williams and the Narragansett Indians*. Smithsonian Institution Press, Washington, DC.

ST. GEORGE, ROBERT BLAIR
2000 Introduction. In *Possible Pasts: Becoming Colonial in Early America*, Robert Blair St. George, editor, pp. 1–29. Cornell University Press, Ithaca, NY.

SALISBURY, NEAL
1982 *Manitou and Providence: Indians, Europeans, and the Making of New England 1500–1643*. Oxford University Press, New York, NY.

SALWEN, BERT
1978 Indians of Southern New England and Long Island: Early Period. In *Handbook of North American Indians*, Vol. 15, *Northeast*, Bruce G. Trigger, editor, pp. 160–176. Smithsonian Institution, Washington, DC.

SILLIMAN, STEPHEN
2001 Agency, Practical Politics, and the Archaeology of Culture Contact. *Journal of Social Archaeology*, 1(2):190–209.

SILVERMAN, DAVID J.
2003 "We Chuse to be Bounded": Native American Animal Husbandry in Colonial New England. *William and Mary Quarterly*, 60(3):511–548.

SMITH, D. S.
1992a Sconticutt Neck and Its Indian Past: Including a Discussion of the Earliest Occupation of Sconticutt Neck by Indians and the Early Arrivals of the White-Man, with a Special Effort to Place the Reader Back in the Days of These Early Times. Manuscript, Genealogy Room, New Bedford Free Public Library, New Bedford, MA.
1992b William Simon at Sconticutt Neck. Manuscript, Genealogy Room, New Bedford Free Public Library, New Bedford, MA.

SOCIETY OF FRIENDS
1785 *Rules and Discipline of the Yearly Meeting*. John Carter, Providence, RI. Microfilm, Lamont Library, Harvard University, Cambridge, MA.

SPIVAK, GAYATRI CHAKRAVORTY
1995 Can the Subaltern Speak? In *The Post-Colonial Studies Reader*, Bill Ashcroft, Gareth Griffiths, and Helen Tiffin, editors, pp. 24–28. Routledge, New York, NY.

STANNARD, DAVID E.
1977 *The Puritan Way of Death: A Study in Religion, Culture, and Social Change*. Oxford University Press, New York, NY.

STOLER, ANN LAURA
1989 Rethinking Colonial Categories: European Communities and the Boundaries of Rule. *Comparative Studies in Society and History*, 31(3):134–161.

TRIGG, HEATHER B.
2003 The Ties That Bind: Economic and Social Interactions in Early-Colonial New Mexico, A.D. 1598–1680. *Historical Archaeology*, 37(2):65–84.

TRIGGER, BRUCE G.
1985 *Natives and Newcomers*. McGill-Queen's University Press, Montreal, Canada.

TUMA, STUART JOHN, JR.
1985 Contact Period (1500–1675) Burials in Southeastern New England. Master's thesis, Department of History and Historical Archaeology, University of Massachusetts at Amherst.

TURNBAUGH, WILLIAM A.
1984 *The Material Culture of RI-1000, a Mid-Seventeenth-Century Narragansett Indian Burial Site in North Kingstown, Rhode Island*. Department of Sociology and Anthropology, University of Rhode Island, Kingstown.
1993 Assessing the Significance of European Goods in Seventeenth-Century Narragansett Society. In *Ethnohistory and Archaeology: Approaches to Postcontact Change in the Americas*, J. Daniel Rogers and Samuel M. Wilson, editors, pp. 133–160. Plenum Press, New York, NY.

UNITED STATES GEOLOGICAL SURVEY
1985 *Westport, Massachusetts–Rhode Island, Quadrangle Map*. 7.5 minute series. U.S. Geological Survey, Washington, DC.

WHITE, RICHARD
1991 *The Middle Ground: Indians, Europeans, and Republics in the Great Lakes Region, 1650–1815*. Cambridge University Press, Cambridge, UK.

WILLOUGHBY, CHARLES C.
1924 Indian Burial Place at Winthrop Massachusetts. *Papers of the Peabody Museum of Archaeology and Ethnology*, 11(1):1–24.

WILSON, HERMAN P.
    1988 The Legend of Destruction Brook (Dartmouth).
          *Spinner: People and Culture in Southeastern
          Massachusetts*, 4:63.

WINTHROP, JOHN
    1826 *The History of New England from 1630–1649*, Vol.
          2, James Savage, editor. Thomas B. Wait and Son,
          Boston, MA.

WORTH, H. B.
    1908 Report of the Historical Research Section. *Old
          Dartmouth Historical Sketches*, 13:6–10.

CHRISTINA J. HODGE
DEPARTMENT OF ARCHAEOLOGY
BOSTON UNIVERSITY
675 COMMONWEALTH AVENUE
BOSTON, MA 02215

Mark E. Mack
Michael L. Blakey

The New York African Burial Ground Project: Past Biases, Current Dilemmas, and Future Research Opportunities

ABSTRACT

The recent excavation of skeletal remains from the African Burial Ground in New York City and their current bioanthropological study and analysis at Howard University is contributing to our understanding of the conditions faced by Africans and their descendants in colonial North America. The complex nature of African enslavement points to the need for interdisciplinary and comparative research on African origins, as well as the biocultural interaction of members of the African Diaspora in the context of European enslavement practices. Research on variation in the biological health status of African-descent communities in the Americas is shown to contribute to knowledge of their social and cultural histories. Through public approval and support, our research team has been able to pursue a more sophisticated and extensive research plan than is usually allowed. The identities thus constructed are complex and compel novel questions. Additionally, our methodological approach empowers the descendant community to engage in its own cultural and historical construction.

Introduction

Approximately five years have passed since the arrival of the New York African Burial Ground skeletal remains at Howard University's Cobb Laboratory for curation and analysis. During this time, cleaning, reconstruction, and recordation of the remains have largely been completed. Historical and archaeological analyses are well advanced, and specialized invasive studies, such as bone and dental chemistry and DNA analysis, have begun. The total research effort contributes to a comprehensive understanding of the conditions faced by Africans and their descendants in colonial North America.

The purpose of this paper is twofold. First of all, based on our scientific findings and the present opportunity to reflect and think beyond the tasks at hand, discussion is focused on the particular areas of skeletal biological research that need to be explored more extensively in the bioarchaeology of the African Diaspora. Secondly, we address the scientific value of public engagement for this particular research project. Special emphasis will be placed on the benefits and challenges of these methodological approaches. Lessons learned along the course of the project might be usefully applied to future bioarchaeological investigations of the African Diaspora.

Areas of Further Research

The African Burial Ground Project's Research Design (Howard University and John Milner Associates 1993) originally pointed to three major research questions regarding those interred at the site: (1) What were their populational and geographical origins; (2) what was the physical quality of life for these largely enslaved Africans; and (3) what can be uncovered about the biocultural transformations of these people from African to African American identities. A fourth question, that of possible modes of resistance, was added in 1995. A wide range of anthropological and interdisciplinary methods is being used to answer these questions. Osteological and dental radiology and chemistry, molecular genetics, history, archaeology, botany, and African art history are but a few of the fields represented in this endeavor. This paper will not address this ongoing interdisciplinary effort in detail but will mainly provide examples of emergent challenges and prospects for biological anthropology that result from the project's biocultural, nonracial, diasporic, and publicly engaged emphases.

An African diasporic perspective locates colonial New York City in relationship to Africa, the American Diaspora, and the Atlantic World. Within this context, the political economy of slavery becomes more apparent, and the identities of African New Yorkers are informed by histories that extend both to and beyond their enslavement experiences. The scientific approach is also biocultural and biohistorical. It examines the historical interactions of biology and culture such that data on each inform the other and, most importantly, such that human biology is interpreted within historically specific, sociocultural contexts. These specifications defy the use of simplistic, static, biological classifications. Finally, the research design was developed through systematic consultation among representatives of the descendant African American community and scholars, following the African American tradition of scholar activism (Hansberry 1923:8; Drake 1980), as well as recent anthropological approaches to "public engagement" (Forman 1994).

Concerning the issue of population origins, initial studies of mitochondrial DNA sequences extracted from bones of 32 individuals show a high probability of maternal ancestors shared with specific living populations in Benin, Nigeria, Senegal, Niger, and elsewhere. Measurements of 26 intact crania are more similar to the Akan-speaking peoples of Ghana and the Ivory Coast than to 36 other worldwide comparative samples (Howells 1973). Dental morphometric data have been collected for the entire population, many of whom exhibit similar morphometric frequencies to those dentitions from sub-Saharan Africa investigated by Joel Irish (1997). Twenty-three adults exhibit dental modifications (deliberate filing or chipping) with at least eight different styles displayed, ranging from a wedge pattern (Burial 23) to an hourglass pattern (Burial 194). Archaeological and historical data further point to a broad range of specific African origins of New York's population.

Far more research needs to be conducted on comparative populations in order to provide clearer genetic and cultural relationships. The dearth of appropriate West and Central African comparative databases has made it more obvious that we are asking quite different questions of our data than those on which most skeletal biologists and geneticists have previously focused, i.e., the cultural origins of the African Diaspora in America. The traditional anthropological focus on race has led to the lumping of diverse groups within single categories for comparison. For example, had we not been able to collect our own comparative craniometric data

on Asante individuals from the collections of the American Museum of Natural History, the population affiliations would have been with some other group with similar morphology or would have been generically "West African." Anthropological questions regarding human origins focus on East and Southern African populations and hunter-gatherers who were peripheral to the Atlantic trade in human captives.

Dental morphological studies are used to ascertain genetic relationships; however, these studies rarely include references to specific African populations. Instead they are lumped into racial or large regional groupings into which populational and cultural identities dissolve (Irish 1997). Available dental morphology reference casts for comparability are based on Asian and Native American populations (Turner et al. 1991), which might not be representative of African and European variations of dental cusp morphology that would be of interest to us. Several previously unreported cusp patterns have already been observed in the African Burial Ground population that are not associated with known Native American and Asian dental samples. Additionally, identifying individual dental modifications with specific African populations is problematic due to a dearth of published comparative data (Handler 1994), and the observation by Donald Ortner (1966) that identical dental modification patterns can be found in a number of different regional populations. Our extensive survey of the literature supports those views. We are proceeding with the use of dental chemistry to establish the childhood ecosystem relationships of African Burial Ground individuals in combination with genetic, cultural, and historical data in an attempt to pin down population origins. However, in the dynamism of African and diasporic history, we expect that maternal genetic lines, phenotypic similarities, locales, and culture may also often be discordant. Clearly, the use of more diverse data sets enhances our ability to get at the complexity of life and culture histories, yet their use may expand the boundaries of interpretation as easily as they can narrow them.

Problems also emerge for the study of the physical quality of life. Those buried at the site showed skeletal evidence of intense labor, high rates of systemic infection, poor dental health, varying degrees of healthy dental development, a high rate of infant mortality, and relatively early adult mortality.

Historical evidence of Africans engaged in strenuous labor activities is abundantly supported by the analysis of the skeletal remains. Nearly 82% (n = 87) of men and 60% (n = 72) of women with reliable age and sex estimates exhibit changes in bony muscle attachments associated with muscle and ligament tears or persistent excessive strain associated with heavy lifting and moving. Many men sustained spinal injuries as a result of arduous labor, including 11 affected by fractures to the cervical and thoracic vertebrae (Hill et al. 1995). Eight others exhibited fractures to the bones of the feet, which might have resulted from work-related trauma.

Comparisons with Europeans and continental Africans are impeded by the dearth of similar work on archaeological populations representing those groups. Anthropologists have traditionally taken little interest in the bioarchaeology of colonial Africa or of European America, whose remains are seldom excavated. Collections that we might ourselves assess are few and small. Comparisons with the more abundant (yet often crude) mortality and fertility data from church and census documents on colonial Europeans have different biases than skeletal populations and cannot be easily compared. Cemetery returns may provide for the most useful comparisons, but an excavation of historic European cemeteries, such as New York's Trinity Church Yard, would give the most scientifically defensible (and perhaps ethically indefensible) means of knowing the difference between the physical quality of life for colonial Africans and Europeans.

Within-group comparisons are also raising questions that require nonanthropological data sets to adequately answer. We recently found that the skeletal distribution of moderate to severe hypertrophy is similar between men and women; indices of muscle groups being used (that is, aspects of elements that tend to be hypertrophic) are similar between the sexes. Although it is uncertain that women were doing the same work as men, a majority of women's bodies were definitely being exerted and stressed by the labor activities they were performing to the same extent as the bodies of men.

While both genders used neck muscles extensively, women's use of the neck and shoulders are distinctive. Men, however, are more involved in work that uses the muscles and bones of the middle and lower back. We need to better understand how lifting took place differently in men and women as well as other work-related behaviors that may have used culturally specific techniques that have influenced the distribution patterns of spinal degenerative disease. Historical and ethnographic research in conjunction with anatomical information might be required to reveal the significance of these differences much beyond mere statistical quantification.

At least five women sustained cranial base ring fractures, which we believe to be the result of carrying loads on the head (axial loading) that were either too heavy or which led to fracturing of the occipital bone because of a misstep (Hill et al. 1995). Other forms of deliberate and accidental trauma are also being explored.

Heavy labor and general exploitation also affected maternal health and consequently impacted neonatal health as well. Intriguing evidence of this can be found in the mother-infant burial of 12/14. Aged at 35–40 years, the woman's skeletal remains reveal evidence of enlarged muscles of the arms and legs. Additionally, as the result of lifting or pushing a load too heavy for her physical capabilities, she suffered a fracture of her 12th thoracic vertebra that split the spinous process down the middle. The fracture healed, but there was nonunion of the spinous process, exposing the spinal cord to further possible injury.

Burial 12 also suffered from a number of dental pathologies. Many of her teeth were affected by severe caries. Periapical abscessing (tissue and possible alveolar inflammation around the tooth root) resulting in the spread of infection would have been likely, lowering her body's immunoresponse system to environmental insults. Reduced dietary intake due to masticatory pain would also contribute to disease risk.

Finally, her skeleton is riddled with sclerotic periostitis (inflammation of the tissue surrounding bone, ultimately causing dense changes on the bone surface) affecting her clavicles, humeri, ribs, vertebrae, and pelvic bones, indicative of a systemic infection. Her poor overall health should have negatively affected her child (Burial 14) both in utero and early life. Poor mineralization of the neonate's deciduous dentition and the simple but sad fact that both the mother and newborn appear to have died shortly after childbirth is consistent with such effects. Our demographic studies show, moreover, that neonates and 30–35 year old females are in the highest risk categories for mortality for this population.

Skeletal analysis of some of the child burials suggests that children suffered the traumatic effects of heavy labor as well. Burial 39, a six year old (+/- 24 months), has dental developmental defects showing that he/she was ill at birth, implying poor maternal health as well. The eye orbits exhibit pitting characteristic of active anemia at the time of death. Periosteal lesions (mild to moderate inflammations of the tissue surrounding bone) indicate generalized infection, and pitting on the inner corpus of the mandible indicates vitamin C deficiency. The child's humeri exhibit a rugose morphology of the deltoid tuberosities (bony buildup at the muscle attachment as a response to prolonged use of those muscles) and enthesopathies (muscle and/or tendon tears, tearing away bone fragments at the muscle attachment site as well) are present at the insertion of the brachialis muscle on both ulnae (both the deltoid and brachialis muscles are used in lifting). Additionally, the first and second vertebrae exhibit asymmetrical, delayed fusion, possibly due to force or axial loading trauma to the top of the skull. Finally, this child exhibits premature sagittal suture closure (craniosynostosis), which may have congenital, nutritional, and/or mechanical causes (Turvey et al. 1996). Our historical data show that older children were actively involved in the labor activities of the colony; however, the pathologies affecting this child suggest that younger children may have labored as well.

Subadults had 24 occurrences of perimortem fractures probably caused by trauma around the time of death. The remaining fractures (four) were comminuted (the affected bone is broken into many places), partial or greenstick (incomplete fracture with the bending of the bone), or unspecified. All fractures occurred in the humerus, ulna, femur, tibia, and fibula. These perimortem fractures to the arms and legs are most suggestive of accidents, some possibly involving work, or they may be the results of abuse. These traumatic injuries may be better indicators of children's exposure to hazardous work environments than the various degenerative changes of adults who lived long enough to show

such changes that require many years of exposure to repetitive tasks. Interestingly, there is little involvement of the vertebral column in subadult trauma when compared with adults, probably relating to greater spinal involvement in adult work, accidents, and other possible violence.

Concerning the biocultural transformation of Africans into African Americans, further research is needed concerning West and Central African burial practices and mortuary patterns, as well as those of the African Diaspora. For instance, how common is Adinkra symbolism, suggested by the heart-shaped symbol on the coffin of Burial 101, within Akan-derived populations in the diaspora? To what extent are heart-shaped symbols used in non-Akan-speaking African burial practices? The genetic evidence of Akan or other West African origin compelled us to begin our investigation there. We are also examining the site for possible Islamic mortuary patterns as well as possible syncretisms of African traditional and Christian burial practices, all of which reflect on the complex interactions of the various cultural origins of these enslaved Africans. Biologically, Burial 101 may be both related to Akan and nearby Islamic populations. Where does this observation lead us? The more we know, the more we need to know.

The skeletal analysis and research questions of the African Burial Ground have opened areas of future research opportunities that have heretofore been neglected, of gaps in comparative data that must be filled, of historical and cultural complexities that must be explained.

Benefits and Challenges of Public Engagement

The gaps in the comparative databases of anthropology which point to new research opportunities result from the unusual nature of our research questions that are strongly influenced by public engagement. Questions from the descendant community needed responses for the justification of research on the African Burial Ground Project.

Cheryl LaRoche and Michael Blakey (1997) detail the level of awareness and feeling that the African American public had for the African Burial Ground. The descendant community demanded respect in handling the remains, a comprehensive scientific analysis of the site, timely reports on the findings, and general progress of the investigation. The community demanded authority in the decision to ultimately reinter the remains. The African American community was uniquely responsible for altering the course of the U.S. General Services Administration's (GSA) plans for the excavation and use of the site and skeletal remains. Journalists brought the glaring attention of the media. Artists, religious leaders, and other concerned individuals formed committees and coalitions in order to take responsibility for the spiritual, physical, and intellectual aspects of the site. That same awareness and depth of feeling for the skeletal remains is still felt and influences the course of the project, whose final disposition remains uncertain.

Acknowledging GSA as our "business client," we also recognize the descendant community as our "ethical client"; we work for them. The descendant community is not a monolithic entity but is comprised of individuals and groups with widely divergent ideologies, cultural backgrounds, and belief systems as well as various age and socioeconomic groups. Visitors to the Cobb Laboratory have included delegates from the Ghanaian National House of Chiefs, delegations from the Nation of Islam and the American Muslim Council, numerous Christian groups, various government officials, interested scholars, university to elementary students, and diverse individuals of the lay public, representing many ethnicities. Those of us who conduct tours must necessarily relate to these various groups from the standpoint of our own sociocultural specificity as we convey knowledge of the site. In this capacity, one takes on a variety of roles from teacher, to tour guide, to "custodian of the ancestors" as some visitors describe our collective role. We are truly both participants and observers of cultural construction, engaged in an interactive process that contributes to a more democratic and ethnically plural production of knowledge. In the end, this knowledge contributes to a broadening of identity and ethnic empowerment.

Many individuals and groups who engage this project come with hidden, and sometimes overt, political and social agendas. The extremes range from those African American cultural nationalists claiming the remains as exclusively their own (not to be touched by whites) to some Euramericans who question our ability to conduct scientifically competent research due to racist beliefs about white objectivity and intelligence that renders the notion of black scientists as oxymoronic. However, most visitors, young and old, leave feeling enlightened and moved by so intimate an experience as interpreting slavery from the physical remains and associated burial artifacts of the enslaved. Some seem pleasantly surprised also by the juxtaposition of technical and ethical principles. We do influence politics by being generators of social knowledge and are influenced in turn, yet we seek greater awareness and choice about how we are being influenced. All anthropologists belong to communities with specific political, cultural, and psychological relationships to the people studied. Such constraints and/or opportunities can be denied or recognized and negotiated.

One avenue towards successfully negotiating this political bias is to endeavor to present evidence, collected and analyzed based on rigorous scientific methods, and to protect the scientific integrity and honesty of the research project. Still, this effort does not exist in a social, political, or cultural vacuum. This does not achieve neutrality. For example, differences simply in the geographical and cultural scope of research (localizing to New York vs. broadening to the diaspora) can alter a population's character, identity, and humanity substantially.

The desire by members of the descendant community for a detailed understanding of the African cultural backgrounds and, therefore, the basic humanity of those who were enslaved, distinguishes these very Africans as people with histories and social lives of their own. The terrible experience of being forcefully taken from their homelands, surviving the horrors of the Middle Passage, and being treated as chattel and forced to labor may take on a different significance depending on whether their previous human experiences are or are not also part of the story. The construction of their humanity becomes clear when one presents them as cultural beings upon whom enslavement is thrust. It is from this understanding that the term "enslaved African" arises as preferred over "slave" by descendants. Diasporic studies of colonial America, Africa, the Caribbean, and South and Central America might also enlarge and enrich the understanding and identity of any local population that lived within the diasporic context. More geographical and cultural areas should be studied in order to compare and contrast the experiences of enslaved and free Africans, their varied interactions with other populations, and their place in the creation of the global economy and "Western" society. If one views those interred in the African Burial Ground simply as slaves, as isolated characters in a local colonial American setting, one would ask different kinds of questions and get different answers regarding local artifacts and skeletal remains. The more we understand about Africa and the Caribbean, the more we can see their influences on the people in New York.

The heart-shaped symbol on the coffin lid of Burial 101, only imagined in the local colonial American context, might be assumed as evidence of acculturation. On the other hand, a present understanding of the historical use of such symbols in West Africa suggests an interpretation of African continuity and resistance (Ofori-Ansa 1995; Willis 1998). Alternatively, it is representative of the "dualism" of W.E.B. DuBois (1903), a possibility requiring familiarity with African American scholarship that archaeologists rarely demonstrate. The difference of this story is the result of inclusion, dialogue, and conscious agreement of scientists and the descendant community who recommended that we pay greater attention to their African origins.

The descendant community also expressed the need for the research project to focus on local outreach and public education; the existence of the African Burial Ground and the African contribution to the development of New York was completely absent in local curricula. Thus, our cooperation with the ethical client in disseminating information, or "spreading the word," to very young audiences is a political choice meant to modify identities, social perceptions, and potentially, behavior (a major goal of the descendant community, especially the elders). As a result, the Office of Public Education and Interpretation (OPEI) was established with Dr. Sherrill Wilson, a cultural anthropologist, as its director. Since its creation, OPEI has provided information through its monthly reports to more than 80,000 people worldwide, conducted archaeological lab tours, and held educators' symposia on how the African Burial Ground phenomenon can be utilized in the classroom (Office of Public Education and Interpretation 1995–1998).

We are also activist scholars by taking the African Burial Ground Project internationally to the United Nations Human Rights Commission, when asked by representatives of our ethical client who were seeking "moral compensation" for descendants of the enslaved.

We constantly have to remind the public that more than likely we will never know the names and the exact identities of those buried at the site. Yet, from our research we are providing a comprehensive body of knowledge on some of the earliest Africans brought to these shores unwillingly. Still, their interest in individual identities, not necessarily of great value for modern skeletal biology, is being accommodated by the most complete individual descriptions we can make. Below we provide two examples.

The first example: Burial 101 was a male aged between 30 to 35 years; his healthy dental development and above-average height (5 ft. 10 in. to 6 ft.) indicated a healthy childhood. He was afflicted with a treponemal infection (probably yaws) during early adulthood, suggesting an early life spent in a tropical environment. This infection might have been syphilis, a scourge of the colonial era, sometimes called "French Pox" by the British. Burial 101 led a strenuously active life from his teens to his relatively early death. Skeletal indicators of heavy labor included robust muscle attachments, nonfusion of the tip of the acromion, and a fracture of the spinous process of the 12th thoracic vertebra. Populational and cultural affiliation evidence points to West African origins. In fact, dental modifications of his maxillary central incisors strongly suggest that he was born in Africa and lived there at least until adolescence. Mitochondrial DNA analysis demonstrates affinity with modern West African people, and craniometric analysis indicates a close affinity to the Asante of Ghana. Importantly, the English noted the involvement of the Asante in New York and Caribbean rebellions. The heart-shaped symbol on his coffin lid, if indeed Asante, represents the Adinkra symbol "Sankofa." We might proceed from this individual description to related historical, biological, and archaeological observations of the population.

The second example: Burial 25 was a female aged in her early twenties who was 5 ft. 1 in. tall (during tours we cradle her skull to show our audience her "face"); she was the victim of a violent death by the hands of a person or persons with access to firearms. During excavation a lead musket ball was found lodged in her ribs. The young woman had been shot from behind; the musket ball entered through and shattered her left scapula and third rib, probably injuring her left lung. Additionally, she sustained an oblique fracture to the proximal end of her right radius as the result of someone violently twisting her right arm. Remodeled bone at the margins of the fracture indicates that she might have lived for several days following the assault. Finally, the woman sustained multiple perimortem blunt-force fractures of the lower face. Archaeologists believe she was buried with an elderly African man who had such extensive osteomyelitis as to suggest grave infirmity and debility. What happened to her and what was their relationship are questions to which future research might add clues, while much will remain unanswered.

These simple yet powerful personalizations of otherwise anonymous remains offer a type of data representation that is both desired and valued by the community. Although contrary to the populational approach, it does not conflict with scientific requirements. Interestingly, this sort of human identification does differ from forensic science (which also emphasizes the individual) in important ways. For instance, the forensic anthropologist, whose business clients are frequently law enforcement units or the courts, usually focuses on reporting height, weight, approximate age, race, and cause of death. There is little emphasis on cultural background, and the details of their reports are not presented to elementary school children! In contrast, with the African Burial Ground Project, the descendant community is interested in where each individual comes from, what their lives were like, whether or not they received enough to eat, how many mothers were buried with their children, and so on. These are questions that go to the heart of the cultural and spiritual connection between these skeletal remains and the descendant community. This connection, as evidenced by the personal stories, is strengthened by the populational and statistical approaches that we are also taking.

Concluding Remarks

Many of the lessons we have learned through our experience with the African Burial Ground Project can be applied to other research efforts. The major lesson is that the descendant community has to be an integral part of any research effort, both to address its concerns and sensitivities and to empower the community to engage in its own cultural and historical construction. Further, with the support of the descendant community, the research effort becomes more diverse, requires more time for public interaction, and is therefore better received and supported. In our case, more extensive research can be conducted than is usually allowed. The project's directions have led to methodological problems that have exposed gaps in the comparative database as a result of past biases in physical anthropology and bioarchaeology.

It is questionable whether the project would have had the same level of visibility and significance were another approach taken, marked by both less community involvement and conflict with the biases of bioarchaeology. The project has greatly contributed to a broadened public knowledge of anthropology and increased public concern for previously neglected African and African American sites. Paying lip service to or providing token involvement of the descendant community is not enough and often is counter-productive (Blakey 1997).

Prior to our involvement and utilization of the approach presented here, immediate reburial appeared to be imminent due to antagonisms among excavators, the government, and the descendant community. The earlier scope of research was both local and narrow rather than diasporic and interdisciplinary. The methodological focus had been on human identification involving racial typology rather than on the culture, history, and specific genetics of the people interred. Anthropologists did not seek out community involvement and direction. In essence, the earlier approach led to public dismay and, ultimately, outrage. Until the discipline views descendant communities as integral participants in the comprehensive research effort, there will always be the real risk of lost research opportunities and scientifically and humanistically problematic and ineffective investigations of the African Diaspora.

ACKNOWLEDGMENTS

The authors wish to acknowledge the dedication and contributions of the scholars who have participated in the multidisciplinary research efforts of the New York African Burial Ground Project: Edna G. Medford, Linda Heywood, and Selwyn Carrington (history); Warren Perry, Jean Howson, Leonard Bianchi, Christopher DeCorse, Kofi Agorsah, and Augustin Holl (archaeology); Kwaku Ofori-Ansa (art history); Fatimah L. C. Jackson and Shomarka O. Y. Keita (biological anthropology).

REFERENCES

BLAKEY, MICHAEL L.
1997 Past Is Present: Comments on "In the Realm of Politics: Prospects for Public Participation in African-American Plantation Archaeology." *Historical Archaeology*, 31(3):140–145.

DRAKE, ST. CLAIR
1980 Anthropology and the Black Experience. *The Black Scholar*, 11:2–31.

DUBOIS, W.E.B.
1903 *The Souls of Black Folk*. Reprinted in 1997 by Bedford Books, Boston, MA.

FORMAN, SHEPARD (EDITOR)
1994 *Diagnosing America: Anthropology and Public Engagement*. University of Michigan Press, Ann Arbor.

HANDLER, JEROME S.
1994 Determining African Birth from Skeletal Remains: A Note on Tooth Mutilation. *Historical Archaeology*, 28(3):113–119.

HANSBERRY, WILLIAM L.
1923 *Howard University Record*, 17:8.

HILL, MARY C., MARK E. MACK, AND MICHAEL L. BLAKEY
1995 Women, Endurance, Enslavement: Exceeding the Physiological Limits. Skeletal Biology IV: Women's Bodies, Women's Lives: Biological Indicators of Labor and Occupation. Abstract, *American Journal of Physical Anthropology, Supplement*, 20:110–111.

HOWARD UNIVERSITY AND JOHN MILNER ASSOCIATES, INC.
1993 Research Design for Archeological, Historical, and Bioanthropological Investigations of the African Burial Ground (Broadway Block) New York, NY. 14 December. Howard University, Washington, DC, and John Milner Associates, Inc., New York, NY.

HOWELLS, W. W.
1973 Cranial Variation in Man. *Peabody Museum of Archaeology and Ethnology Papers*, Vol. 67. Cambridge, MA.

IRISH, JOEL D.
1997 Characteristic High- and Low-Frequency Dental Traits in Sub-Saharan African Populations. *American Journal of Physical Anthropology*, 102:455–467.

LAROCHE, CHERYL J., AND MICHAEL L. BLAKEY
1997 Seizing Intellectual Power: The Dialogue at the New York African Burial Ground. *Historical Archaeology*, 31(3):84–106.

OFFICE OF PUBLIC EDUCATION AND INTERPRETATION
1995–1998 Monthly Reports. Office of Public Education and Interpretation, 6 World Trade Center, New York, NY. [Interim mailing address for OPEI offices is 201 Varick St., Room 1021, New York, NY 10014.]

OFORI-ANSA, KWAKU
1995 Identification and Validation of the Sankofa Symbol. *Update: Newsletter of the African Burial Ground and Five Points Archaeological Projects*, 1(8):3. (Office of Public Education and Interpretation, 6 World Trade Center, New York, NY.) [Interim mailing address for OPEI offices is 201 Varick St., Room 1021, New York, NY 10014.]

ORTNER, DONALD J.
1966 A Recent Occurrence of an African Tooth Type Mutilation in Florida. *American Journal of Physical Anthropology*, 25:177–180.

TURNER, CHRISTY G., II, CHRISTIAN R. NICHOL, AND G. RICHARD SCOTT
1991 Scoring Procedures for Key Morphological Traits of the Permanent Dentition: The Arizona State University Dental Anthropology System. In *Advances in Dental Anthropology*, Marc A. Kelley and Clark S. Larsen, editors, pp. 13–32. Wiley-Liss, New York, NY.

TURVEY, TIMOTHY A., KATHERINE W. L. VIG, AND RAYMOND J. FONSECA (EDITORS)
1996 *Facial Clefts and Craniosynostosis: Principles and Management*. W.B. Saunders, Philadelphia, PA.

WILLIS, W. BRUCE
1998 *The Adinkra Dictionary: A Visual Primer on the Language of Adinkra*. The Pyramid Complex, Washington, DC.

MARK E. MACK
DEPARTMENT OF ANTHROPOLOGY AND SOCIOLOGY
W. MONTAGUE COBB BIOLOGICAL ANTHROPOLOGY LABORATORY
ROOM 230, DOUGLASS HALL
2441 SIXTH ST. NW
HOWARD UNIVERSITY
WASHINGTON, DC 20059

MICHAEL L. BLAKEY
DEPARTMENT OF ANTHROPOLOGY
WASHINGTON HALL 103
THE COLLEGE OF WILLIAM AND MARY
WILLIAMSBURG, VA 23187

EDWARD L. BELL

The Historical Archaeology of Mortuary Behavior: Coffin Hardware from Uxbridge, Massachusetts

ABSTRACT

A popular cultural trend developed in late 18th- and 19th-century American mortuary practices. Called "the beautification of death," this Romantic movement idealized death and heaven through ideological, behavioral, and material transformations. The appearance of mass-produced coffin hardware in archaeological contexts throughout North America may be linked with this popular movement. Archaeological recovery of mass-produced coffin hardware and glass view plates, from cemeteries spanning a range of socioeconomic contexts, demonstrates that certain aspects of popular culture were so pervasive as to find expression, albeit dilute, at even the lowest level of society. The presence of decorated coffins at the Uxbridge Almshouse Burial Ground, as at other cemeteries associated with socioeconomically marginal groups, also suggests that archaeological interpretations that unquestioningly equate socioeconomic status directly to coffin embellishment need to be reviewed in light of socio-historical developments relating to mass consumption and popular culture in industrializing America.

Introduction

Cemetery investigations by historical archaeologists have brought to light an immediate and previously untapped source of data on American mortuary behavior. While historians have studied written accounts of funerals and have shown an interest in surviving examples of related material culture, archaeological evidence from the grave provides direct and compelling evidence of mortuary behavior among many social classes. Strides have also been made toward characterizing the nature of health, morbidity, and mortality among a range of social and economic groups (e.g., Lange and Handler 1985:19–22, 25–27; Reitz et al. 1985: 178–183; Rose 1985a; Parrington et al. 1986; Rose and Rathbun 1987; Wesolowsky 1988, 1989a, 1989b). The emphasis in this article, however, is on the larger socio-historical context of deathways shared among many American groups. Deathways encompasses the whole cultural system of mortuary behavior, involving emotion, ideology, symbolism, technology, and economy. Whether traditional, popular, innovative, or elite, deathways are the customs, rituals, etiquette, and material culture considered appropriate to the treatment and disposal of the dead (cf. Huntington and Metcalf 1979:17–20, 184–186).

The recovery of decorative coffin fittings from geographically and socially diverse archaeological contexts suggests a pervasive material shift that paralleled changes in popular attitudes toward death and burial in industrializing America. Similar forms of mass-produced coffin hardware have been reported throughout North America and are common at archaeological sites dating after the mid-19th century. This distribution testifies to developments in technology, marketing strategies, and transportation. More importantly, the ubiquity of coffin hardware indicates that similar material items were not only popular, but considered appropriate for the burial of the dead by many social and economic groups. The broad archaeological distribution of similar material items, specific to a mortuary context, not only suggests that a material shift had occurred in 19th-century America, but that these objects are the embodiment of a shared ideology.

A popular cultural trend, known as "the beautification of death," developed in the late 18th and 19th century. It was characterized by ritualized behavior and material objects that idealized death and heaven and prolonged the mourning and memorialization of the dead (Douglas 1975:56; Jackson 1977a:298; Stannard 1979:44; Farrell 1980:4–5; Pike and Armstrong 1980:16). Nevertheless, broad patterns of mortuary behavior, such as the beautification of death outlined by social historians, tend to exclude the interesting and significant differences in deathways of socially marginal classes and other divergent groups. Historical research that does address deathways out of the mainstream of American society is wanting for details in the few documentary sources available (Riis 1890: 177; Hoffman 1919:27, 41; Kleinberg 1977:202,

204–205; Buckley 1980:123; Ames 1981:651; Goodwin 1981; Clark 1987; Bell 1987:61–69). Archaeologically recovered mortuary assemblages can provide information, lacking in documentary history, on the deathways of many social and economic groups. Research on the Uxbridge Almshouse Burial Ground, for example, characterized the burial practices associated with a socially and economically marginal group dependent on political structures for economic relief (Elia and Wesolowsky 1989).

Archaeological investigations at historical American cemeteries, focused on traditional death practices among ethnic or economic groups, often fail to recognize the broad impact of popular culture that shaped specific material expressions of mortuary behavior. Mortuary and other behavioral phenomena are often described in terms of discrete, well-defined, and steadfastly maintained ethnic or economic boundaries. Such models often lack the means to show how groups interacted with, participated in, and contributed to larger cultural traditions. By viewing archaeological assemblages in the socio-historical context of 19th-century American mortuary behavior, archaeologists are uniquely able to define the parameters of popular culture of that era within the sphere of traditional deathways practiced by particular social or economic groups.

Mass-produced coffin hardware has been interpreted by historical archaeologists as an indication of socioeconomic rank (cf. Thomas et al. 1977: 410–417; Woodall 1983:17–19; Hacker-Norton and Trinkley 1984:51; Trinkley and Hacker-Norton 1984:13–15; Rose and Santeford 1985b: 135–136, 1985c:156; Bell 1987:15–18, 1989: 340–343; Parrington 1987:57–58; Owsley et al. 1988:90). Drawing from a common disciplinary background in prehistoric archaeology and anthropology, historical archaeologists have viewed coffin hardware as analogous to grave goods in preindustrial cultures. Variable mortuary assemblages are interpreted as evidence of differential rank. Mass-produced and mass-marketed coffin hardware, however, was inexpensive. It was utilized by many socioeconomic classes and not limited to middle-class or upper-class burials. The presence of coffin hardware at sites used to bury nutritionally deficient, physically stressed, low-status groups emphasizes the unsatisfactory and inconsistent conclusions that have been brought forward regarding coffin hardware as an unequivocal indication of high rank.

The beautification of death, an historical paradigm that might be considered equivalent to an archaeological horizon (Willey and Phillips 1958: 32–33), effectively summarizes a large-scale cultural trend. When regarded as an archaeological horizon, the beautification of death is reflected materially in the use of decorative, mass-produced coffin hardware. The interpretation of mass-produced coffin hardware as material evidence of the beautification of death is advantageous since it may serve as a point of departure for the archaeological study of a significant cultural trend.

Mass-produced objects may reflect an aspect of popular culture and function as a strategy of mediating or masking socioeconomic differences. Mass-produced objects are symbolic of apparent wealth; they serve to impart a sense of socioeconomic stature that was not otherwise attainable. Only the middle or upper classes could obtain actually expensive, hand-produced items (cf. Trachtenberg 1982:150; Williams 1982:92). The symbolic function of mass-produced objects, when cast against their role in the popular culture of 19th-century death practices, may account for the appearance of coffin hardware in the graves of low-status, 19th-century groups.

At the Uxbridge Almshouse Burial Ground, a 19th-century paupers' cemetery in southeastern Massachusetts, the recovery of decorative, mass-produced coffin hardware was initially viewed as an anomaly. No such decorative objects were expected at a paupers' cemetery containing the remains of people from the lowest social and economic class. Interpreting the variable mortuary assemblages at the Uxbridge site as a function of differential socioeconomic rank was considered unproductive, given the absolute poverty of the Uxbridge paupers. Interpretations of common coffin accouterments as culturally significant of rank obscure the real nature of socioeconomic disparity at cemeteries used by or for low-status people.

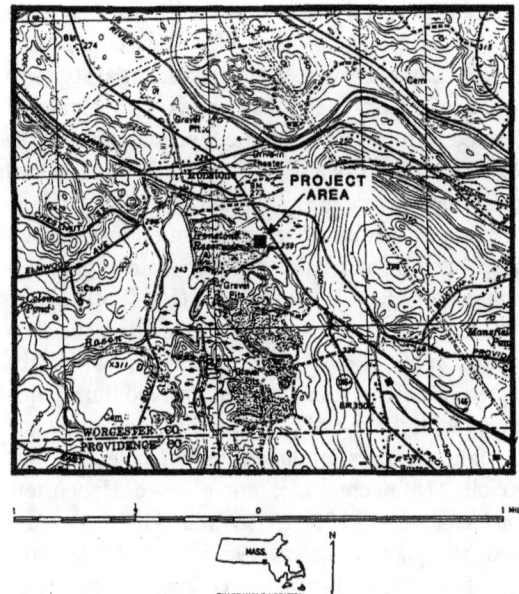

FIGURE 1. Location of the Uxbridge Almshouse Burial Ground (after United States Geological Survey [Blackstone, Massachusetts, Quadrangle] 1979).

Research into 19th-century mortuary behavior provided a context within which to understand the small sample of decorative, mass-produced coffin hardware and glass view plates from Uxbridge as evidence of a larger cultural trend related to the behavioral and material transformation of a way of life and death.

The opportunity for research, excavation, and analyses of materials recovered from the Uxbridge Almshouse Burial Ground was provided by the rediscovery of the site within the proposed right-of-way for the relocation of Route 146 through southeastern Massachusetts (Figure 1). The highway project was carried out by the Massachusetts Department of Public Works, with additional funding from the Federal Highway Administration. Under the direction of Ricardo J. Elia, the Office of Public Archaeology at Boston University excavated the Uxbridge site in 1985. Elia (1986, 1988, 1989a:1–15) has documented the background of the project in greater detail, and the research results are more fully described in the final report of investigations (Elia and Wesolowsky 1989).

Mortuary Behavior in 19th-Century America

A popular ideology, called the beautification of death, began in the late 18th century (cf. Douglas 1975:65–68; Jackson 1977b:5; Pike and Armstrong 1980:16). A related movement occurred in England and on the Continent (Jones 1967; Morley 1971; Gittings 1984). Closely aligned with the Romantic movement, the beautification of death was essentially an ideational shift accompanied by social and material transformations. Late 18th- and 19th-century Americans, unlike their 17th- and early to mid-18th-century counterparts, viewed death and heaven in a sentimental light (Douglas 1975:56; Jackson 1977a:298; Stannard 1979:44; Farrell 1980:4–5; Pike and Armstrong 1980:16). The movement was manifest in the creation of bucolic, landscaped cemeteries, such as Mt. Auburn Cemetery in Cambridge, Massachusetts, and Greenwood Cemetery in Brooklyn, New York (French 1975; Stannard 1979). Perhaps the best-known social expression of the beautification of death was the practice of high mourning among middle-class Victorians. Public mourning became protracted and increasingly formalized and expensive, reaching a pinnacle of ostentation toward the close of the 19th century. By the time this lugubrious period was on the decline (Farrell 1980:5), funeral reform societies began to appear (e.g., Hoffman 1919:26, 41).

The history of funeral directing describes the emergence of a full-time specialist from more generalized occupations. Death and burial involved not only friends and family, but also a number of skilled individuals. Among these were cabinetmakers (who made coffins); "layers out of the dead" (often women who prepared corpses for viewing and burial); sextons (who oversaw more public aspects of funeral ritual, such as supplying coffins and appropriate accouterments, tolling church bells, digging graves, and presiding over funerals and interment); and municipal officers such as coroners, superintendents of burial grounds, and registrars of deaths. Many of these tasks were often carried out by a single person (Habenstein and Lamers 1955: 227–249). The creation of the professional funeral director in the late 19th century capitalized on widely held public perceptions concerning faith in science, technology, and the need for specialized knowledge. The late 19th- and 20th-century popularity of embalming and the relocation of the dead from the family parlor to the funeral parlor reflected "an increased concern for appearances in a consumer culture, a strong and widely publicized sanitary movement, surgical pretensions in an age of respected medicine, [and] a privitization of the home" (Farrell 1980:7).

While the emergence of the funeral directing profession was in many ways responsible for fostering the elaborate nature of funerals into the late 19th century and beyond, the artifacts associated with late 18th- and 19th-century deathways provide evidence of change in popular attitudes toward death. The beautification of death appeared materially in the use of elaborate mourning clothes, decorative mortuary art, ornamental burial containers, and ornate memorial statuary. During this period, mortuary artifacts incorporated classical, biblical, natural, and Romantic motifs, such as seraphs, urns, draped columns, lambs, symbolic flora such as willows, oaks, and evergreens, and deeply grieving mourners. Such motifs departed from earlier depictions of skeletons brandishing scythes or holding hourglasses, as seen on gravestones, mourning rings, palls, and printed broadsides from the 17th and 18th centuries. Spoons and gloves given as funerary tokens in the 17th and 18th centuries also suggest antecedents to the profusion of late 18th- and 19th-century mortuary artifacts, but these earlier death-related artifacts lack the characteristic "melancholy beauty" (Farrell 1980:34) of the material culture associated with the beautification of death (cf. Concord Antiquarian Society 1967; Deetz and Dethlefsen 1967; Earle 1973:365; Schorsch 1976; Pike and Armstrong 1980; Fairbanks and Trent 1982:313–324).

The beautification of death created a social context for the production of funeral-related material culture. The combined forces of mass production and the professionalization of the funeral director eventually gave rise to a fully commercialized funeral industry. Mass-produced coffin hardware, including coffin handles, hinges, plaques, lid fasteners, lid lifters, and tacks, were made specifically for use on coffins. The ornate styles of mass-produced coffin hardware paralleled the sentimental styles so typical of other objects associated with 19th-century mourning. The symbolic representation of the beautification of death inherent in mass-produced coffin hardware can be appreciated in contrast to the plain or restrained styles common to hand-finished handles and plaques made before the mid-19th century (e.g., Fellows n.d. [ca. 1850]). Handles, nameplates or escutcheons, and tacks used on coffins were not 19th-century innovations, but the degree of coffin embellishment peaked during that period with the use of both highly ornamented and specialized, mass-produced items (for earlier, especially 18th-century examples, see Habenstein and Lamers 1955:255–257; Watkins 1962:31; Concord Antiquarian Society 1967; Noël Hume 1969: 158; Bell 1987:54–55). In contrast to the 18th-century use of generalized hardware forms on coffins (i.e., tacks or hinges that would not be out of place on household furniture), 19th-century coffin builders used hinges, tacks, and other fittings that were specifically designed to be used in a mortuary context.

The ubiquity of mass-produced coffin hardware was the result of technological improvements in metal-working machinery that essentially replaced hand finishing; the appearance of inexpensive, malleable alloys such as white metal (also called paktong or German silver) and Britannia metal made decorative coffin hardware affordable to a larger market (Smith 1974:23–25). Illustrated merchandising or trade catalogues, which seem to have first appeared in the United States around the middle of the 19th century (Nelson 1980:iii–ix; McKinstry 1984:xi), influenced popular tastes in hardware styles. Improvements in transportation throughout the 19th century account for the wide geographical distribution of the objects. These transformations in technology, marketing, and transportation can only be fully understood, however, when viewed in the context of cultural changes that define the beautification of death. Stylistically and functionally, mass-produced coffin hardware was clearly a material aspect of the beautification of death. Molded in symbolic and sentimental decorative motifs and culturally specific for a mortuary context, mass-produced coffin hardware perpetuated the identity of the deceased with nameplates and more generic plaques; embellished burial containers; and provided a means to present and view the deceased by enabling hinged coffin lid sections to be lifted or removed. Memorialization and display of the dead in a beautified manner, such as in a decorative coffin, are characteristic of the beautification of death. See Pike (1980:642) for a useful typology.

The trend toward more decorative coffins can also be seen in the use of plate glass on coffin lids, through which the face of the deceased could be viewed. While this particular innovation was used as early as 1848 (Habenstein and Lamers 1955: 263, cited in Rose and Santeford 1985a:68), glass view plates are commonly found at cemeteries dating after the mid-19th century. Glass view plates may simply reflect efforts to ornament burial containers, or their use may be related to concerns about disease, fear of apparent death, or the increasing importance placed on display of the dead (Farrell 1980:7; Ariès 1982:397–404; Mytum 1989:288). Unlike the specially designed coffin hardware, mass-produced by machine, rectangular glass view plates could be fashioned by local coffin makers from windowpane stock. Oval or trapezoidal view plates recovered from some cemeteries may be more specialized forms.

Whether brought about through the persuasion of enthusiastic funeral directors or less formally by family members who saw mass-produced coffin trimmings in merchandising catalogs at the local general store, material aspects of the beautification of death became widely popular. Evidence for the popularity of mass-produced coffin hardware and glass view plates is found in their wide geographical distribution.

Similar styles of coffin hardware have been found at archaeological sites across the United States, including sites in Massachusetts (Faulkner et al. 1978:20–22; Bell 1987:106–137, 1989:351–370), New York (Olafson 1985; Spencer J. Turkel 1986, pers. comm.), Pennsylvania (Parrington 1984:10), Maryland (Rhodes 1987:7–8), Delaware (Payne and Thomas 1988:18), North Carolina (Woodall 1983:8, 15), South Carolina (Combes 1974:54; South 1979:19, 23; Hacker-Norton and Trinkley 1984; Trinkley and Hacker-Norton 1984: 9–12; Orser et al. 1987, 1:398–413), Georgia (Thomas et al. 1977:416–417; Blakely and Beck 1982:192, 202; Garrow 1987), Arkansas (Rose 1985b), Louisiana (Owsley et al. 1988:29, 31, 38, 83), Texas (Fox 1984:40, 43; Taylor et al. 1986), Oklahoma (Ferguson 1983:11, 15), California (Leonardi 1986; Costello and Walker 1987:9, 14–15), Oregon (Brauner and Jenkins 1980:144–152, passim), and Washington (Wegars et al. 1983). Coffin glass view plates, in oval, trapezoidal, and rectangular shapes, have been recovered throughout the United States and in Canada (Combes 1974:54; Brauner and Jenkins 1980:30, 31, 148; Finnigan 1981:41, 45; McReynolds 1981:43–44, 50–51; Blakely and Beck 1982:188, 202; Parrington 1984:13; Rose and Santeford 1985a:58, 90, 114; Rose 1985b:189–193; Taylor et al. 1986: 41, 45; Bell 1987:128–129, 1989:368; Orser et al. 1987, 3:93–106; Payne and Thomas 1988:17, 18, 21). Whether or not glass view plates were simply decorative coffin features, they were popular objects, as shown by their archaeological distribution. The rectangular examples recovered from Uxbridge and from Saskatchewan (Finnigan 1981, James T. Finnigan 1986, pers. comm.) do not appear to be mass-produced, per se, but rather were possibly cut from windowpane stock and fitted by the coffin maker.

The context of late 18th- and 19th-century mortuary behavior has been linked to the advent of an industrialized way of life. ''The nineteenth century brought dramatic change and extreme social stress. Struggling to live in an uncertain world, Americans retreated. They idealized and sanctified the home, the family, and the women who formed them'' (Pike and Armstrong 1980:16; cf. Morley 1971:7). Similarly, death and heaven were idealized in popular literature. Heaven ''became a domesticated haven, a place where all would be welcomed home'' (Pike and Armstrong 1980:17; cf. Douglas 1975:65–68; Stannard 1979:44,46; Farrell 1980:5; Ames 1981:653). The transformation was linked closely with larger social changes:

While Heaven became a more comfortable place, earth had become a less comfortable one. The trauma of uncertainty and change affected the lives of all Americans in the nineteenth century. In the practice of increasingly ritualized mourning customs, they found themselves able to express not only their grief, but their moral and spiritual values as well (Pike and Armstrong 1980:17).

Morley (1971) traced the appearance of the beautification of death to the interplay of industrialization and socioeconomic upheaval:

> The Industrial Revolution brought wealth and death; impartiality in their distribution was not observed.
>
> . . . A new rural and urban middle class arose, accompanied by a new class of rural and urban poor.
>
> . . . An intense social competition was generated . . . [and] the urge towards visible display found ever more opulent expression.
>
> . . . [T]o secure the double crown of respectability in life, and salvation after it, became the aim of the typical Victorian.
>
> . . . [I]t was thought as necessary to maintain the standards of one's class in death as in life, and, if possible, even to use death as a means of further social advancement. This feeling was present with the lowest classes (Morley 1971:10–11).

Morley (1971:11) went on to give examples of these common concerns among England's poor, saving money to ensure against the disgrace of a pauper's grave. A similar anecdote can be related from Easton, Massachusetts (Chaffin 1886:449). To retain social respectability among the living, it was necessary to avoid the mortification of burial at public expense. Morley (1971:10) observed that "the connexion between death and poverty was close . . . [P]overty made it necessary to portray death as the only way to taste even the basic necessities of life."

In selecting decorative, sentimental trappings that represented the beautification of death, late 18th- and 19th-century Americans assimilated certain aspects of this popular movement into their traditional death practices. By transforming their way of death, the new ideology and material culture of the beautification of death allowed 19th-century Americans to find comfort in the loss of a way of life as it helped to overcome the grief naturally associated with the loss of the living. Traditional death practices reinforced group cohesiveness; funerals helped mend the social fabric torn by the loss of group members (cf. Goody 1975; Stannard 1975; Huntington and Metcalf 1979; Yentsch 1981; Brooke 1988:464). When controlled by authority, such as a town or the state, funeral ritual could be exclusionary, seeking to set off one group from another by reserving certain aspects of ritual for the elite. The selective interweaving of popular innovations in mortuary paraphernalia with long-standing, traditional rituals was one way that social groups participated in popular culture without relinquishing group identity. Similar responses in other social events contributed to a pluralistic American culture (cf. Burke 1978:23–64; St. George 1988:11).

"Fit, Proper and Rational": Poverty, Death, and Burial in Uxbridge, Massachusetts

The almshouse system was viewed by the Uxbridge Town Selectmen as a humanitarian effort to provide care for the poor and as a pragmatic means of supporting the poor at the lowest possible cost. One Uxbridge committee concluded in 1870 that "it seems fit, proper and rational, for the Town to have an Asylum for the Poor, a place for the Needy and destitute, it is a humane and laudable act, on the part of the Town" (Uxbridge, Town of, [1848–1870]:456). This passage captures much of the philosophy relating to the mortuary treatment of the Uxbridge paupers during the time that the burial ground was in use (1831–1872): the burial of the poor took place in a context that was "fit, proper and rational" in the eyes of the Overseers of the Poor, commensurate with the poor's marginal status. Poor relief in Uxbridge was shaped by the limitations of the state system of municipal reimbursement, as well as by what the town was willing to pay.

The structure of the poor relief system in Uxbridge, as in other 19th-century American communities, was influenced by many views, sometimes complementary, sometimes contradictory. The broad if somewhat vague notions of Christian charity or Yankee frugality, for example, were both present when decisions were made on how to provide for the "worthy" poor. In Uxbridge, the separation of the needy and the unfortunate into "worthy" and "unworthy" paupers related to the nature of economic support the town was willing to provide (Cook 1988:4–5, 1989:71–76) and mirrors the increasing segmentation of class in 19th-century America. Previous to the establishment of the almshouse, Uxbridge was able to support its poor by providing food, fuel, rent, and labor to residents who required assistance; people without housing were boarded with town families.

The industrialization of the Blackstone River Valley, in which Uxbridge is located, shifted the economic base from a labor, credit, and barter system to one based on labor and cash. Other aspects of regional industrialization played a role in the increasing demand for economic relief among many segments of the community. Cook (1989: 60–64) demonstrated that the development of the almshouse in Uxbridge followed the establishment of similar institutions across the Commonwealth and in other places, where a growing population of the poor put a strain on existing structures of support. The creation of a "poor farm," "town farm," or "poor house," terms by which the Uxbridge Alsmhouse was also known (Elia 1989a: 15), perhaps also embodied certain Romantic values: the idealization of the home and the therapeutic benefits of work at a rural farm while living with other inmates and the superintendent as in a fictive family (Cook 1989:81–82). A centralized institution allowed more efficient control over the unworthy poor and their attendant expenses. Only the worthy poor continued to receive assistance away from the town farm (Cook 1988:5). The Uxbridge Almshouse, like many Massachusetts almshouses, was located away from the town center, near the town's legal boundary (Cook 1989:64; Ricardo J. Elia 1987, pers. comm.). The unworthy poor were institutionalized, kept literally at the margins of town society, and symbolically excluded at their death by burial in a pauper's grave.

Pauper burials were meant to provide decent, Christian interments for those who could not afford them (Hoffman 1919:23–26). According to Hoffman (1919:20) in his treatise on *Pauper Burials and the Interment of the Dead in Large Cities,* pauper burials were simply "interment[s] at public expense" and were generally but not exclusively characterized by minimal funerary treatment (see Elliot 1858:205–211; Earle 1977:34; Bell 1987: 61–69). Interments were often made in plain and simple wooden coffins, brought in a wagon rather than in a hearse to sections of cemeteries set aside for paupers or buried in "potters' fields" in urban areas. The locations of paupers' graves were often indicated by simple markers such as those made of wood (e.g., Hoffman 1919:47–51; Wigginton 1973:318; Leveillee et al. 1981:11; Jordan 1982: 41–43). Pauper burial grounds, wrote Ames (1981:651), were "symbolic and visible manifestations of hierarchical social order." Kleinberg (1977:203) concurred that areas set aside in cemeteries for the burial of paupers "reflected and perpetuated class differences by relegating the poor to undesirable sections and by denying to paupers the right to memorial of their death or resting place."

Paupers who were interred at the Uxbridge Almshouse Burial Ground came from disparate backgrounds. Wesolowsky's (1988, 1989a, 1989b) analyses indicated the presence of at least two blacks and one Native American among the mostly white majority. The cemetery population is an institutional sample, represented by a bimodal distribution of elderly and infirm adults and pre-adolescent children and infants. People who died destitute at the almshouse, and likely other people (such as an unidentified vagrant) who could not pay the costs associated with burial, were interred by the Town of Uxbridge (Cook 1989:75).

The economic and humanitarian rationale of Uxbridge's poor relief system, to provide care for the poor at the lowest possible cost, is embodied in the minimal funerary treatment of paupers. The mention of watching, washing, and dressing the dead in town documents identifies traditional mortuary activities that were carried out in certain cases. Tantalizingly short references found by Cook (1989:106; see Bell 1987:93–95) to "digging graves" and "attending funerals" may have summed up what were possibly quite perfunctory graveside ceremonies.

Burial containers for the poor were purchased by

the town, mostly from a man who also made and repaired furniture for the almshouse (Uxbridge, Town of, 1841–1868:18 February 1847, 20 February 1852). These Selectmen's records indicate that coffin prices varied from a low of less than $2.00 in 1845 (the figure given was for "dig[g]ing [a] grave & [for] a box") to a high of $6.00 in 1867. The usual figure between 1841 and the 1860s was $4.50. (The rise of coffin prices in the mid-1860s was probably the result of widespread economic change during and after the Civil War.) Minor differences in coffin prices evident in town records may also reflect variations in coffin size or style, may indicate discounts given on volume purchases, or may be related to price variations that could be expected when different purveyors supplied coffins to the town. The fact that the person who provided most of the coffins for the town also supplied and repaired furniture for the almshouse, as well as Hansen's (1989:489) identification of wood used for coffin construction, strongly suggests that the chestnut, pine, and yellow poplar coffins were made locally.

Considering the economic stricture imposed by Uxbridge and the limited level of reimbursement set by the Commonwealth in the care and burial of the poor (Cook 1988:4–5, 1989:71–76), it comes as no surprise that paupers were generally interred at the site in simple, inexpensive coffins. In the austere context of pauper burials, the more ostentatious expressions of the beautification of death would have, in fact, been considered a ludicrous, if lamentable, situation (Elliot 1858:209–211).

The Archaeological Evidence of Burial in Uxbridge

Of the 31 graves at the Uxbridge site, 16 were marked with granite quarry spalls or unmodified fieldstone. The permanent commemoration of individuals was not generally followed at this burial ground since a little under half of the graves appear to have been unmarked, and all but one of the graves were marked anonymously. Only one traditional headstone, carved from white limestone,

was present at the site (Elia 1988:11–14, 1989b: 34–36).

The range of variation in the artifacts recovered from the graves at the Uxbridge site is remarkable only for the general lack of highly ornamented burial containers. By and large, the coffins provided for the pauper burials at Uxbridge were quite plain. With the exception of two rectangular burial containers, the graves contained coffins that were hexagonal or roughly so (Figure 2). While in a majority of cases the shape of the container was apparent to excavators, smaller details eluded observation. Deterioration of the coffin wood obliterated carpentry details, save for the fortuitous preservation of a single coffin lid fragment with a beveled edge. Consequently, the hardware from the graves provided most of the data for an analysis of burial practices at the site.

The mortuary assemblages from 17 of the graves (55%) consisted simply of wooden coffin fragments, a handful of cut nails (and sometimes a half dozen or fewer screws), and often one or two common brass hinges (Figure 3d-g). Fourteen graves (45%) contained stylistically specialized, or otherwise unusual, hardware fittings. These items included mass-produced coffin hardware, such as white metal coffin hinges and white metal coffin lid screws and tacks molded in complex designs; white metal coffin hardware was found in 12 graves or nearly 39 percent of the graves (Graves 1, 2, 3, 4, 5, 11, 14, 16, 17, 20, 28, and 30; see Figure 2). Other artifacts found at the site included two rectangular glass view plates (from Graves 1 and 12); five brass tacks (from Grave 27); a brass hook-and-eye fastener (from Grave 12); and five coffin fabric-lining (or covering) tacks, one of white metal (Grave 2), three possible lining tacks of iron or alloy (Graves 12 and 20), and one possible lining tack made of copper or alloy (Grave 4). Straight pins and clothing fasteners were found at the site, as were a few brick fragments and small sherds of refined white earthenware and redware.

The cast plate glass used to fashion coffin view plates and the hardware recovered during excavation were commonly available at general merchandise stores (cf. Clark 1964:228–229; Hacker-Norton and Trinkley 1984). Hacker-Norton and

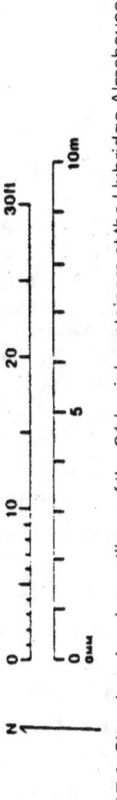

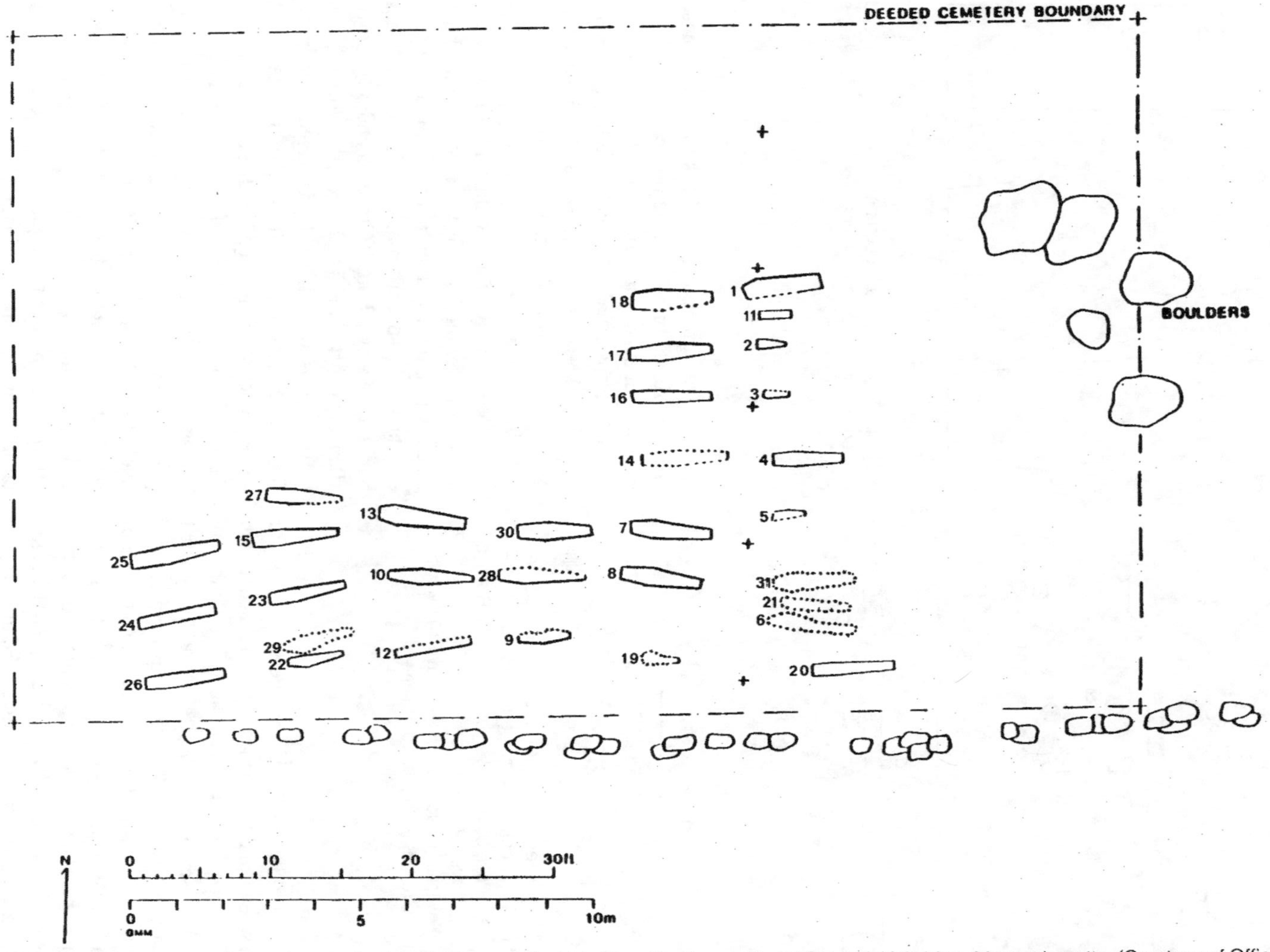

FIGURE 2. Site plan showing outlines of the 31 burial containers at the Uxbridge Almshouse Burial Ground, Uxbridge, Massachusetts. (Courtesy of Office of Public Archaeology, Boston University.)

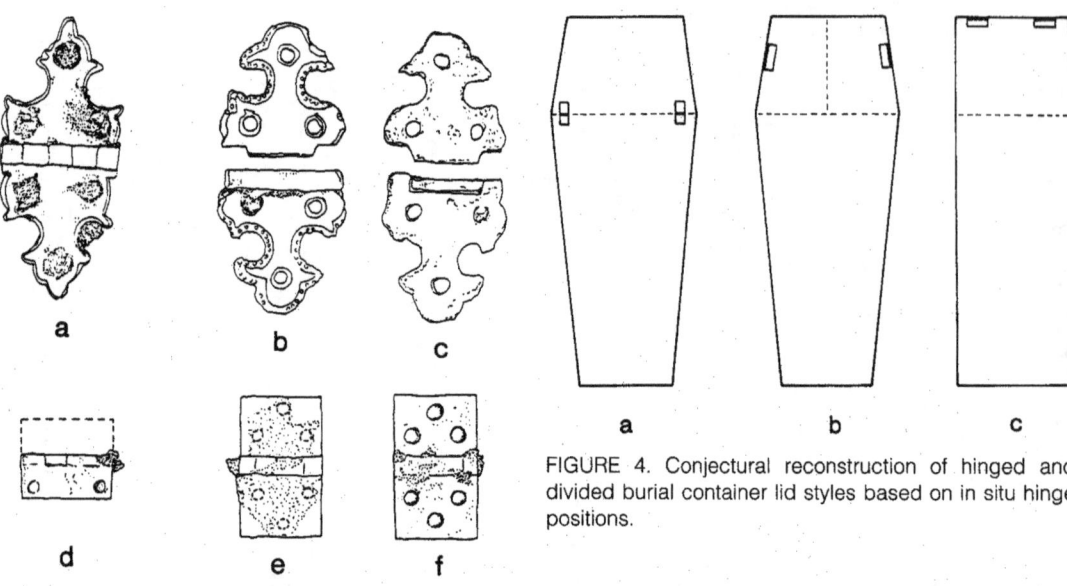

FIGURE 4. Conjectural reconstruction of hinged and divided burial container lid styles based on in situ hinge positions.

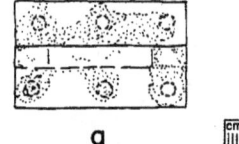

FIGURE 3. Hinge styles recovered at Uxbridge. White metal hinges: a, coffin butt hinge (Grave 1); b-c, dowel-type hinge (Grave 30) [b, obverse; c, reverse]. Brass butt hinges: d, Grave 12 (this example is rusted closed); e, Grave 19 (with iron wood screws); f, Grave 10 (with brass brads); g, Grave 8 (with iron wood screws).

Trinkley (1984:35–37) list wholesale prices for coffin screws and tacks at less than half a cent each (cf. Peck and Walter Manufacturing Company 1853:31; Orser et al. 1987, 1:413), probably what they cost in Uxbridge. The materials used for Uxbridge coffin construction were not expensive, but the cost of labor involved in building coffins is not known. The archaeologically recorded position of hinges suggests that at least three styles of hinged and divided coffin lids were made (Figure 4). One form of coffin lid opened up and forwards toward the feet (Figure 4a); another kind opened like a pair of window shutters (Figure 4b); a third type of lid

seems to have opened up and back toward the head of the coffin (Figure 4c). Two of these forms (Figure 4a-b) are known historically from surviving examples, from patent models, and from depictions in 19th-century documents (Concord Antiquarian Society 1967:Catalogue No. 57; Jones 1967:75; Pike and Armstrong 1980:151).

A close scrutiny of the container fittings reveals that coffins for the Uxbridge poor were sometimes made with a limited attention to detail and a general lack of fine craftsmanship. Two coffin lids bore only a single hinge (Graves 8 and 30); Grave 10 had two different sized hinges; the slots of some coffin screws were severely damaged or stripped (Figure 6e); and, most telling, the articulation of some bodies strongly suggests that decedents were frequently provided with ill-fitting coffins. Wesolowsky (1989a:183) has suggested that "the practice may indicate that coffins were not custom-made to fit the individual, but rather more or less standard sizes were on hand; and if the coffin was a little too narrow for the late departed, a little effort on the part of those preparing the corpse for burial would resolve the matter."

None of the artifacts found with the burials contradicts the historical evidence that the burial ground was probably used between 1831 and 1872

(Cook 1989:58–60, 63–71; Elia 1989c:381–383); diagnostic features of grave markers, nails, wood screws, coffin hardware, clothing fasteners, and the few small ceramic sherds all indicate that the interments span the middle of the 19th century. Attempts to seriate the graves based on general manufacturing dates of these items proved unsuccessful, as the presence or absence of certain artifacts may have resulted from factors other than date of interment, e.g., the use of whatever hardware and coffins were on hand (cf. Habenstein and Lamers 1955:243–244; Hacker-Norton and Trinkley 1984:44, 48–50). White metal coffin hinges (Figures 3a-c and 5), in particular the styles recovered from Uxbridge, are depicted in hardware catalogues as early as 1861 to as late as 1904 (Sargent and Company 1861:107, 1866:129, 1869:155, 1871:277, 1904:46; Russell and Erwin Manufacturing Company 1865:332; Hawley Brothers Hardware Company 1884:409). Coffin screws and tacks (Figures 6 and 7), some identical to the Uxbridge examples, are described or illustrated in manufacturers' trade catalogues from as early as 1853 (Peck and Walter Manufacturing Company 1853:31) until at least 1877 (Hacker-Norton and Trinkley 1984:49–50). Since the styles of mass-produced coffin hardware recovered from Uxbridge appeared in the mid-19th century, only the burial containers manufactured after ca. 1850 would evidence such items. This factor, the *terminus post quem* of mass-produced coffin hardware, certainly modified the incidence of embellished coffins, given the limited temporal span of the Uxbridge series (ca. 1831–1872).

Among all the mortuary assemblages from the site, three graves (Graves 1, 12, and 30) contained the remains of more elaborate coffins. Cluster analyses run on the cemetery sample consistently singled out Graves 1, 12, and 30 for the above-average amount of coffin furniture. Coffin furniture from Grave 1 included two white metal hinges mounted onto a divided lid outfitted with a rectangular glass view plate. The coffin had 16 white metal coffin screws and 29 matching coffin tacks. The coffin from Grave 12 originally had two small brass hinges on a divided coffin lid with a rectangular glass view plate. The Grave 12 coffin also

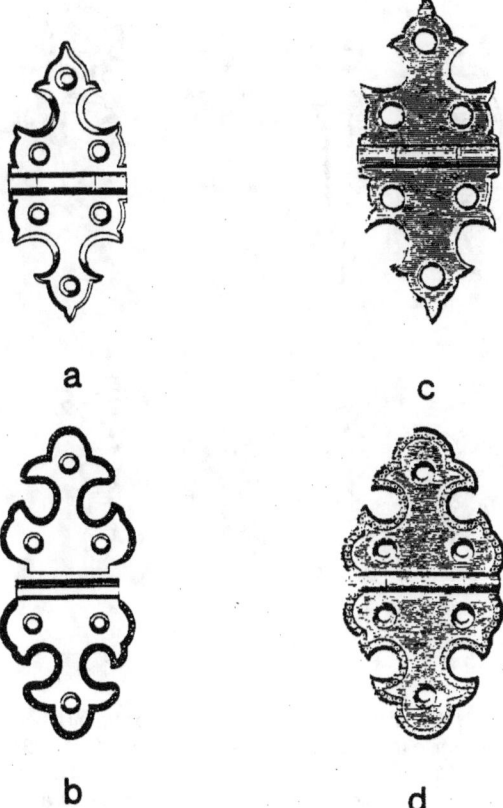

FIGURE 5. White metal coffin hinges, identical to Uxbridge forms, illustrated in 19th-century hardware catalogues (a-b, Russell and Erwin Manufacturing Company [1865:332]; c-d, Sargent and Company [1871:277]. Illustrations identical to c-d can also be seen in Sargent and Company [1866:129, 1869:155]. An illustration identical to d also appears in Hawley Brothers Hardware Company [1884:409] and in Sargent and Company [1904:366]).

had a brass hook-and-eye fastener. Ferrous tacks were possibly used to fasten a fabric lining or covering. Grave 30 contained a single white metal coffin hinge, six white metal coffin screws, and 42 matching coffin tacks. Wesolowsky's (1989a:183) observations of skeletal position for Graves 1, 12, and 30 did *not* indicate that the coffins for these individuals were noticeably ill-fitting. Such a circumstance might support the idea that the three more elaborate coffins were not simply available stock, but may have been specially commissioned

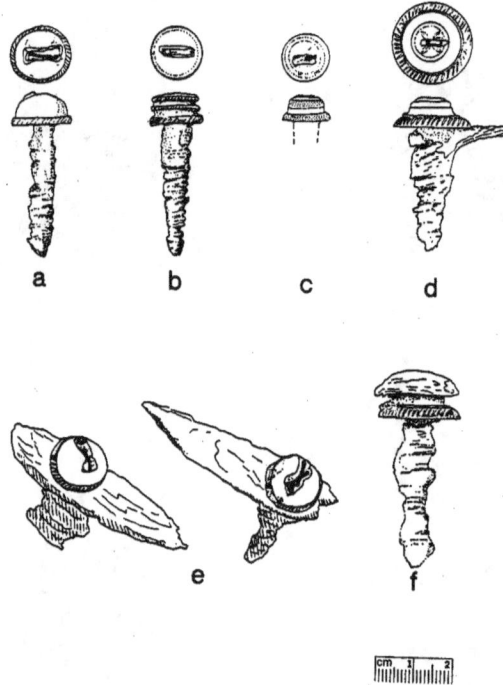

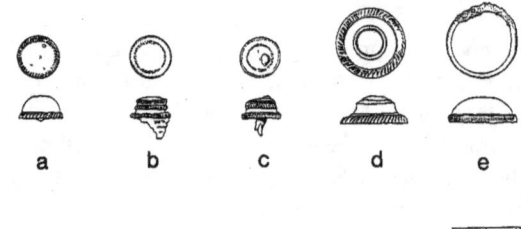

FIGURE 7. Coffin tack styles recovered at Uxbridge: a-d, white metal coffin tacks, plan and profile; e, brass tack, plan and profile. (a, Grave 1; b, Grave 11; c, Grave 2; d, Grave 30; e, Grave 27.)

FIGURE 6. White metal coffin screw styles from Uxbridge: a-d, white metal coffin screws, plan and profile (a, Grave 1; b, Grave 4; c, Grave 2; d, Grave 30); e, coffin screws with stripped slots (Grave 1); f, one example of a wood fragment adhering to the top of a coffin screw (Grave 30), possibly indicating the use of "grave arches" or planks placed laterally across the coffin lid to forestall collapse (cf. Blakely and Beck 1982:188).

for the individuals interred therein. Then again, the normal dimensions of the coffins may only have been fortuitous.

Attempts to interpret intrasite variation in coffin decoration as evidence for differential status positions relating to age, sex, and/or racial categories were unconvincing and subsequently abandoned when faced with a nexus of conundrums that complicate the observation of differentially embellished coffins. Speculation in this regard revolved around a concatenation of events that could have resulted in decedents being provided with whatever burial containers were on hand, and not provided with coffins that matched their (hypothetically) variable status. Considerations included the

practice of using ready-made, stockpiled coffins; the different forms of hardware available at a given time (a function of the vagaries of technological innovation, marketing, supply, and demand [cf. Hacker-Norton and Trinkley 1984:49–51]); the documentary evidence that the Town of Uxbridge paid little money for paupers' coffins; and that particular discrepancies in the relative cost of paupers' coffins may not be directly related to status or decoration but to competitive prices negotiated between coffin purveyors and the town. The lack of internal evidence of a relative chronology among the graves (Elia 1988:17, 1989c:384) further confounded attempts to link coffin embellishment with differential status, as plain coffins may simply date earlier than coffins with decorative hardware. Other variables studied and found to be independent of age, sex, race, and coffin embellishment included grave marking, type of grave markers, and grave location. In sum, interpretations of intrasite variation at Uxbridge were so excessively qualified as to be inconclusive. The socioeconomic baseline of poverty of the almshouse inmates had been established through documentary evidence and later reinforced by conclusions drawn from the osteological data, indicating an institutional sample, generally consisting of "abandoned or orphaned children and . . . the destitute elderly bereft of family" (Elia 1989c:382). Provided with this socioeconomic background of misfortune, the research was not compelled by a search for status among the artifacts from the site. It was clear that relative status in such an adverse socioeconomic situation is culturally meaningless. It was possible, however, to understand the nature of death and burial at the site (generally minimal mortuary treatment) and to characterize the presence of embellished coffins in the cemetery as an aspect of 19th-century popular culture.

Elliot (1858:217), in his sentimental novel *New England's Chattels: or, Life in the Northern Poorhouse*, lamented the conditions under which a pauper's burial took place, saying, "the whole thing was economically arranged." It is widely known that pauper burials were modest (e.g., Elliot 1858: 205–211; Chaffin 1886:449; Hoffman 1919:12, 23–26, 51; Kleinberg 1977:203; Ames 1981:651). The relative paucity of coffin embellishment observed at the Uxbridge site is generally consistent with what one would expect from a paupers' cemetery. The coffin remains studied archaeologically reinforce historical data on the Uxbridge poor relief system: paupers in Uxbridge were generally provided with minimally decent care at low cost. Certainly, economic considerations played a large role in the treatment of the Uxbridge poor, both during life and at death.

The evidence of embellished coffins, however stylistically attenuated, can be understood in the context of the beautification of death movement. The apparent anomaly of embellished coffins in the Uxbridge paupers' burial ground is understandable when the absolute low cost and popularity of mass-produced coffin hardware is taken into consideration. Rectangular glass view plates, white metal hardware, brass tacks, and the brass hook-and-eye were inexpensive and readily available items, and regardless of their low cost, were present on burial containers for the poor. The presence of coffin hardware, such as white metal coffin fittings and glass view plates, demonstrates that the carpenters responsible for coffin construction were familiar with popular, marketable, decorative styles. The presence of these items on 45 percent of the coffins from the Uxbridge Almshouse Burial Ground, then, does not suggest an elevated economic or social status—the sum of evidence from the site denotes just the opposite. The people buried at town expense were, at death, a socially and economically marginal class. Archaeological evidence was invaluable to understanding the material manifestations of death practices accorded a marginal group. The significance of the data, reflecting a popular trend in American death practices, was drawn out by reference to historical and archaeological studies of American deathways. The results of complex social, political, economic, and technological factors were manifest in the mortuary assemblages uncovered at the site.

Implications for Status-Based Approaches to Historical Mortuary Assemblages

Decorative coffin hardware at historical cemetery sites has been considered as evidence to infer rank or status of decedents (cf. Thomas et al. 1977: 410–417; Woodall 1983:17–19; Hacker-Norton and Trinkley 1984:51; Trinkley and Hacker-Norton 1984:13–15; Rose and Santeford 1985b: 135–136, 1985c:156; Bell 1987:15–18; Parrington 1987:57–58; Owsley et al. 1988:90). Nonetheless, such hardware at the Uxbridge site, a paupers' burial ground, suggests that status-oriented archaeological approaches to historical mortuary data need to be reexamined.

First, by comparing the Uxbridge assemblages to sites used by black Americans, the roles of ethnicity and economic or social marginality as they affected material expressions of mortuary behavior can be considered. Next, a comparison of Uxbridge with other marginal burial sites and with a cemetery used by wealthy whites shows that the inference of social status solely based on the presence or absence of coffin furniture may not agree with known historical socioeconomic contexts. The resulting analysis suggests that the unqualified use of status-based interpretive frames is not a tenable approach to surviving material vestiges of historical funerary behavior. Intrasite differences in coffin embellishment may not be solely related to economic factors; a particular grave assemblage may or may not include particular forms of coffin hardware or even any hardware at all, depending on the state of technological development at the time, the vagaries of marketing and supply, the nature of burial (e.g., by a public institution rather than by family, neighbors, or friends), and a host of other factors. Given the nexus of variables that should be considered at the site-level of analysis, status-based approaches alone are not highly productive means to draw out the complexity of mortuary behavior.

Comparisons with Black American Cemeteries

While a little under half of the burial containers at Uxbridge had some decorative elements, even the decorative elements from the three most elaborate coffins from Graves 1, 12, and 30 appear minimal compared to burial containers recovered from most other 19th-century cemeteries, especially those (e.g., Oakland, Cedar Grove, and Mount Pleasant cemeteries) used by blacks. Consider the elaborate coffin handles and oval glass view plates recovered from the Oakland Cemetery in Atlanta, Georgia (Dickens and Blakely 1979; Blakely and Beck 1982:192, 202), or the frequent appearance of coffin handles, engraved plaques, thumbscrews, and escutcheons (lid fasteners), and oval glass view plates at the Cedar Grove Cemetery in Lafayette County, Arkansas (Rose 1985b). The Mount Pleasant Cemetery (38CH778) in Charleston County, South Carolina, yielded ornate coffin handles, decorative thumbscrews, studs, escutcheons, seven stamped brass coffin plaques and a single engraved, tin-plated copper coffin plaque (Trinkley and Hacker-Norton 1984:6, 9, passim). Similar types and quantities of hardware and glass view plates were also noted at the Millwood Cemetery in Abbeville County, South Carolina, possibly used by both black and white tenant farmers (Orser et al. 1987, 1:398–414; 3:93–106). In addition to the assemblages from Oakland, Cedar Grove, Mount Pleasant, and Millwood, compared above, archaeological excavations at other North American and Caribbean black cemeteries have uncovered similarly complex mortuary assemblages, both with and without mass-produced hardware (e.g., Combes 1974; Lange and Handler 1985:25–27; Parrington and Wideman 1986).

In contrast to the mortuary assemblages from other cemeteries, the Uxbridge site contained no coffin handles and no engraved coffin plaques. The two glass view plates were rectangular, unlike the oval or trapezoidal forms found elsewhere. And, while it seems to be a function of the date of the Uxbridge burial ground (cf. Hacker-Norton and Trinkley 1984:46–47), the site contained neither the thumbscrews nor escutcheons common at sites dating to the end of the 19th century. Furthermore, the Uxbridge coffins display none of the ostentation of the high-quality, mass-produced caskets that appeared in the late 19th century (e.g., Crane, Breed & Company 1867; Columbus Coffin Company 1882; National Casket Company 1891).

Deathways, Ethnicity, and Economy

Excavations at black American cemeteries provide insight to mortuary practices and beliefs among some segments of the population. Because at least some of these groups shared a low socioeconomic status (relative to other segments of American society), it is likely that some other factor or factors besides status played a role in the choice of elaborate coffins among some 19th-century blacks, such as persistent traditional beliefs in appeasing peripatetic spirits (cf. Pollak-Eltz 1974; Thompson 1984:132–142; Bell 1987:61–69).

The strength of ethnicity in directing material and social aspects of burial practices (Goodwin 1981; Koch 1983; Parrington and Wideman 1986: 59; Clark 1987:394–395; Thomas 1988) may have had a deciding impact on the presence of ornate burial containers at some black cemeteries. Among others (e.g., Schuyler 1980:viii), Parrington and Wideman (1986:59) recognized the difficulty of "distinguish[ing] between the culture of ethnicity and the culture of poverty," especially as those two "cultures" relate to the material manifestation of burial practices. Their point is most relevant when attempting to differentiate between documentary and material vestiges of ethnic-specific burial practices and mortuary treatment based on economic exigencies. It may be specious, therefore, to compare the artifact assemblages from black cemeteries (presumably used by both the richer and the poorer from more or less *separate* social groups) with the Uxbridge assemblages (from a burial ground used by a municipality to bury only the poor from *many* social groups). Paupers, by definition, occupied the lowest position on the economic scale, but their ranks were made up of people drawn from many social corners.

The selection of decorative coffin trimmings by both mainstream and marginal groups communicates much about these people's perception of their place in the society and economy of 19th-century America. Williams (1982) suggested that mass consumption of mass-produced items, imitative of expensive objects, reinforced a need among some to display the appearance of wealth and to impart a tenuous sense of security. "The outpouring of new commodities . . . created a world where the consumer could possess images of wealth without actually having a large income" (Williams 1982:92; cf. Trachtenberg 1982:130). Williams (1982:58–66) illuminated how this consumer revolution, where most people could acquire objects symbolic of apparent wealth and belonging, actually accentuated the real social and economic distances between classes. Conspicuous and mass consumption are dialectical; while attempting to mask socioeconomic inequality, they reveal larger social conflicts (cf. Douglas and Isherwood 1979:12, 89; Trachtenberg 1982:150–153).

Archaeological reports of burial sites supposedly used exclusively for people on the fringes of society described even sparser burial containers than those recovered from Uxbridge (cf. Dailey et al. 1972; Dethlefsen et al. 1977; Dethlefsen and Demyttenaere 1977; Leveillee et al. 1977; Sargent 1977; Thomas et al. 1977:398–412; Burnston and Thomas 1981; Lutz and Rubertone 1982; Kelley 1984; Piper and Piper 1987; Brian Nagel 1989, pers. comm.). The presence of plain burial containers held together by simple fasteners at these sites is a complex issue, best approached through the site-specific historical contexts. As at Uxbridge, some of the interments at these sites probably predate the introduction of mass-produced hardware. The social contexts of these sites— sometimes difficult to characterize for lack of doc-

umentary information—are also important factors to consider. The Catoctin Furnace Cemetery (Burnston and Thomas 1981) and Cunningham Mound (Thomas et al. 1977) were probably used by or for slaves. Dailey et al. (1972), Piper and Piper (1987), and Kelley (1984) reported on cemeteries used or overseen by the military or the government. Testing at the Bridgewater, Massachusetts, Correctional Institution found areas used to reinter the remains of inmates at a facility that had various uses as an almshouse, an insane asylum, and a prison (Leveillee et al. 1977; Lutz and Rubertone 1982). Brian Nagel (1989, pers. comm.) discussed the excavation of over 300 interments at the Highland Park Cemetery in Rochester, New York, associated with an almshouse and asylum between 1837 and 1862. Only two coffins had brass hinges, and the broken glass in one grave could not be definitively interpreted as a view plate because of disturbance. Personal and religious items—a brass ring, two crucifixes, and two sets of rosary beads—are notably present. A report on limited excavations of burials associated with an almshouse in Montgomery County, Maryland, operating continuously since the late 18th century, indicated that "far more grave goods [including coffin hardware] and differential burial patterns were discovered than expected" (Rhodes 1987:8).

The nature of interment at these sites, reflecting in many cases burial overseen by institutions and not by family or friends, confounds any attempt to interpret the social status of the decedents simply from an observation of plain or embellished coffins. The critical relationship between the historical information of decedents unable to pay burial costs and the observation of minimal burial treatment illuminates the material correlates of poverty, exploitation, and social distance.

To complicate the issue of class and burial treatment, Parrington's reports on the 18th- and 19th-century interments of a group of wealthy white Philadelphians described "various burial techniques . . . from interment in plain wooden coffins with simple iron handles to coffins with metal liners and elaborate and ornate cases and handles" (Parrington 1984:14; see also Parrington 1987:61–62). Again, intrasite differences in coffin styles are related to the dates of interment (Parrington 1987: 62), and the presence of plain containers may also be a function of consumer choices not to purchase elaborate coffins. Perhaps secure in their social and economic positions, and reflecting their Protestant beliefs, members of the Old St. Paul's Episcopal Church may not have been inclined to display the appearance of wealth through ornate burial containers for their dead. As Parrington (1987:62) indicated, however, interment in vaults at Old St. Paul's was more expensive than burial in earth graves and considered to be more prestigious and sanitary.

While the quality or quantity of coffin decoration was often obviously a function of what those responsible were able and willing to pay, the embellishment, per se, of a coffin with fancy hardware does not necessarily correlate with prominent social or economic status of the interred individual. The presence or absence of coffin hardware in a particular grave is a function of a complex chain of events related to date of burial, technological innovation, marketing and supply, stylistic change, and consumer preference (cf. Hacker-Norton and Trinkley 1984:49–51). Intrasite mortuary variability can be approached with explicit reference to the specific socio-historical context of individual cemeteries and the general context of death and burial in historical America. Documents and other kinds of material evidence may complement comparisons of mortuary practices within and between cemeteries and among socioeconomic groups. Grave markers, for example, commemorating individuals or family groups at 19th-century cemeteries conspicuously display relative expenditures in their material and dimensions (Ames 1981; Clark 1987; McGuire 1988). Because grave markers are on display to a community far longer than coffins, the symbolic representation of differential status is more permanently communicated through grave markers than through extravagant burial containers.

Status-Based Interpretations of Historical Mortuary Assemblages

One aspect of recent archaeological investigations at historical cemeteries is the observation of subtle and interesting distinctions in coffin decoration. Hacker-Norton and Trinkley's (1984; Trinkley and Hacker-Norton 1984) influential research on this aspect of material culture persuaded historical archaeologists that formal aspects of coffin hardware represented a productive area of mortuary research. Garrow (1987), for example, seriated coffin hardware in Georgia, providing guidance for synchronic dating of cemeteries and suggestive information on diachronic change in stylistic preferences. Interpretive difficulties are posed, however, by the inference that qualitative or quantitative intrasite differences in coffin hardware may be directly related to the social or economic rank of interred individuals (cf. Thomas et al. 1977:410–417; Woodall 1983:17–19; Hacker-Norton and Trinkley 1984:51; Trinkley and Hacker-Norton 1984:13–15; Rose and Santeford 1985b:135–136, 1985c:156; Bell 1987:15–18; Parrington 1987:57–58; Owsley et al. 1988:90). The unqualified application of status-based interpretive frames to archaeological remains of complex, industrialized cultures is problematic (cf. Beaudry 1988), as many of the researchers just cited have realized, but some have not explicitly acknowledged. The advent of mass production, for example, blurred socioeconomic distinctions based on the possession and control of certain objects because previously expensive articles could be cheaply imitated and globally distributed (Trachtenberg 1982:150–153; Williams 1982:92).

Interpretive models to infer rank at prehistoric mortuary sites (e.g., Bartel 1982) possess only a highly restricted utility when applied in an analogous manner to mass-produced coffin hardware. Mass-produced, inexpensive coffin hardware does not seem analogous to status symbols or grave goods that marked high ranking interments at prehistoric sites. Status symbols in prehistoric mortuary contexts are generally regarded as "exotic material items" (Tainter 1978:120), requiring a great energy expenditure to acquire or produce, and presumably restricted to an elite faction. Traditional mortuary analyses by prehistorians are geared toward inferring rank differentiation, determining descent or affinity groups, characterizing social organization, and elucidating details of emic belief systems (Tainter 1978; Bartel 1982). Tainter (1978:121) was unsatisfied with the "extensive reliance archaeologists place on grave associations", and echoed Brown's (1971) call for more rigorous studies that place the description and explanation of mortuary assemblages within the larger context of mortuary behavior. Brown and Tainter's position on the value of a comprehensive archaeological approach to mortuary behavior is embraced in this analysis. The beautification of death, considered as an archaeological horizon, is particularly apposite to this interpretive vein. Exclusive attention to historical grave assemblages, disregarding the socio-historical context of death and burial, creates some of the same interpretive difficulties addressed by modern pioneers of archaeological mortuary study (see Brown 1971; Tainter 1978; Bartel 1982). Accordingly, rank-based approaches to historical mortuary sites merit reexamination.

Hacker-Norton and Trinkley (1984:51; Trinkley and Hacker-Norton 1984:13–15) suggested that the amount and cost of coffin hardware in a grave are directly related to the decedent's rank. While it is clear that Hacker-Norton and Trinkley were interested in quantifying intrasite mortuary variability, relating the observation to variable cost and linking relative expenditures to differential status (Trinkley and Hacker-Norton 1984:13–15), it is also true that their pioneering research offered a considerably more complex view of coffin hardware in the economic world of the late 19th- and early 20th-century South than their status-based approach suggested. Technological innovation, marketing, supply, and demand in rural communities affected the availability—and, hence, the archaeological representation—of coffin hardware (Hacker-Norton and Trinkley 1984:44). Parrington (1987:57–58), Rose and Santeford (1985b: 135–136, 1985c:156), and Thomas et al. (1977: 410–417) tempered their traditional mortuary analyses by explicitly recognizing that factors other than status (e.g., technological development and pooling group resources to meet burial expenses) can account for variable mortuary assemblages at historical American sites. Consumer preferences, ethnicity, and the institution or group responsible for burial are other mitigating factors

in the nature of coffin embellishment within and between sites. Some investigators (e.g., Woodall 1983:19; Bell 1987:57–58, 65; Owsley et al. 1988: 90) acknowledge the possibility of using elaborate burial containers or personal items interred with the deceased as some measure of status at 19th- or 20th-century sites, but turn to other sources for this information. For example, Bell (1987:15–26, 79–95) gleaned socioeconomic information from primary historical documents and secondary sources as a point of departure for interpretations relating to death and burial of a marginal class; Owsley et al. (1988) focused on variations in grave assemblages, not for identifying status, per se, but as a means to differentiate civilian and military burials; Woodall (1983:7, 17–19) proposed that the relative depth of meticulously dug grave pits, certainly representing considerably effort on the part of grave diggers working in the hard clay of the Carolina Piedmont, is positively correlated to the status of the interred when interpreted in a systemic framework of relative energy expenditure.

Physical evidence of nutritional inadequacy, trauma, and high mortality among 19th-century black American cemetery populations has been detailed using skeletal remains (Rose and Rathbun 1987) at some of the same sites where high rank of individuals has been inferred using coffin hardware. Such evidence accentuates the unsatisfying conclusions drawn from a reductive reliance on status-based models; as Thomas (1988:115) concluded in his overview of mortuary variability in 16th- and 17th-century Spanish Florida, "it is clear that simplistic categorizations such as 'high status' and 'low status' serve to obscure considerably more than they clarify." Lange and Handler (1985), Parrington et al. (1986), Rose (1985a), and Rose and Rathbun (1987) made critically important links between physical evidence from black cemeteries regarding nutrition, health, and mortality with the historical fact of exploitation and discrimination experienced by 19th-century black Americans. Relating these findings to surviving material vestiges of mortuary behavior shows that black Americans, along with other marginal social groups, actively participated in popular cultural traditions. The limited use of coffin hardware in adult graves by two early 20th-century Choctaw families in Oklahoma may be a case in point (Ferguson 1983:7, 11, 15). Even within communities struggling under social, economic, and physical stress, funeral ritual, shaped by popular culture, was used to distinguish highly regarded individuals at their deaths (cf. Bell 1987: 42, 61–68). That such efforts may have included the use of decorative coffin hardware, symbolic of apparent wealth, is likely. Yet, such practices among marginal classes underscore their desires to bridge the real socioeconomic distance between classes by relying on cheap but highly symbolic objects.

Advances in mass production and distribution of coffin fittings, the continuity of local coffin construction after the appearance of ready-made, mass-produced coffins, and consumer strategies (e.g., fraternal burial insurance) followed by different social classes could work alone or in tandem essentially to mask economic distinctions in coffin styles. Toward the end of the 19th century, some firms produced high-quality caskets and silver coffin trimmings that could, one supposes, enable those who wished to reinforce class distinctions to do so through ostentatious display of an expensive casket (Crane, Breed & Company 1867; Columbus Coffin Company 1882; National Casket Company 1891; Bell 1987:17, 42, 57, 63). While an expensive casket can function as conspicuous display, mass-produced coffin hardware was inexpensive and used in the burials of many low-status groups.

Hacker-Norton and Trinkley (1984:50–51) observed that by reducing the number of items on a coffin or using less-expensive hardware styles, coffins could retain a decorative, richer appearance but actually cost less. Such saving measures are one aspect of Hacker-Norton and Trinkley's (1984: 51) understanding that coffin hardware could be used to "denote 'apparent' status as well as 'real' status." Inexpensive coffin hardware, however, did not denote real socioeconomic status at all. Rather, like many mass-produced items, coffin hardware was embraced even by the lower socioeconomic classes in an effort to conceal their real socioeconomic disparity. In Douglas and Isherwood's (1979:11–12) perspective, poverty is not defined by a want or lack of goods, it is defined by a lack of social involvement: "goods are neutral, the issues are social." The profusion of goods created by mass production did not ameliorate socioeconomic distance between classes.

Instead of viewing archaeological assemblages from mortuary sites as directly equated with status, the surviving material evidence from 19th-century cemeteries provides richer interpretations when seen in light of popular changes in mortuary ritual. In the case of the Uxbridge Almshouse Burial Ground, this interpretive angle helped to explain the apparent anomaly of embellished coffins in a paupers' burial ground. The observation that similar material items related to mortuary behavior have been recovered from archaeological contexts throughout North America, coupled with what is known about deathways in 19th-century America, leads to the conclusion that some aspects of a popular movement regarding proper burial of the dead were shared, in various ways, among many social and economic groups. When cast against the technological and social transformations of 19th-century industrialization, mass production and mass consumption can be acknowledged, dialectically, as a means to mediate persistent socioeconomic disparity.

Conclusions

Coffin builders who used popular decorative elements were responding to changes taking place in American deathways, a transformation marked by the increasing commercialization of death-related paraphernalia. Decorative coffin hardware is a small but definite embodiment of the beautification of death, a major cultural phenomenon that had a profound effect on the context of death and burial among most social groups in 19th-century America.

Funerary treatment accorded to some paupers in Uxbridge was consistent with the humanitarian and pragmatic rationale for the support of the poor. Pauper burials were meant to provide minimal Christian burial rites for those who could not pay for them. Decisions by many levels of the town and state government, however, restricted the amount of money available to bury the poor. Unlike the deathways of other social groups, the Uxbridge paupers had no choice in the nature of their funeral rituals. The mortuary assemblages from the site reflect the minimal funerary treatment accorded a marginal group dependent on policial structures for economic relief. Such minimally decent treatment enabled the Town of Uxbridge symbolically and literally to exclude the dependent poor from the community, while reconciling Christian ethics and political mandates. While the town seemingly fulfilled its Christian duties by what it perceived to be "humane and laudable" treatment of the Uxbridge poor, treatment that was "fit, proper and rational," the minimal nature of the burials is a clear testimony of the status accorded the poor, a group that the town made no effort to remember and who were, in fact, forgotten (cf. Cook 1989:48–49; Elia 1989a:5–8).

The absence of any indications of extravagant preparations for burial and the lack of any efforts to memorialize individual deaths suggests that the better known, elaborate aspects of the beautification of death had a negligible role in the death practices associated with the Uxbridge poor. The Uxbridge Almshouse Burial Ground, with its rude markers of quarry waste and fieldstone, stood in stark contrast to the landscaped "rural" cemeteries that were veritable statuary gardens. The Uxbridge coffin builders only expressed their contact with popular culture in the few fittings and minor departures in coffin styles observed at the site.

In comparison to most archaeological grave assemblages at other cemeteries, the Uxbridge examples reinforce the historical conclusions that pauper burials in Uxbridge were minimal. Nonetheless, the presence of any coffin hardware at a paupers' burial ground emphasizes the problematic nature of archaeological inferences directly linking coffin hardware with socioeconomic status. Economic factors alone do not account for the presence of decorated coffins at Uxbridge or at other cemeteries used to inter low-status 19th-century Americans. Given the limitations of status-based approaches to historical mortuary data, less confidence should be placed on the reliability of mass-produced coffin hardware as an unequivocal indication of socioeconomic rank of interred individuals.

In applying a template of traditional archaeological mortuary analyses, originally formulated to discern rank and descent in preindustrial cultures, historical archaeologists must consider the larger historical and cultural context of death and burial in industrializing America. The application of status-based mortuary analyses seems to be confounded by the recognition that coffin hardware is not strictly analogous to grave goods in a prehistoric context. The concomitant development of mass production, mass marketing, and mass consumption, along with advances in distribution systems, allowed inexpensive, decorative coffin hardware to be used in the burials of the socially and economically marginal. As with other inexpensive, mass-produced objects, symbolic of apparent wealth, coffin hardware was embraced by socially disenfranchised groups to mask the real nature of socioeconomic distance between classes.

In tandem, historical and archaeological studies of mortuary behavior can explore traditional deathways among historical America's disparate groups, seeking out the effects of popular culture and mass consumption on behavior and taste. Historical mortuary sites represent a unique source of data on deathways and may provide the only detailed information about the influence of popular culture on American death practices along the social spectrum.

ACKNOWLEDGMENTS

Principals on the Uxbridge Almshouse Burial Ground project included Ricardo J. Elia (Principal Investigator), Al B. Wesolowsky (Physical Anthropologist), and Lauren J. Cook (Project Historian). Some of the research presented in this article was accomplished for the Office of Public Archaeology (OPA) at Boston University under contract with the Massachusetts Department of Public Works. The research benefited from communication among the author, the principals, and the many scholars who generously shared their interest in and knowledge of American death practices. The figures accompanying the article were provided by courtesy of the OPA. The author expresses his appreciation to the staff of the OPA and the Department of Archaeology, in particular Mary C. Beaudry and Ricardo J. Elia, for their guidance and support. Thoughtful comments by three reviewers clarified many points in the article. Responsibility for the interpretations presented here remains solely with the author.

REFERENCES

AMES, KENNETH L.
1981 Ideologies in Stone: Meanings in Victorian Gravestones. *Journal of Popular Culture* 14(4):641–656.

ARIÈS, PHILIPPE
1982 *The Hour of Our Death,* trans. Helen Weaver. Random House, New York.

BARTEL, BRAD
1982 A Historical Review of Ethnological and Archaeological Analyses of Mortuary Practice. *Journal of Anthropological Archaeology* 1(1):32–58.

BEAUDRY, MARY C.
1988 Introduction. In *Documentary Archaeology in the New World,* edited by Mary C. Beaudry, pp. 1–3. Cambridge University Press, Cambridge.

BELL, EDWARD L.
1987 The Historical Archaeology of Mortuary Behavior at a Nineteenth-Century Almshouse Burial Ground. Unpublished M.A. thesis, Department of Archaeology, Boston University, Boston.
1989 Artifacts from the Uxbridge Almshouse Burial Ground. In *Archaeological Excavations at the Uxbridge Almshouse Burial Ground in Uxbridge, Massachusetts,* edited by Ricardo J. Elia and Al B. Wesolowsky, pp. 337–378. Report of Investigations No. 76. Office of Public Archaeology, Boston University, Boston.

BLAKELY, ROBERT L., AND LANE A. BECK
1982 Bioarchaeology in the Urban Context. In *Archaeology of Urban America: The Search for Pattern and Process,* edited by Roy S. Dickens, Jr., pp. 175–207. Academic Press, New York.

BRAUNER, DAVID R., AND PAUL CHRISTY JENKINS
1980 *Archeological Recovery of Historic Burials within the Applegate Lake Project Area, Jackson County, Oregon.* Department of Anthropology, Oregon State University, Corvallis.

BROOKE, JOHN L.
1988 "For Honour and Civil Worship to Any Worthy Person": Burial, Baptism, and Community on the Massachusetts New Frontier, 1730–1790. In *Material Life in America, 1600–1860,* edited by Robert Blair St. George, pp. 463–485. Northeastern University Press, Boston.

BROWN, JAMES A.
1971 Introduction. In *Approaches to the Social Dimensions of Mortuary Practices,* edited by James A. Brown, pp. 1–5. Memoirs of the Society for American Archaeology No. 25. Society for American Archaeology.

BUCKLEY, P. G.
1980 Truly We Live in a Dying World: Mourning on Long Island. In *A Time to Mourn: Expressions of Grief in Nineteenth Century America,* edited by Martha V. Pike and Janice Gray Armstrong, pp. 107–124. Museums at Stony Brook, Stony Brook, New York.

BURKE, PETER
1978 *Popular Culture in Early Modern Europe.* Harper and Row, New York.

BURNSTON, SHARON ANN, AND RONALD A. THOMAS
1981 *Archaeological Data Recovery at Catoctin Furnace Cemetery, Frederick County, Maryland.* Mid-Atlantic Archaeological Research Associates, Newark, Delaware.

CHAFFIN, WILLIAM L.
1886 *History of the Town of Easton, Massachusetts.* John Wilson & Son, Cambridge, Massachusetts.

CLARK, LYNN
1987 Gravestones: Reflectors of Ethnicity or Class? In *Consumer Choice in Historical Archaeology,* edited by Suzanne M. Spencer-Wood, pp. 383–395. Plenum Press, New York.

CLARK, THOMAS D.
1964 *Pills, Petticoats and Plows: The Southern Country Store.* University of Oklahoma, Norman.

COLUMBUS COFFIN COMPANY
1882 *Illustrated Catalogue.* Columbus Coffin Co., Columbus, Ohio. [1984 facsimile edition (microfiche). In *Trade Catalogues at Winterthur,* compiled by E. Richard McKinstry, Item 618. Clearwater Publishing Co., New York.]

COMBES, JOHN D.
1974 Ethnography, Archaeology, and Burial Practices among Coastal South Carolina Blacks. *The Conference on Historic Site Archeology Papers, 1972* 7: 52–61. Columbia, South Carolina.

CONCORD ANTIQUARIAN SOCIETY
1967 *Memento Mori: Two Hundred Years of Funerary Art and Customs in Concord, Massachusetts.* Concord Antiquarian Society, Concord.

COOK, LAUREN J.
1988 A Family of Strangers: Documentary Archaeology and the Uxbridge Town Farm. Paper presented at the 21st Annual Meeting of the Society for Historical Archaeology, Reno, Nevada.
1989 The Uxbridge Poor Farm in the Documentary Record. In *Archaeological Excavations at the Uxbridge Alms-*

house Burial Ground in Uxbridge, Massachusetts, edited by Ricardo J. Elia and Al B. Wesolowsky, pp. 48–107. Report of Investigations No. 76. Office of Public Archaeology, Boston University, Boston.

COSTELLO, JULIA G., AND PHILLIP L. WALKER
1987 Burials from the Santa Barbara Presido Chapel. *Historical Archaeology* 21(1):3–17.

CRANE, BREED & COMPANY
1867 *Wholesale Price List of Patent Metallic Burial Cases and Caskets* . . . Crane, Breed & Co., Cincinnati. [1984 facsimile edition (microfiche). In *Trade Catalogues at Winterthur*, compiled by E. Richard McKinstry, Item 621. Clearwater Publishing Co., New York.]

DAILEY, ROBERT C., L. ROSS MORRELL,
AND W. A. COCKRELL
1972 *The St. Marks Military Cemetery (8WA108).* Bureau of Historic Sites and Properties Bulletin No. 2. Florida Department of State, Tallahassee.

DEETZ, JAMES, AND EDWIN S. DETHLEFSEN
1967 Death's Head, Cherub, Urn and Willow. *Natural History* 76(3):29–37.

DETHLEFSEN, EDWIN S., L. CABOT BRIGGS,
AND LEO P. BIESE
1977 The Clement Site: Analysis of Skeletal Material. *Man in The Northeast* 13:86–90.

DETHLEFSEN, EDWIN S., AND NANCY DEMYTTENAERE
1977 The Clement Site: Features and Artifacts. *Man in the Northeast* 13:90–96.

DICKENS, ROY S., JR., AND ROBERT L. BLAKELY
1979 Preliminary Report on Archaeological Investigations in Oakland Cemetery, Atlanta, Georgia. *The Conference on Historic Site Archeology Papers, 1978* 13:286–314. Columbia, South Carolina.

DOUGLAS, ANN
1975 Heaven Our Home: Consolation Literature in the Northern United States, 1830–1880. In *Death in America*, edited by David E. Stannard, pp. 49–68. University of Pennsylvania Press, Philadelphia.

DOUGLAS, MARY, AND BARON ISHERWOOD
1979 *The World of Goods.* Basic Books, New York.

EARLE, ALICE MORSE
1973 *Customs and Fashions in Old New England.* Charles E. Tuttle Co., Rutland, Vermont.
1977 Death Ritual in Colonial New York. In *Passing: The Vision of Death in America*, edited by Charles O. Jackson, pp. 30–41. Greenwood Press, Westport, Connecticut.

ELIA, RICARDO J.
1986 Death and Burial at a 19th-Century Almshouse. *Context* 5(1-2):1–4. Center for Archaeological Studies, Boston University.
1988 ''Forgotten and Unknown till the Judgement Morn'': Discovery and Excavation of the Uxbridge Almshouse

Burial Ground. Paper presented at the 21st Annual Meeting of the Society for Historical Archaeology, Reno, Nevada.
1989a The Uxbridge Almshouse Burial Ground Project. In *Archaeological Excavations at the Uxbridge Almshouse Burial Ground in Uxbridge, Massachusetts*, edited by Ricardo J. Elia and Al B. Wesolowsky, pp. 1–15. Report of Investigations No. 76. Office of Public Archaeology, Boston University, Boston.
1989b Archaeological Context. In *Archaeological Excavations at the Uxbridge Almshouse Burial Ground in Uxbridge, Massachusetts*, edited by Ricardo J. Elia and Al B. Wesolowsky, pp. 16–47. Report of Investigations No. 76. Office of Public Archaeology, Boston University, Boston.
1989c Conclusions and Recommendations. In *Archaeological Excavations at the Uxbridge Almshouse Burial Ground in Uxbridge, Massachusetts*, edited by Ricardo J. Elia and Al B. Wesolowsky, pp. 379–400. Report of Investigations No. 76. Office of Public Archaeology, Boston University, Boston.

ELIA, RICARDO J., AND AL B. WESOLOWSKY
(EDITORS)
1989 *Archaeological Excavations at the Uxbridge Almshouse Burial Ground in Uxbridge, Massachusetts.* Report of Investigations No. 76. Office of Public Archaeology, Boston University, Boston.

ELLIOT, SAMUEL HAYES
1858 *New England's Chattels: or, Life in the Northern Poor-house.* H. Dayton, New York.

FAIRBANKS, JONATHAN L., AND ROBERT F. TRENT
(EDITORS)
1982 *New England Begins: The Seventeenth Century.* 3 vols. Museum of Fine Arts, Boston.

FARRELL, JAMES J.
1980 *Inventing the American Way of Death, 1830–1920.* Temple University Press, Philadelphia.

FAULKNER, ALARIC, KIM MARK PETERS, DAVID P. SELL, AND EDWIN S. DETHLEFSEN
1978 *Port and Market: Archaeology of the Central Waterfront, Newburyport, Massachusetts.* Interagency Archaeological Services, National Park Service, Atlanta.

FELLOWS, F. P.
n.d. [ca. 1850]
Untitled catalogue. F.P. Fellows, Wolverhampton, England. [1984 facsimile edition (microfiche). In *Trade Catalogues at Winterthur*, compiled by E. Richard McKinstry, Item 1095. Clearwater Publishing Co., New York.]

FERGUSON, BOBBIE
1983 *Final Report on the McGee Creek Cemetery Relocations, Atoka County, Oklahoma.* Bureau of Reclamation, U.S. Department of the Interior, Ferris, Oklahoma. Microfiche.

FINNIGAN, JAMES T.
1981 St. Barnabas Burials: Salvage Excavations at a Late 19th Century Cemetery. *Na'Pao: A Saskatchewan Anthropology Journal* 11(12):41–48.

FOX, ANNE A.
1984 *A Study of Five Historic Cemeteries at Choke Canyon Reservoir, Live Oak and McMullen Counties, Texas.* Choke Canyon Series No. 9. Center for Archaeological Research, University of Texas at San Antonio, San Antonio.

FRENCH, STANLEY
1975 The Cemetery as Cultural Institution: The Establishment of Mount Auburn and the "Rural Cemetery" Movement. In *Death in America,* edited by David E. Stannard, pp. 39–48. University of Pennsylvania Press, Philadelphia.

GARROW, PATRICK H.
1987 A Preliminary Seriation of Coffin Hardware Forms in Late Nineteenth and Early Twentieth Century Georgia. Paper presented at the Annual Meeting of the Eastern States Archaeological Federation, Charleston, South Carolina.

GITTINGS, CLARE
1984 *Death, Burial and the Individual in Early Modern England.* Croom Helm, London.

GOODWIN, CONRAD M.
1981 Ethnicity in the Graveyard. Unpublished M.A. thesis, Department of Anthropology, College of William and Mary, Williamsburg.

GOODY, JACK
1975 Death and the Interpretation of Culture: A Bibliographic Overview. In *Death in America,* edited by David E. Stannard, pp. 1–8. University of Pennsylvania Press, Philadelphia.

HABENSTEIN, ROBERT W., AND WILLIAM M. LAMERS
1955 *The History of American Funeral Directing.* Bulfin, Milwaukee.

HACKER-NORTON, DEBI, AND MICHAEL TRINKLEY
1984 *Remember Man Thou Art Dust: Coffin Hardware of the Early Twentieth Century.* Chicora Foundation Research Series No. 2. Chicora Foundation, Columbia, South Carolina.

HANSEN, JULIE
1989 Analysis of Uxbridge Coffin Wood. In *Archaeological Excavations at the Uxbridge Almshouse Burial Ground in Uxbridge, Massachusetts,* edited by Ricardo J. Elia and Al B. Wesolowsky, pp. 488–495. Report of Investigations No. 76. Office of Public Archaeology, Boston University, Boston.

HAWLEY BROTHERS HARDWARE COMPANY
1884 *Price List and Illustrated Catalogue of Hardware and Agricultural Implements . . .* Hawley Brothers, San Francisco.

HOFFMAN, FREDERICK L.
1919 *Pauper Burials and the Interment of the Dead in Large Cities.* Prudential Press, Newark, New Jersey.

HUNTINGTON, RICHARD, AND PETER METCALF
1979 *Celebrations of Death: The Anthropology of Mortuary Ritual.* Cambridge University Press, Cambridge.

JACKSON, CHARLES O.
1977a American Attitudes to Death. *Journal of American Studies* 11(3):297–312.

JACKSON, CHARLES O. (EDITOR)
1977b *Passing: The Vision of Death in America.* Greenwood Press, Westport, Connecticut.

JONES, BARBARA
1967 *Design for Death.* Bobbs-Merrill, Indianapolis.

JORDAN, TERRY C.
1982 *Texas Graveyards: A Cultural Legacy.* University of Texas Press, Austin.

KELLEY, JEFFREY A.
1984 Skeletal Remains from Chelsea: The U.S. Marine Hospital. Typescript on file, Massachusetts Historical Commission, Boston.

KLEINBERG, SUSAN J.
1977 Death and the Working Class. *Journal of Popular Culture* 11(1):193–209.

KOCH, JOAN K.
1983 Mortuary Behavior Patterning and Physical Anthropology in Colonial St. Augustine. In *Spanish St. Augustine: The Archaeology of a Colonial Creole Community,* edited by Kathleen A. Deagan, pp. 187–227. Academic Press, New York.

LANGE, FREDERICK W., AND JEROME S. HANDLER
1985 The Ethnohistorical Approach to Slavery. In *The Archaeology of Slavery and Plantation Life,* edited by Theresa A. Singleton, pp. 15–32. Academic Press, New York.

LEONARDI, THOM
1986 Casket Furniture from Monroeville. Paper presented at the 19th Annual Meeting of the Society for Historical Archaeology, Sacramento.

LEVEILLEE, ALAN D., BRUCE J. LUTZ, AND DUNCAN RITCHIE
1981 *An Archaeological Assessment of Historic Cemeteries on the Grounds of the Massachusetts Correctional Institution, Bridgewater.* Public Archaeology Laboratory, Department of Anthropology, Brown University, Providence.

LUTZ, BRUCE J., AND PATRICIA E. RUBERTONE
1982 *Archaeological Investigations Relating to Cemeteries Within the Bounds of the Perimeter Fence, Massachusetts Correctional Institution, Bridgewater.* Public Archaeology Laboratory, Department of Anthropology, Brown University, Providence.

McGuire, Randall H.
1988 Dialogues with the Dead: Ideology and the Cemetery. In *The Recovery of Meaning: Historical Archaeology in the Eastern United States,* edited by Mark P. Leone and Parker B. Potter, Jr., pp. 435–480. Smithsonian Institution Press, Washington.

McKinstry, E. Richard (editor)
1984 *Trade Catalogues at Winterthur: A Guide to the Literature of Merchandising, 1750 to 1980.* Garland, New York.

McReynolds, Mary Jane
1981 *Archaeological Investigations at the Laredo Cemetery Site (41WB22), Webb County, Texas.* Reports of Investigations No. 11. Prewitt & Associates, Austin.

Morley, John
1971 *Death, Heaven, and the Victorians.* University of Pittsburgh Press, Pittsburgh.

Mytum, Harold
1989 Public Health and Private Sentiment: The Development of Cemetery Architecture and Funerary Monuments from the Eighteenth Century Onwards. *World Archaeology* 21(2):283–297.

National Casket Company
1891 *National Casket Company, Buffalo, N.Y., 1891.* National Casket Co., Buffalo. [1984 facsimile edition (microfiche). In *Trade Catalogues at Winterthur,* compiled by E. Richard McKinstry, Item 638. Clearwater Publishing Co., New York.]

Nelson, Lee H.
1980 Introduction. In *Illustrated Catalogue of American Hardware of the Russell and Erwin Manufacturing Company,* pp. iii–xi. Association for Preservation Technology, n.p.

Noël Hume, Ivor
1969 *Historical Archaeology.* Alfred A. Knopf, New York.

Olafson, Peter
1985 Breaking Backs for Bones. *Times-Herald Record,* November 10:5, 92. Middletown, New York.

Orser, Charles E., Jr., Annette M. Nekola, and James L. Roark
1987 *Exploring the Rustic Life: Multidisciplinary Research at Millwood Plantation, A Large Piedmont Plantation in Abbeville County, South Carolina, and Elbert County, Georgia.* 3 vols. Russell Papers 1987. Archaeological Services, National Park Service, Atlanta. Mid-Atlantic Research Center, Loyola University of Chicago, Chicago.

Owsley, Douglas W., Mary H. Manhein, and Ann M. Whitmer
1988 *Burial Archaeology and Osteology of a Confederate Cemetery at Port Hudson, Louisiana (16EF68), Report of Investigations.* Division of Archaeology, Louisiana Department of Culture, Recreation, and Tourism, Baton Rouge.

Parrington, Michael
1984 *An Archaeological and Historical Investigation of the Burial Ground at Old St. Paul's Church, Philadelphia, Pennsylvania.* John Milner Associates, Philadelphia.
1987 Cemetery Archaeology in the Urban Environment: A Case Study from Philadelphia. In *Living in Cities: Current Research in Urban Archaeology,* edited by Edward Staski, pp. 56–64. Special Publication Series No. 5. Society for Historical Archaeology.

Parrington, Michael, S. Pinter, and T. Struthers
1986 Occupations and Health Among Nineteenth-Century Black Philadelphians. *MASCA Journal* 4(1):37–41. Museum Applied Science Center for Archaeology, University Museum, University of Pennsylvania, Philadelphia.

Parrington, Michael, and Janet Wideman
1986 Acculturation in an Urban Setting: The Archaeology of a Black Philadelphia Cemetery. *Expedition* 28(1): 55–62. The University Museum, University of Pennsylvania, Philadelphia.

Payne, Ted M., and Ronald A. Thomas
1988 *Relocation of the Nowell Family Cemetery, (7K-E-174, CRS K-6395), Harrington, Delaware, Final Report.* Mid-Atlantic Archaeological Research Associates, Newark, Delaware.

Peck and Walter Manufacturing Company
1853 *Price List.* Peck and Walter Mfg. Co., n.p.

Pike, Martha V.
1980 In Memory Of: Artifacts Relating to Mourning in Nineteenth Century America. *Journal of American Culture* 3(4):642–659.

Pike, Martha V., and Janice Gray Armstrong (editors)
1980 *A Time to Mourn: Expressions of Grief in Nineteenth Century America.* Museums at Stony Brook, Stony Brook, New York.

Piper, Harry M., and Jacquelyn G. Piper
1987 Cultural Response to Stress: An Example from a Second Seminole War Cemetery. Paper presented at the 20th Annual Meeting of the Society for Historical Archaeology, Savannah.

Pollak-Eltz, Angelina
1974 *El concepto de múltiples almas y algunos ritos fúnebres entre los negros americanos.* Instituto de Investigaciones Historicas, Universidad Católica, Caracas.

Reitz, Elizabeth J., Tyson Gibbs, and Ted A. Rathbun
1985 Archaeological Evidence for Subsistence on Coastal Plantations. In *The Archaeology of Slavery and Plantation Life,* edited by Theresa A. Singleton, pp. 163–191. Academic Press, New York.

RHODES, DIANE LEE
1987 *Report on Archeological Investigations at the Poor Farm Cemetery, Montgomery County, Maryland, Summer 1987.* Applied Archeology Center, National Park Service, Rockville, Maryland.

RIIS, JACOB A.
1890 *How the Other Half Lives: Studies among the Tenements of New York.* Charles Scribner's Sons, New York.

ROSE, JEROME C.
1985a Cedar Grove and Black American History. In *Gone to a Better Land: A Biohistory of a Rural Black Cemetery in the Post-Reconstruction South,* edited by Jerome C. Rose, pp. 146–152. Arkansas Archeological Research Series No. 25. Arkansas Archeological Survey, Fayetteville.

ROSE, JEROME C. (EDITOR)
1985b *Gone to a Better Land: A Biohistory of a Rural Black Cemetery in the Post-Reconstruction South.* Arkansas Archeological Research Series No. 25. Arkansas Archeological Survey, Fayetteville.

ROSE, JEROME C., AND TED A. RATHBUN (EDITORS)
1987 Afro-American Biohistory Symposium. *American Journal of Physical Anthropology* 74(2):177–273.

ROSE, JEROME C. AND LAWRENCE GENE SANTEFORD
1985a Burial Descriptions. In *Gone to a Better Land: A Biohistory of a Rural Black Cemetery in the Post-Reconstruction South,* edited by Jerome C. Rose, pp. 39–129. Arkansas Archeological Research Series No. 25. Arkansas Archeological Survey, Fayetteville.
1985b Burial Interpretations. In *Gone to a Better Land: A Biohistory of a Rural Black Cemetery in the Post-Reconstruction South,* edited by Jerome C. Rose, pp. 130–145. Arkansas Archeological Research Series No. 25. Arkansas Archeological Survey, Fayetteville.
1985c Proposed Research Directions for Analysis. In *Gone to a Better Land: A Biohistory of a Rural Black Cemetery in the Post-Reconstruction South,* edited by Jerome C. Rose, pp. 156–157. Arkansas Archeological Research Series No. 25. Arkansas Archeological Survey, Fayetteville.

RUSSELL AND ERWIN MANUFACTURING COMPANY
1865 *Illustrated Catalogue of American Hardware . . .* Russell and Erwin Manufacturing Co., New Britain, Connecticut. [1980 facsimile edition. Association for Preservation Technology, n.p.]

ST. GEORGE, ROBERT BLAIR
1988 Introduction. In *Material Life in America, 1600–1860,* edited by Robert Blair St. George, pp. 3–13. Northeastern University Press, Boston.

SARGENT AND COMPANY
1861 *J.B. Sargent & Co., New Britain, Conn., Sargent & Co., No. 85 Beekman St., New York, New York 1861.* Sargent and Co., n.p.

1866 *Prices of Hardware. . . .* Tuttle, Morehouse, & Taylor, New Haven.
1869 *Illustrated Catalogue and Price List of Hardware and Mechanics' Tools Manufactured and Sold. . . .* Sargent and Co., n.p.
1871 *Price List of Illustrated Hardware Manufactured and for Sale. . . .* Sargent and Co., n.p.
1904 *Coffin and Casket Trimmings. . . .* Sargent and Co., New Haven and New York.

SARGENT, HOWARD R.
1977 The Clement Site: Field Investigation. *Man in the Northeast* 13:79–86.

SCHORSCH, ANITA
1976 *Mourning Becomes America: Mourning Art in the New Nation.* Main Street Press, Clinton, New Jersey.

SCHUYLER, ROBERT L.
1980 Preface. In *Archaeological Perspectives on Ethnicity in America,* edited by Robert L. Schuyler, pp. vii–viii. Baywood Monographs in Archaeology No. 1. Baywood Publishing Co., Farmingdale, New York.

SMITH, CYRIL STANLEY
1974 Reflections on Technology and the Decorative Arts in the Nineteenth Century. In *Technological Innovation and the Decorative Arts,* edited by Ian M.G. Quimby and Polly Anne Earl, pp. 1–64. University Press of Virginia, Charlottesville.

SOUTH, STANLEY
1979 *The General, The Major, and the Angel: The Discovery of General William Moultrie's Grave.* Research Manuscript Series No. 146. University of South Carolina, Institute of Archeology, Columbia.

STANNARD, DAVID E.
1975 Introduction. In *Death in America,* edited by David E. Stannard, pp. vii–xv. University of Pennsylvania Press, Philadelphia.
1979 Calm Dwellings. *American Heritage* 30(5):42–55.

TAINTER, JOSEPH A.
1978 Mortuary Practices and the Study of Prehistoric Social Systems. In *Advances in Archaeological Method and Theory* 1, edited by Michael B. Schiffer, pp. 105–141. Academic Press, New York.

TAYLOR, ANNA J., ANNE A. FOX, AND I. WAYNNE COX
1986 *Archaeological Investigations at Morgan Chapel Cemetery (41 BP 200), A Historic Cemetery in Bastrop County, Texas.* Archaeological Survey Report No. 146. Center for Archaeological Research, University of Texas at San Antonio, San Antonio.

THOMAS, DAVID HURST
1988 Saints and Soldiers at Santa Catalina: Hispanic Designs for Colonial America. In *The Recovery of Meaning: Historical Archaeology in the Eastern*

United States, edited by Mark P. Leone and Parker B. Potter, Jr., pp. 73–140. Smithsonian Institution Press, Washington.

THOMAS, DAVID HURST, STANLEY SOUTH, AND CLARK SPENCER LARSEN
1977 Rich Man, Poor Men: Observations on Three Antebellum Burials from the Georgia Coast. *Anthropological Papers of the American Museum of Natural History* 54(3):393–420.

THOMPSON, ROBERT FARRIS
1984 *Flash of the Spirit: African and Afro-American Art and Philosophy.* Random House, New York.

TRACHTENBERG, ALAN
1982 *The Incorporation of America: Culture and Society in the Gilded Age.* Hill and Wang, New York.

TRINKLEY, MICHAEL, AND DEBI HACKER-NORTON
1984 *Analysis of Coffin Hardware from 38CH778, Charleston County, South Carolina.* Chicora Foundation Research Series No. 3. Chicora Foundation, Columbia, South Carolina.

UNITED STATES GEOLOGICAL SURVEY
1979 Blackstone, Massachusetts, Quadrangle (7.5 minute series). United States Geological Survey, Washington, D.C.

UXBRIDGE, TOWN OF
1841– Selectmen's Records, 1841–1868. Bound ms. volume. Town Clerk's Office, Uxbridge, Massachusetts.
1868 [1848–Town Meetings, etc. Vol. 5 [1848–1870]. Bound ms. 1870] volume. Town Clerk's Office, Uxbridge, Massachusetts.

WATKINS, LURA WOODSIDE
1962 Middleton Buried Its Dead. *Essex Institute Historical Collections* 98(1):26–34.

WEGARS, PRISCILLA, RODERICK SPRAGUE, AND THOMAS M. J. MULINSKI
1983 *Miscellaneous Burial Recovery in Eastern Washington, 1981.* University of Idaho Anthropological Research Manuscript Series No. 76. Laboratory of Anthropology, University of Idaho, Moscow, Idaho.

WESOLOWSKY, AL B.
1988 "A Sort of Journey I Never Thought to Go": The Bones of the Uxbridge Paupers. Paper presented at the 21st Annual Meeting of the Society for Historical Archaeology, Reno, Nevada.
1989a Osteological Analysis. In *Archaeological Excavations at the Uxbridge Almshouse Burial Ground in Uxbridge, Massachusetts*, edited by Ricardo J. Elia and Al B. Wesolowsky, pp. 173–302. Report of Investigations No. 76. Office of Public Archaeology, Boston University, Boston.
1989b The Osteology of the Uxbridge Paupers. In *Archaeological Excavations at the Uxbridge Almshouse Burial Ground in Uxbridge, Massachusetts*, edited by Ricardo J. Elia and Al B. Wesolowsky, pp. 303–336. Report of Investigations No. 76. Office of Public Archaeology, Boston University, Boston.

WIGGINTON, ELIOT (EDITOR)
1973 Old-Time Burial Customs. In *Foxfire 2*, edited by Eliot Wigginton, pp. 304–323. Anchor Press/Doubleday, Garden City, New York.

WILLEY, GORDON R., AND PHILIP PHILLIPS
1958 *Method and Theory in American Archaeology.* University of Chicago Press, Chicago.

WILLIAMS, ROSALIND H.
1982 *Dream Worlds: Mass Consumption in Late Nineteenth-Century France.* University of California Press, Berkeley.

WOODALL, J. NED
1983 *Excavation and Analysis of the Vawter-Swaim Cemetery, 31FY714, Forsyth County, North Carolina.* Archeology Laboratories, Museum of Man, Wake Forest University, Winston-Salem.

YENTSCH, ANNE E.
1981 Death, Misfortune, and Communal Responsibility in Seventeenth Century New England. Paper presented at the 41st Conference on Early American History of the Institute of Early American History and Culture, Millersville, Pennsylvania.

EDWARD L. BELL
MASSACHUSETTS HISTORICAL COMMISSION
80 BOYLSTON STREET
BOSTON, MASSACHUSETTS 02116

www.ingramcontent.com/pod-product-compliance
Lightning Source LLC
Chambersburg PA
CBHW080944120626
46546CB00010B/2831